MANAGEMENT SCIENCE

MANAGEMENT SCIENCE
An Introduction to Quantitative Analysis for Management

William E. Pinney
Donald B. McWilliams

College of Business Administration
University of Texas at Arlington

HARPER & ROW, PUBLISHERS, New York
Cambridge, Hagerstown, Philadelphia, San Francisco
London, Mexico City, São Paulo, Sydney
1817

Sponsoring Editor: Bonnie Binkert
Project Editors: Céline Keating/Jon Dash
Designer: T. R. Funderburk
Production Manager: Willie Lane
Compositor: Syntax International PTE. LTD.
Printer and Binder: The Maple Press Company
Art Studio: Vantage Art, Inc.

MANAGEMENT SCIENCE
AN INTRODUCTION TO QUANTITATIVE ANALYSIS FOR MANAGEMENT

Library of Congress Cataloging in Publication Data

Pinney, William E 1941–
    Management science.

    1. Management—Mathematical models.   2. Decision-
making—Mathematical models.   I. McWilliams, Donald B.,
1936–   joint author.   II. Title.
HD30.25.P56   658.4′033   80-26562
ISBN 0-06-045222-6

To
Suzanne, Mary Allison, Jeffrey, Laura, Mark, and Van

CONTENTS

Chapter 3   MARKOV ANALYSIS   67

Chapter 4   LINEAR PROGRAMMING
—GRAPHICAL ANALYSIS   95

Chapter 5   LINEAR PROGRAMMING
—THE SIMPLEX ALGORITHM   125

Chapter 6   LINEAR PROGRAMMING —COMPUTER APPLICATIONS   182

Chapter 7   THE ASSIGNMENT AND TRANSPORTATION MODELS   204

Chapter 11   INVENTORY AND PRODUCTION MODELS   302

Chapter 12   CPM/PERT   336

PREFACE

An emerging trend in schools of business and public administration in recent years is the inclusion in the curriculum of a required course in quantitative decision models in addition to the introductory statistics course. The course masquerades under various titles, including management science, operations research, decision science, and quantitative methods, and is typically a survey of, and introduction to, a broad spectrum of quantitative decision-making techniques.

Due largely to the lack of mathematical sophistication of students in business administration, the course is a difficult one for both the students and the professor. This text attempts to reduce these difficulties by providing a student-oriented approach to the material, with more emphasis on application (how it works) and problem recognition (when it works) and less on derivation (why it works).

The authors are well aware that the very thought of a course in mathematical optimization techniques strikes terror into the hearts of most business students. Our intent is to allay this terror by keeping the overall tone of the text light. We hope to convince the student, through pragmatic examples, that a basic knowledge of these techniques will be a valuable addition to his/her bag of managerial tools.

The purpose of the text is to provide the student taking a first course in management science with a straightforward, nonthreatening introduction to the decision-making models typically covered in that course. To that end, the following features are incorporated.

The language is aimed at the *student,* rather than the practitioner. Buzz words and technical terms are labeled as such and defined in simple terms. A *summary of key terms and concepts* is included at the end of each chapter for review (or preview, if that approach is preferred). Concise, step-by-step summaries of calculating procedures are included for review and ease of reference later.

Decision models are discussed in the context of *examples,* wherever possible. The method is inductive—from the specific example to the general form—rather than deductive—from a mathematically derived "truth" to a specific example. The examples have been carefully selected to use simple numbers and reduce computational difficulty without sacrificing generality. The authors feel this is particularly important because many texts lose effectiveness by choosing examples that require students to spend an inordinate proportion of time struggling with the numbers, rather than being able to devote their primary attention to problem recognition and to understanding the solution methods employed. A solutions manual is available which contains the complete solutions to all end-of-chapter problems.

Extensive use is made of *visual content.* When students can "see" how and why the model operates, they have much less difficulty achieving an understanding of the solution process.

Chapters on *algebra, matrix algebra,* and *calculus* are included for introduction or review of these key building blocks. Most introductory texts either assume (erroneously, in the authors' experience) the students' familiarity with these topics or studiously avoid their use, to the detriment of the effective learning of much of the material in the course.

Other topics which are frequently omitted in introductory texts include *computer solutions of linear programming problems* (which may be used instead of or in addition to the simplex chapter); a rather extensive section on *duality* and *sensitivity analysis*; a chapter on *goal programming,* which is structured for solution on existing LP software packages; and a simple *contingency table approach to Bayesian revision* of probabilities in decision theory.

The topics are grouped to provide versatility for use in either quarter or semester format. While the primary orientation of the text is to be a one- or two-course sequence in the undergraduate business curriculum, the text is appropriate at the introductory level in most MBA programs. The *modular structure* of the chapters gives flexibility in tailoring text assignments to the special requirements of the particular program. Various topic sequences are suggested in course outline form in the introduction to the Instructor's Manual.

Naturally, the responsibility for any errors rests solely with the authors, but we are indebted to many persons for their interest, encouragement, and assistance during the preparation of the manuscript. We extend our heartfelt thanks to those numerous colleagues and students who reviewed part or all of earlier versions of the text, including Donald L. Adolphson, University of Washington; David Ashley, University of Missouri, Kansas City; Rebecca Baum, Temple University; Edward Baker, University of Maryland; Stanley Brooking, University of Southern Mississippi; I. Keong Chew, University of South Carolina; William Cornette, Texas Tech University; John A. Lawrence, California State University, Fullerton; and Fred Williams, North Texas State University. Their comments and suggestions have been very helpful, and are deeply appreciated. Our sincere appreciation goes to Irene Koby, whose contributions in typing, editing, and drafting went far beyond any reasonable expectations. Special thanks go to Doris Jones (typing), Tim Cheek (proofing solutions), Keith Hatfield (proofreading), Casey Haugland (index), and Joanne Tucker (class testing materials). We also wish to express our thanks to the Systems Analysis Department and the College of Business Administration of the University of Texas at Arlington for the support—financial, professional, and emotional—which was provided by both faculty and staff. Finally, we thank our editor, Bonnie Binkert, and the staff at Harper & Row for their encouragement, understanding, and thoroughly professional attitude during the preparation and publication of the text.

William E. Pinney
Donald B. McWilliams

Chapter 1

INTRODUCTION

WHAT IS MANAGEMENT SCIENCE?

Management science is one of a fairly large family of terms used to describe: (1) an approach to the solution of problems through the application of quantitative, objective, mathematical models and (2) the set of analytical tools, procedures, and techniques that are utilized in solving the problems. The management scientist is a problem solver who applies these tools to solve real problems in the fields of business and public administration.

Other terms frequently encountered and to some extent used interchangeably include decision sciences, quantitative methods or quantitative analysis, operations research, and industrial engineering. We will make the distinction that only management science has an underlying goal of applying the decision-making models and processes to problems in the management of public and private organizations. It is this orientation toward applications in administration that is the principle distinction we wish to make. The actual content, in terms of the analytical models covered, does not vary widely from one of these disciplines to another; the primary differences are in the level of mathematical sophistication required (ours will be relatively low), the mix of emphasis on theory and practice (we emphasize less of the former), and the areas of applications (ours include marketing, finance, accounting, economics, production, and personnel).

HISTORICAL DEVELOPMENT

Management science is a relatively new discipline, with roots going back to the work of Frederick W. Taylor in the late nineteenth century. Taylor is called "the father of scientific management" as a result of his efficiency studies in the steel industry.

A key development of the discipline as we know it came in 1940, when British physicist P. M. S. Blackett was appointed head of an interdisciplinary team of 11 researchers which included physicists, physiologists, army officers, mathematicians, and a surveyor. The group, which came to be known as "Blackett's circus," continued studies begun as early as 1937 on the development and effective deployment of radar systems. The British referred to their studies as "operational research," which was later changed to "operations research."

A Chronology of Model Development

Table 1.1 lists some of the early contributors to the field of management science, their areas of contribution, the approximate dates, and the chapters in which their techniques are treated. Some of the techniques, such as simulation models and cost-volume-profit analysis, are not typically identified with a single individual but have evolved from contributions by a number of authors.

Table 1.1 EARLY CONTRIBUTORS

TECHNIQUE	AUTHOR	APPROXIMATE DATE	CHAPTER(S)
Markov analysis	Markov	1907	3
Linear programming	Dantzig	1947	4–6
Assignment	Egervary	1931	7
Transportation	Hitchcock	1941	7
Goal programming	Charnes and Cooper	1962	8
Classical optimization	Kuhn and Tucker	1951	9
Inventory models	Harris	1918	11
PERT/CPM	Fazar	1958	12
Dynamic programming	Bellman	1957	13
Decision theory	Schlaiffer	1959	14
Game theory	Von Neumann and Morgenstern	1944	15
Waiting lines	Erlang	1917	17

Professional Organizations

There are a number of professional organizations that promote the development of management science. The American Institute for Industrial Engineers (AIIE) was established in 1948. The Operations Research Society of America (ORSA) was founded in 1952. The term *management science* was given official sanction in 1953 with the founding of The Institute of Management Science (TIMS), whereas *decision science* came into being with the establishment of the American Institute for Decision Sciences (AIDS) in 1969.

BEHAVIORAL VERSUS QUANTITATIVE DECISION MAKING

There is a continuing debate over the relationship that should exist between intuitive ("gut feel") behaviorally oriented decision making and quantitatively based ("number cruncher") approaches. Our position is that in the ideal situation the two should complement each other, for almost all nontrivial problems contain both subjective and objective elements.

Decision makers who rely solely upon subjective evaluation are failing to avail themselves of powerful, proven tools of analysis; those who would blindly reduce a complex problem to a set of rigid mathematical formulas ignore potentially crucial behavioral factors. The truly effective executive makes use of both types of analysis, and arrives at decisions that are superior to those obtained by the exclusive application of either intuitive or quantitative analysis.

It has been our experience that it is possible to teach model formulation and solution procedures in an academic environment; it is extremely difficult, however, to teach the art of problem identification, goal setting, and implementation because of the highly subjective, problem-, personality-, and organization-dependent nature of these phases of the problem-solving process.

An introductory treatment such as the one found in this text will not make you an expert in management science, but it will make you a more effective decision maker and give you insights into the overall decision-making process. We intend to provide a sound foundation for a "bag of tools" that can be applied to the problems you will encounter in your specific area(s) of specialization.

THE SYSTEMS APPROACH

The most effective analytical framework for the solution of problems of meaningful scale or the development of new systems is called the *systems approach*. There are six essential elements in the procedure, as shown in Figure 1.1.

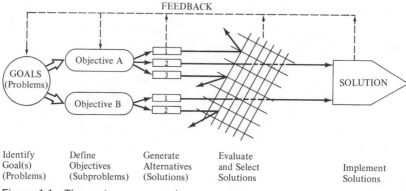

Figure 1.1   The systems approach.

Identify Goals (Problems)

The first step in developing a system or in solving a problem is to identify the goals of the system or to specify the problem to be solved. It is extremely important that this step be undertaken with the goals of the entire system in mind and that care be taken to assure that the real goals (not those which sound nice in press releases) or the real problems (and not merely visible symptoms of those problems) be specified. They should be stated in broad terms applicable to the system as a whole.

Define Objectives

The second step is to translate the general goals or problems into *specific objectives*, defining each objective in precise terms that can be accomplished at a level below the total system level. These will define specific subproblems or components of the new system.

Generate Alternatives

For each objective we generate a number of possible alternate solutions. It is very important that we do not permit preconceived solutions to stifle new approaches and that all feasible alternatives for the solution of the problems be considered. Feasible alternatives are those that do not violate any of the constraints of the problem. These constraints are of two types: internal constraints (those that we impose) and external constraints (those beyond our control that are imposed by the environment).

Evaluate Alternatives and Select Solution(s)

Next we screen the alternatives that have been proposed; evaluate each one, basing our evaluation on the goals and objectives previously defined;

and select the best alternatives(s) from those that are under consideration. It is at this stage of the process that the tools of quantitative analysis find their most frequent use. The models from management science can be used to excellent advantage in measuring the effectiveness of various courses of action in meeting the goals and objectives. Proper application of the models can lead to selection of optimal courses of action.

Implement the Solution

Once the best alternatives for solving the problem or achieving the goals have been identified, the solution must be implemented. It is at this stage that the behavioral skills of the manager–problem solver must be at their best, for an optimal solution or system can, if improperly implemented, lead to worse rather than better results. Recognition of and careful attention to the details and "people problems" are essential if the solution is to be successfully implemented.

The Use of Feedback

Throughout the systems analysis it is necessary that extensive use be made of *feedback*. Feedback is the process which requires that we check at each stage of the process to assure that the alternatives we generate, the criteria we use in evaluating them, and the solutions we select for implementation are in keeping with the goals and objectives we originally specified. It is not uncommon to find that the "solution" initially selected leads to a modification (or clarification) of the original goals or problems, and a second or third iteration of the entire process is required before a final solution can be effectively implemented. Without effective feedback, the "solution" may be the optimal response to the *wrong* problem.

THE ROLE OF MODELS

Types of Models

A model is an abstraction, a simplification, an idealization. There are many ways of classifying models. One general set of categories is: (1) *iconic* models (physical models, such as the scale models used by architects or the toy aircraft we played with as children), (2) *analog* models (which are analogous, or similar, to the thing being modeled, such as road maps or charts and graphs that represent relationships by length of lines or distances between points, or schematic electrical diagrams and the blueprints of a house or building), and (3) *symbolic* models (abstract models which can be verbal or mathematical in form).

The subject material of management science is almost exclusively concerned with the development, design, solution, and interpretation of mathematical models. We will make extensive use of visual (analog) models to assist in our interpretation and understanding of the models, but their foundation will be mathematical.

Mathematical models can be further classified as *deterministic* (having fixed relationships) or *stochastic* (having relationships that behave in an unpredictable or random fashion); as *static* (having relationships that do not change over time) or *dynamic* (having relationships that do change over time); *linear* (having all variables with exponents of zero or one) or *nonlinear* (having variables with exponents other than zero or one, in which cases the functions are curved rather than straight or flat); as *univariate* (reacting to changes in only one factor) or *multivariate* (sensitive to variations in many factors); and as *algorithmic* (having a set solution procedure) or *heuristic* (employing rules of thumb as well as adaptive trial and error procedures that change directions as conditions warrant). Other classifications are possible, but these will serve to demonstrate the major distinctions among the various types of models available.

The Modeling Process

There are five basic elements in the modeling process: (1) *abstraction* (construction), (2) *validation*, (3) *prediction*, (4) *evaluation*, and (5) *revision*. These are suggested in Figure 1.2.

Real-world problems are typically ill-structured and not well defined. Through the process of *abstraction*, management scientists reduce the problem to its important relationships and construct a model that represents the key factors that comprise the essence of the problem. They then must *validate* the model by applying it to known situations that are similar to the problem at hand. If the model appears to work reasonably well, it is used to *predict* the results of various alternative courses of

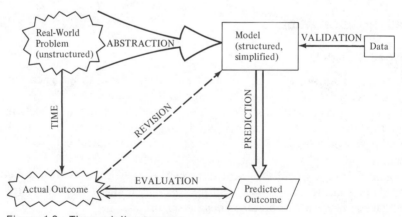

Figure 1.2   The modeling process.

action. These predictions are used as the basis for selecting the preferred alternative(s).

If the model is to be reused, it is essential to *compare* the predicted results with the actual outcome of the decision. If the model was an inaccurate predictor of the outcome, then it is not a valid representation of the real problem and must be modified or *revised* to more accurately reflect the actual situation.

In management science we use models to evaluate the alternative courses of action and to select the optimum decision(s). Although it is often necessary to invent *special purpose* models for unique situations, we will present a selection of the most widely used *standard* optimization models, in the hope that you as a practitioner will be able to utilize them "as is" or to modify them to suit the needs of your particular problems.

MODEL DEVELOPMENT

Although each of the models we will study has its own unique features, there are certain basics that are common to all optimization models.

1. A model must have one or more *objectives*, which must be stated explicitly. These are the factors that we will attempt to optimize in our selection of a solution to the problem.
2. The model will have *variables*, or unknowns, that represent the factors that can change in the problem. Some of the variables are *endogenous* (controllable within our model); others are *exogenous* (take on values from outside our model).
3. In addition to the variables, there will be some values that are known or constant quantities. These are called *parameters*.
4. We express the interplay among our variables and parameters as *relationships*, which we attempt to explain in mathematical terms. Some relationships are *causal* (a change in one actually causes a change in another), and others are *fortuitous* (two variables move together, but not because either controls the other). Also, relationships can be either *direct* or *indirect* in nature.
5. Our model will usually have *boundaries* within which it must operate in order to retain its validity. These are typically expressed as *constraints* on our optimization of the objectives. These constraints frequently represent limitations imposed by scarce resources.
6. In order to construct and validate a model, we must typically have access to *information*. We make an important distinction between *information* and *data*: Data (which is always plural) are just numbers, whereas information has organization, structure, and meaning. For example, the numbers 8175551234 are data; (817) 555–1234 is information.

Although each model organizes these elements in a different fashion, they represent the basic building blocks from which all models are constructed.

OPTIMIZATION

The central concept of management science is *optimization*—the selection of alternatives that constitute the best courses of action under some set of objective criteria. In terms of our mathematical models, this typically takes the form of optimizing (maximizing or minimizing our objectives) subject to a set of constraints. The constraints, taken as a group, serve to define a region of *feasibility* within which we are free to select the optimum outcomes.

One pitfall we wish to avoid is *suboptimization*, which has two connotations, both of which are negative. In the broadest sense, a sub-optimal decision is simply one that is not as good as the optimal one. In a more technical sense, suboptimization refers to optimizing at a level below the total system level—optimizing a subsystem.

A good example of this is the decision on how much inventory to carry. If the marketing department makes the decision, it will opt for high levels of inventory, in order never to lose sales because of shortages of merchandise. The finance department, on the other hand, wishes to carry as little inventory as possible because inventory ties up funds that can be used for other purposes. The production department wishes to plan inventories in such a way that production stays fairly constant and workload scheduling does not fluctuate markedly. The inventory-level decision must be made at the system level in order to balance out the conflicting goals of the three departments. Decisions made at the sub-system level would be suboptimal from the point of view of the overall system.

At the other end of the spectrum we encounter the problem of *overoptimization*. This occurs when diminishing returns result from our attempt to achieve the absolutely best answer when a "quick and dirty" solution would have been, for all practical purposes, just as effective. In this regard, it is extremely useful to know whether the problem we face is a "saucer" or a "funnel." See Figure 1.3.

Saucer   Funnel

Figure 1.3   Two classes of optimum solutions

In "saucer" problems, there is a broad range of solutions with nearly optimal results, and finding the exact optimum is not essential. In "funnel" problems, the determination of the precisely optimal solution is much more crucial, because minor deviations from the optimum lead to major sacrifices in the overall effectiveness of the solution.

The urge to indulge in overoptimization is an occupational hazard for the management scientist. One of your authors once spent over $3 in gasoline going to five different stores to save a total of $0.43 on a grocery bill of $28. (Although I am no longer permitted to grocery shop alone, I am still frequently galvanized into inaction for lengthy periods when presented with several brands and several sizes of an item that varies in quality, such as martini olives.)

A term we use to express the more practical solution to overoptimizing is *satisficing*, which means working until we find a solution that adequately satisfies our needs and then terminating the search for the exact optimum.

After a solution has been obtained, it should be tested for stability in the face of changes in the assumptions that were made in formulating the model. The process is called *sensitivity analysis*. Decision makers strongly prefer to encounter "saucer" type solutions that are insensitive to changes in the assumptions on which the model is based. They are then free to make satisficing decisions that are near optimal, based upon secondary considerations or subjective factors that they were unable to quantify and include in the model expressly.

A final point relating to optimization concerns the subject of *precision*. It is counterproductive to carry out calculations further than the original data warrant. If the data on which the model is formulated are subjective estimates like "around 35 or 40 pounds," it is intellectual and professional heresy to report a solution like 29.3742 pounds. The conscientious management scientist will avoid giving the impression of greater precision than actually exists.

AREAS OF APPLICATION FOR MANAGEMENT SCIENCE

There is almost no area of business or administrative decision making where management science techniques conceivably may not be used. The only requirement for the use of these techniques is that the decision variables be quantifiable to some degree.

Here are some examples of application areas that are representative:

Markov analysis.   Market strategy planning, preventive maintenance program planning, manpower training program design.

Linear programming (LP).   Product mix decisions, oil refinery operation, capital structure planning, capital budgeting, advertising media assignment.

Assignment and transportation models. Physical distribution planning, production planning, manpower assignment, machine assignment, space allocation.

Goal programming. Advertising decisions, municipal resource allocation, product mix decisions.

Inventory models. Raw material inventory planning, retail sales inventory planning.

CPM/PERT. Project scheduling, project budgeting.

Dynamic programming. Complex systems analysis, sales distribution planning, production and inventory planning.

Decision theory. Investment decisions, military strategy planning, medical decisions, gambling (football, basketball, betting).

Game theory. Collective bargaining decisions, bidding strategy planning, military strategy planning.

Simulation. Complex systems analysis, stochastic systems analysis, shop scheduling and planning, inventory policy planning.

Waiting line models (queues). Service facility planning, road and freeway design, plant layout planning.

The foregoing is certainly not an exhaustive list of application areas, but it does give some idea of the pervasiveness of management science techniques. There is some obvious overlap from one technique to another, for it is often true that more than one technique can be successfully applied to a particular problem. Many times *no* standard technique fits a problem perfectly and the management scientist must either modify an existing technique or develop an entirely new one to suit it. A knowledge of the theory upon which the models in this text are based will aid practitioners in recognizing when a model can be used in standard form and when creativity must be their major tool.

QUESTIONS

1. What is management science and how do we differentiate it from operations research, decision sciences, quantitative methods, and industrial engineering?
2. What are the steps in the systems approach?
3. What are the five basic elements in the modeling process?
4. Define suboptimization.
5. Define overoptimization. Explain the saucer and the funnel.

Chapter 2

REVIEW OF MATHEMATICAL TOOLS

INTRODUCTION

This chapter is a very long one (as you have probably noticed), because it attempts to cover a wide range of mathematical fundamentals. Its primary aim is as a refresher or review for those who may not have had occasion to use these mathematical tools for some time. With some help from your instructor, however, it can be used as an introduction to those tools to which you may have had little or no previous exposure. We suggest that only those sections that are appropriate to the particular set of topics to be covered in your course of study be used. These will vary, depending upon the depth desired and your prior experience.

The chapter reviews some basic concepts of algebra, rectangular coordinates, systems of linear equations, matrix algebra and determinants, and probability. Because you will be dealing with mathematical models throughout the text, you will find that a quick review of algebraic operations and their application in solving for the unknown value of a variable will serve you in good stead. Reacquainting yourself with the rectangular coordinate system will prove useful at many points throughout the book, because we have attempted to utilize as much visual material as possible in developing and presenting the various models. Perhaps the most obvious use of this approach is in Chapter 4, which covers the solution of linear programming problems by graphical means.

The background in matrix algebra will be put to use in Chapter 3 on Markov analysis; the method you will learn for finding the inverse of a matrix will form the basis for understanding the simplex method of linear programming in Chapter 5; and the ability to evaluate determinants will enable you to solve sets of linear equations using Cramer's rule.

The review of probability concepts and probability distributions will prove useful in Markov analysis (Chapter 3), CPM/PERT (Chapter 12), decision theory (Chapter 14), game theory (Chapter 15), simulation (Chapter 16), and waiting lines (Chapter 17).

BASIC ALGEBRAIC RELATIONSHIPS

In our discussion of algebraic relationships we begin by defining the three classes of elements that we will use: (1) *parameters,* which in a given relationship have *fixed values;* (2) *variables,* which will be allowed to assume a range of *different values;* and (3) *operators* (such as $+$, $-$, $\times$, $\div$, $\sqrt{}$), which enable us to *manipulate* the parameters and the variables and to express relationships among them. In our present discussion, each parameter and each variable represent a single quantity, and we can refer to this class of relationships as *scalar* algebra. In the next section of the chapter, each parameter or variable will represent a whole *array* of elements, and those relationships are called *matrix* algebra.

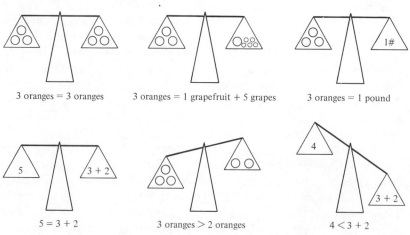

3 oranges = 3 oranges   3 oranges = 1 grapefruit + 5 grapes   3 oranges = 1 pound

5 = 3 + 2   3 oranges > 2 oranges   4 < 3 + 2

Figure 2.1 Examples of equalities and inequalities.

The use of algebra revolves about the concept of *equations*, which are statements that two expressions are equivalent, and *equalities*, which state that one expression or value is greater than (or less than) another. It is useful to think of these concepts as being analogous to the balance scale, as shown in Figure 2.1. The balance uses weight as a measure of value, but in our mathematical models the values can be measured in units of dollars, labor hours, number of units produced, etc. The only requirement is that both sides of the statement be measured in the *same* units.

Addition and Subtraction

If the two sides of an equation (or a balance) are equal in value (or weight) and the same amount is added to or subtracted from both sides, the resulting system will also be an equality. A primary use for this concept is in rearranging, or solving, an equation for one of the variables. The following examples illustrate this procedure.

$$3R - 4 = 9 + 2R$$
$$X - 3 = 5 \qquad (3R - 4) + 4 = (9 + 2R) + 4$$
$$(X - 3) + 3 = 5 + 3 \qquad 3R = 13 + 2R$$
$$X = 8 \qquad (3R) - 2R = (13 + 2R) - 2R$$
$$R = 13$$

$$P + 2S - T + 3 = 7S$$
$$(P + 2S - T + 3) - (2S - T + 3) = (7S) - (2S - T + 3)$$
$$P = 5S + T - 3$$

In the first example, we solve for the value of the unknown variable X by adding 3 to both sides of the equality. The second example requires two steps—first adding 4 to each side and then subtracting $2R$ from each side to find $R = 13$. In the third example, if we wish to solve for the value of P in terms of the other unknowns (S and T), we must subtract the expression ($2S - T + 3$) from both sides.

Multiplication and Division

If the two sides of an expression (or a balance) are equal, then doubling or tripling both sides, or multiplying them both by any value, will leave them still in balance. The same is true of dividing both sides by the same value: If the two sides are of equal value, then one-half of each side or one-fourth of each side will also be equal. Consider the following examples.

$$\frac{L}{9} = 11 \qquad\qquad 4M = 20$$

$$\left(\frac{L}{9}\right) \times 9 = (11) \times 9 \qquad (4M) \div 4 = (20) \div 4$$

$$L = 99 \qquad\qquad \frac{1}{4}(4M) = \frac{1}{4}(20)$$

$$M = 5$$

$$\frac{2V}{3} = \frac{4D + 2R}{7}$$

$$\left(\frac{2V}{3}\right) \times 3 = \frac{(4D + 2R)}{7} \times 3$$

$$2V = \frac{12D + 6R}{7}$$

$$(2V) \div 2 = \frac{(12D + 6R)}{7} \div 2$$

$$V = \frac{6D + 3R}{7}$$

In the first example, we must multiply both sides of the equation by 9 to find the value of L. In the second example, we divide both sides by 4, which is the same as multiplying both sides by $\frac{1}{4}$, to obtain $M = 5$. The third example requires that we multiply both sides by 3 and also divide both sides by 2 to solve for V as a function of D and R. We note that this can be accomplished in a single step by multiplying both sides by $\frac{3}{2}$ or dividing both sides by $\frac{2}{3}$.

Other Operations

As long as the two expressions are of equal value, we can perform any legitimate mathematical operation on both sides without upsetting the equality. These operations include raising to a power, extracting a root, taking the logarithm, taking the absolute value, and others. Some commonly used examples are as follows.

$$Q^2 = 36 \qquad \sqrt{N} = 5D \qquad\qquad 10^W = 84$$
$$\sqrt{Q^2} = \sqrt{36} \qquad (\sqrt{N})^2 = (5D)^2 \qquad \mathrm{Log}_{10}(10^W) = \mathrm{Log}_{10} 84$$
$$Q = \pm 6 \qquad N = 25D^2 \qquad\qquad W = 1.9243$$

The first example requires that we take the square root of both sides to find the values of Q. In the second, we must square both sides to find

N in terms of D. In the third, we can solve for W by taking the logarithm of both sides.

Solving Equations

It is frequently necessary to combine the application of two or more operations in order to solve an equation for one variable in terms of the parameters (constants) and/or other variables. We call the variable that appears by itself on the left side of the equation the *dependent variable*, because its value depends upon the values of the other variable(s). The variables on the right-hand side are called the *independent variables*, and we will assign values to them and observe the corresponding values for the dependent variables. The typical form of a solved equation might be:

$$\underset{\text{Dependent Variable } (Y)}{\underline{Y}} \quad = \quad \underset{\substack{\text{Independent Variables } (X_1, X_2, X_3) \\ \text{and Parameters } (a, b, c)}}{\underbrace{aX_1 + bX_2 + cX_3}}$$

We can describe the procedure of solving an equation for the dependent variable as one involving: (1) *collection* of like terms, (2) *isolation* of the dependent variable, and (3) *solution* for that variable. The following are examples of equations that require application of two or more operations to both sides to solve for the dependent variable.

$$5X + 1 = 2X + 7$$
$$(5X + 1) - 2X = (2X + 7) - 2X$$
$$3X + 1 = 7$$
$$(3X + 1) - 1 = (7) - 1$$
$$3X = 6$$
$$(3X) \div 3 = (6) \div 3$$
$$X = 2$$

$$\sqrt{2Y - 2X + 5} = 4X$$
$$(\sqrt{2Y - 2X + 5})^2 = (4X)^2$$
$$2Y - 2X + 5 = 16X^2$$
$$(2Y - 2X + 5) + (2X - 5) = (16X^2) + (2X - 5)$$
$$2Y = 16X^2 + 2X - 5$$
$$(2Y) \div 2 = (16X^2 + 2X - 5) \div 2$$
$$Y = 8X^2 + X - \tfrac{5}{2}$$

$$\frac{5W + 8}{2G - 3} = 4$$

$$\left(\frac{5W + 8}{2G - 3}\right) \times (2G - 3) = 4(2G - 3)$$

$$5W + 8 = 8G - 12$$

$$(5W + 8) - 8 = (8G - 12) - 8$$

$$5W = 8G - 20$$

$$(5W) \div 5 = (8G - 20) \div 5$$

$$W = \tfrac{8}{5}G - 4$$

$$6R + 7T - M = 8 + R - 3T + 4M$$

$$(6R + 7T - M) - R = (8 + R - 3T + 4M) - R$$

$$5R + 7T - M = 8 - 3T + 4M$$

$$(5R + 7T - M) - (7T - M) = (8 - 3T + 4M) - (7T - M)$$

$$5R = 8 - 10T + 5M$$

$$(5R) \times \tfrac{1}{5} = (8 - 10T + 5M) \times \tfrac{1}{5}$$

$$R = \tfrac{8}{5} - 2T + M$$

In the first example, X is the only unknown; so we collect all of our Xs on the left-hand side and all of the constants on the right-hand side and solve for X. In the second example, we have assumed that Y is the dependent variable; so we square both sides to clear the radical (square root), collect like terms together, isolate Y on the left-hand side, and solve for Y in terms of X. In the third example, we have assumed that W is the dependent variable; so we multiply by $(2G - 3)$ to get all unknowns in the numerator, isolate W on the left, and solve. R is assumed to be the dependent variable in the fourth example. We collect like terms, isolate R on the left, and solve.

At the end of the chapter there are a number of problems that are designed to provide practice in using algebra to solve equations. The student is encouraged to work enough of them so that their solution becomes automatic and requires little effort.

Inequalities

Inequalities are covered in some detail in the chapters on linear programming and goal programming (Chapters 4–8). The principal operations we will utilize in working with inequalities are addition, subtraction, multiplication, and division. Inequalities follow all the same rules as equalities for these operations *except* that multiplication or division by a negative value *reverses* the direction of the inequality.

$$2T - 2 < 8R$$

$$X + 3 < 5$$

$$(2T - 2) + 2 < (8R) + 2$$

$$(X + 3) - 3 < (5) - 3$$

$$2T < 8R + 2$$

$$X < 2$$

$$(2T) \div 2 < (8R + 2) \div 2$$

$$T < 4R + 1$$

$$2 - 3M < 14$$

$$(2 - 3M) - 2 < (14) - 2$$

$$-3M < 12$$

$$(-3M) \div (-3) > (12) \div (-3)$$

$$M > -4$$

In the first example, we subtract 3 from both sides, and the inequality remains in the same direction. In the second example, we add 2 to both sides and divide both sides by 2, with no change in the direction of the inequality. In example three, we subtract 2 from both sides with no effect on the direction of the inequality, but when we divide by -3, the direction of the inequality reverses.

RECTANGULAR COORDINATES

Although there are many systems that are used to locate points in space (polar, cylindrical, and spherical coordinate systems, for example), the most widely used and probably best understood system is the *rectangular*, or *Cartesian*, system of *coordinates*. While the system can be used for three-dimensional representation, most of our work will use only the two-dimensional system.

Points in a Plane

The two-dimensional rectangular coordinate system is illustrated in Figure 2.2. All measurements are distances from the *origin* (the point where $X = Y = 0$). One variable (X) is measured by its distance to the right (positive values) or left (negative values) of the origin; the other (Y), by its distance above (positive values) or below (negative values) the origin. We can identify any point in the plane of the page by specifying its X and Y values (the distance to the right or left and above or below the origin, respectively).

By convention, we write the X value first, followed by the Y value. In Figure 2.2 we have plotted points $A(X = 5, Y = 2)$, $B(X = -1, Y = 4)$, $C(X = -3, Y = -5)$, $D(X = 8, Y = 0)$, $E(X = 0, Y = -4)$, and $F(X = 2, Y = -2)$.

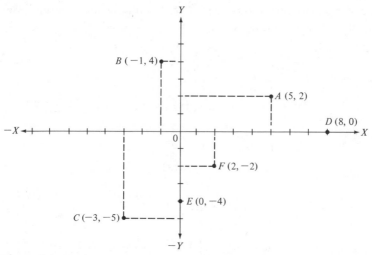

Figure 2.2   Plotting points in rectangular coordinates.

Lines in a Plane

There are two ways of identifying a straight line in a plane—the two-point method and the point-slope method. Because only one straight line can be drawn between two points, knowing the location of any two points on a line enables us to uniquely identify that line.

The equation of a linear function in a plane is

$$Y = a + bX$$

where a is called the *Y intercept* (the place where the line crosses the *Y* axis) and b is called tha *slope* (the amount of rise or fall in *Y* for each unit of increase in *X*). The slope is defined to be the difference in the *Y* values at the two points divided by the difference in the *X* values.

$$b = \text{Slope} = \frac{Y_2 - Y_1}{X_2 - X_1} = \frac{Y_1 - Y_2}{X_1 - X_2}$$

Note that it does not matter which point we call point 1 and which we call point 2.

If we wish to know the equation of the line that passes through the points $G(1, 2)$ and $H(3, -2)$ in the first graph of Figure 2.3, we must determine a (the line crosses the *Y* axis at $Y = +4$) and b.

$$b = \frac{(2) - (-2)}{(1) - (3)} = \frac{(-2) - (2)}{(3) - (1)} = \frac{-4}{2} = -2$$

The equation of the line is therefore $Y = 4 - 2X$.

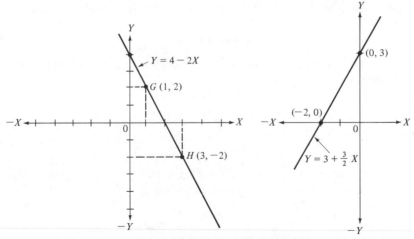

Figure 2.3   Linear functions in a plane (two-point method).

In the second graph of Figure 2.3 we find the equation of the line from its intercept values, $(-2, 0)$ and $(0, 3)$. By inspection

$$a = 3; \qquad b = \frac{(0) - (3)}{(-2) - (0)} = \frac{(3) - (0)}{(0) - (-2)} = \frac{3}{2}$$

The equation is therefore $Y = 3 + \frac{3}{2}X$.

If we know the slope of a line and one point on the line, we can determine the equation of the line by locating a where $X = 0$. In the first graph of Figure 2.4, we wish to find the equation of the line that

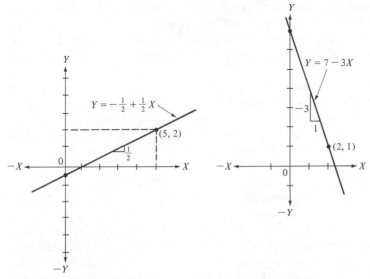

Figure 2.4   Linear functions in a plane (point-slope method).

goes through the point (5, 2) with a slope of $+\frac{1}{2}$. We know that the equation is

$$Y = a + \tfrac{1}{2}X$$

and we know that $Y = 2$ when $X = 5$. Substituting these values into the equation, we can solve for a.

$$2 = a + \tfrac{1}{2}(5)$$
$$a + 2 - \tfrac{5}{2} = -\tfrac{1}{2}$$

Our equation is therefore

$$Y = -\tfrac{1}{2} + \tfrac{1}{2}X$$

In the second example of Figure 2.4, the line through the point (2, 1) with a slope of $b = -3$ has an equation of

$$Y = a - 3X$$

Substituting the point (2, 1) and solving for a

$$(1) = a - 3(2)$$
$$a = 1 + 6 = 7$$

The equation of the line is therefore

$$Y = 7 - 3X$$

Plotting Linear Functions

In our discussion thus far, we have expressed our functions with the dependent variable (Y) on the left-hand side and the independent variable (X) and the constant term (a) on the right-hand side of the equality. We will frequently deal with sets of equations that have the constant term on the right-hand side and both X and Y on the left. Plotting these equations requires locating any two points on the line and connecting them.

Figure 2.5 presents several examples of this procedure. In the first example, the equation is $4X + Y = 8$, and the intercepts can easily be obtained by setting first $X = 0$ to get $Y = 8$, and then $Y = 0$ to get $X = 2$. The second example is similar, except that the X intercept (when $Y = 0$) of $-X + 3Y = 3$ is negative $(-3, 0)$ and the Y intercept (when $X = 0$) is positive $(0, 1)$.

Sometimes it is not practical to plot both intercepts, as shown in the third and fourth examples. For $10X - Y = 50$, we plot the X intercept (5, 0), but the Y intercept is too large to plot. In such cases we merely select any other convenient point, such as $X = 6$ and find $Y = -50 + 10(6) = 10$. These two points (5, 0) and (6, 10) enable us to plot the line.

The final example is similar. The X intercept (40, 0) is off our scale; so we use $X = 8$ and find $Y = 10 - \tfrac{1}{4}(8) = 8$. This point and the Y intercept (0, 10) allow us to plot the line.

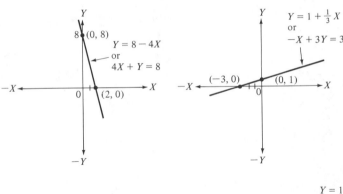

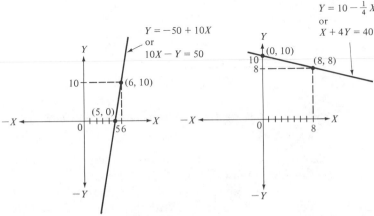

Figure 2.5 Plotting linear functions.

SYSTEMS OF EQUATIONS

Many of our management science models require that we satisfy two or more relationships *simultaneously*. We shall see that there are several different ways to accomplish this, including graphical solution, algebraic methods, and the use of matrices and determinants.

Graphical Solution

If our set of simultaneous equations has only two unknowns, we may solve the equations for the common solution point by plotting the functions and noting their intersection. If a farmer wishes to purchase a total of 12 head of cattle and he specifies that there should be twice as many heifers as steers, his problem can be represented as a set of simultaneous equations with H representing the number of heifers to buy and S the number of steers.

$$H + S = 12$$
$$H = 2S$$

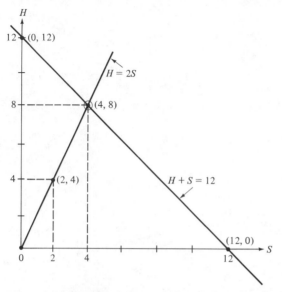

Figure 2.6   Graphical solution of a set of two simultaneous equations.

These are plotted in Figure 2.6. The solution, or point that simultaneously satisfies both equations, is 4 steers and 8 heifers.

Unless two lines in the same plane are parallel, they will eventually cross and have a common solution point. With three equations, however, the problem of simultaneous solutions becomes more difficult. In the first example of Figure 2.7, all three equations pass through the point (3, 3). The more usual case, however, is that of the second example, where each of the three possible *pairs* of equations has a solution, but in each case that point is *not* on the third line. This system has no solution point that is common to all three equations.

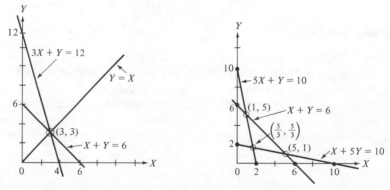

Figure 2.7   Graphical solution of three equations with two unknowns.

Algebraic Solution

The two principal methods of solving simultaneous equations algebraically are *substitution* and *elimination of variables.*

SUBSTITUTION

In substitution, we solve one of the equations for one variable and substitute that expression into the other equation. Using the second example from Figure 2.7, we can find the common solution point of $5X + Y = 10$ and $X + Y = 6$ by first solving the second equation for Y

$$Y = 6 - X$$

and then substituting this expression everywhere Y appears in the other expression.

$$5X + (6 - X) = 10$$

Solving this equation for X gives

$$5X - X = 10 - 6$$
$$4X = 4$$
$$X = 1$$

Using this value for X in either of the original equations gives the solution value for Y.

$$5(1) + Y = 10 \qquad 1 + Y = 6$$
$$Y = 10 - 5 \qquad Y = 6 - 1$$
$$Y = 5 \qquad Y = 5$$

We could have solved the first equation for one of the variables and substituted into the second with the same eventual result.

$Y = 10 - 5X$ (first equation solved for Y)

$X + (10 - 5X) = 6$ (expression for Y substituted into second equation)

$$\left. \begin{array}{c} X - 5X = 6 - 10 \\ -4X = -4 \\ X = 1 \end{array} \right\} \quad \text{(solving for } X\text{)}$$

$$\left. \begin{array}{l} Y = 10 - 5X = 10 - 5(1) = 5 \\ Y = 6 - X = 6 - 1 = 5 \end{array} \right\} \quad \text{(substituting to find } Y\text{)}$$

There is something of an art involved in knowing when to solve for which variable and which equation should be substituted into which. Practice on the problems at the end of this chapter will improve your skills at seeing the easiest route to the solution.

ELIMINATION OF VARIABLES

The second method we shall present for the solution of sets of simultaneous equations is called elimination of variables. The basic idea here is to multiply both sides of one equation by a constant and add the result to another equation, causing one variable to have a zero coefficient and be eliminated from the resulting sum.

Consider these two equations from the second example of Figure 2.7.

$$5X + Y = 10$$
$$X + 5Y = 10$$

If we multiply the second equation by -5 and add it to the first equation, we will eliminate X.

$$
\begin{array}{ll}
5X + Y \quad = \quad 10 & \text{(first equation)} \\
-5X - 25Y = -50 & \text{(-5 times second equation)} \\
\hline
-24Y = -40 & \text{(new equation with X eliminated)} \\
\end{array}
$$

$$Y = \frac{-40}{-24} = \frac{5}{3} \qquad \text{(solving for Y)}$$

$$5X + \left(\frac{5}{3}\right) = 10 \qquad \text{(substituting into the first equation)}$$

$$5X = 10 - \frac{5}{3} = \frac{30 - 5}{3} = \frac{25}{3}$$

$$X = \frac{5}{3} \qquad \text{(solving for X)}$$

$$X + 5\left(\frac{5}{3}\right) = 10 \qquad \text{(substituting into the second equation)}$$

$$X = 10 - \frac{25}{3} = \frac{30 - 25}{3}$$

$$X = \frac{5}{3} \qquad \text{(solving for X)}$$

We could have chosen to eliminate Y by dividing the second equation by -5 and adding it to the first equation.

$$
\begin{array}{ll}
5X + Y = 10 & \text{(first equation)} \\
-\dfrac{1}{5}X - Y = -2 & \left(-\dfrac{1}{5} \text{ times the second equation}\right) \\
\hline
\dfrac{24}{5}X = 8 & \text{(new equation with Y eliminated)} \\
\end{array}
$$

$$X = 8\left(\frac{5}{24}\right) = \frac{40}{24} = \frac{5}{3} \qquad \text{(solving for X)}$$

$$5\left(\frac{5}{3}\right) + Y = 10 \qquad \text{(substituting into the first equation)}$$

$$Y = 10 - \frac{25}{3} = \frac{30 - 25}{3}$$

$$Y = \frac{5}{3} \qquad \text{(solving for } Y\text{)}$$

$$\frac{5}{3} + 5Y = 10 \qquad \text{(substituting into the second equation)}$$

$$5Y = 10 - \frac{5}{3} = \frac{30 - 5}{3}$$

$$Y = \frac{5}{3} \qquad \text{(solving for } Y\text{)}$$

As was the case with the substitution method, practice will improve your ability to decide which variable to eliminate and which equation to multiply to accomplish the desired result.

Other Methods

For larger sets of simultaneous equations, formalized solution models have been developed. One such method, called Gaussian elimination, systematically eliminates variables and solves each equation for a different variable. Another method, Cramer's rule, is based on the use of determinants. Both of these solution procedures are discussed in the sections that follow.

BASIC MATRIX CONCEPTS

We begin with a definition: A *matrix* is a *rectangular array* of *elements*, arranged in *rows* and *columns*. The individual elements of a matrix can be anything, such as the blocks on a map of a city or the cars in a parking garage, but for our purposes they will be mathematical symbols and will be either constants or unknowns. Thus, although all of the examples shown in Figure 2.8 are matrices, only those like (C), (D), and (E) will be of immediate concern to us.

By convention, we will call the lines of elements that are horizontal, *rows* and those that are vertical, *columns*. We will also adopt a convention in numbering the rows and columns and their elements: The rows are numbered sequentially from the top (first) to the bottom (last), and the row elements are numbered sequentially from the left to the right; the

$$
\begin{pmatrix}
\text{Car} & \text{House} & \text{Train} \\
\text{Truck} & \text{Church} & \text{Bus} \\
\text{Bicycle} & \text{Office} & \text{Boat} \\
\text{Skateboard} & \text{Store} & \text{Taxi}
\end{pmatrix}
\qquad
\begin{pmatrix}
\dfrac{\delta^2 W}{\delta X^2} & \dfrac{\delta^2 W}{\delta X \delta Y} & \dfrac{\delta^2 W}{\delta X \delta Z} \\[2mm]
\dfrac{\delta^2 W}{\delta Y \delta X} & \dfrac{\delta^2 W}{\delta Y^2} & \dfrac{\delta^2 Z}{\delta Y \delta Z} \\[2mm]
\dfrac{\delta^2 W}{\delta Z \delta X} & \dfrac{\delta^2 W}{\delta Z \delta Y} & \dfrac{\delta^2 W}{\delta Z^2}
\end{pmatrix}
$$

(A)   (B)

$$
\begin{pmatrix}
4 & 3 & -5 & 2 \\
7 & 0 & 1 & -2 \\
6 & -1 & 8 & -6
\end{pmatrix}
\qquad
(\tfrac{1}{4}, \ \tfrac{3}{8}, \ \tfrac{1}{2}, \ \tfrac{8}{3})
\qquad
\begin{pmatrix}
W \\ X \\ Y \\ Z
\end{pmatrix}
\qquad
\begin{pmatrix}
2X + 1 & Y - 3X \\
2Y + 1 & X + 7Y - 1
\end{pmatrix}
$$

(C)   (D)   (E)   (F)

Figure 2.8   Examples of matrices.

columns are numbered from left (first) to right (last), and the column elements are numbered from top to bottom.

We will stipulate that all matrices be identified by capital letters and that the individual elements of a matrix be identified by the corresponding lower-case letter, subscripted to indicate their location in the matrix. The first subscript refers to the *row* number, and the second to the *column* number. For example, a_{23} refers to the element of matrix A that is in the second row and third column—Bus. Similarly, a_{41} is Skateboard; a_{22} is Church; c_{32} is -1; f_{22} is $X + 7Y - 1$; d_{13} is $\tfrac{1}{2}$; e_{21} is X.

Summation Notation

When we wish to add several terms or elements together, we employ a shorthand that we call *summation notation*. The notation employs the Greek letter $\sum$ (an upper case S, for "summation") and one or more *indices*, each of which is permitted to assume a set of *integer values* from some *initial value* to a *final value*.

For example, if Z were the sum of the values X_1, X_2, X_3, X_4, and X_5, we would write

$$
Z = \sum_{i=1}^{5} X_i = X_1 + X_2 + X_3 + X_4 + X_5
$$

Below the $\sum$ we identify the index and its initial value; above the $\sum$ we specify the final value. To expand the summation, we write the expression to the right of the $\sum$, inserting the initial value of the index every place the index appears in the expression; then we repeat the expression, incrementing the index by 1. This is repeated until the index reaches its final value.

The following examples are illustrative of a few of the possible uses of summation notation.

$$D = \sum_{i=1}^{3} 4R^i = 4R^1 + 4R^2 + 4R^3 = 4 \sum_{i=1}^{3} R^i$$

$$P = \sum_{j=2}^{5} jQ_j = 2Q_2 + 3Q_3 + 4Q_4 + 5Q_5$$

$$T = \sum_{j=1}^{3} (2-j)M^{(j+1)} = (2-1)M^{(1+1)} + (2-2)M^{(2+1)}$$

$$+ (2-3)M^{(3+1)} = M^2 - M^4$$

Matrices and Summation Notation

Summation notation is frequently used in manipulation of matrices, most frequently using the index as one or both of the subscripts on the elements. For example, the sum of the first three elements of the second row of matrix A, which follows, could be expressed by

$$\sum_{j=1}^{3} a_{2j} = a_{21} + a_{22} + a_{23} = 3 - 1 + 2 = 4$$

The sum of all the elements in column 3 of B is

$$\sum_{i=1}^{4} b_{i3} = b_{13} + b_{23} + b_{33} + b_{43} = 3 + 3 - 2 + 2 = 6$$

The sum of the products of the corresponding elements of row 2 of A and column 3 of B (which will come in quite handy a bit later in our discussion) is

$$\sum_{k=1}^{4} a_{2k}b_{k3} = a_{21}b_{13} + a_{22}b_{23} + a_{23}b_{33} + a_{24}b_{43}$$

$$= (3)(3) + (-1)(3) + (2)(-2) + (3)(2) = 8$$

$$A = \begin{pmatrix} 1 & 2 & 1 & 0 \\ 3 & -1 & 2 & 3 \\ 1 & 0 & 2 & 3 \end{pmatrix} \qquad B = \begin{pmatrix} 2 & 1 & 3 & 0 & 3 \\ -1 & 2 & 3 & 2 & 1 \\ 4 & 1 & -2 & 1 & -3 \\ 1 & 0 & 2 & 3 & 2 \end{pmatrix}$$

Row and Column Matrices

Some authors devote a good deal of attention to treatment of two special cases of matrices, the *row matrix* and the *column matrix*. We chose not to do so, other than to explain that a matrix with only one row is called a row matrix (it may also be called a *row vector*) and that a matrix with only one column is called a column matrix (or a *column vector*). As they both obey all of the rules that larger matrices do, no special treatment is required. In Figure 2.8, D is a row matrix, and E is a column matrix.

The Order of a Matrix

One convenient way of classifying matrices is by defining the *order* of a matrix to be the number of rows and columns it has. We usually write the order of a matrix below the matrix as shown in Figure 2.9. It is important to note that the number of rows is always listed *first*, followed by the number of columns. Thus A is of order 4×2; B is a 2×5; D and E are a row vector of order 1×3 and a column vector of order 4×1, respectively; and C and F are *square* matrices of order 2×2 and 4×4.

$$
A = \begin{pmatrix} 2 & 7 \\ 3 & 6 \\ 1 & 5 \\ 4 & 0 \end{pmatrix} \qquad B = \begin{pmatrix} 1 & 3 & 2 & 4 & 7 \\ 3 & 1 & 4 & 2 & 1 \end{pmatrix} \qquad C = \begin{pmatrix} 2 & -1 \\ 4 & 2 \end{pmatrix}
$$
$$
\quad 4 \times 2 \qquad\qquad\qquad 2 \times 5 \qquad\qquad\qquad 2 \times 2
$$

$$
D = (6, \quad -1, \quad 4) \qquad E = \begin{pmatrix} W \\ X \\ Y \\ Z \end{pmatrix} \qquad F = \begin{pmatrix} 1 & 0 & 0 & 0 \\ 0 & 1 & 0 & 0 \\ 0 & 0 & 1 & 0 \\ 0 & 0 & 0 & 1 \end{pmatrix}
$$
$$
\qquad 1 \times 3 \qquad\qquad 4 \times 1 \qquad\qquad 4 \times 4
$$

$$
G = (1) \qquad H = \begin{pmatrix} 1 & 0 \\ 0 & 1 \end{pmatrix} \qquad I = \begin{pmatrix} 1 & 0 & 0 \\ 0 & 1 & 0 \\ 0 & 0 & 1 \end{pmatrix}
$$
$$
1 \times 1 \qquad\quad 2 \times 2 \qquad\qquad 3 \times 3
$$

Figure 2.9 The order of a matrix.

The Identity Matrix

One special matrix that we will single out for a brief mention now is the *identity matrix*. The identity matrix is really a family of matrices, all square (having the same number of rows as columns), with all elements on the principal diagonal (from the upper left corner to the lower right corner) being 1s and all other elements, zeros. The 1×1, 2×2, 3×3, and 4×4 identity matrices are shown as matrices G, H, I, and F, respectively, in Figure 2.9.

The Null Matrix

The *null* matrix has zero for all of its elements. It has the same function in matrix algebra as the zero in scalar algebra.

MATRIX ARITHMETIC AND MATRIX ALGEBRA

We will now turn our attention to four basic arithmetic operations: addition, subtraction, multiplication, and division. (Strictly speaking, division of matrices is not defined, but we will circumvent this difficulty by learning to multiply by the inverse of the matrix (A^{-1}), which will accomplish the same result as division.)

An understanding of these arithmetic operations will enable us to utilize the algebra of matrices in solving entire sets of algebraic equations simultaneously—an extremely powerful tool that we will incorporate into some of our optimization techniques in subsequent chapters.

Addition

In scalar addition, we learned that

$$a + b = c$$

Now we will add matrices—whole arrays of elements—all at once.

In order for us to add two (or more) matrices together, they must be *conformable for addition*. This awesome-sounding restriction simply means that all the matrices involved must be of the *same order*.

We first will state the general rule for matrix addition and then will demonstrate the rule by several examples. The rule is that if

$$A + B = C$$

then

$$a_{ij} + b_{ij} = c_{ij}$$

This means that we must perform R times K separate additions, where R is the number of rows and K is the number of columns in each of the matrices.

One convenient way of visualizing this process is shown in Figure 2.10. If A and B are suspended over C and their respective elements are lined up, each element of C is the sum of the corresponding elements of A and B.

As previously noted, the matrices need not be square, but all three must be of the *same* order. Additional examples of matrix addition are shown in Figure 2.10.

Subtraction

Matrix subtraction has the same conformability requirement as matrix addition: that both matrices and their difference matrix be of the same order. The general rule is that if

$$A - B = C$$

then

$$a_{ij} - b_{ij} = c_{ij}$$

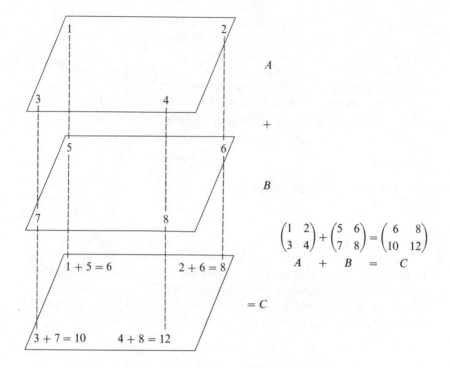

$$\begin{pmatrix} 1 & 2 \\ 3 & 4 \end{pmatrix} + \begin{pmatrix} 5 & 6 \\ 7 & 8 \end{pmatrix} = \begin{pmatrix} 6 & 8 \\ 10 & 12 \end{pmatrix}$$
$$A \quad + \quad B \quad = \quad C$$

$$\begin{pmatrix} 3 \\ 2 \\ 5 \end{pmatrix} + \begin{pmatrix} 1 \\ 2 \\ 4 \end{pmatrix} + \begin{pmatrix} 3 \\ 1 \\ 3 \end{pmatrix} = \begin{pmatrix} 7 \\ 5 \\ 12 \end{pmatrix}$$

$$\begin{pmatrix} X & W \\ Y & Z \\ R & L \end{pmatrix} + \begin{pmatrix} 2 & 5 \\ 1 & 3 \\ -2 & 4 \end{pmatrix} = \begin{pmatrix} X+2 & W+5 \\ Y+1 & Z+3 \\ R-2 & L+4 \end{pmatrix}$$

$$(2, 4, 5, 1) + (3, 2, -2, 4) = (5, 6, 3, 5)$$

$$\begin{pmatrix} 2 & 1 & 2 \\ 4 & 4 & -2 \\ 1 & 0 & 2 \\ -2 & 1 & 6 \end{pmatrix} + \begin{pmatrix} 4 & -2 & 1 \\ -1 & 2 & 3 \\ -4 & 2 & 4 \\ 1 & 0 & 2 \end{pmatrix} = \begin{pmatrix} 6 & -1 & 3 \\ 3 & 6 & 1 \\ -3 & 2 & 6 \\ -1 & 1 & 8 \end{pmatrix}$$

Figure 2.10 Matrix addition.

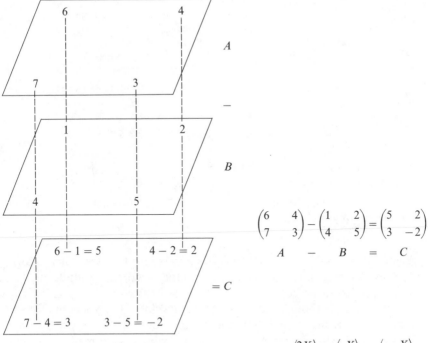

$$\begin{pmatrix} 6 & 4 \\ 7 & 3 \end{pmatrix} - \begin{pmatrix} 1 & 2 \\ 4 & 5 \end{pmatrix} = \begin{pmatrix} 5 & 2 \\ 3 & -2 \end{pmatrix}$$

$$A \quad - \quad B \quad = \quad C$$

$$(2, 1, 5) - (2, 3, -2) = (0, -2, 7)$$

$$\begin{pmatrix} 2X \\ 5Y \\ Z \end{pmatrix} - \begin{pmatrix} X \\ 2Y \\ 3Z \end{pmatrix} = \begin{pmatrix} X \\ 3Y \\ -2Z \end{pmatrix}$$

$$\begin{pmatrix} 2 & 2 & 1 \\ 3 & 1 & 1 \\ 2 & 0 & 1 \\ 4 & 0 & 2 \end{pmatrix} - \begin{pmatrix} 3 & 1 & 0 \\ 2 & 0 & 1 \\ 1 & 2 & 4 \\ 1 & 1 & 0 \end{pmatrix} = \begin{pmatrix} -1 & 1 & 1 \\ 1 & 1 & 0 \\ 1 & -2 & -3 \\ 3 & -1 & 2 \end{pmatrix}$$

$$(11X) - (4) = (11X - 4)$$

Figure 2.11 Matrix subtraction.

The procedure is shown and additional examples are presented in Figure 2.11.

The general rules for addition and subtraction of matrices can now be combined into a single rule as follows: If

$$A \pm B = C$$

then

$$a_{ij} \pm b_{ij} = c_{ij}$$

Applications of Matrix Addition and Subtraction

A simple example of a common usage of matrix addition and subtraction is given in Figure 2.12. On October 1, a new car dealer had on hand various quantities of four different models in five different colors. During

$$
\begin{array}{c}
\begin{array}{cccccc}
 & \text{Red} & \text{White} & \text{Blue} & \text{Yellow} & \text{Green}
\end{array}\\
\begin{array}{c}
\text{Sprint}\\
\text{Cobra}\\
\text{Flash}\\
\text{X-12}
\end{array}
\begin{pmatrix}
4 & 1 & 2 & 1 & 3\\
2 & 0 & 1 & 2 & 3\\
1 & 3 & 0 & 4 & 5\\
5 & 4 & 1 & 3 & 0
\end{pmatrix}\\
\text{October 1 Inventory}
\end{array}
+
\begin{array}{c}
\begin{array}{cccccc}
 & \text{R} & \text{W} & \text{B} & \text{Y} & \text{G}
\end{array}\\
\begin{array}{c}
\text{S}\\
\text{C}\\
\text{F}\\
\text{X}
\end{array}
\begin{pmatrix}
2 & 1 & 2 & 3 & 1\\
0 & 4 & 3 & 1 & 2\\
2 & 1 & 2 & 0 & 1\\
2 & 1 & 5 & 2 & 4
\end{pmatrix}\\
\text{October Deliveries}
\end{array}
$$

$$
-
\begin{array}{c}
\begin{array}{cccccc}
 & \text{R} & \text{W} & \text{B} & \text{Y} & \text{G}
\end{array}\\
\begin{array}{c}
\text{S}\\
\text{C}\\
\text{F}\\
\text{X}
\end{array}
\begin{pmatrix}
5 & 1 & 2 & 3 & 1\\
1 & 1 & 1 & 2 & 2\\
1 & 2 & 0 & 2 & 4\\
3 & 1 & 1 & 0 & 1
\end{pmatrix}\\
\text{October Sales}
\end{array}
=
\begin{array}{c}
\begin{array}{cccccc}
 & \text{R} & \text{W} & \text{B} & \text{Y} & \text{G}
\end{array}\\
\begin{array}{c}
\text{S}\\
\text{C}\\
\text{F}\\
\text{X}
\end{array}
\begin{pmatrix}
1 & 1 & 2 & 1 & 3\\
1 & 3 & 3 & 1 & 3\\
2 & 2 & 2 & 2 & 2\\
4 & 4 & 5 & 5 & 3
\end{pmatrix}\\
\text{November 1 Inventory}
\end{array}
$$

Figure 2.12   Inventory updating.

the month he sold 34 cars and took delivery on 39. He uses matrix addition and subtraction to update his inventory records, resulting in the November 1 status report.

With a little thought, it is possible to develop a fairly lengthy list of applications of matrix addition and subtraction. Several obvious areas are: updating customer accounts in banks (which is normally done by computer on a daily basis), updating tax records (frequently quarterly), inventory systems (such as that of our automobile dealer), tracking vital data on spacecraft, and monitoring the locations of enemy and allied war equipment.

Multiplication

Multiplication of a matrix by a scalar is a simple process, accomplished by multiplying *every* element of the matrix by the constant. For example

$$
\underset{\text{Scalar}}{3} \times \underset{2\times3}{\begin{pmatrix} 2 & 5 & 1\\ 4 & 4 & 3 \end{pmatrix}} = \underset{2\times3}{\begin{pmatrix} 6 & 15 & 3\\ 12 & 12 & 9 \end{pmatrix}}
$$

and

$$
\underset{\text{Scalar}}{-1} \times \underset{4\times2}{\begin{pmatrix} 1 & 2\\ -4 & 3\\ 1 & 7\\ 7 & -6 \end{pmatrix}} = \underset{4\times2}{\begin{pmatrix} -1 & -2\\ +4 & -3\\ -1 & -7\\ -7 & +6 \end{pmatrix}}
$$

This is quite different from matrix multiplication.

Multiplication of matrices is somewhat more complicated than matrix addition and subtraction. The conformability requirement for multiplication is that the number of *columns* in the *first* matrix equal the number of *rows* in the *second* matrix. The product matrix will have the same number of *rows* as the *first* matrix and the same number of *columns* as the *second* matrix. This is not nearly as difficult as it sounds, as is shown in Figure 2.13.

$$
\begin{array}{ccccc}
A & \times & B & = & C
\end{array}
$$

$$
\begin{pmatrix} 2 & 3 & 1 \\ 4 & 0 & 5 \end{pmatrix} \times \begin{pmatrix} 1 & 0 & 2 & 1 \\ 2 & 2 & 1 & 3 \\ 1 & 4 & 0 & 2 \end{pmatrix} = \begin{pmatrix} 9 & 10 & 7 & 13 \\ 9 & 20 & 8 & 14 \end{pmatrix}
$$

②×③ These must be equal. ③×④   ②×④

Number of rows in answer   Number of columns in answer
equals number of rows in A.   equals number of columns in B.

Figure 2.13   Conformability for multiplication.

We will begin with the general mathematical rule and then demonstrate the procedure with a more graphic approach. The rule may be stated as follows: If

$$A \times B = C$$

then

$$c_{ij} = \sum_{k=1}^{m} a_{ik} b_{kj}$$

For manual computation, the following procedure is much clearer. First, check for conformability (columns in A equal rows in B); then lightly circle each *row* of A and each *column* of B. To compute the element that is in the *first row* and the *first column* of C (element c_{11}), we must *multipladd* (multiply and add) the first row of A by the first column of B. This is done as follows.

$$
\begin{array}{ccccc}
A & \times & B & = & C
\end{array}
$$

$$
\begin{pmatrix} 2 & 1 & 2 \\ 1 & 3 & 0 \end{pmatrix} \times \begin{pmatrix} 1 & 0 \\ 1 & 1 \\ 2 & 4 \end{pmatrix} = \begin{pmatrix} 7 & 9 \\ 4 & 3 \end{pmatrix}
$$

$$
\begin{array}{ccc}
2 \times 3 & 3 \times 2 & 2 \times 2
\end{array}
$$

A's First Row B's First Column

$$
\begin{array}{ccccc}
2 & \times & 1 & = & 2 \\
1 & \times & 1 & = & 1 \\
2 & \times & 2 & = & 4 \\
& & & & \overline{7} = c_{11}
\end{array}
$$

To obtain the remaining elements in the product matrix, we multipladd the appropriate row of A by the appropriate column of B.

A's Second Row		B's First Column				A's First Row		B's Second Column		
1	$\times$	1	$=$	1		2	$\times$	0	$=$	0
3	$\times$	1	$=$	3		1	$\times$	1	$=$	1
0	$\times$	2	$=$	0		2	$\times$	4	$=$	8
				$\overline{4} = c_{21}$						$\overline{9} = c_{12}$

A's Second Row		B's Second Column		
1	$\times$	0	$=$	0
3	$\times$	1	$=$	3
0	$\times$	4	$=$	0
				$\overline{3} = c_{22}$

To generalize and summarize the procedure for matrix multiplication:

1. Check for conformability (A's columns equal B's rows).
2. Determine the order of the product matrix (same number of rows as A, same number of columns as B).
3. To calculate the element in C's row i, column j, multipladd A's ith row by B's jth column.

Note that the number of multiplications required for each element of C will be the conformability number (the number of columns in A; the number of rows in B).

Verify the following example for practice. (The second-row, second-column element has been highlighted.)

$$\begin{pmatrix} 1 & 0 \\ 1 & 1 \\ 2 & 4 \end{pmatrix} \times \left(\begin{pmatrix} 2 \\ 1 \end{pmatrix} \begin{pmatrix} 1 \\ 3 \end{pmatrix} \begin{pmatrix} 2 \\ 0 \end{pmatrix} \right) = \begin{pmatrix} 2 & 1 & 2 \\ 3 & 4 & 2 \\ 8 & 14 & 4 \end{pmatrix}$$

$$3 \times 2 \qquad 2 \times 3 \qquad 3 \times 3$$

You probably noticed that these are the same two matrices we used in the previous example, which illustrates the fact that in general

$$B \times A \neq A \times B$$

Two more examples are given below. For additional practice, we urge you to refer to the exercises at the end of the chapter.

$$
\begin{array}{ccc}
A & \times & B & = & C
\end{array}
$$

$$
\begin{pmatrix} ① \\ ② \\ ④ \\ ③ \end{pmatrix} \times \Big(⑤, ③, ②, -1 \Big) =
\begin{pmatrix}
5 & 3 & 2 & -1 \\
10 & 6 & 4 & -2 \\
20 & ⑫ & 8 & -4 \\
15 & 9 & 6 & -3
\end{pmatrix}
$$

$$
④\times① \qquad ①\times④ \qquad\qquad 4 \times 4
$$

$$
\begin{array}{ccccc}
B & \times & A & = & C
\end{array}
$$

$$
\Big(⑤, \quad 3, \quad 2, \quad -1 \Big) \times
\begin{pmatrix} ① \\ 2 \\ 4 \\ ③ \end{pmatrix} = (16)
$$

$$
1 \times ④ \qquad ④\times 1 \qquad 1 \times 1
$$

Applications of Matrix Multiplication

Matrix multiplication is a convenient method of representing a number of repetitive calculations in compact, convenient form. The following simple example from a grocery list illustrates a practical application. The total cost of 2 dozen eggs, 3 cans of soup, 6 green peppers, and 1 quart of milk, with unit prices of 79¢, 35¢, 20¢, and 89¢, respectively, can be represented as follows.

$$
(2, 3, 6, 1) \quad \times \begin{pmatrix} .79 \\ .35 \\ .20 \\ .89 \end{pmatrix} = (\$4.72)
$$

$$
\text{Number of Units} \quad \text{Prices} \quad \text{Total Cost}
$$

A firm makes three sizes of dog houses. Each size uses wood, paint, and labor in the quantities shown in the following matrix.

		Large	Medium	Small
	wood (m)	15	12	9
Unit requirements	paint (l)	4	3	2
	labor (hrs)	6	5	5

$$
\text{Demand} \qquad \text{Total requirements}
$$

$$
\times \begin{pmatrix} 3 \\ 5 \\ 7 \end{pmatrix} = \begin{pmatrix} 168 \\ 41 \\ 78 \end{pmatrix}
\begin{array}{l} \text{meters of wood} \\ \text{liters of paint} \\ \text{hours of labor} \end{array}
$$

They have orders for 3 large, 5 medium and 7 small units. Their total requirements of 168 linear meters of wood, 41 liters of paint, and 78 hours of labor can be determined by matrix multiplication.

In addition to direct applications of these sorts, we will find mathematical applications in the solution of systems of equations later in this chapter.

Division

Division of a matrix by a scalar is simply division of each element by the scalar. Thus

$$\underset{\text{Scalar}}{\tfrac{1}{3}} \times \underset{3 \times 2}{\begin{pmatrix} 2 & 1 \\ 0 & -4 \\ 3 & 5 \end{pmatrix}} = \underset{3 \times 2}{\begin{pmatrix} \frac{2}{3} & \frac{1}{3} \\ 0 & -\frac{3}{4} \\ \frac{3}{3} & \frac{5}{3} \end{pmatrix}}$$

and

$$\frac{\begin{pmatrix} 2 & 4 \\ 1 & 3 \end{pmatrix}}{12 \quad \text{(Scalar)}} = \begin{pmatrix} \frac{1}{6} & \frac{1}{3} \\ \frac{1}{12} & \frac{1}{4} \end{pmatrix}$$

Before we discuss division of matrices, it is necessary to fill in two pieces of background information.

1. The *identity matrix* (*I*), which we discussed earlier, serves the same function in matrix multiplication as the 1 does in scalar multiplication—any matrix multiplied by the appropriately sized identity matrix yields the same matrix we started with. For example

$$\underset{2 \times 2}{\begin{pmatrix} 1 & 0 \\ 0 & 1 \end{pmatrix}} \times \underset{2 \times 1}{\begin{pmatrix} 3 \\ -4 \end{pmatrix}} = \underset{2 \times 1}{\begin{pmatrix} 3 \\ -4 \end{pmatrix}}$$

$$\underset{4 \times 3}{\begin{pmatrix} 2 & 2 & 1 \\ -1 & 3 & -1 \\ 5 & 1 & 3 \\ 1 & 0 & 2 \end{pmatrix}} \underset{3 \times 3}{\begin{pmatrix} 1 & 0 & 0 \\ 0 & 1 & 0 \\ 0 & 0 & 1 \end{pmatrix}} = \underset{4 \times 3}{\begin{pmatrix} 2 & 2 & 1 \\ -1 & 3 & -1 \\ 5 & 1 & 3 \\ 1 & 0 & 2 \end{pmatrix}}$$

2. For every square matrix (except *singular* matrices, which will be discussed later in the section on determinants) there exists another square matrix of the same order, called the *inverse* (A^{-1}), which has the property that when it is multiplied by the original matrix, the product is an identity matrix. For example

$$\begin{pmatrix} 2 & 1 \\ 3 & 4 \end{pmatrix} \begin{pmatrix} \frac{4}{5} & -\frac{1}{5} \\ -\frac{3}{5} & \frac{2}{5} \end{pmatrix} = \begin{pmatrix} 1 & 0 \\ 0 & 1 \end{pmatrix}$$

$$\quad A \qquad \times \qquad A^{-1} \qquad = \qquad I$$

$$\begin{pmatrix} 1 & -\frac{1}{2} & 0 \\ 4 & -\frac{3}{2} & -2 \\ -2 & 1 & 1 \end{pmatrix} \times \begin{pmatrix} 1 \\ 0 \\ 2 \end{pmatrix} \begin{pmatrix} 1 \\ 2 \\ 0 \end{pmatrix} \begin{pmatrix} 2 \\ 4 \\ 1 \end{pmatrix} = \begin{pmatrix} 1 & 0 & 0 \\ 0 & 1 & 0 \\ 0 & 0 & 1 \end{pmatrix}$$

$$\quad A^{-1} \qquad \times \qquad A \qquad = \qquad I$$

As we mentioned at the beginning of this section, division by matrices is not, strictly speaking, possible. It is possible, however, to obtain the desired result by *multiplying by the inverse* of the matrix in question. This process is best described by referring to the corresponding scalar operation and notation.

Scalar Notation	*Matrix Notation*

If

$$ax = b,$$

then

$$\frac{a}{a}x = \frac{b}{a},$$

or

$$a^{-1}ax = a^{-1}b.$$

Since

$$a^{-1}a = 1,$$
$$1x = a^{-1}b,$$

or

$$x = a^{-1}b.$$

If

$$AX = B,$$

then

$$A^{-1}AX = A^{-1}B.$$

Since

$$A^{-1}A = I,$$

$$IX = A^{-1}B,$$

or

$$X = A^{-1}B.$$

Note that in scalar notation, dividing by a is the same as multiplying by a^{-1}, because a^{-n} is another way of expressing $1/a^n$. In matrix notation, instead of *dividing* both sides of the equation by A, we simply *multiply* both sides by A^{-1}, which yields the desired result.

Unfortunately, generating the inverse matrix is not a trivial matter, as it is in the scalar format. There are two widely used methods for finding the inverse: (1) the method of *Gaussian elimination* (sometimes called Gaussian reduction), named for the Dutch mathematician Gauss, and (2) the method involving the *adjoint*. The Gaussian method is probably the most useful because it forms the basis for the SIMPLEX technique in linear programming and is much less complicated, especially for large matrices.

Finding the Inverse by the Method of Gaussian Elimination

The Gaussian method can be generalized as follows. If we begin with a partitioned matrix comprising the matrix A and an identity matrix of the same order, and utilize simple row operations to convert the A matrix into an identity matrix, the original identity matrix will be converted into the inverse of A. We can represent this transformation by

$$(A\,|\,I) \rightarrow (I\,|\,A^{-1})$$

There are only two steps in the procedure, but each must be repeated several times. The steps in generating the kth tableau (or matrix) are

Step 1 Divide row k by a_{kk}. This becomes the *key row* of the kth tableau. (This step is done only once for each new tableau, for a total of N times, where A is of order $N \times N$.)

Step 2 For each other row ($i \neq k$), multiply the key row by $-a_{ik}$. Add this multiple to the old ith row to form the new ith row. (This step is repeated $N - 1$ times, once for each row other than the key row, in each tableau. As there are N tableaux, it is applied a total of $N(N - 1)$ times.)

We will demonstrate the steps with an example. Because we will be finding the inverse of a 3×3 matrix, step 1 will be applied three times (once for each new tableau), and step 2 will be applied twice ($N - 1$ times) at *each* tableau.

This is the initial tableau. We number it 0.

$$\begin{pmatrix} ② & 0 & 1 & | & 1 & 0 & 0 \\ \boxed{1} & 1 & 1 & | & 0 & 1 & 0 \\ \boxed{2} & 1 & 2 & | & 0 & 0 & 1 \end{pmatrix}^0$$

To generate tableau I:

Step 1 Divide row 1 by a_{11} (2, circle in tableau 0). This becomes the key row and gives us the 1 we need in the first column of what is to become our identity matrix.

$$\xrightarrow{\text{Key Row}} \begin{pmatrix} 1 & 0 & \frac{1}{2} & | & \frac{1}{2} & 0 & 0 \end{pmatrix}^{\mathrm{I}}$$

Step 2a   Multiply the key row by $-a_{21}$ (-1, box in tableau 0) to get $(-1\ 0\ -\frac{1}{2}\ |\ -\frac{1}{2}\ 0)$. Add to the old second row to get the new second row.

$$\xrightarrow{\text{Key Row}}\ \begin{pmatrix} 1 & 0 & \frac{1}{2} & \Big| & \frac{1}{2} & 0 & 0 \\ 0 & 1 & \frac{1}{2} & \Big| & -\frac{1}{2} & 1 & 0 \end{pmatrix}^{\text{I}}$$

Step 2b   Multiply the key row by $-a_{31}$ (-2, box in tableau 0) to get $(-2\ 0\ -1\ |\ -1\ 0\ 0)$. Add this to the old third row to get the new third row.

$$\xrightarrow{\text{Key Row}}\ \begin{pmatrix} 1 & \boxed{0} & \frac{1}{2} & \Big| & \frac{1}{2} & 0 & 0 \\ 0 & \textcircled{1} & \frac{1}{2} & \Big| & -\frac{1}{2} & 1 & 0 \\ 0 & \boxed{1} & 1 & \Big| & -1 & 0 & 1 \end{pmatrix}^{\text{I}}$$

Steps 2a and 2b give us the 0's we need in the first column of an identity matrix.

To generate tableau II:

Step 1   Divide row 2 by a_{22} (1, circle in tableau I). This becomes the key row and gives us the 1 in column 2.

$$\xrightarrow{\text{Key Row}}\ \begin{pmatrix} 0 & 1 & \frac{1}{2} & \Big| & -\frac{1}{2} & 1 & 0 \end{pmatrix}^{\text{II}}$$

Step 2a   Multiply the key row by $-a_{12}$ (-0, box in tableau I) and add to the old first row. (As we already have the 0 in the second column, this is unnecessary. Just repeat row 1.)

$$\xrightarrow{\text{Key Row}}\ \begin{pmatrix} 1 & 0 & \frac{1}{2} & \Big| & \frac{1}{2} & 0 & 0 \\ 0 & 1 & \frac{1}{2} & \Big| & -\frac{1}{2} & 1 & 0 \end{pmatrix}^{\text{II}}$$

Step 2b   Multiply the key row by $-a_{32}$ (-1, box in tableau I) to get $(0\ -1\ -\frac{1}{2}\ |\ \frac{1}{2}\ -1\ 0)$.
Add to the old third row to get the new third row. This gives us the remaining 0 in column 2.

$$\xrightarrow{\text{Key Row}}\ \begin{pmatrix} 1 & 0 & \boxed{\frac{1}{2}} & \Big| & \frac{1}{2} & 0 & 0 \\ 0 & 1 & \boxed{\frac{1}{2}} & \Big| & -\frac{1}{2} & 1 & 0 \\ 0 & 0 & \textcircled{\tfrac{1}{2}} & \Big| & -\frac{1}{2} & -1 & 1 \end{pmatrix}^{\text{II}}$$

To generate tableau III:

Step 1   Divide row 3 by a_{33} ($\frac{1}{2}$, circle in tableau II) to obtain the 1 in column 3. This becomes the key row.

$$\xrightarrow{\text{Key Row}}\ (0\quad 0\quad 1\ |\ -1\quad -2\quad 2)^{\text{III}}$$

Step 2a Multiply the key row by $-a_{13}$ ($-\frac{1}{2}$, box in tableau II) to get $(0\ 0\ -\frac{1}{2}|\frac{1}{2}\ 1\ -1)$.

Add to the old first row to obtain the new first row.

$$\underrightarrow{\text{Key Row}}\begin{pmatrix}1 & 0 & 0 & | & 1 & 1 & -1 \\ 0 & 0 & 1 & | & -1 & -2 & 2\end{pmatrix}^{\text{III}}$$

Step 2b Multiply the key row by $-a_{23}$ ($-\frac{1}{2}$, box in tableau II) to get $(0\ 0\ -\frac{1}{2}|\frac{1}{2}\ 1\ -1)$.

Add to the old second row to obtain the new second row. We have an identity matrix on the left, so the inverse of A is on the right.

$$\underrightarrow{\text{Key Row}}\begin{pmatrix}1 & 0 & 0 & | & 1 & 1 & -1 \\ 0 & 1 & 0 & | & 0 & 2 & -1 \\ 0 & 0 & 1 & | & -1 & -2 & 2\end{pmatrix}^{\text{III}}$$
$$\qquad\quad I \qquad\qquad\quad A^{-1}$$

To check our result, we multiply A by A^{-1} to assure that their product is I. We encourage you to multiply in the reverse direction ($A^{-1}A = I$) for practice.

$$\begin{pmatrix}2 & 0 & 1 \\ 1 & 1 & 1 \\ 2 & 1 & 2\end{pmatrix} \times \begin{pmatrix}1 \\ 0 \\ -1\end{pmatrix}\begin{pmatrix}1 \\ 2 \\ -2\end{pmatrix}\begin{pmatrix}-1 \\ -1 \\ 2\end{pmatrix} = \begin{pmatrix}1 & 0 & 0 \\ 0 & 1 & 0 \\ 0 & 0 & 1\end{pmatrix}$$
$$\quad A \qquad\qquad\qquad A^{-1} \qquad\qquad = \qquad I$$

The Gaussian method is not the only method for finding the inverse of a matrix, but for matrices of order 3×3 and larger, it is by far the least difficult computationally. Refer to the texts suggested in the bibliography (Appendix F) for a description of the adjoint method of matrix inversion.

Application of Matrix Division (Use of the Inverse)

One direct application we will have for the Gaussian method of finding the inverse is the simplex algorithm of linear programming, discussed in Chapter 5. If the inverse of a matrix is known, it may be used to solve sets of simultaneous equations. But before we solve any such problems, we must establish the relationship between scalar and matrix notation for the description of sets of linear equations.

Consider the set of three simultaneous linear equations shown in Figure 2.14. Note that as we perform the matrix multiplication, indicated on the left, we generate the three scalar equations on the right. The matrix A comprises the coefficients of the unknowns on the left-hand

Matrix Form	Scalar Form

$$\begin{pmatrix} 3 & 4 \\ 1 & 2 \end{pmatrix} \times \left(\begin{pmatrix} X_1 \\ X_2 \end{pmatrix} \right) = \begin{pmatrix} 4 \\ 0 \end{pmatrix} \Big\} \qquad \left\{ \begin{aligned} \overline{3X_1 + 4X_2 = 4} \\ X_1 + 2X_2 = 0 \end{aligned} \right.$$

$$\quad A \quad \times \quad X \ = \ B$$

$$\begin{pmatrix} 2 & 0 & 1 \\ 1 & 1 & 1 \\ 2 & 1 & 2 \end{pmatrix} \times \left(\begin{pmatrix} X_1 \\ X_2 \\ X_3 \end{pmatrix} = \begin{pmatrix} 1 \\ 0 \\ -1 \end{pmatrix} \right) \Big\} \qquad \left\{ \begin{aligned} 2X_1 + 0X_2 + X_3 &= 1 \\ X_1 + X_2 + X_3 &= 0 \\ 2X_1 + X_2 + 2X_3 &= -1 \end{aligned} \right.$$

$$\quad A \quad \times \quad X \ = \ B$$

Figure 2.14   Matrix and scalar forms of sets of linear equations.

side of the scalar form. Each row represents an equation, and each column contains the coefficients of one variable. The column matrix X consists of the unknowns, listed in the order they appear in the equations. Matrix B is a column matrix of the right-hand side values, just as they appear in the scalar form.

The two forms of representation are completely equivalent, and each may be substituted for the other at any time. We will find it useful from time to time to switch from one form to the other to clarify certain points

If we have a set of simultaneous linear equations such as those in Figure 2.14, then we can use the inverse of matrix A (if A^{-1} exists) to solve for the values of X_1, X_2, and X_3. (Note that the 3×3 matrix is the same one we used in our example of the Gaussian inverse method.)

If

$$AX = B$$

then

$$X = A^{-1}B$$

$$\quad A^{-1} \qquad \times \quad B \ = \ X$$

$$\begin{pmatrix} 1 & -2 \\ -\frac{1}{2} & \frac{3}{2} \end{pmatrix} \times \left(\begin{pmatrix} 4 \\ 0 \end{pmatrix} \right) = \begin{pmatrix} 4 \\ -2 \end{pmatrix} \qquad \begin{aligned} X_1 &= 4 \\ X_2 &= -2 \end{aligned}$$

$$\begin{pmatrix} 1 & 1 & -1 \\ 0 & 2 & -1 \\ -1 & -2 & 2 \end{pmatrix} \times \left(\begin{pmatrix} 1 \\ 0 \\ -1 \end{pmatrix} \right) = \begin{pmatrix} 2 \\ 1 \\ -3 \end{pmatrix} \qquad \begin{aligned} X_1 &= 2 \\ X_2 &= 1 \\ X_3 &= -3 \end{aligned}$$

One extremely powerful use of the inverse is to solve repetitive problems that have the same set of equations (and hence the same inverse) but several different sets of right-hand side values. The solution of two additional problems using the same inverse follows.

$$2X_1 + 0X_2 + X_3 = 4 \qquad \begin{pmatrix} 1 & 1 & -1 \\ 0 & 2 & -1 \\ -1 & -2 & 2 \end{pmatrix} \times \begin{pmatrix} 4 \\ 8 \\ 11 \end{pmatrix} = \begin{pmatrix} 1 \\ 5 \\ 2 \end{pmatrix}$$
$$X_1 + X_2 + X_3 = 8$$
$$2X_1 + X_2 + 2X_3 = 11$$

Scalar Form $\qquad\qquad A^{-1} \qquad \times \quad B \;=\; X$

$$\begin{pmatrix} 2 & 0 & 1 \\ 1 & 1 & 1 \\ 2 & 1 & 2 \end{pmatrix} \times \begin{pmatrix} X_1 \\ X_2 \\ X_3 \end{pmatrix} = \begin{pmatrix} 2 \\ 6 \\ 8 \end{pmatrix} \qquad \begin{pmatrix} 1 & 1 & -1 \\ 0 & 2 & -1 \\ -1 & -2 & 2 \end{pmatrix} \times \begin{pmatrix} 2 \\ 6 \\ 8 \end{pmatrix} = \begin{pmatrix} 0 \\ 4 \\ 2 \end{pmatrix}$$

Matrix Form $\qquad\qquad\qquad A^{-1} \qquad \times \quad B \;=\; X$

DETERMINANTS

Every square matrix has associated with it a scalar quantity or a numerical value called its *determinant*, denoted by det A or $\|A\|$. (Some authors use the symbol $|A|$, but to avoid any possible confusion with the absolute value symbol $|a|$, we will adopt the double-bar notation.)

The Value of a Determinant

The value of a 1×1 determinant is the value of its element. For example,

$$\text{if} \quad A = (-4), \|A\| = \|-4\| = -4$$
$$\text{if} \quad B = (+\tfrac{1}{3}), \|B\| = \|+\tfrac{1}{3}\| = +\tfrac{1}{3}$$

To evaluate a 2×2 determinant, we use what we call the "criss–cross" method. The method consists of three steps:

Step 1 Multiply the two elements on the major diagonal. This product is "criss."

Step 2 Multiply the two elements on the minor diagonal. This product is "cross."

Step 3 The value of the determinant is formed by subtracting "cross" from "criss." ($V = $ criss $-$ cross.)

This process is illustrated in the examples shown in Figure 2.15.

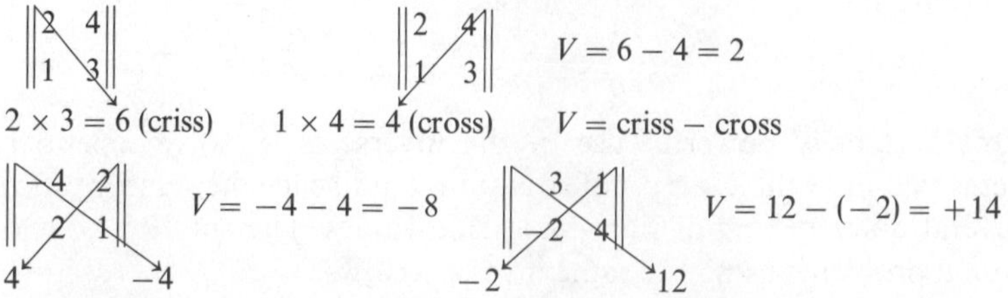

Figure 2.15 The criss-cross method of evaluting a 2×2 determinant.

To evaluate a 3×3 determinant, we expand the idea of the criss–cross.

Step 1   Repeat columns 1 and 2 to the right of the determinant.

Step 2   Multiply all three numbers on the main diagonal together. Move one element to the right and repeat. Move one more element to the right and repeat. The sum of these three products is criss.

Step 3   Multiply all three elements on the minor diagonal together. Move one element to the right and repeat. Move one more to the right and repeat. The sum of these three products is cross.

Step 4   The value of the determinant is criss − cross ($V = $ criss − cross).

This process is summarized and additional examples are shown in Figure 2.16.

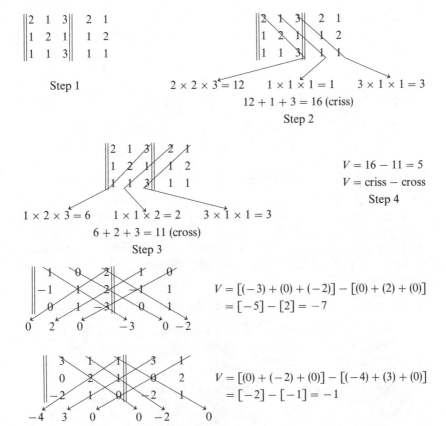

Figure 2.16   The criss-cross method of evaluating 3×3 determinants.

Singular Matrices

A matrix whose determinant has a value of zero is called a *singular matrix*. One of the important features of a singular matrix is that its inverse does not exist. Therefore, division by a singular matrix (multiplication by its inverse), like division by a scalar zero, is not defined.

A Shortcut for Finding the Inverse of a 2 × 2 Matrix

To obtain the inverse of a 2 × 2 matrix:

1. Reverse the *positions* of the elements on the major diagonal.
2. Reverse the *signs* of the elements on the minor diagonal.
3. Divide every element by the value of the determinant of A.

For example, if

$$A = \begin{pmatrix} 3 & 1 \\ 4 & 2 \end{pmatrix}$$

then

$$A^{-1} = \frac{\begin{pmatrix} 2 & -1 \\ -4 & 3 \end{pmatrix}}{\begin{Vmatrix} 3 & 1 \\ 4 & 2 \end{Vmatrix}} = \frac{\begin{pmatrix} 2 & -1 \\ -4 & 3 \end{pmatrix}}{2} = \begin{pmatrix} 1 & -\frac{1}{2} \\ -2 & \frac{3}{2} \end{pmatrix}$$

Check:

$$\underset{A}{\begin{pmatrix} 3 & 1 \\ 4 & 2 \end{pmatrix}} \underset{A^{-1}}{\begin{pmatrix} 1 & -\frac{1}{2} \\ -2 & \frac{3}{2} \end{pmatrix}} = \underset{I}{\begin{pmatrix} 1 & 0 \\ 0 & 1 \end{pmatrix}}$$

Evaluating 4 × 4 and Larger Determinants

Unfortunately, there are no criss-cross methods available for evaluating 4 × 4 and larger determinants. Other methods for their evaluation do exist, but they are rather complicated and will not be treated here. The more advanced texts listed in Appendix F contain discussion of these methods, usually called "expansion of a determinant" about a row or column.

Solving Systems of Equations with Determinants (Cramer's Rule)

The solution of a set of simultaneous linear equations can be obtained by dividing the values of two determinants. The steps in the procedure are as follows:

Step 1 Write the system of equations in matrix form.

Step 2 To solve for a particular variable, set up a numerator determinant by replacing that variable's column in matrix A by the column B. Evaluate this determinant.

Step 3   Divide the value from Step 2 by the value of A's determinant.

Step 4   Repeat Steps 2 and 3 for each variable.

Follow through these steps in the 2×2 and 3×3 systems shown in Figure 2.17. These are the same systems of equations we solved by using the inverse. The results can be verified by substituting the values into the scalar equations.

$$\begin{pmatrix} 3 & 4 \\ 1 & 2 \end{pmatrix} \times \begin{pmatrix} X_1 \\ X_2 \end{pmatrix} = \begin{pmatrix} 4 \\ 0 \end{pmatrix}$$

$$A \quad \times \quad X \ = \ B$$

$$X_1 = \frac{\begin{Vmatrix} 4 & 4 \\ 0 & 2 \end{Vmatrix}}{\begin{Vmatrix} 3 & 4 \\ 1 & 2 \end{Vmatrix}} = \frac{8}{2} = 4$$

$$X_2 = \frac{\begin{Vmatrix} 3 & 4 \\ 1 & 0 \end{Vmatrix}}{\begin{Vmatrix} 3 & 4 \\ 1 & 2 \end{Vmatrix}} = \frac{-4}{2} = -2$$

$$\begin{pmatrix} 2 & 0 & 1 \\ 1 & 1 & 1 \\ 2 & 1 & 2 \end{pmatrix} \times \begin{pmatrix} X_1 \\ X_2 \\ X_3 \end{pmatrix} = \begin{pmatrix} 1 \\ 0 \\ -1 \end{pmatrix}$$

$$A \quad \times \quad X \ = \ B$$

$$X_1 = \frac{\begin{Vmatrix} 1 & 0 & 1 \\ 0 & 1 & 1 \\ -1 & 1 & 2 \end{Vmatrix}}{\begin{Vmatrix} 2 & 0 & 1 \\ 1 & 1 & 1 \\ 2 & 1 & 2 \end{Vmatrix}} = \frac{2}{1} = 2$$

$$X_2 = \frac{\begin{Vmatrix} 2 & 1 & 1 \\ 1 & 0 & 1 \\ 2 & -1 & 2 \end{Vmatrix}}{\begin{Vmatrix} A \end{Vmatrix}} = \frac{1}{1} = 1 \qquad X_3 = \frac{\begin{Vmatrix} 2 & 0 & 1 \\ 1 & 1 & 0 \\ 2 & 1 & -1 \end{Vmatrix}}{\begin{Vmatrix} A \end{Vmatrix}} = \frac{-3}{1} = -3$$

Figure 2.17   Solution of systems of equations by determinants (Cramer's rule).

The Transpose of a Matrix

It is sometimes useful to interchange the rows and columns of a matrix by a procedure called *transposing the matrix*. Every matrix has a *transpose* (denoted by A^T), which is obtained by writing each row of the original matrix as a column, with the same column number as the old row number. An alternate procedure is to write the columns of the original matrix as rows in the transpose matrix. The order of the transpose is always reversed from that of the original matrix. As was the case with the inverse, the transpose of the transpose is the original matrix. That is, $(A^T)^T = A$, just as $(A^{-1})^{-1} = A$. Examples of transposes are shown in Figure 2.18.

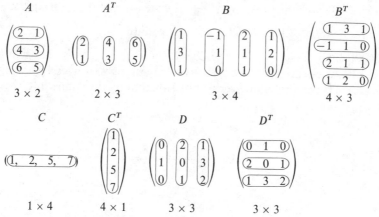

Figure 2.18   The transpose of a matrix.

THE QUADRATIC FORMULA

We often find it useful to determine the location(s) at which a function crosses the horizontal axis (the X intercepts). In linear equations this is easily accomplished by setting the dependent variable equal to zero and solving for the independent variable. For example, if we wish to find the X intercept of

$$Y = 15 - 5X$$

we set $Y = 0$ and solve

$$0 = 15 - 5X$$

for X to obtain

$$X = 3$$

The second-order (or quadratic) function's X intercepts, called the *roots* of the equation (presumably because they represent the points where the function "touches ground"), are more difficult to obtain. The general form of the equation is

$$Y = aX^2 + bX + c$$

and when $Y = 0$, we have

$$0 = aX^2 + bX + c$$

Because we encounter this function quite frequently, its solution has been derived in a general form, called the *quadratic formula*. The roots of

$$0 = aX^2 + bX + c$$

are found at the points

$$X = \frac{-b \pm \sqrt{b^2 - 4ac}}{2a}$$

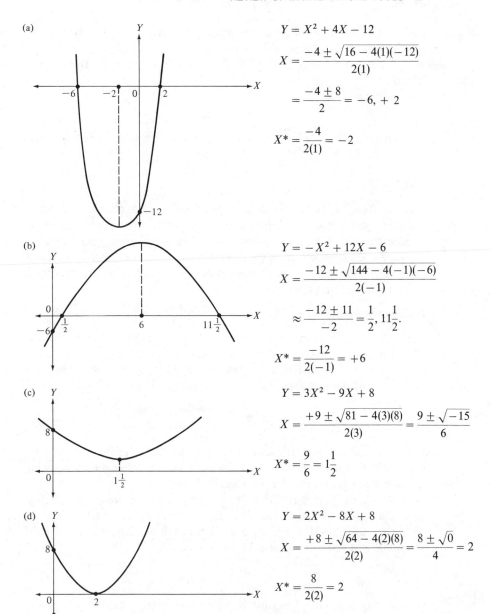

(a)

$$Y = X^2 + 4X - 12$$

$$X = \frac{-4 \pm \sqrt{16 - 4(1)(-12)}}{2(1)}$$

$$= \frac{-4 \pm 8}{2} = -6, +2$$

$$X^* = \frac{-4}{2(1)} = -2$$

(b)

$$Y = -X^2 + 12X - 6$$

$$X = \frac{-12 \pm \sqrt{144 - 4(-1)(-6)}}{2(-1)}$$

$$\approx \frac{-12 \pm 11}{-2} = \frac{1}{2}, 11\frac{1}{2}.$$

$$X^* = \frac{-12}{2(-1)} = +6$$

(c)

$$Y = 3X^2 - 9X + 8$$

$$X = \frac{+9 \pm \sqrt{81 - 4(3)(8)}}{2(3)} = \frac{9 \pm \sqrt{-15}}{6}$$

$$X^* = \frac{9}{6} = 1\frac{1}{2}$$

(d)

$$Y = 2X^2 - 8X + 8$$

$$X = \frac{+8 \pm \sqrt{64 - 4(2)(8)}}{2(2)} = \frac{8 \pm \sqrt{0}}{4} = 2$$

$$X^* = \frac{8}{2(2)} = 2$$

Figure 2.19   Examples of the use of the quadratic formula.

Four examples of the use of the formula are shown in Figure 2.19. The curve in (a) has roots at $X = -6$ and $+2$; in (b) the roots are approximately $X = \frac{1}{2}$ and $11\frac{1}{2}$; (c) has no roots at all (never touches the horizontal axis) because the expression under the radical ($b^2 - 4ac$) is negative, and we cannot take the square root of a negative number; (d) has only one root, at $X = 2$, because $b^2 - 4ac = 0$.

Note that in each case the highest or lowest point on the curve is found at

$$X^* = \frac{-b}{2a}$$

These points, called *maxima* and *minima*, are discussed in more detail in Chapter 9, "Classical Optimization."

PROBABILITY

Most students of business administration will take a course in business statistics, including probability, which is separate from the management science course. There are, however, some statistical concepts required in our study of management science. This section is not intended to replace the study of probability in the statistics course, but it should provide a quick review of some essential concepts.

Definitions

We will use four definitions of the probability that event A will occur. The first is the *a priori* definition, for use when the physical symmetry of the trial makes each of N outcomes equally likely ($P = 1/N$). If event A includes n of the possible outcomes, the probability of A is

$$P(A) = \frac{n}{N}$$

The *a priori* definition can be used to determine probabilities *before* any trials. Examples are tossing a fair coin, rolling a fair die, or drawing a number or card from a hat or a shuffled deck.

We will call the second definition the *frequency theory* of probability. If we do not know the probability, we can have repeated trials and observe the outcomes. If event A occurs S times in N trials, we estimate the probability of A on the next trial by

$$P(A) = \frac{S}{N}$$

We use this approach when faced with a bent coin, a loaded die, or any experiment where the outcomes are not known beforehand.

Note that if after 100 tosses of a bent coin we have 60 heads and 40 tails, we would estimate $P(H) = \frac{60}{100} = .6$. But our estimate will change after every toss. For example, after the next toss, our estimate of $P(H)$ will be either $\frac{61}{101}$ or $\frac{60}{101}$, neither of which equals $\frac{60}{100}$.

The third definition is a theoretical refinement of the frequency theory. It states that the frequency theory gives only an *estimate* of the true probability; if it is extended sufficiently it approaches as a limit the *true value*. Mathematically

$$P(A) = \lim_{N \to \infty} \left(\frac{S}{N}\right)$$

The final concept of probability is *subjective probability*, which is the *best estimate* in the opinion of the individual decision maker after considering what (if any) evidence is at hand. This "gut feel" approach must be employed when objective data are scarce or when different sources of information are in conflict.

Probability Trees

Sometimes the event we wish to describe has more than one element of chance outcome. For example, if we roll a die on a chessboard, the outcomes are a combination of the number on the die and the color of the square on which it lands. To obtain the probabilities of these combinations we might wish to employ *probability trees*, such as those shown in Figure 2.20.

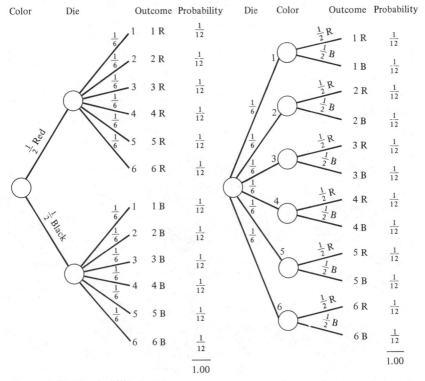

Figure 2.20 Probability trees.

The two trees are equivalent, because our outcomes involve both the die and the color. The probabilities of the outcomes are the products of the probabilities of these two branches.

Venn Diagrams

Another useful way of visualizing the outcome of an experiment is the Venn diagram. It provides a graphic display of the relationships among the various outcomes and their probabilities.

A display of all possible outcomes and their probabilities is called a *sample space*, and the sample space for our die and chessboard experiment is shown in Figure 2.21. In this case we know *a priori* that each of the outcomes is equally likely, and because there are 12 outcomes, each has a probability of $\frac{1}{12}$.

R1 $(\frac{1}{12})$	R2 $(\frac{1}{12})$	R3 $(\frac{1}{12})$
R4 $(\frac{1}{12})$	R5 $(\frac{1}{12})$	R6 $(\frac{1}{12})$
B1 $(\frac{1}{12})$	B2 $(\frac{1}{12})$	B3 $(\frac{1}{12})$
B4 $(\frac{1}{12})$	B5 $(\frac{1}{12})$	B6 $(\frac{1}{12})$

Figure 2.21 A sample space.

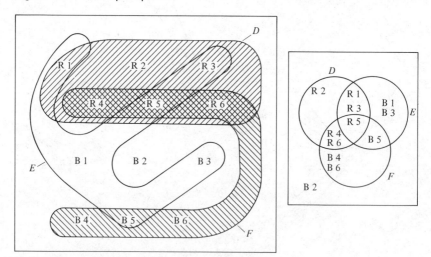

Figure 2.22 Venn diagrams.

A *simple event* is the simplest outcome of a trial. A *compound event* is a combination of two or more simple events. If compound event D is "all outcomes with red squares," event E is "all outcomes with odd numbers," and event F is "all outcomes with numbers 4 or larger," we convert the sample space into a Venn diagram by encircling all the outcomes included in each of the compound events, as shown in Figure 2.22. The left-hand diagram arranges the sample space and makes the Venn figure conform; the right-hand one begins with the Venn circles and moves the sample outcomes to conform.

We can utilize the Venn diagram to discuss concepts such as the probability of D and E (outcomes R1, R3, and R5), D or F (R1, R2, R3, R4, R5, R6, B4, B5, and B6), and *not D* or E or F (only B2). We will use this approach in developing the probability rules in the next section.

Probability Rules

We will review two main rules of probability and two special cases that will be useful in our study in later sections of the text.

THE "AND" RULE

$$P(A \text{ and } B) = P(A) \cdot P(B|A) = P(B \text{ and } A) = P(B) \cdot P(A|B)$$

The probability of A and B is the probability of A times the probability of B *given* A. This is equal to the probability of B and A, which is the probability of B times the probability of A given B. $P(B|A)$ is called the *conditional probability* of B given A. Another symbol with the same meaning as $P(A \text{ and } B)$ is $P(A \cap B)$, which is read "A cap B" or "A intersection B." It is easy to visualize the intersection using the Venn diagram, because the outcome in the area common to both A and B is their intersection. The intersection is also sometimes called the joint probability of A and B. In Figure 2.23 the probability of A is 50/100; the probability of B is 70/100; the probability of $B|A$ is 20/50; the probability of $A|B$ is

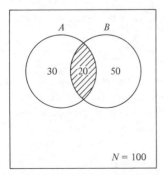

Figure 2.23   *A intersection B.*

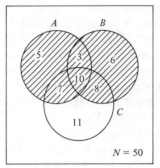

Figure 2.24 *A union B.*

20/70; and the probability of *A* and *B* (or *B* and *A*) is

$$P(A \cap B) = P(A) \cdot P(B|A) = (50/100)(20/50) = 20/100$$
$$P(B \cap A) = P(B) \cdot P(A|B) = (70/100)(20/70) = 20/100$$

THE "OR" RULE

$$P(A \text{ or } B) = P(A) + P(B) - P(A \text{ and } B)$$

The probability of *A* or *B* (or both) is the probability of *A* *plus* the probability of *B* *minus* their joint probability. Another symbol with the same meaning as $P(A \text{ or } B)$ is $P(A \cup B)$, which is read "*A* cup *B*" or "*A* union *B*." In terms of the Venn diagram, we simply add all areas covered by either *A* or *B*. The reason we subtract the intersection is that it has been counted *twice*; once as part of *A* and once as part of *B*. In Figure 2.24

$$P(A) = \frac{5 + 3 + 7 + 10}{50} = \frac{25}{50} \qquad P(B) = \frac{6 + 3 + 8 + 10}{50} = \frac{27}{50}$$

$$P(A \text{ and } B) = \frac{(25)(13)}{(50)(25)} = \frac{13}{50} \quad \text{and} \quad P(A \cup B) = \frac{25}{50} + \frac{27}{50} - \frac{13}{50} = \frac{39}{50}$$

Mutually Exclusive Events

Two events are said to be mutually exclusive if the occurrence of one precludes the occurrence of the other. For example, we cannot draw a heart and a spade on the same draw from a deck of cards, or roll a 2 and a 3 on the same roll of a die, so these are said to be mutually exclusive events. Another way to define mutual exclusivity is to say that two mutually exclusive events have a joint probability of zero, or

$$P(A \cap B) = 0 \qquad \text{(mutually exclusive events)}$$

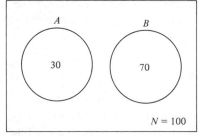 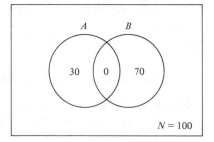

Figure 2.25 Mutually exclusive events.

The Venn diagram of two mutually exclusive events might be as shown in Figure 2.25.

Independent Events

Two events are said to be independent if the occurrence or nonoccurrence of one does not affect the probability of occurrence of the other. This may be written as

$$P\ (B\,|A) = P(B\,|\bar{A}) = P(B)$$

where $\bar{A}$ means "not A."

Revised Probabilities (Bayes' Rule)

We frequently wish to *revise* probability estimates based upon added information. We call this process Bayesian revision, after Rev. Thomas Bayes, who first proposed it in the 1700s. We begin with the AND rule.

$$P(A \cap B) = P(A) \cdot P(B\,|A)$$

Solving for the conditional probability gives

$$P(B\,|A) = \frac{P(A \cap B)}{P(A)}$$

But we know that

$$P(A \cap B) = P(B \cap A) = P(B) \cdot P(A\,|B)$$

and

$$P(A) = P(A\,|B) + P(A\,|\bar{B})$$

Substituting, we obtain the expression

$$P(B\,|A) = \frac{P(B) \cdot P(A\,|B)}{P(A\,|B) + P(A\,|\bar{B})}$$

A more detailed discussion of Bayesian revision and a simple, straightforward, and much "friendlier" approach to revising probabilities using contingency tables is found in Chapter 14, "Decision Theory."

Expected Value of a Discrete Distribution

A discrete probability distribution is one in which the variable is allowed to assume only certain selected values and is not defined between those values. For example, the number of spots showing on a die is a discrete variable limited to the integers 1 through 6; the number of free throws a basketball player sinks in 10 tries is a discrete variable, limited to integer values from 0 to 10.

If we wish to compute the *expected value*, or average, or mean (denoted $\bar{X}$) of the number of successful free throws in 10 tries for the 20 players on a high school basketball team using the data presented in

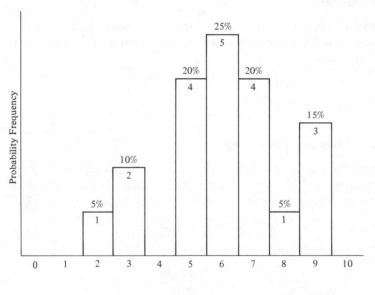

Value (Baskets)	Frequency (Players)	Probability (%)
0	0	0
1	0	0
2	1	5
3	2	10
4	0	0
5	4	20
6	5	25
7	4	20
8	1	5
9	3	15
10	0	0

Figure 2.26   Discrete distribution of free-throw accuracy.

both tabular and graphical form in Figure 2.26, we weight each value of the variable by its frequency and divide the weighted total by the sum of the weights (omitting the terms with zero weights).

$$\bar{X} = \frac{\sum f_i X_i}{\sum f_i} = \frac{(1)(2) + (2)(3) + (4)(5) + (5)(6) + (4)(7) + (1)(8) + (3)(9)}{1 + 2 + 4 + 5 + 4 + 1 + 3}$$

$$= \frac{2 + 6 + 20 + 30 + 28 + 8 + 27}{20} = \frac{121}{20} = 6.05$$

This means that on the average, the players sink slightly over 60% of their free throws.

An alternate approach is to use the percentages (probabilities) of each outcome as weights.

$$\bar{X} = \frac{\sum p_i X_i}{\sum p_i}$$

$$= \frac{(5)(2) + (10)(3) + (20)(5) + (25)(6) + (20)(7) + (5)(8) + (15)(9)}{5 + 10 + 20 + 25 + 20 + 5 + 15}$$

$$= \frac{10 + 30 + 100 + 150 + 140 + 40 + 135}{100} = \frac{605}{100} = 6.05$$

The Binomial Probability Distribution

One very special and widely used discrete probability distribution is the binomial distribution. In order for an event to follow the binomial, it must be a *Bernouli* event, which requires: (1) that there be only two outcomes (heads or tails, success or failure, defective or acceptable) that are mutually exclusive (only one of them may occur on a given trial) and collectively exhaustive (together they account for 100% of the possible outcomes); and (2) that their probabilities in repeated trials be independent. Stated symbolically

$$P(D \ \& \ A) = 0 \qquad \text{(mutually exclusive)}$$
$$P(D) + P(A) = 1 \qquad \text{(collectively exhaustive)}$$
$$P(D_{n+1}) = P(D_{n+1} | D_n) = P(D_{n+1} | A_n) \qquad \text{(independent)}$$

where

D represents defective
A represents acceptable
D_{n+1} represents defective on the $(n + 1)$st trial
A_n represents acceptable on the nth trial, etc.

If these requirements are met, the probability of d defectives in N trials, given the probability of a defective on any given trial (P), can be expressed

$$P(d \mid N, P) = C_d^N P^d (1 - P)^{(N-d)} = \frac{N!}{d!(N-d)!} P^d (1 - P)^{(N-d)}$$

The binomial distribution is tabulated in Appendix A for various values of N, P, and d. The example shown there is the probability of exactly 2 defectives in a sample of 3 when the proportion defective is .40.

$$P(d = 2 \mid N = 3, P = .40) = C_2^3 (.40)^2 (.60)^1 = \frac{3!}{2!1!}(.16)(.6) = .2880$$

The Cumulative Binominal Distribution

It is often useful to determine the probability of D *or more* (or conversely, fewer than D) defective in a sample of N. One way to accomplish this is to add the probabilities of each of the outcomes to arrive at a total probability. Mathematically, this can be expressed as

$$P(d \geq D \mid N, P) = \sum_{d=D}^{N} C_d^N P^d (1 - P)^{(N-d)}$$

An easier method is to utilize the cumulative binominial distribution of Appendix B. The example shown there is the probability of 2 or more defectives in a sample of 3 when $P = .40$. This is the sum of the probability of $d = 2$ (.2880) and $d = 3$ (.0640), or .3520. The probability of fewer than 2 defectives is $1 - P$ (2 or more defectives), or $1 - .3520 = .6480$. We strongly suggest that you sketch the distribution (scale is not important; it is the selection of the appropriate areas that is vital) when working with cumulative binomials.

The Normal Distribution

Perhaps the most widely used probability distribution is the *normal* distribution, which is a continuous (as opposed to discrete) distribution. By continuous, we mean that the variable of interest may assume any value along the X axis, and not just selected values, as in the case of discrete distributions.

The normal curve is the familiar "bell curve" shown in Figure 2.27. It is described by a measure of central tendency (the mean, μ) and a measure of dispersion, or spread (the standard deviation, σ). As shown in the figure, approximately 68% of the area lies within ± 1 σ of the mean; 95% lies within ± 2 σ; and 99.7% lies within ± 3 σ.

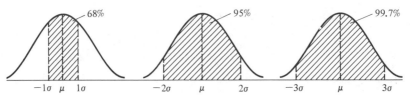

Figure 2.27   The normal distribution.

Appendix C is a tabular compilation of the areas under the "standard" normal curve with a mean of zero ($\mu = 0$) and a standard deviation of 1.0 ($\sigma = 1$). It is a simple matter to transform *any* normal distribution into a standard normal and find the area from any point X to the nearest tail of the curve from the table, using the relationship $Z_X = (x - \mu)/\sigma$

Z_X is the value of the standard normal.
X is the value of the distribution of interest.
μ is the mean of the distribution of interest.
σ is the standard deviation of the distribution of interest.

For example, if income in a particular neighborhood is normally distributed with a mean of $18,000 and a standard deviation of $2,000, we can find the proportion of the population with incomes above $20,000 (15.87%), below $14,000 (2.28%) between $19,000 and $23,000 (30.23%), etc., as shown in Figure 2.28, by using Appendix C. Note that in (c) we must subtract the area above $23,000 (.0062) from the area above $19,000 (.3085) to obtain the area between $19,000 and $23,000 (.3085 − .0062 = .3023).

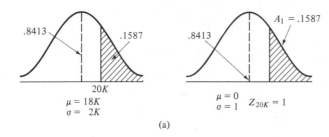

(a)

$$Z_{20K} = \frac{20K - 18K}{2K} = +1$$

$$A_1 = .1587$$
$$P(X \geq 20K) = .1587$$
$$P(X < 20K) = .8413$$

Figure 2.28   Areas under the normal curve.

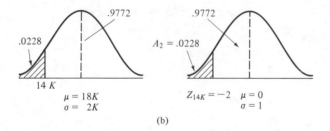

(b)

$$Z_{14K} = \frac{14K - 18K}{2K} = -2$$

$$A_{-2} = .0228$$
$$P(X \le 14K) = .0228$$
$$P(X > 14K) = .9772$$

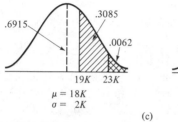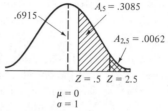

(c)

$$Z_{19K} = \frac{19K - 18K}{2K} = +.5$$

$$A_{.5} = .3085$$

$$Z_{23K} = \frac{23K - 18K}{2K} = 2.5$$

$$A_{2.5} = .0062$$
$$P(19K \le X < 23K) = .3085 - .0062 = .3023$$

Figure 2.28 (*continued*)

SUMMARY OF KEY CONCEPTS

Parameter. A constant; an element having a fixed value.
Variable. An element that may assume a range of different values.
Operators. Symbols $(+, -, \times, \div, \sqrt{},$ etc.$)$ enabling us to express relationships among variables and parameters.

Rectangular coordinates.   A reference system in which any point can be located by its distances from the origin measured along a set of perpendicular axes.

Two-point method.   A means of determining the equation of a straight line ($Y = a + bX$) when any two points on the line are known.

$$b = \frac{Y_1 - Y_2}{X_1 - X_2} \qquad a = Y_1 - bX_1$$

Point-slope method.   A means of determining the equation of a straight line when the slope and any point on the line are known.

$$a = Y - bX$$

Substitution.   A method for solving systems of simultaneous equations by solving one or more of the equations for one unknown and substituting for that unknown in the remaining equations.

Elimination of variables.   A method of solving systems of simultaneous equations by adding (or subtracting) multiples of one equation to another equation to eliminate one or more variables.

Matrix.   A rectangular array of elements arranged in rows and columns.

Summation notation.   A compact, shorthand method of expressing the sum of several terms. Illustration:

$$\sum_{i=1}^{3} a_i = a_1 + a_2 + a_3$$

Index.   An unknown that is permitted to assume integer values from an *initial* to a *final* value in a summation. Example: i is the index in the foregoing illustration.

Row matrix.   A matrix having exactly one row.

Column matrix.   A matrix with exactly one column.

Vector.   A row or column matrix.

Scalar.   A single value; as opposed to a matrix, which can represent many elements at once.

Order of a matrix.   The number of rows and columns in a matrix, in that order ($R \times C$).

Identity matrix.   A square matrix having ones as elements on the principal diagonal and zeros for all other elements.

Null matrix.   A matrix having zeros for all elements.

Conformability for addition and subtraction.   To be conformable for addition and subtraction, two matrices must be of the same order. Their sum or difference also will be of that order.

Conformability for multiplication.   The number of columns of the first matrix must equal the number of rows of the second.

Multipladd.   The process of multiplying the corresponding elements of two vectors and adding the products.

Inverse.   (A^{-1}) A square matrix that, when multiplied by the original matrix, produces an identity matrix: $AA^{-1} = A^{-1}A = I$. It has the function of $1/A$ in matrix algebra.

Gaussian reduction. Also called Gaussian elimination. A method of finding the inverse of a matrix.

Determinant. A scalar value associated with a square matrix.

Criss-Cross. A method of evaluating a 2×2 or a 3×3 determinant.

Cramer's rule. A method of solving sets of simultaneous linear equations by dividing the values of determinants.

Singular matrix. A square matrix that has a zero-valued determinant. Singular matrices do not have inverses.

Transpose of a matrix. (A^T) A new matrix formed by interchanging the rows and columns.

Quadratic formula. A method for finding the roots of a second-order function. If

$$Y = aX^2 + bX + c = 0$$

then

$$X = \frac{-b \pm \sqrt{b^2 - 4ac}}{2a}$$

A priori. When physical symmetry makes each of N outcomes equally likely, the probability of any one is $P = 1/N$; if A includes n of the outcomes, $P(A) = n/N$.

Frequency theory. The probability of an outcome (A) can be estimated by repeating the event N times and recording the number of successes (S).

$$P(A) \approx \frac{S}{N}$$

The true value is found only as the limit when N becomes very large, or

$$P(A) = \lim_{N \to \infty} \left[\frac{S}{N} \right].$$

Probability trees. A graphical representation for determining the probabilities of various outcomes.

Sample space. A graphical representation of each of the outcomes of an event along with the probability of each.

Simple event. The simplest outcome of a trial.

Compound event. A combination of two or more simple events.

Venn diagram. The use of geometric figures to show the relationship among complex events and their probabilities.

Conditional probability. The probability that one outcome will occur given that another outcome occurs: $P(A|B)$.

And rule.

$$P(A \text{ and } B) = P(A \cap B) = P(A) \cdot P(B|A) = P(B \text{ and } A) = P(B) \cdot P(A|B).$$

Or rule.

$$P(A \text{ or } B) = P(A \cup B) = P(A) + P(B) - P(A \text{ and } B).$$

Mutually exclusive events. The occurrence of one event precludes the occurrence of the other.

$$P(A \text{ and } B) = 0.$$

Independent events. The occurrence or nonoccurrence of one event has no effect on the probability of the other.

$$P(B|A) = P(B|\bar{A}) = P(B).$$

Bayes' rule. A means of revising the probability of an outcome, based upon information about other outcomes.

$$P(B|A) = \frac{P(B) \cdot P(A|B)}{P(A|B) + P(A|\bar{B})}$$

Expected value of a discrete distribution.

$$\bar{X} = \frac{\Sigma f_i X_i}{\Sigma f_i} \quad \text{or} \quad \bar{X} = \frac{\Sigma p_i X_i}{\Sigma p_i}$$

Biominal probabilities.

$$P(d|N, P) = C_d^N P^d (1 - P)^{(N-d)}.$$

Values are shown in Appendix A; cumulative values, in Appendix B.

Normal distribution. The "bell curve" with mean μ and standard deviation σ. Areas under the normal curve are shown in Appendix C.

PROBLEMS

Solution of Algebraic Equations

1. Solve the following equations for X.

  a. $X - 7 = 12$

  b. $5X + 2 = 10$

  c. $\dfrac{5}{X} = 7$

  d. $\dfrac{X + 1}{3} = 3X + 2$

2. Solve the following equations for Y and evaluate for $X = 2$.

  a. $X + Y = 7$

  b. $\dfrac{Y - 1}{X} = 7$

  c. $\dfrac{3Y + 4X}{2} = 5X$

  d. $\dfrac{2Y}{X} = X + 5$

  e. $\dfrac{4Y + 2}{X^2 + 6} = 2Y$

  f. $\dfrac{6Y + 4X}{X + 2} = 12X$

  g. $\sqrt{3Y + 4} = X + 3$

  h. $\sqrt{\dfrac{Y - 8}{2X + 4}} = X - 2$

3. Solve for X.

  a. $X + 5 < 11$

  b. $X - 7 \leq 3X$

c. $2X + 4 > 20$

d. $2 - 3X \geq 12$

e. $3 \geq 12 - \dfrac{X}{2}$

f. $\dfrac{2}{X} + 8 \geq 12$

Linear Equations and Rectangular Coordinates

4. Find the X and Y intercepts and plot the lines for the following equations.

a. $Y = 6 - 2X$

b. $2 = \dfrac{X}{2} - Y$

c. $Y = 4 - \dfrac{2X}{3}$

d. $2 = Y - \dfrac{2X}{3}$

5. Find the equations of the lines through the following points.
   a. $X_1 = 4,\ Y_1 = 5;\ X_2 = 8,\ Y_2 = 13$
   b. $X_1 = 6,\ Y_1 = 15;\ X_2 = 12,\ Y_2 = 5$
   c. $X_1 = -2,\ Y_1 = -1;\ X_2 = 6,\ Y_2 = 11$
   d. $X_1 = -4,\ Y_1 = 3;\ X_2 = 8,\ Y_2 = -3$

Systems of Linear Equations

6. Solve the following sets of simultaneous linear equations.
   a. $2X + 4Y = 14$
      $4X + 2Y = 16$
   b. $Y = 14 - 2X$
      $Y = -11 + 3X$
   c. $2 = -X + 2Y$
      $35 = 5X - Y$
   d. $X + 4Y = -8$
      $3X + Y = 9$

7. An investor has $5000 she wishes to divide between Amalgamated bonds, which yield 9%, and Bonaventure bonds, which yield 12%. If she wants to earn 10% on the total investment, how much should she invest in each issue?

8. A stamping machine can produce forks at a rate of 500 per hour or spoons at a rate of 1000 per hour. A forming machine can form 600 forks per hour or 800 spoons per hour.

   Both forks and spoons must be stamped out, then formed. What combination of forks and spoons should be produced to keep both machines busy at all times? (Hint: Solve graphically.)

Matrix Algebra

9. Perform the indicated matrix operations.
   a. $(4 \quad 5 \quad 7) + (6 \quad 2 \quad -2)$

b. $\begin{pmatrix} 2 \\ 9 \\ -8 \\ 4 \end{pmatrix} - \begin{pmatrix} -1 \\ 3 \\ -2 \\ 2 \end{pmatrix}$

c. $\begin{pmatrix} 3 & 4 & 4 \\ 2 & 1 & 5 \\ -2 & 6 & 6 \\ 8 & -4 & 7 \end{pmatrix} + \begin{pmatrix} 1 & 2 & 1 \\ 3 & -2 & 4 \\ 6 & 5 & -3 \\ 2 & 0 & 8 \end{pmatrix}$

d. $\begin{pmatrix} 6 & 1 & 7 \\ 5 & -2 & 6 \end{pmatrix} - \begin{pmatrix} -3 & 2 & 4 \\ 9 & -1 & 3 \end{pmatrix}$

e. $\begin{pmatrix} 7 & 2 & 1 & 6 \\ 4 & 2 & -1 & 3 \end{pmatrix}^T$

f. $\begin{pmatrix} -1 & 6 & 8 & 9 \\ 4 & 3 & 3 & 0 \\ 2 & 1 & 0 & 5 \end{pmatrix}^T$

g. $\begin{pmatrix} 4 \\ 1 \\ 7 \end{pmatrix} \times (2 \quad 2 \quad 3 \quad 1)$

h. $(3 \quad 6 \quad 4 \quad 2) \times \begin{pmatrix} 1 & 0 & 5 \\ 6 & 1 & 1 \\ 4 & 7 & 3 \\ 2 & 0 & -4 \end{pmatrix}$

i. $\begin{pmatrix} 2 & -1 \\ 5 & 3 \end{pmatrix} \times \begin{pmatrix} 4 & 2 \\ 0 & 7 \end{pmatrix}$

j. $\begin{pmatrix} 3 & 4 \\ -1 & 6 \end{pmatrix}^{-1}$

k. $\begin{pmatrix} 2 & 3 & -1 \\ 0 & 4 & 2 \\ 1 & 0 & -1 \end{pmatrix}^{-1}$

Determinants

10. Evaluate the following determinants.

   a. $\|4\|$

   b. $\begin{Vmatrix} 4 & 2 \\ 3 & 1 \end{Vmatrix}$

c. $\begin{Vmatrix} 6 & -1 & 5 \\ 2 & 1 & 0 \\ 3 & 3 & 4 \end{Vmatrix}$

11. Use Cramer's rule to solve the following systems of linear equations.

    a. $2X + 6Y = -7$ b. $2X + Y = 8$
        $3X + 2Y = 7$ $X - 3Y = 12$
    c. $X + Y - Z = 1$ d. $3X - 2Y - Z = -1$
        $X + Y + Z = 5$ $X + Y + 2Z = 0$
        $X - Y - Z = 3$ $2X + Y + Z = 3$

12. Solve for the roots of the following equations using the quadratic formula.

    a. $Y = X^2 + 4X - 5$ b. $Y = 2X^2 - 3X - 5$
    c. $Y = -X^2 + 3X + 4$ d. $Y = -3X^2 + 2X + 5$

13. Find the roots of the following equations.

    a. $Y = X^2 + 6X + 7$ b. $Y = 3X^2 - 2X - 1$
    c. $Y = -X^2 - 5X + 3$ d. $Y = -5X^2 + 6X - 1$

14. Draw the sample space and the probability tree for the compound event of drawing a card from a shuffled poker deck where the first simple event is the color of the card (black or red) and the second single event is the value of the card (A-2-3-4-5-6-7-8-9-10-face card).

15. Draw the sample space and the probability tree for the compound event of a roulette ball landing first on red or black and then, second, on either an odd or an even number.

16. Draw a Venn diagram representing three tosses of a fair coin. Show event A, which is two or more heads; event B, which is two or more tails; and event C, which is heads on the second toss. What are the probabilities of the following:

    a. $P(A)$ f. $P(B \& C)$
    b. $P(B)$ g. $P(A \text{ or } B)$
    c. $P(C)$ h. $P(A \text{ or } C)$
    d. $P(A \& B)$ i. $P(B \text{ or } C)$
    e. $P(A \& C)$ j. $P(A \& C)$

    k. Which of the events A, B, and C are mutually exclusive?

(For a more challenging problem, repeat problem 16 with a bent coin having $P(H) = .6$.)

17. A jar contains equal numbers of red, white, and blue balls. Three balls are to be drawn with replacement. Let event C be two or more blue balls; event D one or more white balls; and event E be all three balls the same color. Find the probability of each of the following:

    a. $P(C)$ f. $P(D \& E)$
    b. $P(D)$ g. $P(D \& E)$
    c. $P(E)$ h. $P(C \text{ or } E)$
    d. $P(C \& D)$ i. $P(C \text{ or } D)$
    e. $P(D \text{ or } E)$ j. Which events are mutually exclusive?

(Notice that if the number of each color of balls is not the same, so that $P(R) \neq P(W) \neq P(B)$, the problem becomes much more difficult, because the probabilities of each of the 27 different outcomes must be computed separately. Notice also that drawing with replacement keeps these probabilities stable and also helps to simplify the problem. For practice in determining probabilities of compound events with unequally likely outcomes and/or experiments in which the successive trials are not independent, repeat problem 17 with a jar containing 2 reds, 3 whites, and 5 blues and drawing without replacement.)

18. What is the average (expected value) length of the boards in the following distribution?

Length (ft)	2	3	4	5	6	7	8
Number	10	15	5	12	9	8	11

19. If *A*s count 4, *B*s count 3, etc., find the grade-point average (expected value) of the student who has 15 *A*s, 11 *B*s, 34 *C*s, 3 *D*s, and 2 *F*s.

20. In drawing with replacement from a jar containing 2 red, 3 white, and 5 blue marbles, what is the probability of each of the following:
   a. 3 reds in 5 draws
   b. 3 whites in 5 draws
   c. 6 blues in 10 draws
   d. 4 reds in 10 draws
   e. no whites in 10 draws
   (Hint: Use the binomial tables in Appendix A.)

21. A manufacturing process produces parts in the following proportion: 10% rejects, 30% repairable, and 60% acceptable. If random samples of parts are taken, determine the probabilities of each of the following:
   a. 2 rejects in a sample of 10
   b. 5 repairables in a sample of 10
   c. 8 acceptables in a sample of 10
   d. 40 repairables in a sample of 100
   e. 70 acceptables in a sample of 100
   (Hint: Use the binomial tables in Appendix A.)

22. In the jar from problem 20, find the following:
   a. at least 2 reds in 5 draws
   b. at most 3 whites in 5 draws
   c. no more than 6 blues in 10 draws
   d. no fewer than 3 reds in 10 draws
   e. more than 20 whites in 100 draws
   (Hint: Use the cumulative binomial tables in Appendix B.)

23. In the sampling of the product in problem 21, compute the probabilities of each of the following:
   a. at least 1 reject in a sample of 5
   b. at most 2 repairables in a sample of 5

    c. no more than 7 acceptables in a sample of 10

    d. no fewer than 12 rejects in a sample of 100

    e. fewer than 65 acceptables in a sample of 100

    (Hint: Use the cumulative binomial tables in Appendix B.)

24. If the incomes of a group of 1,000 professional athletes are normally distributed with a mean of $50,000 and a standard deviation of $10,000, determine how many of them have incomes that are

    a. over $60,000

    b. under $55,000

    c. over $20,000

    d. under $30,000

    e. between $35,000 and $45,000

    (Hint: Use the normal table in Appendix C.)

25. The weights of a group of students are normally distributed with a mean of 150 pounds and a standard deviation of 20 pounds. Determine the percentage of the students you would expect to weigh

    a. under 135 pounds

    b. over 140 pounds

    c. over 180 pounds

    d. under 200 pounds

    e. between 160 and 170 pounds

    (Hint: Use the normal table in Appendix C.)

Chapter 3

MARKOV ANALYSIS

INTRODUCTION

The analysis of first-order Markov chains provides an excellent opportunity to practice some of the skills you have acquired in matrix algebra and the use of determinants for the solution of systems of simultaneous linear equations. Most of our applications of management science models and operations research techniques are designed to predict and deal with the future based on current information. Though the Markov technique was originally developed to predict the behavior of gasses under laboratory conditions, it has many useful and interesting applications in business and the social sciences. For example, given the history of brand-switching by consumers and the current market shares of a group of products, we can predict the market shares of the products in some future period and the market shares that would ultimately be enjoyed by the products. Also, if we know the past history of patient recovery, we can predict patient status at a hospital in a future period. We can predict machine status in a machine shop, performance of trainees in a training program, and many other similar situations.

The computational techniques employed are matrix multiplication, in the case of predicting the state of the system in some finite future period, and the solution of a system of simultaneous equations, for predicting the ultimate state or equilibrium of a system. Both of these techniques were treated in some detail in Chapter 2. The feature that makes Markov analysis different from mere matrix manipulation is the formulation of the matrices and the interpretation of the results of the multiplication.

A Simple 2 × 2 Example

As will be our approach throughout the text, we will introduce the technique with a simple example. Imagine a small town that has two competing barbershops, Sam's and Gino's. At the end of September it was determined that Sam had 50% of the town's customers and that Gino had the same. It was determined further that each month in the past Sam had retained 80% of his customers and had lost 20% to Gino. Gino had managed to retain 70% of his customers each month and had lost 30% of them to Sam. Sam wishes to determine what his market share will be at the end of October and what his market share will be ultimately at some point in the distant future.

Let's see if we can use simple logic to determine what the market shares for each of the shops will be at the end of October. First of all let's give the market a finite size of 100 customers. This means that each of the shops had a total of 50 customers at the end of September. If Sam retains 80% of his customers, then he can expect to have 40 of his old customers at the end of October (.80 × 50 = 40). If Gino loses 30% of his customers to Sam, then Sam can expect to gain an additional 15 customers from Gino (.3 × 50 = 15). The total number of customers that Sam will have at the end of October will be the number retained (40) plus the number gained (15): 40 + 15 = 55.

By the same token, Gino will retain 70% of his customers (.7 × 50 = 35) and will gain 20% of Sam's (.2 × 50 = 10). The total number of customers that Gino will have at the end of October will be 35 + 10 = 45. The market shares that each shop will have at the end of October are then

$$\text{Sam} \quad \tfrac{55}{100} = .55 \text{ or } 55\%$$
$$\text{Gino} \quad \tfrac{45}{100} = .45 \text{ or } 45\%$$

We can also calculate the expected market shares for each of the shops for the end of the next period. This would be done in exactly the same way the first period was done.

Normally Markov calculations are done with percentages rather than with finite numbers, so this time we will use the percentage market shares rather than the actual number of customers. The results derived will be exactly the same as if we had used the number of customers.

We are assuming, of course, that the retention, loss, and gain percentages will be unchanged from the first period. Consequently, at the end of November Sam will have 80% of the customers he had at the end of October (.8 × .55 = .440) and will gain 30% of the customers Gino had at the end of October (.3 × .45 = .135). This would give Sam a total at the end of November of .44 + .135 = .575 or $57\frac{1}{2}$% of the market. This should leave Gino with $42\frac{1}{2}$% of the market. To verify, we complete the calculations. If Gino retains 70% of his customers from October, he should have .7 × .45 = .315 of the total customers and should gain .2 × .55 = .11 of the customers from Sam, for a total of .315 + .11 = .425 or $42\frac{1}{2}$%. The market shares of both shops must total 100%. Our results meet this requirement.

Now that we have explored the logic of the Markov model, let's look at the matrix algebra approach to the calculation of Markov chains.

First of all, we must take the probabilities of retention, gain, and loss and construct a *matrix of transition probabilities* (MTP). We will then construct another matrix, matrix "X_1," from the initial market shares and calculate the expected market shares for the next period. These expected market shares will form matrix "X_2." In simple algebraic form our calculation will be

$$(\text{MTP}) \times (X_1) = (X_2)$$

If we write the equations that we used to calculate the end of October market shares, we have what begins to look like a matrix

$$(.8 \times S_1) + (.3 \times G_1) = S_2$$
$$(.2 \times S_1) + (.7 \times G_1) = G_2$$

where S_1 and G_1 are the end of September market shares for Sam and Gino, respectively, and S_2 and G_2 are the end of October shares. In matrix notation this would look like the following.

FROM

Sam   Gino

$$\text{TO} \quad \begin{matrix} \text{Sam} \\ \text{Gino} \end{matrix} \begin{pmatrix} .8 & .3 \\ .2 & .7 \end{pmatrix} \times \begin{pmatrix} S_1 \\ G_1 \end{pmatrix} = \begin{pmatrix} S_2 \\ G_2 \end{pmatrix}$$

$$\text{MTP} \quad \times \quad X_1 \quad = \quad X_2$$

Remember from our discussion of matrix algebra that we multiply two matrices by multiplying the elements in the columns of one matrix by the corresponding elements in the rows of the other matrix. This operation will give us the Markov predictions for the end of October.

$$\text{TO}\ \begin{array}{c}\text{FROM} \\ \begin{array}{cc}\text{Sam} & \text{Gino}\end{array} \\ \begin{array}{c}\text{Sam} \\ \text{Gino}\end{array}\begin{pmatrix} .8 & .3 \\ .2 & .7 \end{pmatrix} \times \begin{pmatrix} .5 \\ .5 \end{pmatrix} = \begin{pmatrix} .8 \times .5 + .3 \times .5 \\ .2 \times .5 + .7 \times .5 \end{pmatrix} = \begin{pmatrix} .55 \\ .45 \end{pmatrix} \\ \begin{array}{ccc}\text{MTP} & \times\ X_1 = & \qquad\qquad X_2\end{array}\end{array}$$

Previously we calculated the predictions for the end of November by taking the market shares at the end of October and multiplying them by the transition probabilities. In matrix form the calculation looks like the following.

$$\begin{pmatrix} .8 & .3 \\ .2 & .7 \end{pmatrix} \times \begin{pmatrix} .55 \\ .45 \end{pmatrix} = \begin{pmatrix} .8 \times .55 + .3 \times .45 \\ .2 \times .55 + .7 \times .45 \end{pmatrix} = \begin{pmatrix} .575 \\ .425 \end{pmatrix}$$
$$\begin{array}{ccc}\text{MTP} & \times\quad X_2\ = & \qquad\qquad X_3\end{array}$$

This method of using each successive period's market shares to obtain the succeeding period's shares is called "chaining," from one period to the next, and is the basis for the term "Markov chains" to describe the analysis of these systems.

There is an alternative way to calculate Markov predictions. Rather than calculating the first-period shares and then multiplying the results by the original transition probability matrix to obtain the predictions for the next period, we may raise the transition probability matrix to the second power (square it) and multiply by the original market shares. By the same token, we can obtain the predictions for the third period in the future by cubing the transition probability matrix and multiplying it by the original market shares. The answers will be the same as those obtained by multiplying successive market share predictions by the original transition matrix. You will find that the method of multiplying successive market shares by the unchanged transition probability matrix is the easier method. It is always easier to multiply a vector (a matrix with a single row or single column) by a matrix than to multiply a matrix by a matrix.

Equilibrium or Steady-State Market Shares

You may have observed from the previous calculations that in each successive period Sam's share of the market became larger, but in successively smaller bites. If one stops to think of it, it only makes sense. If one shop's share is getting smaller, then, though it is losing the same percentage of its customers to the other shop each month, it is losing a smaller number of customers. Similarly the shop that has a growing share of the market is losing the same percentage, but a larger number of customers, to the other.

Taking this to its natural and logical conclusion, we might guess that eventually the shares of the two shops would be such that the actual number of customers being transferred from one shop to the other would be equal. When this occurs the system is said to have reached *steady state* or *equilibrium*, and each of the shops will have constant shares of the market from that point on. This assumes that the transition probability matrix does not change over time. The likelihood of this kind of stability depends on the particular system being studied.

If we assume that the matrix of transition probabilities is to remain stable, we may wish to determine the equilibrium market shares. One possible approach to the problem is to continue to multiply successive market shares by the transition probabilities matrix until the market shares cease changing. This approach is shown for Sam and Gino's example in Figure 3.1. We note that as the equilibrium condition is approached, the percentage changes from period to period become smaller and smaller, approaching zero at equilibrium.

We know that at equilibrium, the market shares remain the same from one period to the next. Because this is true, we can make the following mathematical statements

Matrix Notation   Scalar Notation

$$\begin{pmatrix} .8 & .3 \\ .2 & .7 \end{pmatrix} \begin{pmatrix} S \\ G \end{pmatrix} = \begin{pmatrix} S \\ G \end{pmatrix} \qquad \begin{aligned} .8S + .3G &= S \\ .2S + .7G &= G \end{aligned}$$

where S and G are the equilibrium market shares for Sam and Gino, respectively.

In addition, we know that the sum of the market shares must be equal to 100%.

$$S + G = 1$$

Collecting like terms in the first two equations, we get

$$\begin{aligned} .8S + .3G &= S \\ .2S + .7G &= G \\ S + G &= 1 \end{aligned} \qquad \begin{cases} -.2S + .3G = 0 \\ .2S - .3G = 0 \\ S + G = 1 \end{cases}$$

Because the first two equations are the same (each is the other multiplied by -1), we delete one of them (it makes no difference which one we delete) to obtain a set of two independent equations and two unknowns.

$$\begin{cases} .2S - .3G = 0 \\ S + G = 1 \end{cases} \quad \text{or} \quad \begin{cases} -.2S + .3G = 0 \\ S + G = 1 \end{cases}$$

In matrix notation, the system on the right can be expressed as follows.

$$\begin{pmatrix} -.2 & .3 \\ 1 & 1 \end{pmatrix} \times \begin{pmatrix} S \\ G \end{pmatrix} = \begin{pmatrix} 0 \\ 1 \end{pmatrix}$$

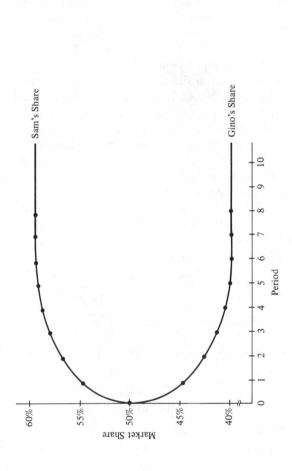

SAM			1	2	3	4	5	6	7	8
	Share	.5	.55	.575	.5875	.59375	.596875	.5984375	.5992187	.599609
	% Change	0	10%	4.5%	2.2%	1.1%	.5%	.3%	.1%	.06%
GINO	Share	.5	.45	.425	.4125	.40625	.403125	.4015625	.4007813	.400390
	% Change	0	10%	5.6%	2.9%	1.5%	.8%	.4%	.2%	.1%
	Period	0	1	2	3	4	5	6	7	8

Figure 3.1   Two firm market share changes.

We can solve this system for the equilibrium market shares using Cramer's rule.

$$S = \frac{\begin{Vmatrix} 0 & .3 \\ 1 & 1 \end{Vmatrix}}{\begin{Vmatrix} -.2 & .3 \\ 1 & 1 \end{Vmatrix}} = \frac{-.3}{-.5} = 60\%$$

$$G = \frac{\begin{Vmatrix} -.2 & 0 \\ 1 & 1 \end{Vmatrix}}{\begin{Vmatrix} -.2 & .3 \\ 1 & 1 \end{Vmatrix}} = \frac{-.2}{-.5} = 40\%$$

The equilibrium market shares are: Sam $= 60\%$ and Gino $= 40\%$. We can check these results by substituting them into the original problem.

$$\begin{pmatrix} .8 & .3 \\ .2 & .7 \end{pmatrix} \times \begin{pmatrix} .6 \\ .4 \end{pmatrix} = \begin{pmatrix} .6 \\ .4 \end{pmatrix} \quad \text{or} \quad \begin{array}{l} .8(.6) + .3(.4) = .6 \\ .2(.6) + .7(.4) = .4 \end{array}$$

EXPANDED EXAMPLE

We can complicate the situation somewhat by assuming the entry into the market of another barbershop, Yohan's. After Yohan has been in the market for 1 year, the behavior of customers has taken on the following characteristics: Sam retains 80% of his customers each month and loses 10% to each of the other shops. Gino retains 70% of his customers and loses 20% to Sam and 10% to Yohan. Yohan retains 90% of his customers and loses 10% to Sam and none to Gino. The matrix of transition probabilities will then be

$$\begin{array}{cc} & \text{FROM} \\ & \begin{array}{ccc} S & G & Y \end{array} \\ \text{TO} \begin{array}{c} S \\ G \\ Y \end{array} & \begin{pmatrix} .8 & .2 & .1 \\ .1 & .7 & 0 \\ .1 & .1 & .9 \end{pmatrix} \end{array}$$

At the end of January it was determined that the market shares of the three shops were: Sam $= 45\%$, Gino $= 30\%$, and Yohan $= 25\%$. What will be the market shares of the three shops at the end of February, assuming the transition probabilities do not change?

Step 1 Set up the two matrixes to be multiplied

$$\begin{pmatrix} .8 & .2 & .1 \\ .1 & .7 & 0 \\ .1 & .1 & .9 \end{pmatrix} \times \begin{pmatrix} .45 \\ .30 \\ .25 \end{pmatrix} = \begin{pmatrix} S_2 \\ G_2 \\ Y_2 \end{pmatrix}$$

$$\text{MTP} \quad \times \quad X_1 \quad = \quad X_2$$

Step 2 Perform the matrix multiplication.

$$S_2 = (.45 \times .8) + (.30 \times .2) + (.25 \times .1) = .445$$
$$G_2 = (.45 \times .1) + (.30 \times .7) + (.25 \times 0) = .255$$
$$Y_2 = (.45 \times .1) + (.30 \times .1) + (.25 \times .9) = .300$$

The new market shares will be: Sam = 44.5%, Gino = 25.5%, and Yohan = 30%.

Logic of the Calculations

Sam's end-of-February market share consists of the percentage of the previous month's market share that was retained (80% of 45%) plus the percentage of Gino's customers that was gained (20% of 30%) plus the percentage of Yohan's customers that was gained (10% of 25%).

$$S_2 = (.8 \times .45) + (.2 \times .3) + (.1 \times .25)$$
$$= .36 + .06 + .025 = .445$$

Gino's end-of-February market share consists of the percentage of Sam's previous month's customers that was gained (10% of 45%) plus the percentage of his own customers that was retained (70% of 30%) plus the percentage of Yohan's customers gained (0% of 25%).

$$G_2 = (.1 \times .45) + (.7 \times .3) + (0 \times .25)$$
$$= 0.45 + .21 + 0 = .255$$

Yohan's end-of-February market share consists of the percentage of Sam's previous month's customers that was gained (10% of 45%) plus the percentage of Gino's customers that was gained (10% of 30%) plus the percentage of his own customers that was retained (90% of 25%).

$$Y_2 = (.1 \times .45) + (.1 \times .3) + (.9 \times .25)$$
$$= 0.45 + .03 + .225 = .300$$

Equilibrium Market Shares

Now we calculate the equilibrium market shares of the three shops, using Cramer's Rule.

Step 1 Set up the equilibrium equations.

$$.8S + .2G + .1Y = S$$
$$.1S + .7G + 0Y = G$$
$$.1S + .1G + .9Y = Y$$
$$S + G + Y = 1$$

Step 2 Put the equations in standard form.

$$-.2S + .2G + .1Y = 0$$
$$.1S - .3G + 0Y = 0$$
$$.1S + .1G - .1Y = 0$$
$$S + G + Y = 1$$

Step 3 Since any one of the first three equations can be obtained by a combination of the other two (for example, adding the first and second equations together yields -1 times the third equation), they are not independent equations. We must arbitrarily eliminate one of the three equations, since all of the information they contain can be obtained from any two of them.[1] Therefore, we throw out the least desirable of the first three equations. It would appear that equation (2) would be the least desirable equation with which to work simply because it has a coefficient of .3 (.1s and .2s are easier to work with). Write the remaining set of equations in matrix form.

$$\begin{pmatrix} -.2 & .2 & .1 \\ .1 & .1 & -.1 \\ 1 & 1 & 1 \end{pmatrix} \times \begin{pmatrix} S \\ G \\ Y \end{pmatrix} = \begin{pmatrix} 0 \\ 0 \\ 1 \end{pmatrix}$$

Step 4 Solve this system of linear equations using Cramer's Rule.

$$S = \frac{\begin{vmatrix} 0 & .2 & .1 \\ 0 & .1 & -.1 \\ 1 & 1 & 1 \end{vmatrix}}{\begin{vmatrix} -.2 & .2 & .1 \\ .1 & .1 & -.1 \\ 1 & 1 & 1 \end{vmatrix}} = \frac{-.03}{-.08} = .375$$

$$G = \frac{\begin{vmatrix} -.2 & 0 & .1 \\ .1 & 0 & -.1 \\ 1 & 1 & 1 \end{vmatrix}}{\begin{vmatrix} -.2 & .2 & .1 \\ .1 & .1 & -.1 \\ 1 & 1 & 1 \end{vmatrix}} = \frac{-.01}{-.08} = .125$$

[1] Note that the 3×3 matrix of coefficients for the first three equations is a *singular* matrix whose determinant has a value of zero (see Chapter 2), and we are unable to divide by zero to obtain the values for S, G, and Y.

$$Y = \frac{\begin{Vmatrix} -.2 & .2 & 0 \\ .1 & .1 & 0 \\ 1 & 1 & 1 \end{Vmatrix}}{\begin{Vmatrix} -.2 & .2 & 1 \\ .1 & .1 & -.1 \\ 1 & 1 & 1 \end{Vmatrix}} = \frac{-.04}{-.08} = .500$$

The equilibrium market shares are therefore

Sam   37.5%
Gino   12.5%
Yohan   50.0%

The set of linear equations from step 3 could also be solved by algebraic methods such as substitution or elimination.

Selecting the method for determining equilibrium conditions is left to the student. The simple elimination method requires somewhat more creativity, but usually requires fewer calculations than solution by determinants. Be cautious. It is easy to make errors in arithmetic using either method.

A Maintenance Management Example Using Markov Analysis

The Duece Trucking Company maintains a fleet of long-haul trucks that are dispatched from company headquarters once each month. At the end of 30 days on the road the trucks return to headquarters for maintenance. The trucks return at staggered periods so that no more than four trucks are in the shop at any one time.

One of the major maintenance expenses is replacement of tires. The current policy is to have the driver call a local tire service company when a tire failure occurs and have the tire replaced. The average cost for this replacement has been $275.00 per tire. Duece has found that it can purchase truck tires in volume and have them replaced at its own shop for $200.00 each.

Duece classifies tire condition as either A (very good condition), B (fair condition), C (marginal condition), or D (failed). An examination of maintenace records showed that 70% of tires found to be in class A condition at one monthly inspection would be in class A at the next inspection, 20% of them would be in class B condition, and that 10% of them would be in class C condition. Eighty percent of the tires found to be in class B condition would remain in that condition until the next monthly inspection, and 20% of them will be in class C condition at the next inspection. Only 20% of the tires found to be in class C condition will remain in that condition through the next inspection, whereas 80% of them will fail while on the road. Naturally the "failed" tires will be replaced with new or class A tires.

Duece wants to know if it would be more economical to change all tires found to be in class C condition during each truck's monthly inspection and maintenance period while the truck is in the company shop. The financial manager argues that the company would be changing some tires that would make it through another month (the 20% of class C tires that would remain in class C). The maintenance foreman argues that the $75.00 saving per tire would more than compensate for the few tires that would be changed unnecessarily. What is the most economical replacement policy?

ANALYSIS

Under the current policy, the matrix of transition probabilities would appear as shown.

$$
\begin{array}{c}
\text{FROM} \\
\begin{array}{cccc}
 & A & B & C & D
\end{array} \\
\text{TO} \quad
\begin{array}{c}
A \\ B \\ C \\ D
\end{array}
\begin{pmatrix}
.70 & .00 & .00 & 1.00 \\
.20 & .80 & .00 & .00 \\
.10 & .20 & .20 & .00 \\
.00 & .00 & .80 & .00
\end{pmatrix}
\end{array}
$$

The D column in the matrix reflects the fact that all tires lost to the "failed" condition are replaced with new tires, and not that "failed" tires are magically resurrected to a class A condition. The equilibrium equations would be

$$.70A + .00B + .00C + 1.00D = A$$
$$.20A + .80B + .00C + .00D = B$$
$$.10A + .20B + .20C + .00D = C$$
$$.00A + .00B + .80C + .00D = D$$
$$A + B + C + D = E$$

Putting the equations in standard form we have the following.

$$-.30A + .00B + .00C + 1.00D = 0$$
$$.20A - .20B + .00C + .00D = 0$$
$$.10A + .20B - .80C + .00D = 0$$
$$.00A + .00B + .80C - 1.00D = 0$$
$$A + B + C + D = 1$$

Now we are ready to solve for the equilibrium conditions. By finding the equilibrium conditions we will know what the expected percentages of tires in each class will be. Once we know this, we can multiply the expected percentages of tires that fail on the road by the cost of having a tire replaced on the road. Actually we could interpret the results of the equilibrium calculations as being the probability of any one tire failing on the road (equilibrium percentage of class D) or of being in any of the other three conditions.

Arbitrarily deleting the third equation (one of the first four must go), we can solve by substitution. (We have not yet learned to evaluate 4×4 determinants, or we could use Cramer's rule). From the first equation we can obtain

$$-.3A + D = 0 \quad \text{or} \quad D = .3A$$

From the second

$$.2A - .2B = 0 \quad \text{or} \quad B = A$$

From the fourth

$$.8C - D = 0 \quad \text{or} \quad C = \frac{D}{.8} = 1.25D$$

Using the first equation and the fourth

$$C = 1.25(.3A) = .375A$$

Substituting all of these into the last equation

$$A + A + .375A + .3A = 1 \quad \text{so} \quad A = \frac{1}{2.675} = .374$$

Therefore

$$B = .374, \qquad C = .140, \qquad D = .112$$

The fact that $D = .112$ means that over the long run any one tire has an 11.2% chance of failing on the road. The expected cost per tire would then be $.112 \times \$275.00$ or $\$30.80$ per month.

If the company elects to stock tires and change all tires in class C condition, all road failures will be eliminated, and therefore the company will be interested in knowing the probability of a tire being in class C condition. This, of course, can be obtained by finding, once again, the equilibrium conditions for the new strategy. If we no longer are going to allow tires to deteriorate to a class D condition, our matrix of transition probabilities will change, and the equilibrium solution values will also change.

Let's analyze the situation. Because no tire found to be in a class A or class B condition ever deteriorates to a class D condition, there will be essentially no change in the transition probabilities for classes A or B.

Seventy percent of the class A tires will remain in class A, 20% will become class B, and 10% will become class C from month to month. Eighty percent of the class B tires will remain class B, and 20% will become class C from month to month. All class C tires will be changed, so that none will remain class C from month to month. One hundred percent of them will become class A. These are the tires that will be changed in the shop at a cost of $200 each. The equilibrium percentage of tires that are class C will also be the probability of any one tire becoming class C and therefore requiring change.

The new matrix of transition probabilities will look like the following

$$
\text{TO}\ \begin{array}{c} \\ A \\ B \\ C \end{array}
\overset{\displaystyle \text{FROM}}{\overset{\displaystyle \begin{array}{ccc} A & B & C \end{array}}{
\begin{pmatrix}
.70 & .00 & 1.00 \\
.20 & .80 & .00 \\
.10 & .20 & .00
\end{pmatrix}}}
$$

The equilibrium equations will be

$$.70A + .00B + 1.00C = A$$
$$.20A + .80B + .00C = B$$
$$.10A + .20B + .00C = C$$

or

$$-.30A + .00B + 1.00C = 0$$
$$.20A - .20B + .00C = 0$$
$$.10A + .20B - 1.00C = 0$$
$$A + B + C = 1$$

Arbitrarily deleting the third equation yields

$$
\begin{pmatrix}
-.3 & 0 & 1 \\
.2 & -.2 & 0 \\
1 & 1 & 1
\end{pmatrix}
\begin{pmatrix} A \\ B \\ C \end{pmatrix}
=
\begin{pmatrix} 0 \\ 0 \\ 1 \end{pmatrix}
$$

Solving using Cramer's rule yields

$$
A = \frac{\begin{pmatrix} 0 & 0 & 1 \\ 0 & -.2 & 0 \\ 1 & 1 & 1 \end{pmatrix}}{\begin{pmatrix} -.3 & 0 & 1 \\ .2 & -.2 & 0 \\ 1 & 1 & 1 \end{pmatrix}} = \frac{.20}{.46} = .4348
$$

$$B = \frac{\begin{pmatrix} -.3 & 0 & 1 \\ .2 & 0 & 0 \\ 1 & 1 & 1 \end{pmatrix}}{.46} = \frac{.20}{.46} = .4348$$

$$C = \frac{\begin{pmatrix} -.3 & 0 & 0 \\ .2 & -.2 & 0 \\ 1 & 1 & 1 \end{pmatrix}}{.46} = \frac{.06}{.46} = .1304$$

To find the expected cost of this new policy, we merely multiply the probability of a tire being in the class C condition by the cost

$$.1304 \times \$200.00 = \$26.08$$

Therefore, the policy that calls for any tire found in the class C condition to be changed is superior to the old policy to the tune of $30.80 − 26.08 = $4.72. As this is the savings per tire per month, we would multiply by the total number of tires to obtain the actual monthly savings.

A Hospital Example

Goodheart County Hospital operates on a charity basis. All expenses are paid by the county. Recently the board of governors of the hospital has been complaining about the size of the budget and insisting that the hospital cut expenses. The major area of concern has been the cost of keeping patients in intensive care. This cost has averaged $1000 per week per person, compared to only $500 per week per person for keeping patients in the wards. Past history shows that of those patients in ICU at the beginning of the week, 50% will be there at the end of the week, and 50% will be moved to a ward. Of the patients in the wards at the beginning of the week, 50% will be there at the end of the week; 10% will get worse and be transferred to ICU; and 40% will become outpatients. Of those persons who are outpatients at the beginning of the week; 85% will remain outpatients at the end of the week; 10% will be admitted to a ward; and 5% will be admitted to ICU.

The board of governors believes the criteria for keeping patients in ICU are too strict and has instructed the ICU staff to relax the criteria so that only 40% of the ICU patients remain in ICU each week and 60% are transferred to wards.

The staff insists that if this is done, 20% of the ward patients will be going into ICU each week and only 30% will be transferred to outpatient status. The percentage of ward patients remaining will still be 50%. There will be no change in outpatient status.

Will the policy advocated by the board of governors actually save money?

ANALYSIS

In this example we are interested in determining the difference in the long-run expected costs of the two situations. This, of course, implies calculation of the equilibrium "shares," or percentages, of patients in each of the three categories—intensive care, ward, or outpatient. There will be no change in the number of categories as in the previous example. Instead there is a change in the actual transition probabilities. At first glance each suggestion of the governing board appears to be economical, but the result is certainly not apparent. We must calculate the probability of a patient's being in each of the two conditions that have a cost to the hospital (intensive care and ward), multiply those probabilities by their respective costs, and then compare the total expected costs for each of the two situations.

Let's look at situation 1, the current situation.

Intensive Care (ICU) Patients

50% remain
50% get better and move to wards (W)
0% get well enough for outpatient status (OP)

The retention and loss column of ICU is then

$$
\begin{array}{c}
 & \text{ICU} \\
\begin{array}{c}\text{ICU}\\ \text{W}\\ \text{OP}\end{array} &
\begin{pmatrix} .5 \\ .5 \\ 0 \end{pmatrix}
\end{array}
$$

Ward Patients

10% go to ICU
50% remain in W
40% go on outpatient status

We can now add the retention and loss column for W to our matrix.

$$
\begin{array}{c}
 & \text{ICU} \quad \text{W} \\
\begin{array}{c}\text{ICU}\\ \text{W}\\ \text{OP}\end{array} &
\begin{pmatrix} .5 & .1 \\ .5 & .5 \\ 0 & .4 \end{pmatrix}
\end{array}
$$

Outpatients

5% go to ICU
10% to W
85% remain outpatients

Adding this column completes the matrix of transition probabilities.

$$
\begin{array}{cc}
 & \text{FROM} \\
 & \begin{array}{ccc} \text{ICU} & \text{W} & \text{OP} \end{array} \\
\text{TO} \quad \begin{array}{c} \text{ICU} \\ \text{W} \\ \text{OP} \end{array} & \begin{pmatrix} .5 & .1 & .05 \\ .5 & .5 & .10 \\ 0 & .4 & .85 \end{pmatrix}
\end{array}
$$

From here on the problem is simply one of mechanics.

First, write the four equilibrium equations

$$.5ICU + .1W + .05OP = ICU$$
$$.5ICU + .5W + .10OP = W$$
$$0ICU + .4W + .85OP = OP$$
$$ICU + W + OP = 1$$

in standard form

$$-.5ICU + .1W + .05OP = 0$$
$$.5ICU - .5W + .10OP = 0$$
$$0ICU + .4W - .15OP = 0$$
$$ICU + W + OP = 1$$

We drop the first one and express the remaining ones in matrix form.

$$
\begin{pmatrix} .5 & -.5 & .1 \\ 0 & .4 & -.15 \\ 1 & 1 & 1 \end{pmatrix}
\begin{pmatrix} ICU \\ W \\ OP \end{pmatrix} =
\begin{pmatrix} 0 \\ 0 \\ 1 \end{pmatrix}
$$

Solving by using Cramer's rule, we obtain the following result.

$$
ICU = \frac{\begin{Vmatrix} 0 & -.5 & .1 \\ 0 & .4 & -.15 \\ 1 & 1 & 1 \end{Vmatrix}}{\begin{Vmatrix} .5 & -.5 & .1 \\ 0 & .4 & -.15 \\ 1 & 1 & 1 \end{Vmatrix}} = \frac{.035}{.310} = .1129
$$

$$
W = \frac{\begin{Vmatrix} .5 & 0 & .1 \\ 0 & 0 & -.15 \\ 1 & 1 & 1 \end{Vmatrix}}{.310} = \frac{.075}{.310} = .2419
$$

$$OP = \frac{\begin{Vmatrix} .5 & -.5 & 0 \\ 0 & .4 & 0 \\ 1 & 1 & 1 \end{Vmatrix}}{.310} = \frac{.200}{.310} = .6452$$

The value for ICU is the probability of a patient being in intensive care, and the value of W is the probability of a patient being in a ward.

By multiplying these probabilities by their respective costs, we obtain the total expected cost per patient.

(Cost of ICU × Probability of ICU) + (Cost of W × Probability of W)

= Expected Cost per Patient

($1000 × .1129) + ($500 × .2419) = $112.90 + $120.95

= $233.85

If the suggestion of the board of governors is followed, there will be some changes in the matrix of transition probabilities. In the ICU column, retention will change from .5 to .4, and ICU's loss to W will change from .5 to .6. In the W column, retention will not change, but loss to ICU will go from .1 to .2, and loss to OP will change from .4 to .3. There will be no change in the OP column.

The new equilibrium equations are

$$.4ICU + .2W + .05OP = ICU$$
$$.6ICU + .5W + .10OP = W$$
$$0ICU + .3W + .85OP = OP$$
$$ICU + W + OP = 1$$

Expressed in standard form, they are

$$-.6ICU + .2W + .05OP = 0$$
$$.6ICU - .5W + .10OP = 0$$
$$0ICU + .3W - .15OP = 0$$
$$ICU + W + OP = 1$$

It appears that elimination of the first equation will yield the easiest matrix with which to work.

Putting the equations in matrix form, we now have

$$\begin{pmatrix} .6 & -.5 & .1 \\ 0 & .3 & -.15 \\ 1 & 1 & 1 \end{pmatrix} \begin{pmatrix} ICU \\ W \\ OP \end{pmatrix} = \begin{pmatrix} 0 \\ 0 \\ 1 \end{pmatrix}$$

and

$$ICU = .1429$$
$$W = .2857$$
$$OP = \underline{.5714}$$
$$1.0000$$

For the purposes of this example we are not really interested in the OP percentages, because there is no cost associated with outpatients. However, it is a good idea to calculate all of the percentages as a check. If all the percentages do not add up to one, then a mistake has been made in calculation.

Calculating the expected cost per patient for these equilibrium conditions; we obtain

$$\$1000 \times .1429 = \$142.90$$
$$+ 500 \times .2857 = \underline{142.85}$$
$$\$285.75$$

Conclusion: The hospital was better off under the old criteria.

Another Method of Predicting
Two or More Periods into the Future

Earlier in this chapter it was stated that in order to predict market shares two or more periods in the future, two approaches could be taken. The easier approach consists of calculating the shares one period in the future by multiplying the current market share matrix by the matrix of transition probabilities, then multiplying the resulting market share matrix by the original transition matrix to obtain shares two periods in the future, then repeating the process for three periods in the future, etc. The more difficult approach is to square the transition matrix and multiply by the current market share matrix to get the shares two periods in the future, or to cube the transition matrix and multiply by the current market share matrix for shares three periods in the future, etc. In this example we will use both methods.

Bigtown has three bakeries, A, B, and C. Research has shown that bakery A retains 80% of its customers from month to month and loses 10% to bakery B and 10% to bakery C. Bakery B retains 70% of its customers and loses 20% to A and 10% to C. Bakery C retains 90% of its customers, loses none to A, and loses 10% to B. At the end of July, A had 40% of the market, and B and C had 30% each. Predict the market shares for the end of August, September, and October.

The matrix of transition probabilities and the July market shares (MS_J) are

$$
\begin{array}{c}
\text{FROM} \\
\begin{array}{ccc}
\text{A} & \text{B} & \text{C}
\end{array} \\
\text{TO}\ \begin{array}{c} \text{A} \\ \text{B} \\ \text{C} \end{array}
\begin{pmatrix} .8 & .2 & 0 \\ .1 & .7 & .1 \\ .1 & .1 & .9 \end{pmatrix}
\begin{pmatrix} .4 \\ .3 \\ .3 \end{pmatrix} \\
\quad\ \text{MTP} \qquad \text{MS}_J
\end{array}
$$

Multiplying the two matrixes to determine market shares at the end of August, we obtain

$$
\begin{pmatrix} .8 & .2 & 0 \\ .1 & .7 & .1 \\ .1 & .1 & .9 \end{pmatrix}
\times
\begin{pmatrix} .4 \\ .3 \\ .3 \end{pmatrix}
=
\begin{pmatrix} .38 \\ .28 \\ .34 \end{pmatrix}
$$
$$
\text{MTP} \qquad\quad \text{MS}_J \quad \text{MS}_A
$$

Now let's square the transition matrix and calculate market shares for the end of September.

$$
\begin{pmatrix} .8 & .2 & 0 \\ .1 & .7 & .1 \\ .1 & .1 & .9 \end{pmatrix}
\times
\begin{pmatrix} .8 & .2 & 0 \\ .1 & .7 & .1 \\ .1 & .1 & .9 \end{pmatrix}
=
\begin{pmatrix} .66 & .30 & .02 \\ .16 & .52 & .16 \\ .18 & .18 & .82 \end{pmatrix}
$$
$$
\text{MTP} \qquad\qquad \text{MTP} \qquad\qquad (\text{MTP})^2
$$

$$
\begin{pmatrix} .66 & .30 & .02 \\ .16 & .52 & .16 \\ .18 & .18 & .82 \end{pmatrix}
\times
\begin{pmatrix} .4 \\ .3 \\ .3 \end{pmatrix}
=
\begin{pmatrix} .360 \\ .268 \\ .372 \end{pmatrix}
$$
$$
(\text{MTP})^2 \qquad\quad \text{MS}_J \quad \text{MS}_S
$$

Let's calculate the market shares for the end of September by multiplying our original transition matrix by our predicted market shares for the end of August and compare the results and the effort.

$$
\begin{pmatrix} .8 & .2 & 0 \\ .1 & .7 & .1 \\ .1 & .1 & .9 \end{pmatrix}
\times
\begin{pmatrix} .38 \\ .28 \\ .34 \end{pmatrix}
=
\begin{pmatrix} .360 \\ .268 \\ .372 \end{pmatrix}
$$
$$
\text{MTP} \qquad\quad \text{MS}_A \quad \text{MS}_S
$$

It is easy to see that the answer is the same, but the effort required is considerably less using the latter method.

To predict market shares for the end of October, we simply repeat the process used to predict shares for the end of September.

$$
\begin{pmatrix} .8 & .2 & 0 \\ .1 & .7 & .1 \\ .1 & .1 & .9 \end{pmatrix} \times \begin{pmatrix} .360 \\ .268 \\ .372 \end{pmatrix} = \begin{pmatrix} .3416 \\ .2608 \\ .3976 \end{pmatrix}
$$

$$
\text{MTP} \qquad\quad \text{MS}_\text{S} \qquad\quad \text{MS}_\text{O}
$$

The Number of Periods Required to Reach Equilibrium

This is a convenient point at which to observe the pattern of change that takes place as predictions are made for periods further and further into the future. Notice that as we begin to approach equilibrium, the amount of change, whether positive or negative, decreases for each subsequent period. If one were to continue the "chain" of matrix multiplications, the change would eventually approach zero. At this point equilibrium will have been reached. In our present example, 3 months' changes have brought us very close to equilibrium. In the earlier example of Sam and Gino, it took 4 periods to reach a similar approximation of equilibrium.

	MS_J	MS_A	$\Delta_\text{J–A}$	MS_S	$\Delta_\text{A–S}$	MS_O	$\Delta_\text{S–O}$
A	.4	.38	−.02	.360	−.020	.3416	−.0184
B	.3	.28	−.02	.268	−.012	.2608	−.0072
C	.3	.34	+.04	.372	+.032	.3976	+.0256

It can be of great interest to a businessperson to know when equilibrium conditions will be reached. Assuming no change in transition probabilities, this can be calculated by simply continuing the multiplication process until the period-to-period changes become negligible and then counting the number of steps that were required to reach that point. The number of periods required is a function of how close the initial market shares are to the equilibrium shares.

Higher-Order Markov Chains

Predictions of future states based on more detailed information can be made by using higher-order Markov processes. A second-order Markov model assumes that choices made in the next future period depend on behavior in the two previous periods. A third-order process assumes the next period's choices depend on behavior in the previous three periods.

Higher-order Markov processes are beyond the scope of this text, but following is a second-order MTP for illustration.

$$
\begin{array}{c}
\text{FROM} \\
\begin{array}{cccc}
A_1A_2 & A_1B_2 & B_1A_2 & B_1B_2
\end{array} \\
\text{TO} \begin{array}{c} A_3 \\ B_3 \end{array}
\begin{pmatrix}
.9 & .6 & .5 & .2 \\
.1 & .4 & .5 & .8
\end{pmatrix}
\end{array}
$$

The upper left-hand element of this matrix shows that 90% of the customers retained by A in periods 1 and 2 will be retained by A in period 3. The lower left-hand element shows that 10% of those customers will be lost to B in period 3. Similarly, the other columns specify period 3 behavior based upon behavior in the two preceding periods.

APPLICATIONS OF MARKOV CHAINS

Marketing Applications

In the first example in this chapter it was pointed out that we were assuming no change in the transition probabilities over time. In most real-life situations this is a rather far-fetched assumption. The retention, loss and gain rates may very well change from period to period.

Transition probabilities change, yet we use the values from a single matrix to calculate equilibrium market shares that are to occur sometime in the uncertain future. What's the sense in this? The answer is that equilibrium shares calculated from a current transition matrix allow a manager to see the *general* direction in which the marketplace is moving *based on current conditions*.

A manager who is pleased with the direction of the marketplace may choose to do nothing that would affect the current transition probabilities, but could simply sit back and wait for the competition to change strategy, and then devise counteracting strategies. On the other hand, the manager who is displeased with the direction can initiate strategies to change the current probabilities.

For example, a manager finds that her product (A) is in an *absorbing state* and at equilibrium the product will capture 100% of the market under current conditions. The current transition matrix might look like this:

$$
\begin{array}{c}
\text{FROM} \\
\begin{array}{ccc}
A & B & C
\end{array} \\
\text{TO} \begin{array}{c} A \\ B \\ C \end{array}
\begin{pmatrix}
1.00 & .1 & .2 \\
0 & .8 & .1 \\
0 & .1 & .7
\end{pmatrix}
\end{array}
$$

Absorbing State

The manager of A could simply rest on her laurels and wait for B and C to change strategies. She is retaining all her customers (losing none) and gaining a few from B and C.

If the manager of product Z viewed the situation below he would see that his market share was in a *disappearing state* and would eventually go to zero. Unless he was planning to retire in the very near future, he would certainly make some strategy changes.

$$
\begin{array}{c}
\text{FROM} \\
\begin{array}{cc}
& \begin{array}{ccc} X & Y & Z \end{array} \\
\text{TO} \begin{array}{c} X \\ Y \\ Z \end{array} & \left(\begin{array}{ccc} .8 & .1 & .2 \\ .2 & .9 & .1 \\ \hline 0 & 0 & .7 \end{array} \right)
\end{array}
\end{array}
$$

Disappearing State

First of all the Z manager might try to increase *brand loyalty*, which is reflected by the percentage shown in row Z, column Z of the matrix (.7). He would want more of the customers who buy his product once to buy it again.

Some possible strategies would be to improve quality, put discount (cents off) coupons in the package, or include some sort of premium certificates in the package.

The next thing the manager would do is try to increase his product's gain from the other products in the market. This might be done with an expanded advertising campaign or with contests and other ploys to bring the brand name to the attention of more potential customers.

Television networks are highly sensitive to market share information on a day-to-day and even an hour-to-hour basis. They have the means to determine (on a sample basis) the behavior of viewers instantaneously. Consequently, they can construct transition matrixes for various nights of the week that show network switching from hour to hour.

What kinds of strategies might a programming manager for a network use to cut losses to the other networks from hour to hour? In other words, how might he or she try to keep viewers "tuned in?"

You have probably noticed one particular strategy—teasers. These are interest-provoking scenes from the subsequent programs scheduled for the same evening. Another is scheduling hour or two-hour programs against groups of shorter programs on the other networks, assuming that a viewer will be caught up in a longer program and stay with it.

A strategy used to increase gains from the other networks would be radio, magazine, and newspaper advertising. Of course, the dominant strategy used, both to cut losses and to increase gains in market share, is simply trying to put programs on that have a wider interest than those of the other networks.

INDUSTRIAL APPLICATIONS

Market information, as it pertains to brand loyalty and brand switching, is difficult and expensive to obtain for the most part. In addition, the transition probabilities change often, because of changes in tastes or changes in market strategies. In many industrial situations, however, information is easy and inexpensive to obtain. Consequently, Markov chains can be used effectively and with very dependable results.

Maintenance Programs

Consider, for instance, the example on truck tire maintenance that we studied earlier. The transition probabilities may be expected to remain quite stable, barring changes in tire technology. The decision maker in a case such as this does not have to contend with counterstrategies of competitors, so his predictions of state changes of tires will be quite accurate.

Markov analysis has also been effectively applied to preventive maintenance programs in large machine shops. Machines, as they wear, tend to become less and less accurate. They move from a state of high accuracy to a state of marginal accuracy and finally to a state of total inaccuracy or failure. Using the Markov approach a maintenance manager could plan his workload requirements and predict the average number of machines that would be out of service during any one period.

Personnel Training

The Markov approach might also be applied to personnel training programs. Of the new trainees who enter the program, a certain percentage will progress to a given skill level after one period; a certain percentage will move to an even higher level during the same period; and still others will fail to progress past the "beginner" level.

Babson Machine and Foundry conducts a welder training program, and trainee progress, historically, has been found to be as follows.

1. After 1 month of training 80% of the trainees have qualified as class B welders; 10% have qualified as class A welders; and 10% are still classified as beginners.
2. Of those trainees classified as B welders at the beginning of the month, 90% become class A by the end of the month, and 10% remain class B.
3. Those welders reaching class A status are replaced in the program by new trainees (beginners).

The matrix of transition probabilities will look like this.

$$
\text{TO} \quad
\begin{array}{c}
 \\
T \\
B \\
A
\end{array}
\begin{array}{c}
\overset{\textstyle\text{FROM}}{} \\
\begin{array}{ccc}
T & B & A
\end{array} \\
\left(\begin{array}{ccc}
.1 & 0 & 1 \\
.8 & .1 & 0 \\
.1 & .9 & 0
\end{array}\right)
\end{array}
\quad
\begin{array}{l}
T = \text{Trainee} \\
B = \text{class B} \\
A = \text{class A}
\end{array}
$$

The one in row T, column A reflects the replacement of welders who have reached class A status and have been replaced by new trainees. No trainees are lost from a higher state to a lower.

Given the preceding matrix and the number of trainees in each classification at any one time, we can easily predict the status of all trainees at the end of the month.

Accounts Receivable

Markov models have been effectively applied in the description of the accounts receivable that a firm carries on its books. The states might be new receivables; 30, 60, 90, and 120 days in arrears; uncollectable; and paid off. The probabilities of moving from one state to the others can be established by analysis of past experience. The "market shares" can be kept in dollar amounts, number of accounts, or as percentages of the total. The model might look like this.

FROM

		New	30	60	90	120	Bad	Paid
	New	0	0	0	0	0	0	0
	30	.3	0	0	0	0	0	0
	60	0	.4	0	0	0	0	0
TO	90	0	0	.6	0	0	0	0
	120	0	0	0	.8	0	0	0
	Bad	0	0	0	0	.9	1	0
	Paid	.7	.6	.4	.2	.1	0	1

Seventy percent of new receivables are paid off within 30 days; 30% move to the "30 days in arrears" state. Each successive state shows a lower probability of being paid and a higher probability of becoming an older debt. After 120 days, they are written off as bad debts. Once written off or paid, the account stays there; so these are absorbing states. New receivables must be added each month.

Health-Care Applications

Markov analysis has been used to predict the movement of blood through a blood bank. New blood comes in and is stored. Either it is used for transfusions, or it ages to the point where it is unusable (about 21 days old). The various states might be defined as "days of age."

In a hospital new patients are admitted daily. Some get better and are released; some get worse before they get better and are released; and, of course, some die. When the transition probabilities are established, a hospital can predict its needs for the following period based on the current distribution of patients. The ICU model discussed in this chapter is one simple example of such an application.

CONCLUSION

The market share example is found in almost every chapter on Markov chains. The reason is simple: The market share model is easy to understand and to visualize. The market share example is not used because it is the best, or even the most common, Markov application.

Machine maintenance, perishable inventory, personnel training, accounts receivable, and other similar areas provide fertile ground for Markov analysis. As long as people or machines or objects within a system move from one status to another with some predictable probability from period to period, Markov chains may be useful in the analysis of those systems.

SUMMARY OF KEY CONCEPTS

Markov chain.   Mathematical model that uses information describing past and present states of variables to predict future states.

Brand switching.   In marketing examples for Markov analysis, major concern is with the probability of customers switching from one brand to another.

Market shares.   The percentage of the total market (in dollars of sales or number of units) held by each of the competing firms. It can be computed for the base period, future periods, and at equilibrium.

Matrix of transition probabilities (MTP).   A matrix that shows the probabilities of staying in the same state (retention probabilities), moving to another state (loss probabilities), and arriving from another state (gain probabilities) from one period to the next.

Retention probabilities.   Found on the principal diagonal of the MTP, they express the probabilities of remaining in the same state from one period to the next.

Loss probabilities.   The remaining entries in the *column* of a particular state. They reflect the likelihood of leaving that state for another. (The sum of the retention probability and the loss probabilities for each state must equal one.)

Gain probabilities. The elements other than the retention rate in the *row* of a state. The likelihood of moving to the state from another state.

Market share vector. A column vector that expresses the absolute or relative share for each state in a given period.

Matrix multiplication. By multiplying the transition probabilities matrix by the market share column vector, market shares for the next period are calculated and appear as a new column vector.

Equilibrium market shares. The market shares that each product would capture after some period of time has passed and that would not change, assuming the transition probability matrix remains unchanged.

Absorbing state. In a matrix of transition probabilities, a state that has no losses to other states but does have gains from other states is an absorbing state. Absorbing states will capture a 100% market share at equilibrium.

Disappearing state. A state that has no gains from other states but does have losses to other states or that exists in a system having an absorbing state is a disappearing state. At equilibrium it will capture a 0% market share.

Brand loyalty. The propensity of a consumer to continue to purchase the same brand of product from period to period.

First-order Markov chains. Markov models that use information from a single period in the past to predict behavior in the future

Higher-order Markov chains. Markov models that make use of information from two or more periods in the past to make predictions of future system behavior.

PROBLEMS

1. In a small midwestern town there are two competing bakeries, Vitamin Plus and Natural Wholesome. Currently Vitamin Plus has 90% of the market, and Natural Wholesome has the remaining 10%. From year to year 80% of Vitamin's customers have remained with Vitamin, and 60% of Natural's have remained with Natural. Calculate the market shares of the two bakeries for five periods in the future.

2. Assume that the current market shares for the bakeries in problem 1 are reversed and calculate the market shares for five periods in the future.

3. Calculate the equilibrium market shares for the bakeries in problem 1.

4. Hank and Rufus are the two car dealers in a small town. Last year Hank sold 80 cars, and Rufus sold 120. In recent years Hank has found that 60% of his sales are repeat customers. Rufus' sales are 90% to return customers. What will be their respective market shares this year if recent trends continue? What will be their shares next year?

5. What will be the equilibrium market shares for Hank and Rufus if current trends continue?

6. There are two barbers, Al and Bob, in Isolated, Montana. Bob performed an analysis that revealed that he retained 70% of his customers over the past year and Al retained 80%. If the matrix of

transition probabilities remains stable and if each now has 50% of the market, what will be their respective market shares next year? The year after? Ultimately?

7. The following table summarizes the brand loyalties of smokers of two brands of cigars, Hempos and Ropos, against the rest of the market. If the current market shares are Hempos 30%, Ropos 10%, and all others 60%, what will Ropos' market shares be next period and two periods in the future? What will Ropos' equilibrium share be?

FROM

$$
\text{TO} \quad \begin{array}{c} \\ H \\ R \\ O \end{array} \begin{array}{ccc} H & R & O \\ \begin{pmatrix} .8 & 0 & .3 \\ .1 & .9 & .1 \\ .1 & .1 & .6 \end{pmatrix} \end{array}
$$

8. One year ago Big Ed's Bright and Flashy disco opened in Boomtown, where two other discos had been in operation for a number of years. After 1 year of operation the disco dancer market was shared as follows:

Uncle Bill's Dignity Plus	40%
Big Ed's Bright and Flashy	20%
Aunt Sally's Restful Repose	40%

An analysis of disco customer loyalty revealed the following matrix of transition probabilities.

FROM

$$
\text{TO} \quad \begin{array}{c} \\ \text{Bill's} \\ \text{Ed's} \\ \text{Sally's} \end{array} \begin{array}{ccc} \text{Bill's} & \text{Ed's} & \text{Sally's} \\ \begin{pmatrix} .8 & 0 & .1 \\ .1 & 1 & .2 \\ .1 & 0 & .7 \end{pmatrix} \end{array}
$$

Assuming the transition probabilities are stable, what will be the equilibrium market shares? What is a state such as Ed's called? Do you think equilibrium will be reached before the MTP is changed? Why?

9. Mr. O. R. Jones is considering the purchase of Ben's Auto Parts Store in a small town served by two other parts stores, Alvin's and Charley's. The big selling point for Ben's store is that it has 60% of the total business in town, whereas the other two stores share the remaining 40% equally. However, Mr. Jones decided to analyze the market behavior of the town's auto parts customers. His findings are summarized in the following MTP.

$$\begin{array}{cc} & \text{FROM} \\ & \begin{array}{ccc} \text{A} & \text{B} & \text{C} \end{array} \\ \text{TO} \begin{array}{c} \text{A} \\ \text{B} \\ \text{C} \end{array} & \begin{pmatrix} .8 & 0 & .3 \\ 0 & .9 & 0 \\ .2 & .1 & .7 \end{pmatrix} \end{array}$$

If the MTP can be considered stable, what are the equilibrium market shares? Should Jones buy Ben's store?

10. Conrad's Credit Jewelry Store classifies credit accounts as current, overdue (30–90 days), and bad debt (over 90 days). An analysis of accounts over the past several years shows that from month to month 90% of current accounts remain current and 10% become overdue. Of the overdue accounts, 50% remain overdue, and 20% become bad debts. Twenty percent of the bad debt accounts are partially paid and are reclassified as overdue, and 10% of them are paid current. If no new accounts are added, what will be the percentage of accounts in each classification at equilibrium?

Chapter 4

LINEAR PROGRAMMING GRAPHICAL ANALYSIS

INTRODUCTION

Linear programming (LP) is the most widely applied quantitative decision-making tool in business and industry. The most commonly used technique for linear programming was developed by George B. Dantzig, a mathematician, in 1947. His original application was in the area of military planning for the U.S. Air Force, but he believed the new approach could be used in the solution of business and industrial problems.

Indeed, the technique of linear programming can be applied to such far-ranging problems as minimizing the cost of "hen scratch" (a combination of cereal grains) while maintaining a proper nutritional balance, or controlling modern oil refineries. It may be used to determine the most profitable product mix in a manufacturing operation or to find the best capital structure for a new corportation.

The procedure is straightforward and mathematically simple. You should find the solving of the examples at the end of this chapter easy enough to be entertaining, yet difficult enough to provide a sense of accomplishment.

A word of warning is necessary at this point. Linear programming is not a panacea. It has limitations, which must be recognized. First and foremost of these limitations is the static nature of LP. The technique does not provide for dynamic situations. It is a snapshot rather than a movie. The solutions obtained hold only as long as the conditions at the time of solution hold. Another limitation is one that, happily, can be overcome by use of a computer. This is the computational limitation. Problems that are simple enough to be worked by hand are usually trivial. In Chapter 6, however, you will see how larger, more complex problems can be handled using preprogrammed ("canned") computer models.

LP MODEL FORMULATION

We are frequently faced with situations in which we wish to fulfill certain objections but find ourselves confronted with barriers which block complete attainment of these goals. We wish to take the most luxurious vacation possible, but we have only 2 weeks off; we have only $100; and we get both airsick and seasick. We wish to make the very best grades possible, but we are required to take several courses that are difficult; we have only 4 hours per day to study; and we are just a little lazy.

Business firms suffer these same dilemmas. A company wishes to make the maximum profit possible, but it has limited production capacity; there is a limit to the number of units the market will absorb; and raw material is difficult to get. An airline wishes to get as many people on a flight as possible, but the plane has a load limit; people rebel at being seated in someone's lap; and there is a competing airline that offers a flight 10 minutes earlier.

Almost all problems encountered in life take this form. There is a recognized wish or goal and a set of limiting factors. In the jargon of the management scientist, the wish or goal is called the *objective function*, and the limiting factors are called *constraints*. Linear programming is simply a method of finding the highest level of goal fulfillment, considering the limitations placed upon that fulfillment. In other words, it allows us to *optimize* (maximize or minimize) the objective function subject to the constraints, as long as the objective function and the constraints can be represented by linear equations. Recall that a linear equation is one that contains only first-order terms, and no squares or cubes, etc.

Before we jump headlong into the mysteries of graphical LP, it would be wise to review the two-dimensional grid in Figure 4.1. Because we will be dealing with real things such as money, corn, tables, chairs, and oil, the least of anything we will be dealing with is nothing, or zero. In other words, if you get an answer that lies in any quadrant other than the first, it is wrong. This is known as the *nonnegativity* constraint.

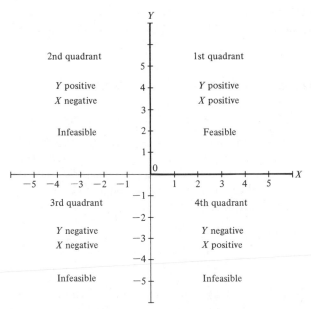

Figure 4.1   Feasible and infeasible quadrants on the two-dimensional grid.

General Form of the LP Problem

We can state the general form of the linear programming problem with n independent variables and m constraints as

$$\text{Optimize } Z = \sum_{j=1}^{n} c_j X_j \quad \text{(objective function)}$$

Subject to

$$\sum_{j=1}^{n} a_{ij} X_j (\lesseqqgtr) b_i, \; i = 1, 2, \ldots, m \quad \text{(constraints)}$$

$$(X_j \geq 0, j = 1, 2, \ldots, n) \quad \text{(nonnegativity constraints)}$$

In this chapter, all problems will be solved graphically and therefore will have only two independent variables. The rather intimidating formulation above becomes

$$\text{Optimize} \quad Z = c_1 X + c_2 Y \quad \text{(objective function)}$$

$$\text{Subject to} \quad \left. \begin{array}{l} a_{11} X + a_{12} Y \, (\lesseqqgtr) b_1 \\ a_{21} X + a_{22} Y \, (\lesseqqgtr) b_2 \\ \quad \vdots \qquad \quad \vdots \qquad \quad \vdots \\ A_{m1} X + A_{m2} Y \, (\lesseqqgtr) b_m \end{array} \right\} m \quad \text{(constraints)}$$

$$(X, Y \geq 0) \quad \text{(nonnegativity constraints)}$$

The symbol ($\lesseqgtr$) indicates that the constraints can be less than or equal to (LTE, $\leq$), greater than or equal to (GTE, $\geq$), or strict equality (EQ, $=$) types.

PLOTTING CONSTRAINTS FOR GRAPHICAL LP PROBLEMS

Less Than or Equal to (LTE) Constraints

In any graphical LP problem, the first step will be to plot the constraints. The problem constraints, in combination with the nonnegativity constraints, will define (or bound) the area containing all *feasible* solution points for the particular problem. We call this area the *feasible region*.

If, for example, we have the constraints

$$4X + 2Y \leq 24$$
$$X + Y \leq 8$$
$$(X, Y \leq 0)$$

we would begin by changing the LTE constraints to equalities.

$$4X + 2Y = 24$$
$$X + Y = 8$$

We would then plot these lines on our graph by establishing the *intercepts* for each line and simply joining the two points. Recall that intercepts are established by setting one of the variables in the equation equal to zero and solving for the value of the other variable.

$$Y = 0: \quad 4X + 2(0) = 24$$
$$X = \tfrac{24}{4} = 6$$
$$X = 0: \quad 4(0) + 2Y = 24$$
$$Y = \tfrac{24}{2} = 12$$

This establishes the points $(6, 0)$ and $(0, 12)$ as the intercepts of the equation $4X + 2Y = 24$.

Following the same procedure with the other constraint, we have

$$Y = 0: \quad X + 0 = 8$$
$$X = 8$$
$$X = 0: \quad 0 + Y = 8$$
$$Y = 8$$

so the intercepts are $(8, 0)$ and $(0, 8)$. Each constraint is plotted in Figure 4.2.

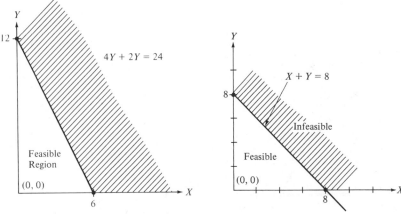

Figure 4.2   Plotting the constraints.

Because all of the points on one side of a constraint line are either feasible or infeasible, testing any *one* point enables us to identify the feasible side of the line. The easiest point is the origin (0, 0). In our example we do this by substituting zero for the X and Y values in the original constraints.

$$X = 0, \quad Y = 0: \quad 4(0) + 2(0) = 0 \le 24$$
$$1(0) + 1(0) = 0 \le 8$$

Neither constraint is violated at this point, so the feasible region is to the left of and below each of the two constraints. We shade in the infeasible area above the constraints. In Figure 4.3 we have plotted both constraints and the nonnegativity constraints.

Note that a part of each constraint bounds the feasible region. Over the range $X = 0$ to $X = 4$ ($Y = 8$ to $Y = 4$) the feasible region is bounded by $X + Y = 8$, and over the range $X = 4$ to $X = 6$ ($Y = 4$ to $Y = 0$) the region is bounded by $4X + 2Y = 24$. The nonnegativity constraints complete the boundary. The remaining, unshaded, area contains all points which do not violate any of our constraints. We call this area the *feasible region*.

Greater Than or Equal to (GTE) Constraints

In the previous example, both constraints were of the LTE variety. How would the problem be set up if these constraints were of the GTE type?

$$4X + 2Y \ge 24$$
$$X + \quad Y \ge 8$$

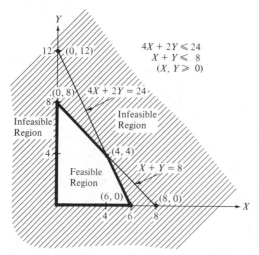

Figure 4.3   A two-variable linear programming (LP) problem with less than or equal to (LTE) constraints.

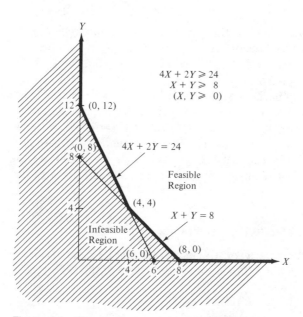

Figure 4.4   Greater than or equal to (GTE) constraints for a two-variable LP problem.

They become exactly the same equalities used in the first example. Consequently, the lines will be plotted on the graph exactly as in Figure 4.3.

The difference in the two situations becomes apparent when we test to find the feasible region. Once again, we substitute the values of X and Y at the origin into the constraint equations

$$4(0) + 2(0) = 0 < 24$$
$$(0) + \quad (0) = 0 < 8$$

Both constraints are violated, so the origin lies outside the feasible region with respect to both constraints. The feasible region is to the right of the constraint lines, as shown in Figure 4.4. Note that the feasible region extends indefinitely upward and to the right, and is said to be *unbounded*, as contrasted with the completely enclosed or bounded feasible region in Figure 4.3.

Thus far, we have examined only constraints and have found the areas in which the answers can and cannot be found. The next step is to find out exactly where within the feasible region the correct answer lies. In order to do this, we must introduce the objective function into our calculations.

Maximizing the Objective Function

The Lampassas Leather Company makes hand-tooled leather jackets (X) and pants (Y). They sell the jackets for a profit of $10 each and the pants for a profit of $6 per pair. Their total profit is $10 times the number of jackets sold plus $6 times the number of pants sold. Expressed mathematically, this becomes

$$\text{Profit} = 10X + 6Y$$

The objective is to maximize this profit, so the foregoing equation is our objective function. Conventionally, in linear programming problems, that which is to be optimized (in this case, profit) is expressed as "Z". Our objective function is, therefore

$$\text{Maximize } Z = 10X + 6Y$$

As you might have guessed, there are factors that keep the company from making infinite profit by simply making an infinite number of jackets and pants. Each of these products requires two operations in construction cutting and sewing. It requires 4 labor hours to cut out a jacket and 2 hours to cut out a pair of pants. The employee who does the cutting can only work 24 hours per week. Consequently, if we multiply the number of jackets cut out by 4 and the number of pairs of pants cut out by 2, the weekly total must be no more than 24. This constraint is stated mathematically as

$$4X + 2Y \leq 24$$

which, by this time, should look quite familiar.

By the same token, the seamstress who sews for the company works only one day (8 hours) per week. She can sew a jacket or a pair of pants in 1 hour. Thus

$$X + Y \leq 8$$

The linear programming problem may now be formally stated as

Maximize $\quad Z = 10X + 6Y \quad$ (profit objective)

Subject to $\qquad 4X + 2Y \leq 24 \quad$ (cutting constraint)

$\qquad\qquad X + \ Y \leq \ 8 \quad$ (sewing constraint)

$(X, Y \geq 0) \quad$ (nonnegativity constraints)

We want to decide how many jackets and how many pants we should make in order to have the greatest profit.

At first glance, it would appear that we should make only jackets, because we make \$4 each more on them than on the pants. As we have already been through the drill of plotting these same constraint equations (they are repeated in Figure 4.5), we can move directly to finding the solution. A simple and straightforward method for doing this is to test the extremities, or corners, of the feasible region, because as we shall see presently, the optimum solution(s) will always occur at one or more of these points.

In Figure 4.5, you can see that the values of X and Y at these corners are

(A) $\quad X = 0, \qquad Y = 0 \qquad$ (the origin)

(B) $\quad X = 0, \qquad Y = 8$

(C) $\quad X = 4, \qquad Y = 4$

(D) $\quad X = 5, \qquad Y = 0$

If we evaluate the objective function at each of these points, we obtain

(A) $\quad 10(0) + 6(0) = 0$

(B) $\quad 10(0) + 6(8) = 48$

(C) $\quad 10(4) + 6(4) = 64$

(D) $\quad 10(6) + 6(0) = 60$

Note the family of parallel dashed lines in Figure 4.5. These lines represent the objective function $Z = 10X + 6Y$ for different values of Z. As our objective function moves up and to the right from the origin, Z takes on greater values. Note that the line $Z = 64$, which passes through the optimum point ($X = 4$, $Y = 4$), just touches the feasible region and is

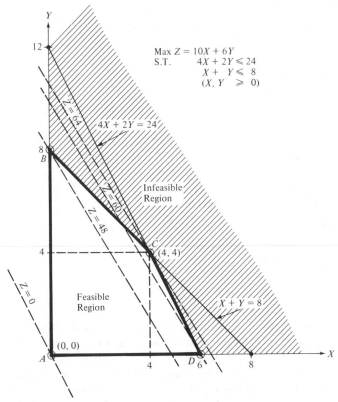

Figure 4.5   A two-variable LP problem with LTE constraints and objective function (maximization problem).

farther from the origin than any of the lines through the other points in the feasible region.

Our optimal solution is to produce 4 jackets and 4 pairs of pants per week. This utilizes all cutting and sewing time and produces the maximum feasible profit of $64 per week.

There is another method of finding the optimum solution graphically. Z represents a *family* of parallel lines, each having a slope equal to $-C_1/C_2$ ($-\frac{10}{6}$ in our example). Therefore, if we can plot *any one* of the family of Z lines, we can "slide over" parallel to it to plot the Z lines through each of the "corners" of the feasible region. Simply assign a convenient value to the objective function by replacing Z with a number that is easily divisible by the coefficients in the equation. Then, follow the same procedure that was used to plot the constraint equations and plot this one member of the objective function family. Plot lines parallel to this line through each of the corners of the feasible region. One of these lines will be farther from the origin than all the others and will pass through the maximum solution point.

Minimizing the Objective Function

Of course, the graphical linear programming approach is not limited to maximization problems. While businesses seek to maximize profit, they also seek to minimize cost. For example, the Econopro Company is considering producing a hamburger meat extender from two synthetic ingredients. The company wishes to minimize the cost of the product while meeting fat and fiber constraints set by their major customer. The two ingredients that may be used are Wondermeal and Tetrafibe.

Each ounce of Wondermeal costs 9¢ and contains 6 units of fiber and 8 units of fat. An ounce of Tetrafibe costs 12¢ and contains 6 units of fiber and 4 units of fat. The customer requires that each portion-controlled package of extender contain at least 36 units of fiber and 32 units of fat. These constraints can be summarized as follows.

	TETRAFIBE	WONDERMEAL	REQUIRED
Fiber	6	6	at least 36
Fat	4	8	at least 32

The first key to the problem is the idea of minimizing the objective function. Obviously, the smallest value of the function is zero if it is unconstrained. If the constraints were the same as those in the last example, the minimum value of the function would still be zero, because the origin is within the feasible region. Unfortunately, the constraints of this problem are of a more mandatory nature. The key words of the constraints are "at least," which means equal to or greater than the value stated. The constraints in the previous example were of the "no more than" nature, or less than or equal to. The shorthand statement of this problem is

$$\text{Minimize} \quad Z = 12T + 9W \quad \text{(cost objective)}$$
$$\text{Subject to} \quad 6T + 6W \geq 36 \quad \text{(fiber constraint)}$$
$$4T + 8W \geq 32 \quad \text{(fat constraint)}$$
$$(T, W \geq 0) \quad \text{(nonnegativity constraints)}$$

As you will see in the following procedure, the constraint lines are plotted in exactly the same manner as in the maximization example.

1. Find the intercepts.

$$6T + 6W = 36 \qquad T = 0, W = 6; W = 0, T = 6$$
$$4T + 8W = 32 \qquad T = 0, W = 4; W = 0, T = 8$$

These constraints are plotted in Figure 4.6.

2. Find the feasible region by testing the origin.

$$T = 0, \qquad W = 0: \quad 6(0) + 6(0) < 36$$
$$4(0) + 8(0) < 32$$

Because these values violate both constraints, the feasible region must be on the other side of the constraint lines as shown in Figure 4.6.

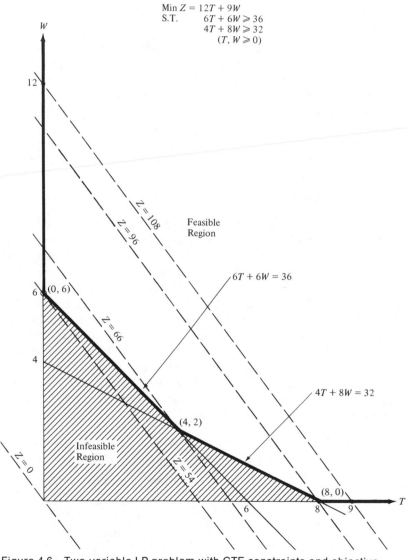

Figure 4.6 Two-variable LP problem with GTE constraints and objective function (minimization problem).

3. Test the extreme points ("corners") of the feasible region.

$$T = 8, \quad W = 0$$
$$Z = 12(8) + 9(0) = 96$$
$$T = 4, \quad W = 2$$
$$Z = 12(4) + 9(2) = 48 + 18 = 66$$
$$T = 0, \quad W = 6$$
$$Z = 12(0) + 9(6) = 54$$

4. Alternatively, we can plot a convenient value of the objective function ($Z = 108$, which divides evenly by both 9 and 12) and slide it along toward the origin until we find the corner where the minimum Z line touches the feasible region $(0, 6)$. This is the only point we actually need to evaluate.

The optimum solution lies at the point where $T = 0$ and $W = 6$, which tells us that the most economical package that meets all requirements is 6 ounces of Wondermeal, no Tetrafibe, and costs only 54¢.

Mixing Constraint Types

A group of investors is planning the construction of a new country club, to be called the Lost Lake Golf and Country Club. They wish to determine the optimum number of two types of memberships—full family and single adult—to offer for sale. They have decided to limit the total number of memberships to a maximum of 900. They have estimated that each family membership will generate 4 customer visits per month in the restaurant and 1 in the bar; each single membership is expected to generate an average of 1 customer visit in the restaurant and 2 in the bar. They project that they must have at least 1200 customers per month in the restaurant and 1000 in the bar to break even on these operations. They wish to maximize the monthly operating profits (including dues), which are estimated at $12 per family membership and $3 per single membership. The problem can be stated as follows.

Maximize $\quad Z = 12F + 3S \quad$ (monthly operating profit objective)

Subject to $\qquad F + S \leq 900 \qquad$ (number of memberships)

$\qquad\qquad 4F + S \geq 1200 \qquad$ (monthly customers in restaurant)

$\qquad\qquad F + 2S \geq 1000 \qquad$ (monthly customers in bar)

$(F, S \geq 0) \quad$ (nonnegativity constraints)

The problem is solved graphically in Figure 4.7. First we plot the three constraints and test the origin to determine the feasible and infeasible

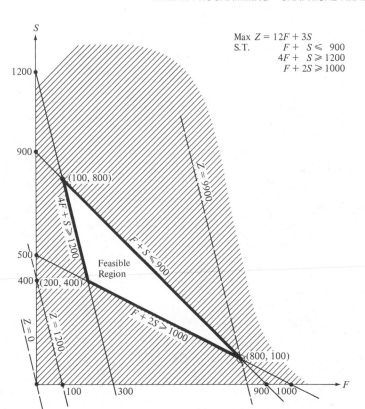

$$\text{Max } Z = 12F + 3S$$
$$\text{S.T.} \qquad F + S \leqslant 900$$
$$4F + S \geqslant 1200$$
$$F + 2S \geqslant 1000$$

Figure 4.7   Solution of the Lost Lake Country Club problem (maximizing monthly operating profit).

sides of each. This leads us to define the feasible region as shown. Then we plot an arbitrary value of Z ($Z = 1200$). Because we know that $Z = 0$ goes through the origin, we can plot it parallel to $Z = 1200$.

Now that we know the slope of the family of Z lines and the direction (up and to the right) in which they attain higher values, we can slide over parallel to $Z = 1200$ to the highest Z line that has at least one point that is feasible. This is $Z = 9900$, which goes through the optimum point (800,100). The solution to the problem is thus to authorize 800 full family memberships and 100 single adult memberships. The maximum monthly operating profit is

$$Z_{\text{MAX}} = 12(800) + 3(100) = \$9900$$

A secondary objective is to minimize the number of delinquent accounts, which average 2% of family memberships and 8% of single memberships. We have done this in Figure 4.8. The feasible region is the

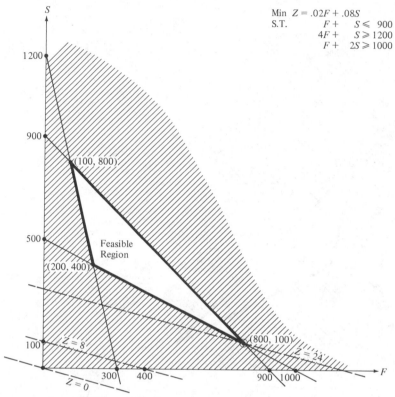

Figure 4.8 Solution to the Lost Lake Country Club problem (minimizing delinquent accounts).

same as before, but the objective function becomes

$$\text{Minimize } Z = .02F + .08S$$

We arbitrarily plot $Z = 8$ to obtain the slope of Z. Then we plot $Z = 0$ through the origin, parallel to $Z = 8$ to check the directions in which Z values increase and decrease. We wish to attain as low a value of Z as possible, but because no point on $Z = 8$ is feasible, we must slide Z upward until we touch the feasible region. This leads us to the optimum point ($F = 800$, $S = 100$) at $Z = 24$.

As it turns out, the same point (800, 100) is optimum for *maximizing* monthly operating profits ($9900) and for *minimizing* delinquent accounts (24). This leads us to the very important point that *it is not possible to determine the optimum point on the perimeter of the feasible region until the slope of the objective function is known.* Naive selection of the point "farthest" from or "nearest" to the origin will lead to incorrect results in a great many cases.

Slacks

Examination of Figure 4.8 reveals that two of the constraints (the number of memberships and the number of bar customers) are *binding*, which means that the optimum solution point lies on their respective lines. The restaurant customer constraint is *nonbinding* because the optimum solution does not lie on its line.

If we substitute the solution point into the binding constraint inequalities, we find that the equality condition holds.

$$F + S \leq 900 \qquad F + 2S \geq 1000$$
$$800 + 100 = 900 \qquad 800 + 200 = 1000$$

Substitution of the optimal point into the nonbinding constraint results in an inequality. A nonbinding constraint, therefore, is said to have *slack*. The amount of this slack is the difference between the two sides of the inequality, or the amount that must be added (in the case of an LTE) or subtracted (in the case of a GTE) to balance the two sides. In our example the slack in the restaurant customer constraint is therefore

$$4F + S \geq 1200$$
$$4(800) + 100 > 1200$$
$$\text{Slack} = 3300 - 1200 = 2100$$

As we shall see, strict equality (EQ) constraints are always binding at the optimum and have no slack.

Equality (EQ) Constraints

An equality constraint requires that we be *on* its line. Thus the feasible region is reduced to that portion of the line that does not violate any of the other constraints. If the investors in the Country Club example had wanted *exactly* 900 memberships, the feasible region would have been reduced to the line segment along $F + S = 900$ between the points (100, 800) and (800, 100). This is shown in Figure 4.9(a).

If there are *two* equality constraints, the feasible region will be reduced to the *point* of their intersection if that point does not violate any of the other constraints. If it does, there is no feasible region, and we say that the problem is *infeasible*. In the Country Club example if both the membership total and the customer count in the restaurant were equalities, the feasible region would be the point of their intersection (100, 800), as shown in Figure 4.9(b).

More than two equality constraints, unless they all happen to pass through the same point, will result in an infeasible problem.

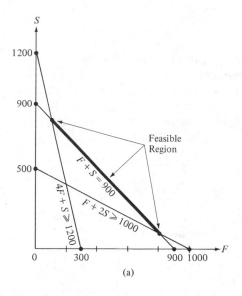

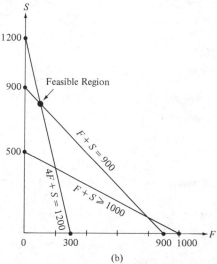

Figure 4.9   (a) One equality constraint; (b) Two equality constraints.

SPECIAL CASES

No Feasible Solution

Any time that the constraints eliminate all feasible points, the problem is overconstrained and is said to have no feasible solution. An example is shown in Figure 4.10. This situation is to be distinguished from the term "infeasible solution," which refers to any point that does not lie inside or on the boundary of the feasible region.

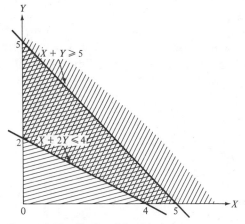

Figure 4.10 No feasible solution.

Unbounded Solution

We have already observed examples of unbounded feasible regions in Figures 4.4 and 4.6. The optimum solution in each of these was bounded. Sometimes we encounter problems with *unbounded optimum solutions*, as in Figure 4.11. We can see from the figure that we can slide our objective function upward and to the right without limit. When this happens in practice, it usually means we have omitted or misinterpreted one or more constraints of the problem.

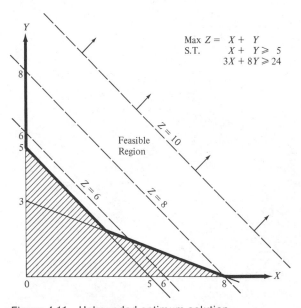

$$\begin{aligned} \text{Max } Z = \ & X + \ Y \\ \text{S.T.} \quad & X + \ Y \geqslant \ 5 \\ & 3X + 8Y \geqslant 24 \end{aligned}$$

Figure 4.11 Unbounded optimum solution.

Degenerate Solution

Degeneracy is a perfectly acceptable condition in which the number of nonzero variables is less than the number of constraints. An example is shown in Figure 4.12. We note that at the optimum solution the only nonzero variable is $Y = 6$, because both constraints are binding and therefore have zero slack.

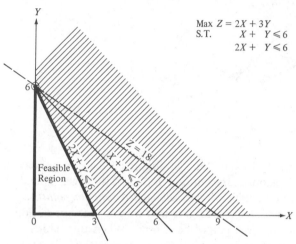

Max $Z = 2X + 3Y$
S.T. $\quad X + \ Y \leqslant 6$
$\quad\quad 2X + \ Y \leqslant 6$

Figure 4.12   Degenerate solution.

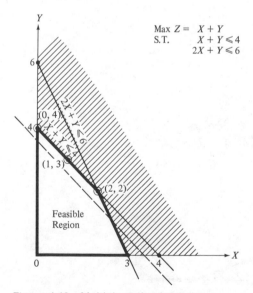

Max $Z = \ X + Y$
S.T. $\quad X + Y \leqslant 4$
$\quad\quad 2X + Y \leqslant 6$

Figure 4.13   Multiple optimal solutions.

Multiple Solutions

If the objective function is parallel to a binding constraint, there is no unique solution. In Figure 4.13 the value of the objective function is the same at (0, 4) and (2, 2) and at any point along the line segment between the two points.

It is important to note that the constraint that is parallel to the objective function must be a *binding* constraint in order for multiple optimality to exist. For example, in Figure 4.7 the objective function is parallel to the restaurant customer constraint, but because this constraint is not binding at the optimum, the solution is unique.

In real-world situations it is often desirable to have multiple optimality because it provides the decision maker with a wider range of optimal choices.

SENSITIVITY ANALYSIS

Earlier it was pointed out that LP solutions are static and can change if problem conditions change. In this section we will explore the sensitivity of the optimal solution to changes in constraints and objective function coefficients. Because the analysis takes place after we have solved the problem, it is also called *postoptimality analysis*. Determining the sensitivity of an LP solution will often be as valuable to the decision maker as the point solution itself.

Changes in Objective Function Coefficients (*C$_j$* Values)

We have seen that the location of the optimum solution in a two-dimensional problem depends upon the slope of the objective function and that this slope is determined by the relative size of the coefficients of the two variables. Consider the following simple example. A farm tractor dealer has ten tractors in his inventory and may sell them in either the foreign or the domestic market. His profit per tractor is $800 in the foreign market and $600 in the domestic. How many tractors should he sell in each market in order to maximize his profit? By inspection we know the optimum solution is to sell all ten tractors in the foreign market for a profit of $8000.

We can represent the problem graphically as shown in Figure 4.14. In this figure the original objective function is plotted, and the optimum solution is clearly shown to be at (10, 0).

Common sense tells us that if the profit on foreign-sold tractors were to increase with no change in domestic profit, the optimum solution would not change, because the slope of the objective function would become steeper. Common sense also tells us that an increase in domestic

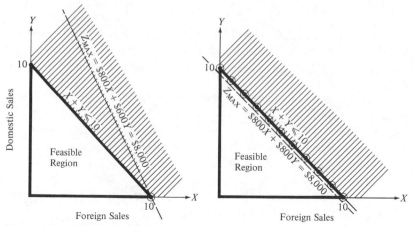

Figure 4.14 Foreign sales optimal.   Figure 4.15 Multiple solutions.

profit would tend to make foreign sales less overwhelmingly desirable and that at some point domestic sales would be just as desirable as foreign sales. This point occurs when the slope of the objective function $-C_1/C_2$ is equal to the slope of the binding constraint $-a_1/a_2$. This is the multiple solution situation shown in Figure 4.15.

If domestic profits continue to increase, it will become more desirable to sell only in the domestic market, as shown in Figure 4.16, where the slope of the objective function is $-\frac{8}{9}$. Any additional increase in domestic profit will only flatten the curve further but will not change the solution. Although the solution point will not change, the value of the objective function will become greater.

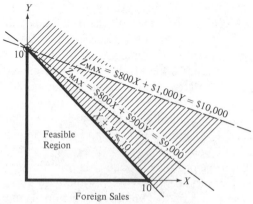

Figure 4.16 Domestic sales optimal.

Consider now the problem shown in Figure 4.17, a somewhat more complicated example than the foregoing. The objective Z_A has a slope of $-\frac{3}{2}$, which puts the optimum solution at point A. If we decrease the coefficient of X_1 until the slope of the objective function is less than that

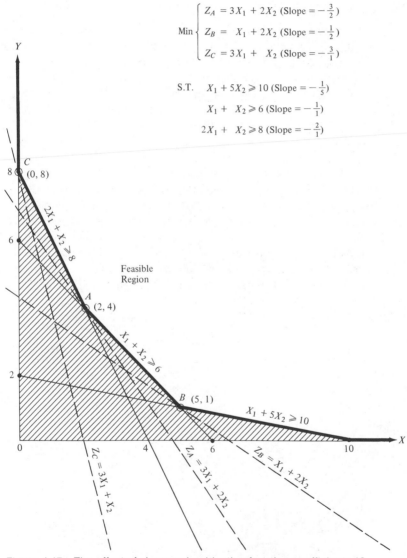

$$\text{Min} \begin{cases} Z_A = 3X_1 + 2X_2 \text{ (Slope} = -\tfrac{3}{2}) \\ Z_B = X_1 + 2X_2 \text{ (Slope} = -\tfrac{1}{2}) \\ Z_C = 3X_1 + X_2 \text{ (Slope} = -\tfrac{3}{1}) \end{cases}$$

$$\text{S.T.} \quad X_1 + 5X_2 \geqslant 10 \text{ (Slope} = -\tfrac{1}{5})$$
$$X_1 + X_2 \geqslant 6 \text{ (Slope} = -\tfrac{1}{1})$$
$$2X_1 + X_2 \geqslant 8 \text{ (Slope} = -\tfrac{2}{1})$$

Figure 4.17 The effect of changes in objective function coefficients (C_j values).

of the second constraint $(-\frac{1}{1})$, we have a situation such as Z_B with a slope of $-\frac{1}{2}$, and the solution moves to point B. If on the other hand we decrease the coefficient of X_2 until the objective function's slope becomes steeper than that of the third constraint $(-\frac{2}{1})$, we will obtain a solution at point C, using Z_C with a slope of $-\frac{3}{1}$.

Moving a Constraint (Changes in b_i Values)

Usually constraints in LP problems represent resource limitations (LTE constraints) or minimum mandates for ingredients or characteristics (GTE constraints). Equality constraints can represent either.

　　If additional amounts of a resource become available or if mandates and restrictions are relaxed, the constraint lines that represent the resources or mandates will move to new positions on the graph. Changes of these types (increasing the b_i value for LTE or decreasing the b_i value for GTE) have the effect of increasing the size of the feasible region. Conversely, when a resource becomes more scarce or a restriction becomes tighter, the b_i values move in the opposite directions (decreasing b_i for LTE and increasing b_i for GTE), and the feasible region's size is reduced.

　　Figure 4.18 shows the changes in the feasible region brought about by changing an LTE constraint. The original feasible region is bounded by points A, B, and C. If we *reduce* the value of b_3 from 5 to 4, it has the effect of *tightening* the constraint and reducing the feasible region to the area bounded by points C, F, and G. *Increasing* the value of b_3 from 5 to 6 *enlarges* the feasible region to the area bounded by C, D, and E.

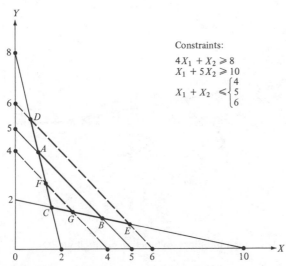

Figure 4.18　Changing b_i for LTE constraint.

Constraints:

$$4X_1 + X_2 \geqslant 8$$
$$X_1 + 5X_2 \geqslant 10$$
$$X_1 + X_2 \leqslant \begin{cases} 4 \\ 5 \\ 6 \end{cases}$$

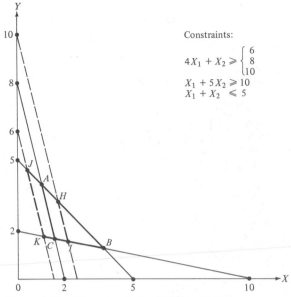

Constraints:

$$4X_1 + X_2 \geqslant \begin{cases} 6 \\ 8 \\ 10 \end{cases}$$

$$X_1 + 5X_2 \geqslant 10$$
$$X_1 + X_2 \leqslant 5$$

Figure 4.19   Changing b_i for GTE constraint.

Changes in GTE constraints are shown in Figure 4.19. The original feasible region is bounded by points A, B, and C. In the first constraint, if we *increase* the value of b_1 from 8 to 10, it has the effect of *tightening* the GTE constraint and reducing the feasible region to the area bounded by points B, H, and I. *Relaxing* the constraint is accomplished by *reducing* the value of b_1 from 8 to 6, which *expands* the feasible region to the area bounded by the points B, J, and K.

It is not possible to generalize about the effects of changes in the b_i values of equality constraints, because the effect is dependent upon the relationship between the equality constraint and the other constraints in the problem.

Sensitivity of the Optimal Solution to Changes in b_i Values

The effect of changes in b_i values on the optimal solution depends upon whether the constraint being changed is binding or nonbinding.

NONBINDING CONSTRAINTS

A nonbinding constraint will always have some slack at the optimum solution. This slack is a measure of the "distance" from the constraint to the optimum point. In Figure 4.20 the feasible region is bounded by

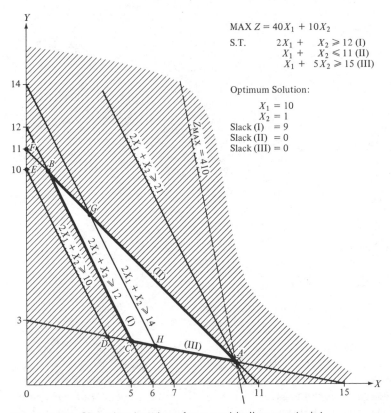

Figure 4.20 Changing b_i values for a nonbinding constraint.

points A, B, and C, and the optimal solution is at point A, where $X_1 = 10$, $X_2 = 1$, and $Z = 410$. There is no slack in the second or third constraints, because they are binding. Constraint 1 has nine units of slack. If we *relax* a *nonbinding* constraint, the optimal solution is *unaffected*. For example, if b_1 is decreased from 12 to 10, S_1 increases from 9 to 11 units, the feasible region expands to A, D, E, F, but the solution does not change.

Tightening a nonbinding constraint by an amount less than or equal to its slack reduces the feasible region but *has no effect* on the optimum solution. If the constraint is tightened by more than the amount of its slack, there are two possible results: (1) the constraint becomes binding, the feasible region is further reduced, the solution point moves, and the optimum value of Z is worse (lower in a maximization problem, higher in a minimization problem); or (2) the feasible region disappears.

In Figure 4.20 tightening the first constraint by less than nine units simply reduces S_1. For example, the only effect of increasing b_1 from 12 to 14 is to reduce the feasible region to A, G, H. The optimum remains at A.

If b_1 is increased by the amount of slack (nine units) to a value of 21, all three constraints are binding; the feasible region becomes a single point at A; and the optimum is unchanged. In this example, if b_1 is tightened by more than nine units, the feasible region vanishes and no feasible solution exists.

BINDING CONSTRAINTS

If a binding constraint is tightened, the solution moves and Z gets worse (lower in a maximization problem, higher in a minimization). If a binding constraint is relaxed, either: (1) the solution does not change, because other constraints still bind the optimum point; or (2) the optimum point moves and Z gets better.

As an example, consider the problem in Figure 4.21. If the second constraint is relaxed by increasing b_2 from 11 to 12, the feasible region expands from A, B, C to L, C, K; the optimum solution moves from point A to point L; and Z_{MAX} increases from 410 to 457.5. If the constraint is tightened by reducing b_2 from 11 to 10, the feasible region is reduced to J, I, C; the optimum point moves to point J; and Z_{MAX} is reduced to 362.5.

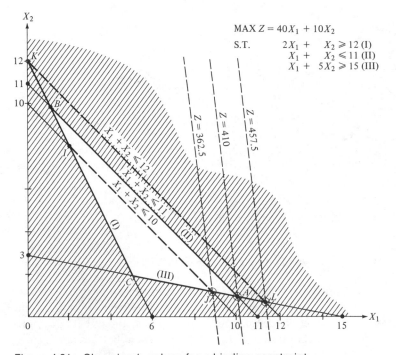

Figure 4.21 Changing b_i values for a binding constraint.

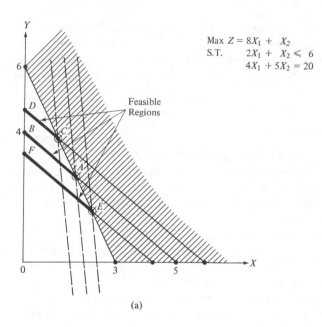

Max $Z = 8X_1 + X_2$
S.T. $2X_1 + X_2 \leqslant 6$
         $4X_1 + 5X_2 = 20$

(a)

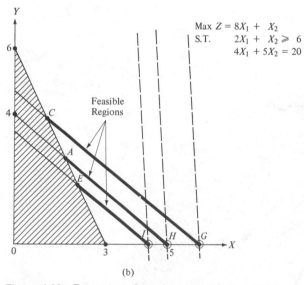

Max $Z = 8X_1 + X_2$
S.T. $2X_1 + X_2 \geqslant 6$
         $4X_1 + 5X_2 = 20$

(b)

Figure 4.22   Examples of moving equality constraints.

Since equality constraints are always binding at the optimum, any movement of an equality constraint results in either: (1) moving the solution point, or (2) eliminating the feasible region altogether. Examples of the types of changes in the solution brought about by shifts in equality constraints are shown in Figure 4.22.

In the first example, increasing b_2 reduces the feasible "region" from the line segment AB to line segment CD and moves the optimum point from A to C, resulting in a worse (lower) value for Z_{MAX}. Decreasing b_2 increases the feasible region to EF, moves the optimum to E, and increases Z_{MAX}.

In the second example, the reverse results are obtained. Increasing b_2 increases the feasible region from AH to CG, moves the optimum point from H to G, and improves (increases) Z_{MAX}. Reducing b_2 reduces the feasible region to EI, moves the solution to point I, and reduces Z_{MAX}. As we have suggested, the effects of moves in equality constraints are determined by the geometry of the particular problem.

Other Changes

Changes in the coefficients of the constraints (a_{ij}), the effects of adding or deleting constraints, and other topics dealing with sensitivity analysis are covered in much greater depth in Chapter 5, when we will have acquired greater analytical capability. We will use the simplex method of linear programming to perform rather extended postoptimality analysis at that point.

SUMMARY OF KEY CONCEPTS

Objective function.   A function (family of lines) that is to be either maximized or minimized, such as profit or cost, respectively. The objective function is the sum of the independent variables multiplied by their respective cost or profit coefficients.

$$\text{Optimize } Z = \sum_{j=1}^{n} c_j X_j$$

Constraints.   Constraints are limitations of resources or mandates of content that prohibit objective functions from going to infinity in the case of maximization or to zero in the case of minimization. Constraints can be of three types: less than or equal to (LTE), greater than or equal to (GTE), or strict equality (EQ). Their respective symbols are $\leq$, $\geq$, and $=$.

$$\sum_{j=1}^{n} a_{ij} X_j (\lesseqqgtr) b_i, \ i = 1, 2, \ldots, m$$

Optimize.   To find the very best solution given the constraints of a system (to maximize or minimize).

Feasible region.   The region within which a solution may occur without violating any of the constraints of the problem. The collection of all allowable solution points.

Infeasible region.   The area outside the feasible region. The collection of points that violate one or more of the constraints.

Infeasible solution. Any solution point that lies outside the feasible region.

Nonnegativity constraint. A constraint implied in every LP problem. It means that negative solution values for any variables are not allowed.

Binding constraint. Any constraint upon which the optimum solution point lies.

Nonbinding constraint. Any constraint upon which the optimum solution point does not lie.

Slack. A measure of the "distance" from a solution point to a nonbinding constraint. Slack is zero for all binding constraints.

No feasible solution. No feasible region exists; the problem is overconstrained.

Unbounded feasible region. A situation in which the feasible region is not completely surrounded by constraints. Solutions with one or more variables having infinite values are feasible. In itself, it is not a problem.

Unbounded solution. If the optimum solution is at an unbounded portion of the feasible region, the problem is probably underconstrained and needs to be reformulated.

Degenerate solution. The number of nonzero variables is less than the number of independent constraints. This situation presents no difficulty and requires no correction.

Multiple solutions. A situation that occurs when the objective function is parallel to (lies on top of) a binding constraint. The two "corners" of the feasible region and all points along the constraint line between them are equally desirable solutions.

Sensitivity analysis (postoptimality analysis). Analysis of the effects on the optimal solution of changes in the original problem.

Tightening a constraint. Moving a constraint in such a direction that it reduces the feasible region. Reducing the b_i value of an LTE or increasing the b_i value of a GTE.

Relaxing a constraint. Increasing the feasible region. Increasing the b_i values of an LTE or decreasing the b_i value of a GTE.

PROBLEMS

1. Solve the following linear programming problem graphically.

$$\text{Maximize } Z = 5X + 5Y$$
$$\text{Subject to} \quad 2X + \ \ Y \leq 8$$
$$X + 3Y \leq 9$$
$$(X, Y \geq 0)$$

2. Solve the following linear programming problem graphically.

$$\text{Minimize } Z = 48X + 8Y$$
$$\text{Subject to} \quad X + 8Y \geq 1600$$
$$2X + \ \ Y \geq 1200$$
$$(X, Y \geq 0)$$

3. Solve graphically.

$$\text{Minimize } Z = 30X_1 + 3X_2$$

$$\text{Subject to} \quad 5X_1 + X_2 \geq 10$$
$$X_1 + X_2 \leq 6$$
$$X_1 + 2X_2 \geq 6$$
$$X_1 \leq 4$$

$$(X_1, X_2 \geq 0)$$

4. Solve graphically.

$$\text{Maximize } Z = 30X_1 + 3X_2$$

$$\text{Subject to} \quad 5X_1 + X_2 \geq 10$$
$$X_1 + X_2 \leq 6$$
$$X_1 + 2X_2 \geq 6$$
$$X_2 \geq 1$$

$$(X_1, X_2 \geq 0)$$

5. Given the following graphical LP problem

$$\text{Minimize } Z = 2X_1 + 8X_2$$

$$\text{Subject to} \quad X_1 + 2X_2 \geq 6$$
$$10X_1 + 2X_2 \geq 20$$
$$4X_1 + 2X_2 = 16$$

$$(X_1, X_2 \geq 0)$$

   a. Plot the constraints and identify the feasible region. (Note that the equality constraint reduces the region to a line segment.)
   b. Solve graphically for Z_{MAX}.
   c. Solve graphically for Z_{MIN}.
   d. What happens to the feasible region if the first constraint becomes an equality constraint?

6. A country club must decide how many lighted and how many unlighted tennis courts to build in order to maximize their total usage by its members. They estimate that an unlighted court will be used an average of 8 hours per day, whereas a lighted court will be used an average of 12 hours per day. They must have a total of at least 6 courts, but have room for a maximum of 10 courts. Unlighted courts cost $10,000 each; lighted ones, $15,000 each. They have a total of $120,000 available to spend on tennis courts. Formulate the objective function and constraints in a linear programming format, and solve graphically.

7. The Authentic Model Car Company produces two toy car models— a roadster and a sedan. The contribution margin for a roadster is

$8.00, and for a sedan it is $10.00. Each car must go through two processes—forming and finishing. Each day there are 28 labor hours available for forming and 48 for finishing. Each roadster requires 2 labor hours in forming and 6 labor hours in finishing. Each sedan requires 4 labor hours in each process. The company president requires that at least two roadsters be produced each day. The company would like to know how many of each type of car they should build each day to maximize profit.

   a. Write the objective function and constraints.

   b. Solve for the optimum product mix graphically.

8. The Bow-Wow Company makes gourmet dog food by combining two ingredients, A and B. Each pound of A costs $4.00, and each pound of B costs $6.00. To maintain a proper nutrition level, each 10-pound bag of dog food must contain at least 30 ounces of protein, 50 ounces of fat, and 32 ounces of fiber. Ingredient A contains 2 ounces of protein, 5 ounces of fat, and 8 ounces of fiber per pound. Ingredient B contains 5 ounces of protein, 5 ounces of fat, and 2 ounces of fiber per pound. Varying proportions of A and B does not change the flavor or appearance of the mixture. The company desires to find the least-expensive combination of A and B that will satisfy all requirements.

   a. Write the objective function and constraints.

   b. Solve the problem graphically.

9. A farmer must decide how many cows and how many pigs to purchase for fattening. He realizes a net profit of $40.00 on each cow and $20.00 on each pig. Cows eat three bushels of feed per week and pigs eat one per week. On the average the farmer can grow and harvest no more than nine bushels per week. He has decided to purchase *at least* four animals, but the number of cows will not exceed four and the number of pigs will not exceed six. He wants to know the most profitable mix of cows and pigs to buy. Solve the problem graphically.

10. A 4-H club member is planning to grow small Christmas trees for a class project. She has 800 square feet of land available that is suitable for growing spruce and fir trees. The profit for each spruce tree is $9.00 and for each fir tree is $7.00. A spruce tree requires 8 square feet of space, and a fir requires 10 square feet. Each spruce tree must have 10 pounds of fertilizer, and each fir, 6 pounds. There are only 600 pounds of fertilizer available.

   a. Find the optimum mix of trees to maximize profit.

   b. If for some reason *no more* than 50 fir trees could be grown, what would the optimum mix be?

   c. How low would the profit on fir trees have to be to cause the planting of fir trees to be unprofitable? (Assume no change in spruce tree profit.)

Chapter 5

LINEAR PROGRAMMING — THE SIMPLEX ALGORITHM

INTRODUCTION

Although the graphical analysis presented in Chapter 4 is an excellent pedagogical tool and works quite well for problems containing one, two, or, with a lot of imagination and hard work, even three independent variables, it is not a practical solution procedure for problems of greater size. Unfortunately, this latter group includes almost all practical applications. It becomes necessary, then, to expand our knowledge of solution procedures to include one that will accommodate problems with many variables and many constraints. The most widely used model for the solution of linear programming (LP) problems is the simplex algorithm, which was originally developed by George B. Dantziz in 1947.

The simplex model handles problems of any size, in terms of number of constraints and number of variables. It accepts all three classes of constraints (LTE, GTE, and EQ). It typically begins at the origin and moves quickly to the perimeter of the feasible region. It begins checking the "corners" of the feasible region and continues systematically, moving to a *better* solution at each iteration, stopping as soon as the optimum is found. It is efficient, in that once it locates the first feasible point, it tests only feasible solutions; it guarantees that each successive solution is better than the previous one; and it recognizes the optimum solution as soon as it is found, whether all the "corners" of the feasible region have been tested or not.

We will begin our discussion of the simplex method by solving a simple, two-variable problem, so that you can relate to the graphical solution method of Chapter 4. Once you have a firm grasp of the solution procedure, we will expand our discussion to slightly larger problems.

In Chapter 6 we will focus on the problem-formulation aspects of linear programming and demonstrate the use of a typical "canned" computer program to solve and analyze some even larger problems. In Chapter 7 solution procedures for two special classes of linear programming problems—the assignment and transportation models—will be demonstrated.

General Problem Statement

In Chapter 4, we stated the general form of the LP problem as follows.

$$\text{Opt } Z = \sum_{j=1}^{n} c_j X_j \quad \text{(objective function)}$$

$$\text{ST} \quad \sum_{j=1}^{n} a_{ij} X_j \; (\lesseqgtr) \; b_i; \; i = 1, 2, \ldots m \quad \text{(constraints)}$$

$$(X_j \geq 0; j = 1, 2, \ldots n) \quad \text{(nonnegativity constraints)}$$

Lest we scare anyone away with the symbols, let us hasten to explain them and offer an example. The X_js are the independent variables, with subscripts from 1 to n ($X_1, X_2, X_3, \ldots, X_n$). The c_js are the coefficients in the objective function. a_{ij} is the coefficient of the jth variable in the ith constraint. For convenience, we number the constraints from 1 to m. Each of the constraints can be of any of the three types ($\leq$, $\geq$, $=$). The b_is are the right-hand sides, or values, of the m constraints.

The following LP problem has been formulated using both letters and numbers to show the symbols more clearly.

$$\text{Max } Z = 3X_1 + 2X_2 \quad \text{(objective function)}$$
$$\text{ST} \quad \left. \begin{array}{l} 2X_1 + 5X_2 \leq 10 \\ 3X_1 + 4X_2 \geq 12 \\ 5X_1 + 3X_2 = 15 \end{array} \right\} \quad \text{(constraints)}$$

$$\text{Max } Z = c_1 X_1 + c_2 X_2 \quad \text{(objective function)}$$
$$\text{ST} \quad \left. \begin{array}{l} a_{11} X_1 + a_{12} X_2 \leq b_1 \\ a_{21} X_1 + a_{22} X_2 \geq b_2 \\ a_{31} X_1 + a_{32} X_2 = b_3 \end{array} \right\} \quad \text{(constraints)}$$

A MAXIMIZATION PROBLEM

We will proceed with our discussion of the simplex method in the context of a specific example. This problem, the simplest type to solve, is a maximization problem containing only LTE constraints. Once you understand the solution procedure, it will be a relatively minor matter to show the differences required to solve minimization problems and to include GTE and EQ constraints.

Ira Painter purchases, paints, and sells plaster yard figures to several local plant nurseries. He handles only two types—dinosaurs and unicorns. He makes a profit of $5 each on the dinosaurs and $4 each on the unicorns. He operates under two restrictions (constraints). First, he carries the unpainted statues up a steep, narrow footpath to his workshop each morning, and because of his bad back, he can only carry a total weight of 12 pounds. The dinosaurs weigh 3 pounds each and the unicorns, 2 pounds each. The second constraint is that it takes him 1 hour to paint a dinosaur and 2 hours to paint a unicorn, and he staunchly refuses to work more than 8 hours per day. If his objective is to maximize his profit, how many of each type should he paint per day?

Let X_1 be the number of dinosaurs per day and X_2 be the number of unicorns per day. Stated in the standard form we outlined earlier, the problem is to

$$\text{Max } Z = 5X_1 + 4X_2 \qquad \text{(profit function)}$$
$$\text{ST} \qquad 3X_1 + 2X_2 \le 12 \qquad \text{(weight constraint)}$$
$$X_1 + 2X_2 \le 8 \qquad \text{(time constraint)}$$

and, as always

$$(X_1, X_2 \ge 0) \qquad \text{(nonnegativity constraints)}$$

Before we can proceed with the solution of the problem, it is necessary that we *augment* the constraints. This requires adding *slack variables* in order to convert each of the constraints into equalities. For LTE constraints, we add a slack variable (S_i) to the left side to "take up the slack" when the two sides are not equal (that is, when the left side is less than the right side). We will number the subscripts to keep track of which S_i belongs to which constraint. In our example the constraints would be augmented as follows.

$$3X_1 + 2X_2 + S_1 = 12$$
$$X_1 + 2X_2 + S_2 = 8$$

Then we must augment the objective function to include these new variables. Because neither a lighter load nor an idle painter contributes to profit, the coefficients of both slack variables are zeros. The augmented objective function thus takes the form

$$Z = 5X_1 + 4X_2 + 0S_1 + 0S_2$$

The augmentation procedure we have followed here is perfectly general. To augment LTE constraints, *always* add a slack to the left side of the constraint, subscripted to indicate to which constraint it belongs (first, second, third, etc.) and add the slack variable to the objective function with a coefficient of zero.

The Initial Tableau

A number of authors have proposed different versions of the simplex table. The recommended reading list for this chapter in Appendix F lists several texts that use a variety of formats. No magic prowess is claimed for the one we have selected; it simply is the one that we feel is the easiest to use and to understand. All of those referenced will perform quite effectively.

Figure 5.1(a) shows the general form of the simplex tableau. The shaded areas contain labels. The numerical data are entered in the locations indicated, where c_j represents the augmented objective function

(a)

(b)

Figure 5.1 (a) General form of simplex table; (b) Initial tableau—objective function and constraints; (c) Initial tableau—basis variables; (d) Completed tableau; (e) Graphical representation.

	c_j	X_1	X_2	S_1	S_2	c_j
c_i		5	4	0	0	b_i
Solution (Basis) Variables S_1	0	3	2	1	0	12
S_2	0	1	2	0	1	8
Z_j						
ΔZ_j						

(c)

	c_j	X_1	X_2	S_1	S_2	c_j
c_i		5	4	0	0	b_i
S_1	0	3	2	1	0	12
S_2	0	1	2	0	1	8
Z_j		0	0	0	0	0
ΔZ_j		5	4	0	0	

(d)

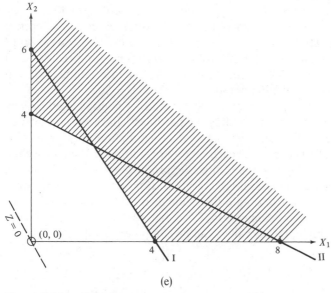

(e)

Figure 5.1 (*continued*)

coefficients; a_{ij}, the augmented constraint coefficients; b_i, the right-hand side values of the constraints; and Z, the value of the objective function. The other values (which will be explained later) are c_i, the objective function values of the nonzero variables; Z_j, the shadow prices; ΔZ_j, the improvement indices; and θ_i, the introduction limits.

To fill in the *initial tableau*, we first write the augmented objective function's coefficients and those of the augmented constraints, which fill everything but the left-hand column and the last two rows [Fig. 5.1(b)].

In every simplex table, there will *always* be an identity matrix of the size $m \times m$, where m is the number of constraints. The variables whose columns make up this identity matrix are the variables that are in the solution at that time. These variables, which are called *basis variables*, form the basis for our solution and can have nonzero values. All other variables are *nonbasic* and have values of zero, for they are not in the current solution. In our initial tableau, the identity matrix is readily found under S_1 and S_2. We enter these basis variables to the left of the tableau, on the appropriate rows (the rows in which the 1 appears), and we enter the coefficient of each from the objective function in the c_i column [Fig. 5.1(c)].

The coefficients within the double lines (the constraint coefficients) are the *exchange ratios* (or substitution ratios) between the variables at the left and those at the top. For example, to bring in 1 unit of X_1, we would have to reduce S_1 by 3 and S_2 by 1. To bring in 1 unit of X_2, we must reduce S_1 by 2 and S_2 by 2. (A look back at the augmented constraints will assure you that this is true.)

The Z_j row entries are the reductions in the profit (shadow prices) associated with the introduction of 1 unit of the variables in their respective columns. To enter 1 unit of X_1, we must lose 3 units of S_1 (at \$0 profit per unit) and 1 unit of S_2 (at \$0 profit per unit) for a total reduction of $(\$0 \times 3) + (\$0 \times 1) = \$0$. To enter 1 unit of X_2, we lose 2 units of S_1 and 2 units of S_2 for a reduction of $(\$0 \times 2) + (\$0 \times 2) = \$0$.

Computationally, we compute the Z_j values by multiplying the c_is by the a_{ij}s for each column and adding the products. This procedure will be similar to the "multipladd" process we used to multiply vectors in Chapter 2. The first elements in each vector are multiplied, then the second elements of each, and so on, and then the products are added. In matrix notation, we are actually multiplying the transpose of column vector C by each column vector to obtain the elements of row Z_j. ($Z_j = C^T \times A_j$, where A_j represents the elements in X_j's column.)

In our example, the Z_j values can be computed as follows.

c_i	X_1	c_i	X_2	c_i	S_1	c_i	S_2
$0 \times 3 = 0$		$0 \times 2 = 0$		$0 \times 1 = 0$		$0 \times 0 = 0$	
$0 \times 1 = 0$		$0 \times 2 = 0$		$0 \times 0 = 0$		$0 \times 1 = 0$	
$0 = Z_1$		$0 = Z_2$		$0 = Z_3$		$0 = Z_4$	

The b_i column contains the values of those variables currently in the solution: $S_1 = 12$ and $S_2 = 8$. Multiplying the c_i column by the b_i column is simply a mechanical way of evaluating the objective function; so the final entry in the Z_j row is the value of Z at this time.

$c_i \quad b_i$

$0 \times 12 = 0 \qquad\qquad Z = 5X_1 + 4X_2 + 0S_1 + 0S_2$

$\underline{0 \times \;\; 8 = 0} \qquad\qquad Z = 5(0) + 4(0) + 0(12) + 0(8) = 0$

$0 = Z$

The elements of the final row of our table (ΔZ_js) show the net change in the objective function that will result from bringing in *1 unit* of the variables in their respective columns. They are called the *improvement indices*, and they are computed by subtracting the loss resulting from the leaving units of the basis variables (Z_j) from the profit from 1 unit of the entering variable (c_j) ($\Delta Z_j = c_j - Z_j$).

$$\Delta Z_1 = c_1 - Z_1 = \$5 - \$0 = \$5$$
$$\Delta Z_2 = c_2 - Z_2 = \$4 - \$0 = \$4$$
$$\Delta Z_3 = c_3 - Z_3 = \$0 - \$0 = \$0$$
$$\Delta Z_4 = c_4 - Z_4 = \$0 - \$0 = \$0$$

Thus, entering 1 unit of X_1 will increase Z by $5, whereas 1 unit of X_2 will increase Z by $4. These values have been entered in our completed initial tableau of Figure 5.1(d). Note that the variables presently in the solution will always have zero ΔZ_j values.

Figure 5.1(e) is a graphical representation of our problem. X_1 and X_2 are shown explicitly, and S_1 and S_2 implicitly. We are at the origin $(0, 0)$, and on the "good" side of both constraints. Our initial solution values are

$$X_1 = 0,\, X_2 = 0,\, S_1 = 12,\, S_2 = 8,\, Z = 0$$

In terms of our original problem, this means that Mr. Painter is painting no dinosaurs and no unicorns and that he has 12 pounds available in his pack and 8 hours of free time per day for a net profit of $0.

Because Z can be improved (increased) by the introduction of either X_1 or X_2, the present solution is not optimal, and we must move to an improved solution.

Improving the Initial Solution

The standard rule of thumb is that the variable with the highest per unit net improvement index (largest ΔZ_j) should enter the solution. In our case this is X_1; so X_1 is designated the *entering variable*, and its column becomes the focus of our attention.

Because we can have only as many variables in the solution at one time as we have equations (constraints), we must determine which of our current basis variables must leave to make room for X_1. Looking at Figure 5.1(e), we can see that we can add 4 units of X_1 before we encounter constraint I and 8 units of X_1 before we reach constraint II. As we do not want any infeasible solutions, we are required to stop as soon as we reach first boundary of the feasible region. At this point (4, 0) we will have brought in 4 units of X_1 and driven out all (12 units) of S_1.

We can accomplish this analysis mathematically by dividing the coefficients in the column of our entering variable (X_1) into the b_i values. The resulting ratios are designated θ_is (for no particular reason) and are entered to the right of the b_is. Because the θ_is, called *introduction limits*, indicate the number of units of X_1 that can be brought in before the corresponding basis variables (S_1 and S_2) are driven out, we must select the variable with the *smallest positive θ value* as the *leaving variable*. Therefore, X_1 will enter the solution, and S_1 will be driven out.

$$
\begin{array}{ccc}
 & b_i & X_1 & \theta_i \\
S_1 & 12 \div 3 & = \textcircled{4} \leftarrow \text{Replace the variable with the} \\
S_2 & 8 \div 1 & = 8 \quad \text{smallest positive } \theta_i \text{ value.}
\end{array}
$$

The initial tableau is shown in Figure 5.2.

To generate the tableau that represents our new solution, two steps are required. Because X_1 will replace S_1 in the solution, X_1's column must become part of the identity matrix. This requires that we obtain a 1 in the first row of X_1's column and 0's in all other rows. The first step produces the 1; the second step is repeated for every other row to obtain the 0's. (You will recognize these steps as those of the Gaussian elimination procedure from Chapter 2.)

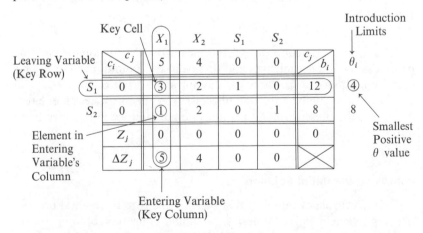

Figure 5.2   Tableau I—entering and leaving variables.

Step 1 Designate the leaving variable's row as the *key row*, and the entering variable's column as the *key column*. The element at their intersection is the *key cell*. Divide each element of the leaving variable's row by the *key cell*. (This produces the 1.)

Step 2 Multiply the *new* key row from step 1 by *minus* the element in the entering variable's column. Add that to the old row to generate the new row. (This generates the 0's in the entering variable's column.)

For our example:

Step 1 New Key Row = Old Key Row ÷ Key Cell (3)

$$(3, 2, 1, 0; 12) \div 3 = (1, \tfrac{2}{3}, \tfrac{1}{3}, 0; 4)$$

Step 2 New Key Row × (−Element in Entering Variable's Column)

$$(1, \tfrac{2}{3}, \tfrac{1}{3}, 0; 4) \times (-1) = (-1, -\tfrac{2}{3}, -\tfrac{1}{3}, 0; -4)$$

$$\text{plus Old 2nd Row} \quad (\ \ 1, \quad 2, \quad 0, 1; \quad 8)$$

$$\text{equals New 2nd Row} \quad (\ \ 0, \quad \tfrac{4}{3}, -\tfrac{1}{3}, 1; \quad 4)$$

The c_i for X_1 is 5, from the objective function.

The Z_js are calculated as before:

c_i	X_1	c_i	X_2	c_i	S_1	c_i	S_2	c_i	b_i
$5 \times 1 = 5$		$5 \times \tfrac{2}{3} = \tfrac{10}{3}$		$5 \times \tfrac{1}{3} = \tfrac{5}{3}$		$5 \times 0 = 0$		$5 \times 4 = 20$	
$0 \times 0 = \underline{0}$		$0 \times \tfrac{4}{3} = \underline{0}$		$0 \times -\tfrac{1}{3} = \underline{0}$		$0 \times 1 = \underline{0}$		$0 \times 4 = \underline{\ 0}$	
$Z_1 = 5$		$Z_2 = \tfrac{10}{3}$		$Z_3 = \tfrac{5}{3}$		$Z_4 = 0$		$Z = 20$	

The new tableau is in Figure 5.3(a), and is shown graphically in Figure 5.3(b). The new solution is

$$X_1 = 4, X_2 = 0, S_1 = 0, S_2 = 4, Z = 20$$

The ΔZ_js are calculated by $\Delta Z_j = c_j - Z_j$. Note the zeros for the variables now in the solution (X_1 and S_2). The negative ΔZ_j for S_1 indicates that entering that variable would *reduce* the objective function. The only variable that will improve our solution is X_2 ($\Delta Z_j = +\tfrac{2}{3}$)—the new entering variable.

To determine the leaving variable, we calculate the θ_is.

$$\begin{array}{ccc} & b_i \quad X_2 & \theta_i \\ X_1: & (4 \div \tfrac{2}{3}) = (4 \times \tfrac{3}{2}) = & 6 \\ S_2: & (4 \div \tfrac{4}{3}) = (4 \times \tfrac{3}{4}) = & ③ \leftarrow \text{Leaving Variable} \\ & & \text{(Key Row)} \end{array}$$

The smallest positive θ is in S_2's row; so S_2 will leave the solution, and 3 units of X_2 will enter.

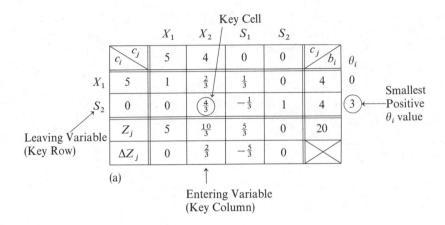

Key Cell

c_i	c_j	X_1 5	X_2 4	S_1 0	S_2 0	c_j / b_i	θ_i
X_1	5	1	$\frac{2}{3}$	$\frac{1}{3}$	0	4	0
S_2	0	0	$\left(\frac{4}{3}\right)$	$-\frac{1}{3}$	1	4	③
	Z_j	5	$\frac{10}{3}$	$\frac{5}{3}$	0	20	
	ΔZ_j	0	$\frac{2}{3}$	$-\frac{5}{3}$	0		

Leaving Variable (Key Row)

Smallest Positive θ_i value

(a)

Entering Variable (Key Column)

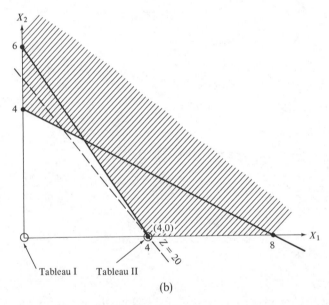

Tableau I   Tableau II

(b)

Figure 5.3 (a) Tableau II; (b) Graphical representation.

To develop the new tableau, we repeat steps 1 and 2.

Step 1   New Key Row = Old Key Row ÷ Key Cell $(\frac{4}{3})$

$$(0, \tfrac{4}{3}, -\tfrac{1}{3}, 1; 4) \div \tfrac{4}{3} = (0, 1, -\tfrac{1}{4}, \tfrac{3}{4}; 3)$$

Step 2   New Key Row × (−Element in Entering Variable's Column)

$$(0, 1, -\tfrac{1}{4}, \tfrac{3}{4}; 3) \times (-\tfrac{2}{3}) = (0, -\tfrac{2}{3}, \tfrac{1}{6}, -\tfrac{1}{2}; -2)$$

plus Old 1st Row $(1, \quad \tfrac{2}{3}, \tfrac{1}{3}, \quad 0; \quad 4)$

equals New 1st Row $(1, \quad 0, \tfrac{1}{2}, -\tfrac{1}{2}; \quad 2)$

Filling in the third tableau and calculating the Z_js and ΔZ_js [Fig. 5.4(a)], we find that we cannot improve the solution. None of the improvement indices (ΔZ_js) are positive; so this solution is optimal (maximum).

$$X_1 = 2, X_2 = 3, S_1 = 0, S_2 = 0, Z \text{ Max} = \$22$$

The graphical equivalent of the optimum solution is in Figure 5.4(b).

Restating the solution in the terms of the original problem, Mr. Painter should paint 2 dinosaurs and 3 unicorns per day. His load to and from his workshop will be

$$3(2) + 2(3) = 12 \text{ pounds} \qquad \text{(constraint I)}$$

and his daily work time will be

$$2 + 2(3) = 8 \text{ hours} \qquad \text{(constraint II)}$$

c_i	c_j	X_1 5	X_2 4	S_1 0	S_2 0	c_j / b_i
X_1	5	1	0	$\frac{1}{2}$	$-\frac{1}{2}$	2
X_2	4	0	1	$-\frac{1}{4}$	$\frac{3}{4}$	3
	Z_i	5	4	$\frac{3}{2}$	$\frac{1}{2}$	22
	ΔZ_j	0	0	$-\frac{3}{2}$	$-\frac{1}{2}$	

(a)

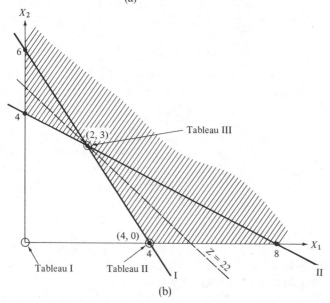

(b)

Figure 5.4   (a) Optimal tableau; (b) Graphical optimal solution.

so there is no slack in either constraint ($S_1 = S_2 = 0$). His maximum daily profit will be

$$Z_{MAX} = 5(2) + 4(3) = \$22$$

A Minimization Problem

Now that you know how to solve maximization problems, the solution of minimization problems will pose little difficulty. Once you learn to augment GTE type constraints, there is but one difference in the computational procedure.

Ima Gardner makes hanging baskets as a hobby and has promised to provide at least 5 for a sale that her home and garden club is having tonight. She has only 8 hours to prepare the baskets. There are two ways she can make the baskets: (1) She can start from scratch, which costs $4 per basket for materials and requires 2 hours of her time for each basket; or (2) she can buy the various pieces ready-made for $7 per basket and arrange them in 1 hour per basket. If she wishes to honor her commitment to make at least 5 baskets, but has only 8 hours to work, and wishes to minimize her cost, how many of each kind should she make?

The objective is to minimize the cost. Let X_1 be the number of less expensive baskets and X_2 the number of more expensive ones.

$$\text{Minimize } Z = \$4X_1 + \$7X_2$$

Her time constraint is $2X_1 + X_2 \leq 8$, and her commitment to the club is $X_1 + X_2 \geq 5$. To augment her first constraint, we add a slack to the left-hand side:

$$2X_1 + X_2 + S_1 = 8$$

Her second constraint is a GTE constraint. To augment it, we *subtract* a slack from the left-hand side:

$$X_1 + X_2 - S_2 = 5$$

Unfortunately, this means that at our initial solution point $(0, 0)$, $S_2 = -5$, which is not allowed. (Remember that no negative values are permitted for any variable.)

To circumvent this difficulty, we add an *artificial variable* to the left side in addition to subtracting the slack.

$$X_1 + X_2 - S_2 + A_2 = 5$$

This artificial variable takes the subscript 2 because it is in the second constraint. It will have a value other than zero only when $X_1 + X_2$ is less than 5. Its physical interpretation is as a *negative slack*, showing by how many units the solution *violates* the second constraint. As soon as we find a solution that does not violate the constraint, A_2 will go to zero and remain there. Its only purpose is to provide us with an initial solution with no negative values. It never appears in the optimal solution but simply helps us get started, hence the name artificial variable. All GTE-type constraints are *always* augmented in this way: subtract a slack variable and add an artificial variable.

As we shall see, artificial variables are also used to augment equality (EQ) constraints. Because the initial solution will generally violate the EQ constraint (unless the constraint passes through the origin, which requires the right-hand side to have a value of zero), an artificial variable, properly subscripted, is *always* added to the left-hand side of a strict equality constraint.

The procedure for augmenting the objective function is to always add the slack variables with zero coefficients, but the method of handling the artificial variables depends on whether the problem is one of maximization or a minimization. The idea is to add the artificial variable to the objective function with a coefficient that makes the variable very unattractive. In our minimization problem, we will add it with a cost of $+\$1$ million per unit (represented by $+M$). This will cause us to force the artificial variable out of solution as quickly as possible and to move into the feasible region of our problem. If we were maximizing, we would add the As with a $-\$1$ million coefficient.

Our augmented LP problem is

$$\text{Min } Z = 4X_1 + 7X_2 + 0S_1 + 0S_2 + MA_2$$
$$\text{ST} \qquad 2X_1 + X_2 + S_1 \qquad\qquad\quad = 8$$
$$X_1 + X_2 \qquad - S_2 + A_2 = 5$$
$$(X_1, X_2, S_1, S_2, A_2 \geq 0)$$

The initial tableau and its graphical representation are shown in Figures 5.5(a) and 5.5(b). Note that $S_1 = 8$ means that we are on the "good" side of constraint I; $A_2 = 5$ means we are violating constraints II; X_1 and X_2 are zero because we are at the origin. The $+M$ coefficient on A_2 causes a large positive value for Z ($\$5M$), and improvement indices of almost a million dollars per unit for X_1 and X_2.

Because we are minimizing, we select the entering variable to be one with the *most negative* ΔZ_j. (Actually, we could select *any* variable with a negative ΔZ_j, but we want the one with the largest improvement per unit introduced.) Because X_1 has a slightly more negative ΔZ_j ($-M + 4$ is more negative than $-M + 7$), X_1 will be our entering variable. The θ_i values ($+4$ and $+12$) lead us to select S_1 as the leaving variable; so 2 (X_1's column and S_1's row) is our key cell.

Dividing the first row by the key cell generates the first row of the second tableau. Multiplying by -1 and adding to the old second row yields the new second row. The new tableau and its graphical location

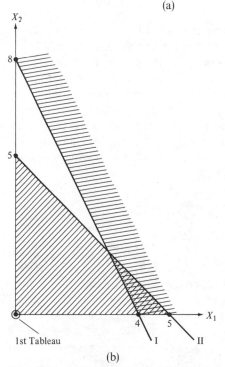

	c_j c_i	X_1 4	X_2 7	S_1 0	S_2 0	A_2 $+M$	c_j b_i	θ_i
S_1	0	2	1	1	0	0	8	④ ←
A_2	$+M$	1	1	0	-1	1	5	12
Z_i		M	M	0	$-M$	M	$5M$	
ΔZ_i		$4-M$	$7-M$	0	M	0		

(a)

(b)

Figure 5.5 (a) Initial tableau; (b) Graphical representation.

are shown in Figures 5.6(a) and 5.6(b). $X_1 = 4$, $X_2 = 0$, and $S_1 = 0$ because we are on constraint 1, and $A_2 = 8$ because we are still violating constraint 2. The value of Z has improved as predicted. We brought in 4 units of X_1 ($\theta_{\text{MIN}} = 4$), and each unit brought in decreased Z by $\$M$ and increased Z by $\$4$.

$$Z_{\text{NEW}} = Z_{\text{OLD}} + (\theta \text{ Min})(\Delta Z_j) = 5M + (4)(4-M) = 5M + 16 - 4M = 1M + 16$$

The only variable that will improve (reduce) our objective function value is X_2; so X_2 becomes our entering variable. Examination of the

c_i \ c_j		X_1	(X_2)	S_1	S_2	A_2	c_j \ b_i	θ_i
		4	7	0	0	$+M$		
X_1	4	1	$\frac{1}{2}$	$\frac{1}{2}$	0	0	4	8
(A_2)	$+M$	0	$(\frac{1}{2})$	$-\frac{1}{2}$	-1	1	1	$(2)\leftarrow$
Z_j		4	$\frac{4}{2}+\frac{1}{2}M$	$\frac{4}{3}-\frac{1}{2}M$	$-M$	$+M$	$M+16$	
ΔZ_j		0	$\left(5-\frac{1}{2}M\right)$	$-2+\frac{1}{2}M$	$+M$	0		

$\uparrow$

(a)

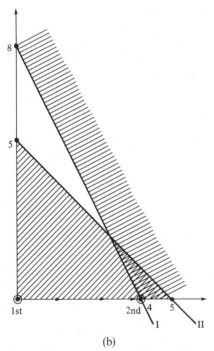

(b)

Figure 5.6   (a) Second tableau—minimization problem; (b) Graphical representation.

θ_is shows the smallest positive value to be 2; so A_2 is the leaving variable, and $\frac{1}{2}$ (the element at the intersection of the leaving variable's row and the entering variable's column) is the key cell. The new value of Z will be the old value $(M+16)$ plus the product of the number of units of X_2

which will enter (2), and the change in Z for each unit of X_2 brought in $(-\frac{1}{2}M + 5)$.

$$Z_{\text{NEW}} = Z_{\text{OLD}} + (\theta_R)(\Delta Z_K)$$

Where R is the row of the leaving variable and K is the column of the entering variable

$$Z_{\text{NEW}} = (M + 16) + (2)(-\tfrac{1}{2}M + 5) = M + 16 - M + 10 = 26$$

c_i \ c_j		X_1 4	X_2 7	S_1 0	S_2 0	A_2 $+M$	c_j \ b_i
X_1	4	1	0	1	1	-1	3
X_2	7	0	1	-1	-2	2	2
Z_j		4	7	-3	-14	10	26
ΔZ_j		0	0	3	14	$M - 10$	

(a)

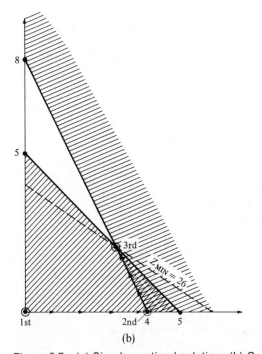

(b)

Figure 5.7   (a) Simplex optimal solution; (b) Graphical optimal solution.

The new second (key) row is the old second row divided by the key cell ($\frac{1}{2}$).

$$(0, \tfrac{1}{2}, -\tfrac{1}{2}, -1, 1; 1) \div \tfrac{1}{2} = (0, 1, -1, -2, 2; 2)$$

The new first row is found by adding the old first row to the new key (second) row times the negative of the element of the old first row that is in the key column.

$$[\text{New Key (Second) Row}] \times [-\text{Element}]$$
$$(0, 1, -1, -2, 2; 2) \times (-\tfrac{1}{2}) = (0, -\tfrac{1}{2}, \tfrac{1}{2}, 1, -1; -1)$$

$$\begin{array}{llll} \text{Old First Row} + (1, & \tfrac{1}{2}, \tfrac{1}{2}, 0, & 0; & 4) \\ \hline \text{New First Row} \quad (1, & 0, 1, 1, -1; & 3) \end{array}$$

These are placed in the third tableau shown in Figure 5.7(a). The graphical location of the third tableau is indicated in Figure 5.7(b).

If we calculate the Z_js and the ΔZ_js, we note that $Z = 26$, as we predicted it would, and also that this is the optimal solution, because there are no ΔZ_j values that are negative. At the optimum, $X_1 = 3$, $X_2 = 2$, $S_1 = 0$, $S_2 = 0$ (both constraints are binding), and $a_2 = 0$ (no violation of constraint 2). Ima should make 3 baskets from scratch and buy the materials for 2; her total cost is $26.

SUMMARY OF THE SIMPLEX PROCEDURE

At this point it is useful to summarize the procedures involved in the solution of linear programming problems using the simplex method.

I. Problem formulation
   State the problem in standard form.

$$\text{Opt } Z = \sum_{j=1}^{n} c_j X_j$$

$$\text{ST} \quad \sum_{j=1}^{n} a_{ij} X_j \ (\lessgtreqqless)\ b_i; \ i = 1, 2, \ldots, m$$

$$(X_j \geq 0)$$

II. Augmentation
   A. Augment the constraints.
      1. Add a slack variable to the left-hand side of each $\leq$ constraint, subscripted to indicate the number of the constraint.
      2. Subtract a slack variable and add an artificial variable to the left-hand side of each $\geq$ constraint, both subscripted with the number of the constraint.

      3. Add an artificial variable to the left-hand side of each $=$ constraint, properly subscripted.

   B. Augment the objective function.

      1. Add all slack variables with zero coefficients

$$Z = \sum c_j X_j + \sum 0 S_i$$

      2. Add each artificial variable with coefficients of $+\$M$ if minimizing and $-\$M$ if maximizing.

$$Z \text{ augmented} = \sum c_j X_j + \sum 0 S_i + \sum (+M) A_i$$
$$\text{(minimizing problem)}$$

$$Z \text{ augmented} = \sum c_j X_j + \sum 0 S_i + \sum (-M) A_i$$
$$\text{(maximization problem)}$$

III. The initial tableau

   A. Enter the augmented objective function coefficients and the augmented constraint equation coefficients in the initial simplex tableau. To determine which variables are in the solution, locate the columns of the identity matrix. *If a constraint has an artificial variable, it will be the variable in the initial solution on that constraint's row. If not, the slack variable for that constraint will be the solution variable on that row.*

   B. Calculate the Z_js by multiplying the c_is (the coefficients of the basic variables) by the a_{ij}s and adding. Example:

$$c_i \qquad X_1$$

First row (S_1) 0 $\times$ 1 $= 0$
Second row (A_2) $+M \times$ 2 $= 2M$
Third row (S_3) 0 $\times$ 3 $= 0$
$$\overline{\hspace{2cm}}$$
$$Z_1 = 2M$$

   C. Calculate the ΔZ_js by subtracting the Z_js from the c_js.

$$\Delta Z_j = c_j - Z_j$$

IV. Entering variable

    Select as the entering variable the one with the largest ΔZ_j of appropriate sign. Consider only the positive ΔZ_js when maximizing; only the negative ones when minimizing. This column is the *key column*. If there are no ΔZ_j values with the appropriate sign, the solution is optimal.

V. Leaving variable

   A. Calculate the θ_is by dividing the b_is by the a_{ij}s in the entering variable's column (key column). Example:

$$
\begin{array}{ccc}
b_i & \text{Key Column} & \theta_i \\
8 \div & 2 & = 4 \\
2 \div & -1 & = -2 \\
12 \div & ④ & = ③ \leftarrow \text{Leaving Variable (Key Row)}
\end{array}
$$

↑
Key
Cell

B. Select the row with the *smallest positive* θ_i as the row of the leaving variable (key row).

C. The element at the intersection of the key row and the key column is the *key element*.

VI. Improving the solution[1]

A. In moving to the next tableau, first calculate the next key row by dividing the old key row by the key element.

$$(\text{New Key Row}) = (\text{Old Key Row}) \div (\text{Key Element})$$

B. To generate the other rows of the new tableau, multiply the *new* key row by minus the element at the intersection of the row you are working on and the key column. Then add this multiple to the old row to obtain the new row.

╱Key Cell

$$
\begin{array}{ccccc}
1 & 3 & ② - 1 & 4 & \leftarrow\text{Key Row} \\
2 & 1 & \boxed{3} & 1 & 7
\end{array}
$$

↑ Intersectional Element
Key
Column

(New Second Row)

$$= [(\text{New Key Row}) \times (-\text{Intersectional Element})]$$
$$+ [\text{Old Second Row}]$$
$$= [(\tfrac{1}{2}, \tfrac{3}{2}, 1, -\tfrac{1}{2}; 2)(-3)] + [2, 1, 3, 1; 7]$$
$$= [-\tfrac{3}{2}, -\tfrac{9}{2}, -3, +\tfrac{3}{2}; -6] + [2, 1, 3, 1; 7]$$
$$= (\tfrac{1}{2}, -\tfrac{7}{2}, 0, \tfrac{5}{2}; 1)$$

C. Calculate the Z_js and ΔZ_js as usual.

VII. Optimal solution

Optimality has been achieved when no ΔZ_j values of the appropriate sign ($-$ for a minimization problem; $+$ for a maximization problem) remain.

---

[1] Note that the steps in improving the solution are exactly the same as those for moving to a new tableau in the Gaussian method of finding the inverse of a matrix, which we discussed in Chapter 2.

Interpretation of the Elements of the Simplex Tableau

Figure 5.8 shows a hypothetical simplex tableau for a problem with three constraints (because there are three rows inside the double lines) and two real variables (X_1 and X_2). From an examination of the slack and artificial variables, we can determine that the first constraint is an LTE-type (only a slack is shown with subscript 1); the second constraint is a GTE-type (both a slack and an artificial have been introduced); and the third constraint is an EQ-type (only an artificial).

The first row of the table (7, 5, 0, 0, $-M$, $-M$) is made up of the coefficients from the augmented objective function (c_js). Because the artificial variables have negative coefficients, this is a maximization problem.

The variables currently in solution are listed at the left of the table. They are S_1, X_1, and A_3. Their coefficients (c_is) are 0, 7, and $-M$, respectively. The values of the solution variables are found in the b_i column: $S_1 = 12$, $X_1 = 10$, and $A_3 = 8$.

The a_{ij} values (all elements within the double lines) represent the exchange ratios between the variables currently in the solution and the entire list of variables at the top of the matrix. For example, for each unit of X_2 that enters the solution, 2 units of S_1, 4 units of X_1, and 3 units of A_3 must leave.

The Z_j values (7, $28 - 3M$, 0, $-14 - 7M$, $14 + 7M$, $-M$) represent the costs of bringing 1 unit of the variables in their respective columns into the solution. This cost is measured in terms of the losses of units of the variables currently in the solution. In the case of X_2, the loss (Z_j) is 2 units of S_1 at \$0 per unit, 4 of X_1 at \$7 each, and 3 of A_3 at \$ $-M$ each, for a total loss of \$28 − \$3M.

		X_1	X_2	S_1	S_2	A_2	A_3		
	c_i ╲ c_j	7	5	0	0	$-M$	$-M$	c_j ╲ b_i	θ_i
S_1	0	0	2	1	6	-6	0	12	2
X_1	7	1	4	0	-2	2	0	10	-5
A_3	$-M$	0	3	0	7	-7	1	8	$\frac{8}{7}$ ←
	Z_j	7	$28 - 3M$	0	$-7M$ -14	$7M$ $+14$	$-M$	70 $-8M$	
	ΔZ_j	0	$3M - 23$	0	$7M$ $+14$	$-8M$ -14	0		

↑

Figure 5.8   Hypothetical simplex table.

To determine the net effect on Z that results from the introduction of 1 unit of X_2, we must subtract this cost (Z_j) from the value added to Z by the addition of a unit of X_2 $(c_2 = \$5)$. We call this net change ΔZ_j and calculate it by $\Delta Z_j = c_j - Z_j$. In the case of X_2, 1 unit adds $5 but reduces Z by $\$28 - \$3M$ for a net change of $\$3M - \$23$. These improvement indices are shown in the bottom line of the tableau $(0, 3M - 23, 0, 7M + 14, -8M - 14, 0)$. Note that all variables currently in the solution have zero ΔZ_j values.

The ΔZ_j values are used to determine which, if any, variables can be introduced into the solution in order to improve the value of Z. In a maximization problem, an improvement in Z is an increase; so we select as the incoming variable the one with the largest positive ΔZ_j value. In our problem, this is S_2. If there were no positive ΔZ_j values, there would be no variable that would improve Z, and our solution would be optimal. In a minimization problem, we select the variable with the most negative ΔZ_j value.

Because only three variables can be in our solution at a time (for we have three constraint equations), one of the solution variables must leave the solution (be reduced to zero) to make room for our entering variable (S_2). Because the a_{ij} values in S_2's column represent the exchange rates between S_2 and the variables presently in solution, if we divide these exchange rates into the number of units of the solution variables $(b_i s)$, we can determine how many units of S_2 will be required to drive out each of the variables currently in the solution $(\theta_i$'s).

$$
\begin{array}{ccc}
b_i & S_2 & \theta_i \\
12 \div & 6 = & 2 \\
10 \div & -2 = & -5 \\
8 \div & 7 = & \tfrac{8}{7}
\end{array}
$$

It would take 2 units of S_2 to drive out all 12 units of S_1, but only $\tfrac{8}{7}$ unit of S_2 to drive out all 8 units of A_3. Negative values of θ_i are ignored, because they indicate that the number of units of the solution variable in that row must be *increased* as the entering variable is introduced. Therefore, X_1 cannot be replaced by S_2 in our problem. The smallest of the positive θ_i values indicates the variable that will leave the solution, and the value of the smallest positive θ_i $(+\tfrac{8}{7})$ is the number of units of S_2 that will enter. The variable in that row (A_3) will leave the solution and be replaced by the entering variable (S_2).

The current value of Z is found by substituting the present solution into the objective function. As all variables except the solution variables have values of zero, this is accomplished by multiplying the number of units of each solution variable (b_i) by the value of each solution variable in the objective function (c_i) and adding the products. The value of Z is found at the bottom of the b_i column and to the right of the Z_j row. The present value of Z is $(0 \times 12) + (7 \times 10) + (-M \times 8) = \$70 - \$8M$.

To determine the total change in the objective function, we multiply the change in Z resulting from the introduction of 1 unit of the entering variable $(+7M + 14)$ by the number of units to be brought in $(\frac{8}{7})$. Thus, the value of Z will change by $(+7M + 14)(\frac{8}{7}) = +8M + 16$. Adding this change to the current value of Z ($\$80 - \$8M$), we obtain the value of Z at the next solution point $(\$70 - 8M) + (\$16 + 8M) = \$86$.

A THREE-VARIABLE PROBLEM

As a final example of the way in which the simplex procedure systematically tests the vertices of the feasible region, let us consider the problem faced by a tailor named A. Taylor, who makes women's, children's, and men's coats, which he sells to a fashionable boutique. His prices are $30 each for the women's and men's, and $20 each for the children's. A woman's coat takes 1 hour to cut out and 3 hours to sew; a child's, 1 hour to cut and 1 hour to sew; a man's, 2 hours to cut and 6 hours to sew. The tailor's son, Rip, works 8 hours a day doing nothing but cutting out garments. His wife, Sue, sews 8 hours a day. Taylor, the tailor, sews 4 hours each day and plays golf the rest of the time. What is the maximum revenue they can generate under this arrangement?

Let R be the revenue; W, the number of women's coats; C, the number of children's; and M, the number of men's. The daily output is constrained by the amount of time available in the cutting operation (8 hours) and by the time available in the sewing operation (12 hours). The problem can be formulated as follows.

$$\text{Max } R = 30W + 20C + 30M$$

ST		$W +$	$C +$	$2M \leq$	8	(cutting constraint)
and		$3W +$	$C +$	$6M \leq$	12	(sewing constraint)

$(W, C, M \geq 0)$ (nonnegativity constraints)

In our discussion of the simplex solution, we will refer to the graphical solution shown in Figure 5.9(a).

In three dimensions, an equation is a plane, rather than a line, as in the two-dimensional case, and the feasible region becomes a volume, rather than an area. In our problem, the feasible region is the tentlike volume bounded by the points $A, B, C, D, E,$ and O. The objective function is a family of planes, including $R = \$120$ (points $D, F,$ and G) and $R = \$180$ (points $H, I,$ and J), that touches the feasible region at the optimal point (C).

As both constraints are of the LTE type, we augment them by adding S_1 and S_2, respectively. The initial simplex tableau is in Figure 5.9(b).

This tableau represents the solution at the origin ($W = C = M = 0$), labeled O in the graph. Because both S_1 and S_2 are in the solution (have values other than zero), we are below both constraint planes.

Note that in selecting the entering variable there is a tie between W and C for the largest positive ΔZ_j. Such ties can be broken arbitrarily,

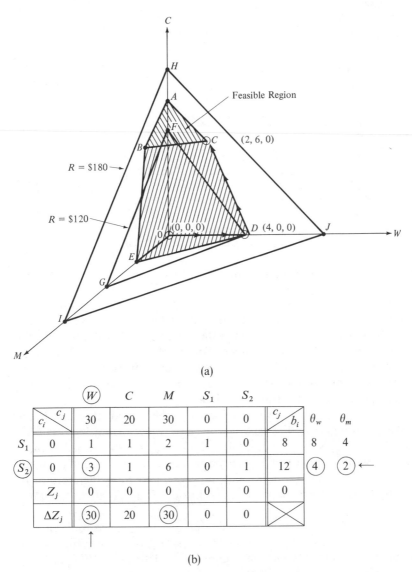

(a)

		W	C	M	S_1	S_2				
	c_i $\quad^{c_j}$	30	20	30	0	0	c_j $\diagdown$ b_i	θ_w	θ_m	
S_1	0	1	1	2	1	0	8	8	4	
S_2	0	③	1	6	0	1	12	④	②	←
	Z_j	0	0	0	0	0	0			
	ΔZ_j	㉚	20	㉚	0	0				
	↑									

(b)

Figure 5.9   (a) Three-variable problem—graphical solution; (b) Initial tableau.

		W	Ⓒ	M	S_1	S_2		
	c_j / c_i	30	20	30	0	0	c_j / b_i	θ_i
(S₁)	0	0	$\frac{2}{3}$	0	1	$-\frac{1}{3}$	4	⑥
W	30	1	$\frac{1}{3}$	2	0	$\frac{1}{3}$	4	12
	Z_j	30	10	60	0	10	120	
	ΔZ_j	0	⑩	-30	0	-10		

↑

(c)

		W	C	M	S_1	S_2	
	c_j / c_i	30	20	30	0	0	c_j / b_i
C	20	0	1	0	$\frac{3}{2}$	$-\frac{1}{2}$	6
W	30	1	0	2	$-\frac{1}{2}$	$\frac{1}{2}$	2
	Z_j	30	20	60	15	5	180
	ΔZ_j	0	0	-30	-15	-5	

(d)

Figure 5.9 (c) Second tableau; (d) Optimum solution.

but a better approach is to calculate the θ_i values for both variables and determine which variable will enter the most units. (Recall that the value of the minimum θ_i is the number of units of the entering variable.) In our case, we select variable W, for we can bring in twice as many units (4, versus 2 for variable M) and thus improve the objective function by twice as much. S_2 is the leaving variable.

Using the 3 as our key cell, we move to the second tableau of Figure 5.9(c). In bringing in 4 units of W, we have moved from the origin out along the W axis to the point ($W = 4$, $C = 0$, $M = 0$), labeled D in the graph. Because this point lies in the plane of constraint 2, $S_2 = 0$. We are still below the first constraint, however, and S_1 is therefore in the solution. The $R = \$120$ plane goes through this point, as shown in Figure 5.9(a).

Following the simplex procedure, we select C as our entering variable and S_1 as our leaving variable. Using $\frac{2}{3}$ as the key cell, we move to the third tableau, shown in Figure 5.9(d). This point ($W = 2$, $C = 6$, $M = 0$) is labeled C in the graphical solution. Because we are on the line that is the intersection of the two constraint planes, both S_1 and S_2 are zero. As can be seen from Figure 5.9(a), the $R = \$180$ plane just touches the feasible region at this point; so this is our optimal solution.

It is interesting to note that if we had selected M as our entering variable in the first tableau, we would have moved to point E in Figure 5.9(a). From there, we would have had to move to either point B or point D before arriving at the optimum. Therefore, our tie-breaking analysis saved us one tableau in the solution of the problem.

SOME SPECIAL PROBLEMS AND THEIR RESOLUTION

You may never be confronted with any of the following problems, but just in case, here are a few hints.

Negative b_i Values

If the simplex procedure is followed properly, no negative values should ever appear in the b_i column. If one or more crops up during the solution of a linear programming problem, you have made a math error. Back up and check your work until you find and correct it.

It is possible, however, to have negative values in the b_i of the original problem. This difficulty is easily remedied by multiplying the entire constraint equation by -1 (which reverses the direction of the inequality). Thus,

$$3X + 2y \leq -8 \quad \text{and} \quad -X + 4y \geq -2$$

become

$$-3X - 2y \geq 8 \quad \text{and} \quad X - 4y \leq 2$$

Tie for the Entering Variable

We have already encountered and overcome this difficulty. Calculate the θ_i values for the variables in question, and choose the variable that will enter the most units and therefore will improve Z the most.

Tie for the Leaving Variable

When there is a tie for the smallest positive θ_i value, it means that both variables will be driven from the solution simultaneously when that number of units of the entering variable is brought in. This leads to a situation known as *degeneracy*. A degenerate solution is one in which there are fewer nonzero variables than there are constraint equations. To solve this problem, we simply allow one of the variables *in* the solution to have a value of zero. A procedure for determining which of the variables leaves and which stays in with a value of zero is discussed in the context of the following example.

$$\text{Max } Z = 3X_1 + 4X_2$$
$$\text{ST} \qquad X_1 + X_2 \leq 4$$
$$2X_1 + X_2 \geq 4$$
$$X_1 \leq 3$$
$$(X_1, X_2 \geq 0)$$

The problem is solved graphically in Figure 5.10(a). The initial tableau is in Figure 5.10(b). X_1 enters and A_2 leaves the solution. The

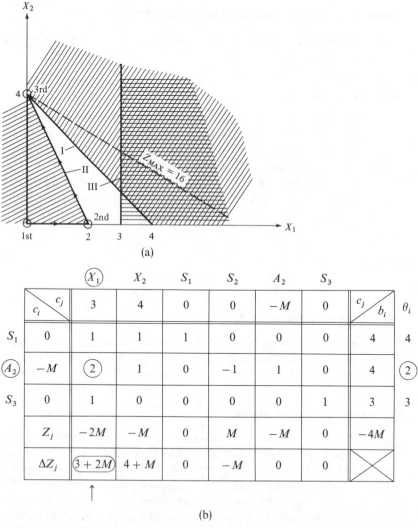

(a)

	c_j	X_1	X_2	S_1	S_2	A_2	S_3	c_j / b_i	θ_i
c_i		3	4	0	0	$-M$	0		
S_1	0	1	1	1	0	0	0	4	4
A_2	$-M$	2	1	0	-1	1	0	4	2
S_3	0	1	0	0	0	0	1	3	3
	Z_j	$-2M$	$-M$	0	M	$-M$	0	$-4M$	
	ΔZ_j	$3 + 2M$	$4 + M$	0	$-M$	0	0		

(b)

Figure 5.10 (a) Degeneracy—graphical solution; (b) Initial tableau.
(c) Tie for the leaving variable; (d) Degenerate solution; (e) Optimal degenerate solution.

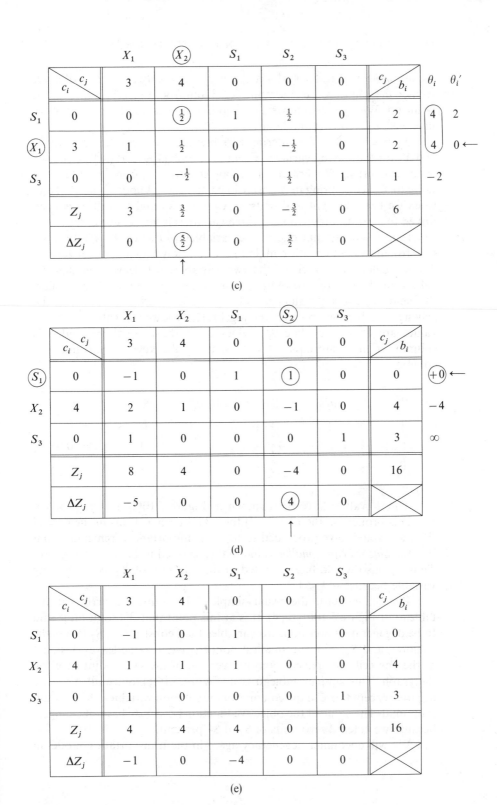

Figure 5.10 (continued)

second tableau [Fig. 5.10(c)] is at $X_1 = 2$, $X_2 = 0$. (Because A_2 will never reenter the solution, we can omit its column from our tableau from this point on. We may not, however, drop out a slack variable, because we may wish to reenter it at a later time.)

X_2 is selected as the entering variable, and there is a tie between S_1 and X_1 for the leaving variable. From the graph [Fig. 5.10(a)] we can see what is occurring. We are moving along constraint 2 from point (2, 0) to point (0, 4). As we bring in X_2, we will be driving out both X_1 and S_1, and when we have brought in 4 units of X_2, both X_1 and S_1 will have been driven to zero. In order to keep three variables in the solution, we resort to trickery and say that one of the variables will leave the solution (go to zero) and the other will remain in the solution with a value of zero.

To determine which of the two variables will leave, calculate θ_i' values for the two tied rows by dividing their key column elements into the elements under the slack variables, beginning with S_1. Select as the leaving variable the one with the algebraically lower θ_i' value. If the θ_i' values are equal, calculate θ_i'' values using the key column and S_2's column. If these are equal, try θ_i''''s, using the key column and S_3's column.

S_1	X_2	θ_i'	S_2	X_2	θ_i''	S_3	X_2	θ_i'''
$1 \div$	$\frac{1}{2} =$	2	$\frac{1}{2} \div$	$\frac{1}{2} =$	1	$0 \div$	$\frac{1}{2} =$	0
$0 \div$	$\frac{1}{2} =$	0	$-\frac{1}{2} \div$	$\frac{1}{2} =$	-1	$0 \div$	$\frac{1}{2} =$	0
0	$-\frac{1}{2}$		$\frac{1}{2}$	$-\frac{1}{2}$		1	$-\frac{1}{2}$	

The θ_i' values have been shown in Figure 5.10(c). In our problem the tie is broken on the first set. If there had been a tie (as in the case of θ_i'''), we would have proceeded to θ_i''. It is important to remember that it is the *algebraically smaller* value that is selected to be the leaving row. Thus, θ_i'' also would have resulted in the selection of X_1 as the leaving variable because $-1 < 1$.

Proceeding with the usual simplex procedure, we arrive at the tableau of Figure 5.10(d) (0, 4). It is at this point that the solution is said to be degenerate (fewer nonzero variables than constraints). S_2 enters the solution, and S_1, with the smallest nonnegative θ_i value leaves. Using 1 as the key cell, we arrive at another version of the same point (0, 4) on the graph. This simplex tableau is in Figure 5.10(e). Since all ΔZ_js are negative except those in the columns of the solution variables, the solution is optimal. The value of the objective function ($Z = \$16$) has not changed, because we entered zero units of S_2 at $\$4$ per unit.

We will encounter degeneracy again in the transportation model in

Chapter 7, where it is handled routinely and with little or no computational difficulty.

Unbounded Solution

Sometimes a problem has no finite optimum. An example will serve to illustrate this point. Our graphical "solution" is presented in Figure 5.11(a), and the simplex tableaux are shown in Figures 5.11(b)–(e).

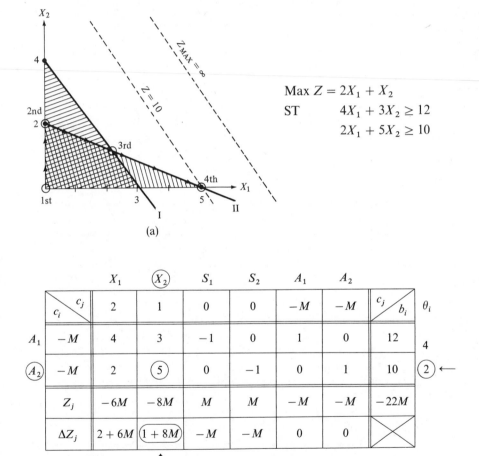

$$\text{Max } Z = 2X_1 + X_2$$
$$\text{ST} \qquad 4X_1 + 3X_2 \geq 12$$
$$\qquad 2X_1 + 5X_2 \geq 10$$

(a)

(b)

Figure 5.11   (a) Graphical representation of unbounded solution; (b) Initial tableau.

c_i \\ c_j		X_1 2	X_2 1	S_1 0	S_2 0	A_1 $-M$	A_2 $-M$	c_j \\ b_i	θ_i
A_1	$-M$	$\left(1\frac{4}{5}\right)$	0	-1	$\frac{3}{5}$	1	$-\frac{3}{5}$	6	$\left(\frac{30}{14}\right)$
X_2	1	$\frac{2}{5}$	1	0	$-\frac{1}{5}$	0	$\frac{1}{5}$	2	5
Z_j		$-2.8M$ $+0.4$	1	M	$-0.6M$ -0.2	$-M$	$0.6M$ $+0.2$	$-6M$ $+2$	
ΔZ_j		$2.8M$ $+1.6$	0	$-M$	$0.6M$ $+0.2$	0	$-1.6M$ -0.2		

(c)

c_i \\ c_j		X_1 2	X_2 1	S_1 0	S_2 0	A_1 $-M$	A_2 $-M$	c_j \\ b_i	θ_i
X_1	2	1	0	$-\frac{5}{14}$	$\frac{3}{14}$	$\frac{5}{14}$	$-\frac{3}{14}$	$\frac{15}{7}$	-6
X_2	1	0	1	$\left(\frac{1}{7}\right)$	$-\frac{2}{7}$	$-\frac{1}{7}$	$\frac{2}{7}$	$\frac{8}{7}$	$\left(8\right)$
Z_j		2	1	$-\frac{4}{7}$	$\frac{1}{7}$	$\frac{4}{7}$	$-\frac{1}{7}$	$\frac{38}{7}$	
ΔZ_j		0	0	$\frac{4}{7}$	$-\frac{1}{7}$	$-M$ $-\frac{4}{7}$	$-M$ $+\frac{1}{7}$		

(d)

c_i \\ c_j		X_1 2	X_2 1	S_1 0	S_2 0	A_1 $-M$	A_2 $-M$	c_j \\ b_i	θ_i
X_1	2	1	$\frac{5}{2}$	0	$-\frac{1}{2}$	0	$\frac{1}{2}$	5	-10
S_1	0	0	7	1	-2	-1	2	8	-4
Z_j		2	5	0	-1	0	1	10	
ΔZ_j		0	-4	0	1	$-M$	$-M-1$		

(e)

Figure 5.11 (c) Second tableau; (d) Third tableau; (e) Fourth tableau.

We note that the solution of the fourth tableau is not optimal, because S_2 is eligible to enter the solution. But there are *no* positive θ_i values, which means that no amount of S_2 will drive either X_1 or S_1 out of the solution. Such a problem is said to have an *unbounded optimal solution.*

Infeasibility

It is possible to overconstrain a linear programming problem so that there exist no solutions that do not violate at least one constraint. Graphically, this means that there is no feasible region. A simple example is illustrated graphically in Figure 5.12(a), and the initial simplex tableau is shown in Figure 5.12(b). To recognize this situation in the simplex format, note that the optimum solution has been reached (all ΔZ_js positive in this minimization problem) with an artificial variable (A_1) in the solution [Fig. 5.12(c)]. When this occurs, the problem should be reexamined, and one or more of the constraints relaxed to create a feasible solution space.

Multiple Solutions

Multiple solutions can occur when the objective function has the same slope as a binding constraint. The existence of alternate solutions is usually of interest only if they are optimal solutions. In the simplex tableau, multiple solutions are identified by ΔZ_j values of zero for variables that are not currently in the solution.

A trivial example demonstrates multiple solutions both at optimality and at suboptimal points.

$$\text{Max } Z = 2X_1 + X_2$$
$$\text{ST} \qquad 4X_1 + 2X_2 \geq 8$$
$$6X_1 + 3X_2 \leq 18$$

Figure 5.13(a) shows the problem graphically. The slopes of both constraints and the objective function are -2. The initial tableau [Fig. 5.13(b)] represents the solution at the origin, which violates the first constraint $(A_1 = 8)$. Two units of X_1 are brought in, and A_1 leaves the solution, moving us to point A, which represents the solution of Figure 5.13(c).

From the graph, we can see that the line representing $Z = 4$ also runs through point B, which is another "corner" of the feasible region. To move to that solution would involve bringing in 4 units of X_2 and driving out X_1. The change in the objective function would be $\Delta Z_j \times \theta_{\text{MIN}} = 0 \times 4 = 0$. A zero in the ΔZ_j row for a variable not in the solution always signals the existence of an alternate solution with the same value of the objective function.

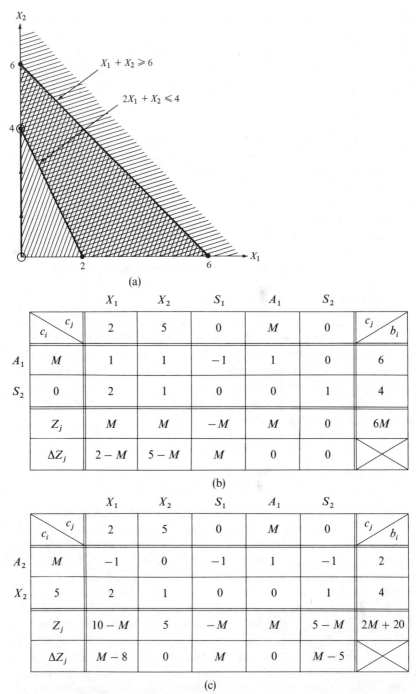

Figure 5.12 (a) Infeasibility—graphical representation; (b) Initial solution—simplex; (c) Infeasible optimum solution.

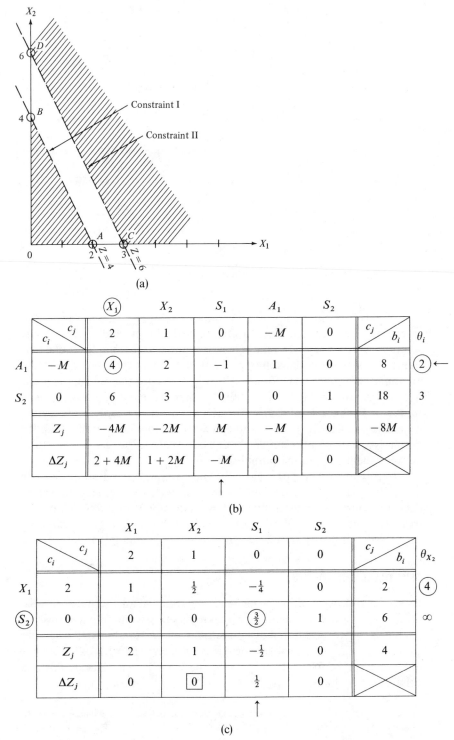

Figure 5.13 (a) Multiple solution; (b) Initial solution; (c) Multiple suboptimal solutions.

		X_1	X_2	S_1	S_2		
θ_{S_1}	c_i \ c_j	2	1	0	0	c_j \ c_i	θ_{X_2}
-8 X_1	2	1	$\frac{1}{2}$	0	$\frac{1}{6}$	3		(6)
(4) ← S_1	0	0	0	1	$\frac{2}{3}$	4		∞
	Z_j	2	1	0	$\frac{1}{3}$	6	
	ΔZ_j	0	[0]	0	$-\frac{1}{3}$		

↑

(d)

Figure 5.13   (d) Multiple optimal solutions.

S_1 has a positive improvement index (ΔZ_j); so it is the variable to enter into the solution. Four units are brought in, and S_2 leaves the solution. This moves us to point C in the graph and the simplex tableau of Figure 5.13(d). Now the solution is optimal, for no positive ΔZ_j values are found. However, as before, we do have a zero for the ΔZ_j of a variable not in the solution (X_2). This tells us that we have *alternate optimal solutions*. To find the solution at the other "corner" of the feasible region, we would bring in X_2 (6 units) and drive out X_1, moving to point D on the graph. Not only points C and D, but all points along the second constraint between them constitute optimal solutions.

In solving practical problems, finding multiple optimal solutions is an especially pleasant circumstance, for it permits the decision maker to decide among the optimal alternatives based upon secondary objectives (personal preferences, personality conflicts, etc.) that have not been quantified and incorporated into the linear programming model.

THE DUAL PROBLEM[2]

Every linear programming problem can be stated in an alternate formulation, called its *dual*. This feature has some very important implications that enable us to gain additional insight into and understanding of the simplex procedure. The dual problem provides another way of looking at and analyzing the problem. It also forms the basis for some more efficient solution procedures.

---

[2] This section contains material which is somewhat more difficult and which is frequently omitted from a first course in management science.

If the original problem, which we call the *primal* problem, is stated as a maximization, then we will construct the dual problem as a minimization problem, and vice versa. The designation of one formulation as the primal and the other as the dual is purely arbitrary, as each is the other's dual. Formally stated, "The dual of the dual is the primal." This is similar to the relationship between a matrix and its transpose, or a matrix and its inverse, discussed in Chapter 2.

An interesting feature of duality is that the optimum solution to the primal is the same as the optimum solution to the dual. If the primal is a maximization problem, then Z_{MAX}(primal) = Z_{MIN}(dual). We will demonstrate the construction and solution of the dual with an example.

Sandy MacHinery runs a small machine shop where she can produce three structural elements for well-drilling companies. The profits on the three items are \$10, \$8, and \$6 per unit. Item 1 takes 2 hours on machine A and 1 hour on machine B. Item 2 requires 1 hour on A and 4 on B; item 3, 1 hour on A and 1 on B. Machine A operates a maximum of 12 hours per day, and machine B operates no more than 8 hours per day. If Sandy wishes to maximize her daily profits, subject to the availability of machine time on the two machines, we can construct the primal problem as follows.

$$\text{Max } Z = \boxed{10X_1} + \boxed{8X_2} + \boxed{6X_3}$$
$$\text{ST} \quad \boxed{2X_1} + \boxed{1X_2} + \boxed{1X_3} \leq \boxed{12}$$
$$\boxed{1X_1} + \boxed{4X_2} + \boxed{1X_3} \leq \boxed{8}$$

$$(X_j \geq 0)$$

To formulate the dual problem, we take the "transpose" of the primal problem, in the sense that each column of the primal becomes a row in the dual, with the c_j values becoming the right-hand sides of the constraints and the b_i values becoming the coefficients of the dual objective function. We also reverse the direction of the inequalities and the intent of the optimization. Each constraint in the primal relates to a variable (Y value) in the dual. Sandy's dual is

$$\text{Min } Z' = \boxed{12Y_1 + 8Y_2}$$

$$\boxed{2Y_1 + 1Y_2 \geq 10}$$

$$\boxed{1Y_1 + 4Y_2 \geq 8}$$

$$\boxed{1Y_1 + 1Y_2 \geq 6}$$

$$(Y_j \geq 0)$$

It is instructive to examine the relationships between the initial and optimal simplex tableaux of the primal and the dual. Both problems have been solved, and the results are shown in Figures 5.14(a) and (b). The optimal solution to the primal occurs in the third tableau after the initial one; the dual takes one step more. You may wish to carry out the calculations as practice problems.

We have already pointed out the relationships between the initial tableaux. Now let us inspect the final (optimal) tableaux. The following relationships will prove helpful in our analysis.

Primal Variable		Dual Variable
X_j	$\Longleftrightarrow$	S_j'
S_i	$\Longleftrightarrow$	Y_j

Primal Parameter		Dual Parameter
$-\Delta Z_j$	$\Longleftrightarrow$	b_i
b_i	$\Longleftrightarrow$	$\Delta Z_j'$

First, we notice that $Z_{MAX} = Z'_{MIN} = 64$. If we ignore the columns of the dual containing the artificial variables (which, you recall, are used to

		c_j	X_1 10	X_2 8	X_3 6	S_1 0	S_2 0	c_j / b_i
	c_i							
S_1	0		2	1	1	1	0	12
S_2	0		1	4	1	0	1	8
	Z_j		0	0	0	0	0	0
	ΔZ_j		10	8	6	0	0	

(a)

		c_j	Y_1 12	Y_2 8	S_1' 0	S_2' 0	S_3' 0	A_1 M	A_2 M	A_3 M	c_j / b_i
	c_i										
A_1	M		2	1	-1	0	0	1	0	0	10
A_2	M		1	4	0	-1	0	0	1	0	8
A_3	M		1	1	0	0	-1	0	0	1	6
	Z_j'		$4M$	$6M$	$-M$	$-M$	$-M$	M	M	M	$24M$
	$\Delta Z_j'$		$12-4M$	$8-6M$	M	M	M	0	0	0	

(b)

Figure 5.14 (a) Sandy MacHinery's primal problem, initial tableau; (b) Sandy MacHinery's dual problem, initial tableau.

		X_1	X_2	X_3	S_1	S_2	
c_i \ c_j		10	8	6	0	0	c_j \ b_i
X_1	10	1	-3	0	1	-1	4
X_3	6	0	7	1	-1	2	4
Z_j		10	12	6	4	2	64
ΔZ_j		0	-4	0	-4	-2	

(c)

		Y_1	Y_2	S_1'	S_2'	S_3'	A_1	A_2	A_3	
c_i \ c_j		12	8	0	0	0	M	M	M	c_j \ b_i
Y_1	12	1	0	-1	0	1	1	0	-1	4
Y_2	8	0	1	1	0	-2	-1	0	2	2
S_2^1	0	0	0	3	1	-7	-3	-1	7	4
Z_j'		12	8	-4	0	-4	4	0	4	64
$\Delta Z_j'$		0	0	4	0	4	$M-4$	M	$M-4$	

(d)

Figure 5.14   (c) Optimal solution, primal; (d) Optimal solution, dual.

obtain an initial feasible solution and will never appear in the optimal feasible solution), the $\Delta Z_j'$ row of the dual gives us the solution to the primal problem.

Column of Dual	Y_1	Y_2	S_1'	S_2'	S_3'
Corresponding Variable in Primal	S_1	S_2	X_1	X_2	X_3
Value	0	0	4	0	4

With a sign change (ΔZ_j values in the optimal tableau of a maximization problem must be zero or *negative*, whereas all b_i values must always be *positive*), the solution values for the dual variables tell us the ΔZ_j values for the primal.

Variable in Dual	Y_1	Y_2	S_1'	S_2'	S_3'
Corresponding Variable in Primal	S_1	S_2	X_1	X_2	X_3
Solution Value (from Dual)	4	2	0	4	0
ΔZ_j Value (from Primal)	-4	-2	0	-4	0

It is possible to construct the a_{ij} values of either tableau from the other by noting that Y_k's row relates to S_k's column; S_k'''s row, to X_k's column; X_k's row, to S_k'''s column; and S_k's row, to Y_k's column. For example, the entry in the Y_2 row, S_3' column of the dual solution (-2) is the same as that in the X_3 row, S_2 column of the primal solution $(+2)$ *with the sign reversed.* Our primary interest, however, is in the ΔZ_j rows and the b_i columns.

These comparisons can be reversed to construct the solution to the dual problem from the final tableau of the primal problem. Knowledge of the primal–dual relationships can greatly simplify the solution of linear programming problems. A problem containing five unknowns and two constraints can be converted into its dual problem, and the optimal value of Z can be obtained *graphically*, because the dual will have five constraints but only two unknowns. Conversely, a minimization problem with three variables and ten GTE constraints would require addition of ten slacks and ten artificial variables and ten iterations (of a 10×23 tableau) to get a *feasible* (not necessarily optimal) solution. Its dual can usually be solved in fewer iterations of a 3×13 tableau.

ECONOMIC INTERPRETATION OF THE PRIMAL AND THE DUAL[3]

The Primal

c_j VALUES

The c_j values represent the *contribution* to the objective function of 1 unit of their respective variables. For example, each unit of product 1 that Sandy produces and sells increases her profit by $10.

c_i VALUES

The c_i values are the c_j coefficients of the variables in the solution (basic variables).

b_i VALUES

The b_i values are the *solution values* of the basic variables ($X_1 = 4, X_3 = 4$). All nonbasic variables have zero values. Sandy should produce 4 units each of products 1 and 3 and none of product 2. The fact that the slack variables both have values of zero means that all of the resources are being utilized fully. Slack values indicate available, unused capacity on the machines.

[3] This section contains material which is somewhat more advanced than the rest of the text, and can be omitted without loss of continuity.

a_{ij} VALUES

The values within the double lines of the simplex table are *exchange rates* of one variable for another. The coefficient in X_3's row and X_2's column of the optimal primal tableau (7) means that each unit of X_2 that enters the solution displaces or drives out 7 units of X_3. The -3 in X_1's row indicates that 3 units of X_1 must *enter* for each unit of X_2 that is brought in.

Z_j VALUES

The numbers in the Z_j row represent the *costs* of bringing in 1 unit of the variables in their respective columns. For example, introducing 1 unit of X_2 requires *adding* 3 units of X_1 at \$10 profit each and *removing* 7 units of X_3 at \$6 profit each for a *net cost* of $(-3 \times \$10) + (7 \times \$6) = \$12$ for each unit of X_2 added. If S_2 were brought in, each unit added would bring in 1 additional unit of X_1 and drive out 2 units of X_3 for a net cost of $(-1 \times \$10) + (2 \times \$6) = \$2$ per unit of S_2 added. The final element of the Z_j row is Z, the value of the objective function.

$\Delta Z_j (c_j - Z_j)$ VALUES

The final row is the difference between the profit added by the introduction of 1 unit of that variable and the cost associated with the addition of that unit. Thus it represents the net change in the objective function (hence our notation ΔZ_j) from 1 unit of that variable. It is, in effect, the price paid or profit received for 1 unit of the variable in its column and is therefore commonly referred to as the *shadow price* or *implicit cost*.

The Dual

Economic interpretation of the variables and the coefficients of the dual problem is a difficult task, for the interpretation depends upon the nature and form of the primal and just what the primal represents. This discussion relates to the dual in our example.

Y_j VALUES

We always have one Y variable for each constraint in the primal, and the value of Y_k in the optimal solution is the same (adjusted for sign) as the ΔZ_j value of the S_k in the primal. So the value of Y_k represents the per-unit contribution of the kth resource (constraint) to the objective function. Thus, if $Y_1 = 4$, 1 additional hour of capacity on machine A would provide an additional \$4 profit. We know this from the primal, because S_1's ΔZ_j value of -4 tells us that to bring in 1 hour's slack (reduce our utilization of the machine by 1 hour) would reduce our profit by \$4.

S_i' VALUES

There is always one slack variable (S_1') in the dual for each real variable (X_j) in the primal. The value of S_k' in the dual represents the shadow price (ΔZ_k value) of X_k in the primal.

c_i VALUES

The coefficient of Y_k in the dual objective function is the b_k value from the primal. It represents the availability of the kth resource. Y_2's coefficient (8) represents the 8 hours of machine time available on machine B.

b_i VALUES

b_k is the per-unit profit contribution of the kth primal variable in the initial dual tableau, and the values the b_is assume in the optimal dual tableau are the shadow prices or per-unit contribution to profit of their respective variable at the optimal solution.

a_{ij}' VALUES

As in the primal problem, these represent exchange rates between variables.

$\Delta Z_j'$ VALUES

The improvement indices for Y_k and S_k' are the solution values of the primal variables S_k and X_k, respectively.

SENSITIVITY ANALYSIS[4]

Now that you have learned how to find the optimal solution to a linear programming problem, it is tempting to close out the discussion and move on to conquer other classes of problems. But in attempting to apply the model to real problems, we usually must stop to ask some "what if?" types of questions.

Frequently, the numerical values we have used in our model are not known with absolute certainty. As decision makers we well may wish to know the effects that changes in some of these values will have on the solution we have obtained. Because we are measuring the *sensitivity* of the solution to these changes in input values and because this analysis takes place *after* we obtain the optimal solution to the original problem, it is called *sensitivity analysis* or *postoptimality analysis*.

---

[4] Some parts of this section are relatively more difficult than others. Your instructor may wish to have you omit some of the material.

We will investigate the sensitivity of the optimal solution to changes in the following:

1. Objective Function Coefficients (c_js)
   a. Coefficients of variables *not in* the optimal solution (nonbasis)
   b. Coefficients of variables *in* the optimal solution (basis)
2. Constraint Values (b_is)
   a. Nonbinding in the optimal solution ($S_i > 0$)
   b. Binding in the optimal solution ($S_i = 0$)
3. Coefficients of the constraint equations (a_{ij}s)

The changes will be made in one element at a time, with all other elements retaining their original values. Simultaneous variation is too complex a problem to be considered here. We will use the following simple example problem as the context of our discussion.

$$\text{Max } Z = X_1 + 4X_2$$
$$\text{ST} \qquad 2X_1 + X_2 \le 8$$
$$X_1 + X_2 \le 6$$

Objective Function Coefficients (c_js)

NONBASIS VARIABLES

First, we will consider the impact of changes in the coefficient of one of the variables *not* included in the optimal solution. We focus our attention on the c_j and the ΔZ_j rows of the optimal tableau [Fig. 5.15(a)].

If the problem is a maximization problem, the basis variables will have $\Delta Z_j = 0$, and the nonbasis variables will have $\Delta Z_j < 0$. Because nonbasis variables have values of zero (e.g., $X_1 = 0$), any change that does not bring them into the solution will have *no* effect on the optimal solution; that is, as long as $\Delta Z_j = c_j - Z_j$ remains negative, the original solution is still optimal.

Thus, in a maximization problem, c_j values of nonbasis variables may decrease without bound or increase by as much as the absolute value of ΔZ_j with no effect on the optimal solution. In general terms, $-\infty < \Delta c_j \le |\Delta Z_j|$ is the permissible range of changes in c_j. In our example, the coefficient of X_1 may vary over the range $-\infty < c_1 \le 3$. Graphically [Fig. 5.15(b)] this changes the slope of Z. Decreasing c_1 "tilts" Z upward with no effect on the optimal solution. Increasing c_1 tilts Z downward toward constraint II.

In a minimization problem, the ΔZ_js will be positive; so the c_js may increase without bound or may drop by as much as ΔZ_j

$$\Delta Z_j \le \Delta c_j < +\infty$$

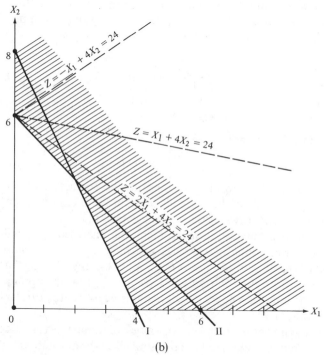

	c_j	X_1	X_2	S_1	S_2	
c_i		1	4	0	0	c_j / b_i
S_1	0	1	0	1	-1	2
X_2	4	1	1	0	1	6
Z_j		4	4	0	4	24
ΔZ_j		-3	0	0	-4	

(a)

(b)

Figure 5.15   (a) Final tableau; (b) Changes in C_1.

If the coefficient of a nonbasis variable changes by more than the allowable amount ($|\Delta Z_j|$), the old solution becomes nonoptimal (because ΔZ_j will have reversed in sign), and the new value of ΔZ_j indicates the change in Z_{OPT} for each unit of that variable that enters the solution. We make the change in the "final" tableau and iterate to obtain the new optimal solution.

BASIS VARIABLES

Since the coefficients of basis variables are used in the computation of Z, any change in their values will result in a change in the value of Z_{OPT}. But small changes in c_js may not change the *set* of basis variables. Larger changes, however, will cause a change in the basis and will move the solution point on our graph. The easiest way to handle a proposed change in the coefficient of a basis variable is to make the change in the final tableau (both c_j and c_i) and recompute the Z_js and ΔZ_js. If the solution is still optimal, stop; if not (one or more ΔZ_js reverse sign), iterate to obtain the new optimal solution. Figures 5.16(a) and 5.16(b) show a change in the value of C_2 (from 4 to 3) that results only in a change in the value of Z_{MAX}. Figures 5.17(a) and 5.17(b) show a change (from 4 to $\frac{1}{6}$) that causes a move to a new solution. From the graph we can see that two iterations will be required to arrive at the new solution.

A more general approach is to calculate the amount of change in the c_j of the basis variable required to drive each of the nonzero ΔZ_js to

	c_j	X_1	X_2	S_1	S_2	c_j
c_i		1	③	0	0	b_i
S_1	0	1	0	1	−1	2
X_2	③	1	1	0	1	6
	Z_j	③	3	0	3	18
	ΔZ_j	−2	0	0	−3	

(a)

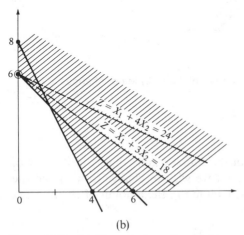

(b)

Figure 5.16   (a) Changes in optimal tableau; (b) Minor changes in C_2.

	c_j	X_1	X_2	S_1	S_2	
c_i		1	$\left(\frac{1}{6}\right)$	0	0	c_j / b_i
S_1	0	1	0	1	-1	2
X_2	$\left(\frac{1}{6}\right)$	1	1	0	1	6
	Z_j	$\left(\frac{1}{6}\right)$	$\frac{1}{6}$	0	$\frac{1}{6}$	$\left(1\right)$
	ΔZ_i	$\left(+\frac{5}{6}\right)$	0	0	$\left(-\frac{1}{6}\right)$	✕

(a)

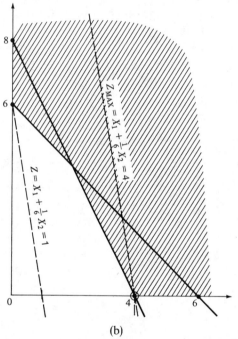

(b)

Figure 5.17   (a) Changes requiring new solution; (b) Major changes in C_1.

zero. If we locate the element of the simplex table that is in the row of the basis variable whose coefficient we wish to change (row k) and the column of the nonbasis variable (column j), the amount of change in c_k required to drive ΔZ_j to zero is

$$\Delta c_k = \frac{\Delta Z_j}{a_{kj}}$$

If you will refer again to the final tableau of Figure 5.16(a), you will see that the change in c_2 required to drive ΔZ_1 to zero is

$$\Delta c_2 = \frac{-2}{1} = -2$$

For S_2, the required change in c_2 is

$$\Delta c_2 = \frac{-3}{1} = -3$$

In this example, changes in a positive direction change only the value of Z_{MAX}; so the permissible range of values for c_2 is

$$+1 \leq c_2 < +\infty$$

Constraint Values (b_is)

Before we begin our discussion of the sensitivity of our solution to changes in the b_i values, we must understand the meaning of *relaxing* and *tightening* constraints. To relax a constraint is to change the right-hand side (b_i) value in a direction that *enlarges* the feasible area. Thus an increase in the b_i value of an LTE constraint is a relaxation, and a decrease is a tightening of the constraint. Conversely, decreasing the b_i value of a GTE expands (relaxes) the feasible region, and an increase reduces (tightens) it. Figures 5.18(a) and 5.18(b) show this graphically.

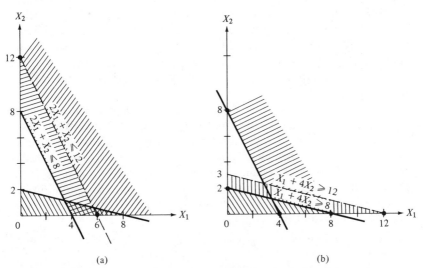

(a)   (b)

Figure 5.18   (a) Increasing b_i on LTE constraint expands feasible region;
(b) Increasing b_i on GTE constraint reduces feasible region.

NONBINDING CONSTRAINTS

If we relax a constraint that is *not* binding, there will be no change in the optimal solution. The amount of slack in that constraint will simply increase by the amount of the change in b_i.

If we tighten a nonbinding constraint by an amount that does not exceed its slack, no change will occur except that the slack will be reduced by the amount of the change.

If we tighten a nonbinding constraint by more than the available slack, the slack will assume a negative value (indicating *violation* of that constraint) in the b_i column of the final tableau. Because this is not allowed,[5] we must resolve the problem. The range of changes in b_i that do not change the solution is therefore

$$-S_i \leq \Delta b_i < +\infty \qquad \text{(LTE)}$$
$$-b_i \leq \Delta b_i \leq S_i \qquad \text{(GTE)}$$

In our example problem, $S_1 = 2$ in the final solution. Because this constraint ($2X_1 + X_2 \leq 8$) is an LTE, it may be expanded (b_1 increased) without bound, and it may be tightened (b_1 reduced) by as much as 2 units; so the limits on b_1 if optimality is not to be changed are

$$6 \leq b_1 < +\infty$$

BINDING CONSTRAINTS

A binding constraint has zero slack. Because its slack is zero, the *column* containing its slack will have a nonzero ΔZ_j value. If a binding constraint is changed, the solution point will move, and the value of Z_{OPT} will, in general, change. If the constraint is tightened (b_i reduced for an LTE or increased for a GTE), the feasible region will become smaller, and the value of Z_{OPT} will become worse (lower for a maximization problem, higher for a minimization problem). If the constraint is relaxed, Z_{OPT} will become better.

We can determine, from the final tableau, the range within which the b_i value of a binding constraint may change without driving out a basis variable. If the b_i value of binding constraint k is changed, the impact on the solution values of the basis variables can be found by multiplying the amount of the change (Δb_k) by the coefficient from S_k's column. If ΔX_i is the change in the value of the solution variable on the ith row of the final matrix, the change brought about by a change in the b_i value of the kth constraint is

$$\Delta X_i = a_{ik} \Delta b_k$$

---

[5] There is an algorithm called *dual simplex* that does permit negative b_i values, but our regular simplex does not.

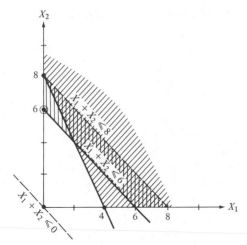

Figure 5.19 Limits on changes in b_2.

Because we may not drive any solution variable negative, we can use this relationship to find the allowable range for Δb_k (and, therefore, b_k).

$$X_i + a_{ik}\Delta b_k \geq 0$$

$$\Delta b_k \geq \frac{-X_i}{a_{ik}}, \qquad (a_{ik} > 0)$$

$$\Delta b_k \leq \frac{-X_i}{a_{ik}}, \qquad (a_{ik} < 0)$$

From our example, $S_2 = 0$; so the second constraint is binding. S_2s column is $\binom{-1}{1}$; so the allowable Δb_2 values are

$$\begin{aligned} S_1 &: 2 + (-1)\Delta b_2 \geq 0, & -\infty < \Delta b_2 \leq +2 \\ X_2 &: 6 + (1)\Delta b_2 \geq 0, & -6 \leq \Delta b_2 < +\infty \end{aligned}$$

Therefore the allowable range for Δb_2 is

$$-6 \leq \Delta b_2 \leq +2$$

and the corresponding range for b_2 (the original value was 6) is

$$0 \leq b_2 \leq 8$$

This result is shown graphically in Figure 5.19.

EQUALITY CONSTRAINTS

Equality constraints are *always* binding in the optimum feasible solution. Increases in their b_i values usually lead to improved solutions (higher

Z_{MAX} values) in maximization problems and worse solutions (higher Z_{MIN} values) in minimization problems. Decreases in their b_i values usually have the reverse effect (lower Z_{OPT} values).

Constraint Coefficients (a_{ij}s)

BINDING CONSTRAINTS

Changing an a_{ij} value changes the slope and one intercept of the constraint. If the constraint is binding, an increase in a_{ij} will result in reducing X_j's intercept. Therefore: (1) if the constraint is an LTE, Z_{OPT} will remain the same or get worse because the feasible region will be reduced; or

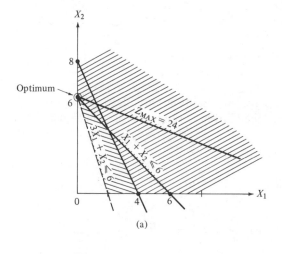

(a)

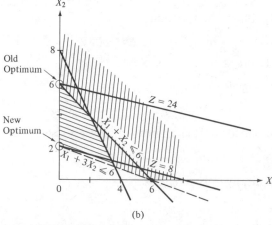

(b)

Figure 5.20 (a) Change in a_{ij} for a nonbasic variable; (b) Change in a_{ij} for a basic variable.

(2) if the constraint is a GTE, Z_{OPT} will remain the same or get better because the feasible region will be increased. The effects of a reduction in a_{ij} have the reverse effects of an increase.

When an a_{ij} value is changed, only one intercept of the function changes in value. In two dimensions, this leads to a "swinging gate" movement of the line about the other (fixed) intercept. If the optimum solution is at the fixed end (the variable whose a_{ij} is changed has a value of zero and is not in the basis), the solution does not change. This situation is illustrated in Figure 5.20(a), where X_1's coefficient in the second constraint is changed from 1 to 3. The feasible region is reduced by the movement of a binding constraint, but the optimum is unaffected.

When the a_{ij} of a basis variable is changed, the optimum shifts, as shown in Figure 5.20(b), where X_2's coefficient in the second constraint is changed from 1 to 3. The feasible region is reduced, and Z_{MAX} decreases from 24 to 8.

EQUALITY CONSTRAINTS

Because a strict equality constraint is the equivalent of a GTE and an LTE with the same a_{ij} and b_i values, changing its coefficients is like changing *both* a GTE and an LTE at once. If the variable whose a_{ij} is changed is nonbasic, the solution will be unchanged. If the variable is basic, a decrease in a_{ij} will increase Z_{OPT}, and an increase in a_{ij} will decrease Z_{OPT}.

NONBINDING CONSTRAINTS

If the constraint is not binding, a change in a_{ij} that increases the feasible area (relaxes the constraint) will have no effect upon the solution. This change would be an increase in an a_{ij} in a GTE or a decrease in an a_{ij} in an LTE. Changes in the opposite direction lead to reductions in the feasible area. If the change is large enough, the new solution will be worse than the old one; if not, the slack in the constraint will be reduced.

The range of values for a_{ij}s that will not affect the solution can be determined, but the mechanics of the calculations require a great deal more sophistication and a greater understanding of the simplex than we have provided in our brief treatment. Such analysis is better left for more advanced texts.

Adding a Constraint

If we wish to impose an additional constraint on the problem, our first step should be to evaluate the constraint at the optimal solution. If it is not binding, we can calculate its slack and relax. If it is binding, the slack is zero, and we have a degenerate solution (still no problem). If the new constraint is violated by the optimum point, it will be binding, and Z_{OPT} will be worse than before, or it will wipe out our feasible region, and there will be no feasible solution. To find out which, we must resort to the use of the dual simplex method or rework the problem.

Removing a Constraint

If we wish to remove a nonbinding constraint, we simply strike the row containing its slack, which leaves the solution unchanged. If the constraint is binding, removing it will improve Z_{OPT}. We increase b_i for an LTE (decrease b_i for a GTE) until the constraint becomes nonbinding. An alternate approach is to retrace our steps backward through the simplex tableaux to the last one in which the slack for our constraint appeared, strike its row from the tableau, and iterate as necessary to find the new optimum. If its slack never entered the solution (this could happen with a GTE), we remove it from the initial problem and resolve.

Deleting a Variable

If we wish to delete a nonbasis variable, we simply remove its column, which leaves the solution unchanged. If we wish to delete a basis variable, we can backtrack to a tableau where it was not in the solution, delete its column, and iterate to the new optimum.

Adding a Variable

If we wish to add a variable, it is possible to update the final tableau and proceed from there, but this requires advanced procedures such as the *revised simplex*. The simplest approach is just to restate the problem and resolve it.

Summary

Tables 5.1–5.3 attempt to summarize the main concepts of sensitivity analysis that we have covered.

Table 5.1 SENSITIVITY ANALYSIS
SUMMARY: c_js

NONBASIS VARIABLES	BASIS VARIABLES
MAXIMIZATION PROBLEMS $-\infty < \Delta c_j \le \lvert \Delta Z_j \rvert$ No change in optimum	$\Delta c_k \le \dfrac{\Delta Z_j}{a_{kj}}$
MINIMIZATION PROBLEMS $\Delta Z_j \le \Delta c_j < +\infty$ No change in optimum	No change in basis

Table 5.2   SENSITIVITY ANALYSIS
SUMMARY: b_is

NONBINDING CONSTRAINTS	BINDING CONSTRAINTS
LTE CONSTRAINTS $-S_i \leq \Delta b_i < +\infty$ No change in optimum	$\Delta b_k \geq \dfrac{-X_i}{a_{ik}}, (a_{ik} > 0)$
GTE CONSTRAINTS $-b_i \leq \Delta b_i \leq S_i$ No change in optimum	$\Delta b_j \leq \dfrac{-X_i}{a_{ik}}, (a_{ik} < 0)$ No change in basis
EQUALITY CONSTRAINTS If the solution is feasible, the equality constraint(s) must be binding.	MAXIMIZATION PROBLEMS $\Delta b_i > 0, Z_{MAX}$ improves $\Delta b_i < 0, Z_{MAX}$ gets worse
	MINIMIZATION PROBLEMS $\Delta b_i < 0, Z_{MIN}$ improves $\Delta b_i > 0, Z_{MIN}$ gets worse

Table 5.3   SENSITIVITY ANALYSIS SUMMARY: a_{ij}s

NONBINDING CONSTRAINTS	BINDING CONSTRAINTS
LTE CONSTRAINTS $\Delta a_{ij} < 0$, no change in optimum S_i reduced, $\Delta a_{ij} > 0$, Z_{OPT} can get worse	NONBASIS VARIABLE No change in optimum BASIS VARIABLE $\Delta a_{ij} < 0$, Z_{OPT} improves $\Delta a_{ij} > 0$, Z_{OPT} gets worse
GTE CONSTRAINTS $\Delta a_{ij} > 0$, no change in optimum S_i reduced, $\Delta a_{ij} < 0$, Z_{OPT} can get worse	NONBASIS VARIABLE No change in optimum BASIS VARIABLE $\Delta a_{ij} > 0$, Z_{OPT} improves $\Delta a_{ij} < 0$, Z_{OPT} gets worse
EQUALITY CONSTRAINTS If the solution is feasible, the equality constraint(s) must be binding.	NONBASIS VARIABLE No change in optimum BASIS VARIABLE $\Delta a_{ij} > 0$, $\Delta Z_{OPT} < 0$ $\Delta a_{ij} < 0$, $\Delta Z_{OPT} > 0$

SUMMARY OF KEY CONCEPTS

Simplex.   A systematic, iterative procedure for solving linear programming (LP) problems.

Augmentation.   Adding appropriate slack and artificial variables with appropriate signs and magnitudes to convert the constraints into equalities and to assure a feasible optimum solution, if one exists.

Slack variable. A variable added to the left-hand side of LTE ($\leq$) type constraints and subtracted from GTE ($\geq$) constraints during augmentation. The value of a slack variable is the amount of leeway in its constraint or the amount by which the constraint could be tightened without affecting the optimal solution.

Artificial variable. A variable added to the left-hand side of EQ ($=$) and GTE ($\geq$) type constraints to permit an initial solution in the simplex procedure. The value of the artificial variable indicates the amount by which the constraint is violated or the amount by which it must be relaxed in order to make the solution feasible. If a feasible solution exists, no artificial variables will appear in the optimal solution.

Big M Method. A procedure whereby the artificial variables are added to the objective function with very large coefficients ($M = \$1,000,000$) to assure that the artificial variables will not appear in the optimal solution. The Ms are given positive signs in minimization problems and negative signs in maximization problems.

Basis variables. Those variables (real, slack, and artificial) that appear in the solution at a particular point. These variables have nonnegative values, whereas all others have values of zero.

Exchange ratios. The a_{ij} values in the augmented constraint equations. They represent the number of units of the solution variable in row i that will be driven out of the solution if 1 unit of the variable in column j is brought into the solution. (Also called *substitution ratios*.)

Improvement indices. The ΔZ_j values that indicate the net change (increase) in the objective function that results from the introduction of 1 unit of the variables in their respective columns. A negative ΔZ_j indicates a drop in Z; a positive ΔZ_j indicates an increase in Z.

Entering variable. The nonbasis variable that will be introduced into the solution at the next iteration—the one with the largest positive (maximization problem) or most negative (minimization problem) ΔZ_j value.

Leaving variable. The basic variable that will be driven to zero (out of the solution) by the introduction of the entering variable—the variable with the smallest positive θ_i value.

Introduction limits. The θ_i values that indicate how many units of the entering variable are required to drive out the basis variable in their respective rows.

Key column. The column containing the entering variable.

Key row. The row containing the leaving variable.

Key cell. The element at the intersection of the key row and the key column.

Degeneracy. A solution at the intersection of more than two constraints, where the number of nonzero variables is less than the number of constraints.

Infeasibility. A problem in which no feasible solutions exist. All possible solutions violate one or more of the constraints.

Alternate optimality. When the objective function is parallel to a constraint, it passes through more than one "corner" of the feasible region at once. If this occurs at the optimum solution, then all of the feasible solutions on that objective function are optimal.

Primal problem. Original LP problem. ("The dual of the dual is the primal.")

Dual problem. An alternate formulation of the primal problem used to reduce the calculation required to find the solution.

Sensitivity analysis. Examination of the parameters (coefficients, constants) to determine the effect of changes in their values on the optimum solution.

PROBLEMS

1. Augment the constraints and objective function for the following LP problem and set up the initial simplex tableau.

$$\text{Max } Z = 3X_1 + 5X_2 + 7X_3$$
$$\text{ST} \quad 2X_1 - 4X_2 + 5X_3 \le 12$$
$$X_1 + 6X_2 - 3X_3 \ge 16$$
$$5X_1 + 2X_2 + X_3 = 7$$
$$(X_j \ge 0)$$

2. Augment the following LP problem and set up the initial simplex tableau.

$$\text{Min } Z = 4X_1 - 12X_2 + 5X_3$$
$$\text{ST} \quad X_1 + 3X_2 - 8X_3 = 5$$
$$2X_1 - 9X_2 + 4X_3 \le 14$$
$$3X_1 + 5X_2 - X_3 \ge 7$$
$$X_2 = 2$$
$$(X_j \ge 0)$$

3. A retailer wishes to determine the optimum number of each of three sizes of artificial trees to order. The large trees cost $35 and sell for $60 each; the medium trees cost $30 and sell for $50 each; the small ones cost $15 and sell for $25 each. He wishes to order at least 20 of each type. He has only $3000 to spend on inventory of the trees. His space limitations are such that he cannot exceed 60 units of the large and medium trees combined. He wants a gross revenue from the sale of trees to be at least $5000. If he wishes to maximize his profit, state his problem in the form of a linear programming problem and set up the first tableau.

4. A little-league baseball coach has divided his players into three groups: 3 Infielders (I); 2 Outfielders (O); and 6 Utility players (U); who can play either infield or outfield with equal effectiveness. His pitcher and catcher have already been selected (the Sponsor's kid and the only one with a mask). There are 4 infield positions (1st, 2nd, 3rd, and short), and 3 outfield positions (1, c, r) to be filled. In order to have any defensive strength at all, at least 2 infielders and at least 1 outfielder must start. The coach wishes to maximize offensive potential, as measured by batting averages. The infielders average .193; the outfielders, .227; the utility players, .284. The solution to this problem is achievable by inspection. Your task is *not* to solve the problem but rather to formulate it in standard form as a linear programming problem and set up the first tableau. (Hint: Let U_I = number of utility players who start in the infield and U_O = number who start in the outfield.)

5. A truck driver who charges for intracity hauling by the pound wishes to load the maximum possible amount of weight into her truck. She has three types of cargo available: air conditioners, bean bags, and crates of candles. The weights of 1 unit of each are 100#, 5#, and 25#, respectively. The respective volumes of 1 unit of each type of cargo are 7, 5, and 6 cubic feet. The total usable cargo space in the truck is 130 cubic feet. The total number of units of each type cargo she needs to move are 10, 50, and 30 units. She only has time to load a total of 30 units, and she has promised to deliver at least 5 units of each kind. Her objective is to maximize revenue and, therefore, weight. Set up the problem for solution by simplex and develop the first tableau.

6. Balls, Inc. manufactures and sells tennis balls and racquet balls. Their net profit is $4 per dozen on tennis balls and $2 per dozen on the racquet balls. It takes 1 labor hour to manufacture, package, and ship a dozen tennis balls, and 2 labor hours for a dozen racquet balls. The firm has 4 workers, who work a 40-hour week. Management has determined that it needs a combined production rate (both types added together) of at least 2 dozen per hour to break even. How many dozens of each type ball should they produce each hour to maximize profits? What is their maximum profit for a 40-hour week? Set up the problem as a linear programming problem. Augment the constraints and the objective function. Solve by simplex and graphically. Relate each tableau to a point on the graphical solution.

7. A retailer wishes to determine the optimum allocation of 1000 square feet of floor space between Christmas decorations and toys. The toys return $2 per square foot during the month of December; the decorations, $1 per foot. ("Return" means net profit.) He must have at least 200 square feet for decorations and at least 400 square feet for the toys. Furthermore, he wishes the space devoted to the toys to be at least twice that devoted to decorations. Let X represent the square footage devoted to decorations; Y denote that left over for toys. Formulate the problem as a linear programming problem and solve it graphically and by simplex, relating each tableau to a point on the graphical solution.

8. A farmer-rancher produces three products on his farm-ranch—corn, cotton, and cattle. He wishes to optimize the amount of acreage

devoted to each. Let the number of acres (in thousands) of corn, cotton, and cattle be designated by X_1, X_2, and X_3, respectively. The constraints on the problem are:

1. Total available land is 10,000 acres, and all is to be used.
2. In order to feed the cattle and still have a corn crop left over, the acreage devoted to corn must exceed that devoted to cattle by at least 4000 acres.
3. In order to qualify for a government subsidy, he must have no more than 3000 acres of cotton.

His anticipated profit per thousand acres is estimated to be (in thousands) $2 for corn, $3 for cotton, and $5 for cattle. Set up and solve by simplex to maximize his profit.

9. A wholesaler of Christmas trees has four warehouses, which she refers to as W_1, W_2, W_3, and W_4. The number of trees in each of the warehouses is 4000, 3000, 6000, and 5000, respectively. She supplies three large retailers with trees: R_1, R_2, and R_3. They have ordered 1000, and 4500, and 6500 large trees, respectively. If it costs $.01 per tree per mile to transport the trees and the distances are as shown in the diagram, set up a linear programming problem with X_{ij} representing the number of trees shipped from warehouse i to retailer j and with the objective being to find her minimum cost shipping schedule.

(Hint: There will be 12 variables—1 for each possible path from a warehouse to a retailer—and 7 constraints—1 for each warehouse (limited by capacity) and 1 for each retailer (limited by number of trees ordered). We will learn a more efficient method for solving this problem (called a *transportation problem*) in Chapter 7.

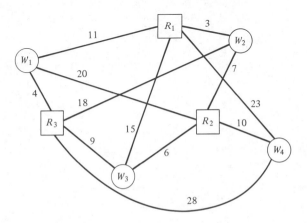

10. Frank's Friendly Fine Foods has a scheduling problem involving the checkers and baggers. They operate from 6:00 A.M. to 10:00 P.M., and schedule personnel on 8-hour shifts beginning at 6:00 A.M. (shift A), 10:00 A.M. (shift B), and 2:00 P.M. (shift C). The minimum number of employees by function required during the various parts of the day are as shown in the following table. Stocking can be done by either checkers or baggers, but because checkers cost $5 per hour and baggers cost $3 per hour, they would rather have stocking done by baggers. Set up the problem as a linear programming problem to minimize the total cost.

	6–10	10–2	2–6	6–10
Checking	3	5	6	3
Stocking	4	2	1	3
Bagging	1	4	6	2

Shift A	Shift C

Shift B

11. Given the following LP problem, formulate and solve both the primal and dual problems by SIMPLEX. Show the correspondence between initial tableaus of the primal and dual problems and the final tableaux of each.

Min $Z = 2X_1 + 3X_2$
ST $\qquad\qquad 2X_2 \geq 4$
$\qquad X_1 \qquad\quad \geq 3$
$\qquad X_1 + X_2 \geq 8$
$(X_j \geq 0)$

12. Formulate the primal and the dual of the following problem and show the augmented form of the objective function and the constraints in each case. Solve the dual problem and fill in the perimeter values of the final tableau of the primal solution (omitting artificial variables).

Min $Z = 3X_1 + X_2$
ST
(1) $\qquad X_1 + 5X_2 \geq 15$
(2) $\qquad 2X_1 + 4X_2 \geq 24$
(3) $\qquad 3X_1 + 3X_2 \geq 18$
(4) $\qquad 4X_1 + 2X_2 \geq 24$
(5) $\qquad 5X_1 + X_2 \geq 15$
$(X_j \geq 0)$

13. Given the optimal tableau from problem 1 (see the tableau below), the range of values within which each of the following variables can vary without changing the basis of the optimum solution. Indicate the main effects of each change.

a. c_1 b. c_2 c. b_1 d. b_2

	c_j	X_1	X_2	X_3	S_1	A_2	S_2	A_3	c_j
c_i		3	5	7	0	$-M$	0	$-M$	b_i
S_1	0	-4.333	0	0	1	1.167	-1.167	-1.500	20.167
X_2	5	1.333	1	0	0	0.083	-0.083	0.250	3.083
X_3	7	2.333	0	1	0	-0.167	0.167	0.500	0.833
Z_j		23.000	5	7	0	-0.754	0.75	4.75	21.250
ΔZ_j		-20.000	0	0	0	$-M + 0.754$	-0.750	$-M$ 4.75	

Chapter 6

LINEAR PROGRAMMING— COMPUTER APPLICATIONS

INTRODUCTION

In Chapter 5 the simplex method of linear programming was introduced. The technique was shown to be a straightforward and logical optimizing tool. Unfortunately it becomes rather laborious from a computational standpoint when there are more than four structural variables.

This drawback is easily overcome by the use of the digital computer. The user need not be an expert in computer operation or be a computer programmer in order to solve linear programming problems of significant complexity by this method. However, the user must understand the simplex algorithm and be able to set up the problem in proper form. To make use of the solution, the user must also be able to interpret the results supplied by the computer.

There are many "canned" linear programming computer programs available. The one explained here is representative of most of them.

Let's review the steps required to set up a linear programming problem for solution by the simplex method.

1. Identify the structural variables.
2. Construct the objective function and determine whether it is to be maximized or minimized.
3. Construct the constraint equations, specifying the type (LTE, EQ, GTE) of each.
4. Augment the constraints by supplying slack and artificial variables as needed. Remember, if the constraint is an (LTE) type, add a slack variable. If it is an (EQ) type, add an artificial variable. If it is a (GTE) type, subtract a slack and add an artificial.
5. Augment the objective function with zero coefficients on all slack variables and + or − M (depending on whether you are minimizing or maximizing) on all artificial variables.

Most computer LP packages will perform steps 4 and 5 automatically. You should read the user's manual to be sure of this.

GETTING THE PROBLEM READY FOR THE COMPUTER

First obtain the instructions for the particular LP program available on your computer. Next, obtain some program coding sheets. It does not matter if the sheets are designed for COBOL or FORTRAN, as long as they contain 80 numbered columns. Almost all canned LP programs will require that numbers be placed properly on the data cards that are to be fed into the computer. Many institutions have available *interactive computer terminals* that may be used to solve LP problems, but in this chapter we will deal with "batch mode" only. This means that all input to the computer is by punched card and that all output will be printed on a line printer.

Each line on your coding sheet represents one data card. Keep this in mind when you are transcribing information onto the coding sheets and when you are punching your cards. The best way to illustrate the actual *encoding* of the LP problem is, as always, by example, one step at a time.

Let's assume that the ABC company produces three products, which we will designate $X(1)$, $X(2)$, and $X(3)$. The *contribution margins* (profits per unit produced) of these products are $10, $15, and $20, respectively. Obviously we would wish to maximize profit; so our objective function is

$$\text{Maximize } Z = 10X(1) + 15X(2) + 20X(3)$$

There are three processes through which each of the products must progress. In process I, product $X(1)$ requires 10.7 hours per unit; product $X(2)$ requires 5 hours per unit; and product $X(3)$ requires 2 hours per unit. There are 2705 hours available in process I each month. In process II,

$X(1)$ requires 5.4 hours per unit; $X(2)$ requires 10 hours; and $X(3)$ requires 4 hours. There are 2210 hours available in process II. In process III, $X(1)$ requires 0.7 hours; $X(2)$ 1 hour; and $X(3)$ 2 hours. There are 445 hours available. There are no other constraints that need be considered, so we can now construct the three relevant constraints.

$$10.7X(1) + 5.0X(2) + 2.0X(3) \leq 2705.0 \quad \text{(Process I)}$$
$$5.4X(1) + 10.0X(2) + 4.0X(3) \leq 2210.0 \quad \text{(Process II)}$$
$$0.7X(1) + 1.0X(2) + 2.0X(3) \leq 445.0 \quad \text{(Process III)}$$

Because all three constraints are of the LTE type, the computer will add a slack variable to each to transform the inequalities into equations. In keeping with the usual convention, we will call the slack for process I $S(1)$; for process II, $S(2)$; and for process III, $S(3)$. The resulting equations are then

$$10.7X(1) + 5.0X(2) + 2.0X(3) + 1.0S(1) + 0.0S(2) + 0.0S(3) = 2705.0$$
$$5.4X(1) + 10.0X(2) + 4.0X(3) + 0.0S(1) + 1.0S(2) + 0.0S(3) = 2210.0$$
$$0.7X(1) + 1.0X(2) + 2.0X(3) + 0.0S(1) + 0.0S(2) + 1.0S(3) = 445.0$$

Because of programming considerations, most LP programs will label the foregoing matrix as follows.

$$10.7X(1) + 5.0X(2) + 2.0X(3) + 1.0X(4) + 0.0X(5) + 0.0X(6) = 2705.0$$
$$5.4X(1) + 10.0X(2) + 4.0X(3) + 0.0X(4) + 1.0X(5) + 0.0X(6) = 2210.0$$
$$0.7X(1) + 1.0X(2) + 2.0X(3) + 0.0X(4) + 0.0X(5) + 1.0X(6) = 445.0$$

where $X(4)$, $X(5)$, $X(6)$ are $S(1)$, $S(2)$, $S(3)$, respectively. In other words, there is no distinction made between structural variables, slack variables, or artificial variables as far as labeling is concerned. Consequently the objective function will look like this

$$Z = 10.0X(1) + 15.0X(2) + 20.0X(3) + 0.0X(4) + 0.0X(5) + 0.0X(6)$$

instead of this

$$Z = 10.0X(1) + 15.0X(2) + 20.0X(3) + 0.0S(1) + 0.0S(2) + 0.0S(3)$$

TELLING THE COMPUTER WHAT TO DO

Now that we know what we want to do, we must tell the machine. Let's consider what the machine has to know if it is to do the job,

1. *Job name and user account number.* At most installations, especially universities, a user must insert a card that assigns a name to the job to be run and provides the machine with proof that the user is authorized to use the machine.

2. *Program name.* There will probably be many programs stored in the computer; so the user will have to specify that the LP program is the one that is wanted.
3. *Number of independent variables in the problem.*
4. *Number of constraints in the problem.*
5. *Number of tableaux to be printed.* The options will normally range from having the values of the objective function in the final solution printed to having all tableaux plus the results printed.
6. *Type of problem—maximize or minimize.*
7. *Layout of the input data cards.* In many programs it is necessary only to enter values on the data input cards and separate them with commas. However, in some programs it is necessary to place variable coefficients in particular columns of the cards and to alert the computer beforehand where each of the values is to be found.
8. *Coefficients of the variables of the objective function* (C_j).
9. *Coefficients of the variables of the constraint equations* (A_{ij}). Normally each constraint starts on a new card and is continued on successive cards if necessary. A well-designed program will allow the user to enter the coefficients of the structural variables, the stipulation (b_i) values, and a code that identifies the constraint as LTE, GTE, or EQ and does not require that the coefficients of slack or artificial variables be entered.

Figure 6.1 depicts the deck of cards that would be used to input our example problem.

In Figure 6.1, card 1 indicates the job name is LINPRO, that it is a "job" card, that the user account number is A116, and that the user's name is "Doe." Card 2 indicates that the program desired is in the FORTRAN library and is named SIMPLEX. Card 3 tells the machine that there are three independent variables, three constraints, that only the first and last tableaux are to be printed, and that it is a maximization problem. If we had wanted all the tableaux printed, we would have placed a zero in the third position rather than a one. A two in the third position would have caused every second tableau to be printed; a three, every third; etc. Card 4 contains the coefficients of the objective function. Cards 5, 6, and 7 contain the coefficients of the three constraints, the stipulation values, and the type of constraint. L means "LTE"; E means "EQ"; and G means "GTE". The last card, 8, simply indicates the end of the input.

The deck in Figure 6.1 contains no card to show the layout of the input data cards because none is required for the program we are using. Some LP packages permit the user to specify the format (column by column layout) of the data; others require a preset format (such as 10 columns per variable). Check your user's manual to be sure which arrangement your program utilizes.

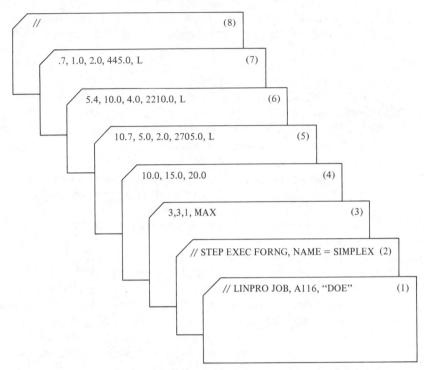

Figure 6.1   Card deck for example problem.

OUTPUT AND INTERPRETATION

After the cards are properly punched and entered into the machine, all that is left to do is to collect and interpret the results. The program we are using here will yield the output in Table 6.1.

Note that in the output for the example problem, the original input is reproduced in the standard simplex form.

In the sensitivity portion of the output, the variables in the optimal solution are shown with their values and with their boundary $C(J)$ values. The minimum $C(J)$ value indicates the contribution margin such that any value below it will cause the solution to move to another point. The maximum $C(J)$ value indicates the contribution margin such that any value greater than it will cause the solution point to move to another point. If the contribution margin for any particular variable is equal to either the minimum or maximum $C(J)$, there will be multiple solutions. This will be explained graphically in the next section.

The constraint sensitivity merely shows essentially the same information for each constraint. $W(1)$ is constraint 1, $W(2)$ is constraint 2, and

Table 6.1 OUTPUT FOR EXAMPLE PROBLEM

PROBLEM—LINPRO
TABLEAU NUMBER 1

C(J)		0.0	10.0	15.0	20.0	0.0	0.0	0.0
C(I)	BASIS	X(0)	X(1)	X(2)	X(3)	X(4)	X(5)	X(6)
0.0	X(4)	2705.00	10.70	5.00	2.00	1.00	0.00	0.00
0.0	X(5)	2210.00	5.40	10.00	4.00	0.00	1.00	0.00
0.0	X(6)	445.00	0.70	1.00	2.00	0.00	0.00	1.00
C(J)–Z(J)		0.00	10.00	15.00	20.00	0.00	0.00	0.00

TABLEAU NUMBER 4 (OPTIMAL SOLUTION)

C(J)		0.0	10.0	15.0	20.0	0.0	0.0	0.0
C(I)	BASIS	X(0)	X(1)	X(2)	X(3)	X(4)	X(5)	X(6)
10.0	X(1)	200.00	1.00	0.00	0.00	0.125	−0.063	0.000
15.0	X(2)	65.00	0.00	1.00	0.00	−0.065	0.156	−0.250
20.0	X(3)	120.00	0.00	0.00	1.00	−0.012	−0.056	0.625
C(J)–Z(J)		5375.00	0.00	0.00	0.00	−0.063	−0.594	−8.750

SENSITIVITY

STRUCTURAL VARIABLES	VALUE	MINIMUM C(J)	C(J)	MAXIMUM C(J)
X(1)	200.0	9.5	10.0	19.5
X(2)	65.0	11.2	15.0	16.0
X(3)	120.0	6.0	20.0	25.0

CONSTRAINT SENSITIVITY

CONSTRAINT NUMBER	SLACK VALUE	MINIMUM B(I)	B(I)	MAXIMUM B(I)
W(1)	0.0	1105.0	2705.0	3745.0
W(2)	0.0	1794.0	2210.0	4343.3
W(3)	0.0	253.0	445.0	705.0

W(3) is constraint 3. The stipulation values of the constraints may change within the range between the minimum B(I) and maximum B(I) without changing the variable set that is in solution. However, any change from the actual B(I) value will change the value of Z if the constraint is binding. A detailed discussion of sensitivity analysis is given in Chapter 5.

A GRAPHICAL EXAMPLE

Let's consider a very simple example with only two independent variables so that we can solve the problem graphically and compare results with the computer solution.

Assume that a company produces two products known simply as A and B. The profit per unit of A is $5.00, and per unit of B, $8.00. Assume also that the two products must go through two processes. Product A requires 2 hours per unit in process I, and product B requires 4 hours. In process II product A requires 6 hours, and product B requires 3 hours. Each week there are 40 hours available in process I and 42 hours available in process II.

With the foregoing information we can set up the problem for the computer. The objective function will be

$$\text{Max } Z = 5A + 8B$$

and the constraints will be

$$2A + 4B \leq 40 \quad \text{and} \quad 6A + 3B \leq 42$$

Following the computer-variable naming convention, we write the objective function as

$$Z = 5X(1) + 8X(2) + 0X(3) + 0X(4)$$

and the constraints as

$$2X(1) + 4X(2) + X(3) + 0X(4) = 40$$

and

$$6X(1) + 3X(2) + 0X(3) + X(4) = 42$$

X(3) and X(4) are, of course, the slack variables for process I and process II, respectively.

Refer to Figure 6.1 and verify that input cards 3, 4, 5, and 6 will be as shown in Figure 6.2.

If we now input the problem into the computer and specify that all tableaux be printed, we will get three tableaux and a sensitivity analysis. The first tableau and its graphical representation are shown in Figure 6.3.

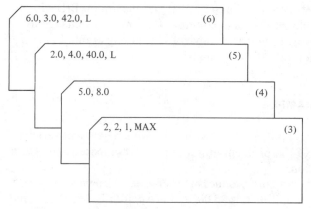

Figure 6.2 Data input cards.

PROBLEM—LINPRO

TABLEAU NUMBER 1

C(J)		0.0	5.0	8.0	0.0	0.0
C(I)	BASIS	X(0)	X(1)	X(2)	X(3)	X(4)
0.0	X(3)	40.00	2.00	4.00	1.00	0.00
0.0	X(4)	42.00	6.00	3.00	0.00	1.00
C(J)–Z(J)		0.00	5.00	8.00	0.00	0.00

INCOMING VARIABLE IS X(2) OUTGOING VARIABLE IS X(3)

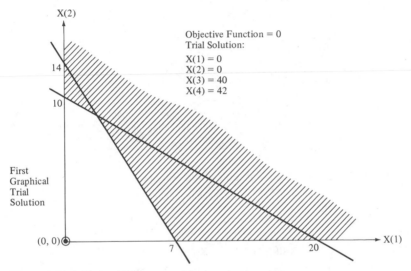

Figure 6.3   Initial solution—graphical and computer.

In the first tableau the two slack variables X(3) and X(4) are in solution with values of 40 and 42, respectively. This solution corresponds to a point at the origin, which is certainly a feasible (if not very profitable) solution. The printout also indicates that X(2) will come into solution in the next tableau as X(3) goes out of solution.

The second tableau (Fig. 6.4) shows a solution where all of the X(2) possible is being produced and no X(1) is being produced. Process I is the limiting factor for production of X(2). This is indicated by the fact that none of the slack for process I is now in solution [X(3)]. The printout shows X(1) coming into solution in the next tableau as X(4) goes out.

Figure 6.5 shows the final (optimal) solution tableau and its corresponding graph. In this figure you can see the progress of trial solutions and the final maximizing solution at the intersection of the two constraints.

TABLEAU NUMBER 2

C(J)		0.0	5.0	8.0	0.0	0.0
C(I)	BASIS	X(0)	X(1)	X(2)	X(3)	X(4)
8.0	X(2)	10.00	0.50	0.00	0.25	0.00
0.0	X(4)	12.00	4.50	0.00	−0.75	1.00
C(J)−Z(J)		80.00	1.00	0.00	−2.00	0.00

INCOMING VARIABLE IS X(1)   OUTGOING VARIABLE IS X(4)

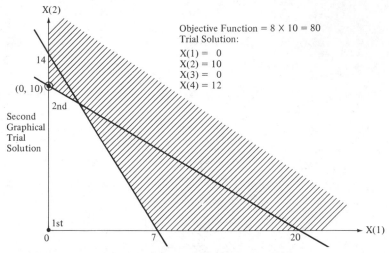

Objective Function = 8 × 10 = 80
Trial Solution:

X(1) = 0
X(2) = 10
X(3) = 0
X(4) = 12

Second Graphical Trial Solution

Figure 6.4   Second solution—graphical and computer.

TABLEAU NUMBER 3 (OPTIMAL SOLUTION)

C(J)		0.0	5.0	8.0	0.0	0.0
C(I)	BASIS	X(0)	X(1)	X(2)	X(3)	X(4)
8.0	X(2)	8.66	0.00	1.00	.166	−.111
5.0	X(1)	2.66	1.00	0.00	−.166	.222
C(J)−Z(J)		82.66	0.00	0.00	−.499	−.222

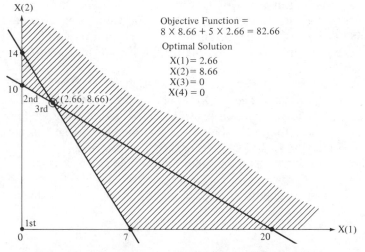

Objective Function =
8 × 8.66 + 5 × 2.66 = 82.66

Optimal Solution

X(1) = 2.66
X(2) = 8.66
X(3) = 0
X(4) = 0

Figure 6.5   Optimal solution—graphical and computer.

Structural Variables	Value	Minimum C(J)	C(J)	Maximum C(J)
X(1)	2.66	4.00	5.00	16.00

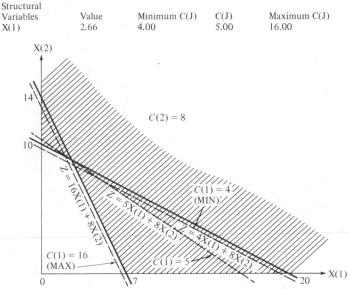

Figure 6.6   Sensitivity analysis of C(1).

SENSITIVITY

Figure 6.6 illustrates the numerical sensitivity information provided by the computer program along with a graphical representation. The broken lines in each graph show the positions of the objective function lines for the boundary values of the objective function coefficients. We see the objective function line as originally specified and at its optimum value $(C(1) = 5)$. The maximum and minimum values that the X(1) coefficient can take on (coefficient of X(2) remains constant) are the values that maintain the slope of the objective function line between the slopes of the two constraint lines. If the value of the X(1) coefficient were less than 4, the slope of the objective function would be greater than the line $2X(1) + 4X(2) = 40$, and the optimum solution would then move to the point where $X(1) = 0$ and $X(2) = 10$. If the X(1) coefficient were greater than 16, then the slope of the objective function would be less than the slope of $6X(1) + 3X(2) = 42$, and the optimum solution would move to $X(1) = 7$ and $X(2) = 0$.

Figure 6.7 is exactly the same as Figure 6.6 except that the boundary values of the X(2) coefficients have been substituted in the objective function.

Although the optimum mix does not change in these cases, the value of the objective function does. In our example substitution of the minimum

Structural Variables	Value	Minimum C(J)	C(J)	Maximum C(J)
X(2)	8.66	2.50	8.00	10.00

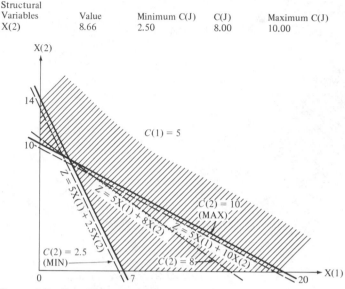

Figure 6.7   Sensitivity analysis of C(2).

value of the X(1) coefficient yields a Z value of

$$4(2.66) + 8(8.66) = 79.92$$

and substitution of the maximum value yields a Z value of

$$16(2.66) + 8(8.66) = 111.84$$

The one shortcoming of the sensitivity analysis provided by the program is that the boundary values of each coefficient are given, assuming a constant value of the other variable's coefficient.

We can derive a valuable relationship from the information provided by the program. If the X(2) coefficient remains constant, the X(1) coefficient may vary from 4 to 16. This means the relationship between the X(1) coefficient and X(2) coefficient may vary between $\frac{4}{8} = .5$ and $\frac{16}{8} = 2$. This means that the slope of the objective function may vary within a range of 1.5 without affecting the optimum mix. With this relationship we may test simultaneous changes in both coefficients to determine effect.

Figures 6.8 and 6.9 show the sensitivity analysis for the right-hand side (B_i) values of the constraints. We see that B(1) can tighten to a low of 14 or loosen to a high of 56 before the mix of solution variables in the optimum changes. B(2) can vary from 30 to 120. Note that because both constraints are binding (the values of their slack variables are zero) at the optimum, *any* movement causes a shift in the *location* of the optimum and a change in the value of Z.

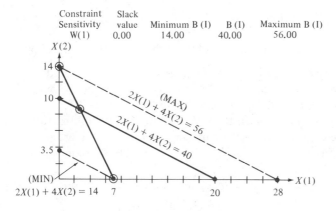

Constraint Sensitivity W(1)	Slack value	Minimum B (I)	B (I)	Maximum B (I)
	0.00	14.00	40.00	56.00

Figure 6.8 Sensitivity analysis of B(1).

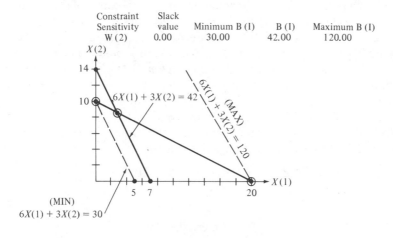

Constraint Sensitivity W (2)	Slack value	Minimum B (I)	B (I)	Maximum B (I)
	0.00	30.00	42.00	120.00

Figure 6.9 Sensitivity analysis of B(2).

A FINANCE EXAMPLE

The Apex Manufacturing Company, Inc., is planning an expansion program that will require $50 million of new capital. Naturally the company desires to acquire the new capital at the absolute minimum cost while staying within the guidelines established by the board of directors.

Apex may acquire the new funds through the sale of bonds, preferred stock, common stock, or through a combination of any of these. Currently, the company's bonds are selling at par with a coupon rate of 8.5%. Preferred stock issued by Apex is yielding 9%, and the common stock dividend is $\frac{1}{2}$ of the earnings of the company after debt service and taxes.

This has averaged approximately 10% of the price of the stock for the past 5 years.

The guidelines for the capital structure of the company are as follows.

1. The debt/equity ratio of the company shall never exceed 25%. (Preferred stock is considered as $\frac{1}{2}$ debt, $\frac{1}{2}$ equity for the purpose of this calculation.) The current debt/equity ratio is 25%.
2. There must be no more than 10% of the total capitalization in preferred stock. (This is the current percentage of preferred.)
3. There must be at least 5% of any new capital acquisition in preferred stock.
4. The entire planned amount of any capital acquisition must be subscribed.

Note also that the tax rate for Apex is 50%. Bond interest is deductible, but preferred stock dividends and common stock dividends are not. Bonds are sold for a period of 20 years, and each year $\frac{1}{40}$ of the value of the bonds must be set aside in a sinking fund for repayment of the bonds.

The problem facing us is to minimize the cost of the capital the company is trying to acquire. What is the cost of a bond? The interest (less tax deductions) plus the contribution to the sinking fund. The interest is .085, but with a 50% tax rate the actual interest cost is .0425 times the amount of bonds sold. The sinking fund contribution is $\frac{1}{40}$ or .025 for a total bond cost of .0675. The cost of preferred stock is the dividend, or 9% (.09). We can assume that the cost of common stock is also the yearly dividend of 10%. Therefore the objective function is

$$\text{Min } Z = .0675(B) + .09(P) + .10(C)$$

where

$$B = \text{Bonds}$$
$$P = \text{Preferred}$$
$$C = \text{Common}$$

The first constraint concerns the ratio between debt issues and bonds and preferred stock and between equity issues and common stock. Conceivably, two constraints could be constructed from the information in the first guideline, but one would be redundant. Let's approach this constraint from the debt limitations angle and say that total debt may not exceed 25% of $50 million, or $12.500 million. The total debt will be all of the bonds issued plus half the preferred or

$$B + .5P \le 12,500,000$$

Guideline 2 states that there may be no more than 10% of the total capitalization in preferred stock, or simply

$$P \le 5,000,000$$

Guideline 3 mandates that there be at least 5% of the capitalization in preferred. Thus

$$P \geq 2,500,000$$

The last guideline simply states that the entire $50 million must be subscribed, so the constraint is

$$B + P + C = 50,000,000$$

All that remains to be done is to punch the cards. Cards 1 and 2 are exactly like 1 and 2 in Figure 6.1. Card 3, you will recall, tells the machine how many independent variables, how many constraints, which tableaux are to be printed, and whether the problem is a maximization or a minimization problem. We have three independent variables, four constraints,

Table 6.2   OUTPUT FOR EXAMPLE PROBLEM

PROBLEM—LINPRO
TABLEAU NUMBER 1

C(J)			0.0	.0675	.090	.100	0.0	0.0	9.00	0.0	9.00
C(I)	BASIS	X(0)	X(1)	X(2)	X(3)	X(4)	X(5)	X(6)	X(7)	X(8)	
0.00	X(4)	12500000.0	1.0	0.5	0.0	1.0	1.0	0.0	0.0	0.0	
0.00	X(5)	5000000.0	0.0	1.0	0.0	0.0	0.0	0.0	0.0	0.0	
9.00	X(6)	2500000.0	0.0	1.0	0.0	0.0	0.0	1.0	−1.0	0.0	
9.00	X(8)	50000000.0	1.0	1.0	1.0	0.0	0.0	0.0	0.0	1.0	
C(J)–Z(J)		***********	−8.9	−17.9	−8.9	0.0	0.0	0.0	9.0	0.0	

TABLEAU NUMBER 4 (OPTIMAL SOLUTION)

C(J)			0.0	.067	.090	.100	0.0	0.0	9.00	0.0	9.00
C(I)	BASIS	X(0)	X(1)	X(2)	X(3)	X(4)	X(5)	X(6)	X(7)	X(8)	
0.07	X(1)	11250000.0	1.0	0.0	0.0	1.0	0.0	−0.5	0.5	0.0	
0.00	X(5)	2500000.0	0.0	0.0	0.0	0.0	1.0	−1.0	1.0	0.0	
0.09	X(2)	2500000.0	0.0	1.0	0.0	0.0	0.0	1.0	−1.0	0.0	
0.10	X(3)	36250000.0	0.0	0.0	1.0	−1.0	0.0	−0.5	0.5	1.0	
C(J)–Z(J)		4609374.0	0.0	0.0	0.0	0.03	0.0	9.0	0.0	8.9	

SENSITIVITY

STRUCTURAL VARIABLES	VALUE	MINIMUM C(J)	C(J)	MAXIMUM C(J)
X(1)	11250000.0	0.080	0.0675	−INF
X(2)	2500000.0	+INF	0.0900	0.0837
X(3)	36250000.0	0.1125	0.1000	0.0675

CONSTRAINT SENSITIVITY

CONSTRAINT NUMBER	SLACK VALUE	MINIMUM B(I)	B(I)	MAXIMUM B(I)
W(1)	0.0	1250000.0	12500000.0	48750000.0
W(2)	2500000.0	2500000.0	5000000.0	+INF
W(3)	0.0	0.0	2500000.0	5000000.0
W(4)	0.0	13750000.0	50000000.0	+INF

and a minimization problem. If we want just the first and last tableaux printed, our number 3 card will look like this.

$$(3) \quad 3,4,1,\text{MIN}$$

Card 4 contains the objective function coefficients

$$(4) \quad .0675,.09,.10$$

Cards 5, 6, 7, and 8 contain the constraint coefficients, the stipulation values, and the constraint types.

$$(5) \quad 1.0,.5,0.0,12500000,L$$

$$(6) \quad 0.0,1.0,0.0,5000000,L$$

$$(7) \quad 0.0,1.0,0.0,2500000,G$$

$$(8) \quad 1.0,1.0,1.0,50000000,E$$

Card 9 will be the // card that signals the end of the input.

Table 6.2 shows the results of the computer run for this example. In the table $X(1)$ represents bonds; $X(2)$ represents preferred stock; $X(3)$ represents common stock; $X(4)$ is the slack variable associated with $B + .5 P \leq 12,500,000$; $X(5)$ is the slack variable associated with $P \leq 5,000,000$; $X(6)$ is the artificial variable associated with $P \geq 2,500,000$; $X(7)$ is the slack variable associated with that constraint; and $X(8)$ is the artificial variable associated with $B + P + C = 50,000,000$. The $*****$ value for Z indicates that the value is too large to fit in the space allotted on the printout. From the optimum solution we see that the company should issue \$11.25 million in bonds, \$2.5 million in preferred stock, and \$36.25 million in common stock. The cost of this capital will be \$4,609,374.

A MARKETING EXAMPLE

The Huckster Advertising Company is putting together an advertising campaign for Scrubby Wubby Soap. The Scrubby Company wants exposure in newspapers and magazines and on radio, TV, and billboards, but they want the very best return for dollars spent on the program. The budget that the Scrubby Company has given Huckster is \$5 million. The president of Scrubby fancies herself an expert on advertising and has insisted on some rough limitations on how the advertising budget be spent. Written ads (newspapers, magazines, and billboards) must consume no more than 50% of the total advertising budget; unwritten ads (radio and television) must account for at most 60%. TV should be at least 40%, billboards at least 10%, and magazines at least 20%.

Huckster has learned from years of experience that every dollar spent on newspaper ads results in \$11.00 in sales; each dollar spent on radio results in \$10.00; \$12.00 per dollar for TV; \$6.00 per dollar for magazines; and \$10.00 per dollar for billboards. The manufacturer has set a sales target of at least \$45 million worth of Scrubby Wubby Soap.

Is this a maximization or minimization problem? Do we want to minimize advertising cost or maximize sales? Our advertising budget is not an unknown; our sales are. Consequently, our problem is one of maximizing sales within the limitations of budget. How can we express the objective function? What is the measure of sales? We can express the dollar sales volume by summing the dollars spent on each medium multiplied by the respective resulting sales dollars per advertising dollar spent.

If N is the dollar amount spent on newspaper ads, then the resulting sales would be 11N. The same logic holds for radio, R; TV, T; magazines, M; and billboards, B. The objective function is

$$\text{Max } Z = 11N + 10R + 12T + 6M + 10B$$

There are seven constraints. First, the budget constraint

$$N + R + T + M + B \leq 5,000,000$$

and then the sales target

$$11N + 10R + 12T + 6M + 10B \geq 45,000,000$$

The last five constraints are those dealing with the media mix

$$N + M + B \leq 2,500,000$$
$$R + T \leq 3,000,000$$
$$T \geq 2,000,000$$
$$B \geq 50,000$$
$$M \geq 100,000$$

You should verify that the following are the cards necessary to make the computer do the rest of the work.

```
 (1) //LINPRO JOB, A116, "DOE"
 (2) //STEP EXEC FORNG,NAME=SIMPLEX
 (3) 5,7,1,MAX
 (4) 11.0,10.0,12.0,6.0,10.0
 (5) 1.0,1.0,1.0,1.0,1.0,5000000,L
 (6) 11.0,10.0,12.0,6.0,10.0,45000000,G
 (7) 1.0,0.0,0.0,1.0,1.0,2500000,L
 (8) 0.0,1.0,1.0,0.0,0.0,3000000,L
 (9) 0.0,0.0,1.0,0.0,0.0,2000000,G
(10) 0.0,0.0,0.0,0.0,1.0,50000,G
(11) 0.0,0.0,0.0,1.0,0.0,100000,G
(12) //
```

Our last example, which dealt with finance, would have taken some time to work by hand but was not of bone-crushing proportions. This marketing media problem, however, could consume an afternoon and a handful of pencils using the hand method.

Because there are seven constraints, we know there will be seven rows in each tableau. Also there will be five columns for the structural variables and 11 for slack and artificial variables for a total of 16 columns. Because only one structural variable enters the solution per trial, we would have at least five tableax. In fact, as can be seen in the program output in Table 6.3, seven tableax were required to obtain the optimum solution. Table 6.4 is a list of the structural, slack, and artificial variables showing their interpretations and approximate solution values.

The optimal strategy is to spend approximately $1.85 million on newspaper ads, $3 million on TV, $100,000 on magazines, and $50,000 on billboards to obtain maximum sales for the advertising money spent. The actual values from the final tableau (for example, $X(1) = 1,849,997$ and $X(9) = 500,001$) show examples of rounding errors inside the computer.

Table 6.4   INTERPRETATION OF VARIABLES

VARIABLE	DESIGNATION	INTERPRETATION	APPROXIMATE VALUE
$X(1)$	Structural	Newspaper Expenditure	$1.85 million
$X(2)$	Structural	Radio Expenditure	0
$X(3)$	Structural	TV Expenditure	$3.00 million
$X(4)$	Structural	Magazine Expenditure	$0.10 million
$X(5)$	Structural	Billboard Expenditure	$50 thousand
$X(6)$	Slack	Budget Constraint	0
$X(7)$	Artificial ⎱		0
$X(8)$	Slack ⎰	Sales Target Constraint	$12.45 million
$X(9)$	Slack	Written Ads Constraint	$0.50 million
$X(10)$	Slack	Unwritten Ads Constraint	0
$X(11)$	Artificial ⎱		0
$X(12)$	Slack ⎰	TV Constraint	$1.00 million
$X(13)$	Artificial ⎱		0
$X(14)$	Slack ⎰	Billboard Constraint	0
$X(15)$	Artificial ⎱		0
$X(16)$	Slack ⎰	Magazine Constraint	0

Sensitivity Analysis

The sensitivity analysis is shown in Table 6.5. The minimum and maximum $C(J)$ values for the structural variables show the range of permissible variation for each objective function coefficient without changing the location of the optimum solution. The minimum and maximum $B(I)$ values for the constraints show the allowable relaxation or tightening which can occur without changing the mix of solution variables in the optimum solution.

Table 6.3 INITIAL AND FINAL TABLEAUX

| C(J) | 0.0 | 11.0 | 10.0 | 12.0 | 6.0 | 10.0 | 0.0 | −99.0 | 0.0 | 0.0 | 0.0 | −99.0 | 0.0 | −99.0 | 0.0 | −99.0 | 0.0 |
BASIS	P(0)	P(1)	P(2)	P(3)	P(4)	P(5)	P(6)	P(7)	P(8)	P(9)	P(10)	P(11)	P(12)	P(13)	P(14)	P(15)	P(16)
TABLEAU NUMBER 1																	
P(6)	5000000	1.0	1.0	1.0	1.0	1.0	1.0	0.0	0.0	0.0	0.0	0.0	0.0	0.0	0.0	0.0	0.0
P(7)	45000000	11.0	10.0	12.0	6.0	10.0	0.0	1.0	−1.0	0.0	0.0	0.0	0.0	0.0	0.0	0.0	0.0
P(9)	2500000	1.0	0.0	0.0	1.0	1.0	0.0	0.0	0.0	1.0	0.0	0.0	0.0	0.0	0.0	0.0	0.0
P(10)	3000000	0.0	1.0	1.0	0.0	0.0	0.0	0.0	0.0	0.0	1.0	0.0	−1.0	0.0	0.0	0.0	0.0
P(11)	2000000	0.0	0.0	1.0	0.0	0.0	0.0	0.0	0.0	0.0	0.0	1.0	0.0	0.0	0.0	0.0	0.0
P(13)	50000	0.0	0.0	0.0	0.0	1.0	0.0	0.0	0.0	0.0	0.0	0.0	0.0	1.0	−1.0	0.0	0.0
P(15)	100000	0.0	0.0	0.0	1.0	0.0	0.0	0.0	0.0	0.0	0.0	0.0	0.0	0.0	0.0	1.0	−1.0
C(J)−Z(J)	*********	1100.0	1000.0	1299.0	699.0	1099.0	0.0	0.0	−99.0	0.0	0.0	0.0	−99.0	0.0	−99.0	0.0	−99.0
TABLEAU NUMBER 7 (OPTIMAL SOLUTION)																	
P(8)	12449990	0.0	2.0	0.0	0.0	0.0	11.0	−1.0	1.0	0.0	1.0	0.0	0.0	−1.0	1.0	−5.0	5.0
P(1)	1849997	1.0	0.0	0.0	0.0	0.0	1.0	0.0	0.0	0.0	−1.0	0.0	0.0	−1.0	1.0	−1.0	1.0
P(9)	500001	0.0	0.0	0.0	0.0	0.0	−1.0	0.0	0.0	1.0	1.0	0.0	0.0	−0.0	0.0	−0.0	0.0
P(12)	1000000	0.0	1.0	0.0	0.0	0.0	0.0	0.0	0.0	0.0	1.0	−1.0	1.0	0.0	0.0	0.0	0.0
P(3)	3000000	0.0	1.0	1.0	0.0	0.0	0.0	0.0	0.0	0.0	1.0	0.0	0.0	0.0	0.0	0.0	0.0
P(5)	50000	0.0	0.0	0.0	0.0	1.0	0.0	0.0	0.0	0.0	0.0	0.0	0.0	1.0	−1.0	0.0	0.0
P(4)	100000	0.0	0.0	0.0	1.0	0.0	0.0	0.0	0.0	0.0	0.0	0.0	0.0	0.0	0.0	1.0	−1.0
C(J)−Z(J)	57449952	0.0	−2.0	0.0	0.0	0.0	−11.0	−99.0	0.0	0.0	−1.0	−99.0	0.0	−98.0	−99.0	−94.0	−5.0

Table 6.5 SENSITIVITY ANALYSIS

STRUCTURAL VARIABLES	VALUE	MINIMUM C(J)	C(J)	MAXIMUM C(J)
X(1)	1849997.0	10.0	11.0	12.0
X(2)	0.0	−INF	10.0	12.0
X(3)	3000000.0	11.0	12.0	+INF
X(4)	100000.0	−INF	6.0	11.0
X(5)	50000.0	−INF	10.0	11.0

CONSTRAINTS	SLACK VALUE	MINIMUM B(I)	B(I)	MAXIMUM B(I)
W(1)	0.0	3868184.0	5000000.0	5500001.0
W(2)	12449990.0	−INF	45000000.0	57449984.0
W(3)	500001.0	1999999.0	2500000.0	+INF
W(4)	0.0	2499999.0	3000000.0	4849997.0
W(5)	1000000.0	−INF	2000000.0	3000000.0
W(6)	0.0	0.0	50000.0	1899997.0
W(7)	0.0	0.0	100000.0	1949997.0

Running linear programming problems on the computer is easy, and the information received is useful and concise. However, we encourage you to take the time to study the chapter on the simplex method of linear programming for a deeper understanding of the real power of the technique.

SUMMARY OF KEY CONCEPTS

Canned programs.   Programs that are written and stored in the computer so that only data input is necessary to work a particular problem.

Interactive computer terminal.   A typewriterlike device that allows the user to "talk" directly to the computer.

Batch mode.   Input to the computer is prepunched on data cards and is fed to the computer at one time.

Encoding.   Writing the problem in the form that can be fed into the computer.

Contribution margin.   Gross profit per unit produced.

PROBLEMS

1. Solve problem 5.1 by computer.
2. Solve problem 5.2 by computer.
3. Solve problem 5.3 by computer.
4. Solve problem 5.4 by computer.
5. Solve problem 5.5 by computer
6. Precip, Inc., manufactures 10 industrial fluids by distilling a natural liquid substance obtained from South America and the Middle East. The amount of each fluid produced in proportion to the others can be varied by controlling the temperatures and pressures in the distilling process. Precip would like to use an LP approach to determine

the optimum proportions of their products X_1 through X_{10} to produce each week, based on beginning of the week prices each is commanding on the open market. This week's prices per gallon are: $X_1 = \$4$, $X_2 = \$3$, $X_3 = \$6$, $X_4 = \$1$, $X_5 = \$4$, $X_6 = \$7$, $X_7 = \$3$, $X_8 = \$10$, $X_9 = \$5$, $X_{10} = \$3$. Physical restrictions on proportions are as follows.

Product	Range
X_1	.05–.1
X_2	.02–.2
X_3	.1–.2
X_4	.02–.1
X_5	.04–.25
X_6	.1–.3
X_7	.01–.05
X_8	.02–.05
X_9	.1–.5
X_{10}	.25–.5

Formulate the LP problem and solve by computer. (Be sure to include a constraint requiring $\sum_{i=1}^{10} X_i = 1$.)

7. The Keyway Company has three engine manufacturing plants and four regional distribution warehouses to which the plants ship engines. The plant capacities, per unit transportation costs from the plants to the various warehouses, and the warehouse demands are as follows.

Plant	Capacity (units)
I	2000
II	3500
III	3000

Warehouse	Demand
A	1500
B	2200
C	3300
D	1000

TRANSPORTATION COSTS TO WAREHOUSE (PER UNIT)

		A	B	C	D	E
	I	X_1 15	X_4 18	X_7 21	X_{10} 30	X_{13} 0
FROM PLANT	II	X_2 26	X_5 20	X_8 14	X_{11} 12	X_{14} 0
	III	X_3 17	X_6 30	X_9 22	X_{12} 16	X_{15} 0

Set up the problem and solve by computer. (Hint: the objective is to minimize the total transportation cost $Z = \sum C_j X_j$.)

8. The Job-Away Machine Shop has four jobs in house each of which can be performed on any one of five machines. The times required for each job on each machine are as follows. Find the optimum job/machine assignment schedule that minimizes the total machine times, using the computer LP model.

TIMES (MINUTES)

		JOBS			
		1	2	3	4
MACHINE	A	X_1 35	X_6 18	X_{11} 105	X_{16} 60
	B	X_2 42	X_7 17	X_{12} 90	X_{17} 70
	C	X_3 26	X_8 22	X_{13} 85	X_{18} 55
	D	X_4 19	X_9 30	X_{14} 70	X_{19} 27
	E	X_5 50	X_{10} 15	X_{15} 95	X_{20} 18

9. Leisure Time Patio Accessory Company distributes six items in Houston. The company has a 10,000-square-foot warehouse where the entire season's stock must be stored. Their contractual arrangement with suppliers requires that they purchase at least 500 of each item except chairs and patio umbrellas. They must purchase at least 1000 chairs and 100 umbrellas.

The items along with their costs, selling prices, square feet of floor space required per stack, and the number of units that can be stacked vertically in the warehouse are shown in the following matrix.

ITEM	PRICE	COST	FLOOR AREA (sq ft)	NUMBER IN STOCK
X_1 Large Smoker	$80	$50	12	4
X_2 Small Smoker	22	15	4	6
X_3 Patio Table	75	50	16	8
X_4 Umbrella	40	25	6	8
X_5 Patio Chair	30	20	9	5
X_6 Chaise Lounge	50	30	18	5

Past experience has shown that no more umbrellas than tables are sold, that at most four times as many chairs as tables are sold, that at least as many chaise lounges are sold as tables, and that the total of large and small smokers sold will be greater than or equal to the number of tables sold.

The company will not be able to reorder until after the season, and the warehouse is now empty. They know they can sell their entire stock by the end of the season and would like to maximize their profit. Find the optimum number of each product Leisure Time should now order.

10. Solve problems 5–9 using the computer.

Chapter 7

THE ASSIGNMENT AND TRANSPORTATION MODELS

INTRODUCTION

There are two special classes of linear programming problems that are encountered so frequently that special, more efficient computational models have been developed to solve them. They are called the *transportation model* and the *assignment model*. As suggested by Figure 7.1, the assignment problem is actually a special case of the transportation problem and can be solved using the solution procedures developed for the transportation problem. As you will see, however, the assignment model is much simpler and easier to solve. Both classes of problems can be solved as LP problems by simplex, but they are much more easily solved using the methods presented in this chapter. The two models can be considered in either order, but as the assignment model is the easier of the two, it is presented first.

THE ASSIGNMENT MODEL

The model we present for the solution of this class of problems was published in 1955 by H. W. Kuhn. Because it is based upon a theorem by

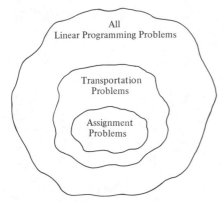

Figure 7.1   Relationship of assignment, transportation, and linear programming problems.

König and the work of Egervary, both of whom were Hungarian mathematicians, Kuhn called it the "Hungarian method," and this is the name still used today.

The essence of the assignment problem can be illustrated by the example of the State Director of the Texas Rangers, who must assign four new Texas Rangers to four available territories. His objective is to minimize the total relocation cost to the organization. The relocation costs for each of the personnel and each of the territories are summarized in Figure 7.2. Since there are 4! = 24 possible sets of assignments even for a small problem such as this one, the total enumeration approach has little appeal.

The problem is to make exactly one assignment in each row (a person can be assigned to only one territory) and exactly one assignment in each

	Territories			
	I	II	III	IV
Mary	26	40	22	31
Alphred	30	27	26	20
Sam	18	29	20	23
Theola	25	38	32	33

Figure 7.2   Relocation cost table ($ hundreds).

column (each territory is assigned only one person) in such a way that the total cost of the assignments is minimized. All assignments must be in whole units; so each cell has either a one or a zero value, and there must be one and only one assigned cell in each row and one and only one in each column. The transportation model can be used to solve this problem, but the Hungarian method is faster and easier. Likewise, the problem can be formulated in the general linear programming format and then solved, but this is also rather cumbersome. There would be 16 unknowns (one for each cell) plus artificial variables for each of the 7 equality constraints (one for each row and column, less one because the total for rows must equal the total for columns).

The Hungarian Method

The solution procedure begins by locating the least expensive cell in each row and the least expensive cell in each column. We will consider the rows first, but the method would also work quite well if the columns were first.

Step 1(a)   Subtract the smallest value in each row from every value in that row. This leaves zeros in the cheapest cell (or cells, if more than one has the same lowest value in a given row) and positive values for all other cells in the row. These values represent the penalties we will pay if we fail to assign the unit on that row to the cheapest cell. This step leads to the values shown in Figure 7.3(a).

Step 1(b)   Using this revised tableau, subtract the smallest number in each column from each value in that column. If there is a zero in the column, no change will take place in that column; so only

	I	II	III	IV
M	4	18	0	9
A	10	7	6	0
S	0	11	2	5
T	0	13	7	8

(a)

	I	II	III	IV
M	4	11	0	9
A	10	0	6	0
S	0	4	2	5
T	0	6	7	8

(b)

Figure 7.3   (a) After subtracting the smallest value in each row of 7.2; (b) After subtracting the smallest value in each column of 7.3(a).

the second column requires any change. This leads to the tableau of Figure 7.3(b).

Step 2 To find out whether an optimal assignment can now be made, determine the *minimum* number of horizontal and/or vertical lines required to cover all the zeros. If we can cover all the zeros with *fewer* lines than there are rows (or columns, for there must always be the same number of each), then we cannot yet make optimal assignments, and we must go on to the next step. Figure 7.4(a) shows *one* set of three lines that could be used to cover all of the zeros (the line through the first row could have been drawn through the third column, instead).

Step 3(a) Subtract the smallest value *not* covered by one or more lines [2 in Fig. 7.4(a)] from *each* value *not* covered by one or more lines.

Step 3(b) Add that number (2) to each cell covered by *two lines*. (The 4 and the 10 in the first column of [Fig. 7.4(a)].)

Step 3(c) Repeat the values covered by *only one line* with *no change*. These steps lead to the revised table of Figure 7.4(b).

Step 4 Return to step 2, using the revised tableau. If it is not possible to cover all zeros with fewer than N lines (where N is the number of rows or the number of columns), optimal assignments can be be made. If it is possible, return to step 3.

Two problems arise at this point: (1) How do we know that we cannot cover all the zeros with fewer lines than we have used? (This question is immaterial if we have done the job with fewer than N lines, but if it requires N lines, how can we be sure that there is not another set of $N - 1$ lines?) (2) How do we go about making the optimal assignments once we reach the point where N lines are required? We can resolve both of these problems by using what we will call the "Lone Ranger" technique.

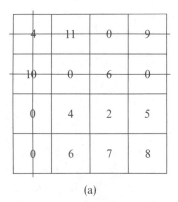 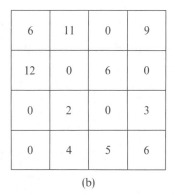

(a) (b)

Figure 7.4 (a) Covering the zeros; (b) Revised tableau.

The "Lone Ranger" Technique

Continuing our example problem from the revised tableau of Figure 7.4(b), we can make tentative assignments of personnel to territories and draw a minimum number of covering lines by proceeding as follows. Let us designate a cell containing the only uncovered zero in its row (*or* in its column) as a "Lone Ranger" cell. (If there is more than one zero, none of them is a Lone Ranger.) Our optimal assignments will all be in Lone Ranger cells because they represent the cheapest cells in their respective rows or columns.

Examination of our most recent tableau reveals Lone Rangers in the first and the last rows. We therefore assign each of these cells and designate the fact that assignments have been made by placing an asterisk (∗) in the cells. For each assignment we make in a *row*, we draw a line through that cell's *column* [Fig. 7.5(a)]. For clarity, we have numbered the lines to indicate the order in which we drew them, but in practice this is not necessary. This leaves two zeros uncovered, but no Lone Rangers in any rows (no uncovered zeros in rows 1, 3, and 4, and two zeros uncovered in row 2).

We now repeat (or continue) the procedure, focusing on the *columns*. We see that we have Lone Rangers in both column 2 and column 4. Assigning either one of these (we arbitrarily selected column 2, but it makes absolutely no difference) and drawing a line through its *row* (because it was a Lone Ranger in its column) completes the covering of the zeros.

The Lone Ranger method guarantees that all assignments will be made optimally and that the smallest possible number of lines will be used. We have used three lines to cover all zeros, and $N = 4$; so we must repeat step 3 to generate the rerevised tableau of Figure 7.5(b). Our smallest

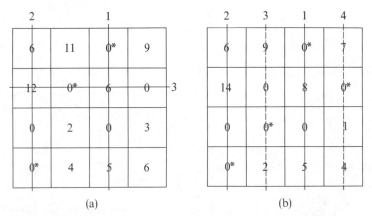

(a)   (b)

Figure 7.5   (a) Covering the zeros again; (b) Rerevised tableau.

Territories

	I	II	III	IV
Mary	26	40	(22)	31
Alphred	30	27	26	(20)
Sam	18	(29)	20	23
Theola	(25)	38	32	33

Figure 7.6   Optimum assignments.

uncovered number is 2; so we subtract that value from each uncovered cell, add it to each double covered cell, and repeat all singly covered cells unchanged.

Proceeding with the Lone Ranger method, we assign cells (1, 3) and (4, 1) as Lone Rangers in their rows, striking their columns (3 and 1, respectively). This makes cell (3, 2) a Lone Ranger in its row. Assigning it and striking its column leaves cell (2, 4) as a Lone Ranger in both its row and its column. Assigning it and striking its column (or row, whichever way you choose to view it) completes the coverage of the zeros. The number of lines required is equal to N; so our set of assignments is optimal. They are cells (1, 3), (2, 4), (3, 2), and (4, 1). Locating these cells in the original tableau (repeated in Figure 7.6) shows that the minimum total cost of assignment is

Mary to Territory III for a cost of	$2200
Alphred to Territory IV for a cost of	2000
Sam to Territory II for a cost of	2900
Theola to Territory I for a cost of	2500
Total Cost	$9600

Unbalanced Problems

We will not always be fortunate enough to have the supply and demand sides exactly equal. We handle this problem by adding dummy rows or columns (with zero costs) as required to achieve balance. Because the assignment problem must always be square, with the number of rows and columns equal, we may need to add several rows or several columns to achieve balance. (But never both rows *and* columns.)

Examples of balancing unbalanced problems are shown in Figures 7.7(a) (adding 1 row), 7.7(b) (adding 2 rows), and 7.7(c) (adding 3 columns). Note that if some assignments are infeasible, we assign a very high cost or simply "X out" these cells and ignore them throughout the analysis. If dummy column(s) are added, step 1(a) becomes unnecessary because the smallest value in every row is zero. Similarly, if dummy row(s) are added, we may skip step 1(b) because every column already will have at least one zero. (But note that if some entries are *negative*, these short cuts will not work.)

JOBS

	Sales	Clerical	Driver	Steno	Janitor
Ray	5	15	2	✕	3
Sue	✕	0	2	1	3
Tom	7	3	2	5	2
Ulon	10	2	3	4	1
Dummy	0	0	0	0	0

APPLICATIONS

(a)

MACHINES

	J	K	L	M	N
A	4	7	✕	12	3
B	6	✕	9	15	✕
C	10	13	11	8	6
Dummy	0	0	0	0	0
Dummy	0	0	0	0	0

JOBS

(b)

Figure 7.7 (a) Training costs; (b) Processing costs; (c) Hours of preparation required on term projects.

STUDENTS

	Bob	Linda	Jay	Dummy		
Markov Chains	6	4	7	0	0	0
PERT	5	8	2	0	0	0
SIMPLEX	3	2	5	0	0	0
Game Theory	4	6	7	0	0	0
Simulation	5	3	8	0	0	0
Inventory	4	3	2	0	0	0

TOPICS

(c)

Figure 7.7 (*continued*)

We then proceed to apply steps 2, 3, and 4, using the Lone Ranger method, until an optimal set of assignments has been made. Whichever rows or columns wind up being "assigned" to dummys are interpreted as being unassigned in the interpretation of the final result.

Multiple Solutions

It should come as no surprise to discover that there are many assignment problems in which no unique optimal solution exists. We have already seen that there are frequently more than one set of K lines ($K \leq N$) that will cover the zeros, but as long as we followed the Lone Ranger procedure, this did not cause any problems because any set of lines we developed was equally effective.

As was the case in the simplex procedure, we can find multiple sets of assignments that are equally desirable, and this situation can develop at an intermediate tableau or in the optimal tableau. If it is at a nonoptimal stage, we simply ignore the alternate solution(s) and proceed to a better set of assignments, but if it is in the final solution, we usually will wish to list all alternate optimal assignment sets.

The existence of alternate solutions is indicated in assignment problems when we run out of Lone Rangers before we run out of uncovered zeros. This situation is depicted in the intermediate tableau of Figure 7.8(a). The only uncovered zeros appear in rows or columns that have more than one uncovered zero.

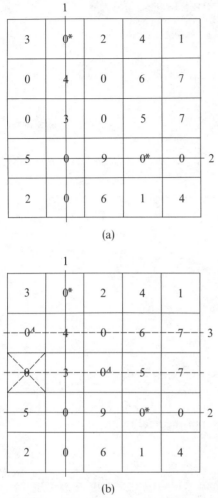

(a)

(b)

Figure 7.8   (a) Alternate intermediate solutions; (b) One of the alternate solutions.

We solve this dilemma [Fig. 7.8(b)] by: (1) arbitrarily assigning any one of the uncovered zeros, using an *A* rather than an asterisk [we select cell (2, 1)]; (2) adding *one* line in that cell's column or its row (this is also purely arbitrary, and we elect the row); and (3) "covering" the remaining zero(s) in our assigned cell's row or column that remain uncovered by "Xing them out" temporarily. This leaves cell (3, 3) as a Lone Ranger in its column; so we assign it and add a line in its row. This covers all of the zeros with 4 lines, and as $N = 5$, we proceed to the next tableau. Because this solution is not optimal, we do not bother to find the alternate solution.

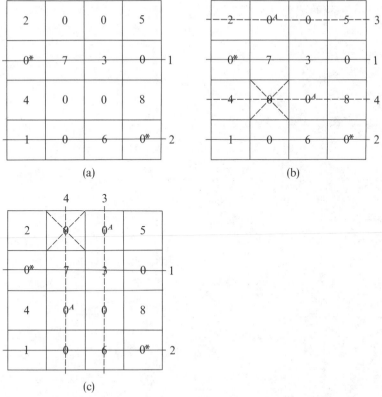

Figure 7.9 (a) Alternate optimal solutions; (b) One optimal solution;
(c) Another optimal solution.

If it had taken N lines to cover all the zeros, we would probably wish
to determine the alternate optimal solution(s). Consider the tableau of
Figure 7.9(a). Arbitrarily assigning cell (1, 2), lining out its row, and
"covering" the zero in its column (3, 2), we have a Lone Ranger in cell
(3, 3). Assigning this cell and striking its row, we have an optimal set of
assignments (number of lines equals N), as shown in Figure 7.9(b).

To determine the alternate optimal solution, we return to Figure
7.9(a) and select an uncovered cell that did *not* appear in the first solution
[either (1, 3) or (3, 2)]. Assigning this cell [we chose (1, 3)], we strike its
row or column and "cover" the zeros in its column or row. This leaves
cell (3, 2) as a Lone Ranger in its row; so we assign it and strike its column,
which yields the second solution, shown in Figure 7.9(c).

In some problems there can be several alternate optimal solutions.
An example of an innocent-looking problem with four alternate solutions
is shown in Figures 7.10(a)–(f).

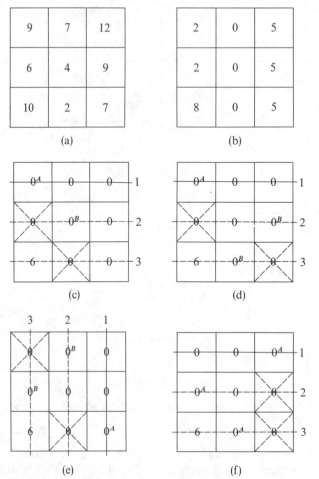

Figure 7.10 (a) Original problem; (b) After subtracting rows; (c) After subtracting columns (first optimal solution); (d) A second optimal solution; (e) Yet a third optimal solution; (f) Still a fourth optimal solution.

After subtracting in the rows and the columns, we arrive at the tableau of Figure 7.10(c). We can see that there are two possible choices in the first column, then two in the second, and one in the third; so there will be $2 \times 2 \times 1 = 4$ possible solutions. Because no Lone Rangers are available, we arbitrarily assign cell (1, 1), striking its row and "covering" cell (2,1). We still have no Lone Rangers; so we must *reapply* the arbitrary selection, selecting cell (2, 2), striking its row, and "covering" cell (3, 2) in its column. Now we assign Lone Ranger cell (3, 3) and strike its row.

Recall that we made an arbitrary choice after selecting cell (1, 1). We must return to that point and select one of the remaining cells that did not wind up in the solution [cells (2, 3) and (3, 2)]. Selecting either one makes the other a Lone Ranger and leads to the solution in Figure 7.10(d).

Returning to the beginning, if we had selected cell (3, 3) first, we could have been left with a second arbitrary choice, as in Figure 7.10(e). If we had selected either cell (1, 1) or cell (2, 2), we would have obtained the same solution as we did in Figure 7.10(c). Selecting cell (1, 2) (as we did) or cell (2, 1) leads to a new solution. Finally, cell (1, 3) has yet to be included in any solution. If we begin with it, we can follow the Lone Ranger method to obtain the solution of Figure 7.10(f).

Although each of the solutions has the same total cost in cases of multiple optimality, it can be extremely useful to a decision maker to know all of the solutions. When several solutions are equally attractive from a cost point of view, the choice of a particular result can then focus on secondary criteria such as personal preferences, time considerations, and organizational idiosyncrasies.

Maximization Using the Assignment Model

While most of the literature focuses on the minimization properties of the assignment model, it is a simple matter to utilize this method to solve problems when the objective is to maximize the sum of the elements assigned. The *only* modification required is to reverse the signs of every element in the initial tableau.

As an example, consider the case of the plant manager who must assign three vending machines to four coffee-break stations in her plant. The projected profits and losses from each assignment are indicated in Figure 7.11(a). Adding the dummy machine (row) and reversing all signs results in the tableau of Figure 7.11(b). Subtracting the smallest value in each row (Be careful! The most negative value is the smallest one.), we obtain the tableau of Figure 7.11(c). Using the Lone Ranger method, we

		STATIONS								
		A	B	C	D		-5	-2	0	-4
	Soft Drinks	5	2	0	4		-3	-6	-2	-3
MACHINES	Coffee	3	6	2	3		-3	$+2$	-3	-4
	Candy	3	-2	3	4		0	0	0	0

(a)   (b)

Figure 7.11   (a) Profits and losses form machine assignments ($100's per month); (b) Reversing signs and adding dummy machine.

0	3	5	1
3	0	4	3
1	6	1	0
0	0	0	0

(c)

1	2	4	3
0*	3	5	1
3	0*	4	3
1	6	1	0*
0	0	0*	0

(d)

Figure 7.11   (c) After subtracting the rows; (d) Optimal solution.

find the optimal assignments [Fig. 7.11(d)] to be

Soft Drinks to Station A for a profit of	$ 500 per month
Coffee to Station B for a profit of	600 per month
Candy to Station D for a profit of	400 per month
No vending machine at Station C for a profit of	0 per month
Total Profit	$1500 per month.

THE TRANSPORTATION MODEL

The transportation problem can be viewed as an assignment problem in which we have relaxed the requirement that one and only one assignment must be made in each row and in each column. F. L. Hitchcock was the first to publish an analysis of the problem in 1941. In 1953 George Dantzig presented the linear programming formulation. Charnes and Cooper developed the *stepping stone method*, and the *MODI*, or *modified distribution* method, was presented in 1955.

The basic problem is to determine the optimum (least cost) method of transporting a product produced at several *sources* to a set of *destinations*. It is perhaps best described within the context of a simple concrete example.

The Ace Concrete Company has two locations (S_1 and S_2) at which they produce the concrete their trucks are to haul, and they currently are supplying three large construction projects (D_1, D_2, and D_3) with concrete. The production capacities are 50 truckloads per day at S_1 and 100 per day at S_2. The quantities demanded for today are 40 truckloads at D_1, 80 at D_2, and 30 at D_3. It costs $1 per mile round trip to transport the concrete to the sites. The distances between the production facilities and the destinations are shown in Figure 7.12. The problem is to determine the number of truckloads (X_{ij}) to send from the ith source to the jth destination in order to satisfy the requirements for the least total cost.

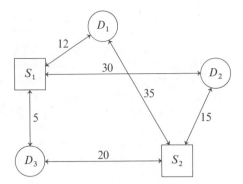

Figure 7.12   Distances for the concrete example.

Standard Transportation Formulation

The problem can be formulated concisely as shown in Figures 7.13(a) and (b). The sources and their respective capacities are each assigned a row; the destinations and their demands each have a column. In this example, the total supply and the total demand are equal (150 truckloads), and the problem is said to be *balanced*. This happy coincidence is not usually found in real problems, but the procedure for balancing an unbalanced problem, as you shall soon see, is quite simple.

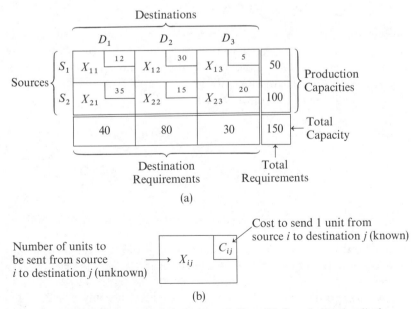

Figure 7.13   (a) Concrete example formulation; (b) Generalized cell of transportation model formulation.

Each cell of the table in Figure 7.13(a) has the general form of the cell in Figure 7.13(b). We use a double subscripted notation in which the first number designates the row (in our example, the source) and the second, the column (destination). C_{ij} is the cost to send 1 unit from source i to destination j and will be known before we attempt to solve the problem. For example, the cost of shipping from S_1 to D_3 is \$5 per truckload. X_{ij} is the number of units that will be sent from source i to destination j and is not known. Our problem is to determine a set of X_{ij} values that will satisfy all of our demands without violating any of our supply restrictions.

Note that the cost for each cell is the product of the number of truckloads from source i to destination j (X_{ij}) and the cost of moving one truckload (C_{ij}). Our objective function therefore could be written as follows.

$$\text{Min } Z = 12X_{11} + 30X_{12} + 5X_{13} + 35X_{21} + 15X_{22} + 20X_{23}$$

The constraints on our problem are of two types—those imposed by production capacities and those imposed by demand quantities. We will exactly meet these constraints, so they will all be equalities.

$$\text{Source 1}: X_{11} + X_{12} + X_{13} = 50$$
$$\text{Source 2}: X_{21} + X_{22} + X_{23} = 100$$
$$\text{Destination 1}: X_{11} + X_{21} = 40$$
$$\text{Destination 2}: X_{12} + X_{22} = 80$$
$$\text{Destination 3}: X_{13} + X_{23} = 30$$

Because the total supply and the total demand are equal, only four of these five equations are independent. Thus, in solving the problem, we must delete one (any one) of the constraints. If we have R rows, or sources, and K columns, or destinations, the general form of the linear programming formulation of the transportation problem is

$$\text{Min} \qquad Z = \sum_{i=1}^{R} \sum_{j=1}^{K} C_{ij} X_{ij}$$

$$\text{ST} \quad \sum_{j=1}^{K} X_{ij} = S_i, i = 1, 2, \ldots, R$$

$$\sum_{i=1}^{R} X_{ij} = D_j, j = 1, 2, \ldots, K$$

Recall however, that we must delete any one of the $R + K$ constraints.

The number of variables in our linear programming problem is $R \times K$ (one for each cell), or six in the concrete example. The number of *independent* constraints is $R + K - 1$, or 4. Therefore only $R + K - 1$ of the $R \times K$ variables can be in the solution at any time, including the final or optimal solution. Manual solution of a linear programming problem with six variables and four equality constraints would quite obviously be a tedious and time-consuming exercise. For more realistically sized problems, the magnitude of the computational problem (even for the tireless computer) is quite formidable.

The simpler computational methods we shall present here are of two distinct types. We shall learn three methods of obtaining an *initial solution*—these are called the *Northwest corner rule*, the *best cell method*, and *Vogel's approximation method* (*VAM*). We shall also present two methods for obtaining improved solutions, to enable us to move from the initial solution to the optimal one—the *stepping stone method* and the **Mo***dified* **Di***stribution* (*MODI*) *method*.

Balancing the Problem

If our problem had not been balanced (total supply equal to total demand), we would have had to balance it before proceeding further. Assume that total supply exceeds total demand by 20 units, as shown in Figure 7.14(a). To balance the problem, we simply add a fictitious or "dummy" destination that has just enough demand to equal the excess supply and balance the problem [Fig. 7.14(b)]. The variables in this column are the slack variables we would have added in the linear programming solution. Because this destination does not exist, we will not actually ship any concrete to it, and the values of S_1 and S_2 will simply represent excess unused capacity at plants 1 and 2, respectively. As no shipping takes place to this destination, the costs are always zeros.

Similarly, if we had had an excess of demand over supply, as in Figure 7.14(c), we would add a dummy source (row 3), and whatever portion of the demands is met from this source will not be delivered [Fig. 7.14(d)]. As in the case of the fictitious destination, the costs associated with the dummy source are all zeros.

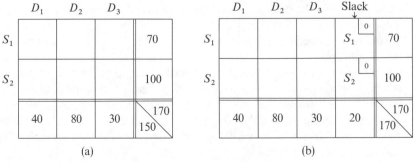

(a) (b)

Figure 7.14 (a) Excess supply; (b) Addition of dummy destination.

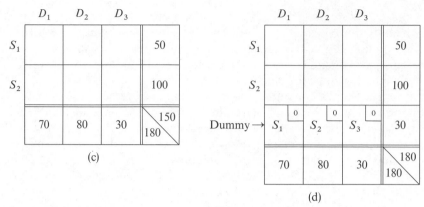

Figure 7.14   (c) Excess demand; (d) Addition of a dummy source.

It should be apparent that only one row or one column need ever be added and that there will never be more than one dummy source or one dummy destination and never one of each.

Northwest Corner Rule

This method is purely arbitrary and makes no attempt at even approaching optimality. Its sole purpose is to obtain an initial feasible solution to the problem. We set up our problem as we did in Figure 7.13(a) but with no X_{ij}s or C_{ij}s [Fig. 7.15(a)]. The X_{ij}s are omitted because we do not know them yet, and the C_{ij}s are omitted for clarity because we do not use them in obtaining the initial solution. We will start at the upper left-hand cell, hence the name, northwest corner. (We could just as easily have begun at the southwest, or northeast, or southeast corner, and if you have strong regional biases, you may wish to begin at a different corner in subsequent problems—they all work equally well.)

First we assign as many units as the row (50) and column (40) con-straints will allow to X_{11}. The row constraint will allow us to assign up to 50 units, but the column constraint only permits 40; so 40 units is the most we can assign. This completely satisfies the first column; so no more units can be assigned in that column. (Therefore X_{21} will be zero in our initial solution.)

Because column 1 is sold out, we move over to column 2, staying in row 1, and assign all we can to X_{12}. The column constraint will permit 80 units, but because the row cannot exceed 50 and we have already assigned 40 in the row, only 10 can be assigned at X_{12}. This completes the first row (X_{13} will be zero); so we move down to the second row, staying in column 2.

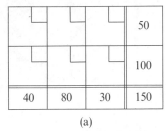
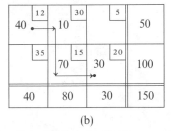

(a)   (b)

Figure 7.15   (a) Blank tableau; (b) Completed initial solution.

We have 70 left to assign in this column and 100 available in the second row; so X_{22} is assigned a value of 70, and we move to the third column. Because 30 units are available in column 3 and 30 are also left in row 2, X_{23} is assigned a value of 30, and our initial solution is complete, as shown in Figure 7.15(b).

It is wise at this point to recheck each row and each column to assure yourself that your solution is indeed feasible.

$$\text{Row 1: } 40 + 10 = 50$$
$$\text{Row 2: } 70 + 30 = 100$$
$$\text{Column 1: } 40 \qquad = 40$$
$$\text{Column 2: } 10 + 70 = 80$$
$$\text{Column 3: } 30 \qquad = 30$$

The value of the objective function (total cost) is found by adding the products of the unit cost and the number of units for each cell. For our solution, this becomes

$$40(12) + 10(30) + 0(5) + 0(35) + 70(15) + 30(20) = \$2430$$

To reinforce the procedure, let us practice on the larger problem shown in Figure 7.16(a). Note that once a dummy row (or column) has been added to balance the problem, it is treated exactly the same as any other row (or column). The answers for northwest corner and for southwest corner initial solutions are shown in Figures 7.16(b) and 7.16(c). A feasibility check shows that either of these assignments provides an initial solution that satisfies all the constraints.

The Best Cell Method

As the northwest corner method of initial assignment is purely arbitrary and makes no use at all of the cost information, it is reasonable to assume that a better initial solution could be obtained if these values were considered. One simple, intuitively attractive method is to locate the best cell

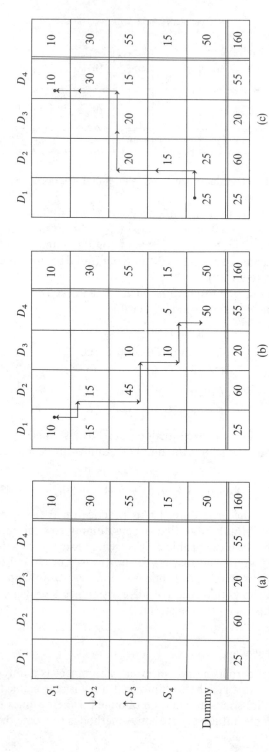

Figure 7.16 (a) Practice problem; (b) Northwest corner initial solution; (c) Southwest corner initial solution.

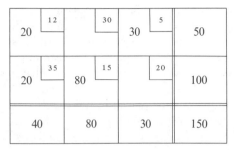

20 [12]		30 [30]	30 [5]	50
20 [35]	80 [15]	[20]	100
40	80	30	150

Figure 17.7   Best cell method.

(least cost, in a minimization problem) in the matrix and place as many units as possible there, then move to the next cheapest *available* cell, and so forth, until all the supply and demand requirements are met.

Figure 7.17 shows an application of this method to our concrete example. First, 30 units are placed in the best ($5) cell. This fills the requirements of that column and removes the $20 cell from consideration. The cheapest remaining cell is the $12 cell, and so we place 20 units there, which fills the first row's requirements and removes the $30 cell from contention. Next we put 80 units in the $15 cell, which fills its column. Finally we put 20 units in the last remaining cell ($35) to complete our initial assignments.

This method is simple, fast, and in most cases leads to a relatively good (reasonably close to the optimum) initial solution. In this case, the total cost is $2290, which is an improvement over the northwest corner initial solution cost of $2430.

Vogel's Approximation Method (VAM)

A more powerful method is the Vogel method (VAM), which deals with *first differences*. The idea behind the VAM is that we should determine the penalty that we would pay if we fail to place the entire supply or demand in the cheapest cell in each row and column. Having found the row or column that assesses the greatest penalty, we place as many units as possible in the cheapest cell and reevaluate the penalties for the cells that remain available. We repeat this process until a feasible solution has been established.

Let us illustrate the VAM by applying it to our concrete example, which is repeated in Figure 7.18(a). We examine each row and each column and record the difference between the cheapest and second cheapest cells in the row or column. The largest of these "first differences," or penalties, is the one for the first column. This tells us that if we fail to place some of the demand in that column into the $12 cell, we will pay a penalty of $35 − $12 = $23 for each unit that we must place in the $35 cell. As no other row or column has that high a penalty, we place all the units we can (40) into the $12 cell. This has been done in Figure 7.18(b).

Note that because all 40 units in column 1 have been assigned, the \$35 cell cannot be used. We have indicated this by placing a small "x" in that cell as a reminder. For the remaining cells, we recompute the first differences, finding the largest is now in row 1. We place all we can in the cheapest remaining cell (\$5) in that row, which is 10 units. This fills up row 1, as is shown in Figure 7.18(c). Because only one cell remains in columns 2 and 3, the remaining units must be placed in these cells. The completed tableau is shown in Figure 7.18(d). The total cost of this set of assignments is only \$2130. (Note that we now remove the small *X*'s.)

[12]	[30]	[5]	50	12 − 5 = 7
X [35]	[15]	[20]	100	20 − 15 = 5
40	80	30	150	
35 − 12 = (23)	30 − 15 = 15	20 − 5 = 15		

(a)

40 [12]	[30]	[5]	50	30 − 5 = (25)
X [35]	[15]	[20]	100	20 − 15 = 5
40	80	30	150	
	30 − 15 = 15	20 − 5 = 15		

(b)

40 [12]	X [30]	10 [5]	50
X [35]	[15]	[20]	100
40	80	30	150

(c)

40 [12]	[30]	10 [5]	50
[35]	80 [15]	20 [20]	100
40	80	30	150

(d)

Figure 7.18 (a) First step—VAM; (b) Second step—VAM; (c) Third step—VAM; (d) Feasible solution by VAM.

As is frequently (but by no means always) the case with small problems, the VAM has given us the optimal solution on the first try. In fact, the VAM is so powerful that it yields the optimum solution directly in many of the problems to which it is applied.

Let us practice the VAM on the slightly larger problem in Figure 7.19(a). The first differences are computed as shown. Note that the zero values in the dummy row are treated just the same as any other values. Also notice that when the lowest and second-lowest values are the same (as 0 and 0 in row 4), the difference is zero. The largest penalty is 6; so we place as many units as possible (7) in the cheapest cell in column 3. This completely fills that column; so we "X out" the remaining cells. Recalculating the differences for the rows gives us the second column of values

11	3	6 X	10	$6 - 3 = 3$	$11 - 3 = \boxed{8}$
4	12	9 X	20	$9 - 4 = 5$	$12 - 4 = \boxed{8}$
7	2	16 X	10	$7 - 2 = 5$	$7 - 2 = 5$
0	0	0 7	10	$0 - 0 = 0$	$0 - 0 = 0$
12	31	7	50		

$$4 - 0 \quad 2 - 0 \quad 6 - 0$$
$$= 4 \qquad = 2 \qquad = \boxed{6}$$

(a)

11 10	3	6	10
4 12	12 8	9	20
7 10	2	16	10
0	0 3	0 7	50
12	31	7	50

(b)

Figure 7.19   (a) Larger problem—VAM; (b) Feasible solution.

to the right of the tableau. The first and second columns need not be recalculated, for no cells have been changed in either of them.

Note that we now have a tie for the row or column with the largest penalty (8 for row 1 and row 2). This tie can be broken arbitrarily or by any of a number of rules of thumb. The results are usually not greatly affected by the method of tie breaking. We will arbitrarily select the first row and therefore place 10 units into the $3 cell. This closes off the first row to further additions and causes us to reevaluate the column differences. The new column penalties are still 4 and 2 (column 3 is full and should not be considered). Now we select row 2 with a penalty of 8 and place 12 units in the $4 cell, filling up the first column. As there is only one available cell in each of rows 2, 3, and 4, the remaining requirements are placed in these cells to complete the assignments as shown in Figure 7.19(b). The total cost of these assignments is $194.

Although the best cell method and the VAM are more complicated than the corner rules (northwest, southeast, etc.), they pay dividends by enabling a better initial solution and by reducing the number of tableaux required to find the optimum solution. The added effort at this stage pays large dividends in saving time and effort later.

The Stepping Stone Method ("Ring-Around-the-Rosie")

Now that we have a method of obtaining an initial feasible solution, we need a procedure for testing that solution (and any subsequent ones we may develop) to determine whether or not it is optimal and, if it is not, a method for improving our solution. We will be able to accomplish both of these objectives with the stepping stone method, which, for reasons that will become obvious, was nicknamed the "ring-around-the-rosie" method by a somewhat irreverent former student.

As in the simplex method, we will first determine which, if any, of the variables not presently in the solution could be introduced in order

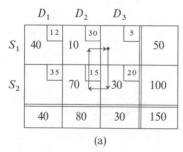 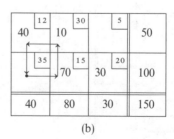

(a)   (b)

Figure 7.20   (a) Stepping stone path for cell (1, 3); (b) Stepping stone path for cell (2, 1).

to improve the solution. Figures 7.20(a) and 7.20(b) show our initial (northwest corner) solution to the concrete example. Cells (1, 3) and (2, 1) are the only ones not presently in the solution.

Let us analyze the effects of bringing *1 unit* of X_{13} into the solution. Begin in cell (1, 3) and follow the path indicated by the errors in Figure 7.20(a). If we introduce a unit of X_{13}, we must reduce X_{23} by that same amount in order to keep the total number in column 3 equal to 30. But if we reduce X_{23} by 1, we must add 1 to X_{22} in order to keep the total in row 2 equal to 100. Increasing X_{22} requires a similar decrease in X_{12} so that column 2 still has a total of 80. Decreasing X_{12} requires an increase in one of the cells in row 1 to keep the total of 50 for the row, but we have already done that when we began by introducing 1 unit into cell (1, 3). This closed path, from (1, 3) to (2, 3) to (2, 2) to (1, 2) and back to (1, 3), is called the *stepping stone path* for cell (1, 3).

To find the stepping stone path for any empty cell, we move horizontally and vertically (like the rook or castle in chess) as far as we wish in straight lines, turning *only* on cells that are in the solution ("stone" cells). The name derives from the age-old practice of crossing a stream by stepping on exposed rocks, or stepping stones. We may jump as far as we wish, but we may only turn when we are standing on a "stone" cell. *There will be one and only one stepping stone path for each empty cell in our table, and no stone cell will ever have such a closed path.*

If we traverse the stepping stone path, alternately adding and subtracting 1 unit at each cell where we *turn*, we can determine the net effect on the total cost of our introducing 1 unit of variable X_{13} into the solution. Looking at the costs of the cells on our path, we add $5 at X_{13}, subtract $20 at X_{23}, add $15 at X_{22}, and subtract $30 at X_{12} for a net change of $+5 - 20 + 15 - 30 = -\$30$. This means that every unit of X_{13} we bring into the solution will reduce our objective function (total cost) by $30. In simplex notation, this number is *exactly* the ΔZ_{ij} for variable X_{13}.

The stepping stone path for the other empty cell (X_{21}) is shown in Figure 7.20(b). It is (2, 1), (2, 2), (1, 2), (1, 1), (2, 1); and the ΔZ_j is $+\$35 - \$15 + \$30 - \$12 = +\$38$. This means that each unit of X_{21} we introduce into the solution will *increase* our total cost by $38.

Because we are minimizing, the presence of an empty cell with a negative ΔZ_{ij} implies that we do not have an optimal solution, and we should bring in as many units as possible of the variable with the most negative ΔZ_{ij} (X_{13} in our case).

Our next step is to determine which variable will leave the solution to make room for X_{13} (remember, only $R + K - 1 = 4$ variables in solution at a time). At the same time, we will determine how many units of X_{13} will enter the solution, which will be the number required to drive out the leaving variable, because the variables trade at a one-to-one ratio. (This is the θ_i value in the simplex table.)

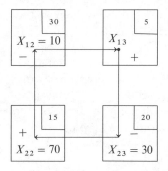

Figure 7.21   Stepping stone path for X_{13}.

Figure 7.21 shows the "stone cells" that are on the stepping stone path for cell $(1, 3)$. Note that we are adding units into cells $(1, 3)$ and $(2, 2)$, and subtracting units from $(1, 2)$ and $(2, 3)$. Since our objective is to drive one of the variables presently in the solution to zero, we will continue to move units around the stepping stone path until one of the "minus" variables $[(1, 2)$ and $(2, 3)]$ is driven to zero. As there are 10 units of X_{12} and 30 units of X_{23}, X_{12} will be depleted first. Therefore 10 units of X_{13} will enter the solution; all 10 units of X_{12} will leave; 10 units will be added to X_{22}; and 10 units will be taken from X_{23}. The resulting new table is shown in Figure 7.22(a). Note that all the constraints (both rows and columns) are satisfied and that there are exactly $R + K - 1 = 4$ stone cells. Our new value of the objective function (total cost) is $40(12) + 0(30) + 10(5) + 0(35) + 80(15) + 20(20) = \$2130$, which is a $300 improvement from our previous value of $2430. We could have predicted this because we knew that each unit of X_{13} that entered the solution would save us $30 (our ΔZ_{ij} value), and we brought in 10 units for a net change of $300.

To determine whether this new solution is optimal, we must reevaluate all empty cells by finding their stone paths. These are shown in Figure 7.22(b). Notice that in finding the path for X_{21} we have "jumped over" both empty and stone cells. This is perfectly proper because our

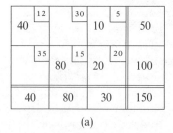

(a)

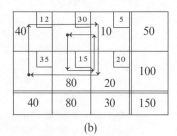

(b)

Figure 7.22   (a) Second table; (b) Stepping stone paths for X_{12} and X_{21}.

only rule is that we move in straight lines and only turn on stone cells. Also note that the direction in which we traverse the path is immaterial. The improvement index (ΔZ_{ij}) for X_{12} is

$$+30 - 5 + 20 - 15 = +30$$

which is not useful to us at all. For X_{21} it is

$$+35 - 12 + 5 - 20 = +8$$

which is likewise unattractive. As there are no negative ΔZ_{ij} values, we have reached the optimum solution, which is to send 40 truckloads from plant 1 to destination 1, 10 from plant 1 to job 3, 80 from plant 2 to job 2, and 20 from plant 2 to job 2.

For practice, find the stone paths and calculate the ΔZ_{ij}s for the empty cells in Figures 7.23(a) and 7.23(b). Some of the more difficult ones have already been done, and the ΔZ_{ij}s are circled so you can check your results. Be certain to check for feasibility (all row and column totals check) and for the proper number of stone cells $(R + K - 1)$.

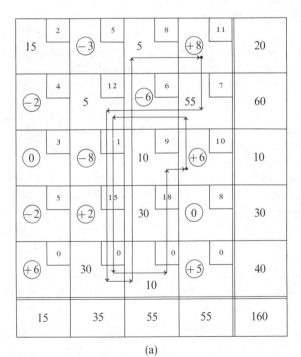

(a)

Figure 7.23   (a) Practice problem with dummy source.

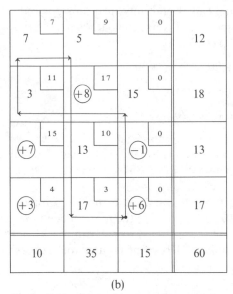

(b)

Figure 7.23   (b) Another practice problem with dummy destination.

The Modified Distribution (MODI) Method

Just as the best cell method and the VAM are more powerful replacements for the corner rule in obtaining an initial feasible solution, the MODI method is a much faster and easier method than the stepping stone method for evaluating the ΔZ_{ij}s of the empty cells. It is especially attractive for larger problems, because it does not require that the stepping stone *paths* be determined, except for the one cell that will enter the solution.

The MODI method requires that a set of numbers be assigned, one for each row (R_i) and one for each column (K_j), such that the cost value of each stone cell is the sum of the cell's R and K values. Mathematically, $R_i + K_j = C_{ij}$, for the stone cells only.

Since we must always have a number of stone cells equal to one less than the total number of rows and columns, we do not have enough equations to uniquely determine the values for the R_i and K_j variables. We can, however, obtain a set of relative values for the R_is and K_js by simply assigning an arbitrary value to any one of them and then calculating the values for the rest.

Returning to the concrete example [see Fig. 7.24(a)], we have four equations (one for each stone cell) and five unknowns (one for each row and each column). These equations are

$$R_1 + K_1 = 12$$
$$R_1 + K_3 = \ 5$$
$$R_2 + K_2 = 15$$
$$R_2 + K_3 = 20$$

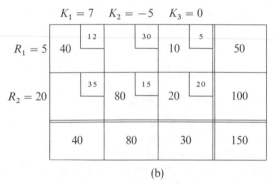

$$K_1 = 12 \quad K_2 = 0 \quad K_3 = 5$$

	$K_1 = 12$	$K_2 = 0$	$K_3 = 5$	
$R_1 = 0$	40 [12]	[30]	10 [5]	50
$R_2 = 15$	[35]	80 [15]	20 [20]	100
	40	80	30	150

(a)

$$K_1 = 7 \quad K_2 = -5 \quad K_3 = 0$$

	$K_1 = 7$	$K_2 = -5$	$K_3 = 0$	
$R_1 = 5$	40 [12]	[30]	10 [5]	50
$R_2 = 20$	[35]	80 [15]	20 [20]	100
	40	80	30	150

(b)

Figure 7.24　(a) Concrete example—MODI numbers; (b) Concrete example—another set of MODI numbers.

If we arbitrarily assign a value (any value will be just fine, but because we are lazy, we will always assign the value zero) to R_1, we have four unknowns and four equations and can solve for the other values. These become

$$K_1 = 12 - R_1 = 12 - 0 = 12$$
$$K_3 = 5 - R_1 = 5 - 0 = 5$$
$$R_2 = 20 - K_3 = 20 - 5 = 15$$
$$K_2 = 15 - R_2 = 15 - 15 = 0$$

We do not need to write out the equations to find the MODI numbers. Referring to Figure 7.24(a), if we let $R_1 = 0$, then, using stone cell (1, 1), we obtain $K_1 = 12$ because the row and column MODI numbers for that stone cell must add up to the cost value ($R_1 + K_1 = C_{11} = 12$). Using stone cell (1, 3), we get $R_1 + K_3 = 5$; so $K_3 = 5 - R_1 = 5 - 0 = 5$. From K_3 and stone cell (2, 3), we obtain $R_2 = 20 - K_3 = 20 - 5 = 15$. Finally, from stone cell (2, 2) we get $K_2 = 15 - R_2 = 15 - 15 = 0$.

There are an infinite number of sets of values that will satisfy our equations, depending upon which unknown we choose to assign a value and the actual value we assign. Any of these sets will work quite well. As an exercise, develop the set of MODI numbers for Figure 7.24(b), beginning with $K_3 = 0$.

Having developed a set of MODI numbers, we can now proceed to use them to evaluate the ΔZ_{ij} values for the empty cells. We do so by utilizing the relationship

$$\Delta Z_{ij} = C_{ij} - (R_i + K_j)$$

This relationship holds for all cells, but we forced it to be zero for each of our stone cells (remember that $\Delta Z_i = 0$ for all variables in the solution) when we generated our MODI numbers; so we need only calculate a value for each of the nonstone cells. Using the values from Figure 7.24(b), we obtain

$$\Delta Z_{12} = C_{12} - (R_1 + K_2) = 30 - [5 + (-5)] = +30$$

and

$$\Delta Z_{21} = C_{21} - (R_2 + K_1) = 35 - [20 + 7] = +8$$

which are the same values we found using the stepping stone method. At this point you should verify that the same improvement index values can be obtained using the MODI numbers of Figure 7.24(a).

Let us now use the MODI method to test the VAM initial solution we obtained in Figure 7.19(b) for optimality. That solution is repeated in Figure 7.25(a).

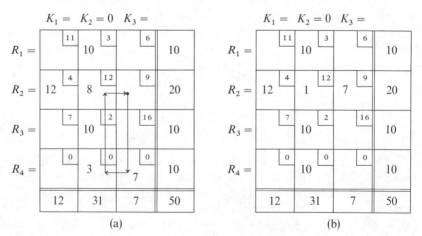

(a)   (b)

Figure 7.25   (a) MODI numbers and stone path; (b) MODI numbers and optimum solution.

In deciding which of the MODI numbers to assign a value of zero, one rule of thumb that is useful is to assign the zero value to the row or column that contains the greatest number of stone cells. In this problem, that is the second column, which has 4 stone cells. This leads immediately to the values of $R_1 = 3$, $R_2 = 12$, $R_3 = 2$, and $R_4 = 0$. Using stone cells (2, 1) and (4, 3), we obtain $K_1 = -8$ and $K_3 = 0$. [Begin with $K_2 = 0$ and develop these for yourself in Fig. 7.25(a).]

The ΔZ_{ij} values are calculated from these MODI numbers as follows.

$$\Delta Z_{11} = C_{11} - [R_1 + K_1] = 11 - [3 + (-8)] = +16$$
$$\Delta Z_{13} = 6 - [3 + 0] = +3$$
$$\Delta Z_{23} = 9 - [12 + 0] = -3$$
$$\Delta Z_{31} = 7 - [2 + (-8)] = +13$$
$$\Delta Z_{33} = 16 - [2 + 0] = +14$$
$$\Delta Z_{41} = 0 - [0 + (-8)] = +8.$$

Only the -3 for cell (2, 3) is negative; so we find its stone path and determine where and how many units will be moved and which stone cell drops out of the solution. (Seven units will be moved, and X_{43} drops out of the solution.) This revised tableau is shown in Figure 7.25(b). Because 7 units are added at \$3 savings each, the new value of the objective function should be \$21 lower than before. This is the case, as Z dropped from $3(10) + 4(12) + 12(8) + 2(10) + 0(3) + 0(7) = 194$ to $3(10) + 4(12) + 12(1) + 9(7) + 2(10) + 0(10) = 173$.

Checking for optimality, beginning with $K_2 = 0$, we get $R_1 = 3$, $R_2 = 12$, $R_3 = 2$, $R_4 = 0$. From the second row we find $K_1 = -8$ and $K_3 = -3$. (Fill these in on Figure 7.25(b) for practice.) The ΔZ_{ij}s are

$$\Delta Z_{11} = 11 - [3 + (-8)] = +16$$
$$\Delta Z_{13} = 6 - [3 + (-3)] = +6$$
$$\Delta Z_{31} = 7 - [2 + (-8)] = +13$$
$$\Delta Z_{33} = 16 - [2 + (-3)] = +17$$
$$\Delta Z_{41} = 0 - [0 + (-8)] = +8$$
$$\Delta Z_{43} = 0 - [0 + (-3)] = +3$$

and, as all are positive, we have found the optimum solution.

SPECIAL PROBLEMS AND THEIR SOLUTIONS

There are a number of difficulties that crop up from time to time to complicate the solution procedures that have been outlined here. These include the degenerate solution, which may be encountered in the initial, intermediate, or optimal tableau; the multiple solution, or alternate optimality, case; the nonfeasible cell; and the transshipment problem.

Degeneracy in the Initial Tableau

Degeneracy, or the degenerate solution, is simply the situation where there are fewer nonzero variables in the solution than there are independent equations. The solution is to carry one or more variables "in the solution" with values of zero.

In the initial solution, the condition occurs when the placing of units in a cell results in the simultaneous fulfilling of both its row and its column constraints (except in the case of the last cell filled, which always does this). The result is that the number of stone cells is less than the number of independent equations $(R + K - 1)$. The solution to this problem is quite simple—"bring in" an available cell with zero value in the row or the column which was simultaneously filled.

Consider the initial solution shown in Figure 7.26(a). Using the northwest corner rule, 10 units have been assigned to (1, 1), satisfying the first column requirement. Then 10 units are assigned to (1, 2), completing the assignments for the first row. Our next step is to assign 10 units to (2, 2), which simultaneously completes both the second row and the second column. This signals that the initial solution will be degenerate (too few stone cells). If the solution is completed by adding 15 in (3, 3) and 25 in (3, 4), the number of stone cells is five, which is less than $R + K - 1 = 3 + 4 - 1 = 6$. This makes it impossible to assign MODI numbers or to complete the stone paths for some of the empty cells.

To get around this difficulty, we assign a zero to one of the available cells in the row or column of the cell that caused the problem (2, 2). (In general, *any cell that has no stone path* is acceptable for use as the "dummy" cell.) If we select cell (2, 3), as shown in Figure 7.26(b), all empty cells will then have valid stone paths. In this problem, any of the empty cells except

10	10	x	x	20
x	10			10
x		15	25	40
10	20	15	25	70

(a)

10	10			20
	10	0		10
		15	25	40
10	20	15	25	70

(b)

Figure 7.26 (a) Degeneracy in the initial tableau; (b) Solution of degeneracy problem in initial tableau.

(2, 1) would be equally good locations. Once the zero has been added, stone paths and MODI numbers are possible, and the analysis proceeds as usual.

Degeneracy in a Subsequent Tableau

Degeneracy can occur at any point during the solution. It takes place when two or more of the cells that are being reduced on the stone path are depleted simultaneously. Consider the example shown in Figure 7.27(a). Assume cell (2, 3) is the entering cell with stone path as shown. As we move units around the path, cells (2, 2) and (3, 3) are both depleted as the tenth unit is removed. As only one cell (2, 3) enters the solution and two cells leave, we will have a degenerate solution at the next tableau. The problem is easily solved by permitting either one of the "leaving" cells to remain in solution with a value of zero. Therefore either Figure 7.27(b) or 7.27(c) will be our next solution.

30			30
	10		10
	20	10	30
5	5		10
35	35	10	80

(a)

30			30
	0	10	10
	30		30
5	5		10
35	35	10	80

(b)

30			30
		10	10
	30	0	30
5	5		10
35	35	10	80

(c)

Figure 7.27 (a) Degeneracy after initial tableau; (b) Resolving degeneracy; (c) Another possible resolution.

Improving a Degenerate Solution

If a degenerate solution is not the optimal solution (one or more ΔZ_{ij} is negative), three possibilities exist with respect to the effect of degeneracy on the next (improved) solution.

1. The dummy cell may not be involved in the changes and will remain as is. Figure 7.28(a) shows a partial tableau in which this is the case. This will always be true if the dummy cell is not one of the turning cells on the stone path.
2. The dummy cell may cease being a dummy and become an active variable, providing a nondegenerate solution (assuming there are not any other dummys in the solution). This situation is shown in Figure 7.28(b). This always occurs when the dummy cell is a turning cell that is in an "adding" position on the stone path. The new solution will have the proper number of active stone cells, unless two of the "subtracting" cells drop out at the same time to create a new degenerate solution.
3. The dummy cell may simply move to a new location, leaving the "new" solution unchanged from the previous one. As shown in Figure 7.28(c), this results when the dummy cell is in a "subtracting" position on the stone path. Zero units are moved around the path, and the hoped-for improvement in the solution does not materialize.

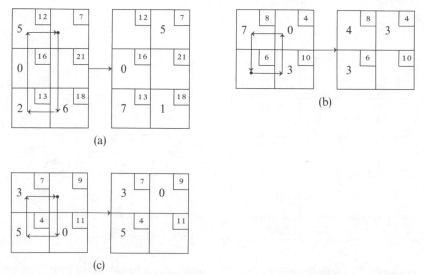

Figure 7.28 (a) Dummy cell not involved; (b) Dummy cell vanishes; (c) Dummy cell moves.

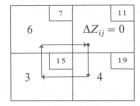

Figure 7.29   Multiple solutions.

MULTIPLE SOLUTIONS

As was the case in the general linear programming problem and the assignment problem, there is sometimes more than one solution that yields the same value of the objective function. This situation will occur when a variable (cell) not in the solution has a zero value for the improvement index (ΔZ_{ij}). If there are other empty cells with negative improvement indices, we simply ignore the fact that alternate solutions exist (who needs more suboptimal solutions?) and proceed to the improved solution. If no empty cells have negative ΔZ_{ij} values, then we have more than one optimal solution, and we will typically wish to obtain all such solutions. This is accomplished by bringing in the cell with the zero improvement index value, as shown in Figure 7.29. The new solution will also have a cell with $\Delta Z_{ij} = 0$, indicating the existence of the other solution(s).

THE NONFEASIBLE CELL

In many applications of the transportation problem it will not be possible to supply the demands of all the destinations from each of the sources. This leads to the existence of one or more nonfeasible cells in the tableau. This situation is handled quite easily by specifying an extremely high cost for those cells (like the "big M" method of guaranteeing that artificial variables not stay in the solution of simplex problems). If the problem

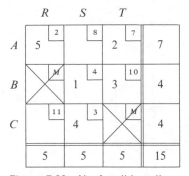

Figure 7.30   Nonfeasible cells.

is being worked by hand, it is convenient to "X-out" the cell and ignore it completely. In Figure 7.30, cells BR and CT are infeasible cells.

THE TRANSSHIPMENT PROBLEM

Many times it is possible to route shipments in such a way that one carrier stops at several points along a route, making some sources act temporarily as destinations and making some destinations act as sources. This routing of shipments through intermediate points is known as *transshipment*.

This situation is treated in detail in the Wagner and the Hillier and Lieberman texts referenced in Appendix F. The essence of the solution method is to expand the tableau to include each location as both a source and a destination, using nonfeasible cells to account for any route segments that do not actually exist in the real problem.

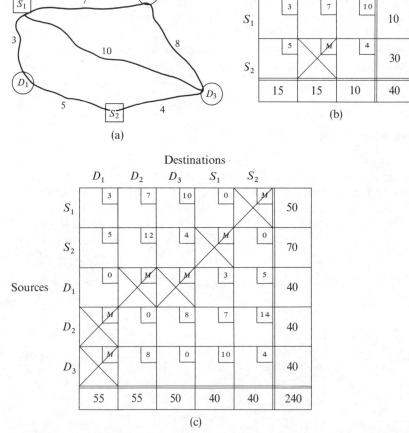

Figure 7.31 (a) Transshipment example; (b) Tableau without transshipment; (c) Tableau with transshipment.

A simple example of such a problem and its expanded tableau are shown in Figures 7.31(a), (b), and (c). Note that we have added the total number of units supplied (demanded) to the existing supply and demand values and have given each fictitious supply and demand point this many as well. This is to assure that each location will have enough available units to meet the requirements, even if the entire total were to be shipped through the point. Notice also that Ms are assigned wherever direct links do not exist and that "self-shipments" from a point to itself have zero transportation costs. These self-shipment cells are ignored in the solution and represent slack variables that act to "soak up" the 40 fictious units we have added to each row and column. The problem can now be solved using the regular transportation algorithm.

MAXIMIZATION WITH THE TRANSPORTATION MODEL

Although the model is typically presented as a minimization technique, there is no reason that the procedure cannot handle sales, or profits, or other variables that would generally be subject to maximization. In obtaining an initial solution by the best cell method or the VAM, we use the largest values rather than the smallest. The only differences in the working of the stepping stone or MODI procedures is that nonfeasible cells would have values of $-M$ and the empty cells to be considered for entry into the solution would be those with *positive* rather than negative improvement indices (ΔZ_{ij}s).

SUMMARY OF KEY CONCEPTS

Assignment model. An efficient computational method for solving problems in which one set of items must be matched one-for-one with another set in order to minimize or maximize the total value of the assignments.

Hungarian method. The general name for the computational procedure used in solving assignment problems.

Dummy rows (or columns). Device used to balance a problem that has more in one set to be assigned than in the other set.

Lone Ranger method. A procedure for making optimal assignments and testing for optimality.

Transportation model. A special case of the linear programming model in which a homogeneous product is shipped from two or more sources to two or more destinations in such a way as to minimize total shipping cost.

Balanced problem. Problem in which total supply equals total demand.

Dummy variables. Artificial supply or demand to balance a problem in which the two are unequal.

Northwest corner rule. An arbitrary method of obtaining an initial feasible solution to the problem.

Best cell method. A method of obtaining a "good" initial solution.

Vogel's approximation method (VAM). A more efficient method of obtaining an initial solution, based on the concept of first differences.

Vogel number. The difference between the cost of the cheapest and the second cheapest cells in a given row or column. Used to make initial assignments in the VAM.

Stepping stone method. A technique for determining: (1) whether the solution is optimal, (2) which variable (if any) should enter the solution, (3) how many should enter, and (4) which one(s) will leave the solution.

Stone cell. A cell representing a variable that is in the solution. The number of stone cells must be one less than the total number of rows and columns.

Stone path. A closed loop that turns only on stone cells. Used to evaluate the desirability of introducing a new variable into the solution. Each empty cell has one and only one stone path.

Improvement index. The change in the objective function resulting from the introduction of 1 unit of a particular variable.

Modified distribution (MODI) method. A simpler method than the stepping stone method for calculating the improvement indices.

MODI numbers. A set of values (Rs and Ks) assigned to the rows and columns such that the improvement index for any cell is $\Delta Z_{ij} = C_{ij} - (R_i + K_j)$.

Degenerate solution. One in which one or more basis variables has a zero value.

Multiple solutions. More that one solution exists with the same value of the objective function.

Nonfeasible cells. Cells indicating that it is not possible to ship directly from that source to that destination. Assigned a large positive value ($+M$).

Transshipment problem. A problem allowing intermediate stops on the routes used to ship the goods.

PROBLEMS

1. WXYZ-TV's news director has four major news stories to develop and only three reporters available to cover them. The total number of hours (including travel, research, editing, etc.) required for each reporter to prepare each story are as follows. (Note that Mel refuses to cover the rape trial.) Which stories should be covered by which reporters; which story will go uncovered; and what is the minimum total number of hours expended by the reporters?

	REPORTERS		
	DIANA	OLIVIA	MEL
Rape Trial	7	9	X
Airline Crash	10	7	12
Drug Bust	8	10	11
Apartment Fire	6	4	3

2. T. R. Bixby has three rush jobs to be done on the four machines in his machine shop. Determine a schedule that will minimize the machine-hours required to process all of the jobs on the machines. The machine-

hours required to perform the work on each job are shown in the following table. Note that some of the jobs cannot be done on some of the machines. What is the minimum number of machine-hours?

	MACHINE A	MACHINE B	MACHINE C	MACHINE D
Job X	8	2	7	X
Job Y	X	4	5	6
Job Z	5	3	8	9

3. A casino operator has three dealers available and must have them cover three of her tables. Over a period of time she has developed an efficiency rating for each of the dealers on each of the tables. The best rating is 1, and the worst is 10. A matrix of these ratings follows. Use the assignment method to determine the *two* best sets of assignments.

DEALER	BLACK JACK	POKER	BACARAT
Lucky	7	9	8
Gus	8	5	8
Slick	6	4	9

4. The Coarse Beer Company, based in Goldenrod, Colorado, is attempting to expand their market into Kansas, Oklahoma, Utah, and Nevada. This will require assigning a regional manager to each of the new states. So far, they have only been able to come up with three qualified managers. If their objective is to assign the personnel to the territories in such a way as to minimize the cost of relocation, which managers will they assign to which states and which state will be left without a manager? The relocation costs are as follows (in thousands). There are two optimal solutions.

	KANSAS	OKLAHOMA	UTAH	NEVADA
Benson	9	8	5	6
Jackson	12	7	2	4
Munson	8	5	1	10

5. Maxi, Inc., is an advertising agency that has four advertising account managers to be assigned to four accounts. The commissions that can be expected to be made from each of the assignments is shown in the following matrix. Find the most profitable assignment scheme.

	ACE CONCRETE	BOB'S GROCERY	CAL'S BAKERY	DON'S DONUTS
Sheri	50	70	20	80
Mort	100	60	10	40
Zelda	30	60	60	40
Thurman	60	40	30	30

6. LUV, Inc., is a small but highly profitable publishing firm that sells Bibles and other religious material on a door-to-door basis. They plan to expand into four new states—Georgia, Mississippi, Alabama, and Louisiana. They have been able to hire only three new sales representatives—Jones, Smith, and Polonski—so they will be forced to leave one of the new states uncovered temporarily. The sales manager has estimated the sales potential (in thousands) for each of the representatives in each of the territories, and these are shown in the following table. Using the assignment model and showing all work, determine which representatives should be assigned to which states in order to *maximize* total sales. Which state will be left uncovered? What is the value of the maximum total sales?

	GEORGIA	MISSISSIPPI	ALABAMA	LOUISIANA
Jones	10	4	3	5
Smith	4	3	5	2
Polonski	5	6	8	7

7. Industructo Steel Company operates four mines (A, B, C, and D), and four smelters (W, X, Y, and Z). Production, demand, and transportation costs are as follows. Use the northwest corner method to find an initial feasible solution.

PRODUCTION (TONS)	DEMAND (TONS)
A–35	W–70
B–50	X–30
C–80	Y–75
D–65	Z–55

TRANSPORTATION COSTS

From	A	A	A	A	B	B	B	B	C	C	C	C	D	D	D	D
To	W	X	Y	Z	W	X	Y	Z	W	X	Y	Z	W	X	Y	Z
Cost	10	7	6	4	8	8	5	7	4	3	6	9	7	5	4	3

8. Nationwide Auto Rental rents one-way to any major U.S. city. They presently have an imbalance in the number of cars available and the number required in various locations. There are 12 extra cars in Los Angeles, 6 in Miami, and 5 in New York. There are too few cars available in Atlanta (3), Boston (8), Chicago (3), and Detroit (8). Using the following mileage chart, they wish to determine the lowest total mileage arrangement to remedy their imbalance. Set up the problem and find an initial feasible solution using the northwest corner rule.

	Atlanta						
Atlanta	0	Boston					
Boston	11	0	Chicago				
Chicago	7	10	0	Detroit			
Detroit	7	7	3	0	Los Angeles		
Los Angeles	23	31	22	24	0	Miami	
Miami	7	16	14	14	29	0	New York
New York	9	2	8	6	29	15	0

Figure 7.32

9. Set up an initial solution for problem 7 using the VAM. Compare the total cost for the VAM with that from the northwest corner rule.
10. Set up problem 8 using VAM. Compare the total mileage with the mileage from using the northwest corner rule.
11. Use the stepping stone or the MODI method to find the optimum solution to problem 7. (Hint: Begin with the VAM solution from problem 9.)
12. Solve problem 8 for the minimum total mileage. (Hint: Begin with the VAM solution from problem 10, and add a dummy cell to make the number of stone cells equal $R + K - 1 = 7$.)
13. Solve problem 9 using the transportation model. (We set it up in Chapter 5 as an LP problem.)
14. Three orders have been received by True-Test-R, a chemical analysis firm. Ten samples are submitted by a chemical producer, 8 by a hospital, and 2 by a government agency. The effort required varies with the type of test requested and by which of three processes are used. Chemical analysis takes 3 hours per sample on the new machine, cannot be performed on the old machine, and takes 2 hours by hand. Hospital samples require 1 hour on the new machine, or 4 hours on the old machine, or 6 hours by hand. Government agency reports take 3 hours on the new machine, or 7 hours on the old machine, or 9 hours by hand. True-Test-R has enough chemicals on hand to analyze 7 samples on the new machine, 4 samples on the old machine, and 5 samples by hand. Which samples should be analyzed by which process in order to minimize total time spent in analysis?
15. The chairperson of the Management Science Department in a school of business is making out the line schedule for the coming semester. There are four full-time faculty members who must each teach 4 sections, and they wish to offer 6 sections each of Statistics and

Management Science, 3 sections of Queuing, and 2 sections of Simulation. Depending on the background and interests of the faculty members, it will take them differing amounts of time to prepare and teach the courses as shown in the following table. Use the transportation model to determine the schedule of offerings that will minimize the total preparation time for the whole department and maintain all of the faculty's full-time teaching status. What is the *average* preparation for the full-time faculty?

	STAT	MG/S	QUEUES	SIMULATION
Ponney	2	1	5	8
McWilson	4	4	1	5
Barker	6	8	10	9
Broberts	9	9	5	1

16. Howard Ashbrook, owner of Honest Abe's Cut-Rate Auto Emporium ("three convenient locations to serve you—we tote the note—no credit check required") has purchased 4 sports cars, 7 sedans, and 9 subcompacts at an automobile dealers' auction. He wishes to distribute them to the three lots he owns in such a way as to maximize his profit on them. He has room for 3 of them at the downtown lot, 5 at the suburban lot, and 6 at the rural location. Any cars not placed will be resold to other dealers at no profit. Due to the different car-buying habits of the clientele at the three lots, the profits he expects vary by type of car and location as follows.

		LOCATION		
		DOWNTOWN	SUBURBAN	RURAL
	Sportscar	40	70	90
MODEL	Sedan	80	160	110
	Subcompact	120	40	100

Which lot should receive which car; how many of which types should be wholesaled; and what is his maximum total profit on the cars?

17. Earl N. Meier, chemistry student and political anarchist, is manufacturing explosives for an attack on the state capitol building. He has 4 bases (X, R, P, and D) and 3 activators (M, S, and Q). The explosive force (in thousands of pounds of TNT equivalent) created by mixing 1 pound of a certain base with a pound of a particular activator varies, and certain combinations produce no explosive result. Earl has on hand 60 pounds of M, 50 of S, 20 of Q, 40 of X, 50 of R, 35 of P, and 35 of D.

The explosive combinations and their forces generated are as follows (other combinations are duds).

Combination	MX	MR	MD	SR	SP	SD	QX	QR	QP
Thousands of Pounds Force for 1 Pound of Base and Activator	4	7	12	2	9	8	11	6	4

How many pounds of which combinations should he mix in order to maximize his explosive arsenal? How much of which ingredient is left over? How many thousand pounds of force can he create?

Chapter 8

GOAL PROGRAMMING

PROBLEMS THAT DO NOT QUITE FIT THE LP MODEL

Although linear programming is an extremely useful and widely applied problem-solving tool, there are many types of problems that do not lend themselves to direct solution through its use. Many of these can be solved by application of one of the special purpose algorithms that have been developed to attack certain types of problem structures. Following is a list of some of these special models and the types of problems they are designed to solve.

Problem Type	*Solution Model*
Second-order objective function	Quadratic Programming
Equations are products (rather than summations) of terms.	Geometric Programming
All variables must be integers.	Integer Programming
Some variables are integers and some are continuous.	Mixed-Integer Programming
Variables are either included (value of 1) or not (value of 0).	0–1 Programming

Problem has no feasible solution.   Goal Programming
Problem is linear but has more than   Goal Programming
one objective to optimize at same
time.

The discussion of most of these models is beyond the scope of an introductory text such as this one, but the relative simplicity and wide applicability of goal programming make it an important addition to the problem-solving arsenal of the beginning management scientist. The references in Appendix F suggest other texts that treat these other models.

PROBLEMS WITH NO FEASIBLE SOLUTION

Consider the linear programming problem shown in Figure 8.1. The problem is clearly overconstrained, and no feasible region exists. If we view the constraints not as absolute requirements but as *goals* that we wish either to meet or to violate by as little as possible, we can cast the problem in the goal programming format. This requires three steps:

1. Augment the goals (constraints) with appropriate slack (S) and violation (V) variables.

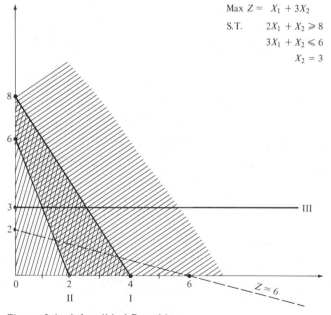

$$\text{Max } Z = X_1 + 3X_2$$
$$\text{S.T.} \quad 2X_1 + X_2 \geqslant 8$$
$$3X_1 + X_2 \leqslant 6$$
$$X_2 = 3$$

Figure 8.1   Infeasible LP problem.

2. Augment the objective function by the addition of the appropriately signed and weighted slack and violation variables from (1).
3. Solve this expanded problem on any standard LP package.

Augmenting the Goals (Constraints)

Any constraint that is not absolute and inviolable can be considered a goal, subject to deviations in either direction. We will use the symbol S_i to indicate slack and V_i to indicate violation. These variables will be assigned subscripts to indicate the constraint to which each refers.

GTE GOALS

The greater-than-or-equal-to (GTE) goals are augmented by subtracting a slack variable $(-S_i)$ and adding a violation variable $(+V_i)$. In our example problem,

$$2X_1 + X_2 \geq 8$$

becomes

$$2X_1 + X_2 - S_1 + V_1 = 8$$

The slack variable (S_1) represents the amount in excess of the boundary value, and the violation variable (V_1) represents underachievement of the original constraint.

LTE GOALS

Less-than-or-equal-to (LTE) goals are augmented by adding slack $(+S_i)$ and subtracting violation $(-V_i)$ variables. In the second goal of the example,

$$3X_1 + X_2 \leq 6$$

becomes

$$3X_1 + X_2 + S_2 - V_2 = 6$$

Here, the slack variable (S_2) represents shortfall of the limiting value, and the violation variable (V_2) represents oversubscription of the constraint boundary.

EQ GOALS

Strict equality (EQ) goals are augmented by adding a violation variable (V_i) and subtracting a second violation variable $(-V_i')$. For the third goal in our example,

$$X_2 = 3$$

becomes

$$X_2 + V_3 - V_3' = 3$$

In the case of EQ goals, the shortage variable $(+V_i)$ represents violation on the same side of the goal as the origin $(X_i = 0)$, whereas the surplus variable $(-V_i')$ indicates violation on the opposite side of the goal.

Augmenting the Objective Function

Augmenting the objective function to include the deviation variables that we have added to the problem requires consideration of two factors— the *signs* and the *magnitudes* of the coefficients of the variables.

SLACK VARIABLES

Those deviations that represent *slacks* in the original constraints have no impact on the value of the objective function and are assigned zero coefficients. In our example, the objective function is increased by the addition of

$$0S_1 + 0S_2$$

VIOLATION VARIABLES

The deviations that represent *violations* of their respective constraints $(V_i$ and $V_i')$ are treated in much the same way as were the artificial variables in the simplex. They are given a sign that makes them move in the *opposite* direction from that desired for Z ($-$ if we are maximizing; $+$ if we are minimizing). The magnitudes of their coefficients are more difficult to assign. They should be an order of magnitude (at *least* ten times) larger than the largest coefficient in the original objective function. Furthermore, because violations of the various goals may not be equally undesirable, we may express the relative importance of each goal by the size of its coefficient, relative to the others.

If the first goal in our example was twice as important as the second, which was three times as important as the third, our weights might be 600, 300, and 100, respectively, and the augmented objection would be

$$Z = X_1 + 3X_2 + 0S_1 - 600V_1 + 0S_2 - 300V_2 - 100V_3 - 100V_3'$$

Solution

The augmented problem can now be summarized as follows

$$
\begin{aligned}
\text{Max} \quad & Z = X_1 + 3X_2 + 0X_3 - 600X_4 + 0X_5 - 300X_6 - 100X_7 - 100X_8 \\
\text{ST} \quad & 2X_1 + X_2 - X_3 + X_4 = 8 \\
& 3X_1 + X_2 + X_5 - X_6 = 6 \\
& 0X_1 + X_2 + X_7 - X_8 = 3
\end{aligned}
$$

where X_3 through X_8 represent the deviation variables. The solution (by computer) values are interpreted as follows:

Computer Solution	Goal Programming Solution	Original Problem Interpretation
$X_1 = 0$	$X_1 = 0$	$X_1 = 0$
$X_2 = 8$	$X_2 = 8$	$X_2 = 8$
$X_3 = 0$	$S_1 = 0$	First constraint is
$X_4 = 0$	$V_1 = 0$	binding.
$X_5 = 0$	$S_2 = 0$	Second constraint is
$X_6 = 2$	$V_2 = 2$	violated by 2 units.
$X_7 = 0$	$V_3 = 0$	Third constraint is
$X_8 = 5$	$V_3' = 5$	violated by 5 units on side away from the origin.

$$Z_{MAX} = -1076 \qquad Z_{MAX} = 24$$

The solution is shown as point A in Figure 8.2.

To interpret Z_{MAX}, it is necessary to remove the effects of the violation variables.

$$Z_{MAX} = Z_{COMPUTER} - \sum_{j=3}^{8} C_j X_j = -1076 - [(2)(-300) + (5)(-100)] = 24$$

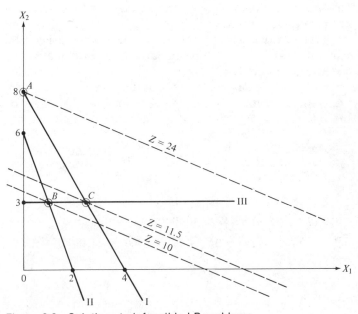

Figure 8.2 Solutions to infeasible LP problems.

If we had assigned different weights to the goals, we could have arrived at a different solution. For example, if the first and third goals were equally important and the second goal were twice as important as either of them, the objective function might become

$$\text{Max } Z = X_1 + 3X_2 + 0X_3 - 100X_4 + 0X_5 - 200X_6 - 100X_7 - 100X_8$$

and the solution would move to point B in Figure 8.2, where constraints II and III are binding, constraint I is violated by 3 units, and $Z = 10$.

If one or more of our constraints were absolute while others remained violable (but at a penalty), we would not need to augment the fixed constraints before submitting the problem for solution. Thus, if the first constraint could not possibly be relaxed, but the others were negotiable, with the second constraint twice as important as the third, the problem that we would submit to the computer would reduce to

$$\text{Max} \quad Z = X_1 + 3X_2 + 0X_3 - 200X_4 - 100X_5 - 100X_6$$
$$\text{ST} \quad 2X_1 + X_2 \geq 8$$
$$3X_1 + X_2 + X_3 - X_4 = 6$$
$$X_2 + X_5 - X_6 = 3$$

with X_3 through X_6 representing S_2, V_2, V_3, and V_3', respectively. The solution is shown at point C in Figure 8.2. $Z = 11.5$ and constraint II is violated by 1.5 units.

PROBLEMS WITH MULTIPLE GOALS (AND NO OBJECTIVE FUNCTION)

A more classic goal programming problem is one in which no single objective is stated, but several (usually competing) objectives are listed.

A Portfolio Problem

Consider the dilemma of the portfolio manager. He wishes to earn an overall return of at least $20,000; at least half of the funds should be invested in bonds; he does not wish to invest any more than $200,000 of the funds presently available; no more than $50,000 should be invested in common stocks. His investment alternatives are bonds (B), common stocks (S), and home mortgages (M). Bonds usually come in denominations of $10,000 (but smaller face values are available) and carry a 6% interest rate; the stocks on his list average $30 per share, are normally purchased in round lots of 100 shares, and have an expected return of 12% the mortgages are for $50,000 each at an interest rate of 9%.

His goals can be written as follows.

$$(\$10{,}000)(.06)B + (\$3{,}000)(.12)S + (\$50{,}000)(.09)M \geq \$20{,}000 \qquad \text{(I)}$$
$$\$10{,}000B - \qquad \$3{,}000S - \qquad \$50{,}000M \geq \$0 \qquad \text{(II)}$$
$$\$10{,}000B + \qquad \$3{,}000S + \qquad \$50{,}000M \leq \$200{,}000 \qquad \text{(III)}$$
$$\$3{,}000S \qquad\qquad\qquad \leq \$50{,}000 \qquad \text{(IV)}$$

Augmenting the constraints, we obtain

$$600B + \;\; 360S + \;\; 4{,}500M - S_1 + V_1 = \;\; 20{,}000 \qquad \text{(I)}$$
$$10{,}000B - 3{,}000S - 50{,}000M - S_2 + V_2 = \qquad 0 \qquad \text{(II)}$$
$$10{,}000B + 3{,}000S + 50{,}000M + S_3 - V_3 = 200{,}000 \qquad \text{(III)}$$
$$3{,}000S \qquad\qquad + S_4 - V_4 = \;\; 50{,}000 \qquad \text{(IV)}$$

The violation variables are V_1, V_2, V_3, and V_4. We can attempt to satisfy all our of our goals simultaneously by minimizing an objective function comprising a weighted sum of these violation variables. The weights indicate the relative importance to us of each of the goals. If the first goal is twice as important as the third, which is five times as important as either the second or fourth goals, the objective function is

$$\text{Min } Z = 10V_1 + V_2 + 5V_3 + V_4$$

If we designate B, S, and M as X_1, X_2, and X_3, and S_1 through V_4 as X_4 through X_{11}, we can now solve the problem on the computer. The solution is

$$B = 10 \qquad S = 16.67 \qquad M = 1 \qquad V_1 = \$3{,}500$$

which tells the portfolio manager to purchase 10 of the $10,000 bonds, 1667 shares of stock, and 1 home mortgage. All of the goals are met except the most important one—the profit is only $16,500, which falls short of the $20,000 target by $3,500. This result points out both strengths and weaknesses inherent in the relative weighting approach. The advantage is that it permits interaction and trade-offs among the various goals— if the penalty for violating a high priority goal is more than balanced by the reduction in penalties in other goals, then the higher priority goal will be unrealized. The disadvantage is that when this happens, we frequently find that we must reevaluate the weights we have assigned, for we are uncomfortable with the result. This leads to a very important point.

The sensitivity analysis provided by most canned linear programming programs can yield important insights into the relative importance of the goals. In this example, the weight of variable V_1 would have to be at least three times its present value to force the solution to another corner of the feasible region. This means that we must consider the profit goal to be at least 30 times as important as the second and fourth goals to force it to be met.

If we reformulate the problem, giving the profit goal a weight of 100, the result becomes

$$B = 6.67, \qquad S = 44.4, \qquad V_2 = 66,666, \qquad V_4 = 83,333$$

This solution meets the profit goal, but violates the goals of having half of the portfolio in bonds and of keeping the investment in stock below $50,000.

A Marketing Media Mix Problem

The marketing vice president of a bank must decide on the optimal mix of media to use in the bank's advertising campaign promoting a new "instant loan" program. The media she is considering are billboards (B), newspapers (N), radio (R), and TV (T). The costs, number of families reached, and expected exposure units (a marketing term that expresses the anticipated response to the ad) are estimated in the following table.

MEDIA	COST PER UNIT	NUMBER OF FAMILIES REACHED	EXPECTED EXPOSURE UNITS
Billboards	$10,000	1,000	80
Newspapers	500	5,000	90
Radio	200	250	20
TV	3,000	4,000	150

The goals she hopes to attain are

   (I) stay below her $50,000 budget for the first month;
  (II) reach or exceed 6,000 expected exposure units;
 (III) reach or exceed 200,000 families exposed to the ads;
 (IV) spend no more than $20,000 for TV advertising;
  (V) run no more than one newspaper ad per day.

which can be expressed as follows.

$$
\begin{array}{rl}
\$10,000B + \$500N + \$200R + \$3,000T \le \$50,000 & \text{(I)} \\
80B + 90N + 20R + 150T \ge 6,000 & \text{(II)} \\
1,000B + 5,000N + 250R + 4,000T \ge 200,000 & \text{(III)} \\
\$3,000T \le \$20,000 & \text{(IV)} \\
N \le 30 & \text{(V)}
\end{array}
$$

If the first goal is an absolute requirement and the second through fifth goals are each twice as important as the one below it, the problem can be expressed thus.

$$\text{Min } Z = 8V_2 + 4V_3 + 2V_4 + V_5$$
$$\text{ST} \quad 10{,}000B + \quad 500N + 200R + 3{,}000T \le 50{,}000$$
$$80B + \quad 90N + \quad 20R + \quad 150T - S_2 + V_2 = \quad 6{,}000$$
$$1{,}000B + 5{,}000N + 250R + 4{,}000T - S_3 + V_3 = 200{,}000$$
$$3{,}000T + S_4 - V_4 = \quad 20{,}000$$
$$N \qquad\qquad\qquad + S_5 - V_5 = \quad 30$$

We have left the first goal (constraint) in the LTE form, which will *require* any solution to meet the budget constraint. An alternate approach would be to augment the constraint in the usual way and to assign V_1 a weight that is very large in comparison with the other weights (as we did in the second formulation of the portfolio problem).

The solution to the media mix example is

$$N = 31.3, \qquad R = 146.3, \qquad T = 1.69, \qquad S_4 = \$14{,}934, \qquad V_5 = 1.3$$

This mix relies heavily on newspapers (slightly violating the one ad per day goal) and radio spots (almost five per day), makes no use of billboards, and uses little television ($S_4 = \$14{,}934$). The solution values must be integers; so to obtain the nearest practical solution, we increase T to 2, reducing newspaper and radio ads slightly to stay within the budget.

$$N = 30, \qquad R = 145, \qquad T = 2, \qquad S_4 = \$14{,}000$$

Note that this solution violates none of the goals, for S_4 is a slack variable.

A Production Problem

The Apex Manufacturing Co. makes four products, and each requires a different mix of raw materials and types of labor, as shown in the following table.

	LABOR (HOURS)			
	CARPENTERS	MACHINISTS	ASSEMBLERS	INSPECTORS
Couches	3	0	2	$\frac{1}{2}$
Bar-B-Que Pits	0	2	1	$\frac{1}{2}$
Reclining Chairs	2	2	2	1
Patio Furniture	2	1	2	1

	UNIT COSTS			RAW MATERIALS		
	LABOR	MATERIALS	TOTAL	WOOD (ft)	METAL (#)	FABRIC (yd)
Couches	\$57	\$55	\$112	50	0	10
Bar-B-Que Pits	\$40	\$16	\$ 56	0	20	0
Reclining Chairs	\$78	\$64	\$142	20	30	10
Patio Furniture	\$66	\$53	\$119	30	10	10

Carpenters cost $11 per hour; machinists, $12; assemblers $8; inspectors, $16. Wood costs $0.50 per board foot; metal is $0.80 per pound; fabric is $3 per yard.

Abe Tannenbaum, the owner of Apex, has the following goals.

   (I) Maximize the number of employees.

  (II) Minimize variable costs.

 (III) The absolute minimum output that will cover fixed costs is 100 units (of all types added together) per week.

 (IV) Three carpenters have seniority and must be paid whether they work or not, but there are plenty of others who can be added as needed.

  (V) A maximum of six machinists is available, and they will work overtime (at time and a half) if needed.

These goals can be used to formulate a goal-programming problem. X_1 through X_4 will be the number of units of each of the four products produced per week. Each employee works 40 hours per week. Notice that we have three different types of goals.

STANDARD INEQUALITY GOALS

$$\text{Number of carpenters: } 3X_1 + 0X_2 + 2X_3 + 2X_4 \geq 120 \qquad \text{(IV)}$$

Goal IV is based on the number of hours of carpentry required per unit produced for each product and on the desire to keep at least three carpenters employed full time (120 hours per week). There is no penalty using additional carpenters (the cost goal will address that problem), but idle time for the three regulars cost $11 per hour. ($C_{S_4} = 0$, $C_{V_4} = 11$.)

$$\text{Number of machinists: } 0X_1 + 2X_2 + 2X_3 + 1X_4 \leq 240 \qquad \text{(V)}$$

To achieve goal V, the number of machinists' hours cannot exceed 240 per week (6 full-time machinists), or a penalty of $6 per hour (overtime penalty) will be encountered. Using fewer than this number envokes no penalty. ($C_{V_5} = 6$, $C_{S_5} = 0$.)

ABSOLUTE REQUIREMENTS

$$\text{Number of units of output: } X_1 + X_2 + X_3 + X_4 \geq 100 \qquad \text{(III)}$$

Because a minimum output (goal III) *must* be achieved, no deviational variables will be assigned, and this goal will be input as a GTE constraint.

MAXIMIZATION OR MINIMIZATION OF GOALS

Goal I is based on the percentage of a week's work (e.g., $\frac{3}{40}$ of a carpenter, 0 machinists, $\frac{2}{40}$ of an assembler, and $\frac{1}{80}$ of an inspector to make a couch) required for each product. Because we wish to maximize the total number employed, we use the GTE inequality. The goal value (3) is purely arbitrary—we could have used *any* value (3 is a logical one, in order to keep the 3 carpenters, but as we shall see, the number does not matter). ($C_{S_1} = -500$, $C_{V_1} = +500$.)

Number of Employees:

$$(\tfrac{3}{40} + \tfrac{2}{40} + \tfrac{1}{80})X_1 + (\tfrac{2}{40} + \tfrac{1}{40} + \tfrac{1}{80})X_2$$
$$+ (\tfrac{2}{40} + \tfrac{2}{40} + \tfrac{2}{40} + \tfrac{1}{40})X_3 + (\tfrac{2}{40} + \tfrac{1}{40} + \tfrac{2}{40} + \tfrac{1}{40})X_4 \geq 3$$
$$= \tfrac{11}{80}X_1 + \tfrac{7}{80}X_2 + \tfrac{14}{80}X_3 + \tfrac{12}{80}X_4 \geq 3$$
$$= .1375X_1 + .0875X_2 + .175X_3 + .15X_4 \geq 3 \qquad \text{(I)}$$

ASSIGNING THE COEFFICIENTS

In assigning the coefficients to the deviation variables in an "optimize" goal, we assign a *desirable* value to the *overachievement* of the goal (rather than a zero, as in the standard inequality goal) and an *undesirable* value to the *violation* variable. In this case, we assign the same value, reversed in sign, but in some cases the violation variable would be more costly than the overachievement is desirable.

$$\text{Cost: } \$112X_1 + \$56X_2 + \$142X_3 + \$119X_4 \leq \$5,600 \qquad \text{(II)}$$

As was the case for goal I, the goal value is immaterial. We picked $5600 as the cheapest way to meet the absolute requirement for 100 units of output from III (all 100 units would be Bar-B-Que pits). ($C_{S_2} = -1$, $C_{V_2} = 1$.)

PROBLEM FORMULATION

It is now possible to state the problem in its goal programming format.

$$\text{Min } Z = -500S_1 + 500V_1 - S_2 + V_2 + 11V_4 + 6V_5$$

ST	$.1375X_1 + .0875X_2 + .175X_3 + .15X_4 - S_1 + V_1 =$			3	(I)
	$112X_1 + 56X_2 + 142X_3 + 119X_4 + S_2 - V_2 =$			5600	(II)
	$X_1 + X_2 + X_3 + X_4$		$\geq$	100	(III)
	$3X_1 + 0X_2 + 2X_3 + 2X_4 - S_4 + V_4 =$			120	(IV)
	$0X_1 + 2X_2 + 2X_3 + 1X_4 + S_5 - V_5 =$			240	(V)

In assigning the coefficients in the objective function, it is important that we keep in mind the units represented by each of the violation variables. Goal II is expressed in dollars (total cost); so the objective is to *minimize the violation variable (V_2) and maximize the slack variable (S_2)*, and the coefficients are a $1-bonus for each dollar saved and a $1-penalty for each dollar spent.

Goal I is expressed in numbers of employees; so each unit represents 1 week of labor added or reduced. Because Tannenbaum wishes to maximize the number of employees, we will assume that a worker is worth more than his or her wages (which average about $470 per week) and assign a benefit of $500 for each worker added and a penalty for each one dropped. Note that goal I is not 500 times as important as goal II, but only about 5% more important because of the difference in units of V_1 and S_1 (number of employees) and V_2 and S_2 (dollars). Goal III does not appear in the objective function because it is an absolute requirement and must be met. Goals IV and V receive $11 and $6 penalty values, because each is expressed in hours of labor. The rates for the violation variables (V_4 and V_5) already have been discussed.

Given the foregoing set of facts in this example, it is a simple task to postulate an entirely different set of weights for the goals. Those described here are meant to represent one such set but by no means the only logical or reasonable one. A further discussion of the art of weighting the deviation variables is given at the end of this chapter.

SOLUTION

The optimum solution from the computerized LP program is to produce 40 couches and 60 barbecue pits. $S_1 = 7.75$; so the total number of employees is 10.75. $V_2 = 2240$; so total variable cost is $7840. $S_5 = 120$ hours; so 3 machinists will be hired.

To produce 40 couches and 60 barbecue pits requires 3 carpenters, 3 machinists, $3\frac{1}{2}$ assemblers, and $1\frac{1}{4}$ inspectors. These fractional employees can be obtained by hiring part-time workers, or an integer solution can be found.

COMMENTS ON FORMULATING GOAL PROGRAMMING PROBLEMS

Notation

The notation we have chosen to use in this chapter represents a distinct improvement over the standard notation found in the goal programming literature. Most authors use "deviational variables," represented by $d_i{}^+$ (a surplus variable) and $d_i{}^-$ (a shortage variable) to augment the constraints and the objective function.

The augmentation procedure is straightforward—always subtract the surplus variable $(-d_i{}^+)$ and add the shortage variable $(+d_i{}^-)$. The difficulty with this notation is that d_i^+ represents slack in a GTE goal and violation in a LTE goal, and this necessitates continual referring to the original problem to interpret the results.

The S_i and V_i notation greatly reduces this confusion and, in our experience, is much simpler, easier, faster to interpret and leads to fewer errors.

Assigning Weights

Although augmenting the goals is a simple matter, assigning the weights is much more difficult and can be highly subjective. In actual practice the management scientist and the decision maker (if the two are not one and the same) should collaborate in this crucial step.

Frequently a heuristic approach will be the most fruitful one. An initial set of weights can be assigned and the solution obtained. The solution should be examined carefully by the decision maker for "reasonableness," and the sensitivity analysis should be examined by the management scientist to determine the stability of the solution and to suggest trade-offs between various goals. Additional constraints (goals) can be added to the original problem, and different sets of weights can be examined until a solution that is compatible with both the mathematical model *and* the original problem it attempts to describe can be found.

SUMMARY OF KEY CONCEPTS

Goals.   Targets that we attempt to reach in solving goal programming problems. They correspond to the constraints in linear programming.

Slack variables (S_i).   Variables that are subtracted from GTE and added to LTE goals in augmenting. They have the same meaning as slacks in ordinary linear programming problems.

Violation variables (V_i).   Variables that are added to GTE and EQ and subtracted from LTE goals in augmenting. (V_i' variables are subtracted from EQ goals.) They have the same meaning as artificial variables in ordinary linear programming problems.

Relative weights.   The coefficients assigned to the variables in augmenting or constructing the objective function in a goal programming problem. Their values are set relative to the importance of their goals.

Absolute goals.   Those that may not be violated at any price. These are not augmented prior to inputting the problem for solution by a computerized linear programming package.

Priority levels.   The ranking of goals (or groups of goals) according to their necessity of being met. Coefficients of each level of priority are assigned so that an order of magnitude (at least 10 times) separates adjacent priortiy-level goals.

Deviation variables.   Shortage (d_i^-) and surplus (d_i^+) variables that are added and subtracted, respectively, to augment the goals (an alternative to S_i and V_i values).

Shortage variables (d_i^-).   Variables that are added to make the left-hand side equal the target value. These represent slack in LTE constraints and violation in GTE and EQ constraints.

Surplus variables (d_i^+).   Variables subtracted from the left-hand side to make it equal the target value. They represent slack in GTE constraints and violation in LTE and EQ constraints.

PROBLEMS

1. Set up the following infeasible LP problem as a goal programming problem for solution by a computerized LP package. Make the weights 10 times the largest value in the original objective function.

$$\text{Max } Z = 4X_1 + 3X_2 + 5X_3$$
$$\text{ST} \qquad X_1 + X_2 + X_3 \le 10$$
$$2X_1 + X_2 + 2X_3 \ge 50$$

2. Formulate this infeasible LP problem as a goal programming problem and solve it on a computerized LP package.

$$\text{Max } Z = 2X_1 + X_2 + 4X_3 + 5X_4$$
$$\text{ST} \qquad 3X_1 + 2X_2 + X_3 + 4X_4 \ge 100$$
$$X_1 + 2X_2 + 3X_3 + X_4 \le 50$$
$$2X_1 + 3X_2 + 4X_3 + 2X_4 = 40$$

3. All American Autos, Inc., plans to enter the U.S. automobile market with a full line of cars, from subcompact to luxury sizes. They plan to build 100,000 vehicles (exactly). DOE regulations require that the average mileage rating be at least 28 mpg for their total production. These two requirements *must* be met. In addition, they would like to achieve a gross profit of at least $80 million and total sales of at least $700 million. The profit goal is twice as important as the sales goal. Set up their problem as a goal programming problem for solution by standard LP routines, and run it to find their optimum solution.

	GROSS PROFIT	PRICE	MPG
Subcompact	$ 300	$4000	40
Compact	$ 500	$5000	30
Standard	$ 800	$6000	20
Luxury	$1500	$9000	15

4. The City Council of Rock Bluff, a rapidly growing town in the Sunbelt, is planning a bond issue, which will be submitted to the voters. There are five different categories in which money will be spent—water,

sewers, streets, parks, and city hall improvements. From past experience, they know that the total bond issue cannot exceed $8 million if it is to have a reasonable chance of passing. If city services are to be continued, they feel they must have at least $2 million for water and $1.5 million each for sewers and streets. These form constraints are absolute. They would *like* to have a total of at least $3 million for water, $2 million for sewers, $3 million for streets, $0.3 million for parks, and $0.2 million for city hall repairs. Of these added amounts, the city hall repairs and parks have the highest priority; the added amounts for streets and sewers are $\frac{1}{10}$ as vital as parks or city hall; and added water funds are half as crucial as those for streets or sewers. Set up as a goal programming problem and solve on a computerized LP package.

5. E. Z. Windfall has inherited $250,000 from his hermit uncle and wishes to invest it so that he can retire and live modestly (but not work). He has asked you to help him determine how to invest his legacy in order to meet the following objectives.

  1. He has a maximum of $250,000 to invest (absolute).
  2. He wants a yearly income from dividends and interest of at least $18,000.
  3. In addition, he wants a capital gain each year of at least $10,000 for vacations and special purchases.
  4. He wants to invest at most $100,000 in stocks.
  5. He wants to invest at least $100,000 in bonds.
  6. He wants to invest no more than $25,000 in preferred stock.
  7. He wants to invest no more than $10,000 in commercial paper.
  8. He wants at least $20,000 in a bank savings account for liquidity.

The expected income and capital gains rates for each of the five investment vehicles he is considering are as follows. The income of $18,000 is the most important goal; the $10,000 capital gain is only half that important; the other goals are $\frac{1}{10}$ as important as the capital gains goal. Set up the problem as a goal programming problem for solution by LP, and solve on a computerized LP package.

	INCOME	CAPITAL GAINS
Stocks	3%	10%
Bonds	8%	—
Preferred	5%	5%
Paper	9%	—
Savings	6%	—

6. Slummaker Associates is a land developer who wishes to subdivide a 300 acre tract, which they have recently acquired, into luxury home lots (2 homes per acre), tract home lots (5 homes per acre), and duplex

lots (8 homes per acre). Zoning restrictions require that any new development have an average of no more than 6 families per acre (a total of no more than 1800 homes). They would like to have a minimum of 50 acres devoted to each of the three types of homes. Although these minimums are not absolute, the luxury target is ten times as important as either of the other two. If these quotas are exceeded, additional tract homes are three times as desirable as additional luxury homes, and additional duplex homes are five times as desirable as additional luxury homes. Set up as a goal programming problem, and solve on a computerized LP package. (Hint: let L, T, and D represent the number of *homes* of each type. Note that the *slacks* in the last three constraints are desirable and will appear in the objective function with *negative* weights.)

Chapter 9

CLASSICAL OPTIMIZATION

INTRODUCTION

To most undergraduate students studying business administration, the term "classical optimization" would be classified as one of those nebulous terms that they have heard before but do not know the exact meaning of. If, in an attempt to clarify the concept, the words "calculus" or "derivatives" are used, then we move from vagueness into the "stark terror" category. In this chapter our aim is to make all three of these terms understandable and usable.

We begin by reviewing briefly the determination of the slope of a linear function and proceed with an intuitive discussion that extends this idea to include the slope of nonlinear functions. Rules for obtaining the derivatives of the more commonly encountered functional forms are given, and the concept of the slope function is introduced. Through the use of a graphical illustration, the procedures for determining local maxima and minima are developed. Finally, we present the concept of constrained classical optimization and boundary values.

Chapters 10 and 11 deal with applications of classical optimization in microeconomics and production and inventory models; so the time we spend now in laying these foundations will reap benefits as we progress into these applications areas.

THE SLOPE OF A FUNCTION

Linear Functions

Recall from Chapter 2 that a linear function of the form

$$Y = a + bX$$

has a slope (b), which can be determined by

$$b = \frac{Y_2 - Y_1}{X_2 - X_1}$$

where (X_1, Y_1) and (X_2, Y_2) represent two points on the line.

If we refer to the difference between the two Y values as ΔY and the difference between the two X values as ΔX, then

$$\Delta Y = Y_2 - Y_1$$
$$\Delta X = X_2 - X_1$$

$$b = \frac{\Delta Y}{\Delta X}$$

This notation is illustrated in Figure 9.1, where two points (4, 5) and (7, 11) have been selected, and

$$\Delta Y = Y_2 - Y_1 = 10 - 6 = 4$$
$$\Delta X = X_2 - X_1 = 16 - 8 = 8$$

$$b = \frac{\Delta Y}{\Delta X} = \frac{4}{8} = +\frac{1}{2}$$

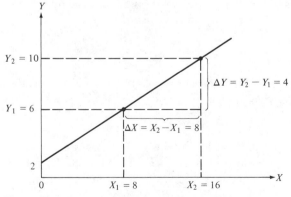

Figure 9.1 Determination of the slope of a linear function.

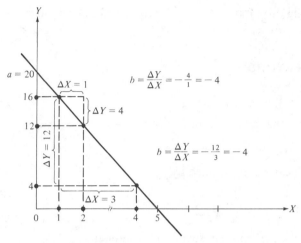

Figure 9.2   Linear function with a negative slope.

This means that for every 1-unit increment we take along X, the line moves upward 2 units in Y.

The intercept (a) can be found by using the slope (b) and any one point on the line, such as (8, 6).

$$6 = a + \tfrac{1}{2}(8)$$
$$a = 6 - 4 = 2$$

It is important to note that the slope of a linear function is the same at every point along the line and that the length of ΔX is unimportant in finding b. Figure 9.2 illustrates a linear function with a *negative* slope that is calculated using both a wide interval for ΔX and a narrow one. The function is

$$Y = 20 - 4X,$$

and the slope is the same whether the two points are relatively close together [(1, 16) and (2, 12)] or far apart [(1, 16) and (4, 4)].

Slopes of Nonlinear Functions

Suppose we attempt to apply this same approach to the calculation of the slope of a nonlinear function, such as

$$Y = 3 + 2X + X^2$$

which is shown in Figure 9.3. First, let us take $X_1 = 1$ and $X_2 = 5$. Substituting into the equation, we obtain $Y_1 = 6$ and $Y_2 = 38$. Therefore ΔX equals 4, and ΔY is 32, and the "slope" is 8. From Figure 9.3 we

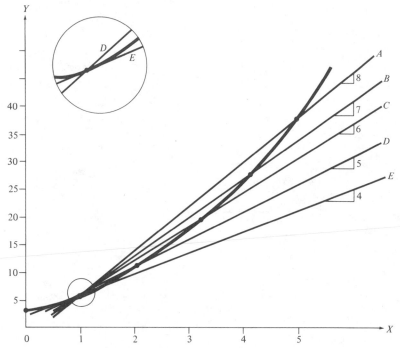

Figure 9.3   Approximating the slope of a nonlinear function by a straight line.

observe that what we actually have done is to approximate the slope of the curve by that of a straight line (A) through the two points $(1, 6)$ and $(5, 38)$.

Observe that as we select progressively smaller ΔX values (the calculations are summarized in Table 9.1), the slope of the line becomes progressively flatter, until finally the two points on the curve are so close that the line (E) through the points just touches the curve but does not cut through it (see inset). This limiting case is called the *tangent* to the curve, and we will define the slope of a curve at any point to be equal to the slope of the tangent to the curve at that point.

To arrive at the slope at our point $(1, 6)$, we selected X_2 at a point just slightly greater than X_1 (i.e., $X_2 = X_1 + \Delta X$, or $X_2 = 1 + \Delta X$). The value of Y_2 was found by substituting X_2 into the equation for Y

$$Y_2 = 3 + 2(1 + \Delta X) + (1 + \Delta X)^2 = 6 + 4\,\Delta X + (\Delta X)^2$$

Subtracting, we obtain

$$\Delta Y = Y_2 - Y_1 = 4\,\Delta X + (\Delta X)^2$$

The ratio of ΔY to ΔX becomes

$$\frac{\Delta Y}{\Delta X} = \frac{4\,\Delta X + (\Delta X)^2}{\Delta X} = 4 + \Delta X$$

Table 9.1 SLOPE CALCULATIONS

CASE	X_1	X_2	Y_1	Y_2	ΔX	ΔY	"SLOPE"
A	1	5	6	38	4	32	8
B	1	4	6	27	3	21	7
C	1	3	6	18	2	12	6
D	1	2	6	11	1	5	5
E	1	$1 + \Delta X$	6	$6 + 4\Delta X + (\Delta X)^2$	ΔX	$4\Delta X + (\Delta X)^2$	$\displaystyle \operatorname*{Limit}_{\Delta X \to 0} \left\{ \frac{4\Delta X + \Delta X^2}{\Delta X} \right\} = 4$

As ΔX becomes smaller, the value of $\Delta Y/\Delta X$ approaches the slope of the tangent line (E). We call this process taking the *limit* of $\Delta Y/\Delta X$ as the value of ΔX approaches zero, and denote it by

$$\underset{\Delta X \to 0}{\text{Limit}} \{4 + \Delta X\} = 4 + 0 = 4$$

This should be obvious that the tangent to a nonlinear function, and therefore the slope of the function, will be different at different points along the curve. To arrive at a general expression for the slope at any point along the curve, we simply repeat the procedure just outlined for a general point X. If $X_1 = X$ and $X_2 = X + \Delta X$, then $Y_1 = Y(X)$ and $Y_2 = Y(X + \Delta X)$. Taking as an example the function $Y = a + bX + cX^2$, the values of Y_1 and Y_2 would be

$$Y_1 = Y(X) = a + bX + cX^2$$
$$Y_2 = Y(X + \Delta X) = a + b(X + \Delta X) + c(X + \Delta X)^2$$

Expanding, we obtain

$$Y_2 = a + bX + b(\Delta X) + cX^2 + 2cX(\Delta X) + c(\Delta X)^2$$

ΔY therefore becomes

$$Y_2 - Y_1 = b(\Delta X) + 2cX(\Delta X) + c(\Delta X)^2$$

and

$$\frac{\Delta Y}{\Delta X} = \frac{b(\Delta X) + 2cX(\Delta X) + c(\Delta X)^2}{\Delta X} = b + 2cX + c(\Delta X)$$

Finally, taking the limit of $\Delta Y/\Delta X$ as ΔX approaches zero, we obtain an expression for the slope of the function at any point. We denote this expression by the symbol dY/dX and call it the *derivative* of the function Y.

$$Y' = \frac{dY}{dX} = \underset{\Delta X \to 0}{\text{Limit}} \{b + 2cX + c\Delta X\} = b + 2cX$$

We will also use the symbol Y', called "Y prime," to indicate the derivative. The two symbols have exactly the same meaning and may be used interchangeably.

RULES FOR TAKING DERIVATIVES

Fortunately, we will not be required to work our way through this rather tedious process for each new function we encounter, for there are some "shortcut" rules that have been developed by those who have gone before us. These rules are available for a wide range of functional forms, but we will require the use of only two rules. (We have limited the scope of our discussion to functions of only one independent variable. For a list of the rules for other functional forms and functions of more than one independent variable, see the list of suggested supplemental readings in "Selected References."

RULE I

If the function has the form $Y = aX^n$, its derivative will be

$$Y' = \frac{dY}{dX} = anX^{n-1}.$$

Examples:

$$Y = 2X^3, \; Y' = 2(3)X^{3-1} = 6X^2$$

$$M = \frac{7}{Q^3} = 7Q^{-3}, \frac{dM}{dQ} = (7)(-3)Q^{-4} = \frac{-21}{Q^4}$$

$$R = 4\sqrt{T} = 4T^{\frac{1}{2}}, \; R' = 4(\tfrac{1}{2})T^{-\frac{1}{2}} = \frac{2}{\sqrt{T}}, \qquad \text{(assuming } T > 0)$$

$$B = \frac{1}{5\sqrt[3]{D^2}} = \tfrac{1}{5}D^{-\frac{2}{3}}, \; B' = \tfrac{1}{5}(-\tfrac{2}{3})D^{-\frac{5}{3}} = \frac{-2}{15\sqrt[3]{D^5}}$$

$$T = 3M = 3M^1, \; T' = 3(1)M^\circ = 3$$

$$W = 10 = 10P^0, \frac{dW}{dP} 10(0)P^{-1} = 0$$

The last two examples are of particular interest because they are examples of two cases often singled out for special treatment. They are: (1) the derivative of aX is a, and (2) the derivative of a constant is zero. We will make no further ado over them, for they both obey the general rule quite nicely. We encourage you to adopt the practice of rewriting the functions in aX^n notation before taking the derivative, at least for the time being. It will reduce algebraic error remarkably.

RULE II

If the function has several terms, the derivative of the function is simply the sum of the derivatives of each term.

$$Y = u(X) + v(X) - w(X)$$

$$Y' = \frac{dY}{dX} = \frac{du}{dX} + \frac{dv}{dX} - \frac{dw}{dX}$$

Examples:

$$N = 2 + 3C, \frac{dN}{dC} = 0 + 3 = 3$$

$$U = 500 - 20T, U' = 0 - 20 = -20$$

$$Y = 3 + 2X + X^2, \frac{dY}{dX} = 0 + 2 + 2X = 2 + 2X$$

$$Y = a + bX + cX^2, Y' = 0 + b + 2cX = b + 2cX$$

$$V = \frac{3}{S^2} + \frac{4}{S} - \frac{1}{3} + 8S - 4S^2 + 2S^3$$

$$= 3S^{-2} + 4S^{-1} - \tfrac{1}{3}S^0 + 8S^1 - 4S^2 + 2S^3$$

$$\frac{dV}{dS} = 3(-2)S^{-3} + 4(-1)S^{-2} - \tfrac{1}{3}(0)S^{-1} + 8(1)S^0$$

$$- 4(2)S^1 + 2(3)S^2 = \frac{-6}{S^3} - \frac{4}{S^2} + 8 - 8S + 6S^2$$

You will recognize the first four functions as four of those we have already examined in this chapter. Note that in each case, the derivative obtained using the rules is the same as the slope or derivative found earlier by other methods.

Second Derivatives

We will find it useful presently to talk about the slope of the derivative function. This slope is determined in the same way we find the slope of any function—by taking the derivative—only in this case, we will be taking the derivative of the derivative. We call this the *second derivative* of the original function and denote it by Y'' or d^2Y/dX^2.

It is really much simpler than it may sound. Consider the following examples.

If

$$Y = 4 + X^3$$

then

$$\frac{dY}{dX} = 3X^2$$

and

$$\frac{d^2Y}{dX^2} = 6X.$$

If

$$L = \tfrac{1}{4}T + 4T^3 - \frac{1}{T^2}$$

then

$$L' = \frac{1}{4} + 12T^2 + \frac{2}{T^3}$$

and

$$L'' = 24T - \frac{6}{T^4}$$

We will examine additional examples later on in this chapter, when we consider second derivative applications.

Maxima and Minima

In discussing maxima and minima, we must first distinguish between several different types of optimum points. In the chapters on linear programming, you learned about *constrained optimization* of linear functions. If there are constraints or *boundaries* on a nonlinear function, we must investigate the boundary conditions as possible maximum or minimum values of the function. This is discussed at the end of this chapter.

In dealing with nonlinear functions, we must also deal with *local optima*, which are the highest or lowest points in their immediate neighborhoods, such as the "hill" at point A and the "valley" at point B in Figure 9.4. We will define the *global optima* to be the highest and lowest points over the entire permissible range of the function. These points are the highest of all local maxima and boundary values and the lowest of all local minima and boundary values.

The primary motive for this study of derivatives and slopes is to prepare you for the task of locating local maximum and minimum points of functions. The process of determining the rate of fuel burn that achieves maximum thrust, or the production rate that minimizes costs, or the output that maximizes profits is called *optimization*. When the optimiza-

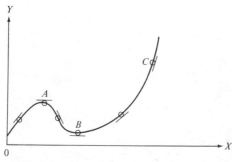

Figure 9.4　Tangents to a function.

tion is achieved using derivatives, the method is called *classical optimization*.

Classical optimization makes use of the fact that, in order for a function to achieve a local maximum or a minimum value, it must change directions, and *at the local maximum or minimum point, the slope of the function must be zero*. In Figure 9.4 we have shown the tangent lines to the function at several points. Note that only at the local maximum and minimum points is the slope of the tangent line (and hence the value of the derivative) equal to zero. This property enables us to use the derivative of a function to locate *critical points* (maxima and minima) of the function.

Consider the function

$$Y = 3 + 8X - X^2$$

and its slope function (first derivative)

$$Y' = 8 - 2X$$

To locate the point where the slope of the function is zero, we set the derivative equal to zero and solve for X. We will use the asterisk (*) to indicate an optimum value.

$$Y' = 8 - 2X = 0$$
$$2X = 8$$
$$X^* = 4$$

This tells us that $dY/dX = 0$ at $X = 4$ and that the critical point of the function occurs at that point. To find the value of Y at its maximum point, we substitute $X = 4$ into the equation for Y and obtain $Y_{MAX} = 19$. The function is shown in Figure 9.5.

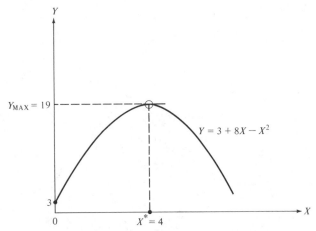

Figure 9.5 Locating the maximum.

Let's consider a second example. Find the critical point of the function

$$R = 27 - 12M + 2M^2$$

Taking the derivative, we obtain

$$\frac{dR}{dM} = -12 + 4M$$

Setting it equal to zero and solving the critical value of M produces

$$R' = -12 + 4M = 0$$
$$4M = 12$$
$$M^* = 3$$

Referring to Figure 9.6, we observe that this time our critical point is a local minimum. Solving for the value of the function, we arrive at

$$R_{MIN} = 27 - 12(3) + 2(3)^2 = 9$$

Note that we have used exactly the same procedure for locating a local maximum in one case and a local minimum in another:

1. Take the first derivative of the function.
2. Set the derivative equal to zero.
3. Solve for the value of the independent variable.

Since these three steps are required of every critical point, they are called the *necessary condition*. As we shall see, there can be other points that

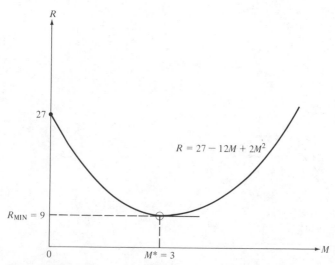

Figure 9.6 Locating the minimum.

also satisfy the necessary condition. We therefore denote all points that meet this condition as *critical points*.

To avoid confusion and to be certain that we have found what we set out to find, we need a procedure for determining whether the critical point we have found is a maximum or a minimum (or neither). This can best be done by referring to Figure 9.7, where we show the relationships that exist between the function and its first and second derivatives.

If we take a point to the left of a maximum point (e.g., $X = 3$), the slope of the function must be positive, and so the value of the slope function Y' will be positive ($Y' = +2$); at a point to the right of the maximum (e.g., $X = 6$), the function will have a negative slope, and Y' will be negative ($Y' = -4$). It is very important to note the *progression* of the slope values from left to right as we cross through the maximum: *positive to zero to negative*. If the slope function (Y') must go from a positive value to zero

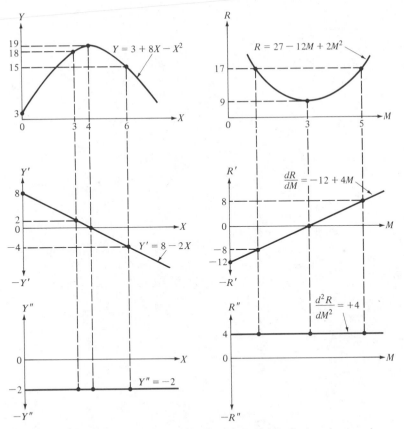

Figure 9.7   Relationship between the function and its first and second derivatives.

Table 9.2 EVALUATION OF CRITICAL POINTS

FUNCTION	EXAMPLE	FIRST DERIVATIVE	CRITICAL POINT	SECOND DERIVATIVE	$Y''(X^*)$	DESCRIPTION
$Y = X^{2n}$	$Y = X^4$	$Y' = 4X^3$	$X^* = 0$	$Y'' = 12X^2$	$Y'' = 0$	Minimum
$Y = -X^{2n}$	$Y = -X^6$	$Y' = -6X^5$	$X^* = 0$	$Y'' = -30X^4$	$Y'' = 0$	Maximum
$Y = X^{2n+1}$	$Y = X^3$	$Y' = 3X^2$	$X^* = 0$	$Y'' = 6X$	$Y'' = 0$	Point of Inflection
$Y = -X^{2n+1}$	$Y = -X^5$	$Y' = 5X^4$	$X^* = 0$	$Y'' = -20X^3$	$Y'' = 0$	Point of Inflection
$Y = \sum a_i X^i$	$Y = 1 + 12X - 6X^2 + X^3$	$Y' = 12 - 12X + 3X^2$	$X^* = 2$	$Y'' = -12 + 6X$	$Y'' = 0$	Point of Inflection

to a negative value for the original function (Y) to pass through a maximum, then the *slope* of Y', which we call Y'', must be *negative* at the point where Y' equals zero, because the value of Y' is continually decreasing.

Now consider the situation that must occur in order that we have a minimum point. At a point to the left of the minimum of $R(M = 1)$, the slope of R is negative; therefore R' is negative ($R' = -8$). At the minimum point ($M = 3$), the slope of R is zero, and $R' = 0$. At a point to the right of the minimum ($M = 5$), the slope of R must be positive, so R' is positive ($R' = +8$). Again, observe the progression of slopes required for a minimum: *negative to zero to positive*. For R' to achieve the progression, its slope must be *positive*; so the value of its derivative (R'') must also be positive ($R'' = +4$).

We can now summarize these rules:

1. At a *maximum*, the second derivative is *negative*.
2. At a *minimum*, the second derivative is *positive*.
3. If the second derivative is *zero*, the test *fails*.

Because (1) and (2) guarantee that the critical points that satisfy them are maxima and minima, respectively, they are called the *sufficient conditions* for maxima and minima.

Critical points that fall under (3) can be either maxima, minima, or *neither*. Those that are neither are *points of inflection*. An inflection point is a place where the curvature of the function reverses from a "dish" to a "dome," or vice versa. As the point is approached from one side it looks like a maximum, but from the other direction it appears to be a minimum. Examples of these types of functions are shown in Table 9.2 and Figure 9.8.

For another example, let us analyze the following functions

$$D = 5 - 3V + 2V^2 - \tfrac{1}{3}V^3$$
$$D' = -3 + 4V - V^2$$
$$D'' = +4 - 2V$$

which are shown in Figure 9.9. We know that the critical point(s) will be found where $D' = 0$. D' is a *quadratic function* of the form $aV^2 + bV + c = 0$; so we can use the quadratic formula (discussed in Chapter 2) to determine the values of V for which $D' = 0$.

$$V^* = \frac{-b \pm \sqrt{b^2 - 4ac}}{2a} = \frac{-4 \pm \sqrt{16 - 4(-1)(-3)}}{2(-1)} = \frac{-4 \pm \sqrt{4}}{-2}$$

$$= \frac{-2}{-2}, \frac{-6}{-2} = 1, 3$$

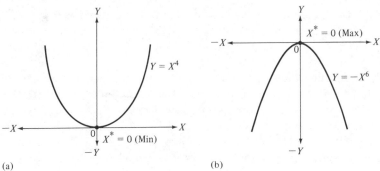

Figure 9.8   Special cases with $Y'' = 0$.

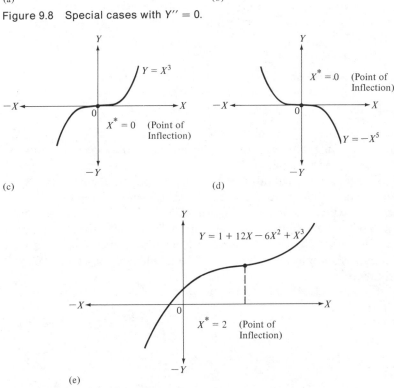

Figure 9.8   Special cases with $Y'' = 0$.

At $V = 1$, $D'' = +2$; so D achieves a minimum at $V = 1$. At $V = 3$, $D'' = -2$; so D is a maximum at this point.

Note that the slope of the function D goes from negative to zero to positive as we move through the minimum and from positive to zero to negative as we move through the maximum. Notice also that at $V = 2$, the second derivative is zero, indicating a point of inflection in the function D. This is the point at which the nature of the curve changes from a

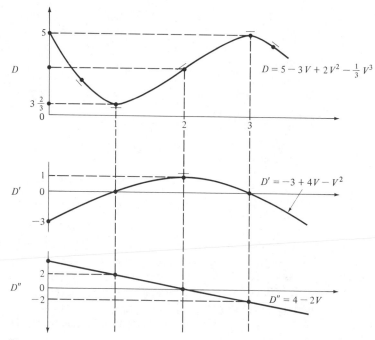

Figure 9.9 A function that has both a maximum and a minimum.

"dish" (convex to the horizontal axis) to a "dome" (concave to the horizontal axis). We also note that it is not necessary for the curve (D) to have a slope of zero at a point of inflection, but merely that D'' be zero. We will ignore points of inflection and focus our attention on the maxima and minima.

Global Optima

The extreme points we have identified thus far all have been *local* optimum points; that is, they have been the highest or lowest points in their particular region of the curve. As we investigate functions with higher powers of the independent variable, we may find more than one local maximum and more than one local minimum. The total number of extreme points cannot exceed $N - 1$, where N is the highest power to which the independent variable is raised.

For example, the function

$$M = a + bR - cR^2 + dR^3 - eR^4 + fR^5$$

can have a maximum of four extreme points, because the highest power of R is 5. Such a function might be similar to the one in Figure 9.10. This

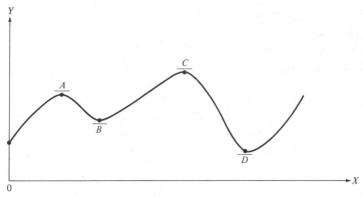

Figure 9.10 A function with several local optima.

function has local maximum values at A and C and local minima at B and D. The highest point of all is called the *global maximum*, and the lowest is the *global minimum*. In this example, points C and D are the global optima of the function over the range shown. If several local extremes are located, it is normally required that the value of the function at each of the points be calculated in order to determine the global maximum or minimum.

Constrained Optimization

Frequently, we are interested in the behavior of a function only over a limited range rather than over the entire spectrum from $-\infty$ to $+\infty$. When this is the case, we find it useful to apply constraints to the problem. For example, we may wish to determine the maximum and minimum values of the function

$$Z = 9 + 63S - 15S^2 + S^3$$

between the values $S = 0$ and $S = 10$. The function has been graphed in Figure 9.11. Using calculus, we find the first derivative to be

$$Z' = 63 - 30S + 3S^2$$

Applying the quadratic equation yields the critical points

$$S^* = \frac{-(-30) \pm \sqrt{900 - 4(3)(63)}}{2(3)}, \frac{30 \pm \sqrt{144}}{6} = \frac{18}{6}, \frac{42}{6} = 3, 7$$

which satisfy the necessary condition (that the first derivative be zero). The second derivative is

$$Z'' = -30 + 6S$$

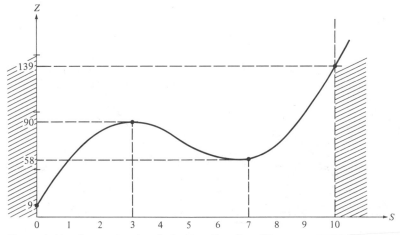

Figure 9.11   Constrained optimization ($0 \leq S \leq 10$).

Applying the sufficiency condition (that the second derivative be negative for a maximum and positive for a minimum), we find the function has a local maximum at $S = 3$ $[Z''(3) = -12]$ and a local minimum at $S = 7$ $[Z''(7) = +12]$.

However, if we seek the highest point attained by Z over the range from $S = 0$ to $S = 10$, we must identify the point $S = 10$, where $Z = 139$. Similarly, the global minimum occurs not at $S = 7$, where $Z = 58$, but at $S = 0$, where $Z = 9$.

Without belaboring the point any further, we will state that *if a function is bounded or constrained to a certain feasible region, the global optima will occur at either the local extreme points or at the boundaries.* Thus, if we wish to find the lowest point on Z between $S = 4$ and $S = 10$ (Fig. 9.12), we must find the smallest of the local minimum $[Z(7) = 58]$ and the two boundaries $[Z(4) = 85$ and $Z(10) = 139]$. Over this region, the local minimum is the global minimum. To find the global maximum over the same region, we need only examine the two boundaries, because no local maximum occurs within the region. The global maximum is the larger of $Z(4) = 85$ and $Z(10) = 139$.

Since it is not necessary to have a local optimum in order to locate a global optimum in a constrained problem, we can talk about finding the maximum or minimum of a linear function, as long as it is bounded. Figure 9.13 shows some examples of bounded linear functions and their maxima and minima. In each case the area to be searched, or the *feasible region*, is in white, whereas the *area outside the constraint*, or the infeasible region, has been cross-hatched. The maxima are $Q_{MAX} = 17$ at $C = 5$, $W_{MAX} = 15$ at $T = 0$, and $H_{MAX} = 61$ at $P = 7$; the minima are $Q_{MIN} = 8$ at $C = 2$, $W_{MIN} = 7$ at $T = 8$, and $H_{MIN} = 6$ at $P = 12$.

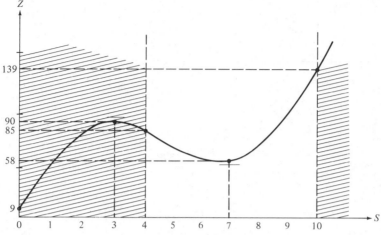

Figure 9.12 Constrained optimization ($4 \leq S \leq 10$).

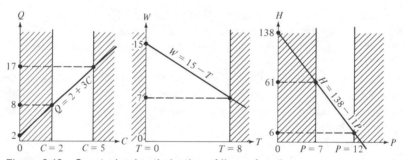

Figure 9.13 Constrained optimization of linear functions.

APPLICATIONS OF MAXIMA AND MINIMA

The purpose of this chapter has been to review the theory and principles of classical optimization. The next two chapters will build on your knowledge of optimum points. Chapter 10 discusses some topics from microeconomics—the cost, volume, profit analysis—and Chapter 11 analyzes inventory and production models and the calculation of the economic order quantity (EOQ). Both chapters are applications aimed at utilizing and extending your newfound capabilities in classical optimization.

SUMMARY OF KEY CONCEPTS

Function. A mathematical expression of the relationship that exists between two or more unknowns or variables.

Linear function. A function in which the independent variable is raised to the power zero or one. The function graphs as a straight line.

Nonlinear function. A function in which the independent variable is raised to a power other than zero or one. The graph of the function will be curved rather than a straight line.

Independent variable. The unknown for which we are free to assume values. It is typically written on the right-hand side of the equation $Y = f(X)$ (e.g., $Y = 12 + 3X - X^2$). X is the independent variable.

Dependent variable. The unknown whose value depends upon the specific value we select for the independent variable. It is typically found on the left-hand side of the equation $Y = f(X)$.

Intercept. The value of one variable when the other variable has a value of zero. The location(s) of the point(s) where the function crosses (intercepts) the X or Y axis. Unless otherwise noted, it usually refers to the Y intercept, or the value of the dependent variable when the independent variable equals zero. This will always be the same as the value of the constant term in the equation (e.g., the intercept of $Y = a + bX^2$ is a).

Slope. The rate of change in the dependent variable (Y) for a unit change in the independent variable (X). The slope of a linear function is $\Delta Y / \Delta X$. The slope of a nonlinear function is taken to be the tangent to the curve at any point and is expressed by

$$\text{Slope} = Y' = \frac{dY}{dX} = \operatorname*{Limit}_{\Delta x \to 0} \left\{ \frac{Y(X + \Delta X) - Y(X)}{\Delta X} \right\}$$

Tangent. A straight line that touches a nonlinear function at only one point, not cutting through the curve at the point. The slope of the tangent line is used as a measure of the slope of the curve at that point.

Derivative. A function that expresses the slope of another function at every point.

Rules for differentiation. (1) If $Y = aX^n$, $dY/dX = Y' = anX^{n-1}$. (2) If $Y = U(X) \pm V(X)$, $dY/dX = Y' = dU/dX \pm dV/dX$.

Second derivative. The derivative of the first derivative. If $Y' = \dfrac{d}{dX}(Y)$,

$$Y'' = \frac{d^2 Y}{dX^2} = \frac{d}{dX}(Y')$$

Local maximum. A point on a curve that is higher than the points on both sides of itself. A point where $Y' = 0$ and $Y'' < 0$.

Local minimum. A point on a curve that is lower than the points on each side of itself. A point where $Y' = 0$ and $Y'' > 0$.

Point of inflection. A point on a curve at which the direction of curvature changes ($Y'' = 0$; Y' may or may not be 0).

Classical optimization. Locating the maximum and/or minimum value(s) of a function through the application of differential calculus.

Necessary condition. The first derivative of the function is equal to zero, and the slope of the function is zero.

Critical point. Any point that satisfies the necessary condition. These points may be maxima, minima, or points of inflection.

Sufficient condition. For a maximum, a critical point at which the value of the second derivative is negative ($Y'' < 0$); for a minimum, a critical point at which the value of the second derivative is positive ($Y'' > 0$).

Root(s) of a function. Any point(s) at which the value of the function is zero. The X intercept(s) of a function. The point(s) at which the function crosses the X axis.

Quadratic function. A function of second order, having the form $Y = aX^2 + bX + c$.

Quadratic equation. A method of determining the roots of a quadratic function. If $Y = aX^2 + bX + c$, $Y = 0$ at

$$X^* = \frac{-b \pm \sqrt{b^2 - 4ac}}{2a}$$

Constrainted maximum. The highest point on a curve within a given region of the independent variable.

Constrainted minimum. The lowest point on a curve within a given region of the independent variable.

Boundary values. The values of a function at the ends (boundaries) of the feasible region.

Global optimum. The highest or lowest point of a curve, taking into account both local optima and boundary values.

PROBLEMS

1. Find the first derivatives of the following functions.

a. $T = 5 + 11S$

b. $B = 6 - 4M + 5M^2$

c. $F = \sqrt{R} + 6$

d. $D = \dfrac{2}{3L} - 9\sqrt{L^3} + \dfrac{6L}{5} - 8$

e. $V = 44 + 6S + 13S^2 - .80S^3$

f. $Q = \dfrac{12}{\sqrt{N}} + 3N + 5\sqrt{2N}$

g. $C = \dfrac{7}{P} + 4P^2 - P^3 + 6$

2. Compute the value of the second derivative of each of these functions at the point where the independent variable has a value of $+2$.

a. $R = 6 + 2T + 3T^2$

b. $U = 14 - 5Y + \dfrac{4}{Y} + Y^2$

c. $A = \sqrt{3E} + \dfrac{1}{\sqrt{3E}}$

d. $Z = 4\sqrt{J^3} - 11J^2$

e. $W = 2 + 9G + 7G^3$

3. Locate the local maxima and/or minima of each of the following functions. State whether each is a max or a min.

a. $Y = 3 + 12X - 2X^2$

b. $S = 4 - 7T + 3T^2$

c. $M = \dfrac{8}{P} + 2P + 8$

d. $E = 18L - 2L^3 - 7$

e. $W = 23 - 9D + 5D^2 - \frac{1}{3}D^3$

$R = 17 + 8V - 5V^2 + V^3$

4. State the Kuhn-Tucker conditions for local optima (for functions of one independent variable).

5. Determine the highest *and* lowest points on each of the following functions over the ranges indicated. (Be sure to check the boundaries.) Sketch the curves.

a. $Y = 5 - 8X + X^2, 0 \le X \le 5$

b. $W = \dfrac{8}{C} + 2C, 1 \le C \le 10$

c. $Q = 6 + T^2, -3 \le T \le +2$

d. $Z = 2 + 12B - B^3, 0 \le B \le 3$

e. $P = -8 + 10Q - Q^2, 0 \le Q \le 10$

6. A 10-meter-long manifold in a heat venting system is subjected to temperatures that vary (approximately) according to the equation

$$T = 30X + X^2 - \tfrac{1}{3}X^3 + 500$$

where T is temperature in °F and X is distance (in meters) from the left-hand end of the manifold. What is the highest temperature achieved and where is it located?

7. Find the compression ratio (C) that *minimizes* the fuel consumption rate (R) in an experimental engine if the relationship between C and R can be expressed as $R = 40 - 12C + C^2$.

8. If income (I) varies with labor hours (H) according to the expression $I = 5H - \frac{1}{4}H^2$, and expenses (E) vary according to the expression $E = 2 + 3H$, (where H, I, and E are all in hundreds), between what two values of H will income exceed expenses? (Hint: Find the values of H for which $E = I$.) At what value of labor hours does income exceed expenses by the largest margin? (Hint: Maximize the expression for $I - E$.)

9. If profit (P) can be estimated as a function of quantity produced (Q) by $P = -4 + 6Q - Q^2$, what level of output produces the maximum profit? What is the value of profit at this output?

10. If government revenue (R) is related to the effective tax rate (T) by the expression $R = T/2 - T^2$, at what effective tax rate does the government generate its maximum revenue?

Chapter 10

ECONOMIC ANALYSIS OF THE FIRM

INTRODUCTION

This chapter focuses on analysis of the firm as an example of the classical optimization procedures you learned in Chapter 9. We will investigate the relationships that exist among the *revenue*, *cost*, *output*, *price*, and *profit* of a firm. This analysis will provide a framework within which managers can evaluate the courses of action open to them and a method of determining the likely impact of pricing and volume decisions on the future profitability of their firms.

A SIMPLE LINEAR MODEL OF THE FIRM

Let us begin by formulating a simple model of the firm, within which we can define the terms we will need in order to move on to more complicated models. In its simplest form, the total costs of doing business can be thought of as being broken down into two primary components.

1. *Fixed costs.* Those that do not vary directly with output (such as rent, insurance, utilities, and many administrative costs).

2. *Variable costs.* Those that are directly related to the level of output (or sales) and that vary with changes in volume (such as labor, materials, shipping costs, and sales commissions).

In practice, some costs may be considered as having both a fixed component (the salaries of the president and his or her secretary, for example) and a variable component (the president's bonus, which depends on profit, and the wages of temporary office workers who may be required during periods of high work load). For our simple model, we will assume that we can distinguish these and represent the complex real situation reasonably well by our two categories of fixed and variable costs. Graphically, these can be represented as shown in Figure 10.1(a). Mathematically, they can be expressed as follows.

$$\text{Total Cost} = \text{Fixed Cost} + \text{Variable Cost}$$

or

$$TC = f + vQ$$

where Q is the quantity, or number of units of output or sales; f is the dollar amount fixed cost; and v is the dollar amount of variable cost *per unit* of output or sales.

The *revenue*, or income to the firm, usually has only a variable component. This is the price received by the firm for each unit sold. The total revenue function for our model is shown in Figure 10.1(b), and can be expressed as

$$TR = pQ$$

where p is the price of 1 unit of the product and Q is the number of units sold.

If we combine the total cost and the total revenue functions, as has been done in Figure 10.1(c), we can identify a *profit region* and a *loss region*, separated by a *break-even point* (Q_B). The break-even point is the quantity at which the total revenue equals the total cost. At outputs below this level, cost exceeds revenue, and a loss is sustained; at outputs greater than the break-even quantity, revenue exceeds cost, and a profit is earned.

If "profit" is defined as total revenue less total cost, we can express the level of profit as a function of sales, as has been done in Figure 10.1(d). Mathematically, it is expressed as

$$\text{Profit} = \text{Total Revenue} - \text{Total Cost}$$
$$P = pQ - (f + vQ)$$
$$= -f + (p - v)Q$$

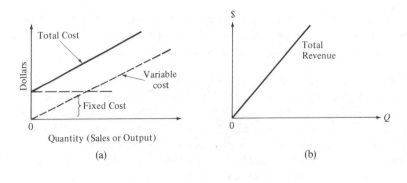

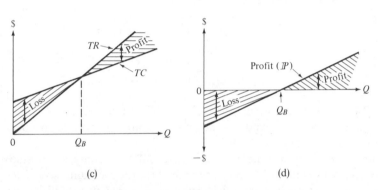

Figure 10.1 (a) Fixed, variable, and total cost; (b) Total revenue; (c) Break-even point; (d) Profit function.

where $\mathbb{P}$ is the profit (we would have used P, but we have already used p for price, and we do not want any more confusion over symbols than is absolutely necessary) and $f, p, v,$ and Q are fixed cost, price, variable cost per unit, and quantity, respectively.

The profit at zero output is $-f$ because no variable cost is incurred and no revenue is generated. The slope of the profit function is $(p - v)$, the difference between sales price and variable cost. The accountants refer to this difference as the "*contribution* to overhead and profit." At the break-even point, we have sold just enough units so that the difference between revenue and variable cost exactly equals the fixed cost. At volumes below Q_B, the excess of revenue over variable cost contributes toward paying the fixed costs; at volumes above Q_B, the difference becomes profit.

Let us use our model to analyze an example.

Example

An enterprising business administration major named Morris is attempting to decide whether he should go into business producing and selling a highly effective battery-operated fishing lure he has developed which emits fishy sounds and flashes off and on and which he calls the Superfly. He has located a building that would be suitable for producing the lure, and the he estimates that the rent on the facility plus his utilities and telephone expenses would be approximately $2000 per month ($f = 2000). His materials cost approximately $2 per unit. He can hire students at $4 per hour who can turn out 4 units per hour; so his variable costs are $3 per unit ($v = 3). A survey of local hardware and sporting goods stores reveals that he can wholesale the Superfly at $4 each ($p = 4). He wishes to determine how many units per month he would have to produce and sell in order to break even.

Figure 10.2(a) shows his cost and revenue functions. His break-even point occurs where total cost and total revenue are equal.

$$TC = 2000 + 3Q$$
$$TR = 4Q$$
$$TR = TC$$
$$4Q = 2000 + 3Q$$
$$Q_B = 2000 \text{ units}$$

His profit function is shown in Figure 10.2(b). Note that his contribution to overhead and profit is $p - v = 1 per unit. To locate Q_B, we set $= 0$ and solve for Q.

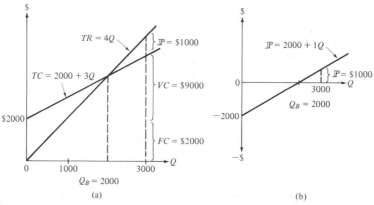

Figure 10.2 (a) Cost and Revenue for Superfly; (b) Profits for Superfly.

$$P = TR - TC = 4Q - (2000 + 3Q) = -2000 + (4 - 3)Q$$
$$= 0 = -2000 + Q$$
$$Q_B = 2000$$

Thus, Morris would have to produce and sell 2000 Superflys per month to break even. This means he would have to hire 500 student hours (2000 units ÷ 4 units per hour = 500 worker hours) per month, or just over 3 workers (500 hours ÷ 160 hours per month = $3\frac{1}{8}$ workers) to break even. If he wishes to make a profit of $1000 per month, he must produce and sell an additional 1000 units per month for a total of 3000 Superflys per months and hire almost 5 full-time workers [(3000 ÷ 4) ÷ (160) = $4\frac{5}{8}$].

Sensitivity Analysis

One of the most important lessons a would-be builder of quantitative decison-making models can learn is the necessity of testing his or her solution to determine the sensitivity of the result to possible variations in the assumptions implicit in the model. Variations are of two types—changes in the underlying assumptions and changes in the values of the parameters of the model.

Generalities about the first type are difficult because the assumptions are often unique to the particular situation being analyzed and to the scope of the current investigation. However, the impact of parameter variations on the solution is a straightforward matter, and this sort of analysis should be undertaken whenever there is uncertainty about the appropriate values for the parameters of the model.

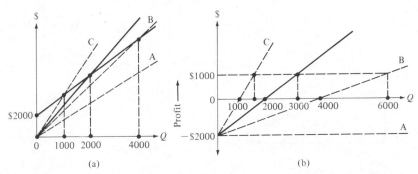

Figure 10.3   (a) Break-even point sensitivity to price; (b) Profit sensitivity to price.

The general approach is to vary each of the parameters over its relevant range and resolve the model for the optimal decision. The changes in the effectiveness measure and the decision variable (profit and output, in our example) for given changes in the input parameters are called their *sensitivities*.

For example, what would be the changes in break-even output and potential profit if Morris were to find that he could sell the Superflys for $3 or $3.50 or $5, instead of $4? Figures 10.3(a) and 10.3(b) show the results graphically. At $p = \$3$, the contribution to overhead and profit is ($p - v = 3 - 3 = 0$), and the total revenue function parallels the total cost function; so profits are never made at any volume (case A). At $p = \$3.50$, the contribution is $0.50, and the break-even output is found to be

$$P = -2000 + .50Q = 0$$
$$Q_B = 4000$$

This is shown as case B in Figures 10.3(a) and (b). The output required to reach a monthly profit of $1000 is 6000 units.

$$P = -2000 + .50Q = 1000$$
$$Q = 6000$$

At $p = \$5$ (case C), the contribution is $2 for each unit sold, and the Q_B is

$$P = -2000 + 2Q = 0$$
$$Q_B = 1000$$

The $1000 profit output is reduced to

$$P = -2000 + 2Q = 1000$$
$$Q = 1500$$

A similar analysis can be made for possible variations in the values of fixed cost (f) and variable cost per unit (v). An example of each is shown in Figures 10.4(a) and 10.4(b).

In case D, Morris has found an alternate location in which to produce the Superflys at a monthly fixed cost of $1000. This causes his Q_B to drop from 2000 to 1000 units, and his $1000 per month profit output to drop from 3000 to 2000 units.

Case E demonstrates the effects of an increase in the variable cost per unit (v) from $3 to $3.50. His Q_B increases to

$$P = -2000 + .50Q = 0$$
$$Q_B = 4000$$

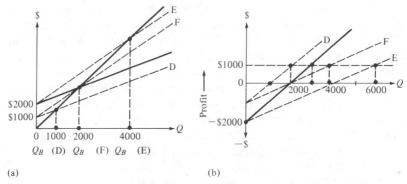

(a)   (b)

Figure 10.4   (a) Breakeven point sensitivity to cost; (b) Profit sensitivity to cost.

and his $1000 profit output increases to

$$\mathbb{P} = -2000 + .5Q = 1000$$
$$Q = 6000 \text{ units}$$

Note that increasing v by $0.50 has exactly the same effects as reducing p by $0.50 because in each case the contribution (the slope of the profit function) is reduced from $1 to $0.50.

In case F, both of the changes (D and E) have taken place: f has become $1000 and v, $3.50. This results in the original break-even point

$$\mathbb{P} = -1000 + .50Q = 0$$
$$Q_{\text{B}} = 2000$$

but a higher output is required for $1000 profit

$$\mathbb{P} = -1000 + .50Q = 1000$$
$$Q = 4000$$

Obviously, an entire spectrum of combinations of changes in the parameters of the model is possible, and those that are relevant should be analyzed. One of the major advantages of quantitative modeling is that it enables the decision maker to perform this sort of "What if . . .?" analysis *prior* to making decisions and to evaluate the impact of the various contingencies without the adverse effects resulting from poor decisions.

For example, what would have been the effect on profit of each of the six possibilities we have just suggested if Morris had gone ahead as the original model suggested and produced 3000 units? The results are shown in Table 10.1. His monthly profits could range from a $2000 per month loss to a $4000 per month gain.

Table 10.1 PROFITS UNDER THE ORIGINAL DECISION

Case	Original	A	B	C	D	E	F
Monthly Profit	$1000	−$2000	−$500	+$4000	+$2000	−$500	+$500

ECONOMIC APPLICATIONS OF CLASSICAL OPTIMIZATION

One of the key assumptions underlying our simple model was that the firm could sell as many units as it wished at $4 per unit. Economists tell us that in practice this is usually not the case. Generally, the higher the price, the fewer units will be sold; conversely, the more we wish to sell, the lower must be our price. They call the function relating the price charged to the number of units sold a *demand function*.

For our model, let us assume that the relationship between price and quantity can be represented by the demand function of Figure 10.5. We note that at Morris' break-even quantity (2000), the price he must charge to clear the market is $5. But if he wishes to sell 3000 units, he can charge only $4 per unit, the value we assumed initially.

If our objective is to maximize the monthly profits, we must incorporate this demand function into our model. This can be accomplished by reformulating our total revenue curve, substituting $P = 7 - .001Q$ for the function $P = \$4$, which we used before.

$$TR = PQ = (7 - .001Q)Q = 7Q - .001Q^2$$

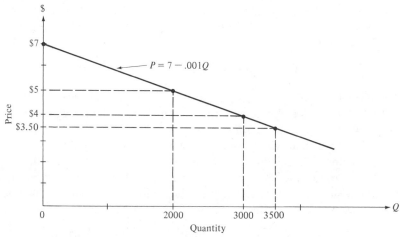

Figure 10.5 Demand curve for Superfly.

Looking at the problem in a slightly different way, another name for the demand curve is the *average revenue* function, because it expresses the average revenue received (the price) for a given volume of sales. To arrive at an expression for the total revenue function, we simply multiply the average revenue (price) by the number of units sold (quantity) and arrive at the same expression we developed previously.

$$TR = AR \times Q = (7 - .001Q)Q = 7Q - .001Q^2$$

Morris may wish to know how many Superflys to sell in order to achieve maximum total revenue. As we learned in Chapter 9, this is readily accomplished by locating the point at which the slope of the *TR* curve is zero. We call the slope of the total revenue function the *marginal revenue* (*MR*). It represents the additional revenue that will be realized from the sale of an additional unit. Morris would continue to increase sales as long as the next unit sold adds to total revenue (until *MR* equals zero). Mathematically, we can accomplish this by setting *MR* (or *TR'*) equal to zero and solving for *Q*.

$$TR = 7Q - .001Q^2$$
$$TR' = 7 - .002Q = 0$$
$$Q^* = 3500 \text{ units}$$

Checking the second derivative to assure that the point we have found is indeed a maximum, we find that

$$TR'' = -.002$$

As the second derivative is less than zero at $Q^* = 3500$, we know the point is a maximum. The value of the total revenue is determined by evaluating the *TR* function at $Q = 3500$.

$$TR(3500) = 7(3500) - .001(3500)^2 = \$12,250$$

These values are illustrated in Figure 10.6. The price to charge in order to sell 3500 units is found by substituting 3500 into the price (average revenue, demand) function (Fig. 10.5) $P = 7 - .001(3500) = \$3.50$.

Before we send Morris out to set up shop, planning to make 3500 units per month, let us consider the costs as well as the revenues. Although producing and selling 3500 units per month generates the greatest revenue, he may wish to go a step further and determine the output at which he maximizes profit. Rewriting his profit function, we obtain

$$P = TR - TC = (7Q - .001A^2) - (2000 + 3Q)$$
$$= -2000 + 4Q - .001Q^2$$

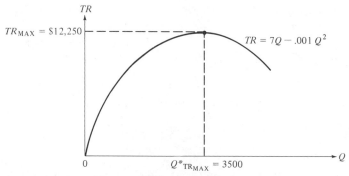

Figure 10.6   Maximizing total revenue.

To optimize, we take the first derivative, set it equal to zero, and solve for the optimum quantity. Just as we defined marginal revenue to be the first derivative of the total revenue function, we can refer to the first derivative of the total cost function as the *marginal cost* (MC), which represents the added cost of producing one more unit.

Since profit is the difference of two terms ($\mathbb{P} = TR - TC$), the first derivative of the profit function will be the difference of the first derivatives of these functions ($\mathbb{P}' = TR' - TC'$), and profit is maximized where $\mathbb{P}' = TR' - TC' = 0$, or where $MR = MC$. Thus it is always true that profit is maximized where marginal revenue equals marginal cost.

$$\mathbb{P}' = 4 - .002Q = 0$$
$$Q^*_{\pi_{MAX}} = 2000 \text{ units}$$

As the second derivative is negative ($TR'' = -.002$), we know this is a maximum point.

The amount of profit to be generated at the profit-maximizing output is

$$\mathbb{P}_{MAX} = \mathbb{P}(2000) = -2000 + 4(2000) - .001(2000)^2$$
$$= -2000 + 8000 - 4000 = \$2000 \text{ per month}$$

whereas the profit to be made at 3000 units per month is only

$$\mathbb{P}(3000) = -2000 + 4(3000) - .001(3000)^2 = \$1000 \text{ per month}$$

and the profit at 3500 units of output is

$$\mathbb{P}(3500) = -2000 + 4(3500) - .001(3500)^2 = -\$250$$

or a \$250 loss each month. These values are shown in Figures 10.7(a) and 10.7(b).

The break-even points are located where $TR = TC$ [Fig. 10.7(a)] or $\mathbb{P} = 0$ [Fig. 10.7(b)]. Using the quadratic formula from Chapter 2, we obtain

$$\mathbb{P} = -2000 + 4Q - .001Q^2 = 0$$

$$Q_B = \frac{-4 \pm \sqrt{(4)^2 - 4(-.001)(-2000)}}{2(-.001)} = \frac{-4 \pm \sqrt{8}}{-.002} = 585; 3414$$

Thus any output between 585 and 3414 will generate some profit. The optimum point is at 2000 units ($\mathbb{P}_{MAX} = \$2000$ per month), and Morris' earlier strategy of 3000 per month yields a profit of only \$1000 per month.

In addition to varying the selling price with the output, we might also find it useful to let variable cost be expressed as a nonlinear function of quantity. For example, if materials or labor were in short supply, Morris' variable cost per unit might increase as more units were produced (because of reduced productivity of overworked workers or shortages requiring higher labor rates or more expensive alternate sources for raw materials). Perhaps his variable costs per unit would be expressed by

$$v = 2 + .002Q$$

His total cost function then would become

$$TC = f + vQ = 2000 + (2 + .002Q)Q$$
$$= 2000 + 2Q + .002Q^2$$

To determine the output at which he minimizes the average cost per unit produced, he would find the expression for average cost (total cost

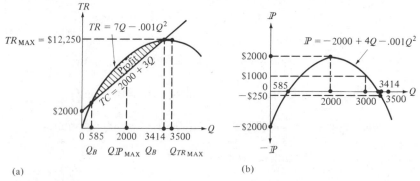

Figure 10.7   (a) Total revenue and total cost; (b) Profit.

divided by quantity produced)

$$AC = TC \div Q = \frac{2000}{Q} + 2 + .002Q$$

and optimize

$$AC' = \frac{-2000}{Q^2} + .002 = 0$$

$$Q^*_{AC_{MIN}} = 1000 \text{ units per month}$$

This point is shown in Figure 10.8(a). As $AC''(1000) = 2000/(1000)^3$ is positive, we know this is a minimum point. But Morris' profit is a function of how much each unit sells for as well as its cost. To determine his profit-maximizing output, we generate the profit function

$$\mathbb{P} = TR - TC = (7Q - .001Q^2) - (2000 + 2Q + .002Q^2)$$
$$= -2000 + 5Q - .003Q^2$$

and optimize

$$\mathbb{P}' = 5 - .006Q = 0$$
$$Q^*_{\pi_{MAX}} = 833 \text{ units per month}$$

The profit maximization is shown in Figure 10.8(b). The amount of the maximum profit is \$83.33, and the break-even points are at $Q = 667$ and $Q = 1000$.

Thus we see that Morris' optimum output will vary in response to changes in the parameters of the model as well as to changes in the objective he seeks to optimize.

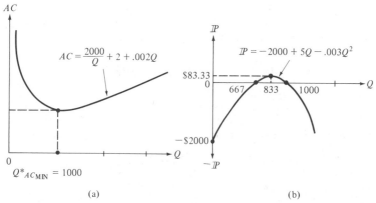

(a) (b)

Figure 10.8 (a) Minimizing average cost; (b) Maximum profit and break-even points.

Example

Let us analyze the various options available to a firm facing the following demand and total cost functions.

$$AR = 8 - \tfrac{1}{6}Q^2 \qquad TC = 4 + 2Q + \tfrac{1}{9}Q^2$$

Their revenue-maximizing output is

$$TR = AR \times Q = 8Q - \tfrac{1}{6}Q^3$$
$$TR' = 8 - \tfrac{1}{2}Q^2 = 0$$
$$Q^2 = 16$$
$$Q^*_{TR_{MAX}} = 4$$
$$TR_{MAX} = 8(4) - \tfrac{1}{6}(4)^3 = \$21.33$$
$$TR'' = -\tfrac{2}{2}(4) = -4,$$

so the point is a maximum.

$$\mathbb{P}_{TR_{MAX}} = \$7.55$$
$$P_{TR_{MAX}} = \$5.33$$

Their average-cost–minimizing point is

$$AC = \frac{TC}{Q} = \frac{4}{Q} + 2 + \frac{1}{9}Q$$

$$AC' = \frac{-4}{Q^2} + \frac{1}{9} = 0$$

$$Q^2 = 36$$
$$Q^*_{AC_{MIN}} = 6$$

$$AC'' = \frac{8}{(6)^3} = +.037 \qquad \text{(Min)}$$

$$AC_{MIN} = \tfrac{4}{6} + 2 + \tfrac{1}{9}(6) = \$3.33$$
$$\mathbb{P}_{AC_{MIN}} = -\$8.00$$
$$P_{AC_{MIN}} = \$2.00$$

The profit-maximizing output is

$$\mathbb{P} = TR - TC = [8Q - \tfrac{1}{6}Q^3] - [4 + 2Q + \tfrac{1}{9}Q^2]$$
$$= -4 + 6Q - \tfrac{1}{9}Q^2 - \tfrac{1}{6}Q^3$$
$$\mathbb{P}' = 6 - \tfrac{2}{9}Q - \tfrac{1}{2}Q^2 = 0$$

$$Q^*_{\mathbb{P}_{MAX}} = \frac{-(-\tfrac{2}{9}) \pm \sqrt{(-\tfrac{2}{9})^2 - 4(-\tfrac{1}{2})(6)}}{2(-\tfrac{1}{2})} = \frac{\tfrac{2}{9} \pm \sqrt{12\tfrac{4}{81}}}{-1} = -3.69, +3.25$$

Checking out the second derivative at each of these points, we obtain

$$P'' = -\tfrac{2}{9} - Q$$
$$P'' @ (-3.69) = -\tfrac{2}{9} - (-3.69) = +3.47 \text{ (Min)}$$
$$P'' @ (+3.25) = -\tfrac{2}{9} - (+3.25) = -3.47 \text{ (Max)}$$

Because a negative output ($Q = -3.69$) is impossible, this point is of only academic interest. The other point ($Q = +3.25$) does prove to be a maximum, with

$$P_{MAX} = -4 + 6(3.25) - \tfrac{1}{9}(3.25)^2 - \tfrac{1}{6}(3.25)^3 = \$8.61$$

The price they should charge to achieve maximum profit is

$$P = AR = 8 - \tfrac{1}{6}(3.25)^2 = \$6.24$$

The total revenue will be

$$TR = 8(3.25) - \tfrac{1}{6}(3.25)^3 = \$20.28$$

To check this, multiply price by quantity

$$TR = AR \times Q = (6.24)(3.25) = \$20.28$$

Average cost is

$$AC = \frac{4}{3.25} + 2 + \frac{1}{9}(3.25) = \$3.59$$

Total Cost is

$$TC = 4 + 2(3.25) + \tfrac{1}{9}(3.25)^2 = \$11.67$$

checking, we obtain

$$TC = AC \times Q = (3.59)(3.25) = \$11.67$$

As a final check, test to see that total revenue less total cost equals profit.

$$P = TR - TC = 20.28 - 11.67 = \$8.61$$

We end up with the same value we determined previously. The revenue, cost, and profit curves are shown in Figure 10.9.

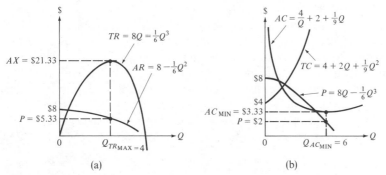

Figure 10.9   (a) Revenue maximization; (b) Average cost minimization.

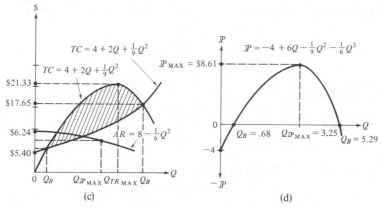

Figure 10.9 (c) Cost, revenue, and price; (d) Profit maximization.

WHERE DO THE EQUATIONS COME FROM?

The analyses we have performed in this chapter have been based on demand and cost functions that were "given" to us. The obvious question this raises for most students is: "Where do the equations come from?"

As theorists, this problem does not concern us because our purpose is simply to develop logical analytical frameworks, leaving the "trivial" task of obtaining the exact equations to the practitioner in the real world. As practicing consultants and professional analysts, however, we recognize that this question is crucial to successful application of the theoretical models to real problems.

The functions used in the analysis can come from several sources. Sometimes they are merely educated guesses by someone with experience in the business involved. When more rigor is desired, the accounting system can usually provide very good estimates of the fixed and variable costs required to specify the cost functions.

The demand functions are more difficult to approximate because they depend on the responses of many different customers to changes in the price of a product and can be influenced by changes in advertising, sales location, competitors' prices and promotions, and the whims of the consumer. A good market research department or outside consultant can generate data on quantities sold at different price levels in test markets, and statistical analysis of these data by linear or nonlinear regression will develop one or more demand functions having relatively good fit to the data.

As always, it is important that we have a good idea of how well the equations describe the real problem, because the most exacting analysis of incorrect data leads to meaningless results.

CONCLUSION

In this chapter we have investigated the relationships among cost, output, price, revenue, and profit. We learned to determine the break-even output for a simple linear model of the firm, and we applied the concepts of classical optimization from Chapter 9 to find the optimum output and price under three different objectives (maximizing revenue, minimizing average cost, and maximizing profits) for some more interesting, nonlinear models. It is our fervent hope that we will have succeeded in dispelling some of the uncertainty and fear many students have in regard to both microeconomic models and classical optimization. Chapter 11 continues our application of the optimization principles by analyzing inventory and production models.

SUMMARY OF KEY CONCEPTS

Output or volume.   The number of units produced and/or sold by the firm per unit time, normally per month or per year. This is the independent variable in all of our models.

Average revenue.   The average amount received for each unit sold. If all units are sold at the same price, then that price is the average revenue.

Demand curve.   The function that expresses the relationship between the price charged and the quantity sold (demanded). Another name for the average revenue function.

Total revenue.   The gross income to the firm before any expenses. Price (or average revenue) times quantity.

Marginal revenue.   The income generated by one more unit of sales. The marginal revenue function is the first derivative of the total revenue function.

Fixed costs.   The expenses that are independent of sales or production volume. These will be incurred even if no output is produced or sold.

Variable costs.   The expenses directly attributable to production or sales. The value of variable cost depends on the quantity sold or produced.

Total cost.   The sum of fixed and variable costs.

Marginal cost.   The cost of producing or selling one more unit. The marginal cost function is the first derivative of the total cost function.

Profit.   Total revenue minus total cost.

Profit maximization.   Occurs where marginal revenue equals marginal cost.

Break-even point.   The output at which total revenue equals total cost and profit is zero. At this volume, the firm "breaks even." Nonlinear models may have two break-even points.

Contribution to overhead and profit.   The revenue from one more unit minus the cost of producing that unit. Marginal revenue minus marginal cost.

Sensitivity analysis. The process of testing to determine the manner in which changes in the assumptions on which the model is constructed or variations in the values used in the model affect the results.

PROBLEMS

1. Continental Amalgamated is a small firm (despite the implications of their name) that manufactures ski poles. They sell the poles for $5 per pair; the variable cost of materials is $2.50 per pair; the cost of direct labor is $1.50 per pair; their monthly fixed cost is $5000.
   a. Let Q represent the number of thousands of pairs they make and sell in a month, and write the equations for a simple linear model of the firm, including monthly total cost (TC) in thousands of dollars, total revenue (TR) in thousands of dollars, and Profit (P) in $ thousands.
   b. Calculate their break-even output (Q_B).
   c. Sketch TR, TC, P, and show Q_B.
   d. What happens to Q_B if fixed cost increases?
   e. What happens to Q_B if variable cost per unit drops?
   f. What happens to Q_B if sales price increases?

2. In the simple linear model of the firm with

$$TR = 8Q \quad \text{and} \quad TC = 6 + 5Q$$

   find the break-even output (Q_B) for each of the following.
   a. the original model
   b. the original model with price changed from $8 to $6
   c. the original model with fixed cost changed from $6 to $5
   d. the original model with variable cost changed from $5 to $7
   e. the original model with price changed from $8 to $9, with variable cost changed from $5 to $4, *and* with fixed cost changed from $6 to $10

3. Dora Cluck, an egg rancher, has reviewed her operating records for the past 2 years and has determined that her fixed costs are approximately $40 per day and her variable cost to produce a dozen eggs is $.06. The county agricultural agent has shown her a study that proposes her demand (average revenue) function for eggs can be estimated by the equation

$$AR = .50 - .001Q$$

   where Q is in dozens sold. Find Dora's maximum revenue, her maximum profit, the price to charge in order to accomplish each, and calculate her break-even outputs.

4. The Open Arms, a small hotel with 60 rooms in a somewhat run-down neighborhood near downtown Boston, has been purchased by a group

of management science graduate students. Some market research has led them to estimate the demand for hotel rooms of the quality they have by the function

$$P = 24 - \tfrac{1}{4}Q$$

where Q is the number that will be rented at price P. If their objective is to achieve full occupancy, what price should they charge? If they wish to maximize their total revenue, what price should they charge? How many rooms will they rent, on the average?

Analysis of the accounting records of the previous owner suggests that daily costs can be estimated by the function

$$TC = \$100 + 4Q$$

where Q is the number actually rented. What is their maximum daily profit, and what price should they charge to achieve it? Find their break-even *prices*.

5. Given the following demand and total cost functions

$$D = 12 - 2Q \qquad TC = 2 + 2Q^2$$

   a. Assuming your objective is to maximize total revenue, find the output (Q), price (P), total revenue (TR), average cost (AC), total cost (TC), and profit ($\mathbb{P}$).
   b. Repeat part (a) assuming your objective is to minimize average cost (AC).
   c. Repeat part (a) assuming your objective is to maximize profit ($\mathbb{P}$).
6. Repeat problem 5, given these demand and total cost functions.

$$D = 12 - 3Q \qquad TC = 2 + Q^3$$

Chapter 11

INVENTORY AND PRODUCTION MODELS

INTRODUCTION

Inventory can be viewed as a shock absorber or buffer between the supply function and the production function and between the production function and the sales function. If a company were able to receive its raw materials at the same rate at which it produced its finished products and if it were able to sell the finished products at the same rate at which they were produced, no inventory would be necessary. Material would simply flow through the company like water through a pipe. This situation is best illustrated with an example.

A small town recently installed a municipal water system and did away with all the private wells in town. The new system consisted of a large electric pump connected to the primary water main. The pump was capable of furnishing up to 1000 gallons of water per hour, which was more than adequate during the fall and winter months. However, when spring arrived and the local townsfolk began watering their lawns, they frequently received no more than a trickle of water. Even during the summer months, though, the pump was often idle during the late night and early morning hours.

An examination of the facts showed that total water usage for the town, even during the hottest period, was only 15,000 gallons per day, 9,000 gallons less than the daily capacity of the pump. The problem was that the hourly demand peaked in the early evening at about 3,000 gallons per hour, three times the capacity of the pump.

The answer to the problem was simple—inventory. The town built a 25,000-gallon water tower (which was considerably cheaper than buying a 3,000-gallon-per-hour pump) and let their old pump operate to fill the tower as water was used from it. During the night and early moning when demand was low, the tower was filled to near capacity, so that plenty of water was available when lawn-watering time came in the afternoon and evening.

In this example the pump represents the production function, and the water usage by the townspeople represents the sales or demand function. The water tower acts as a buffer between the sharply varying demand and the constant rate of production.

This system is an example of a class of inventory problems known as *quantity-based* systems. These systems are generally used where the demand fluctuates and is difficult to predict. When the stock reaches some predetermined level (reorder level), enough stock to refill the bins or storage space is ordered. In the example, a float could be installed in the water tower. When the float reached, say, the 10,000-gallon level, the pump would be turned on and would begin to refill the tower.

As a second example, consider a lathe operator who machines pulleys for use in air conditioners. He uses a quantity-based inventory system called the "two-bin" system. In this scheme one bin is provided for the primary inventory supply, and another smaller bin is provided for lead-time inventory. In other words, the smaller bin holds an amount of material that will last during the period between the placing of the order for more material and its arrival. When the larger bin is emptied, enough material is ordered to fill both bins, and the order arrives just as the smaller bin is depleted.

Another basic inventory system is the *time-based* system. The time based system is used most often in situations where demand is fairly constant and predictable. Here orders for material are placed at the end of some regular period—every 90 days, for instance. If demand is constant, the same amount of raw material may be ordered each time. If not, enough is ordered to replenish the stock level to some predetermined maximum level. Different items will have different order cycles because of differences in usage rates and costs.

COSTS OF INVENTORY

At this point you are probably convinced that inventory, like sliced bread, is a great idea. But, we never get something for nothing unless the something is undersirable. The benefits that inventory obviously provides have costs. In other words, there are trade-offs involved.

Stockouts

Some of the costs associated with carrying too little inventory or carrying no inventory at all are fairly obvious. In the foregoing machine shop example, it is clear that if the lathe operator were to run out of raw material, he would stop producing pulleys but would still be on the payroll. The cost of running out of stock (having a *stockout*) would be the pay of the idle operator. It is more difficult to place a dollar cost on a stockout of a particular item in a retail operation, however. If a customer comes in to purchase that item and there are none, he or she may go elsewhere. A sale will be lost, and the cost will be the profit lost on that item. On the other hand, the clerk may *back order* the item, and the customer may be willing to return later when it becomes available. If an airline runs out of seats on a particular flight, a potential passenger may wait until a later flight or he or she may go to another airline. The point is that stockout costs are an important factor in inventory analysis, but the assessments of these costs are situation-dependent.

Holding Costs

The first solution that might come to mind for avoiding stockout costs is simply to carry more stock—fill the shelves to the ceiling and the raw material bins to the very rafters. Certainly this would eliminate any stockout costs, but there are costs associated with simply having the stock in inventory. These are commonly referred to as *holding costs*.

Holding costs are made up of several components. There is the cost of the space where the stock is stored or warehoused (including the building, utilities, insurance, security, etc.), the cost of looking after the stock and maintaining the warehouse, and the cost of money (either your own or borrowed) used to finance the inventory.

It is easy to see why warehouse space would cost money, and it is easy to see why it would cost money to hire someone to look after the warehouse. Understanding why the cost of money has any effect is a bit more difficult. Perhaps an example will help to clear the mist.

Consider Little's Machine Shop, where the owner, Bubba Little, has $1000 at the start of the month with which to buy raw material and to pay the rent and the help. The products the shop produces this month will not be paid for for another month; so even though he will receive more than $1000 for the finished products (he operates at a profit), he may run short of money before his customers pay up. Because of this situation he cannot afford a large inventory. What he can do in order to increase his inventory is borrow money from the bank and repay it when he gets his money from his customers.

There is one problem, however. The bank charges interest on the money it lends. The larger the inventory the shop wishes to carry, the more money it must borrow and the more interest it must pay. Interest, then, is the cost of money. Even if the shop owner had plenty of cash on hand, there would be a cost of money involved. If he put his cash in a savings account, he could draw interest on it. By using the cash to buy inventory, he gives up that interest. The cost of money in this case would be the interest payments foregone.

Ordering Costs

Another cost associated with inventory is the cost of actually placing the orders. Someone has to spend time making out the order and deciding how much to order and from whom to order. There may also be some minimum freight charge associated with each order. It will come as no surprise to the reader that these costs are lumped into a cost factor called *ordering costs*.

The objective of any inventory system should be to provide adequate amounts of the proper items at the proper time at minimum cost. The question is, what are the proper amounts? To minimize the chances of stockouts, one needs to order large amounts of inventory. To minimize the holding cost, one should order small amounts. To minimize the ordering cost, one should order large amounts but not very often. Obviously, one cannot order both large amounts and small amounts at the same time. The answer to this dilemma is found in balancing the trade-offs and finding that order quantity that yields the least *overall* cost.

A SIMPLE INVENTORY MODEL

First, let us assume that the firm uses the raw material being ordered at a constant, known rate. Second, the length of time for the order to arrive from the supplier is constant and known. This is commonly called *lead time*. Third, the order arrives all at one time and is immediately available for use. This is referred to as the *instantaneous replenishment* assumption. Fourth, ordering costs and per-unit holding costs are known and are constant.

Figure 11.1(a) is a graphical depiction of the behavior of the supply of the raw material when usage rate is constant and the supply of material is replenished instantaneously. When the workers show up on Monday morning, there are 5 boxes of parts ready and waiting for use. The usage rate is 1 box per day; so Tuesday morning there are 4 boxes left. At this rate, the order clerk knows that if lead time for the supplier is 2 days, he

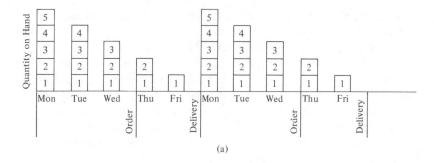

(a)

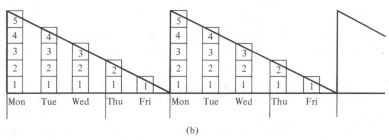

(b)

Figure 11.1   (a) Inventory usage; (b) Linear approximation.

needs to order material the first thing Thursday morning. The last part from the last box is used at quitting time Friday. The truck delivers the next week's supply of 5 boxes of material Monday morning and the process begins all over again. With this routine, the time between orders is 1 week, and the order quantity is 5 boxes. Let's plan the ordering for a 4-week (1-month) period and determine the optimum ordering strategy.

In Figure 11.1(b), we move to a somewhat more abstract illustration of the same situation by drawing a line from a point representing the amount of material available at the start of work on Monday (5 boxes) to a point representing the amount of material available at the end of work on Friday (0 boxes). The slope of this line represents the usage rate of the material. From this figure, it is simple to compute the average amount of inventory carried for the week. It is the maximum in inventory (5) plus the minimum in inventory (0) divided by 2 or $2\frac{1}{2}$ boxes. This is the amount of inventory on which holding cost will be based.

If we set the holding cost (C_H) at $.25 per box per week or $1.00 per box for the 4 weeks, and the ordering cost (C_O) at $10.00 per order, our total cost would be $(2.5 \times \$1) + (4 \times \$10) = \$42.50$, because we would have placed 4 orders during the 4 weeks and would have had an average inventory of 2.5 boxes. Perhaps we can improve upon this scheme.

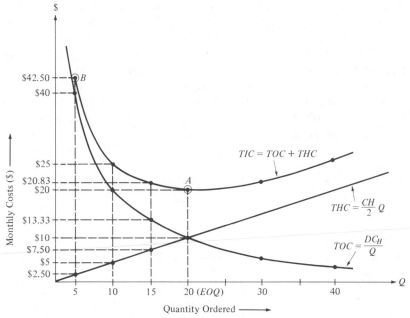

Figure 11.2 Economic order quantity (*EOQ*).

Figure 11.2 shows how the two costs, holding and ordering, behave with variations in order quantity. The horizontal scale represents the quantity ordered each time—in our case, the number of boxes of material ordered. The vertical scale represents the cost in dollars.

The line labeled *THC* (total holding cost) is located by calculating the total holding cost for each order quantity using the equation

$$THC = \frac{Q}{2} C_H$$

where Q is the amount ordered, $Q/2$ is the average amount on hand, and C_H is the monthly holding cost per box. For example, when 5 boxes (a 1-week supply) are ordered

$$THC_5 = \tfrac{5}{2}(\$1) = \$2.50$$

In the same way, when the order quantities are 10, 15, and 20, the holding costs for the month are

$$THC_{10} = \tfrac{10}{2}(\$1) = \$5$$
$$THC_{15} = \tfrac{15}{2}(\$1) = \$7.50$$
$$THC_{20} = \tfrac{20}{2}(\$1) = \$10$$

Subsequent points are calculated in the same manner. Note that THC slants upward to the right, because as orders become larger, there is a larger average amount in inventory and holding cost increases.

The line could have been established easily by simply calculating two points and drawing a straight line through them and the origin. Unfortunately, the total ordering cost (TOC) curve cannot be drawn that easily, because the relationship between TOC and the quantity ordered (Q) is not described by a first-order (linear) equation. TOC *is* a linear function of the number of orders (N) per month,

$$TOC = NC_O$$

If we represent the total monthly demand by D, then the number of orders is

$$N = \frac{D}{Q}$$

We can use this relationship to obtain an expression for ordering cost as a function of quantity

$$TOC = \frac{D}{Q} C_0$$

If we evaluate TOC for several different values of Q (using $D = 20$ units per month and $C_O = \$10$ per order), we can plot the values and sketch in the curve as shown in Figure 11.2. For example,

$$TOC_5 = \tfrac{20}{5}(\$10) = \$40$$
$$TOC_{10} = \tfrac{20}{10}(\$10) = \$20$$
$$TOC_{15} = \tfrac{20}{15}(\$10) = \$13.33$$
$$TOC_{20} = \tfrac{20}{20}(\$10) = \$10$$

Optimum Order Size

The *total incremental cost* (TIC) is the sum of the total ordering cost and the total holding cost

$$TIC = TOC + THC$$

Points on this curve are established by adding total holding cost and total ordering cost at various order quantities. Note that at the point chosen in the example for order quantity (5 units, point B in Figure 11.2), the incremental cost of $42.50 is considerably above the low point of the aggregate curve.

To find the quantity that minimizes the total incremental cost, we utilize the classical optimization procedure from Chapter 9.

$$TIC = \frac{D}{Q} C_O + \frac{Q}{2} C_H = DC_O Q^{-1} + \frac{C_H}{2} Q$$

Taking the first derivative with respect to the unknown (Q) and setting it equal to zero, we obtain

$$\frac{dTIC}{dQ} = \frac{-DC_O}{Q^2} + \frac{C_H}{2} = 0$$

Solving for the optimum value of Q gives us

$$\frac{DC_O}{Q^2} = \frac{C_H}{2}$$

$$Q^2 = \frac{2DC_O}{C_H}$$

$$Q^* = \pm \sqrt{\frac{2DC_O}{C_H}}$$

To be certain this is a minimum, we take the second derivative.

$$\frac{d^2 TIC}{dQ^2} = \frac{2DC_O}{Q^3}$$

Because D, C_O, and Q must all be positive, the second derivative must also be positive, and the point is a minimum. In our example, the optimum order size, or *economic order quantity* (*EOQ*) is

$$Q^* = \sqrt{\frac{2(20)(\$10)}{\$1}} = \sqrt{400} = 20 \text{ units per order}$$

This is point A in Figure 11.2. Substituting this value into the expressions for TIC, TOC, and THC yields

$$TOC = \frac{D}{Q} C_O = \frac{20}{20}(\$10) = \$10$$

$$THC = \frac{Q}{2} C_H = \frac{20}{2} (\$1) = \$10$$

$$TIC = TOC + THC = \$10 + \$10 = \$20$$

Note that the low point of the aggregate curve occurs at the point where the holding cost curve and the ordering cost curve intersect. This means, simply, that the minimum total cost of ordering and holding occurs where the two are equal. Unfortunately, this is true only under the conditions that have been stated for this example (unfortunate because the minimum cost is very easy to calculate when the minimum occurs at the intersection—one needs only to set the two costs equal and solve for quantity). Thus,

$$THC = TOC$$

$$\frac{D}{Q} C_O = \frac{Q}{2} C_H$$

$$2DC_O = Q^2 C_H$$

$$Q^* = \sqrt{\frac{2DC_O}{C_H}}$$

which is the same result we obtained using calculus. It should be re-emphasized that this approach (equating ordering and holding costs) works *only* because of the special nature of the functions used in this model and that, in general, we determine local maxima and minima by classical means (calculus).

Optimum Number of Orders

Now that we know the total monthly demand (D) and the optimum order size (Q^*), we can determine the optimum number of orders per month (N^*).

$$N^* = \frac{D}{Q^*}$$

In our example,

$$N^* = \tfrac{20}{20} = 1 \text{ order per month}$$

Length of the Inventory Cycle (T)

The number of working days in the *inventory cycle* (T) can be determined by calculating the number of days the inventory will last before running out. Because we order 20 units and use 1 per day, we must resupply each 20 days.

$$T^* = \frac{Q^*}{d} = \frac{20}{1} = 20 \text{ days}$$

Alternately, we can determine the length of the inventory cycle by dividing the total number of working days by the number of orders

$$T^* = \frac{\text{Total Days}}{N^*} = \frac{20}{1} = 20 \text{ days}$$

Reorder Point

It is important that we allow sufficient lead time when placing an order to guarantee that the goods will arrive before we run out of stock. We call

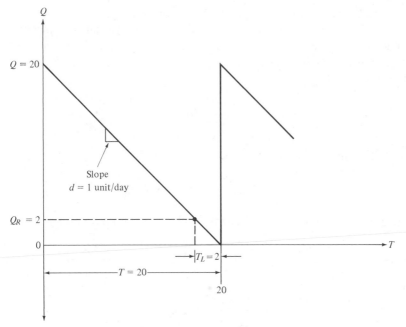

Figure 11.3   Inventory cycle and reorder point.

the time between the placing of the order and the receipt of the goods the *lead time* and denote it by T_L. To know when to place the order, we must determine how many units will be sold during lead time. If our daily demand is d, then the number of units required between the placing of an order and the receipt of the goods is d times T_L. Therefore, we define the *reorder point* or *reorder level* (Q_R) as the number on hand when we place an order.

$$Q_R = T_L d$$

In our example, if lead time is 2 days and we use 1 unit per day, $Q_R = (2)(1) = 2$ units. Thus, we simply watch the number of units on hand and place an order whenever the number drops to 2 units. These relationships are shown in Figure 11.3, which shows our optimum order quantity of 20; usage rate, or demand, of 1 unit per day; lead time of 2 days; and reorder level of 2 units.

Length of the Planning Horizon

In our example we have used 4 weeks, or 20 working days, as the period of time over which we wished to minimize our *TIC*. We will refer to this length of time as the *planning horizon*, expressed in working days. We could have used any other planning horizon, and we would have arrived at the same result. For example, if the planning horizon is chosen as 1 year, or 52 weeks (260 working days), the holding cost (at $.25 per box per week) becomes $C_H = \$13$ per box per year; the total demand over the period is $D = 260$ boxes; ordering cost remains $C_O = \$10$ per order; and the *EOQ* is

$$Q^* = \sqrt{\frac{2DC_O}{C_H}} = \sqrt{\frac{2(260)(\$10)}{\$13}} = 20 \text{ boxes per order}$$

The optimum number of orders per year (N^*) is

$$N^* = \frac{D}{Q^*} = \frac{260}{20} = 13 \text{ orders per year}$$

The optimum length of the inventory cycle (T^*) can be found by

$$T^* = \frac{Q^*}{d} = \frac{20}{1} = 20 \text{ days}$$

or

$$T^* = \frac{\text{days per year}}{N^*} = \frac{260}{13} = 20 \text{ days}$$

A year is the most frequently used planning horizon, but the outcome is unaffected by its length as long as the holding cost (C_H) is expressed in dollars per unit for the entire period.

AN ALTERNATE SOLUTION

Rather than concentrate on the quantity (Q), we could have formulated the problem in terms of the number of orders (N). Recall that

$$N = \frac{D}{Q}$$

so

$$Q = \frac{D}{N}$$

and

$$TIC = NC_O + \frac{Q}{2} C_H$$

can now be written as

$$TIC = NC_O + \frac{D}{2N} C_H$$

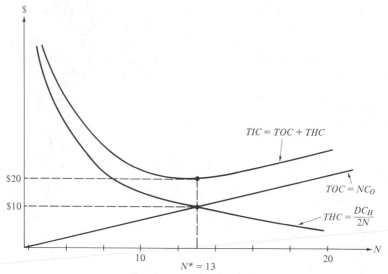

Figure 11.4   Simple inventory model as a function of N.

Applying the calculus, we find

$$TIC' = C_O - \frac{DC_H}{2N^2} = 0$$

$$N^* = \sqrt{\frac{DC_H}{2C_O}} = \sqrt{\frac{(260)(\$13)}{2(\$10)}} = 13 \text{ orders per year}$$

$$TIC'' = \frac{DC_H}{N^3} \; (>0, \text{ minimum})$$

$$Q^* = \frac{D}{N^*} = \frac{260}{13} = 20 \text{ units per order}$$

This solution is shown in Figure 11.4. Note that, as was the case when Q was chosen as the independent variable, the optimum occurs when $TOC = THC$. Also, note that now it is TOC which is linear and THC which is hyperbolic.

MORE COMPLICATED MODELS

Remember that in the previous example we assumed that the ordering cost was constant ($10 per order) and that the holding cost was also constant ($.25 per unit per week). Also recall that the usage rate was constant (1 unit per day) and known. *Only* under these conditions are we able to calculate *EOQ* by setting total ordering cost equal to total holding cost.

When these conditions are relaxed somewhat (for example, if we allow the holding cost rate to vary with the quantity ordered or if we allow the ordering cost rate to vary with the number of orders placed during our planning period) we will find that the minimum point on the aggregate cost curve does not occur at the intersection of the holding cost and ordering cost curves.

Consider a more complex case where the cost per order varies with the number of orders, according to the expression

$$C_O = \frac{100}{N} + 20$$

Total ordering cost is therefore the more complex expression

$$TOC = NC_O = N\left(\frac{100}{N} + 20\right) = 100 + 20N$$

where N is the number of orders during the period.

Holding cost is a constant at $C_H = \$6$ per unit per year and the annual requirement is $D = 600$ units per year, demand is $d = 2$ units per day, and there are 300 working days per year.

Formulating the total holding costs in terms of N,

$$THC = \frac{Q}{2}\, C_H = \frac{DC_H}{2N}$$

and total incremental cost is

$$TIC = 100 + 20N + \frac{DC_H}{2N}$$

Solving for the N^* that minimizes TIC, we obtain

$$TIC' = 20 - \frac{DC_H}{2N^2} = 0$$

$$N^* = \sqrt{\frac{DC_H}{40}} = \sqrt{\frac{(600)(6)}{40}} = \sqrt{90} \approx 9.5 \text{ orders per year}$$

$$TIC'' = \frac{DC_H}{N^3} \qquad (>0, \text{ minimum})$$

$$Q^* = \frac{D}{N^*} = \frac{600}{9.5} \approx 63 \text{ units per order}$$

$$T^* = \frac{Q^*}{d} = \frac{63}{2} \approx 32 \text{ days per cycle}$$

or

$$T^* = \frac{300}{N^*} = \frac{300}{9.5} \approx 32 \text{ days per cycle}$$

$$TIC = [100 + 2(9.5)] + \frac{(600)(6)}{2(9.5)} = 290 + 190 = \$480 \text{ per year}$$

This model is shown in Figure 11.5. Note that equating TOC and THC leads to an incorrect answer of $N = 7.3$ orders per year, which implies $Q = 600/7.3 \approx 82$ units per order and $TIC = \$490$ per year. Although the size of the annual cost difference is small (\$10 per year) in this example, it can be quite sizable.

As a second example of a complicating factor, let the cost of holding a unit vary with the size of the order according to the following relationship

$$C_H = .01Q \text{ \$ per unit per year}$$

with C_o constant at \$300 per order, daily demand (d) of 20 units, and 360 working days per year. Annual demand is

$$D = 360(20) = 7200 \text{ units per year}$$

$$TIC = NC_o + \frac{Q}{2}C_H = \frac{D}{Q}C_o + \frac{Q}{2}(.01Q) = \frac{DC_o}{Q} + .005Q^2$$

$$TIC' = \frac{-DC_o}{Q^2} + .01Q = 0$$

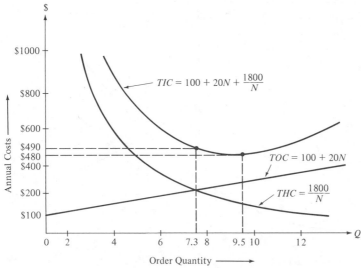

Figure 11.5 Example of TIC_{MIN} where $TOC \neq THC$.

$$Q^* = \sqrt[3]{\frac{DC_O}{.01}} = \sqrt[3]{(7200)(300)(100)} = 600 \text{ units per order}$$

$$TIC'' = \frac{2DC_O}{Q^3} = +.02 \qquad (>0, \text{ minimum})$$

$$N^* = \frac{D}{Q^*} = \frac{7200}{600} = 12 \text{ orders per year}$$

$$T^* = \frac{360}{N^*} = \frac{360}{12} = 30 \text{ days per cycle}$$

or

$$T^* = \frac{Q^*}{d} = \frac{600}{20} = 30 \text{ days per cycle}$$

$$TIC_{\text{MIN}} = 12(\$300) + \frac{600}{2}(.01)(600) = \$5400 \text{ per year}$$

Equating *TOC* and *THC* gives $Q \approx 756$ units per order and $TIC = \$5715$ per year. The graph of Figure 11.6 summarizes these results.

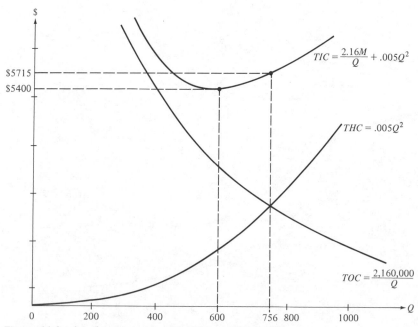

Figure 11.6   Another example with $TOC \neq THC$ at TIC_{MIN}.

The whole thrust of this discussion is that you can never go wrong if you calculate the *EOQ* by taking the first derivative of the *TIC* curve, setting it equal to zero, and solving for *EOQ*. If you can write the expression for the *TIC* curve, this will always work.

IMPLICATIONS OF VARIABLE DEMAND AND LEAD TIME

Except in a few isolated situations, either lead time or demand for an item (or both) will be variable. Up to this point in the chapter we have assumed constant and known demand and lead time. What are the implications of variations in usage rate (demand) and delivery (lead time)? When stock arrives later than expected or when more stock than expected is used, you run out of stock, or have a *stockout*.

Stockouts cost money. In some cases it is easy to calculate how much. In other cases it may be more difficult. In a manufacturing operation, for example, if an order of raw material fails to arrive on time, an entire assembly line may be idled, resulting in wages paid for nonproductive time. We simply count the hours and multiply by the wage rate to compute the stockout cost. Conversely, in a retail operation it may be very difficult to determine how much of a particular item might have been sold had the supply not been exhausted. The cost, of course, would be the profit per unit unsold.

Variations in Lead Time

Let's assume that the nominal (average) lead time Fabco, Inc., experiences with sheet metal orders is 15 days and that the company uses 100 pieces of the sheet metal each day. The reorder point for sheet metal is 1500 pieces. When the stock level reaches 1500 pieces, the company places an order with the supplier for 4500 pieces (their *EOQ*). Fifteen days later the order arrives. This happens just as the last piece in stock is used. This is the ideal situation, and graphically it looks like time period 1 in Figure 11.7(a).

If the steel supplier gets behind on orders and Fabco's order cannot be delivered until 25 days after the order is placed, there will be 10 work days in which no production can take place because Fabco will have run out of stock on the fifteenth day. This is shown in time period 2 of Figure 11.7(a). In period 3, the lead time is only 10 days, and no stockout occurs.

The first time a stockout occurs and causes a break in production several things are likely to happen at Fabco (after the purchasing agent is fired). The most logical action will be the raising of the reorder point so that there will be a *buffer stock* or *safety stock* (Q_s) on hand in case lead time extends past the 15-day average.

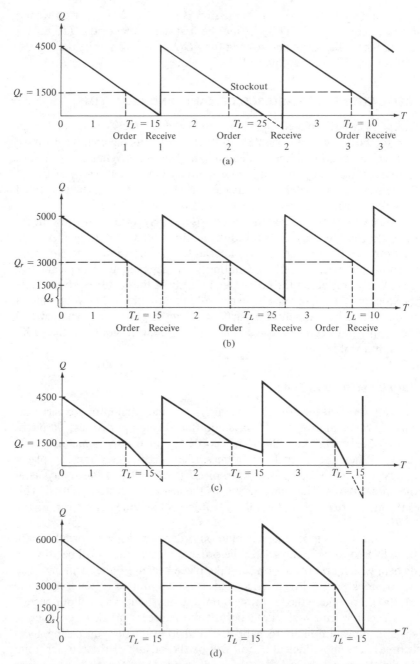

Figure 11.7 (a) Variable lead time with no safety stock; (b) Variable lead time with safety stock; (c) Variable usage with no safety stock; (d) Variable usage with safety stock.

If the company decides to order when stock levels reach 3000 units, they will have a safety stock of 1500 units and a reorder quantity of 4500 units. Note in Figure 11.7(b) that a lead time of 25 days does not cause a stockout under these conditions. Note also that the area of Figure 11.7(b) is much greater than that of Figure 11.7(a); so holding cost will be higher.

Variations in Demand

Figure 11.7(c) depicts the inventory profile where lead time is a constant 15 days but the usage rate or demand during the lead time period varies. Fabco is vulnerable to a stockout only during lead time. Obviously there is stock on hand when the reorder point is reached. The effect of accelerated demand during lead time is exactly the same as that of an extended lead time—they run out of stock. The remedy for this is the same also: carry some safety stock. In Figure 11.7(d) the reorder point has been raised once again from 1500 to 3000 units, while the reorder quantity has remained constant at 4500 units. The usage rate can go as high as 200 units per day without a stockout occurring.

Variations in Both Lead Time and Demand

When lead time *and* demand vary, the model becomes at least twice as volatile as when only one of the two is variable. Imagine the impact of an extended lead time and accelerated demand occurring at the same time. If stockouts are to be totally eliminated, sufficient safety stock must be carried to allow for this extreme situation.

Determining Optimum Safety Stock

In the simple *EOQ* model the optimum order quantity is determined by finding the order quantity that minimizes the total cost of ordering and carrying the inventory. The same approach is used for determining optimum safety stock, except that the expected cost of stockouts plus the carrying cost of the safety stock is minimized.

In the *EOQ* model, the carrying cost was calculated based on the average amount of inventory held ($Q/2$, where Q was the order quantity). However, the cost of carrying safety stock must be based on the total amount of safety stock carried, because it is an amount of stock over and above the annual usage. Chapter 16 contains a more detailed discussion of safety stock calculation.

VOLUME PRICE DISCOUNTS

In the discussion so far, there has been one assumption that has not been discussed. That assumption is that price remains constant and need not be considered. In industry it is common practice for vendors (sellers) to give volume price breaks. In other words, a supplier will offer a lower per-unit price for large orders than for small orders.

For example, the foundry that makes the pulley blanks for the machine shop might charge $1.00 each for the blanks when fewer than 100

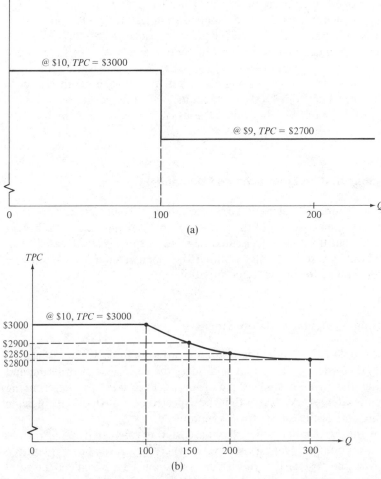

Figure 11.8   (a) *TPC* with cumulative volume discount; (b) *TPC* with incremental volume discount.

are ordered at one time and only $.90 when 100 or more are ordered. Prices might be further reduced for orders of 200 or more, 300 or more, etc.

These price breaks may also be structured in two different ways. They may be *cumulative* (as illustrated in Figure 11.8(a)) or *incremental*, (as illustrated in Figure 11.8(b)). If the price break is cumulative, the buyer pays the same price for all units ordered, and the price drops when order size reaches the break point. The Finch Winch & Wrench Company uses 3000 pulley blanks per year. If the base price of the pulley blanks is $1.00 each for orders of fewer than 100 and a 10% cumulative price break is offered for orders of 100 or more, they will pay $.90 if they purchase 100 or more at a time. With total annual demand of 3000 units, the total purchasing cost will be $3000 for lot sizes of $Q < 100$ per order and $2700 for larger lots.

The incremental price break is figured differently. If the situation just described were the same except for the fact that the price breaks were incremental rather than cumulative, the buyer would pay $1.00 for the first 100 units and $.90 for all units over 100 in each order. For example, at $Q \leq 100$, total annual purchasing cost would be $3000 \times \$1 = \$3000$. A 150-unit order would cost $(100 \times \$1) + (50 \times \$.90) = \$145$. This would require $3000/150 = 20$ orders per year for an annual TPC of $20 \times \$145 = \$2900$. Lots of 200 units would cost $100(\$1) + 100(\$.90) = \$190$ and would require $3000/200 = 15$ orders per year for a TPC of $2850. For $Q = 300$, $TPC = [(100 \times \$1) + 200(\$.90)](3000/300) = \$2800$.

Total Annual Cost (TAC)

The only difference between the total annual cost curve (TAC) and the total incremental cost curve (TIC) is the addition of the total annual cost of purchasing the inventory. Because one component of the cost of holding inventory is the cost of money invested in inventory and because volume price breaks are the rule rather than the exception, unit price will be an important factor in actual EOQ calculations.

Unfortunately, when price breaks are introduced into the EOQ problem, the total annual cost curve is discontinuous. In other words, the curve cannot be described with a single equation. Therefore, the EOQ cannot be calculated by taking the first derivative and setting it equal to zero. Under these conditions, an *initial* solution is obtained for *minimum* TIC by using the method previously shown, based on the original price. If the price break quantity is larger than the EOQ, the TAC must be calculated for the EOQ and for the price break quantity and then compared. If the TAC at the price break quantity is lower, then the proper order quantity is the price break quantity.

Consider the Finch Winch and Wrench Co. If their holding cost is $10 per unit per year and their ordering cost is $13.50 per order, their *EOQ* is

$$Q^* = \sqrt{\frac{2DC_O}{C_H}} = \sqrt{\frac{(2)(3000)(\$13.50)}{\$10}} = \sqrt{8100} = 90 \text{ units per order}$$

At $Q = 90$

$$TOC = \tfrac{3000}{90} \times \$13.50 = \$450$$
$$THC = \tfrac{90}{2} \times \$10 = \$450$$
$$TIC = \$450 + \$450 = \$900$$
$$TPC = 3000 \times \$1 = \$3000$$
$$TAC = \$900 + \$3000 = \$3900$$

At $Q = 100$

$$TOC = \tfrac{3000}{100} \times \$13.50 = \$405$$
$$THC = \tfrac{100}{2} \times \$10 = \$500$$
$$TIC = \$405 + \$500 = \$905$$
$$TPC = 3000 \times \$.90 = \$2700$$
$$TAC = \$905 + \$2700 = \$3605$$

Finch's cost curves are shown in Figure 11.9. The lowest point on their *TAC* curve is at $Q = 100$; so they should take the discount. Annual savings will be $3900 - \$3605 = \$295$.

As a second example, consider the Memorial Casket Company, which has annual sales (*D*) of 20,000 units. Ordering cost is $200 per order ($C_O = \$200$). Their purchase cost per unit (C_P) is $80, and inventory holding cost is 10% of the price per unit per year ($HC = \$8$). Solving for the *EOQ*, we obtain

$$TIC = \frac{Q}{2}(C_H) + \frac{D}{Q}(C_O)$$

$$\frac{dTIC}{dQ} = \frac{C_H}{2} - \frac{D(C_O)}{Q^2} = \frac{8}{2} - \frac{20,000(200)}{Q^2} = 0$$

$$Q^* = \sqrt{\frac{(2)(20,000)(200)}{8}} = 1000 \text{ units per order}$$

$$N^* = \frac{D}{Q^*} = \frac{20,000}{1,000} = 20 \text{ orders per year}$$

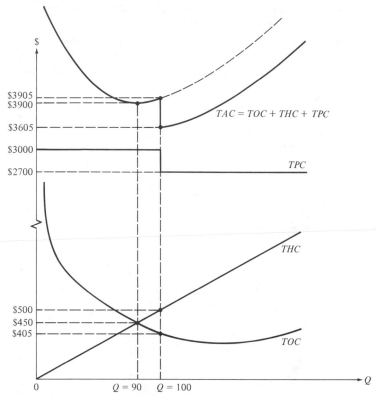

Figure 11.9   Finch's *TAC* curve for incremental volume discount.

Given the 1000-order quantity, the total annual cost would be

$$TAC = TOC + THC + TPC$$

$$= NC_O + \frac{Q}{2}C_H + DC_P$$

$$= (20 \times \$200) + (\tfrac{1000}{2} \times \$8) + (20{,}000 \times \$80)$$
$$= \$1{,}608{,}000$$

Now consider the situation where Memorial's supplier offers a 5% volume discount (price break) on orders of 2000 units or more. If $Q = 2000$, $N = 20{,}000/Q = 10$, $C_P = .95(\$80) = \$76$, and $C_H = .1(\$76) = \$7.60$, then the total annual cost would be

$$TAC_{1000} = 10(\$200) + \tfrac{2000}{2}(\$7.60) + 20{,}000(\$76) = \$1{,}529{,}600$$

In this case, the *TIC* increased from \$8,000 to \$9,600, but the total price decreased by \$80,000 for a net decrease of \$78,400. The proper choice is clear: Take the discount and increase order size to 2000. This problem is illustrated in Figure 11.10(a).

If the volume discount were .5% for orders of 5000 and over, the number of orders would drop to 4; purchasing cost would drop to $79.60; C_H would drop to $7.96, and the total annual cost at the break point

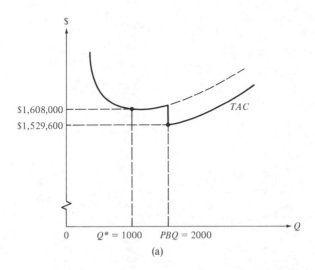

(a)

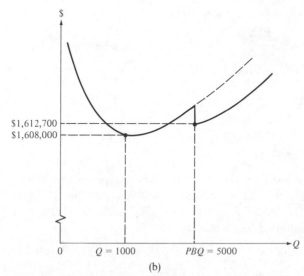

(b)

Figure 11.10 (a) Advantageous volume discount; (b) Insufficient volume discount; (c) *TAC* price break quantity less than Q^*.

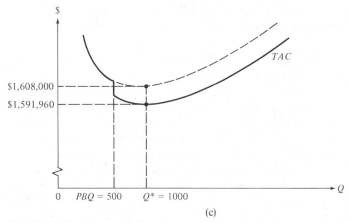

Figure 11.10   (*continued*)

would be

$$TAC_{5000} = 4(\$200) + \frac{5000(\$7.96)}{2} + 20,000(\$79.60) = \$1,612,700$$

The decrease of $8,000 in total price is not enough to overcome the increase of $12,700 in *TIC*; so the proper choice would be to decline the offer of the volume discount and continue to order in quantities of 1000. This situation is shown in Figure 11.10(b).

If the break point is below the *EOQ* quantity, it will automatically be taken, and the *EOQ* is the optimum order size. If Memorial's supplier were to offer a 1% discount on orders of 500 or more, *TAC* at the *EOQ* value of 1000 units per order would be

$$TAC = (20 \times \$200) + (\tfrac{1000}{2} \times \$7.92) + 20,000(\$79.20) = \$1,591,960$$

This is shown in Figure 11.10(c).

These examples assume a cumulative discount. The total discount on price would have been less had an incremental discount been used (see Figure 11.8). Whether the discount system used is cumulative or incremental, the objective is to find that order quantity that minimizes the total annual cost to the purchaser. That quantity is truly the "*EOQ*."

THE ECONOMIC PRODUCTION RUN

Let's assume that Little's Machine Shop expands its product line to include an additional pulley but still has only the one lathe on which to produce both pulleys. We will also assume that the demand for the two pulleys is equal at 500 each per month, that it costs $.20 per unit per year to hold a unit in inventory, and that it costs $200 to change over from the production of one pulley to the other. If the production capacity of the lathe is 2000 of either pulley per month, what is the *economic production run (EPR)*?

The problem is certainly similar to the *EOQ* problem, and it is tempting to approach it in exactly the same manner. There is involved, however, a new dimension that you may have noticed. While the lathe is turning out pulleys to be stacked in the warehouse, pulleys are being taken from the warehouse and sold. The rate of inventory build-up is, therefore, the difference between the production rate and the sales rate. From Figure 11.11, which shows the production/inventory cycle, you can see that at a production rate of 2000 per month (100 per day) and a sales rate of 500 per month (25 per day), there is a build-up in inventory of 1500 units per month (75 per day). Figure 11.11 shows a production run of 4000 units, which is the economic production run size whose calculation follows. The maximum number of units in inventory, the number on which holding cost is based, is equal to 3000 (4000 produced and 1000 sold in the 40-day period). Recall that the calculation of *EOQ* involves balancing the cost between annual order cost and annual holding cost. In this case the calculation of economic production run involves balancing annual holding cost and annual set-up cost.

We will define an *inventory build-up ratio* as

$$R = \frac{p - d}{p} = 1 - \frac{d}{p}$$

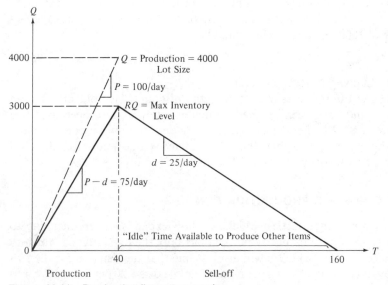

Figure 11.11 Production/inventory cycle.

where

$$p = \text{production rate (100 units per day)}$$
$$d = \text{demand or sales (25 units per day)}$$

(Note that if the production rate is infinite, which is the instantaneous replenishment assumption of our simple EOQ model, $R = 1$.) If we multiply the build-up ratio by the production run size (Q), we see that in our example there is an inventory build-up of

$$Q_{MAX} = \frac{100 - 25}{100}(Q) = .75Q$$

units remaining in inventory for each unit produced during the production run.

As in the EOQ model, the total holding cost will be the average number of units in inventory multiplied by the cost per unit of holding inventory. The average number of units in inventory will, of course, be the maximum number of units inventoried divided by 2. Thus, total annual cost (TAC) will be the sum of total manufacturing cost, total set-up cost, and total holding cost.

$$TAC = DC_M + \frac{D}{Q}(C_S) + \frac{p - d}{p}\left(\frac{Q}{2}\right)(C_H) = DC_M + \frac{DC_S}{Q} + \frac{RC_H}{2}Q$$

where

$D = \text{total annual usage}$

$C_M = \text{manufacturing cost per unit (corresponds to } C_P)$

$C_S = \text{set-up cost per production lot (corresponds to } C_O)$

$C_H = \text{holding cost per unit per year}$

$Q = \text{number produced per run}$

$p = \text{production rate in units per day}$

$d = \text{sales rate in units per day}$

$R = \text{build-up ratio}$

Taking the first derivative of TAC with respect to Q results in

$$\frac{dTAC}{dQ} = 0 - \frac{DC_S}{Q^2} + \frac{RC_H}{2}$$

Setting this expression equal to zero and solving for Q (in this case the economic production run), we find

$$Q^* = \sqrt{\frac{2DC_S}{RC_H}}$$

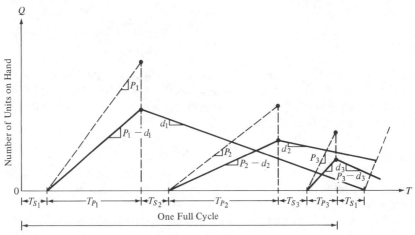

Figure 11.12 Multiple-product production/inventory cycle.

(Note that when $R = 1$, this is our *EOQ* equation.) When we substitute the numbers from our example into this equation, we find that

$$Q^* = \sqrt{\frac{2(6000)(200)}{(.75)(.20)}} = 4000 \text{ units per production run}$$

The idle time shown in Figure 11.11 will be used to manufacture the second type of pulleys. A set-up time (T_S) must be accounted for between different production runs. A plant that manufactures three products with different production and sales rates, lot sizes, and set-up times might look like Figure 11.12.

MORE COMPLICATIONS

In many cases in industry there are factors to be considered in inventory planning that are very difficult to quantify. For example, we might calculate our *EOQ* for a particular item to be 5000 units, a three-month supply. We may have some advance information on a possible new substitute for the item that will be much less expensive. Naturally we do not want a warehouse full of the old item when the new one becomes available. We would, therefore, tend to purchase less than our *EOQ*.

On the other hand, we may have advance information on a possible price increase of an item. If we know when it will become effective and how much the increase will be, we can easily determine the quantity we should buy now. On the other hand, if our information is inexact (rumor), we will have a more difficult time deciding on a strategy. We might have to guess the probabilities of when and how much and make our decision on the basis of expected value.

We might also be faced with a situation where shortages of a particular item are expected and we might want to "stock up."

The message here is that inventory management is not always a cut-and-dried situation. Many times one must depend on intuition and experience to provide guidance when hard facts and convenient numbers are unavailable.

ABC ANALYSIS

In the management and control of inventory items it is possible to expend levels of effort ranging from total neglect to in-depth analysis. The decision as to what level to apply to a particular inventory item should be based on the item's relative economic importance to the firm. It would not be desirable or economically feasible to spend the same amount of time and effort controlling the purchase and inventory of screws and fasteners as in controlling expensive electronic components. Ten to 15% of the items inventoried by a manufacturing firm can represent as much as 80% of the dollar value of items inventoried. The majority of the items in inventory, therefore, will represent as little as 20% of inventory value.

ABC analysis can be used to rank or group the items inventoried by a firm by the relative importance of those items. The technique is very simple, and the resulting ranked list provides a useful guide for control.

The mechanics of ABC analysis are as follows:

1. List all items carried in inventory.
2. List the number of dollars spent each year for each of the items.
3. Arrange the list of items in order of descending cost per year.
4. Designate the top 10–15% as A inventory, the next 20–30% as B inventory, and the remainder as C inventory.

The percentages selected for each classification are flexible. For a particular firm there may be a well-defined natural break between A and B and between B and C. In other situations the line between classifications may be vague and must be set arbitrarily by the decision maker.

Once the analysis has been completed, its use is obvious. The most sophisticated techniques and the greatest control effort are applied to A inventory and attention is given to B and C items only to the degree necessary to avoid crisis situations.

Example

The inventory items in Table 11.1 have been listed in order of yearly cost.

Table 11.1 ABC ANALYSIS

		ITEM NUMBER	YEARLY COST		
A	1	050	2,949,000	7,697,000	Total Cost
	2	121	2,763,000		
	3	005	1,985,000	71.56%	Percentage of Total Inventory
B	4	110	865,000		
	5	130	240,000		
	6	020	235,000		
	7	212	210,000	1,939,000	Total Cost
	8	001	204,000	18.03%	Percentage of
	9	625	185,000		Total Inventory
C	10	318	138,000		
	11	420	110,000		
	12	198	101,000		
	13	225	101,000		
	14	615	94,000		
	15	512	90,000		
	16	612	88,000		
	17	465	86,000		
	18	381	52,000		
	19	475	48,000		
	20	003	47,000		
	21	090	32,000		
	22	013	30,000		
	23	622	19,000		
	24	740	19,000		
	25	311	18,000		
	26	410	17,000	1,120,000	Total Cost
	27	019	14,000		
	28	070	8,000	10.4%	Percentage of
	29	560	6,000		Total Inventory
	30	401	2,000		

In this example there is a natural break between A and B inventory after the third item (10%), but the break between B and C is set arbitrarily after the ninth item (20%). Here the A inventory represents 71.56%, B 18.03%, and C 10.4% of the total cost of inventory.

CONCLUSION

Effective inventory management can increase the profitability of a firm with no increase in sales or productivity. The management program need not be highly quantitative to be effective, as long as the decision makers understand the relationship between cost factors such as holding and ordering costs and make their decisions in light of their knowledge of the cost behavior.

Naturally, the more precise the quantitative approach can be, the nearer purchasing and inventory decisions will be to optimum, but the decision maker must make the choice between the value of his or her time and the potential savings obtainable.

SUMMARY OF KEY CONCEPTS

Inventory. That which is held or stored against future need.

Quantity-based inventory system. A system in which orders for replacement stock are placed when stock reaches a predetermined level and order quantity remains more or less constant.

Time-based inventory system. A system in which orders are placed at predetermined time intervals (once each month, for example) and order quantities may vary.

Stockout. Having a zero inventory level while a positive demand exists.

Back order. An order that is placed against stock available at some future date but not available at the time of the order.

Safety stock or buffer stock (Q_s). An amount of stock over and above expected use in order to reduce or eliminate the chance of a stockout.

Holding cost (C_H). The cost associated with having inventory on hand. Cost of capital, warehouse space, and warehouse maintenance are examples. Expressed as a percent of unit cost or in dollars per unit per year.

Ordering cost (C_O). The cost associated with placing an order. Administrative or clerical time and minimum freight charges are examples. Expressed in dollars per order.

Total holding cost (THC). Holding cost (C_H) multiplied by average number of units on hand.

Total ordering cost (TOC). Ordering cost (C_O) multiplied by number of orders (N).

Total incremental cost (TIC). Total order cost plus total holding cost. $TIC = TOC + THC$. Expressed in dollars per planning period.

Economic order quantity (EOQ). That order quantity which minimizes TIC. The value of Q that satisfies the relationship

$$\frac{dTIC}{dQ} = 0 \quad \text{when} \frac{d^2TIC}{dQ^2} > 0$$

Lead time (T_L). The time between order placement and receipt of the stock ordered.

Reorder level (Q_R). When the reorder level of stock is reached, a new order is placed. The Q_R should allow enough stock to last through the lead time.

Inventory cycle (T). That period during which inventory goes through one complete change in profile. This may be the period between orders or the period between zero inventory levels or maximum inventory levels.

Planning horizon. The period covered by current plans when order quantities are set. This may be any time between 1 day and 1 century. Typically the inventory planning horizon is 1 year.

Acquisition or total purchase cost (*TPC*).   The price per unit of an item multiplied by the number of units purchased per year.

Volume price discounts.   A reduction in the list price of an item that is granted when the item is purchased in large quantities.

Cumulative volume price discount.   When a cumulative discount is given, all units purchased are priced at the discount price level.

Incremental volume price discount.   When an incremental discount is given, the discount price applies only to the number of items over the discount quantity.

Total Annual Cost (*TAC*).   The sum of total purchasing cost and total incremental cost.

$$TAC = TPC + TIC$$

Set-up costs (*C_S*).   In a production operation, set-up costs are those costs associated with changing a production line from one product to another. Idle time for production employees and salaries for personnel who adjust the machinery are examples. This is the same as C_O in the basic model.

Inventory build-up ratio (*R*).   The relationship between production rate and usage rate of a product.

$$R = \frac{p - d}{p} \quad \text{or} \quad 1 - \frac{d}{p}$$

where p is the production rate and d is the usage or demand rate.

Economic production run size or economic lot size (*ELS*).   That number of units produced in a continuous run which minimizes the total of set-up cost and holding cost. The maximum number of units in inventory will be $ELS \times R$. The number of runs per year will be D/ELS.

Manufacturing cost.   The cost per unit to manufacture an item. This includes labor cost, material cost, and overhead.

ABC analysis.   A method for classifying inventory items by economic activity.

Useful relationships

D = annual demand (units/year)

Q = order quantity or production lot size

N = number of orders per year

d = usage or sales rate (units/day)

p = production rate (units/day)

C_O = order cost (\$/order)

C_H = holding cost (\$/unit/year)

C_S = set-up cost (\$/cycle)

Q^* = economic order quantity or lot size

$$N = \frac{D}{Q} = \frac{\text{units per year}}{\text{units per order}} \text{ (orders per year)}$$

$$\frac{12}{N} = 12\left(\frac{Q}{D}\right) \text{ months supply per order or number of months between orders}$$

$$\frac{52}{N} = 52\left(\frac{Q}{D}\right) \text{ weeks supply per order or number of weeks between orders}$$

$\dfrac{365}{N} = 365\left(\dfrac{Q}{D}\right)$ calendar days supply per order or number of days between

orders

$Q^* = \sqrt{\dfrac{2DC_O}{C_H}}$ optimum number of units per order (EOQ) per year and C_O and

C_H expressed in dollars.

$Q^* = \sqrt{\dfrac{2DC_sp}{(p-d)C_H}}$ = optimum production lot size when D is expressed in units

per year, C_S and C_H are expressed in dollars, and p and d are expressed in units per day.

$Q_{\text{MAX}} = Q^*\left(\dfrac{p-d}{p}\right)$ = maximum inventory stored

PROBLEMS

1. Given the following costs, find
   a. the economic order quantity
   b. the cost per order
   c. the daily demand
   d. the length of the inventory cycle (working days)

Yearly Demand	100,000 units
Unit Cost	$25
Ordering Cost	$200 per order
Carrying Cost	$10 per unit per year (1 year = 250 working days)

2. Given the following information
   a. What is the EOQ?
   b. How many orders per year?
   c. If the year is 360 days, how many days between orders?

Yearly Demand	60,000
Ordering Cost	$200
Carrying Cost	$1.50 per unit per year

3. The Brown Company purchases a preassembled electronic component for use in a voltmeter that it manufactures. Annual usage is 72,000 units. The company's cost of capital is $16\frac{7}{8}\%$, and administrative ordering cost is $30 per order. Components cost $10 each.
   a. Find the optimum order quantity.

b. If lead time (T_L) is 2 days, what is the reorder level (Q_R)? (Assume 360 days per year.)

c. What is the number of orders per year.

4. The Ajax Engine Company distributes farm tractor engines. Each year Ajax sells 20,000 B model engines at a uniform rate. The administrative ordering cost is $250, and carrying cost is 5% of purchase price. Engines cost $200 each. How many month's supply should Ajax order each time?

5. Soundo, Inc.; purchases 4800 turntables per year from a Japanese manufacturer and uses them as part of a stereo system marketed under the Soundo label. Soundo's ordering cost is $120, and carrying cost is $5 per average unit per year. What is Soundo's optimum number of orders per year?

6. Each year Casemate Company uses 150,000 small electric motors in the manufacture of humidifiers. It costs Casemate $93.75 to place an order, and it costs $.50 per year for each unit held in inventory (average). How many week's supply of motors should Casemate order? (52-week year)

7. In problem 3 the Brown Company has been offered a 2% cumulative discount if they will order once each month. Should the company accept? If the discount is taken, what will be the cost or savings?

8. In problem 4 what percentage cumulative discount would be necessary to cause Ajax to order one time each quarter? (Assume each unit costs $200.)

9. In problem 5 what is the largest amount the company will order if the cumulative volume discount offered by the turntable manufacturer is 3%? (Assume turntables cost $50.)

10. Peak Manufacturing produces, among other items, room air conditioners. The company sells 24,000 of these units per year at a fairly uniform rate. The air conditioners are made on the same assembly line as several other products. Set-up of the line costs $500 per set-up. Holding cost for the air conditioners is $24 per average unit in inventory per year. The inventory build-up ratio for the air conditioners is 25% per unit. What is the optimum production run size for air conditioners?

11. The Jones Company manufactures and sells several models of CB radios. One model, the Big Mouth, is the most popular model and sells 52,000 units per year at a more or less uniform rate. The assembly line is capable of producing 1,800 units per week, and the cost of setting up the line for the Big Mouth is $300 per set-up. Holding cost for this unit is $5 per year per average unit in inventory. How many weeks' supply should be produced at each production run?

12. Listed below are 20 inventory items carried by Atlas, Ltd., along with the economic activity for each item. Rank the items by dollar activity

and separate them into A, B, and C inventory classifications. What is the value of each class?

ID	ECONOMIC ACTIVITY ($)	ID	ECONOMIC ACTIVITY ($)
1211	45,000	1582	10,000
1053	28,000	1717	27,000
2625	157,000	2419	176,000
1101	250,000	1112	19,500
2207	18,000	1111	8,500
2725	4,500	1413	148,000
1666	2,500	1341	17,000
1608	3,000	1220	6,000
1390	94,000	1782	5,000
1984	82,000	1510	22,000

Chapter 12

CPM/PERT

INTRODUCTION

Who has not, at some time or other, undertaken a project and had it suddenly turn from harmony to chaos because of some small task that was overlooked early in the project? This usually happens when the project planner fails to consider the interrelationships between the project activities. The planner may have carefully listed each job that had to be done to complete the project and may have estimated the time required and assigned each job to a group or individual. Still someone forgot, or put off, a small detail that eventually became *critical* to the entire project.

There are, as you may have guessed by now, methods that aid planners in avoiding such foul-ups. These techniques fall under the generic heading of *network models* and under the general group of network models known as *critical path method* (CPM) models.

One of the best-known and most widely used CPM techniques is the *program evaluation and review technique* (PERT). PERT is a specialized (three-estimate) model of CPM that was developed by the Navy in 1957–1958 for use on the Fleet Ballistic Missile (Polaris) program. The technique is credited with having aided in completing the program well ahead of schedule. PERT is best applied to those projects that are nonrepetitive and have a high degree of uncertainty.

CRITICAL PATH METHOD (CPM)

In using CPM, each activity or task is first identified, and then the tasks that must precede each subsequent task are defined. Once this has been done, a network is constructed where each activity or task is represented by an arrow (Fig. 12.1) pointing in the direction of work flow. The length of the shaft of the arrow has no significance.

An activity *takes time* to accomplish. Time estimates for each of the activities must be made by the individual best qualified to estimate the required time accurately. The time estimate for each activity is called the *expected time* and is indicated by t_e.

The points where activities begin and end are called *events* or *nodes* and are represented by circles (Fig. 12.2). Events *mark points in time*; they do not take time to accomplish.

Once the activities have been put together into a network, it will look like a roadmap. The first event in any project network will be "start," and the last event will be "project complete." There will always be a single start event and a single end event.

An event that is the termination point for more than one activity is called a *sink point* (Fig. 12.3). An event from which more than one activity starts is called a *burst point* (Fig. 12.4).

Figure 12.1   Activity (arrow).

Figure 12.2   Event (circle).

Figure 12.3   Sink point.

Figure 12.4   Burst point.

Figure 12.5   Earliest time (T_E).

Figure 12.6   Beginning and ending
events for activity 1-2.

There are several schemes currently used for labeling events and
activities. The convention that we will use here will be to label only the
events, starting with the number 1. The number of the event is in the left-
hand part of the circle, and the *earliest event occurrence time* (T_E) is in the
right-hand part, as shown in Figure 12.5. Event 1 will always be the starting
event. When the events are labeled in this way, then the activities can be
identified by the number of the event where they start, followed by the
number of the event where they end. The activity that starts at event 1
and ends at event 2 is activity 1-2 (Fig. 12.6).

Building the Network

When all the activities have been identified and labeled, we can begin
building the network. Let's look at simple example and examine the logic
that is used (see Table 12.1).

In this example there are 10 events and 12 activities. Event 1 is the
first event, and event 10 is the last. Note that only one activity starts at
event 1 (activity 1-2) and that three activities begin at event 2 (activities

Table 12.1   NETWORK DATA

ACTIVITY LABEL	BEGINNING EVENT	ENDING EVENT	ACTIVITY NOTATION	EXPECTED TIME
A	1	2	1- 2	3
B	2	3	2- 3	5
C	2	5	2- 5	2
D	2	7	2- 7	5
E	3	4	3- 4	6
F	4	6	4- 6	9
G	4	10	4-10	7
H	5	6	5- 6	4
I	6	9	6- 9	2
J	7	8	7- 8	1
K	8	9	8- 9	5
L	9	10	9-10	8

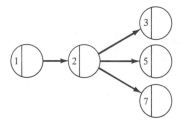

Figure 12.7   Activities beginning at burst node 2.

2-3, 2-5, and 2-7). Obviously the first activity in the network will look like Figure 12.6, and when we add the next three activities, the network will begin to take shape (Fig. 12.7).

We continue to build the network by observing the events that are left hanging in mid-air, finding the unused activities that begin at those events and drawing them in. Events 3, 5, and 7 each have only one activity beginning from them (3-4, 5-6, and 7-8) (Fig. 12.8). Now we repeat the process for events 4, 6, and 8 (Fig. 12.9). Add the last activity, and we have the complete network shown in Figure 12.10.

Note that an activity never begins at an event having a number larger than that of the event where it ends. Also note that the arrows always point nominally "downstream" in the direction of work flow.

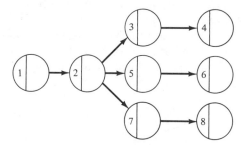

Figure 12.8   Building the network.

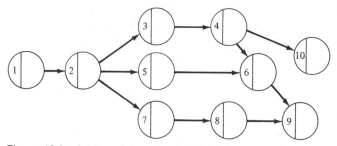

Figure 12.9   Adding sink nodes 6 and 9.

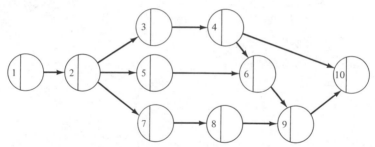

Figure 12.10   Completed activity network.

Time Estimates

With the network completed we can assign time estimates to the various activities and calculate the time necessary to complete the entire project.

Taking the time estimates from Table 12.1 and transcribing them onto the respective activities on the network as shown in Figure 12.11 will allow us to progress to the next step in the analysis, which is to determine the *earliest time* (T_E) that each event can occur. This will be done starting at event 1, which usually occurs at time 0, and progressing sequentially through the network until the last event is reached. *No event can occur until all the activities that end at that event have been completed, and no activity that begins at an event can begin until that event has occurred.*

Event 2 occurs at time 3 because activity 1-2 is its only predecessor. We place a 3 in the right side of event 2 (Fig. 12.12). Using the same technique, we determine that event 3 occurs at time 8 (2-3 begins at time 3 and takes 5 units of time). By the same logic we establish that event 5 occurs at time 5, event 7 occurs at time 8, event 4 occurs at time 14, and event 8 occurs at time 9 (Fig. 12.13).

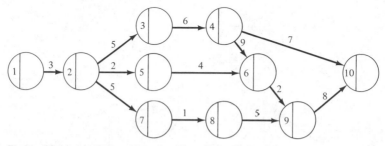

Figure 12.11   Activity network with activity times (t_e).

Figure 12.12 T_E for event 2.

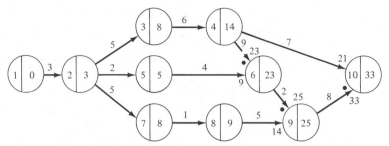

Figure 12.13   Complete network with earliest times (T_E) for all events.

Establishing the time of occurrence of events 6 and 9 requires that we determine the completion times of all activities that end at those events. An event does not occur until *all* the activities ending there are complete. Activity 4-6 will be complete at time 23, and 5-6 will be complete at time 9. Write 23 near the 4-6 arrowhead and 9 near the 5-6 arrowhead. Because 23 is the *latest* completion time, enter 23 in the right side of event 6 and place a *dot* near the head of the 4-6 arrow. (The reason for the dots will be explained later.) The same technique is used to establish the times for event 9 and event 10. Because each of these events has more than one immediate predecessor activity, be sure to place the dots by the latest one to arrive.

Event 9 will occur at time 25 because that is when the last activity ending at 9 (activity 6-9) will be complete. Only two activities end at event 10, 4-10 and 9-10. Activity 4-10 will be complete at time 21, but 9-10 will not be finished until time 33. Time 33, then, is the earliest completion time for the total project.

The Critical Path

The *critical path* for a CPM network is that sequence of activities that establishes the earliest project completion time. Any time added to a critical path activity will be added to the project completion time. This is why it is called the *critical* path.

At this point the critical path is very easy to find. The dots that we have been placing at the points of the activity arrowheads establish a clear route from the ending event to the beginning event and trace the sequence of activities that takes the greatest length of time.

Starting at event 10, find the activity arrow with a dot at its point (9-10) and darken in the arrow until you reach event 9. At event 9 there is a choice between activities 6-9 and 8-9. Activity 6-9 has the dot; so darken it. Repeat the process for event 6 and darken activity 4-6. There are no more choices to make, for there is only one path from event 4 back to the beginning (event 1). When you reach event 1 you will have darkened

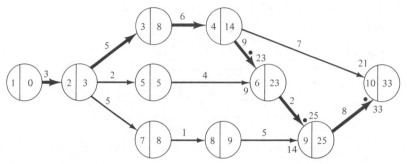

Figure 12.14   Critical path.

Figure 12.15   Expanded notation.

all the activities on the critical path; the critical path is 1-2-3-4-6-9-10. This is shown in Figure 12.14.

SLACKS

An Improved Notation Scheme

We will now expand the node notation scheme to include two additional pieces of information. The node is shown in Figure 12.15. Where T_E is the *earliest time* for the node to be realized, T_L is the *latest time*, and S_E is the *event slack* at event N.

Earliest Time

The earliest time an event can be realized is the time its last immediate predecessor activity is completed. We have already utilized this concept in developing the critical path.

Latest Time

The latest time an event can be realized is the time its *first* immediate successor activity must begin in order not to delay the completion of the entire network. Thus, in the partial network shown in Figure 12.16, if event 12 is the final event, it must be completed by $T_L = T_E = 38$. To find the latest start time for its predecessor activities, we subtract their expected duration (t_e) from their latest finish times. Activity 11-12 must

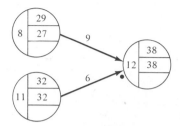

Figure 12.16   Establishing T_L values.

occur no later than time $38 - 6 = 32$, but activity 8-12 need not start before $38 - 9 = 29$. These are the T_L values for their respective beginning events.

If there are two or more activities beginning at an event, the *earliest* one to leave determines the T_L for the event. Thus, in the partial network shown in Figure 12.17, activity 6-7 must begin by $24 - 10 = 14$, and activity 6-9 must begin by $27 - 12 = 15$; so event 6 must occur no later than time $T_L = 14$.

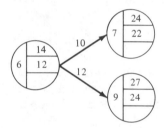

Figure 12.17 T_L for a burst node.

If we apply these rules to the network we used to find the critical path, the T_L values would be as shown in Figure 12.18.

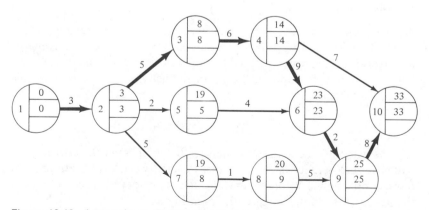

Figure 12.18   Latest times (T_L) for all network events.

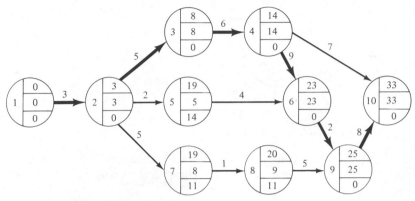

Figure 12.19   Event slacks.

Event Slacks

The slack (also sometimes called "float") at an event (S_E) is the difference between its latest time (T_L) and its earliest time (T_E).

$$S_E = T_L - T_E$$

It is a measure of how much later than expected a particular event could occur without delaying the completion of the entire project. It should be obvious that, by definition, all events on the critical path have zero slack.

For our example network the event slacks are as shown in Figure 12.19.

Activity Slack

Another concept of slack is the slack in the activity time estimates, which we call *activity slack* (S_A). It is the difference between the time available to perform the activity (measured from the earliest start time to the latest finish time) and the expected length of the activity. For activity ij, this can be expressed as follows.

$$S_{A_{ij}} = (T_{L_j} - T_{E_i}) - t_{e_{ij}}$$

As was the case with event slacks, all activities on the critical path will have zero activity slack. Examples of activity slack calculations from our example network follow, and the activity slacks for each activity in the network are shown in parentheses in Figure 12.20.

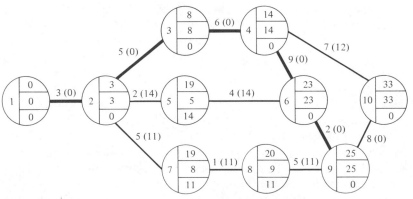

Figure 12.20 Activity slacks.

$$S_{A9\text{-}10} = (33 - 25) - 8 = 0 \qquad S_{A4\text{-}10} = (33 - 14) - 7 = 12$$
$$S_{A2\text{-}5} = (19 - 3) - 2 = 14 \qquad S_{A5\text{-}6} = (23 - 5) - 4 = 14$$
$$S_{A2\text{-}7} = (19 - 3) - 5 = 11 \qquad S_{A7\text{-}8} = (20 - 8) - 1 = 11$$
$$S_{A8\text{-}9} = (25 - 9) - 5 = 11 \qquad S_{A3\text{-}4} = (14 - 8) - 6 = 0$$

Branch Slack (Distributed Slack)

When we have a series of activities such as 2-5-6 or 2-7-8-9 in our example, each activity will have the same activity slack. This does not imply that *every one* of them can be delayed by this amount, but that the total amount of slack along that branch can be distributed among the activities. This is therefore referred to as *branch slack* or *distributed slack*.

In the example, activities 2-5 and 5-6 may take up to an additional 14 weeks between them without delaying the project completion date of 33 weeks. It could be split 10-4, 3-11, 14-0, $5\frac{1}{2}$-$8\frac{1}{2}$, etc. Similarly, activities 2-7, 7-8, and 8-9 can divide 11 weeks of slack among themselves in any manner as long as the total of their overruns does not exceed the available branch slack.

Negative Slack

Often, we complete our analysis only to find that a deadline has been imposed and the total time available is less than our expected project completion time. This necessitates recalculating the slacks, based on this new T_L for the final event.

There are two methods of accomplishing this. One is to begin at the final event, using the revised T_L value, and to calculate the slacks as we did before. A simpler method is to determine the amount of change from the expected time and then simply to decrease (if the target is earlier than the expected completion date) or increase (if the target is later) every event slack and activity slack in the network by this difference.

If the schedule has been tightened, this results in *negative slack* along the critical path (and possibly on other paths as well). Negative slack indicates events or activities that are behind schedule (based on the target date) and alerts us to the fact that the target completion date is in jeopardy. Action is required to reduce all negative slacks to zero in order to get back on schedule.

Another way negative slack can occur is by having an activity take longer than expected. This increases the earliest times and has the same effect as shortening the latest times.

In determining which activities to shorten, we must look at the cost consequences, which will be covered in a later section called PERT/COST. The project manager should have the CPM charts updated regularly to compare actual programs with planned completion dates. In this way, she or he will be alerted to any schedule problems as soon as they develop and will be able to take early action to minimize their impact on the program completion schedule.

PROGRAM EVALUATION AND REVIEW TECHNIQUE (PERT)

PERT differs from the standard CPM analysis in that PERT requires three time estimates for each activity rather than just one. These three estimates are the *optimistic* (*a*), the most *most likely* (*m*), and the *pessimistic* (*b*).

The optimistic time is the time it would take to complete the activity if everything went just right. If the activity were performed 100 times, the optimistic time would be the one shortest performance time of the 100. The most likely time would be that one time out of the 100 that occurs most frequently (the modal time). The pessimistic time is that one out of 100 times that would be the longest.

In most cases the individual who is putting the PERT analysis together will not be making the time estimates for the individual activities. This will be a supervisor, a designer, a group leader, or some other individual familiar with the particular task. The best time estimates will be obtained if the time estimator is asked to give the most likely estimate first, then the optimistic estimate, and finally the pessimistic estimate.

Once the three estimates have been made for each activity we can calculate the expected time (t_e) for the activities using a weighted average of the *a*, *m*, and *b* values, expressed by the equation

$$t_e = \frac{a + 4m + b}{6}$$

or by an easier form for manual computation,

$$t_e = m + \frac{(b - m) - (m - a)}{6}$$

For example, if $a = 3$, $m = 5$, and $b = 10$ and we substitute these values into the first equation, then

$$t_e = \frac{3 + 4(5) + 10}{6} = \tfrac{33}{6} = 5\tfrac{1}{2}$$

with the second equation

$$t_e = 5 + \frac{(10 - 5) - (5 - 3)}{6} = 5 + \tfrac{3}{6} = 5\tfrac{1}{2}$$

Manually, the second equation is applied as follows.

1. Find the difference on the left (2).

$$3 \qquad 5 \qquad 10$$

2. Find the difference on the right (5).

$$m - a = 2 \qquad b - m = 5$$

3. Find the difference between these two differences, and note its direction ($+3$ because the larger difference is to the right).

$$(b - m) - (m - a) = +3$$

4. Add or subtract this value from m to obtain t_e ($5\tfrac{1}{2}$).

$$t_e = 5 + \tfrac{3}{6} = 5\tfrac{1}{2}$$

t_e is the *mean* of the *beta* probability distribution. The beta distribution is flexible. If the distance from a to m is equal to the distance from m to b, the distribution is symmetrical. If the distance from a to m is greater than the distance from m to b, the distribution is skewed left. If the distance from a to m is less than the distance from m to b, the distribution is skewed right. Examples of these three types of distributions are shown in Figure 12.21.

When the t_e has been calculated, it is used as the single time estimate for the activity duration, and the analysis proceeds exactly as in a CPM analysis, through the determination of T_Es and T_Ls, finding the critical path, and calculation of the slacks.

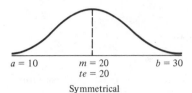

$a = 10$ $m = 20$ $b = 30$
$te = 20$

Symmetrical

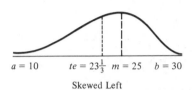

$a = 10$ $te = 23\frac{1}{3}$ $m = 25$ $b = 30$

Skewed Left

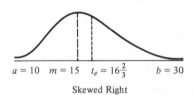

$a = 10$ $m = 15$ $t_e = 16\frac{2}{3}$ $b = 30$

Skewed Right

Figure 12.21   Beta distributions.

Example

Let's look at an example using the PERT model with three time estimates. The precedence relationships and time estimates are shown in Table 12.2. Both of the equations for calculating t_es are used. (With a little practice, you will find that the second method is easier and faster.)

We must first build the network using the same logic that was used in the CPM example. Then we add the activity expected times (t_es) as shown in Figure 12.22.

The next step is to work our way from event 1 to event 9, establishing the T_Es for each event as we go and marking the latest arrivals with dots. This gives us the network in Figure 12.23.

The dots enable us to identify the critical path as 1-4-5-7-9. Working backward through the network we can calculate the T_Ls. From these we compute the S_Es and S_As. The completed network is shown in Figure 12.24. You should perform these calculations to verify the solution. Note that there is $\frac{1}{2}$ week of branch slack is the network segment 5-8-9, that segment 4-6-9 contains 7 weeks of slack, and that segments 1-2-7 and 1-3-5 contain $12\frac{1}{2}$ units and $5\frac{1}{2}$ weeks, respectively.

Table 12.2 TIME ESTIMATES

ACTIVITIES	a	m	b	t_e
1-2	3	5	7	$\dfrac{3 + 4(5) + 7}{6} = 5$
1-3	6	7	8	$7 + \dfrac{0}{6} = 7$
1-4	4	8	12	$\dfrac{4 + 4(8) + 12}{6} = 8$
2-7	2	3	13	$3 + \dfrac{9}{6} = 4.5$
3-5	1	2	3	$\dfrac{1 + 4(2) + 3}{6} = 2$
4-5	4	6	11	$6 + \dfrac{3}{6} = 6.5$
4-6	2	4	6	$\dfrac{2 + 4(4) + 6}{6} = 4$
5-7	3	8	10	$8 - \dfrac{3}{6} = 7.5$
5-8	1	3	5	$\dfrac{1 + 4(3) + 5}{6} = 3$
6-9	7	9	11	$9 + \dfrac{0}{6} = 9$
7-9	1	6	11	$\dfrac{1 + 4(6) + 11}{6} = 6$
8-9	5	10	15	$10 + \dfrac{0}{6} = 10$

(For activity 1-3: differences 1, 1, net 0. For 2-7: 1, 10, net 9. For 4-5: 2, 5, net 3. For 5-7: 5, 2, net 3. For 6-9: 2, 2, net 0. For 8-9: 5, 5, net 0.)

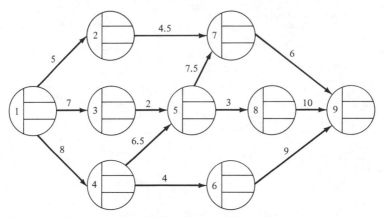

Figure 12.22   Completed PERT network with t_e values.

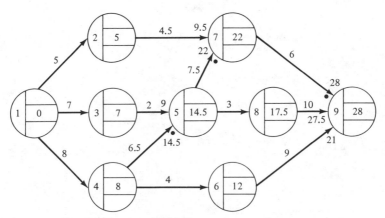

Figure 12.23   PERT network with T_Es.

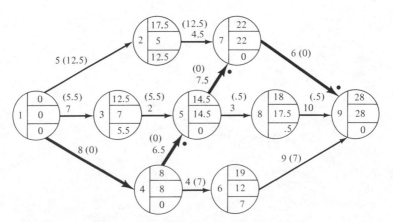

Figure 12.24   PERT network with slacks and critical path.

Probability Determinations for Project Completion Time

Thus far in our discussion of PERT we have made no use whatsoever of the added information provided by the three time estimates (a, m, and b). We represented the activity time distributions by their mean values (t_es) and performed a CPM analysis. Now we will put the added information to use in making probability statements about the project completion time.

Because the project completion time is determined by the sum of the times for the critical path activities and each critical path activity's time is represented by a probability distribution; the project completion time can be represented by a distribution that has a mean T_{CP} and a standard deviation σ_{CP} and is approximately *normal*. T_{CP} is the T_E value of the final event, or 28 in our example.

Each activity in a PERT network has a *standard deviation* that is calculated by the formula $\sigma = (b - a)/6$. The distance from a to b is the distance from one extreme of the beta distribution to the other, or approximately 6 standard deviations. Thus

$$b - a = 6\sigma \quad \text{and} \quad \sigma = \frac{b - a}{6}$$

We can calculate the mean and variance for the entire critical path by taking the sums of the means and variances for all the activities on the critical path. Thus

$$T_{CP} = \sum^{CP} te$$

and

$$\sigma_{CP} = \sqrt{\sum^{CP} \sigma^2} = \sqrt{\sum^{CP} \left(\frac{b - a}{6}\right)^2} = \frac{1}{6}\sqrt{\sum^{CP} (b - a)^2}$$

Calculation of the mean and standard deviation for the total program completion time distribution is shown in Table 12.3.

Knowing the mean and standard deviation of the distribution of project completion times, we can make probability estimates for various

Table 12.3 CALCULATION OF MEAN AND STANDARD DEVIATION OF TOTAL PROGRAM COMPLETION TIME DISTRIBUTION

ACTIVITY	t_e	b	a	$b - a$	$(b - a)^2$
1-4	8.0	12	4	8	64
4-5	6.5	11	4	7	49
5-7	7.5	10	3	7	49
7-9	6.0	11	1	10	100
	28.0				262

$T_{CP} = 8 + 6.5 + 7.5 + 6.0 = 28$

$\sigma_{CP} = \frac{1}{6}\sqrt{64 + 49 + 49 + 100} = \frac{1}{6}\sqrt{262} \approx 2.7$

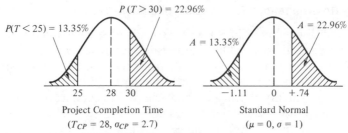

Figure 12.25   PERT probability computations.

completion times using the normal distribution table in Appendix C. If, for example, we wanted to determine the probability that the project would be completed within 25 weeks, we need only use the normalizing equation and calculate a Z value.

$$Z_T = \frac{T - T_{CP}}{\sigma_{CP}}$$

where T is the desired completion time. Substituting our values gives

$$Z_{25} = \frac{25 - 28}{2.7} = \frac{-3}{2.7} = -1.11$$

This means 1.11 standard deviations to the left of the mean. From the normal table the probability if found to be .1335, or about a 13% probability the project will be finished by the twenty-fifth week.

If we wish to determine the probability that the project will take longer than 30 weeks, we compute

$$Z_{30} = \frac{30 - 28}{2.7} = .74$$

The area to the right of $Z = .74$ is .2296; so there is approximately a 23% probability that the program will take longer than 30 weeks. These calculations are illustrated in Figure 12.25.

A Note of Caution

Note that in computing the probability, we implicitly assumed that our critical path would remain critical. In actual practice, when the activities on the critical path take longer than their expected times, the total project is delayed. However, when the critical path activities take less than their expected times, the critical path may change, as other paths become critical.

This results in an *optimistic bias* in the total program time estimates using the PERT methodology. To obtain an unbiased estimate of the total program duration, we can turn to various network simulation models of which the graphical evaluation and review technique (GERT) is the best known and most widely used.

A PRACTICAL EXAMPLE

Designing and Building a Car

Up to this point you have been required to work only a simple puzzle. The activities were well defined and labeled in such a way as to make building the network a step-by-step procedure. The use of the PERT technique in a real industrial situation requires a great deal more creativity on the part of the practitioner.

In this simplified example we are going to start from scratch. We will decide what activities and events must take place and then determine their precedence relationships. We will also discover along the way that we need to add one more tool to our kit—the *dummy activity*.

In designing and building a car we have to determine how the work can logically be subdivided. In this example we are going to assume there are three major assemblies; the body, the frame and wheels, and the engine/transmission. All three of these assemblies must be designed and matched up on paper before any parts can be built.

After all the parts are completed, the interior of the car must be finished and the car tested. Completion of the test phase will be the final event in the project. The first event will, of course, be "start." This type of exercise should begin with the listing of all the activities required to complete the project. Let's break down the activities into four major groups: design, fabrication, assembly, and wrap-up.

In the design phase we must:

A. Design the body
B. Design the frame
C. Design the engine
D. Design the body-to-frame coupling
E. Design the engine-to-frame coupling

At this point we can:

F. Build the body
G. Build the frame
H. Build the engine

With the fabrication completed we then:

I. Install the engine in the frame
J. Install the body on the frame

Finally we:

    K. Finish the interior
    L. Test the car

Now we must determine the precedence relationships among the various activities by taking each activity and asking ourselves what activity must be completed immediately before this one can start.

In the design phase we can assume that size and power parameters have been previously set. Consequently, activities A, B, and C have no precedents. We can denote this by setting up a table of activities and precedents as shown in Table 12.4.

The next group of activities do, however, have precedents. We cannot design the body-to-frame coupling until both the body and the frame have been designed. By the same token, the engine-to-frame coupling design cannot proceed until the frame and engine designs are complete. Therefore, A and B must precede D and A, B, and C must precede E.

We cannot build the body until the body/frame coupling has been designed; we cannot build the engine until the engine/frame coupling has been designed; and we cannot build the frame until both couplings have been designed. Therefore, D must precede F; E must precede H; and D and E must precede G.

Before we install the engine in the frame, both body and frame must be fabricated, and before the body can be mounted on the frame, the body must be fabricated. Thus G and H precede I, and I and F precede J.

When the body is mounted, the interior can be finished, and after that, the car can be tested. Therefore, J precedes K, and K precedes L.

Table 12.4 PRECEDENCE RELATIONSHIPS

Activity	Description	Precedents
A	Design body	—
B	Design frame	—
C	Design engine	—
D	Design body/frame coupling	A, B
E	Design engine/frame coupling	A, B, C
F	Build body	D
G	Build frame	D, E
H	Build engine	E
I	Install engine in frame	G, H
J	Mount body on frame	I, F
K	Finish interior	J
L	Test	K

Figure 12.26   Activities with no predecessors.

This is not the nice, neat activity table that we had in earlier examples, and constructing the network is not going to be as easy. After a little practice, though, the technique can be mastered. To start with, we know that an activity starts and ends at an event. We can number the events as we go through the network.

Activities A, B, and C have no activities preceding them, so they must all start at event 1 (Fig. 12.26). We number the ending events of each of the three 2, 3, and 4. Now we confront a confusing situation. Activity D is preceded by both A and B, and they end at separate events. The fact that an activity is preceded by two activities would seem to indicate a situation like that shown in Figure 12.27(a). But A and B start at the same event. We could solve the problem by bending one of the activities and making the network segment look like Figure 12.27(b).

For various reasons, including "which one is activity 1-2?", we do not permit two activities to begin and end at the same pair of events. A neater way to handle this situation is to use a *dummy activity* that makes no time but indicates the precedence relationships [Fig. 12.27(c)].

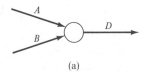

(a)

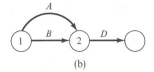

(b)

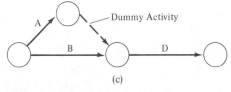

(c)

Figure 12.27   (a) An activity with two predecessors; (b) Improper contruction for two parallel activities; (c) Proper construction for parallel activities using dummy activity.

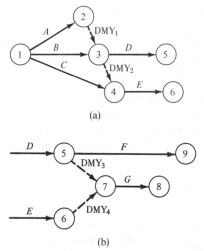

(a)

(b)

Figure 12.28   (a) Partial network with two dummy activities; (b) Partial network with third and fourth dummy activities.

RULE

When you encounter two or more activities that logically begin at the same event and end at the same event, give each a separate ending event and join the ending events with dummy activities.

When we look at activity E we encounter a similar problem.   Activity E follows A, B, and C, whereas activity D follows only A and B. This problem is solved by the addition of a second dummy activity as shown in Figure 12.28(a). Activities F and G bring up another problem.

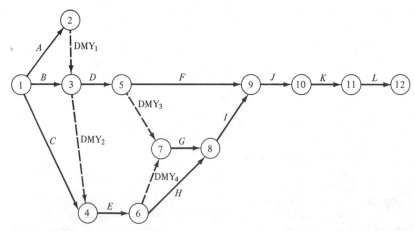

Figure 12.29   Example network.

G is preceded by both D and E, but F is preceded by D only. We can indicate this by joining G's beginning event with dummy activities from the ending events of D and E [Fig. 12.28(b)].

H is preceded by E only, and I is preceded by both G and H. No other activities are preceded by either G or H so they can both end at event 8. The rest of the network is straightforward, and the completed network is shown in Figure 12.29.

We can now place time estimates on the various activities, calculate the T_Es, and find the critical path and earliest completion time for the project (see Table 12.5). The expanded notation scheme can be used now that all the events have been established.

Verify that the T_Es, T_Ls, and slacks in the network are as shown in Figure 12.30. Note that we do not compute activity slacks for the dummy activities. The critical path is 1-2(A), 2-3, 3-5(D), 5-7, 7-8(G), 8-9(I), 9-10(J), 10-11(K), 11-12(L), with an earliest completion time of 52 weeks. The standard deviation of the critical path can now be calculated. Naturally 2-3 and 5-7 can be ignored because they are dummies.

$$\sigma_{CP} = \tfrac{1}{6}\sqrt{16 + 0 + 16 + 0 + 4 + 64 + 4 + 4 + 64}$$
$$= \tfrac{1}{6}\sqrt{172} \approx 2.2 \text{ weeks}$$

With this information we can calculate the probability of completing the project at a particular time. If we start on January 1, for example, the probability we will finish by Christmas (1 week early), is 32.64%.

$$Z = \frac{51 - 52}{2.2} = -.45 \qquad A_{.45} = .3264$$

Table 12.5   EXPECTED TIMES

	ACTIVITY	a	m	b	t_e
A	1-2	4	6	8	6
B	1-3	3	5	7	5
C	1-4	4	6	8	6
DMY$_1$	2-3*	0	0	0	0
DMY$_2$	3-4*	0	0	0	0
D	3-5	2	4	6	4
E	4-6	1	2	3	2
DMY$_3$	5-7*	0	0	0	0
F	5-9	8	10	12	10
DMY$_4$	6-7*	0	0	0	0
H	6-8	7	8	9	8
G	7-8	6	7	8	7
I	8-9	3	7	11	7
J	9-10	8	9	10	9
K	10-11	10	11	12	11
L	11-12	4	8	12	8

* Indicates dummy activity.

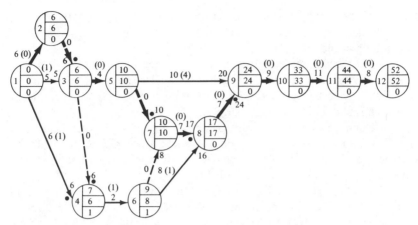

Figure 12.30 Completed network.

PERT/COST

Up to this point in our discussion of PERT we have talked only in terms of the time required to complete activities. PERT/COST includes cost considerations and the relationship between time and cost for each activity. In almost any activity undertaken there will be a trade-off between the time required and the resources allocated to the activity. For example, a contractor may estimate that her present crew can roof a particular house in 2 days, but if she can add more people to the crew, the job can be finished in a single day.

If she doubles her daily cost and cuts the required time in half, she will pay no premium for the time saved. On the other hand, if she more than doubles her cost per day and cuts the time in half, she pays a premium for *crashing* the activity. Crashing an activity is completing the activity in the shortest possible time by allocating additional resources to it.

In PERT/COST we will use two time estimates, the normal time (T_N) and the crash time (T_C), and two cost estimates, $\$_N$ and $\$_C$, as shown in Figure 12.31. For the sake of simplicity we will assume a linear relationship between time and cost. To calculate the cost per week saved (R), we use the relationship

$$R = \frac{\$_C - \$_N}{T_N - T_C}$$

If we have an activity that would normally take 6 weeks to complete at a cost of $2000 and we determine that the activity could be completed in 3 weeks at a cost of $5000, we can achieve a time reduction at a cost of $1000 per week.

$$R = \frac{\$5000 - \$2000}{6 - 3} = \$1000$$

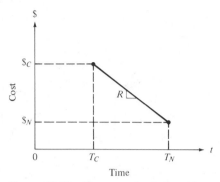

Figure 12.31 Time–cost relationship.

Once the times and costs for the project activities have been established, we have the ability to determine where time can be saved at the least cost. If the project is running behind schedule or if the earliest project completion time under normal conditions is unsatisfactory, we look for the activity on the critical path that has the least cost per week for time reduction. This would be the first activity to be compressed. If we need still more time reduction, the next cheapest activity would be compressed, and so on. A simple example of how the technique can be used is illustrated by the data in Table 12.6. The network is shown in Figure 12.32.

Setting up the network and calculating the earliest completion time under normal conditions gives T_E for event 10 of 33 weeks with a critical path 1-2-3-4-6-9-10. The normal cost for the total project is $65,000.

Table 12.6 PERT/COST DATA

ACTIVITY	NORMAL TIME	CRASH TIME	NORMAL COST	CRASH COST	MAXIMUM WEEKS SAVED	COST PER WEEK SAVED
*1-2	3	1	$ 6,000	$ 8,000	2	$1,000
*2-3	5	2	8,000	14,000	3	2,000
2-5	2	1	2,000	4,000	1	2,000
2-7	4	1	4,000	5,500	3	500
*3-4	6	4	10,000	13,000	2	1,500
*4-6	9	6	8,000	14,000	3	2,000
5-6	4	2	6,000	12,000	2	3,000
*6-9	2	1	2,000	4,000	1	2,000
7-8	1	1	1,000	1,000	0	—
8-9	5	2	3,000	3,600	3	200
4-10	7	3	7,000	11,000	4	1,000
*9-10	8	5	8,000	14,000	3	2,000
$T_{E_N} = 33$		$T_{E_C} = 19$	$65,000	$104,000		

* Critical path activities.

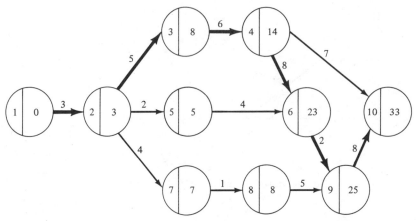

Figure 12.32   Network for PERT/COST example.

What if the project had to be completed in 30 weeks? Of all the activities on the critical path, 1-2 has the least cost for time reduction; so we start there. Unfortunately we can save only 2 weeks; so we must go to the next cheapest activity (3-4) for the remaining week of time reduction. The additional cost for the 3 weeks reduction is then $2 \times \$2000 + 1 \times \$1500 = \$4500$.

What would happen if we wanted to complete the project in the least possible time? Would the critical path change? What would the cost be? To answer these questions we need only construct the network and use the crash times for all activities, as has been done in Figure 12.33.

Crashing *all* activities allows us to finish the project in 19 weeks but costs us $39,000 more. It is not really necessary to crash all activities, only those on the critical path. We need to reduce the time for the non-

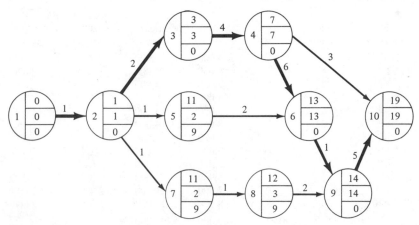

Figure 12.33   All crash times.

critical activities only so that they do not become critical. For example, activity 4-10 can be completed in normal time and still be complete by week 19. This saves $4000. Verify that segments 2-7-8-9 and 2-5-6 can also be completed in normal time without extending the 19-week completion time. Consequently we need only spend an additional $25,000 to crash the project.

Parallel Critical Paths

In many cases we will not be able to complete the noncritical activities in normal time without extending the total project completion time. Any time the completion time for critical path activities is reduced by the amount of slack in a noncritical branch, that branch becomes critical. Then in order to gain further time reduction in the project, we must reduce the time in *both* of the parallel branches, or we must reduce the time in a part of the network that is common to both branches. Consider the network of Figure 12.34(a).

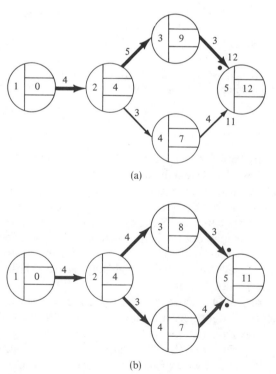

(a)

(b)

Figure 12.34 (a) Original network; (b) One-week reduction, parallel critical paths.

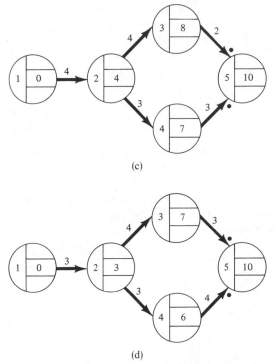

(c)

(d)

Figure 12.34   (c) Two-week reduction, reducing both parallel paths; (d) Two-week reduction, reducing common path activity.

The critical path in this network is 1-2-3-5. We wish to reduce the project completion time by 2 weeks. If we reduce the time of 2-3 by 1 week, we have two paths that are critical, 1-2-3-5 and 1-2-4-5. This is shown in Figure 12.34(b). Now we have to reduce both 2-3-5 and 2-4-5 by 1 week each to gain 1 more week *or* we can reduce 1-2 by 1 week for the same result. The latter choice may or may not be the best strategy. If a 1-week reduction costs $1500 and a 1-week reduction for 2-3-5 and 2-4-5 costs $500 each, we would, of course, choose the cheaper alternative. These are shown in Figures 12.34(c) and 12.34(d).

Some networks may be "tight" networks where there is very little slack in noncritical branches. A tight network may be very expensive to reduce, because reduction may have to take place in several branches. On the other hand, a "loose" network, one that has a great deal of slack in noncritical branches, may be relatively inexpensive to reduce, for we may concentrate on reducing the critical path only.

A PERT/COST EXTENSION

If the completion time for an activity can be reduced by adding resources (money), then the cost of an activity can possibly be reduced by adding time. For those activities for which this is true and that are not on the critical path, we can take advantage of the activity slack for cost reduction. Also, resources can be shifted from those noncritical activities that yield the highest cost saving to critical activities in order to reduce the total completion time at little or no additional cost over normal cost.

SUMMARY OF KEY CONCEPTS

Network model. A graphical description of a problem that shows the relationships between activities in the problem. Activities are represented by lines connecting the events, which are represented by circles.

Critical path method (CPM). A network model that uses only one time estimate for each activity.

PERT. Program evaluation and review technique (3-estimate CPM).

Activity. A single task or closely associated tasks that are part of a total project. Depending on the level of the network, individual activities may be more or less specific. A network for a large project might list the entire design activity as one activity. Activities are represented by arrows in network diagrams.

Expected time (t_e). The best estimate of the time required to complete an activity.

Events. The beginning and ending points for activities. An event takes no time but merely signals the beginning or ending of an activity or group of activities. Events are represented by circles in the PERT network.

Sink point. An event that terminates more than one activity.

Burst point. An event that is the beginning of more than one activity.

Earliest event occurrence (T_E). The latest ending time for activities terminating at a particular event.

Critical path. That particular sequence of activities beginning at the first event and ending at the last event in a network that determines the earliest project completion time or the longest path.

Latest event occurrence (T_L). The time that an event must occur so as not to extend the project completion time.

Event slack. The time by which an event's occurrence can be delayed without extending the project completion time. The time difference between when an event must occur and when it may occur. ($S_i = T_{L_i} - T_{E_i}$).

Activity slack. The difference between the time in which an activity may be completed and the time in which it must be completed in order not to extend the project completion time. $S_{ij} = (T_{L_j} - T_{E_i}) - t_{ij}$.

Branch slack (distributed slack). Activity slack that may be distributed among or shared by a sequence of activities in a branch of a network.

Negative slack. An indication of impending project overrun; shows that the project is behind schedule.

Optimistic time (a). If an activity were performed 100 times, the time estimated for the shortest completion time of the 100 would be the optimistic estimate.

Most likely time (m). The modal completion time estimate if an activity were performed 100 times; the most likely time.

Pessimistic time (b). The longest completion time estimate if an activity were performed 100 times.

Mean of the beta distribution.

$$t_e = \frac{a + 4m + b}{6} = m + \frac{(b - m) - (m - a)}{6}$$

Activity standard deviation.

$$\sigma = \frac{b - a}{6}$$

Standard deviation of the total project completion time distribution.

$$\sigma_{CP} = \sqrt{\sum^{CP} \left(\frac{b - a}{6}\right)^2} = \tfrac{1}{6} \sqrt{\sum^{CP} (b - a)^2}$$

Z transformation.

$$Z = \frac{T - T_{CP}}{\sigma_{CP}}$$

GERT. Graphical evaluation and review technique. An extension of PERT where certain assumptions, such as nonrepetition of events, completion of all activities, and others, are relaxed.

Dummy activity. A zero-time activity used to show precedence relationships.

PERT/COST. A network analysis technique that includes cost ramifications for time saving.

Crashing. Reducing the completion time of activities to a minimum by increasing the resources (money) for the activities.

Time–cost trade-off rate.

$$R = \frac{\$_C - \$_N}{T_N - T_C}$$

PROBLEMS

1. Given the following activities and times
   a. Draw and label the network.
   b. Find the earliest project completion time.
   c. Find the critical path.

Activity	Time
1-2	2
1-3	5
2-3	8
2-5	9
3-4	4
4-5	6
4-6	3
5-6	3

2. Draw the network and find T_E and the critical path for the following activities and times.

Activity	Time
1-2	5
1-3	3
2-4	7
2-5	7
3-4	8
3-6	9
4-7	2
5-8	12
6-7	8
6-8	10
7-8	10

3. Draw the network and find T_E and the critical path for the following project.

Activity	Time
1-2	4
1-3	6
1-4	12
2-4	7
2-5	11
3-4	7
3-7	8
4-6	8
4-7	13
5-6	4
6-7	4

4. In problem 2 find the event slack for events 2 and 5.
5. In problem 2 find the activity slack for activity 6-8.
6. In problem 3 find the slack for the path 2-5-6.

7. Given the following activities and time estimates

Activity	a	m	b (Weeks)
1-2	2	3	4
1-3	6	8	10
1-4	4	4	4
2-5	7	10	10
2-7	4	7	10
3-5	5	8	8
3-6	4	7	13
4-6	6	7	8
5-7	4	5	6
5-8	11	11	14
6-8	7	8	9
6-9	3	5	7
7-9	5	8	14
8-9	9	11	13

 a. Draw the network.
 b. What is the expected project duration?
 c. What is the critical path?
 d. How much slack is there at event 5?
 e. How much slack is there in activity 5-7?

8. For the project described as follows
 a. Draw the network.
 b. What is the expected project duration?
 c. What is the critical path?
 d. What is the standard deviation of the critical path?
 e. What is the probability of completing the project in 22 weeks or less?

Activity	a	m	b
1-2	4	7	10
1-3	2	7	9
1-4	8	10	12
2-3	1	2	3
2-4	2	4	9
3-5	4	5	6
3-6	7	8	15
4-6	6	8	13
5-6	2	5	8

9. In problem 7 what is the probability of completing the project at least 2 weeks ahead of the expected time?

10. In problem 8 there is a $1000 penalty for each week the project requires past the calculated T_E. How much should be included in the project cost estimate to cover the possibility of being 1 week late?

11. Following is a list of project activities, times, maximum time savings, and cost per week of time saved for each activity.

Activity	Time (weeks)	Possible Time Savings	Cost per Week
1-2	10	3	$ 500
1-3	8	1	700
1-4	3	2	1000
2-5	7	2	200
3-4	4	1	400
3-5	6	2	300
4-5	8	2	800

    a. Draw the network and find T_E and the critical path.

    b. Find the most economical strategy for reducing T_E by 3 weeks.

12. In problem 11 find the most economical strategy for reducing T_E by 4 weeks.

Chapter 13

DYNAMIC PROGRAMMING

INTRODUCTION

Unlike other management science techniques that have been covered thus far, dynamic programming does not have a rigid structure or set of equations associated with it. Rather than a technique, it is a procedure for systematically making a set of interrelated decisions that yield an optimum solution.

Like linear programming problems, dynamic programming problems have objective functions and constraints, but the form of these functions may vary from problem to problem or even from one part of a problem to the next. The common characteristic of all dynamic programming problems is that they are complex, with many variables, but they can be broken down into several small problems and solved in such a way as to optimize the overall objective function.

It is often difficult to identify those problems that can be solved with dynamic programming, and once identified, setting up the problem can require a measure of ingenuity. The best way to gain the insight required for proficiency in dynamic programming is through examples. Those contained in this chapter will give you an idea of the breadth of applications for the technique, but they do not, by any means, represent the entire spectrum of dynamic programming problems.

The first example is a variation of the classic stagecoach problem. Note the many similarities between this problem and the CPM problems in the preceding chapter.

UP THE SPLATTERHORN

Mack plans to climb the renowned east face of Splatterhorn Peak in central Kansas. He has purchased a climber's map like that shown in Figure 13.1 which shows the various paths, estimated climbing times, and rest stops which are located at strategic points up the east face, usually at intersections of paths.

Mack's objective is to get from Base Camp to Peak as quickly as possible. Since there are only seven possible routes to the Peak, he knows he could easily add up the hours for each route and choose the shortest. However, Mack wants to try out his new-found quantitative skills and apply the principles of dynamic programming (DP) to the problem. His first step is to redraw his map as shown in Figure 13.2. Note that Mack has divided the map into four *stages* to simplify his calculations.

Analysis Details

With the new map in hand Mack imagines himself to be at the Peak. Obviously, just before getting there, he had to be either at (R7) or (R8). The question is "What are the best routes from each of these stage 1 stops?" In each case there is only one route, so there is no choice. The peak is three hours from (R7) and two hours from (R8).

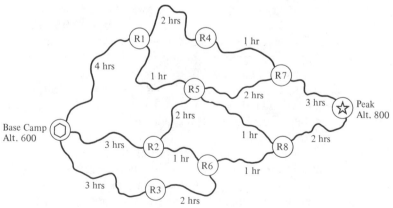

Figure 13.1 East face of the Splatterhorn.

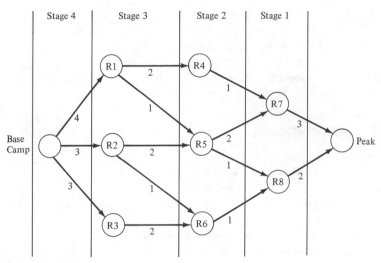

Figure 13.2 Simplified Splatterhorn map.

Now to have reached (R7) or (R8), Mack would have had to have come from a stage 2 stop—(R4), (R5), or (R6). From (R4) there is only one route to stage 1—(R4) → (R7)—with a travel time of 1 hour and a total of 4 hours to the peak. From (R5) there are two possible routes to stage 1—(R5) → (R7) and (R5) → (R8)—with times of 2 and 1 hour, respectively. If Mack were to find himself at (R5), what would be the shortest time to the peak—(R5) → (R7) → (Peak) or (R5) → (R8) → (Peak)? The latter, of course, with a total time of 3 hours as opposed to the former, with a total time of 5 hours. From (R6) there is only one route to stage 1 and on to the peak—(R6) → (R8) → (Peak)—with a total time of 3 hours.

To have reached any stage 2 rest stop, Mack would have had to have departed from a stage 3 rest stop—(R1), (R2), or (R3). From (R1) there are two choices—(R1) → (R4) or (R1) → (R5). If he goes to (R5), he knows he can get to the peak in 3 hours; from (R4) it takes 4 hours. (R1) → (R4) takes 2 hours for a total time to the peak of 6 hours, compared to a total time of 4 hours by way of (R1) → (R5) → (R8) → (Peak). The optimum routing from (R1), then, is to (R5). The same process is used to determine the optimum routing from (R2) and (R3).

The last step in the analysis places Mack at base camp in stage 4. He has already determined the optimum routing from each of the rest stops in stage 3 and is left with only the decision between (Base) → (R1), (Base) → (R2), and (Base) → (R3). At this point the decision is easy. Because the shortest time from each of the stage 3 stops to the peak is known, Mack simply adds the times from base to each of the stage 1 stops to the times from the stops to peak and chooses the route with the shortest total time.

ELEMENTS OF THE DP APPROACH

Let's go back over the example step by step and identify the unique characteristics of the decision process.

Separation of a Single Complex Problem into Several Simpler Problems

The optimum route to the peak from base camp could have been determined by viewing it as a single problem and enumerating the times for all possible paths. However, Mack divided the map into stages, thereby creating four simple problems that could be solved independently, using the output from one stage as input into the next stage.

Backward Pass

Once the problem is segmented into several problems, or stages, the most common approach is to start at the end, or goal, and work backward toward the beginning. We move from the goal into the first stage preceding the goal, and from each state in that stage we calculate the cost of reaching our goal. In our example, the states are the rest stops, and the costs are the times required to complete each leg.

In Table 13.1 the results of each stage are tabulated. Note that in each stage only single legs of the climb are evaluated. The total optimum time for each state is carried over to the next successive state. When we finally get to the last stage, the beginning, we simply trace our way back through the system, progressing from one optimal solution to the next until we reach the goal (the peak).

Principle of Optimality

If we make the optimal decision in each stage, the combination of decisions will be optimal. This follows Bellman's principle of optimality, which states:

> An optimal policy has the property that whatever the initial state and initial decision are, the remaining decisions must constitute an optimal policy with regard to the state resulting from the first decision.

In our example this means that no matter which path we used to arrive at a given rest stop, our optimal decision at *that* point is to select

Table 13.1 SPLATTERHORN DECISION TABULATIONS

STAGE 1 TABULATIONS

(STATE) REST STOP	ALTERNATE ROUTES	TIME TO PEAK	BEST TIME
(R7)	*(R7)→(Peak)	3	3
(R8)	*(R8)→(Peak)	2	2

STAGE 2 TABULATIONS

(STATE) REST STOP	ALTERNATE ROUTES	TIME TO STAGE 1	BEST TIME TO PEAK	TOTAL TIME	BEST TIME
(R4)	*(R4)→(R7)	1	3	4	4
(R5)	(R5)→(R7)	2	3	5	
	*(R5)→(R8)	1	2	3	3
(R6)	*(R6)→(R8)	1	2	3	3

STAGE 3 TABULATIONS

(STATE) REST STOP	ALTERNATE ROUTES	TIME TO STAGE 2	BEST TIME FROM STAGE 2 TO PEAK	TOTAL TIME	BEST TIME
(R1)	(R1)→(R4)	2	4	6	
	*(R1)→(R5)	1	3	4	4
(R2)	(R2)→(R5)	2	3	5	
	*(R2)→(R6)	1	3	4	4
(R3)	*(R3)→(R6)	2	3	5	5

STAGE 4 TABULATIONS

(STATE) REST STOP	ALTERNATE ROUTES	TIME TO STAGE 3	BEST TIME FROM STAGE 3 TO PEAK	TOTAL TIME	BEST TIME
(Base)	(Base)→(R1)	4	4	8	
	*(Base)→(R2)	3	4	7	7
	(Base)→(R3)	3	5	8	

OPTIMUM ROUTE

$$(Base) \xrightarrow{3} (R2) \xrightarrow{1} (R6) \xrightarrow{1} (R8) \xrightarrow{2} (Peak)$$

Shortest Time: $3 + 1 + 1 + 2 = 7$ hours

the shortest path from the point to the peak. If a rest stop is on the optimal path, the shortest route from that rest stop to the peak is also on the optimal path.

The Objective Function

We examined the objective function in our discussion of linear programming. It was always stated as

$$\text{Max } Z = C_1 X_1 + C_2 X_2 + \cdots + C_n X_n$$

or

$$\text{Min } Z = C_1 X_1 + C_2 X_2 + \cdots + C_n X_n$$

where the X_js were the real variables and the C_js were constants representing contribution margins for maximization problems or costs for minimization problems. Objective functions for DP problems may be stated in much the same way, but they need not be linear as long as the function can be separated by stages.

In our Splatterhorn example we might express the objective function as

$$\text{Min } Z = X_1 + X_2 + X_3 + X_4$$

where Z is the total time for the climb and X_1–X_4 are the times required in stages 1–4, respectively.

DP may be employed for solving problems that have either maximization or minimization objective functions. Actually each stage has its own objective function, which is:

$$\text{Opt } Z_i = X_i + Z_{i-1}^*$$

where X_i represents the choices in stage i and Z_{i-1}^* represents the *optimal* decision from stage $i - 1$ to the end of the problem. The overall objective function is then

$$\text{Opt } Z = \sum Z_i$$

which agrees with Bellman's principle. If each stage is optimized, the total system will be optimized.

Transformation Function

The transformation function is the mathematical relationship that ties the stages of a DP problem together. This function will be discussed in more detail in the following examples.

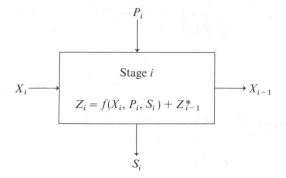

X_i = Input to stage i from stage $i + 1$

P_i = Input to stage i independent of previous stages

S_i = Output at stage i

X_{i-1} = Input to stage $i - 1$ from stage i

Z_{i-1}^* = Optimum value of objective function for stages $i - 1$ to the end of the problem

Z_i = Objective function for stage i in terms of X_i, P_i, S_i, and Z_{i-1}^*

The decision at stage i may be in terms of P_i, S_i, or both.

Figure 13.3   Dynamic programming model.

General Structure of DP Problems

Figure 13.3 illustrates the general layout of a DP problem. This layout is typical for all DP problems. The letter symbols may change from problem to problem to facilitate understanding or simply for convenience. This structure will become clearer after we examine a few more examples.

SALES DISTRIBUTION EXAMPLE

Assume that a farmer has 10 pigs to sell and a choice of 4 markets in which to sell them. Each of the markets has a different demand function (price quantity relationship), and each has a limited demand for pigs. The demand functions are shown in Figure 13.4. The farmer desires to maximize his profit on the 10 pigs; so he must decide how many to sell at each market. The 4 markets are the stages; the X_is are the number of pigs available for sale at each stage; and the S_is are the number sold at each stage.

Because there is no time relationship between the stages, it is irrelevant which stage represents which market. It is relevant that the decision at each stage depends on the decisions for all other stages.

To make the problem conform more closely to our previous example, we may assume that the farmer is going to load up his pigs in a truck and

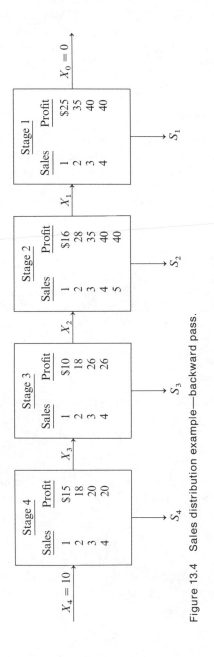

Figure 13.4 Sales distribution example—backward pass.

drive from stage 4 to stage 3, then to stage 2, and finally to stage 1, dropping off the optimum number of pigs at each stage. $X_4 = 10$ indicates the number of pigs on the truck when he reaches stage 4. X_3, X_2, and X_1 represent the number of pigs left on the truck as he reaches stage 3, stage 2, and stage 1, respectively. The fact that $X_0 = 0$ means he must sell all the pigs.

Transformation Function

The relationship between the stages in this example is a simple one: The number of pigs left over to be distributed among the remaining stages (X_{i-1}) is equal to the number on hand when we entered the ith stage (X_i) minus the number we decide to sell at stage i (S_i). Mathematically, this relationship is expressed as follows.

$$X_{i-1} = X_i - S_i$$

Decision Variable

Our decision in each stage is: "How many should I sell in this stage (S_i) in order to maximize my profit for this stage and all subsequent stages?" Because X_i is determined by the choices in previous stages, our only decision variable is S_i.

Objective Function

Because our objective is to maximize profit for this *and* subsequent stages, we must consider both the profit in this stage and the impact our decision has on the profits for the following stages.

$$\mathbb{P}^*_{(X_i)} = \text{Max}\{\mathbb{P}_{(S_i)} + \mathbb{P}^*_{(X_{i-1})}\}$$

To accomplish this we must calculate the profit for each feasible combination of X_i and S_i values that is possible at each stage.

Feasible Solution

Frequently the structure of the problem will dictate that certain values for X_i and/or S_i are not possible. We will use this information to form a sort of "feasible region" and reduce our computational difficulty.

Payoff Tables

Tables 13.2(a)–(d) are the payoff tables for each stage. Starting with 13.2(a), let's examine what they mean and how they are constructed.

Table 13.2   PAYOFF TABLES (BACKWARD PASS)

(a) STAGE 1

X_1 \ S_1	0	1	2	3	4	P_1^*	S_1^*	S_0^*
0	⓪	—	—	—	—	0	0	0
1	—	㉕	—	—	—	25	1	0
2	—	—	㉟	—	—	35	2	0
3	—	—	—	㊵	—	40	3	0
4	—	—	—	—	㊵	40	4	0

(b) STAGE 2

X_1 \ S_2	0	1	2	3	4	5	P_2^*	S_2^*	X_1^*
2	35	㊷	28	—	—	—	41	1	1
3	40	51	㊝	35	—	—	53	2	1
4	40	56	㊫	60	40	—	63	2	2
5	—	56	68	㉘	65	40	70	3	2
6	—	—	68	㊛	㊛	65	75	3, 4	3, 2
7	—	—	—	75	㊿	75	80	4	3
8	—	—	—	—	㊿	㊿	80	4, 5	4, 3
9	—	—	—	—	—	㊿	80	5	4

(c) STAGE 3

X_3 \ S_3	0	1	2	3	4	P_3^*	S_3^*	X_2^*
6	75	80	㊵	79	67	81	2	4
7	80	85	88	⑧⑨	79	89	3	4
8	80	90	93	⑨⑥	89	96	3	5
9	80	90	98	⑩①	96	101	3	6
10	—	90	98	⑩⑥	101	106	3	7

(d) STAGE 4

X_4 \ S_4	0	1	2	3	4	P^*	S^*	X_3^*
10	106	⑪⑥	114	109	101	116	1	9

Stage 1　The numbers across the top represent the number of pigs it will be possible to sell at stage 1 (0–4). The numbers down the left-hand side represent the possible number of pigs that may be on the truck when the farmer arrives at stage 1. The numbers within the body of the table are the values of the objective function for every possible combination of X_1 and S_1. Because he must leave stage 1 with no pigs, he must sell exactly the number he bring to stage 1. If he brings no pigs, he sells no pigs, and the payoff is 0. If he brings 1, he sells 1, and the payoff is $25. The $25 comes from the demand function for stage 1. The other payoffs are found in the same way.

The column headed P_1^* contains the optimum payoff for each X_1 and the S_1^* column lists the decision that yields that optimum. Because there is only one decision possible for each X_1, there is only one payoff for each.

Stage 2　In Table 13.2(b) the situation becomes more complicated because of the increased combinations of X_2 and S_2. For example, the smallest number of pigs that can be on the truck when it reaches stage 2 is 2, because the farmer could have sold a maximum of 8 pigs at stages 4 and 3. If there are 2 pigs on the truck, the farmer has three choices at stage 2. He may sell none at stage 2 and 2 at stage 1 for a return of $35, 1 at stage 2 and 1 at stage 1 for a profit of $16 + $25 = $41, or both at stage 2 for a profit of $28.

The maximum number of pigs that can be on the truck when it reaches stage 2 is 9, because that is all that can be absorbed in stages 2 and 1. In this case there is only one decision possible, sell 5 pigs at stage 2 and 4 at stage 1 for a return of $40 + $40 = $80.

The value of S_2 that yields the highest *combined* profit for stages 1 and 2 is selected for each possible value of X_2. Note that when $X_2 = 6$ or 8, there are two equally attractive values for S_2.

Stage 3　The smallest number of pigs that can be on the truck at stage 3 is 6, because the maximum number that can be sold prior to that is 4. The largest number that can be on the truck is 10, because it is possible to sell none at stage 4 and the following three stages can absorb 10 or more.

Here is how the payoffs for stage 3 are determined [see Table 13.2(c)]. For $X_3 = 6$ and $S_3 = 0$, $X_2 = 6 - 0 = 6$, and the optimum payoff for $X_2 = 6$ is $75 [from Table 13.2(b)]. The payoff, then, for ($X_3 = 6$, $S_3 = 0$) is $75 (0 + 75). For $X_3 = 6$ and $S_3 = 1$, $X_2 = 6 - 1 = 5$. The payoff is $10 for the 1 pig sold in stage 3, plus $70 (which is the optimum payoff for $X_2 = 5$) for a total of $80. When this row is completed, we find that the best strategy when

Table 13.3 SOLUTION

STAGE	X_i^*	S_i^*	X_{i-1}^*	PROFIT (STAGE i ONLY)
4	10	1	9	15
3	9	3	6	26
2	6	3, 4	3, 2	35, 40
1	3, 2	3, 2	0	40, 35
		Total Profit		$116

$X_3 = 6$ is to sell 2 in stage 3 and pass 4 to stage 2. The payoff and optimum decision are shown in the P_3^* and S_3^* columns ($81, 2 pigs).

The remainder of the table is filled in the same manner. Note that the S_3^* column contains the optimum decisions for all possible values of X_3.

Stage 4 The stage 4 table [Table 13.2(d)] is simple, because there is only one possible value of X_4. If the farmer sells no pigs in stage 4, he carries all 10 pigs to stage 3 ($X_3 = 10$), and we find that the optimum return for $X_3 = 10$ is $106 [Table 13.2(c)]. If 1 pig is sold at stage 4, 9 pigs are passed to stage 3 ($X_3 = 9$) for a return of $101 + $15 = $116. When the rest of the table is filled in, we see that the optimum strategy at stage 4 is to sell 1 pig and pass the rest on to the other stages.

The Total Strategy

When we complete the table for stage 4, we know our optimum decision for that stage and the total return for all stages. Now we need to determine the optimum number of pigs to sell at each stage to yield the overall optimum solution.

The complete solution can now be determined to be that shown in Table 13.3. Note the multiple optimal choices for S_1^* and S_2^*. If we set S_2 equal to 4, then $X_1 = 2$ and $S_1 = 2$. If we set S_2 equal to 3, then $X_1 = 3$ and $S_1 = 3$. In either case the return is the same and is optimal.

SALES DISTRIBUTION EXAMPLE WITH A NEW TWIST

Earlier in the chapter we mentioned that the "backward pass" was the most common approach to solving DP problems; it is also possible to use a "forward pass" approach when it is more convenient. In the following example the major change from previous examples is notational. X_i, for example, is the output from stage i rather than the input to it, so

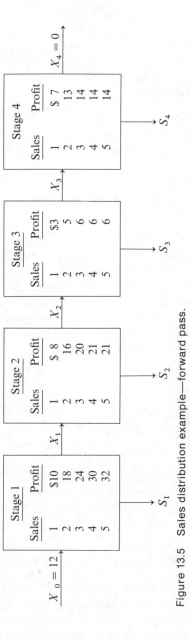

Figure 13.5 Sales distribution example—forward pass.

that the transformation function is

$$X_i = X_{i-1} - S_i$$

The objective function at each stage must include the profit for that stage and all *previous* stages.

$$P^*_{(X_i)} = \text{Max}\{P_{(S_i)} + P^*_{(X_{i-1})}\}$$

The primary philosophical difference between the forward pass and the backward pass is that in the backward pass we focus on the number *entering* the stage, whereas in the forward pass we concentrate on the number *leaving* the stage.

In this example let's assume that our farmer has 12 pigs to sell in the next 4 weeks. The profit functions for each week are shown in Figure 13.5. Week 1 is stage 1, week 2 is stage 2, etc. Obviously, the farmer's objective is to maximize his profit.

The first step in solving this DP problem is to construct the stage 1 table. Because the market will absorb 5 pigs in the first week, the farmer has the option of selling 0, 1, 2, 3, 4, or 5 of his pigs that week. The largest number of pigs he can withhold from the market until the following 3 weeks is 12, because more than 12 can be absorbed in weeks 2, 3, and 4. The smallest number of pigs that he can wait to sell is 7. This is the number left if he decides to sell 5 in the first week. Table 13.4(a) is the completed table for week 1 with the payoffs for all possible combinations of X_1 and S_1.

In constructing the table for week 2 (stage 2) the possible values of S_2 are 0–5, as in Stage 1. However, the possible values for X_2 are different. If all possible pigs are sold in weeks 1 and 2, there will be only 2 left to sell in weeks 3 and 4; so the minimum value of X_2 is 2. Only a possible total of 10 pigs can be sold in the last 2 weeks; so X_2 has a maximum value of 10.

Table 13.4(a)   PAYOFF TABLE (FORWARD PASS): STAGE 1

X_1 \ S_1	0	1	2	3	4	5	P_1^*	S_1^*	X_0^*
12	⓪	—	—	—	—	—	0	0	12
11	—	⑩	—	—	—	—	10	1	12
10	—	—	⑱	—	—	—	18	2	12
9	—	—	—	㉔	—	—	24	3	12
8	—	—	—	—	㉚	—	30	4	12
7	—	—	—	—	—	㉜	32	5	12

The stage 2 calculations are summarized in Table 13.4(b). As an example, consider the profits for $X_2 = 8$. If 8 pigs are passed to stage 3, the farmer would have to have sold 4 pigs in weeks 1 and 2. When $S_2 = 0$, all 4 would have been sold in week 1, and X_1 would have been $X_2 + S_2$ or $8 + 0 = 8$ and $S_1 = 4$. From Figure 13.5, we find the profit for the sale of 4 pigs in week 1 is \$30.

Table 13.4(b) PAYOFF TABLE (FORWARD PASS): STAGE 2

S_2 \ X_2	1	1	2	3	4	5	$P_2{}^*$	$S_2{}^*$	$X_1{}^*$
10	(18)	(18)	16	—	—	—	18	0, 1	10, 11
9	24	(26)	(26)	20	—	—	26	1, 2	10, 11
8	30	32	(34)	30	21	—	34	2	10
7	32	38	(40)	38	31	21	40	2	9
6	—	40	(46)	44	39	31	46	2	8
5	—	—	48	(50)	45	39	50	3	8
4	—	—	—	(52)	51	45	52	3	7
3	—	—	—	—	(53)	51	53	4	7
2	—	—	—	—	—	(53)	53	5	7

Table 13.4(c) PAYOFF TABLE (FORWARD PASS): STAGE 3

S_3 \ X_3	0	1	2	3	4	5	$P_3{}^*$	$S_3{}^*$	$X_2{}^*$
5	(50)	49	45	40	32	24	50	0	5
4	52	(53)	51	46	40	32	53	1	5
3	53	(55)	(55)	52	46	40	55	1, 2	4, 5
2	53	56	(57)	56	52	46	57	2	4
1	—	56	(58)	(58)	56	52	58	2, 3	3, 4
0	—	—	58	(59)	58	56	59	3	3

Table 13.4(d) PAYOFF TABLE (FORWARD PASS): STAGE 4

S_4 \ X_4	0	1	2	3	4	5	$P_4{}^*$	$S_4{}^*$	$X_3{}^*$
0	59	65	(70)	69	67	64	70	2	2

TABLE 13.5 SOLUTION (FORWARD PASS)

STAGE	X_i^*	S_i^*	X_{i-1}^*	PROFIT (STAGE i ONLY)
4	0	2	2	13
3	2	2	4	5
2	4	3	7	20
1	7	5	12	32
		Total Profit		$70

When X_2 is 8 and S_2 is 1, it means 1 pig is sold in week 2 and 8 are held for sale in weeks 3 and 4. The profit for 1 pig sold in week 2 is $8. The other three must have been sold in week 1 for a profit of $24; $24 + $8 = $32.

When $X_2 = 8$ and $S_2 = 2$, then 2 pigs are sold in week 2 and 2 in week 1 for profits of $16 and $18, respectively, for a total of $34. In the same manner the payoff of $30 for $X_2 = 8$ and $S_2 = 3$ is the profit for 3 pigs sold in week 2 ($20) plus the profit for 1 pig sold in week 1 ($10). Similarly, the $21 profit results from selling 4 pigs in week 2.

The remainder of the table and the tables for stage 3 and stage 4 are constructed in the same manner as the stage 2 table. These results are summarized in Tables 13.4(c) and 13.4(d).

Beginning with the optimum choice in stage 4 ($X_4^* = 0$, $S_4^* = 2$, $X_3^* = 2$), we work backward to stage 3 ($X_3^* = 2$, $S_3^* = 2$, $X_2^* = 4$); stage 2 ($X_2^* = 4$, $S_2^* = 3$, $X_1^* = 7$); and stage 1 ($X_1^* = 7$, $S_1^* = 5$, $X_0^* = 12$). These results are summarized in Table 13.5. The optimum strategy is to sell 5 pigs the first week, 3 the second week, 2 the third week, and 2 the fourth week for a total profit of $70.

As an exercise you may wish to resolve these two problems in the reverse directions to show that the results are the same regardless of whether the forward or the backward approach is used. When only one end value is known (either starting or finishing) we would begin at the opposite end and work toward the known value. In these examples, both end values were known, so either method could be used.

PRODUCTION PLANNING EXAMPLE

In this example the objective will be to minimize the total cost of production and inventory over a 3-month period when sales for each month are known. Let P_i represent the number of units produced in period i; X_i represent the number of units transferred into period i; and S_i represent sales in period i.

There is a cost (inventory cost) associated with the X_is. This cost is expressed as a mathematical relationship rather than as a tabulation.

Constraints

$2 \leq p_i \leq 7$ $\qquad$ $X_0 = 2$ $\quad$ $X_3 = 2$ $\quad$ $S_1 = 5$ $\quad$ $S_2 = 7$ $\quad$ $S_3 = 3$

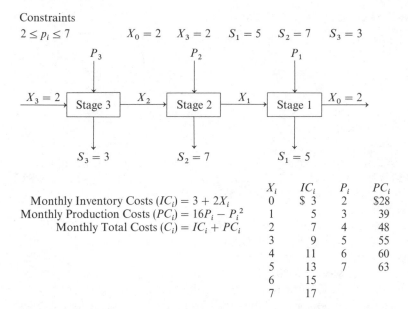

	X_i	IC_i	P_i	PC_i
Monthly Inventory Costs $(IC_i) = 3 + 2X_i$	0	\$ 3	2	\$28
Monthly Production Costs $(PC_i) = 16P_i - P_i^2$	1	5	3	39
Monthly Total Costs $(C_i) = IC_i + PC_i$	2	7	4	48
	3	9	5	55
	4	11	6	60
	5	13	7	63
	6	15		
	7	17		

Cumulative Total Cost $= TC_i^* = \text{Min}\{C_i + TC_{i-1}^*\}$
(Objective Function)

Figure 13.6   Production planning example.

For units produced in one period and not sold until a later period, the cost is $IC_i = 3 + 2X_i$ per month. The production cost for each period is $PC_i = 16P_i - P_i^2$.

In addition to the sales constraints, we have the additional restrictions that $X_3 = 2$, $X_0 = 2$, and $2 \leq P_i \leq 7$. All of the essentials for this example are summarized in Figure 13.6.

The transformation function for this example is

$$X_i + P_i = S_i + X_{i-1}$$

which means that the amount entering a stage $(X_i + P_i)$ is equal to the amount leaving a stage $(S_i + X_{i-1})$. For our purposes, we express this as

$$X_{i-1} = X_i + P_i - S_i$$

The calculations for the problem are shown in Table 13.6. They follow exactly the same steps as the previous examples. Note that we have used the backward pass approach and that we have ignored the cost of carrying 2 units of X_0. (Had we included this cost, it would have simply added \$7 to every entry in the entire table.) The solution to the problem is summarized in Table 13.7.

Table 13.6 CALCULATIONS FOR PRODUCTION PLANNING PROBLEM

(a) STAGE 1

X_i \ P_i	2	3	4	5	6	7	$TC_1{}^*$	$P_1{}^*$	S_i	$X_0{}^*$
0	—	—	—	—	—	(66)	66	7	5	2
1	—	—	—	—	(65)	—	65	6	5	2
2	—	—	—	(62)	—	—	62	5	5	2
3	—	—	(57)	—	—	—	57	4	5	2
4	—	(50)	—	—	—	—	50	3	5	2
5	(41)	—	—	—	—	—	41	2	5	2

(b) STAGE 2

X_2 \ P_2	2	3	4	5	6	7	$TC_2{}^*$	$P_2{}^*$	S_2	$X_1{}^*$
1	—	—	—	—	(131)	133	131	6	7	0
2	—	—	—	(128)	132	132	128	5	7	0
3	—	—	(123)	129	131	129	123	4	7	0
4	—	(116)	124	128	128	123	116	3	7	0
5	(107)	117	123	125	123	117	107	2	7	0
6	(108)	116	120	120	116	—	108	2	7	1

(c) STAGE 3

X_3 \ P^3	2	3	4	5	6	7	$TC_3{}^*$	$P_3{}^*$	S_3	$X_2{}^*$
2	(166)	174	178	178	174	178	166	2	3	1

Table 13.7 SOLUTIONS TO PRODUCTION PLANNING PROBLEM

STAGE	$X_i{}^*$	$P_i{}^*$	S_i	$X_{i-1}{}^*$	IC_i	PC_i	$C_i{}^*$
3	2	2	3	1	7	28	35
2	1	6	7	0	5	60	65
1	0	7	5	2	3	63	66
						Total Cost	$166

AN INVESTMENT EXAMPLE

In this example we will recap the steps in the DP approach to reinforce what you have learned so far.

Let us assume that a company has $100,000 available to invest for the next year and that there are four alternatives available.

1. Only $40,000 or less may be invested in corporate bonds (I_1) that will return 4%.
2. Venture A may be financed at various levels and will return 10% on all investment above the $20,000 machinery lease $[.1(I_2 - $20,000)]$. No more than $70,000 may be invested in venture A.
3. Venture B may be financed at various levels and will return 8% on all investment above the $10,000 franchise fee $[.08(I_3 - $10,000)]$. Investment in venture B may not exceed $60,000.
4. Investment C may be financed at various levels and will return .05% (I_4). Investment C may not exceed $30,000.

All $100,000 must be invested, and decisions are restricted to $10,000 increments.

In Figure 13.7 the investment opportunities as well as the tabulated return functions are shown graphically. The order in which we listed the four investments is purely arbitrary and will *not* affect our solution at all. Any other ordering would lead us to the same optimal result.

If R_i represents the return from stage i, X_i represents available funds passed from stage to stage, and I_i represents the amount invested in alternative i, the objective is to maximize total return (TR) for stage i and all subsequent stages.

$$TR_i^* = \text{Max}\{R_i + TR_{i-1}^*\}$$

The transformation function is

$$X_{i-1} = X_i - I_i$$

In words, the amount passed out of a stage is equal to the amount passed in less the amount invested. The calculations are summarized in Table 13.8.

For the stage 1 table, the limits of X_1 and I_1 are both $0 minimum and $40,000 maximum. X_1 may be as little as $0, because it is possible to exhaust the entire $100,000 in the other three stages. I_1 may be $0, because we are not required to invest in bonds. There is only one value of I_1 for each value of X_1, because the same amount must be invested as is passed in.

In stage 2, I_2 may range from $0 to $70,000, and X_2 may range between $10,000 and $100,000. Ten thousand dollars is the amount that would be passed if the maximum amount were absorbed in stages 3 and 4, and $100,000 would be passed if none were absorbed in stages 3 and 4. There are no entries for $X_2 = 20$ and $I_2 = 30$, because the amount invested cannot exceed the amount passed in. The same holds true for $X_2 = 30$, $I_2 = 40$ and on down the table to $X_2 = 60$, $I_2 = 70$.

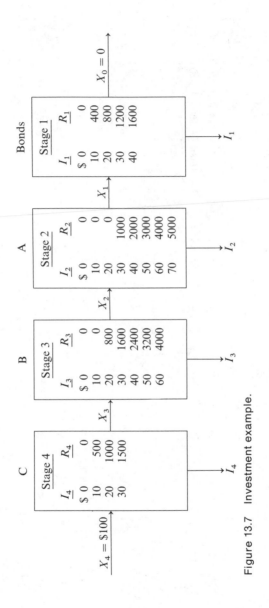

Figure 13.7 Investment example.

Table 13.8 CALCULATIONS FOR THE INVESTMENT PROBLEM

(a) STAGE 1

X_1 \ I_1	0	10	20	30	40	TR_1^*	I_1^*	X_0^*
0	(0)					0	0	0
10		(400)				400	10	0
20			(800)			800	20	0
30				(1200)		1200	30	0
40					(1600)	1600	40	0

(b) STAGE 2

X_2 \ I_2	0	10	20	30	40	50	60	70	TR_2^*	I_2^*	X_1^*
10	(400)	0	—	—	—	—	—	—	400	0	10
20	(800)	400	0	—	—	—	—	—	800	0	20
30	(1200)	800	400	1000	—	—	—	—	1200	0	30
40	1600	1200	800	1400	(2000)	—	—	—	2000	40	0
50	—	1600	1200	1800	2400	(3000)	—	—	3000	50	0
60	—	—	1600	2200	2800	3400	(4000)	—	4000	60	0
70	—	—	—	2600	3200	3800	4400	(5000)	5000	70	0
80	—	—	—	—	3600	4200	4800	(5400)	5400	70	10
90	—	—	—	—	—	4600	5200	(5800)	5800	70	20
100	—	—	—	—	—	—	5600	(6200)	6200	70	30

(c) STAGE 3

I_3 / X_3	0	10	20	30	40	50	60	TR_3^*	I_3^*	X_2^*
70	(5000)	4000	3800	3600	3600	4000	4400	5000	0	70
80	(5400)	5000	4800	4600	4400	4400	4800	5400	0	80
90	(5800)	5400	5800	5600	5400	5200	5200	5800	0	90
100	6200	5800	6200	(6600)	6400	6200	6000	6600	30	70

(d) STAGE 4

I_4 / X_4	0	10	20	30	TR_4^*	I_4^*	X_3^*
100	(6600)	6300	6400	6500	6600	0	100

Table 13.9 SOLUTION TO
INVESTMENT PROBLEM

STAGE	$X_i{}^*$	$I_i{}^*$	S_{i-1}^*	$R_i{}^*$
4	100	0	100	0
3	100	30	70	1600
2	70	70	0	5000
1	0	0	0	0
			Total Return	$6600

There are no entries from $X_2 = 50$, $I_2 = 0$ to $X_2 = 100$, $I_2 = 50$, because X_1 may not exceed 40 and $X_1 = X_2 - I_2$. Thus $X_2 - I_2$ may not exceed 40.

When the returns for all feasible combinations of X_i and I_i have been calculated for each table, determine the optimum value in each row and record it in the TR^* column. In the I^* column record the I value for which the optimum R value occurs.

After completing the tables for all stages, we begin with the last table completed and work back through the tables to identify the overall optimum strategy, shown in Table 13.9.

A KNAPSACK EXAMPLE

The knapsack example is a classic application of the DP approach. In this type of problem there is a limited amount of space or carrying capacity and a variety of items that have some volume or weight and some value. The value may be nutritional value in the case of food items or utility in the case of camping items, NASA space probes, and the like.

In our example we will assume that we have a carrying capacity of 13 lbs maximum and 4 varieties of food items we may carry. The items are prepackaged and may not be broken down to packages smaller than specified. The items are as follows.

A   Weight 2 lbs per package; 500 nutritional units per package.
B   Weight 3 lbs; 850 nutritional units.
C   Weight 4 lbs; 1100 nutritional units.
D   Weight 1 lb; 225 nutritional units.

The objective is to load the knapsack in such a way as to maximize the nutritional units without exceeding the 13-lb maximum load. Notationally we will use K_i to indicate available capacity at stage i; N_i, the number of units of item i loaded in the pack; W_i, the weight of N units; V_i, the nutritional value in stage i; and $TV_i^* = \text{Max}\{V_i + TV_{i-1}^*\}$, the total nutritional value for stage i and all subsequent stages. The transfer function is $K_{i-1} = K_i - W_i$.

The problem is formulated in Figure 13.8, and the calculations and the solution are summarized in Tables 13.10 and 13.11.

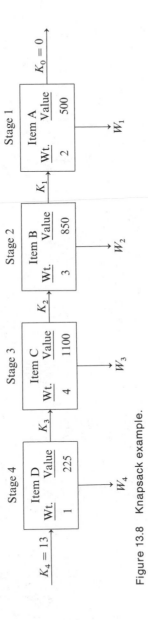

Figure 13.8 Knapsack example.

Table 13.10 CALCULATIONS FOR KNAPSACK PROBLEM

(a) STAGE 1

K_1	N_1: 0 / W_1: 0	1 / 2	2 / 4	3 / 6	4 / 8	5 / 10	6 / 12	TV_1^*	W_1^*	N_1^*	K_0^*
0	(0)	—	—	—	—	—	—	0	0	0	0
1	(0)	—	—	—	—	—	—	0	0	0	1
2	—	(500)	—	—	—	—	—	500	2	1	0
3	—	(500)	—	—	—	—	—	500	2	1	1
4	—	—	(1000)	—	—	—	—	1000	4	2	0
5	—	—	(1000)	—	—	—	—	1000	4	2	1
6	—	—	—	(1500)	—	—	—	1500	6	3	0
7	—	—	—	(1500)	—	—	—	1500	6	3	1
8	—	—	—	—	(2000)	—	—	2000	8	4	0
9	—	—	—	—	(2000)	—	—	2000	8	4	1
10	—	—	—	—	—	(2500)	—	2500	10	5	0
11	—	—	—	—	—	(2500)	—	2500	10	5	1
12	—	—	—	—	—	—	(3000)	3000	12	6	0
13	—	—	—	—	—	—	(3000)	3000	12	6	1

(b) STAGE 2

K_2 / N_2,W_2	0, 0	1, 3	2, 6	3, 9	4, 12	TV_2^*	W_2^*	N_2^*	K_1^*
0	(0)	—	—	—	—	0	0	0	0
1	(0)	—	—	—	—	0	0	0	1
2	(500)	—	—	—	—	500	0	0	2
3	500	(850)	—	—	—	850	3	1	0
4	(1000)	850	—	—	—	1000	0	0	4
5	1000	(1350)	—	—	—	1350	3	1	2
6	1500	1350	(1700)	—	—	1700	6	2	0
7	1500	(1850)	1700	—	—	1850	3	1	4
8	2000	1850	(2200)	—	—	2200	6	2	2
9	2000	2350	2200	(2550)	—	2550	9	3	0
10	2500	2350	(2700)	2550	—	2700	6	2	4
11	2500	2850	2700	(3050)	—	3050	9	3	2
12	3000	2850	3200	3050	(3400)	3400	12	4	0
13	3000	3350	3200	(3550)	3400	3550	9	3	4

(c) STAGE 3

K_3 / N_3,W_3	0, 0	1, 4	2, 8	3, 12	TV_3^*	W_2^*	N_3^*	K_2^*
0	(0)	—	—	—	0	0	0	0
1	(0)	—	—	—	0	0	0	1
2	(500)	—	—	—	500	0	0	2
3	(850)	—	—	—	850	0	0	3
4	1000	(1100)	—	—	1100	4	1	0
5	(1350)	1100	—	—	1350	0	0	5
6	(1700)	1600	—	—	1700	0	0	6
7	1850	(1950)	—	—	1950	4	1	3
8	(2200)	2100	(2200)	—	2200	0, 8	0, 1	8, 0
9	(2550)	2450	2200	—	2550	0	0	9
10	2700	(2800)	2700	—	2800	4	1	6
11	2050	2950	(3050)	—	3050	8	2	3
12	(3400)	3300	3200	3300	3400	0	0	12
13	3550	(3650)	3550	3300	3650	4	1	9

(d) STAGE 4

K_4 / N_4,W_4	0,0	1,1	2,2	3,3	4,4	5,5	6,6	7,7	8,8	9,9	10,10	11,11	12,12	13,13
13	(3650)	3625	3500	3475	3450	3325	3300	3275	3150	3125	3100	2975	2700	2925

TV_4^*	W_4^*	N_4^*	K_3^*
3650	0	0	13

Table 13.11 SOLUTION TO KNAPSACK
PROBLEM

STAGE	K_i^*	W_i^*	N_i^*	K_{i-1}^*	V_i^*
4	13	0	0	13	0
3	13	4	1	9	1100
2	9	9	3	0	2550
1	0	0	0	0	0
				Total Value	3650

CONCLUSION

As we have seen, the mathematics of dynamic programming are elementary, and DP is a philosophy rather than an algorithm. In DP, you create your own algorithm to fit the specific problem under consideration.

The major feature of DP is the process of separating a large, complex problem into a number of manageable segments or stages and solving the segments sequentially. Sometimes the stages fall logically into place, especially when time periods are involved. In other cases the stages must be artifically created. In the example where the farmer sold his pigs over a 4-week period, it was obvious which week was the first stage and which was the last. In the example where he sold pigs in 4 different markets, it really made no difference which market was which stage. The important consideration was identifying points at which decisions were to be made.

Other major factors in DP are the transformation function and the cost or payoff function. The transformation function ties the stages together to show the relationship of a decision in one stage to decisions in other stages. The cost or payoff function allows you to calculate the result of a decision.

The examples that we have explored in this chapter have all been discrete. This is not a requirement for using the DP approach. It is possible for a continuous function to be involved, but the mathematics for solution are much more complex in this case. Also, in our examples, the optimum decisions in each stage have been easy to identify. This is not always the case. It is possible for some optimization technique such as linear programming to be required to determine the optimum stage decisions.

The purpose of this chapter is to acquaint you with the DP philosophy and not to enumerate all possible DP applications. Few problems in business will perfectly fit any of the quantitative techniques that have been discussed previously because their requirements are fairly rigid. DP, on the other hand, has "rubber walls" and can be stretched to fit the needs of the decision maker.

SUMMARY OF KEY CONCEPTS

Stage. One of the segments into which a complex problem is divided.

State. A possible condition within a stage. In a sales distribution problem the states might be sell 1, sell 2, sell 3, etc.

Backward pass. A method of solving a DP problem by starting at the last stage and working back toward the first stage.

Forward pass. A method of solving a DP problem by starting at the first stage and working forward toward the last stage.

Immediate goal. The optimum solution between stages.

Long-range goal. The overall optimum solution for all stages.

Bellman's principal of optimality. "An optimal policy has the property that whatever the initial state and initial decision are, the remaining decisions must constitute an optimal policy with regard to the state resulting from the first decision."

Objective function. The function that is to be optimized. (Maximize profit, minimize cost, etc.)

Transformation function. The function that ties the various stages of a DP problem together. In a sales distribution problem, for example, the transformation function is the relationship between the units carried over from the previous stage, the number sold in the current stage, and the number passed on to the following stage.

PROBLEMS

1. The Lyk-Nu Golf Ball Company sells refurbished golf balls. The demand curve for the balls varies with the seasons, so they vary their price in an attempt to maximize their profits. They wish to maintain a fairly stable range of prices, so they do not permit the price to change by more than $1 from one season to the next. Their anticipated profits at various prices for the four quarters of the year are as follows. What should be their prices in each quarter, and what is their maximum total profit for the year? If the $1 shift restriction is removed, what would be their maximum annual profit?

	QUARTER			
PRICE/DOZEN	WINTER	SPRING	SUMMER	FALL
$5	400	400	600	1200
$6	500	500	700	800
$7	600	1000	900	500
$8	700	800	900	600
$9	1000	700	700	900
$10	800	500	500	1200

2. The numbers in the grid represent miles between the lettered points. Find the shortest route from point *A* to point *P*, using dynamic programming. Repeat the problem finding the *longest* route by dynamic programming.

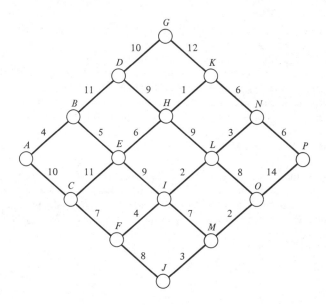

3. A manufacturer of fiberglass swimming pools has 2 pools in stock and has made commitments to build 4 more this month. He has a firm commitment to sell 5 pools next month for $6000 each, and he wishes an inventory of 3 pools at the end of next month. Use discrete dynamic programming to determine the following.
   a. How many pools should he sell this month?
   b. How many pools should he carry on hand as inventory into next month?
   c. How many pools should he produce next month?
His production cost per unit next month can be expressed by

$$PC_N = \$5K + \$3KP_N$$

His sales price per unit this month can be expressed

$$SP_T = \$20K - \$2KS_T$$

His per-unit holding cost from this month to next follows the equation

$$HC_N = \$1K + \$2KX_N$$

The problem may be represented schematically as shown.

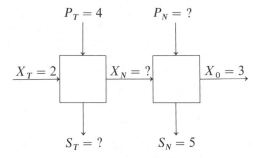

4. Cal's Custom Auto Shop specializes in replicas of vintage automobiles. They have 5 autos avilable to sell in 3 different locations. The demand curve is different in each location, as indicated by the following equations.

Dallas	Houston	Atlanta
$D = AR = 17 - 4X$	$D = AR = 15 - 3X$	$D = AR = 11 - 2X$

If Cal's son Hal is in charge of sales and he receives 10% of the total revenue as commission, how many cars does he send to which location? How much is his maximum commission? (Set up as a dynamic programming problem—complete with box diagram.)

5. The owner of a small manufacturing concern faces the demand for his product as shown in the following table. He has 2 units on hand at the start of the year. Inventory storage cost is $4 per month for 1 unit, $7 per month for 2 units, $9 per month for 3 units, and $10 per month for 4 or more units, payable in advance. The 2 units now in storage were paid for when they were stored last December. Due to seasonal problems in the wage structure, production costs vary as shown in the table. To keep the permanent staff on hand, at least 1 unit must be produced each month. Due to limitations of the facility size, the maximum monthly production rate is 3 units. No inventory is needed beyond June. Determine the owner's optimal production schedule.

Month	Jan	Feb	Mar	Apr	May	Jun
Demand	2	1	4	2	3	2
Unit Production Cost	$3	$5	$2	$4	$3	$2

6. A firm that sells used aircraft is now planning its next 3-year inventory picture. Sales projections for each year have been made as shown in the following diagram. Two units are on hand now (I_0). Inventory at the end of a year is not to fall below 2 units, and the number on hand at the end of the third year (I_3) must be 4. The total procurement cost in each year (TPC) is indicated in millions of dollars. The storage

and maintenance cost (HC) for each year are figured on the year-end inventory and vary from year to year as shown. Determine the optimum number of units to procure in each year and the minimum total (3-year) cost.

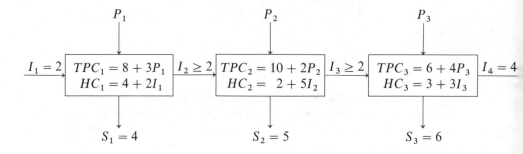

Chapter 14

DECISION THEORY

INTRODUCTION

In order to discuss the classes of decisions we will consider in this chapter, it is useful to introduce a framework or model for the process of decision making. In its simplest form, the decision model we will use can be reduced to three elements: (1) *choice*, (2) *chance*, and (3) *consequence*.

$$\text{Choice} + \text{Chance} \rightarrow \text{Consequence}$$

Choice is the central element in any problem solution model. It involves the selection of the alternative (or alternatives) that the decision maker's analysis has shown to be the "best" approach to the solution of the problem.

Chance refers to the uncertain nature of the outcomes (which are usually measured at some time in the future) resulting from the choices (which are made in the present). We will single out three different classes of decisions, based on the degree of our knowledge (or lack of it) of the likelihoods of occurrence of the various outcomes. Specifically, we will distinguish among decision-making under conditions of *certainty*, *uncertainty*, and *risk*.

Under conditions of *certainty*, we know at the time of the decision what the eventual outcome of each alternative will be, and the decision-making process involves systematic evaluation of the available alternatives and selection of the alternative with the most attractive result. This type of analysis is the domain of the deterministic models we have studied in previous chapters. In this chapter and those that follow, we shall turn our attention to *stochastic* models, in which the link between action and result is not known with certainty but which includes the element of chance.

Decision making under conditions of *uncertainty* requires that decisions be made with no knowledge of the likelihoods of the various outcomes. Obviously, the chances of making a less than optimal decision under these conditions are substantial. We shall investigate several approaches to making decisions under uncertainty conditions that provide different decision criteria for use given differing sets of assumptions, attitudes, and goals for the decision maker.

The largest part of our discussion will be devoted to the consideration of decisions that are made under conditions of *risk*. We will define this class of decisions to be those all of whose outcomes are known and to each of which we are able to assign *probabilities* of occurrence. Because our solution procedures involve the application of some elementary statistics, these methods are frequently called *statistical decision theory*.

The third element of our simplified model of the decision process is *consequence*. The consequence of an action (choice) and an event (chance) forms the objective function that we wish to optimize (maximize or minimize) in making our selection among the available alternatives. The nature of these consequences or payoffs may be positive (profit, sales, revenues, utility) or negative (cost, time, regret), which will determine the direction of our optimization, but our procedures will apply regardless of the form of the payoffs.

DECISIONS UNDER CERTAINTY

As an example of a decision made under certain conditions, consider an investor who is contemplating three fixed-return instruments: (1) certificates of deposit (CDs), which yield 9%, (2) treasury notes, which carry a 7% return, and (3) tax-free municipal bonds, which have a 5.5% interest rate. Her objective is to maximize her long-term, after-tax return; she assumes the instruments to be equally safe; her marginal tax rate is 50%; and the consequences of each alternative are known with certainty. Her decision can be summarized as shown in Table 14.1.

Paying no tax on the municipals and reducing the return on the other instruments by her 50% marginal tax rate leads to a predictable consequence for each alternative. Her optimal choice is the municipals,

Table 14.1 DECISION UNDER CERTAINTY

CHOICE	CONSEQUENCE		
	NOMINAL RATE —	TAXES	= NET AFTER-TAX RATE
1. CD's	9%	— (50%)(9%) =	4.5%
2. T Notes	7%	— (50%)(7%) =	3.5%
3. Municipals	5.5%	— 0 =	5.5% ←— optimal choice

Table 14.2 PAYOFF TABLE FOR CONCESSIONAIRE

		CHANCES		
		WARM (W)	COLD (C)	RAINY (R)
	Beer (B)	$60	$20	$30
CHOICES	Soft Drinks (D)	$50	$30	$50
	Hot Dogs (H)	$50	$50	$40

with an effective after-tax yield of 5.5%. Note that we have omitted the "chance" element from the model because the outcome of each alternative is known with certainty.

We will have more to say about this class of decisions when we discuss decisions under perfect information in the section on decisions under risk.

DECISIONS UNDER UNCERTAINTY

To illustrate decision making under conditions of uncertainty, we shall investigate the dilemma facing a concessionaire at the Texas Rangers' baseball games. He has the option of selling beer (B), soft drinks (D), or hot dogs (H). The profits he can expect to earn will depend on the weather conditions at the time of the game, which can be reduced to three: warm (W), cold (C), or rainy (R). The profits for each choice–chance combination are shown in Table 14.2.

The Criterion of Optimism

If our concessionaire is an unfettered optimist and assumes that events will turn out well no matter what course of action he elects, he will choose the criterion of optimism. Using this criterion, he determines the best possible outcome for each of his alternatives and then selects the alternative that has the *best* of these best outcomes (Table 14.3). Mechanically, this requires that the best (in our case, the maximum) outcome in each row be listed, and then the maximum of these maximums (also called the *maximax* for what should be obvious reasons) be selected as the optimal act or choice. An alternative method is to locate the best

Table 14.3 THE CRITERION OF OPTIMISM

	W	C	R	ROW MAXIMA (BEST OUTCOMES)
B	60	20	30	$60 ←—Optimal Choice
D	50	30	50	$50 (Maximax)
H	50	50	40	$50

Table 14.4 CRITERION OF PESSIMISM

	W	C	R	ROW MINIMA (WORST OUTCOMES)
B	60	20	30	$20
D	50	30	50	$30
H	50	50	40	$40 ←— Optimal Choice (Maximin)

(in our case, largest) value in the table, and select the act corresponding to that row.

The Criterion of Pessimism

Although most of us have known someone who has operated using the optimist criterion, the criterion of pessimism is by far the more widely used of the two. It is for those of us who believe Murphy's law (If anything can go wrong, it will!"). It is generally attributed to statistician Abraham Wald, and is often called the Wald criterion.

Mechanically, it requires that we find the *worst* outcome (the lowest profit, in this example) for each alternative and then select the alternative with the *best* of these worst outcomes (Table 14.4). Another name for the pessimist's criterion is the *maximin* criterion.

This is as much a criterion of conservatism as it is one of pessimism because the decision maker is *guaranteed* that the outcome will be no worse than the minimum value he or she has selected. If any but the worst outcome occurs, the payoff will be *better* than this value.

If the payoff has a negative connotation, such as cost or penalty, the *worst* outcome is the *largest* value, and we select the alternative with the smallest of these; so it would be called the *minimax* criterion.

The Hurwicz Criterion

Both the maximax and the maximin strategies suffer from the same shortcoming: Each looks at only one end of the spectrum of payoff values.

Table 14.5 THE HURWICZ CRITERION

	W	C	R	H VALUE
B	60	20	30	$(.6)(60) + (.4)(20) = \$44$
D	50	30	50	$(.6)(50) + (.4)(30) = \$42$
H	50	50	40	$(.6)(50) + (.4)(40) = \$46$ ⟵ Optimal Choice
				(Hurwicz, $\alpha = .6$)

The optimist fails to consider the downside risk, whereas the pessimist ignores the possibility of large gains from favorable outcomes.

Hurwicz suggested that a more flexible and realistic approach is to look at both ends of the continuum and take a *weighted average* of the best and worst outcomes for each. The weights attached to the two outcomes will depend on the degree of optimism (α) of the decision maker. If we let $\alpha = 0$ represent the pessimist and $\alpha = 1$ represent the pure optimist, then the Hurwicz value for an alternative can be computed by the following equation.

$$H = (\alpha)(\text{best}) + (1 - \alpha)(\text{worst}) \qquad 0 \leq \alpha \leq 1$$

Our optimum choice is the alternative with the best (largest, in our example) H value. If our concessionaire is slightly optimistic ($\alpha = .6$), his choice will be the hot dogs ($H = \$46$) (Table 14.5).

Examination of the equation for calculating H shows that for a totally pessimistic decision maker ($\alpha = 0$), the Hurwicz model becomes the Wald criterion; for the total optimist ($\alpha = 1$), it becomes the maximax. Thus the more general Hurwicz criterion encompasses both the optimistic and the pessimistic criteria as special cases.

The Savage Criterion

This criterion focuses on the regret (also called "conditional opportunity loss") matrix rather than on the original payoff matrix. To construct the *regret matrix*, we subtract each element of a column from the best (in our example, largest) value in that column. The reasoning behind this approach is as follows: If the weather is warm and he selects beer, he will have no regret because this is the optimal choice; if he chooses either of the other two alternatives, he will regret his choice by the amount of profit foregone ($\$60 - \$50 = \$10$). If the weather is cold, his optimal choice is hot dogs, because the other alternatives cause regrets of $30 ($\$50 - \$20$) for beer and $20 ($\$50 - \$30$) for soft drinks. If the weather is rainy, soft drinks is the optimal choice, because beer has a regret of $20 ($\$50 - \$30$), and hot dogs, $10 ($\$50 - \$40$). Thus the savage criterion

Table 14.6 THE SAVAGE CRITERION

	PROFIT MATRIX W	C	R	REGRET MATRIX W	C	R	ROW MAXIMA (MOST REGRET)
B	60	20	30	0	30	20	30
D	50	30	50	10	20	0	20
H	50	50	40	10	0	10	10 ←— Optimal Choice (Minimax Regret)

uses the pessimist approach and selects the alternative that *minimizes* the *maximum regret* (Table 14.6).

DECISIONS UNDER RISK

Under conditions of uncertainty, we have no knowledge of the probabilities of the chance events. Knowledge of these probabilities is what differentiates decisions under *risk* from those under *uncertainty*. The probabilities can be obtained from historical data, by market research or similar analyses, by intuitive or subjective assessment, or in the absence of any of these, by use of the LaPlace principle.

The LaPlace Principle

Also known as the "principle of insufficient reason," the LaPlace principle provides us with a means of moving from uncertainty to risk. Briefly stated, it says that "in the absence of sufficient reason to do otherwise, we may assume each of the possible outcomes of a chance event has an equal likelihood of occurrence." Thus if there are n outcomes, each is assigned a probability of occurrence of $1/n$. Although it is not a strategy or a criterion in itself, it does enable us to apply the solution methods for decisions under risk to problems for which they would otherwise be unavailable.

Table 14.7 MAXIMIZING EXPECTED PROFIT USING THE LAPLACE PRINCIPLE

	W	C	R	EXPECTED PROFIT
B	60	20	30	$\frac{1}{3}(60)+\frac{1}{3}(20)+\frac{1}{3}(30)=\$110/3$
D	50	30	50	$\frac{1}{3}(50)+\frac{1}{3}(30)+\frac{1}{3}(50)=\$130/3$
H	50	50	40	$\frac{1}{3}(50)+\frac{1}{3}(50)+\frac{1}{3}(40)=\$140/3$ ←— Optimal Choice (Max E. V. Profit)
Probabilities:	$\frac{1}{3}$	$\frac{1}{3}$	$\frac{1}{3}$	

PROFIT MATRIX

Optimize Expected Value

The most frequently applied decision criterion in decisions under risk is that of optimizing the expected value of the payoff. When our payoffs are positive in nature (profits, sales, output), we maximize the expected value; for negative types of payoffs (costs, regret, penalties), we minimize expected value. In our example, assigning probabilities by the LaPlace principle, we obtain the result shown in Table 14.7.

The probabilities could have been assigned by the vendor after obtaining a weather forecast. If he assigned probabilities of 60%, 10%, 30%, the solution would be as shown in Table 14.8.

Minimize Expected Regret

We can combine the criterion of optimizing expected value with the concept of regret, which we introduced with the Savage criterion under uncertainty. We can recompute the regret matrix and apply the probabilities we assigned under the criterion of maximizing expected profit (Table 14.9). It is an interesting (and very useful, as we shall see later) fact that the alternative that is the best under the criterion of *minimizing expected regret* will always be the same as that selected by *optimizing expected payoff*.

Table 14.8 MAXIMIZING EXPECTED PROFIT USING ASSIGNED PROBABILITIES

	W	C	R	EXPECTED PROFIT	
B	60	20	30	$.6(60)+.1(20)+.3(30) = \$47$	
D	50	30	50	$.6(50)+.1(30)+.3(50) = \$48$	← Optimal Choice (Max E. V. Profit)
H	50	50	40	$.6(50)+.1(50)+.3(40) = \$47$	
Probabilities:	.6	.1	.3		
		PROFIT MATRIX			

Table 14.9 MINIMIZING EXPECTED REGRET

	W	C	R	EXPECTED REGRET	
B	0	30	20	$.6(0) + .1(30) + .3(20) = \$9$	
D	10	20	0	$.6(10) + .1(20) + .3(0) = \$8$	← Optimal Choice (Min E. V. Regret)
H	10	0	10	$.6(10) + .1(0) + .3(10) = \$9$	
Probabilities:	.6	.1	.3		
		REGRET MATRIX			

Maximize Expected Utility

Still another criterion that can be employed under risk is that of maximizing expected utility. This requires that each payoff be replaced with its equivalent utility value. Obtaining these values requires that the decision maker develop a *utility curve* such as the one in Figure 14.1. The straight diagonal line is the curve for the purely rational decision maker, who uses expected monetary value as the payoff. She or he is said to be *risk neutral*. The broken curve below the risk neutral line is that of a *risk seeker*. She or he will enter into ventures or select alternatives that have expected payoffs below the expected monetary value in the hope that the higher outcome will be the one that occurs. The optimist (maximax criterion) of our previous discussion and the habitual gambler are examples of individuals who have these types of utility curves.

Most of us are *risk averse* and tend to have utility curves more like the upper solid curve. We are willing to take a sure payoff of somewhat less value than the actual expected value of a chance outcome. We are willing to sacrifice our chance at the higher payoff in order to avoid the possibility of facing the lower payoff. In general, we are more willing to take a risk neutral attitude for small payoffs (the $.50 Nassau bet on the golf course or a $1 bet on a football game), but we become more risk averse as the value of the payoffs increases. We also tend to become much more risk averse when the lower payoff becomes negative, as opposed to situations where all payoffs are positive.

If we use the curve for the risk avoider in Figure 14.1 for our concessionaire, we can convert the profit payoffs into utility values as shown

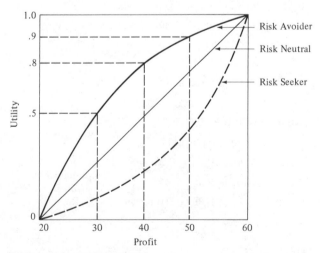

Figure 14.1   Utility curves.

Table 14.10   MAXIMIZING EXPECTED UTILITY

	W	C	R	EXPECTED UTILITIES
B	1.0	.0	.5	$.6(1) + .1(0) + .3(.5) = .75$
D	.9	.5	.9	$.6(.9) + .1(.5) + .3(.9) = .86$
H	.9	.9	.8	$.6(.9) + .1(.9) + .3(.8) = .87$ ←—Optimal Choice
Probabilities:	.6	.1	.3	(Max E. V. Utility)

UTILITY
MATRIX

in Table 14.10. We can use these values to maximize expected utility by using the same probabilities as before.

In actual practice, the decision maker's utility curve may take one of the classical shapes, or it can assume a form that is a combination of risk seeker and risk avoider, such as an "S" curve. Because the shape of the curves varies from individual and even from day to day for one decision maker (with changes in outlook and available resources), utility theory is not widely utilized in actual practice.

DECISION TREES

One very useful framework for the analysis of decisions is the decision network or *decision tree*. It provides the decision maker with a standard approach and a visual frame of reference that permits him or her to "see" the entire problem and the interrelationships among its various parts, both literally and conceptually.

Decision trees are constructed from two primary building blocks: *decision nodes* or *choice points* and *event nodes* or *chance points*. We will represent the choice points by squares and the chance points by circles. Examples of both types are shown in Figure 14.2.

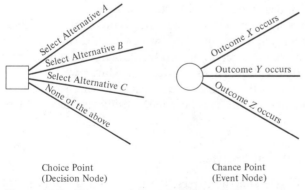

Choice Point
(Decision Node)

Chance Point
(Event Node)

Figure 14.2   Chance points and choice points.

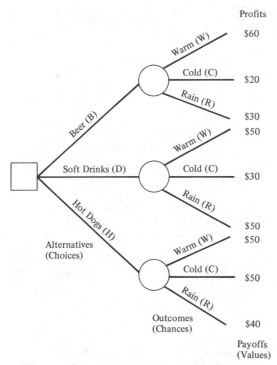

Figure 14.3   Decision tree for concessionaire.

When a choice point is encountered, the decision maker must select one (or more) of the alternatives and reject the others. She or he controls what happens—the selection of the alternative(s) is not subject to outside factors. At a chance point, on the other hand, the decision maker does *not* control which outcome will occur. This selection is done by outside forces (nature or other individuals), and the decision maker can only estimate the probabilities associated with each outcome.

Figure 14.3 illustrates the concessionaire's decision problem. He must first make a decision (choice point), after which nature will select an outcome (chance point). Each act–event combination has a payoff (in this case, profit) associated with it. These are the same values we had in the earlier tabular versions of the problem, and each of the decision criteria that we used under uncertainty can be applied using the decision tree representation.

Optimize Expected Payoff Criterion

The most common use of decision trees, however, is in the analysis of decisions under conditions of risk. We will add the probability information

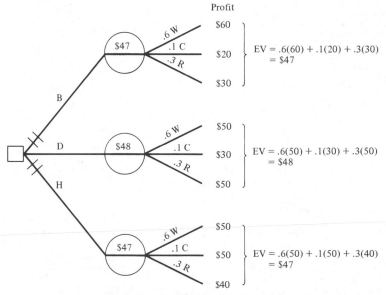

Figure 14.4 Maximizing expected profit.

for each chance point [note that only chance points (circles) have probabilities; the choice points require us to make a decision and select the best alternative] by noting the probability of occurrence for each outcome. Once we have done this, we can apply the maximize expected profit criterion.

Beginning at the right-hand side of the tree, we *replace each choice point with its expected payoff*, placing this value in the top half of the circle representing the event. This has been done in Figure 14.4.

After each chance point has been replaced by its expected profit, we move to the left to the next node, which in our case is a choice point. Here we compare the expected profits from each alternative ($47, $48, $47) and select the alternative with the best (in this example, highest) expected value. We indicate our choice by chopping off the branches that were not selected.

Minimize Expected Regret Criterion

An alternative approach we used in selecting the best alternative under risk is that of minimizing expected regret. These calculations are shown in Figure 14.5. We have placed the expected value of regret in the bottom half of the circle representing the event. The optimal alternative is *always* the one with the minimum expected regret.

We shall see that *the alternative selected by **optimizing** expected payoff will always be the same one selected by **minimizing** expected regret.*

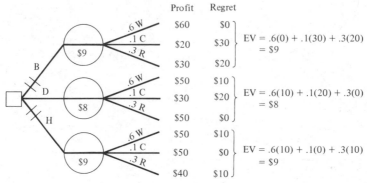

Figure 14.5   Minimizing expected regret.

Table 14.11   PAYOFF MATRIX FOR DEVELOPER

	SINGLE-FAMILY DWELLINGS (SFD)	APARTMENTS (A)	CONDOMINIUMS (C)	SELL
Factory (F)	$-5M	$20M	$10M	$2M
Golf Course (GC)	$25M	$15M	$20M	$2M

Furthermore, *the **difference** between any two alternatives measured by their expected **payoffs** will always be the same as the difference measured by their expected **regrets***.

Example

As another example, consider a land developer who must decide how to develop a particular plot of land. He can build single-family dwellings (SFD), apartments (A), or condominiums (C), or he can sell the land. His profits will vary depending on whether the land next to his is selected as the site for a major manufacturing plant or on whether it is retained by the city for a golf course. His best estimates of potential profit (in millions) under each set of circumstances are shown in Table 14.11.

If he feels that there is a 50% chance of the site being a factory, his decision tree is shown in Figure 14.6. Note that comparisons between alternatives yield the same results whether expected profits or expected regrets are used. The only difference between the two measures is in the direction—higher profits are "better" and lower regrets are "better."

The optimum decision (highest profit, lowest regret) is to build apartments; condominiums is second best (by $2.5 million); single-family dwellings is third ($5 million behind apartments); and selling is a distant fourth ($8 million worse than single-family dwellings). These findings are summarized in Table 14.12.

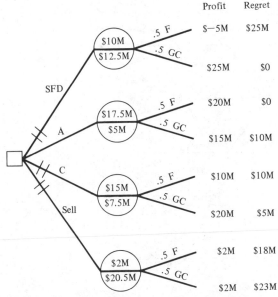

Figure 14.6   Developer/builder's decision tree.

Table 14.12 SUMMARY OF DIFFERENCES BETWEEN ALTERNATIVES
(EXPECTED PROFIT AND EXPECTED REGRET)

	A	C	SFD	Sell
EV Profit	$17.5M	$15M	$10M	$2M
EV Regret	$5M	$7.5M	$12.5M	$20.5M

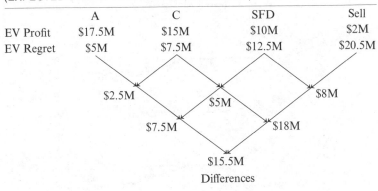

EXPECTED VALUE OF PERFECT INFORMATION

Let us suppose that we do not have to make our decision under *prior
information* as we have done thus far but can purchase additional information about which of the chance outcomes will actually occur. Let us
also postulate that there is available a *perfect indicator* that can foretell
the outcome of chance events with 100% accuracy. The decision trees
for the concessionaire and the developer must be expanded to include
these new conditions, as shown in Figures 14.7 and 14.8.

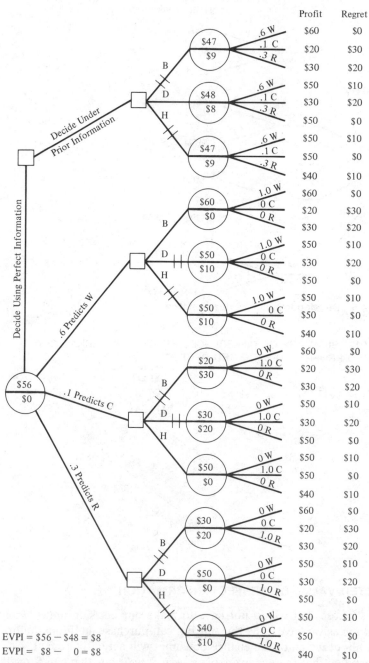

	Profit	Regret
.6 W	$60	$0
.1 C	$20	$30
.3 R	$30	$20
.6 W	$50	$10
.1 C	$30	$20
.3 R	$50	$0
.6 W	$50	$10
.1 C	$50	$0
.3 R	$40	$10
1.0 W	$60	$0
0 C	$20	$30
0 R	$30	$20
1.0 W	$50	$10
0 C	$30	$20
0 R	$50	$0
1.0 W	$50	$10
0 C	$50	$0
0 R	$40	$10
0 W	$60	$0
1.0 C	$20	$30
0 R	$30	$20
0 W	$50	$10
1.0 C	$30	$20
0 R	$50	$0
0 W	$50	$10
1.0 C	$50	$0
0 R	$40	$10
0 W	$60	$0
0 C	$20	$30
1.0 R	$30	$20
0 W	$50	$10
0 C	$30	$20
1.0 R	$50	$0
0 W	$50	$10
0 C	$50	$0
1.0 R	$40	$10

EVPI = $56 − $48 = $8
EVPI = $8 − 0 = $8

Figure 14.7 Decision tree for concessionaire with perfect information.

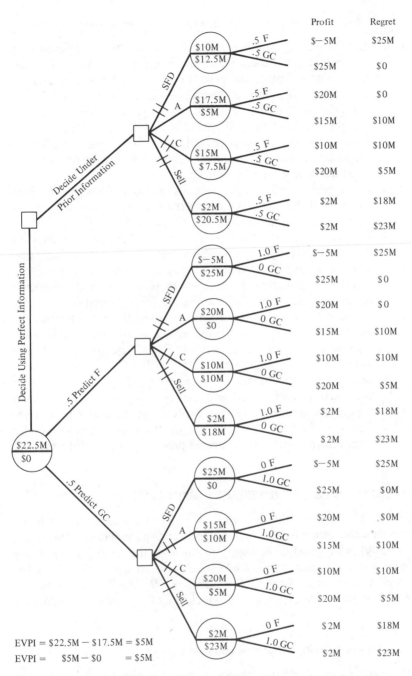

	Profit	Regret
$10M / $12.5M (.5 F / .5 GC)	$-5M / $25M	$25M / $0
$17.5M / $5M (.5 F / .5 GC)	$20M / $15M	$0 / $10M
$15M / $7.5M (.5 F / .5 GC)	$10M / $20M	$10M / $5M
$2M / $20.5M (.5 F / .5 GC)	$2M / $2M	$18M / $23M
$-5M / $25M (1.0 F / 0 GC)	$-5M / $25M	$25M / $0
$20M / $0 (1.0 F / 0 GC)	$20M / $15M	$0 / $10M
$10M / $10M (1.0 F / 0 GC)	$10M / $20M	$10M / $5M
$2M / $18M (1.0 F / 0 GC)	$2M / $2M	$18M / $23M
$25M / $0 (0 F / 1.0 GC)	$-5M / $25M	$25M / $0M
$15M / $10M (0 F / 1.0 GC)	$20M / $15M	$0M / $10M
$20M / $5M (0 F / 1.0 GC)	$10M / $20M	$10M / $5M
$2M / $23M (0 F / 1.0 GC)	$2M / $2M	$18M / $23M

EVPI = $22.5M − $17.5M = $5M

EVPI = $5M − $0   = $5M

Figure 14.8   Decision tree for developer/builder with perfect information.

Examination of these figures reveals several important points.

1. Because we are hypothesizing a *perfect* indicator, the probability of a prediction is the same as the prior probability of that outcome. For example, the prior probability of warm weather is .6; so the probability of getting a warm prediction is also .6. The prior probability of a golf course is .5; so the probability of a prediction of the golf course is also .5.

2. Because the prediction is perfect, after we receive a prediction, the probability of that outcome becomes 1.0, and the probabilities of all other outcomes become 0.

3. Using perfect information is the same as making the decision under conditions of certainty, so the expected regret will always be 0 for the optimum choice.

4. The *expected value of perfect information (EVPI)* can be computed in two ways: (1) by determining the improvement the information made in the expected value of the payoff (profit, in our examples), or (2) by calculating the amount of reduction in the expected regret brought about by the use of the information. Because the expected regret using a perfect indicator is always zero, the *EVPI is always equal to the expected value of regret under prior information*, which means we will never have to construct the lower portion of the tree to obtain *EVPI!*

5. Because the differences between expected profit under prior and perfect information and expected regret under the same conditions are the same, the expected profit under perfect information can be found by adding the expected regret under prior information to the expected profit under prior information.

EXPECTED VALUE OF IMPERFECT INFORMATION

Because it is unlikely that any of us will ever be able to earn a living (or even a consulting fee) for making decisions under perfect information (certainty), what good is the ability to calculate the *EVPI*? The primary reason for wanting to know *EVPI* is to form an upper bound for the expected value of *imperfect* information (*EVII*) and to set a standard against which we can compare the efficiency of the imperfect indicator.

Revising Probability Estimates (Bayes' Rule)

The primary use of additional information is in *revising the prior probability estimates*. In the case of perfect information, the prior estimates were revised to values of 0 or 1.0. An imperfect indicator does not permit this drastic a reduction in the uncertainty expressed by the probabilities and leaves us under conditions of risk.

The standard approach to the revision of prior probability estimates is to apply Bayes' rule, which can be developed as follows.

If
$$P(A \& B) = P(A) \cdot P(B|A),$$

then
$$P(B|A) = \frac{P(A \& B)}{P(A)}$$

But
$$P(A) = P(A \& B) + P(A \& \bar{B}),$$

and
$$P(A \& B) = P(B \& A) = P(B) \cdot P(A|B),$$

so
$$P(B|A) = \frac{P(A \& B)}{P(A \& B) + P(A \& \bar{B})} = \frac{P(B) \cdot P(A|B)}{P(B) \cdot P(A|B) + P(B) \cdot P(A|\bar{B})}.$$

All of which, in our experience, leaves most business administration students gasping for breath and sends many out to the departmental office to look up the procedure for dropping the course. One approach we have found that takes most of the "stark terror" out of Bayesian revision is the contingency table approach.

Contingency Tables

We shall illustrate this approach through the use of an example involving a senior faculty member, a distinguished scholar who has published widely and has been retained by a publisher of college textbooks to review manuscripts and predict whether or not they will be successful in the marketplace. In order to know just how much weight to give his advice, we must first obtain some indication of his track record.

Suppose that of all the books that he has reviewed that eventually became successful he has given positive recommendations on 80% and has been wrong (given negative recommendations) on 20%, and that of those that were not successful, he was right (predicted poor reception) 60% of the time and wrong (predicted good reception) 40% of the time. If the publisher thought a particular manuscript had a 50:50 chance of success (prior probabilities), what would be his *revised* probabilities (after receiving the reviewer's recommendation)? We may state the problem as follows:

Prior Probability of Success	$P(S) = .5$
Prior Probability of Failure	$P(F) = .5$
Track Record on Successful Books	$P(\text{Predicted S} \mid \text{Actually S}) = .8$
	$P(\text{Predicted F} \mid \text{Actually S}) = .2$
Track Record on Failures	$P(\text{Predicted F} \mid \text{Actually F}) = .6$
	$P(\text{Predicted S} \mid \text{Actually F}) = .4$

Find

$$P(\text{Predict S}) = ?$$
$$P(\text{Predict F}) = ?$$
$$P(\text{Actually S} \mid \text{Predicted S}) = ?$$
$$P(\text{Actually F} \mid \text{Predicted S}) = ?$$
$$P(\text{Actually F} \mid \text{Predicted F}) = ?$$
$$P(\text{Actually S} \mid \text{Predicted F}) = ?$$

To solve the problem we set up a contingency table. We pretend that the reviewer will review 100 books like the one in question (grand total in the table). Using the prior probabilities, we split this total into 50 successful books and 50 failures. [Table 14.13(a)].

Using the track record for successful books we can break down the 50 that are actually successful into those to which he will give good recommendations ($50 \times .8 = 40$ books) and those to which he will give bad reviews ($50 \times .2 = 10$ books). The 50 that will actually be failures can also be separated into favorable recommendations ($50 \times .4 = 20$ books) and unfavorable ones ($50 \times .6 = 30$ books) [Table 14.13(b)]. Adding the columns tells us the number (out of 100) of books to which he will give good reviews (60) and the number of bad reviews (40) [Table 14.13(c)]. Thus the probability of a good review is

$$P(\text{Predict S}) = \tfrac{60}{100} = 60\%$$

and that of a bad review is

$$P(\text{Predict F}) = \tfrac{40}{100} = 40\%$$

The table also permits us to determine the *revised* probabilities of success and failure after we receive the scholar's advice. Of the 60 books he recommends, 40 will be winners; so

$$P(\text{Actually S} \mid \text{Predicted S}) = \tfrac{40}{60} = \tfrac{2}{3}$$

The other 20 will be failures; so

$$P(\text{Actually F} \mid \text{Predicted S}) = \tfrac{20}{60} = \tfrac{1}{3}$$

Table 14.13 CONTINGENCY TABLES

PRIOR PROBABILITIES
PREDICTIONS

		S	F	
ACTUAL	S			50
	F			50
				100

(a)

JOINT PROBABILITIES
PREDICTIONS

		S	F	
ACTUAL	S	40	10	50
	F	20	30	50
				100

(b)

COMPLETED
PREDICTIONS

		S	F	
ACTUAL	S	40	10	50
	F	20	30	50
		60	40	100

(c)

Of the 40 to which he gives bad reviews, 10 will actually be successful, and 30 will not.

$$P(\text{Actually S} \mid \text{Predicted F}) = \tfrac{10}{40} = \tfrac{1}{4}$$
$$P(\text{Actually F} \mid \text{Predicted F}) = \tfrac{30}{40} = \tfrac{3}{4}$$

The probability values can be incorporated into a decision tree as shown in Figure 14.9.

Examples

Returning to our previous examples, we can use the contingency table approach to develop the revised probability estimates.

Let us assume that the developer knows of a real estate professor at a local university who has an enviable record in performing land-use studies and in predicting development patterns. She claims to have been 90% successful in correctly forecasting areas that eventually were devoted to recreational use and 60% correct in predicting the fate of land that eventually came to be industrialized. Using the developer's 50:50 prior probabilities, we can develop the contingency table shown in Table 14.14.

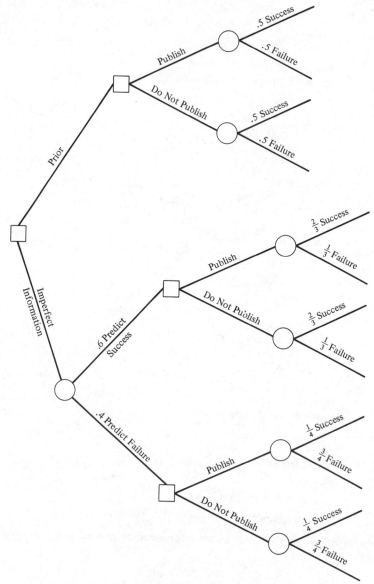

Figure 14.9   Publisher's decision tree with revised probabilities.

Table 14.14   CONTINGENCY TABLE FOR DEVELOPER

		PREDICTIONS				
		F	GC			
ACTUAL	F	30	20	50	50(.6) = 30	50(.4) = 20
	GC	5	45	50	50(.1) = 5	50(.9) = 45
		35	65	100		

418

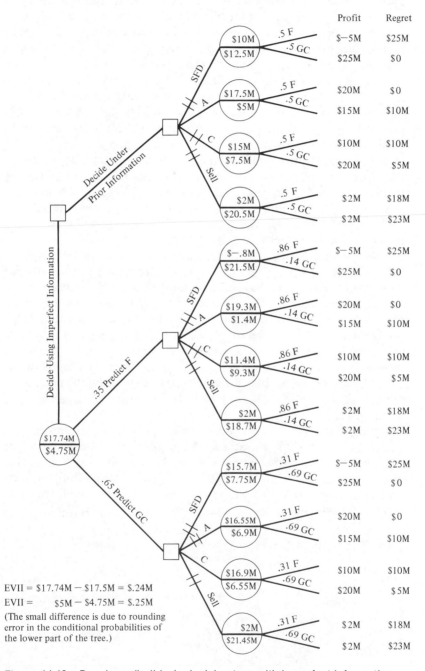

	Profit	Regret
SFD — $10M / $12.5M	.5 F	$-5M	$25M
	.5 GC	$25M	$0
A — $17.5M / $5M	.5 F	$20M	$0
	.5 GC	$15M	$10M
C — $15M / $7.5M	.5 F	$10M	$10M
	.5 GC	$20M	$5M
Sell — $2M / $20.5M	.5 F	$2M	$18M
	.5 GC	$2M	$23M

EVII = $17.74M − $17.5M = $.24M
EVII = $5M − $4.75M = $.25M
(The small difference is due to rounding error in the conditional probabilities of the lower part of the tree.)

Figure 14.10   Developer/builder's decision tree with imperfect information.

From the table we can obtain the probabilities we need for the lower portion of the decision tree of Figure 14.10. The probability of the professor predicting that the factory will go in is $\frac{35}{100}$ or 35%; the odds she will predict a golf course are $\frac{65}{100}$ or 65%. The conditional probability that the factory will be built if she predicts it is $\frac{30}{35} = 86\%$; the probability that the golf course will go in if she predicts it is $\frac{45}{65} = 69\%$.

Using the information optimally, the builder's decision rule is to build apartments if the professor predicts that the factory will be built and to build condominiums if she predicts the golf course. The expected value of the imperfect information ($EVII$) is the amount by which it increases expected profit or reduces expected regret (approximately \$250,000—the small discrepancy is due to rounding errors in the revised probabilities). The builder should be willing to pay up to this amount for her study. The *relative efficiency* of this indicator (relative to a perfect indicator) is the percentage of the regret it removes, or $EVII/EVPI$. Our indicator leaves most of the expected regret and is therefore not very efficient \$250K/\$5M = 5%.

Suppose the concessionaire decides to consult the National Weather Service to revise his probability estimates. He makes a study of their performance during last season and finds that on days when it was actually warm, they predicted warm 80% of the time, cold 10% of the time, and rainy 10% of the time; on days that were actually cold, they predicted warm 20% of the time, cold 60% of the time, and rainy 20% of the time; on rainy days they predicted warm 10% of the time, cold 20% of the time, and rainy 70% of the time. Using these probabilities to spread the 60 warm, 10 cold, and 30 rainy days (from the prior probabilities of .6, 1.0, and .3), we obtain the contingency table shown in Table 14.15.

We use the table to obtain the revised probabilities for the decision tree in Figure 14.11. For example, the probability of a cold prediction is $\frac{18}{100}$ or 18%; the probability of actually having rain after a prediction of rain is $\frac{21}{29} = .72$; the probability of its actually being cold after a warm prediction is $\frac{2}{53} = .04$. (We will use two decimal places in all the probabilities. This results in slight rounding errors, as we will see.)

Table 14.15 CONTINGENCY TABLE FOR CONCESSIONAIRE

		PREDICTION						
		W	C	R				
ACTUALLY	W	48	6	6	60	60(.8) = 48	60(.1) = 6	60(.1) = 6
	C	2	6	2	10	10(.2) = 2	10(.6) = 6	10(.2) = 2
	R	3	6	21	30	30(.1) = 3	30(.2) = 6	30(.7) = 21
		53	18	29	100			

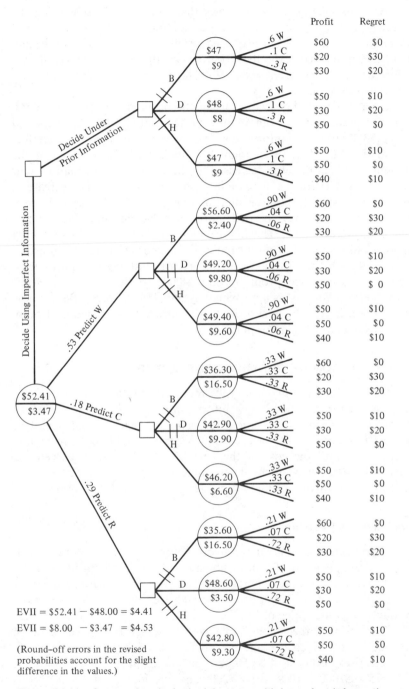

	Profit	Regret
	$60	$0
	$20	$30
	$30	$20
	$50	$10
	$30	$20
	$50	$0
	$50	$10
	$50	$0
	$40	$10

EVII = $52.41 − $48.00 = $4.41

EVII = $8.00 − $3.47 = $4.53

(Round-off errors in the revised probabilities account for the slight difference in the values.)

Figure 14.11   Concessionaire's decision tree with imperfect information.

Analysis of Figure 14.11 shows that our decision rule using the weather predictions to revise our probabilities will be to sell beer if warm weather is predicted (expected profit = $56.60), hot dogs if cool weather is predicted (expected profit = $46.20), and soft drinks if rain is forecast (expected profit = $48.60). The expected regrets for each act are shown as well.

If we combine these values using the probabilities of warm, cool, and rainy predictions, we obtain the expected profit ($52.41) and expected regret ($3.47) using the information. The expected value of the imperfect information (*EVII*) is the amount by which profit is increased or the amount by which regret is decreased by the use of the information. Our two values ($4.41 for the increase in profit and $4.53 for the decrease in regret) differ slightly because of rounding errors in the revised probabilities. We could have carried more than two decimal places if this difference were critical. The important point is that our vendor only improves his expected profit (or reduces his expected regret) by approximately $4.50 by using the weather forecast. But perfect information increased his expected profit by only $8.00; so the *relative efficiency* of the weather forecast is approximately 56% ($4.50/$8.00). Because the information is free, he would do well to utilize it. If it had cost more than its value, he should not purchase it.

DETERMINATION OF OPTIMUM SAMPLE SIZE

Sometimes information comes in discrete packages, and we, as decision makers, must decide how much information we wish to obtain before we make a decision. If we know the *value* of each additional unit of information and the *cost* of each unit, we can simply continue to buy information until the cost of the next bit of information exceeds its value. This is referred to as determining the *optimal sample size*. We shall illustrate this procedure with reference to specific examples.

Wholesaler's Example

A. T. Farbuckle is a wholesaler of hydrothermopheumostat valves, which are key components of the antidefibulator control mechanisms in widespread use in industry. He purchases the valves from the manufacturer in lots of 100 units at a unit cost of $10.00. He sells them to the control producers at a unit price of $12.75.

The lots are either "good" lots, which average 10% defective units, or "bad" lots, which average 50% defectives. Farbuckle must repair any defectives at a cost of $7.50 per unit; so his profit on a "good" lot is $1275 - $1000 - 10($7.50) = $200, and his loss on a "bad" lot is $1275 - $1000 - 50($7.50) = $100. If he rejects a good lot, he must pay a $50 penalty to the manufacturer. Half the lots he receives are bad. A

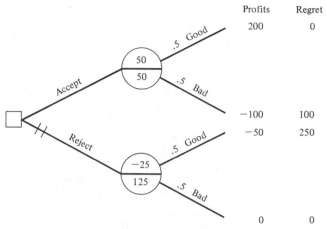

Figure 14.12   Farbuckle's decision tree with prior information.

portable X-ray device, which can test the units on the loading dock, is available. It costs $10 per unit to test for defectives. Farbuckle wishes to determine the optimum number to sample from each lot and the decision rule to employ in accepting or rejecting a lot.

Farbuckle's decision tree, profit values, and regret under prior information are shown in Figure 14.12. His optimal choice is to accept every lot, as he has been doing in the past, and his expected profit is $50 per lot.

If Farbuckle decides to use the X-ray device to sample 1 unit randomly from each lot, his decision tree and contingency table are shown in Figure 14.13. If he sampled 1 unit from each of 100 lots, 50 lots would be good ($P_D = .1$) and 50 would be bad ($P_D = .5$). Of the 50 good lots, 5 (10%) would yield a defective sample, and 45 would have an acceptable unit sampled. Of the 50 bad lots, 25 (50%) would have a defective unit sampled, and 25 would have a good unit sampled. Thus, the probability of getting a defective unit in a sample of 1 is .30, and the probability of the sampled unit being acceptable is .70.

If the unit sampled is defective, the probability that it came from a good lot is $\frac{5}{30} = \frac{1}{6} \approx .17$. If the sample is not defective, the probability that it came from a good lot is $\frac{45}{70} \approx .64$. (This rounding of the probabilities will cause a minor problem later, as we shall see.)

Farbuckle's decision rule is to reject the lot if the sample is defective and to accept the lot if the sample is not defective. Using the rule, his expected profit is $61.85; and his expected regret is $37.95. The *expected value of the sample information* for a sample of one unit ($EVSI_1$) is $61.85 - $50 = $11.85 using profit; it is $50 - $37.95 = $12.05 using regret. This discrepancy is due to the rounding error previously mentioned.

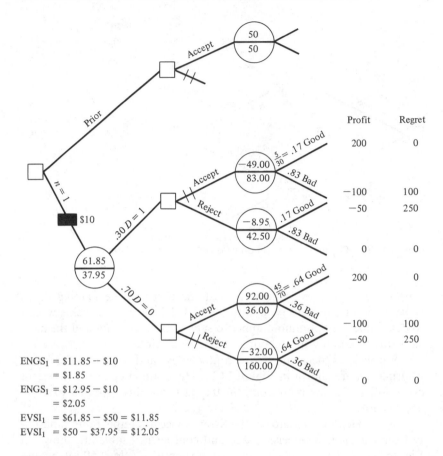

$ENGS_1 = \$11.85 - \$10$
$\quad = \$1.85$
$ENGS_1 = \$12.95 - \$10$
$\quad = \$2.05$
$EVSI_1 = \$61.85 - \$50 = \$11.85$
$EVSI_1 = \$50 - \$37.95 = \$12.05$

(Differences due to rounding error)

	$D = 1$	$D = 0$	
Good ($P_D = .1$)	5	45	50
Bad ($P_D = .5$)	25	25	50
	30	70	100

Figure 14.13   Farbuckle's decision tree using a sample of 1 unit.

The *expected net gain from sampling* ($ENGS_1$) is the $EVSI_1$ less the cost of the sample: $ENGS_1 = \$11.85 - \$10 = \$1.85$ or $ENGS_1 = \$12.05 - \$10 = \$2.05$. Thus, the value of the information in the sample exceeds the cost of the information, and Farbuckle would be wise to use the sampling procedure.

Next, we will determine the net gain from a sample of 2 units ($ENGS_2$). The contingency table and the decision tree are shown in Figure 14.14.

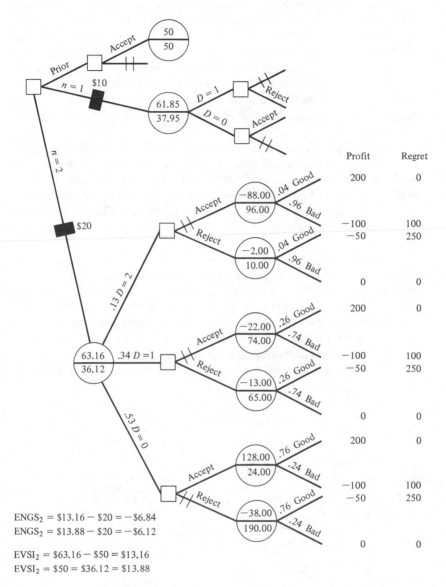

$ENGS_2 = \$13.16 - \$20 = -\$6.84$
$ENGS_2 = \$13.88 - \$20 = -\$6.12$

$EVSI_2 = \$63.16 - \$50 = \$13.16$
$EVSI_2 = \$50 = \$36.12 = \$13.88$

(Differences due to rounding error)

	$D = 2$	$D = 1$	$D = 0$	
Good ($P_D = .1$)	5	90	405	500
Bad ($P_D = .5$)	125	250	125	500
	130	340	530	1000

Figure 14.14   Farbuckle's decision tree using a sample of 2 units.

The contingency table is based on sampling 1000 lots, of which 500 would be good. If a lot is good ($P_D = .1$), the probability of 2 defectives in a sample is $P(D = 2 | n = 2, P_D = .1) = .01$ (using the binomial or from the tables in Appendix A); so in 500 good lots there would be 5 in which both units sampled were defective. From the completed table we find, for example, that the probability of a sample of 2 with 1 defective $[P(D = 1)]$ is .34 and that after a sample of 2 units yields no defectives, the probability that the lot is good is .76 $[P(\text{Good} | D = 0)] = 405/530 \approx .76)$.

Farbuckle's decision rule is to reject the lot if 1 or both units sampled are defective and to accept only if both are good units. The expected profit is \$63.16; the expected value of the sample information ($EVSI_2$) is \$13.16 using profit and \$13.88 using regret. (As before, the discrepancy is due to rounding error in the revised probabilities.) The net gain from sampling ($ENGS_2$) is $-\$6.84$ or $-\$6.12$, depending on which measure is used.

Because the sampling cost exceeds the $EVSI$ and $ENGS_2$ is negative, Farbuckle should not use samples of 2 units. His optimum sampling plan is to use samples of 1 unit per lot. This is a typical result—that the *marginal* value of sample information (the increase in $EVSI$ from the addition of one more to sample size) is a *decreasing* function, and each increase in sample size adds less than the previous one to $EVSI$.

The general relationship among size of sample, cost of sampling, and the value of the sample information is illustrated in Figure 14.15.

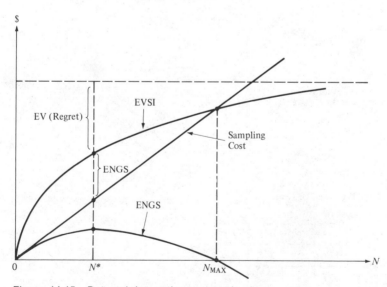

Figure 14.15 Determining optimum sample size.

As N increases, each additional unit sampled adds less than the previous one to the value of sample information ($EVSI$), with $EVSI$ approaching $EVPI$ for every large N. Sampling costs are usually fairly linear with sample size. $ENGS$ is the difference between the value of the sample information and its cost. The optimum sample size (N^*) is at the point where this difference reaches its greatest value and where $ENGS$ is at its maximum.

Notice that the expected value of regret, which is a measure of risk or uncertainty, is the difference between $EVPI$ and $EVSI$. In some situations it may be desirable to increase sample size to the point N_{MAX}, where the value of the sample information equals the cost of sampling and $ENGS$ equals zero. Although the net gain from sampling is zero and the expected profit is the same as that under prior information, the expected regret (risk) is much lower, and decisions can be made with greater confidence of favorable outcomes. Any sample larger than N_{MAX} results in lowering the expected profit.

Not all problems in sampling use profit maximization as the objective, and some decisions must be based on subjective comparisons. For example, in health-care situations patient well-being and even lives can be at stake (e.g., how much testing should be done before certifying a new drug or vaccine for human use). In military situations the lives of soldiers and even civilians can rest on the effectiveness of a new weapons system. How much testing should be done on a new pesticide, the effectiveness of which is measured in terms of insect control and the detriments in terms of harm to wildlife?

CONCLUSION

In this chapter, as in Chapter 13, we have discussed problems that do not fall neatly into categories that can be solved by the application of the highly structured optimizing techniques such as linear programming or CPM/PERT. In practice, very few problems fall into these categories. Usually the future is uncertain, and information is either nonexistent or prohibitively expensive to gather.

Our aim in this chapter has been to suggest a general structure or framework within which we can analyze a broad spectrum of problems. We have attempted to show, in the context of a few simple examples, that the basic nature of the decision process can be applied to the solution of problems of widely differing size and scale, employing various degrees of knowledge, in diverse application areas, using many different types of decision criteria. Our hope is that you will be able to transfer this general framework into the specific decision situations you will encounter both on the job and in your personal life.

SUMMARY OF KEY CONCEPTS

Choice. Evaluation of alternatives to select the one(s) that can be shown to be "best" by some criterion.

Chance. An outcome controlled not by the decision maker but by outside forces, nature, or other people.

Consequence. The payoff or value of some measure that results from the combination of a choice and a chance.

Certainty. The outcomes of the chance events are known to the decision maker at the time of the decision.

Uncertainty. The decision maker can not even assign the probabilities of the outcomes of the chance events.

Risk. The decision maker is able to assign probabilities to the outcomes of the chance events.

Criterion of optimism (maximax). Selection of the alternative with the best best outcome.

Criterion of pessimism (maximin or minimax). Selection of the alternative with the best worst outcome. Also called the Wald criterion.

Hurwicz criterion. Selection of the alternative with the highest H value for the given level of optimism, where $H = (\alpha)\text{Best} + (1 - \alpha)\text{Worst}$.

Coefficient of optimism (α). A value between zero and one that expresses the degree of optimism of the decision maker. If $\alpha = 0$, the Hurwicz criterion becomes the Wald criterion; if $\alpha = 1$, it becomes the Maximax.

Savage criterion. Minimax regret, where regret is the difference between the payoff of the optimum alternative and the one in question. Regret is sometimes called "conditional opportunity loss."

LaPlace principle. The principle of insufficient reason. A method of moving from decision making under uncertainty to decision making under risk by assigning equal probabilities to all outcomes.

Risk avoider. One who will accept a sure payment of less than the expected value of a chance payoff.

Risk seeker. The optimist, or gambler, who will pay more than the expected value for a chance payoff.

Risk neutral. The "economic man" who neither seeks nor avoids risk but makes decisions based on expected values.

Decision tree. A graphical presentation of a decision, using chance points and choice points.

Choice point. In a decision tree, a point that represents a decision among alternative courses of action. ($\square$)

Chance point. A representation of an event the outcomes of which are not under control of the decision maker. ($\bigcirc$)

Expected value of perfect information (EVPI). The difference between the expected payoff under prior information and the expected payoff under perfect information (certainty). Equal to the expected regret under prior information.

Bayes' rule. A method of revising prior probabilities in light of added information.

$$P(B|A) = \frac{P(B) \cdot P(A|B)}{P(A)}.$$

Contingency table. A simple tabular method of obtaining revised probabilities.

Expected value of imperfect information (*EVII*). The reduction in expected regret or improvement in expected payoff achieved by using imperfect indicators.

Expected value of sample information (EVSI). The same as *EVII*, except that the imperfect information is obtained by sampling.

Efficiency of imperfect information. The percentage of the uncertainty (expected regret) removed by an imperfect indicator.

$$\frac{EVII}{EVPI}.$$

Sampling cost (SC). The expenses required in obtaining sample information.

Expected net gain from sampling (ENGS). The difference between the value of sample information and the cost of obtaining it ($ENGS = EVSI - SC$).

Optimum sample size (N*). The sample size for which *ENGS* is greatest.

Maximum feasible sample size (N_{MAX}). The sample size for which the value of the sample information equals the cost of sampling and *ENGS* equals zero.

PROBLEMS

1. T. J. Bullfeathers is one of six candidates who have entered the Democratic primary to select a candidate to replace the retiring senator from their state. He feels he must decide whether to select a central issue on which to base his campaign or to skirt all issues and not offend anyone. His projected vote count (in millions) depending on his choice of issues and the public's responses, are shown in the following table.

	PUBLIC SENTIMENT		
ISSUES	ANTIGOVERNMENT	ANTITAX	PERSONAL FREEDOM
Cut federal spending	1.2	.7	.7
Decrease federal taxes	.5	1.5	.8
Antiabortion	.6	.7	1.1
No central issue	.8	.6	.9

a. Under certainty, what would be T. J.'s optimal choice of theme for his campaign and how many votes would he expect if he knew that the public mood would be antigovernment? Antitax? For personal freedom issues?

b. Compare his alternatives using the criterion of optimism.

c. Compare his alternatives using the criterion of pessimism.

d. Compare the alternatives using the Hurwicz criterion and a coefficient of optimism of .6.

e. What value of α makes him indifferent to either of the first two alternates?

f. Compare the alternatives using the Savage criterion (minimax regret).

g. What is the expected number of votes for the optimal choice using the LaPlace criterion?

2. Hoopla, Inc., has developed a toy that can be used as a hulahoop, sails like a Frisbee, glows in the dark, and is edible. They must decide whether to promote the product locally, regionally, or nationally. (They cannot do it in stages, because as soon as it comes out, someone will copy it and promote it in the remaining markets.) Their expected net profit (in millions of dollars) on the project as a function of the degree of customer acceptance is shown in the following table.

| DISTRIBUTION | CUSTOMER ACCEPTANCE | | |
	GOOD	FAIR	POOR
Local	.8	.2	− .2
Regional	1.2	.7	− .8
National	5.0	.6	−2.0

What is the optimal choice and the payoff (profit) under each of these criteria?

a. Certainty of good customer acceptance.
b. Certainty of fair customer acceptance.
c. Certainty of poor customer acceptance.
d. The criterion of optimism.
e. The criterion of pessimism.
f. The Hurwicz criterion with $\alpha = .5$.
g. The Savage criterion.
h. The LaPlace criterion.

3. The highly successful and prosperous law firm of Dewey, Cheatum, and Howe is faced with a decision of whether to take a patent infringement suit to trial or to accept an out-of-court settlement. They are asking $2 million; the defendant has offered $600,000. The probable court-ordered settlement amounts and their subjective probabilities are as follows.

Amount	$2M	$1M	$.5M	$0
Probability	.1	.2	.3	.4

a. Construct their client's decision tree.
b. Add the payoff values and regrets to the tree.
c. What is the expected regret and the expected payoff of the optimal cost?
d. What is the *EVPI*?

4. An American auto manufacturer is considering adding a new subcompact, either diesel or electric-powered. The expected acceptability and, therefore, profit hinge on the availability of oil, the government's

EPA clean air standards, and the success of researchers in developing a new, more compact battery. Various combinations of these three factors have been analyzed, and the results are summarized in five scenarios. These, along with their profits (in millions of dollars) and probabilities of occurrence are as follows.

ACTION	SCENARIO				
	I	II	III	IV	V
Diesel	30	20	− 20	− 5	10
Electric	− 10	5	20	10	− 5
Neither	0	0	0	0	0
Probability	.2	.3	.2	.2	.1

a. Draw their decision tree.
b. Add their payoffs and regrets.
c. What are the optimal alternative's expected profit and expected regret?
d. What is the *EVPI*?

5. A management consultant must place an order for a computer in anticipation of receiving one or more of three consulting contracts he has bid. If he orders the small machine, he can service no more than one contract, whereas the larger machine can handle as much business as he is likely to ever have. The small machine costs $10,000; the large one, $50,000. If he buys the small one and obtains more than one contract, he must switch to the large machine, and the salvage value of the small one just covers the short-notice penalty for converting at the last minute. He could decide to rent on a time-shared basis and cover his needs that way for $40,000. The profit, exclusive of computer costs, will be $30,000 per contract received. His estimates of the probabilities are summarized as follows.

Outcome	1 contract	2 contracts	3 contracts
Probability	.5	.4	.1

a. Draw his decision tree.
b. Add his profits to the tree.
c. Find his optimal act and expected profit.
d. Use the utility functions of Figure 14.1 to determine his utility for each payoff (risk seeker and risk avoider). Change the horizontal scale from (20, 30, 40, 50, 60) to (− 20, 0, 20, 40, 60).
e. Determine the optimal act and expected utility for each of the two (risk seeker and risk avoider) in part (e).

6. Short Hop Airways is considering adding one or two new routes. The profits from the routes will depend on how heavily the flights are booked. The annual profit figures (in millions of dollars) are as shown.

	CUSTOMER USE	
	HEAVY	LIGHT
Add Route A	2	−1
Add Route B	3	−2
Add both A and B	5	−2
No new routes	0	0
Prior probability	.5	.5

a. Draw and label the decision tree.
b. What is the expected profit from the optimal act under prior information?
c. What is $EVPI$?

  A marketing research firm will predict the passenger traffic density for a fee. Their past record suggests that they have predicted "heavy" in 60% of the cases where actual traffic turned out to be "heavy" and "light" in 80% of the cases where actual traffic was "light."
d. Add the tree for imperfect information.
e. Develop the revised probabilities using a contingency table and label the tree from (d).
f. What is the optimal act and its expected profit *after* a "heavy" prediction?
g. What is the imperfect predictor worth ($EVSI$)?
h. How efficient is the predictor (compared with perfect information)?
7. A college professor, I. R. Teacher, has bought a condominium and is moving out of his small home near the university, which he will either lease to students or sell. His income from leasing would depend on competition from nearby apartment houses, changes in enrollment, how well the leasees treat the house, whether he can find renters for the summer, and other factors. He has studied the matter carefully and has grouped all these factors into composite measures of "good" and "bad." If he sells the home, he will invest the profit and receive $1000 per year in interest. His annual returns on the options available are as follows.

	RENTING CLIMATES	
	GOOD	BAD
Sell home	$1000	$1000
Rent home	$2000	$500
Probability	.4	.6

a. Construct and label the decision tree.
b. What is the optimal act under prior information and its expected profit?
c. What is the $EVPI$? (Base this on only 1 year's income.)

The Department of Real Estate and Economics at the University will predict the rental climate for Professor Teacher. In the past, they have correctly predicted "good" climate in 80% of the cases when "good" actually happened; when the climate was "bad," they correctly predicted "bad" 70% of the time.

d. Add the tree for imperfect information.

e. Calculate the revised probabilities using a contingency table and label the tree from (d).

f. What is the decision rule, using the imperfect indicator?

g. What is the *EVSI* (based on 1 year's income)?

h. How efficient is the information (compared with perfect information)?

8. Ekswhyzee Corp. buys flange bearings in lots of 1000. Eighty percent of the lots have traditionally been acceptable, which means about 10% have been defective. The rest were unacceptable and averaged about 40% defectives.

It costs $2 to examine and test a bearing. If an unacceptable lot is accepted, it costs $400 to repair the defectives. If a lot is refused and is subsequently found to be acceptable, Ekswhyzee must pay the manufacturer's inspection cost of $1000. There is no cost for accepting a good lot or rejecting a bad one.

a. What is the optimal choice (accept or reject) under prior information?

b. What is the expected cost under prior information?

Try different sample sizes and evaluate the expected net gain from sampling (*ENGS*) for each until you find the optimum sample size.

d. What is the optimal decision rule?

e. How efficient is the optimal sample size (relative to perfect information)? (Do not take sampling cost into account in the calculation of efficiency.)

Chapter 15

GAME THEORY

INTRODUCTION

Not all decisions involving the selection of an optimum alternative have the implacable face of Nature or the blind chance of random events as the force that determines the payoff. There are times when we as decision makers face one or more real, intelligent, and malevolent adversaries who will attempt to maximize their utility at our expense. This vicious, dog-eat-dog scenario is analyzed by the application of a framework with the innocuous title of game theory.

Game theory is the body of knowledge concerned with determining optimum courses of action under the sorts of conditions we have just described. In Chapter 14 we discussed decisions under uncertainty, which are sometimes called one-person games or games against Nature. Here we shall limit our discussion to the simplest set of assumptions—*two-person, zero-sum games*. The two-person assumption restricts the number of participants in the problem to ourselves and one adversary. This is not as restrictive as it may sound, because several opponents can be assumed to act in concert with the effect of one adversary. The zero-sum

Minimizing Player (B)

$$
\begin{array}{c}
 & \begin{array}{cccccc} b_1 & b_2 & b_3 & \cdots & b_n \end{array} \\
\begin{array}{c} a_1 \\ a_2 \\ a_3 \\ \vdots \\ a_m \end{array} &
\left(\begin{array}{ccccc}
p_{11} & p_{12} & p_{13} & \cdots & p_{1n} \\
p_{21} & p_{22} & p_{23} & \cdots & p_{2n} \\
p_{31} & p_{32} & p_{33} & \cdots & p_{3n} \\
\vdots & \vdots & \vdots & & \vdots \\
p_{m1} & p_{m2} & p_{m3} & \cdots & p_{mn}
\end{array}\right)
\end{array}
$$

Maximizing Player (A)

Figure 15.1 Payoff matrix.

assumption specifies that what one player wins, the other loses, and vice versa. No side payments, tariffs, subsidies, or taxes are involved.

The payoffs are presented in the form of a payoff matrix such as the one in Figure 15.1. The entries in the matrix are, by convention, the values paid *to* the player on the left (Player A) *by* the player at the top (Player B). Thus a value of $+3$ designates a \$3 payment to A from B; a value of $-\$5$, a \$5 payment to B from A. Because Player A receives the amount in the table, A wishes to *maximize* the value and is referred to as the maximizing player. Player B views the values in the matrix as payments *from* him or her; B wishes to keep the value of the payoff as low as possible and is called the minimizing player. These designations are in no way discriminatory against B but are merely the result of the decision to let the payoff matrix be stated in terms of payoffs to A. If we had stated them in terms of payments to B (by reversing all the signs), the players' roles would reverse. Therefore, no generality is lost by these designations.

The actual amount of the payoff is determined by the strategies selected by the two players. If A chooses a_2 and B chooses b_3, the payoff will be p_{23}. Obviously, foreknowledge of the opposing player's selection results in an unfair advantage and moves the decision from uncertainty to certainty. We will not permit that, but we will be able to move from uncertainty to risk by specifying the optimal probabilities for *both* players as well as the expected value of the game. Because we have postulated an intelligent adversary, we will assume that she or he will also know the complete solution and that she or he will act in an optimum fashion. We hope, of course, that this is not the case, because suboptimal play by our opponent will result in increased profits to us if we play optimally.

Pure Strategy (Saddle Point) Games

The simplest (from an analytical point of view) and dullest (from a player's point of view) games are those in which each player has a single "best" strategy and will play only that strategy. The name "saddle point" derives from the fact that these games have a single cell that is both the smallest value in its row and the largest value in its column. Player A views the column and sees the cell as the highest point from the horse's vantage point; Player B observes the row and finds it to be the lowest point from the rider's point of view. Any game having this property has a pure strategy, or saddle point, solution.

Consider the examples shown in Figure 15.2. In the first game, A has three strategies and B has four. Player A examines each strategy, determines the worst (in this case, lowest) possible outcome, and lists these at the right of the payoff matrix. A then selects the best of these worst outcomes (strategy a_2). This is the maximum of the row minimums and is called the *maximin*. Player B lists the worst (highest, because the values represent payments) outcome for each strategy (column) and selects the best (lowest) of these. This is the *minimax*. Because both players have selected the same value, this is the solution value for the game: A will play only a_2, and B will play only b_3. The payoff will always be $3 to A. Both players have used the pessimist approach from Chapter 14 to arrive at their optimum strategies.

Note that whenever either player moves to a strategy *other than* his or her optimum strategy, she or he will do *worse*, in terms of payoff, than the optimum value. If B moves to a different strategy, B will pay more ($4, $6, or $5); if A moves, A will receive less ($-3 or $1). For this reason, the solution is optimal for *both* players, and any deviation by one player is punished by worse payoffs for that player.

In the second game, A plays a_2 and B plays b_1; the value of the game (-2) is a $2 payment from A to B. Notice that a move by either one of the players to a different strategy results in a penalty (worse payoff) for the offending player.

Because the solution of saddle point games is so simple, we should always check for the existence of such a solution as the first step in solving any game. If a pure strategy solution exists, it obviates the need to use the more difficult solution procedures outlined in the following discussion.

Mixed-Strategy Solutions

If a single-strategy solution does not exist, a combination of two or more strategies must be employed. We will present a numerical approach for solution of the simplest (2×2) games, a graphical procedure for slightly larger ($2 \times M$ and $M \times 2$) games, a matrix method for larger square games, and finally, a general linear programming method and a simulation approach for use on games of any size and shape.

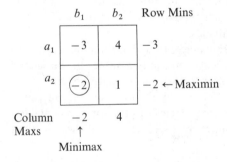

	b_1	b_2	b_3	b_4	Row Mins
a_1	2	8	−3	4	−3
a_2	4	6	③	5	3 ← Maximin
a_3	1	−9	1	−2	−9
Column Maxs	4	8	3	5	

↑
Minimax

	b_1	b_2	Row Mins
a_1	−3	4	−3
a_2	⊝−2	1	−2 ← Maximin
Column Maxs	−2	4	

↑
Minimax

Figure 15.2 Saddle point games.

2 × 2 Games

We will call the method for solution of 2 × 2 games the "swap the differences" method. Our objective is to determine the *relative frequencies* with which each player should play the two strategies available over a large number of plays. These relative frequencies are then used as the *probabilities* with which a player should play the strategies on a single play of the game.

First, we always check for the existence of a pure strategy (saddle point) solution. Consider the following game.

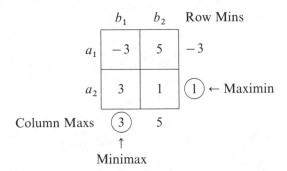

Because the maximin and the minimax do not refer to the same cell, there is no saddle point, and we must devise a *mixed strategy* that involves the possibility of playing both strategies.

To determine the relative frequencies, find the differences between the two values in the first row and between the two values in the second row and "swap the differences"—write the first row difference by the second row and the second row difference by the first row. These values now represent the optimal relative frequencies of play for A's strategies. They may be converted to probabilities by dividing each of them by their sum.

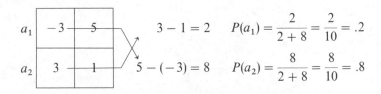

To find B's optimal mix of strategies, find the differences in each column and switch the values. Dividing each by their total yields the probabilities.

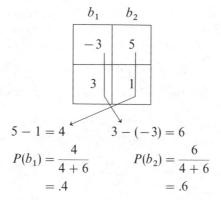

$$5 - 1 = 4 \qquad\qquad 3 - (-3) = 6$$

$$P(b_1) = \frac{4}{4 + 6} \qquad\qquad P(b_2) = \frac{6}{4 + 6}$$

$$= .4 \qquad\qquad\qquad = .6$$

The complete solution is that A should play a_1 20% of the time, or with a 20% probability on any one play of the game; B should play b_1 40% of the time, or with 40% probability on any given play.

Following are two additional examples of 2 × 2 games with mixed-strategy solution.

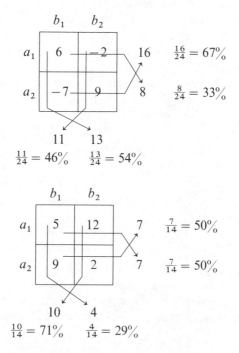

We now need a method of determining the value of the game. The method we will use serves as a check to verify the correctness of our solution and forms the basis for testing the solution to larger games later.

First, we will assume that A plays his or her strategies in their optimal mix, but that B plays b_1 only. We compute the expected value of this play, and call it V_{b_1}, the value against a pure strategy b_1.

$$V_{b_1} = .2(-3) + .8(3) = -.6 + 2.4 = \$1.80$$

Next, we compute the expected payoff against a pure strategy of b_2.

$$V_{b_2} = .2(5) + .8(1) = 1.0 + .8 = \$1.80$$

Now assume that B plays optimally, while A plays only a_1.

$$V_{a_1} = .4(-3) + .6(5) = -1.2 + 3.0 = \$1.80$$

Finally, let A play only a_2.

$$V_{a_2} = .4(3) + .6(1) = 1.2 + .6 = \$1.80$$

The value of the game (\$1.80 to A) is the same in each case, which leads us to observe that *either* player can assure the value of the game by playing his or her optimal mix of strategies no matter *what* the other player chooses to do. If playing the optimal mix results in the same expected value against either of the opponent's pure strategies, it will do so against *any combination* of those strategies.

A note of caution is in order at this point. If a 2×2 game has a saddle point, the "swap the differences" method yields an erroneous result. The error will be detected when we test the value of the game, however. As an example of this, consider the following saddle point game.

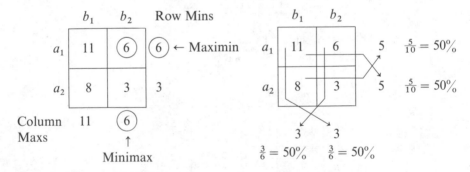

If we fail to find the saddle point solution (\$6 to A), we obtain the "solution" of a 50:50 mix for both players. When we attempt to find the value of the game, however, we obtain the following:

$$V_{a_1} = .5(11) + .5(6) = \$8.50$$
$$V_{a_2} = .5(8)\ + .5(3) = \$5.50$$
$$V_{b_1} = .5(11) + .5(8) = \$9.50$$
$$V_{b_2} = .5(6)\ + .5(3) = \$4.50$$

Because the value is not the same against each of the pure strategies, our "solution" is incorrect.

Dominance

Some games have strategies that are superior to others regardless of what the opposing player does. These strategies are said to *dominate* the less attractive strategies. In the saddle point games we have examined this is true, and each player plays only the dominant strategy. In games larger than 2×2, it is wise to attempt to reduce the size of the game by eliminating dominated strategies.

To player A, a dominant strategy is one that is as good as or better than the dominated strategy for *all* of player B's possible choices. In the following game, for example, a_2 yields a payoff that is equal to or greater than that for a_1 against each of B's strategies; so a_1 is dominated by a_2 and can be removed from consideration. a_2 also dominates a_3 but does not dominate a_4.

Player B tries to minimize the payoff; so she or he thinks of dominance in the opposite direction. A dominant column is one that is the same as or less than another for each of A's possible strategies. In the example, b_3 dominates b_1 but not b_2. Using dominance, the 4×3 game can be reduced to the 2×2 shown.

	b_1	b_2	b_3
a_1	8	5	-1
a_2	10	5	2
a_3	-1	3	-2
a_4	12	-4	7

	b_2	b_3
a_2	5	2
a_4	-4	7

$2 \times M$ Games

$2 \times M$ games are those in which player A has two available strategies and player B has more than two. We will employ a graphical solution method to solve these games. As an example, consider the 2×4 game in Figure 15.3.

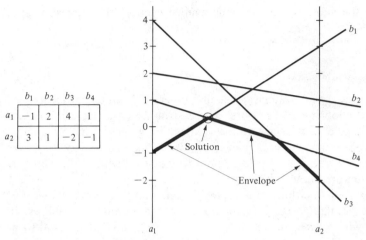

	b_1	b_2	b_3	b_4
a_1	-1	2	4	1
a_2	3	1	-2	-1

Figure 15.3 Graphical solution of optimal strategies in a 2 × 4 game.

We can represent the game graphically by constructing a pair of parallel scales, labeled a_1 and a_2, and then plotting each of B's strategies as shown. Dominance can be readily observed by noting that b_4 is below b_2 at every point; so we remove b_2 from consideration. Because B is the player with the M strategies and B wishes to minimize the value of the game, we find the *envelope* consisting of the lowest line at every point across the interval. A then locates the *highest* point on this envelope, as shown in the figure.

Because this point is at the intersection of strategies b_1 and b_4, these are the strategies B should play, and the game reduces to a 2 × 2.

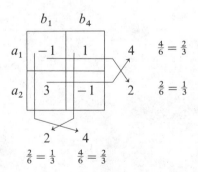

A should play a_1 two-thirds of the time and a_2 one-third of the time; B should play b_1 one-third of the time and b_4 two-thirds of the time. B should *not* play b_2 or b_3, even though b_3 forms a part of the envelope.

To test the solution, we play it against each strategy in the original game.

$$V_{a_1} = \tfrac{1}{3}(-1) + 0(2) + 0(4) + \tfrac{2}{3}(1) = \tfrac{1}{3}$$
$$V_{a_2} = \tfrac{1}{3}(3) + 0(1) + 0(-2) + \tfrac{2}{3}(-1) = \tfrac{1}{3}$$
$$V_{b_1} = \tfrac{2}{3}(-1) + \tfrac{1}{3}(3) = \tfrac{1}{3}$$
$$V_{b_2} = \tfrac{2}{3}(2) + \tfrac{1}{3}(1) = \tfrac{5}{3}$$
$$V_{b_3} = \tfrac{2}{3}(4) + \tfrac{1}{3}(-2) = \tfrac{6}{3}$$
$$V_{b_4} = \tfrac{2}{3}(1) + \tfrac{1}{3}(-1) = \tfrac{1}{3}$$

Against each of A's strategies and against both of B's *active strategies* (b_1 and b_4) the value is one-third. Against B's *inactive strategies* (b_2 and b_3), the value is higher or worse for B. This shows that if B plays a strategy other than the ones in the optimal mix, she or he will be penalized.

This leads us to a *definition* of an optimal solution: *An optimal solution is one that yields the game value when played against each of the active strategies and yields the same value or worse against any inactive strategies.* "Worse" means a *higher* expected value against B's inactive strategies and a *lower* expected value against A's inactive strategies. Any solution that meets these requirements is an optimal one.

Much of the solution can be obtained directly from the graphical solution. If a vertical line is constructed through the solution point, we can read $V(V_{a_1}, V_{a_2}, V_{b_1}, V_{b_4})$, V_{b_2}, and V_{b_3} from the scale. A's optimum mix is read as the relative distances of the solution point from the opposite sides of Figure 15.4.

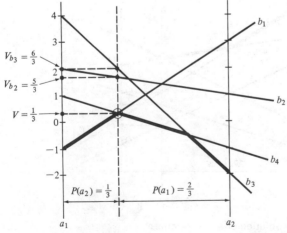

Figure 15.4   Complete graphical solution to the 2 × 4 game.

$M \times 2$ Games

Games in which A has more than two strategies and B has exactly two strategies are solved by the same procedure as that for $2 \times M$ games, except that A selects the *upper envelope* and B chooses *the lowest* point on the envelope. Consider the 5×2 game in Figure 15.5. The lowest point on the upper envelope is at the intersection of a_3 and a_4. If we extract this 2×2 subgame, we find the solution is $(\frac{1}{4}, \frac{3}{4})$ for B and $(0, 0, \frac{1}{4}, \frac{3}{4}, 0)$ for A. The value of the game is

$$V = V_{a_3} = V_{a_4} = V_{b_1} = V_{b_2} = \tfrac{5}{4}$$

and the values against A's inactive strategies are

$$V_{a_1} = -\tfrac{5}{4}, \qquad V_{a_2} = 0, \quad \text{and} \quad V_{a_5} = -\tfrac{2}{4}$$

We can see that both a_2 and a_4 dominate a_1, and that both a_3 and a_4 dominate a_5.

If a $2 \times M$ or an $M \times 2$ game has a saddle point, the graphical solution will allow us to see it. The games in Figure 15.6 demonstrate saddle point games and their solutions.

In the first game, a_2 clearly dominates both a_1 and a_3, and the solution could be obtained by dominance from the game matrix. In the second game b_3 dominates b_1 and b_4, but not b_2. The row dominance is not apparent until column b_1 has been removed. Even though b_2 forms part of the lower envelope, the solution is at the intersection of b_3 and a_2, and is obviously a saddle point.

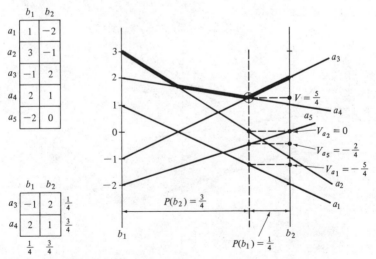

Figure 15.5 Graphical solution of a 5×2 game.

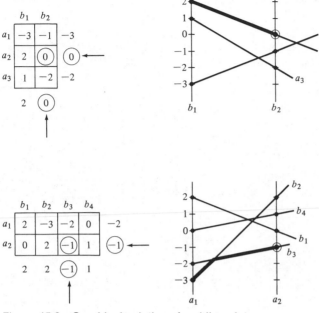

Figure 15.6   Graphical solution of saddle point games.

SOLUTION METHODS FOR LARGE GAMES

Although there are numeric methods available for solutions of 3 × 3 games, they require more work than they save. The methods presented here are useful for games from 2 × 2 on up. The matrix algebraic method requires the game to be square and involves development of the adjoint matrix, which can be a tedious chore for anything larger than a 3 × 3. The linear programming solution assumes the availability of a computerized LP program for solution of larger games and is the most practical approach, useful for games of any size and shape. The simulation method is simple and easy to apply, relatively easy to program, and can yield approximations to optimum solutions for large games with extremely simple calculations.

Matrix Algebra Solution

If G is a square game matrix, we can determine the optimal solution, frequencies for A and B, as well as the values of the game by the following method.

$$A = \frac{(1, 1, \ldots, 1)(\text{adj } G)}{(1, 1, \ldots, 1)(\text{adj } G)\begin{pmatrix} 1 \\ 1 \\ \vdots \\ 1 \end{pmatrix}}$$

$$B = \frac{(\text{adj } G)\begin{pmatrix} 1 \\ 1 \\ \vdots \\ 1 \end{pmatrix}}{(1, 1, \ldots, 1)(\text{adj } G)\begin{pmatrix} 1 \\ 1 \\ \vdots \\ 1 \end{pmatrix}}$$

$$V = \frac{\|G\|}{(1, 1, \ldots, 1)(\text{adj } G)\begin{pmatrix} 1 \\ 1 \\ \vdots \\ 1 \end{pmatrix}},$$

where

$(1, 1, \ldots, 1)$ is a row matrix with as many ones as the

rows of G; $\begin{pmatrix} 1 \\ 1 \\ 1 \\ \vdots \\ 1 \end{pmatrix}$ is a column matrix with the same number of

ones.

$\|G\|$ is the value of G's determinant.

Adj G is the adjoint of G.

The *adjoint* is the transpose of the matrix formed by replacing each element with its *cofactor* or by multiplying each element of the inverse by the value of the original matrix's determinant. The adjoint of a 2×2 can be obtained by simply reversing the positions of the elements on the main diagonal and reversing the signs of the elements on the minor diagonal.

As an example of this method, we will use it to solve the following 2×2 game.

	b_1	b_2	
a_1	2	3	$\frac{3}{4}$
a_2	4	1	$\frac{1}{4}$
	$\frac{2}{4}$	$\frac{2}{4}$	

$$\text{adj } G = \begin{pmatrix} 1 & -3 \\ -4 & 2 \end{pmatrix}$$

$$\|G\| = -10$$

$$V = \tfrac{10}{4}$$

$$A = \frac{(1,1)\begin{pmatrix} 1 & -3 \\ -4 & 2 \end{pmatrix}}{(1,1)\begin{pmatrix} 1 & -3 \\ -4 & 2 \end{pmatrix}\begin{pmatrix} 1 \\ 1 \end{pmatrix}} = \frac{(-3,-1)}{-4} = (\tfrac{3}{4}, \tfrac{1}{4})$$

$$B = \frac{\begin{pmatrix} 1 & -3 \\ -4 & 2 \end{pmatrix}\begin{pmatrix} 1 \\ 1 \end{pmatrix}}{(1,1)\begin{pmatrix} 1 & -3 \\ -4 & 2 \end{pmatrix}\begin{pmatrix} 1 \\ 1 \end{pmatrix}} = \frac{\begin{pmatrix} -2 \\ -2 \end{pmatrix}}{-4} = \begin{pmatrix} \tfrac{2}{4} \\ \tfrac{2}{4} \end{pmatrix}$$

$$V = \frac{\begin{Vmatrix} 2 & 3 \\ 4 & 1 \end{Vmatrix}}{(1,1)\begin{pmatrix} 1 & -3 \\ -4 & 2 \end{pmatrix}\begin{pmatrix} 1 \\ 1 \end{pmatrix}} = \frac{-10}{-4} = \frac{10}{4}$$

As a second example, we will solve a 3×3 game.

	b_1	b_2	b_3
a_1	4	1	3
a_2	5	0	2
a_3	1	4	2

$$\text{adj } G = \begin{pmatrix} -8 & 10 & 2 \\ -8 & 5 & 7 \\ 20 & -15 & -5 \end{pmatrix}$$

$$\|G\| = 20$$

$$A = \frac{(1,1,1)\begin{pmatrix} -8 & 10 & 2 \\ -8 & 5 & 7 \\ 20 & -15 & -5 \end{pmatrix}}{(1,1,1)\begin{pmatrix} -8 & 10 & 2 \\ -8 & 5 & 7 \\ 20 & -15 & -5 \end{pmatrix}\begin{pmatrix} 1 \\ 1 \\ 1 \end{pmatrix}} = \frac{(4,0,4)}{8} = \frac{1}{2}, 0, \frac{1}{2}$$

$$B = \frac{\begin{pmatrix} -8 & 10 & 2 \\ -8 & 5 & 7 \\ 20 & -15 & -5 \end{pmatrix}\begin{pmatrix} 1 \\ 1 \\ 1 \end{pmatrix}}{8} = \frac{\begin{pmatrix} 4 \\ 4 \\ 0 \end{pmatrix}}{8} = \frac{1}{2}, \frac{1}{2}, 0$$

$$V = \frac{20}{8} = 2\frac{1}{2}$$

This solution tells us that a_2 and b_3 should not be active strategies. Testing the solution, we find

$$V_{a_1} = \tfrac{1}{2}(4) + \tfrac{1}{2}(1) + 0(3) = \tfrac{5}{2}$$
$$V_{a_2} = \tfrac{1}{2}(5) + \tfrac{1}{2}(0) + 0(2) = \tfrac{5}{2}$$
$$V_{a_3} = \tfrac{1}{2}(1) + \tfrac{1}{2}(4) + 0(2) = \tfrac{5}{2}$$
$$V_{b_1} = \tfrac{1}{2}(4) + 0(5) + \tfrac{1}{2}(1) = \tfrac{5}{2}$$
$$V_{b_2} = \tfrac{1}{2}(1) + 0(0) + \tfrac{1}{2}(4) = \tfrac{5}{2}$$
$$V_{b_3} = \tfrac{1}{2}(3) + 0(2) + \tfrac{1}{2}(2) = \tfrac{5}{2}$$

which tells us that our solution is valid, because the "inactive" strategies yield the same expected payoff as the active ones. (Recall that our definition of an optimum was that we would have the same or worse payoff against inactive strategies as against active strategies.)

Linear Programming Solution

Solution of games by linear programming is the best approach for large games, assuming that a linear programming package is available.

To set up the problem for solution by the computer, we first assume that A wishes to determine a set of values (playing frequencies) that will, when played against each of B's strategies, yield V (the value of the game, which is unknown) against B's active strategies and V or more (worse for B) against B's inactive strategies. Consider the following examples.

	b_1	b_2	b_3	
a_1	2	4	−5	X_1
a_2	3	1	−2	X_2
a_3	1	−3	0	X_3
a_4	−3	5	1	X_4

$$V_{b_1} = \quad 2X_1 + 3X_2 + 1X_3 - 3X_4 \geq V$$

$$V_{b_2} = \quad 4X_1 + 1X_2 - 3X_3 + 5X_4 \geq V$$

$$V_{b_3} = -5X_1 - 2X_2 + 0X_3 + 1X_4 \geq V$$

If we divide both sides of each of these inequalities by V to remove the unknown from the right-hand side, we obtain

$$2\frac{X_1}{V} + 3\frac{X_2}{V} + 1\frac{X_3}{V} - 3\frac{X_4}{V} \geq 1$$

$$4\frac{X_1}{V} + 1\frac{X_2}{V} - 3\frac{X_3}{V} + 5\frac{X_4}{V} \geq 1$$

$$-5\frac{X_1}{V} - 2\frac{X_2}{V} + 0\frac{X_3}{V} + 1\frac{X_4}{V} \geq 1$$

We now define a new set of variables

$$X_i' = \frac{X_i}{V}$$

Substituting, we have

$$2X_1' + 3X_2' + 1X_3' - 3X_4' \geq 1$$
$$4X_1' + 1X_2' - 3X_3' + 5X_4' \geq 1$$
$$-5X_1' - 2X_2' + 0X_3' + 1X_4' \geq 1$$

These are our constraint equations. To obtain an objective function, we begin with a statement of the fact that the sum of the original variables (X_i) is unity.

$$X_1 + X_2 + X_3 + X_4 = 1$$

If we divide both sides by V, we obtain

$$\frac{X_1}{V} + \frac{X_2}{V} + \frac{X_3}{V} + \frac{X_4}{V} = \frac{1}{V}$$

Using the same transformation as we did in the constraints $(X_i' = X_i/V)$, we find

$$X_1' + X_2' + X_3' + X_4' = \frac{1}{V}$$

Since we are looking for A's playing frequencies and A wishes to find a set of X_is that *maximize* V, we will have as our objective to *minimize* $1/V$, or

$$\text{Min } Z = X_1' + X_2' + X_3' + X_4' = \frac{1}{V}$$

The results of the linear programming solution are

$$X_1' = 0, \quad X_2' = 4, \quad X_3' = 16, \quad X_4' = 9, \quad \text{and} \quad Z_{\text{MIN}} = 29$$

Transforming these values into X_is by

$$V = \frac{1}{Z} \quad \text{and} \quad X_i = VX_i'$$

we obtain the solution

$$V = \tfrac{1}{29} = .0345, \qquad X_1 = 0, \qquad X_2 = \tfrac{4}{29} = .138,$$
$$X_3 = \tfrac{16}{29} = .552, \qquad X_4 = \tfrac{9}{29} = .310$$

Solving for B's strategies requires formulation of a new linear programming problem. From our definition of an optimal solution, we know that there exists a set of values for B's playing frequencies that, when played against A's pure strategies, will yield the value of the game (V) for A's active strategies and V or "worse" (lower) for A's inactive strategies. Writing these out, we obtain

$$
\begin{aligned}
V_{a_1} &= & 2Y_1 + 4Y_2 - 5Y_3 &\leq V \\
V_{a_2} &= & 3Y_1 + 1Y_2 - 2Y_3 &\leq V \\
V_{a_3} &= & 1Y_1 - 3Y_2 + 0Y_3 &\leq V \\
V_{a_4} &= -3Y_1 + 5Y_2 \quad 1Y_3 &\leq V
\end{aligned}
$$

Dividing both sides of each equation by V and transforming ($Y_1' = Y_i/V$) yields our constraints

$$
\begin{aligned}
2Y_1' + 4Y_2' - 5Y_3' &\leq 1 \\
3Y_1' + 1Y_2' - 2Y_3' &\leq 1 \\
1Y_1' - 3Y_2' + 0Y_3' &\leq 1 \\
-3Y_1' + 5Y_2' + 1Y_3' &\leq 1
\end{aligned}
$$

The sum of the Y_i equals one.

$$Y_1 + Y_2 + Y_3 = 1$$

Dividing by V gives us

$$\frac{Y_1}{V} + \frac{Y_2}{V} + \frac{Y_3}{V} = \frac{1}{V}$$

Transforming, we have

$$Y_1' + Y_2' + Y_3' = \frac{1}{V}$$

which becomes our objective function. Because B wishes to *minimize* V, she or he will wish to *maximize* $1/V$.

$$\text{Max } Z = Y_1' + Y_2' + Y_3'$$

The results of this linear program problem are

$$Y_1' = 10, \qquad Y_2' = 3, \qquad Y_3' = 16, \qquad S_1' = 49, \qquad Z_{\text{MIN}} = 29$$

Transforming these back into Y_is yields

$$V = \tfrac{1}{29} = .0345, \qquad Y_1 = \tfrac{10}{29} = .345, \qquad Y_2 = \tfrac{3}{29} = .103, \qquad Y_3 = \tfrac{16}{29} = .552$$

The slack in the first constraint ($S_1' = 49$) can be transformed by multiplying by V to show how much less than V player A would win if she or he plays strategy a_1. $S_1 = VS_1' = \frac{49}{29} = 1.69$ below V, or an expected value $V_{a_1} = V - S_1 = \frac{1}{29} - \frac{48}{29} = -1.655$.

We advise you to practice the linear programming solution on several small problems for which the correct answers have been developed by other methods to gain familiarity with the procedure.

Solution of Games with Nonpositive Game Values—A Warning

In the procedure for solution of games by linear programming, we divide both sides of the inequality constraints by V. If V happens to be negative, this has the unwanted effect of *reversing* the direction of the inequalities, which leaves us with an LP problem in which we minimize Z subject to a set of LTE constraints (for the X_i' values) and maximize Z subject to a set of GTE constraints (for the Y_i' values). This means $X_i' = 0$, and Y_i' is unbounded. If $V = 0$, X_i' and Y_i' are undefined ($X_i/0$ and $Y_i/0$).

To avoid these problems, when there are any negative elements in the game matrix, we add one more than the most negative element ($E + 1$) to each element of the matrix and solve in the usual way. This assures that $V > 0$ and avoids the problems we have just mentioned. The X_i and Y_i values are the same as those for the original game, and V is increased by the amount added to the elements. After the solution to the new game is obtained, we find the value of the original game by subtracting $E + 1$ from the value of the new game.

As an example, we will solve the following game.

	b_1	b_2
a_1	3	-5
a_2	-2	0

Adding 6 (one more than the most negative element) to each element gives the new game.

	b_1	b_2
a_1	9	1
a_2	4	6

The LP problems are

$$\text{Min } Z = X_1' + X_2' \qquad \text{and} \qquad \text{Max } Z = Y_1' + Y_2'$$
$$\text{ST} \qquad 9X_1' + 4X_2' \geq 1 \qquad \qquad \text{ST} \qquad 9Y_1' + Y_2' \leq 1$$
$$X_1' + 6X_2' \geq 1 \qquad \qquad \qquad 4Y_1' + 6Y_2' \leq 1$$

The LP solutions to the new game are $Z = .20$, $X_1' = .04$, $X_2' = .16$, $Y_1' = .10$, $Y_2' = .10$. Thus the actual solution to the new game is $V = 5$, $X_1 = .2$, $X_2 = .8$, $Y_1 = .5$, $Y_2 = .5$.

These are the true solution values of X_i and Y_i for *both* games, but the value of the original game is found by *subtracting* 6 from the value of the new game to get $V = -1$. These results can be verified by solving both games by the "swap the differences" method.

Solution of Games by Simulation

Confronted by a large game in the absence of a computerized linear programming package, the decision maker has a last resort—to approximate the solution by a simulation approach sometimes referred to as the *method of fictitious play*. We will outline all the steps in this method, demonstrating each in an example. The example problem is the same one we just solved using linear programming; so we will be able to check the results of our simulation against the actual solution.

1. Select any row and write it below the matrix. We have selected the fourth row. (We could just as easily begin with a column; it does not really matter.)

	b_1	b_2	b_3
a_1	2	4	-5
a_2	3	1	-2
a_3	1	-3	0
a_4	-3	5	1
	-3	5	1

2. Circle the minimum value in that row and write the column above it to the right of the matrix (column 1 in our example).

2	4	-5	2
3	1	-2	3
1	-3	0	1
-3	5	1	-3

$\widehat{-3}$ 5 1

3. Circle the largest value in that column and add its row to the last line below the matrix.

2	4	-5	2
3	1	-2	$\bigcirc 3$
1	-3	0	1
-3	5	1	-3

$\widehat{-3}$ 5 1
  0   6 -1

4. Circle the smallest value in the new row and add its column to the last column to the right of the matrix.

2	4	-5	2	-3
3	1	-2	$\bigcirc 3$	1
1	-3	0	1	1
-3	5	1	-3	-2

$\widehat{-3}$ 5 1
  0   6 $\widehat{-1}$

5. Repeat steps 3 and 4 as many times as you wish to simulate playing of the game. (The first five iterations are shown.)

2	4	−5	2	−3	−8	−13	−9	$\frac{0}{5}$
3	1	−2	(3)	1	−1	−3	−2	$\frac{1}{5}$
1	−3	0	1	(1)	(1)	(1)	−2	$\frac{3}{5}$
−3	5	1	−3	−2	−1	0	(5)	$\frac{1}{5}$

$$
\begin{array}{ccc}
(-3) & 5 & 1 \\
0 & 6 & (-1) \\
1 & 3 & (-1) \\
2 & 0 & (-1) \\
3 & (-3) & -1 \\
\hline
\frac{1}{5} & \frac{1}{5} & \frac{3}{5}
\end{array}
$$

6. Break ties for the lowest or highest value by using a random device.
7. Estimate the optimum playing frequency for each strategy by the percentage of times it was played (circled).
8. If the last two circled values are divided by the number of iterations, the value of the game will lie between those two values.

$$-\tfrac{3}{5} \le V \le \tfrac{5}{5}$$

The method works by having each player, in turn, examine the playing history of his or her opponent and select the strategy that has the best (highest for A, lowest for B) average payoff. (We use the totals, but this has the same effect as using the average.) The solution to the game as estimated after 5, 10, 20, and 30 iterations is compared with the true solution in Table 15.1. (If you carry this out, you may obtain a slightly different solution because of differences in breaking ties.)

The method of fictitious play provides us with a very simple but quite powerful tool for approximating the solution to large games without

Table 15.1 SIMULATION SOLUTIONS

	ITERATIONS				ACTUAL SOLUTION
	5	10	20	30	
$P(a_1)$	0	0	0	0	0
$P(a_2)$	$\frac{1}{5} = .20$	$\frac{3}{10} = .30$	$\frac{4}{20} = .20$	$\frac{4}{30} = .133$	.138
$P(a_3)$	$\frac{3}{5} = .60$	$\frac{3}{10} = .30$	$\frac{10}{20} = .50$	$\frac{17}{30} = .567$	.552
$P(a_4)$	$\frac{1}{5} = .20$	$\frac{4}{10} = .40$	$\frac{6}{20} = .30$	$\frac{9}{30} = .300$	.310
$P(b_1)$	$\frac{1}{5} = .20$	$\frac{3}{10} = .30$	$\frac{6}{20} = .30$	$\frac{10}{30} = .333$	.345
$P(b_2)$	$\frac{1}{5} = .20$	$\frac{1}{10} = .10$	$\frac{1}{20} = .05$	$\frac{2}{30} = .066$	.103
$P(b_3)$	$\frac{3}{5} = .60$	$\frac{6}{10} = .60$	$\frac{13}{20} = .65$	$\frac{18}{30} = .600$	.552
V	$-.6$ to 1.0	$-.2$ to $.2$	$-.05$ to $.15$	$-.066$ to $.133$	.0345

the use of computers or sophisticated mathematics. It can be tedious, but it guarantees that we can *always* arrive at a solution for any game.

SUMMARY OF KEY CONCEPTS

Games. Adversary situations in which each player selects a strategy and these selections determine a payoff.

Game theory. Analytical framework for determination of optimal strategy selection.

One-person games. Games against Nature. Decision making under conditions of uncertainty. Discussed in Chapter 14.

Two-person games. The game is assumed to have only two players. One or both may actually be groups of individuals.

Zero-sum games. Payoffs to the winning player are paid by the losing player. No subsidies or tariffs.

Payoff matrix. A table showing the net value to the maximizing player (A) for each combination of strategies for the two players.

Value of a game. The expected payoff (to player A) from optimal play of the game.

Pure strategy games (saddle point games). Games in which each player optimizes by always playing the same strategy. If one player chooses a different strategy, she or he will do worse than the value of the game.

2 × 2 games. Games in which each player has exactly two strategies.

Mixed-strategy games. Games in which the optimum solution involves each player playing more than one strategy (if the game is played repeatedly) or selecting from "active" strategies on a probability basis.

"Swap the differences." A method of solving 2 × 2 games with mixed-strategy solutions.

2 × M games. Games in which the maximizing player (A) has exactly two strategies and the minimizing player (B) has more than two.

M × 2 games. B has two strategies, and A has more than two.

Graphical solution. A method of solving M × 2 and 2 × M games.

Dominance. When one strategy is as good or better against each of the opponent's strategies than another, the second strategy is dominated by the first and is never played. The dominating strategy between two rows (A's strategies) is the larger-valued one; between columns (B's strategies), it is the one with lower values.

Active strategies. Those that have nonzero probabilities (or frequencies) of play in the optimum solution.

Inactive strategies. Those that are not played in the optimum mix.

Matrix algebra solution. A method that can be applied to any square game but used mostly for smaller games. Computationally tedious for games larger than 4×4.

Adjoint of a matrix. The transpose of the matrix of cofactors, or the product of $\|A\|$ and A^{-1}. Used in the matrix algebra solution for square games.

Linear programming solution. The most powerful method of solution for large games. Typically involves use of a computerized linear programming package.

The method of fictitious play. A simulation method for approximating the solution of games of any size.

PROBLEMS

1. Solve for A and B's optimal strategies and the value of the games.

	b_1	b_2
A_1	7	3
A_2	−4	2

	b_1	b_2	b_3	b_4
A_1	3	2	−2	−6
A_2	4	5	−1	7
A_3	−8	14	−5	8

2. Find the solutions to the following games.

	b_1	b_2
A_1	10	−5
A_2	2	−4

	b_1	b_2	b_3
A_1	6	4	−3
A_2	5	7	−4
A_3	10	8	15
A_4	9	2	18

3. "Racetrack" Holmes, a prominent defense attorney, has frequent legal skirmishes with the local district attorney, "White Hat" Wilson. He has researched the results of past cases tried before juries and has found that his probability of winning depends on the type of case he presents (aggressive versus conservative) and the stance taken by the prosecutor (hard line or moderate) in addition to the actual facts of the case at hand. "Racetrack" would like to maximize his probability of winning the case, whereas "White Hat" would like to minimize it. If "Racetrack's" win probabilities are as follows, what are the optimal strategies and the expected win probability?

	"WHITE HAT" WILSON	
	HARD LINE	MODERATE
"RACETRACK" HOLMES Aggressive	.4	.6
Conservative	.5	.2

4. In a union–management confrontation at Ulysses Freight Haulers, management can either stand firm on its offer or compromise; the union can either go out on strike or compromise. Management has computed its expected cost for each set of actions as follows. What is the optimum strategy for each side? As the choice is to be made only once this year, what does this imply?

		MANAGEMENT	
		STAND FIRM	COMPROMISE
UNION	Strike	$60K	$100K
	Compromise	$80K	$40K

5. The blue forces are launching a series of attacks on the well-entrenched red forces, and the red general must decide on a strategy that will maximize the attacking force's losses. He can split his forces 90% in the north and 10% in the south; or 10%:90%, or 50%:50%. The attacking force will attack either the north or south position. Blue's losses are as shown. Find the optimum strategies and the average losses per attack for blue.

			BLUE FORCES	
			N	S
	90% N,	10% S	200	50
RED FORCES	50% N,	50% S	120	80
	10% N,	90% S	60	180

6. Two competing firms are bidding for several consulting contracts. Bates has three strategies under consideration—low, moderate, and high bids, whereas Armstrong is considering only low and high bids. The contracts are not awarded solely on price but on a complicated combination of price and perceived (by the issuing agency) contractor competence and understanding of the project. The following table represents Armstrong's probabilities of getting a contract for different sets of bid strategies. Find the optimum strategies for each company and the value of the game.

		BATES		
		LOW	MODERATE	HIGH
ARMSTRONG	Low	.5	.4	.6
	High	.2	.5	.1

7. Solve the following game. (Hint: Check saddle point and dominance.)

	b_1	b_2	b_3	b_4
A_1	8	0	-3	-2
A_2	4	5	2	-1
A_3	3	1	3	-2
A_4	6	0	4	2

8. Solve for the optimal strategies for A and B and check your answer.

	b_1	b_2	b_3	b_4
A_1	-1	8	-2	3
A_2	5	6	6	-1
A_3	4	7	5	6

9. Daisy Dairy and Vita Moo brands of milk compete in a certain market. Each is considering several different strategies to increase their profits. The expected monthly net profit (loss) in thousands of dollars for each combination of moves is shown as follows. What is the solution to the game? What action should Daisy take? (Use LP for solution.)

		VITA MOO			
		PRICE CUT	INCREASE ADVERTISING	BOTH	NEITHER
DAISY DAIRY	Price Cut	-1	2	-3	2
	Increase Advertising	0	-2	1	3
	Both	2	1	-1	4
	Neither	-1	-1	-2	0

10. Appleton, Berry City, and Cornville are three small towns with 100 voters each that are situated along a remote country road 10 miles apart, with Baldwin in the middle. "Honest Abe" Sackowitz and Bob "Sharkey" Brown are locked in a tight senatorial race, and each can afford only one short stop in one of the three towns during the last weeks of the campaign. The number of votes Abe gets will depend

on which town each visits, as shown in the following table. Travel plans for both candidates must be made in advance, with no knowledge of the other's plans. Solve the game by linear programming.

		BOB			
		A	B	C	NONE
ABE	A	70	85	80	90
	B	80	110	75	110
	C	80	75	85	100
	None	40	30	40	50

11. After reducing the size of problem 9 by dominance, simulate by the method of fictitious play for ten iterations, beginning with the first row. Break any ties in favor of the lower-numbered row or column.
12. After reducing problem 10 by dominance, simulate for ten iterations, beginning with the first column. Break any ties in favor of the lower-numbered row or column. (Hint: You may wish to reduce the size of the numbers by subtracting the smallest value from every cell. Remember to add it back to V at the end of the simulation.)

Chapter 16

SIMULATION

SIMULATION OF SYSTEMS

Webster says that *simulation* is the act of assuming the appearance of, without the reality. Simulation, then, is imitation of reality. When taken in its broadest sense, any model—physical, graphical, pictorial, or mathematical—is a simulation of reality.

For example, from geometry we know that for a right triangle the length of the hypotenuse squared is equal to the sum of the squared lengths of the other two sides (see Figure 16.1). If we know the lengths of sides B and C, we can substitute the values into the given equation and calculate the length of side A. This is simulation. We could, of course, actually construct the triangle and measure side A. This is reality.

Simulation is not simply plugging values into equations, however. It is typically applied to problems that are so complex that they cannot be described by a single equation or probability distribution. Usually a complex system can be subdivided into a sequence of smaller models, typically mathematical models, that use the output of a previous stage

$$A^2 = B^2 + C^2$$

Figure 16.1   Right triangle and a mathematical simulation of the relationship among the lengths of its sides.

as input and whose output becomes the input of a following stage. The behavior of the individual models is predictable, with some degree of accuracy, and, when observed along with the other system parts, allows the experimenter to study the behavior of the entire system.

Obviously simulation of a system has certain advantages. Simulation is less expensive than manipulation of a real system and is more timely— not faster, necessarily, because some real systems are too fast to observe and must be simulated at a slower rate.

Simulation also has disadvantages. The accuracy of the simulation model may be very difficult to validate because of the complexity of the real system. In other words, the essential characteristics of the real system may not be accurately portrayed by the simulation model.

In management science, simulation most often refers to the use of *stochastic* models to imitate reality. A stochastic model is one in which the outputs are not strictly predictable from the inputs but whose results are dependent on some probability distribution. The act of tossing a coin is such a process. We cannot predict whether the result of each toss will be heads or tails, but we can predict over time that the results will be 50% heads are 50% tails if the coin is fair.

In Chapter 17 we will see examples of simulation of stochastic models for queuing systems. The models we will explore will all be *discrete* models, meaning there are a finite number of outcomes or values. Simulation models may also be *continuous*, where the possible values are unlimited within the bounds of the distribution.

A good contrast between a discrete distribution and a continuous distribution would be a jar containing red, green, blue, white, black, and yellow marbles and a jar containing beans. If a marble is chosen at random from the marble jar, it will have one of six colors. The distribution is discrete. If a bean is chosen at random from the other jar and is weighed, it may have a value different from that of any other bean in the jar, and the range of possible values, within the bounds of possibility for bean weights, is infinite. The distribution of weights is continuous.

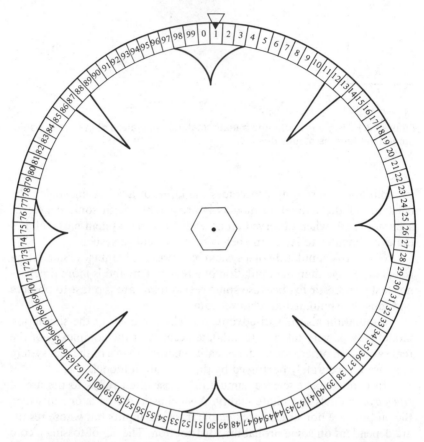

Figure 16.2 The wheel of fortune.

The method of simulation on which we will focus in this chapter will be "Monte Carlo" simulation. The method is named after the famous gambling establishment because it employs a "wheel of fortune" technique to generate values for the various models.

The wheel shown in Figure 16.2 should be adequate for simulating most discrete probability distributions. There are 100 numbers on the wheel, and each number has an equal probability of coming up (1/100). As long as a particular event has a probability of occurrence that is an even percentage (not a fraction, such as 1.5%), we can use this wheel. However, as the number of possible events increases, the wheel would have to have more subdivisions. For example a wheel with 1000 numbers could be used when events had probabilities measured to 0.1%.

To approach a continuous distribution we would have to use a wheel with many thousands of numbers. The same results can be obtained by

Table 16.1   PROBABILITY DISTRIBUTION
OF LEMONADE SALES

A SALES (NUMBER OF GLASSES)	B PROBABILITY	A × B
10	.05	.50
15	.05	.75
20	.15	3.00
25	.15	3.75
30	.25	7.50
35	.25	8.75
40	.05	2.00
45	.03	1.35
50	.02	1.00
	Expected Value =	28.60

using a table of *random numbers*, such as that found in Appendix E, or one of the many random number generators available for computer use.

Example 1: Single-Stage Simulation

Let's look at a simple example of simulation for a lemonade stand. Assume that several years' past history for the stand has provided us with the probabilities in Table 16.1. Assume also that the ingredients for each day must be purchased that day before the stand opens and any leftover lemonade must be thrown out at the end of the day.

Ingredients cost $.10 per glass, and each glass sells for $.20. The strategy that has been followed in the past has been to purchase enough ingredients to make 30 glasses each day. The owner has found that he often runs out of lemonade with this strategy. The table shows that 35% of the time demand exceeds 30 glasses. The owner would like to know what would happen to his profit picture if he makes up 35 glasses or 40 glasses.

He can actually make up 35 glasses each day for a month and check his profit, and then make up 40 glasses each day for a month and again check his profit. This will take time and might cost money. Therefore the owner has decided to see what effects these two strategies will have by simulating the system. Although the more days simulated the more accurate the model will be, only 30 days will be simulated for the sake of brevity.

The first step in the simulation is to decide how to divide up the "wheel" in Figure 16.1. We could, of course, have the first five numbers represent the 5% probability of selling 10 glasses. It would seem that a

Table 16.2 PROBABILITY DISTRIBUTION
AND RANDOM NUMBER RANGES
FOR LEMONADE SALES

SALES (GLASSES)	PROBABILITY	RANDOM NUMBER ASSIGNMENTS (1 FOR EACH 1%)
10	.05	0–4
15	.05	5–9
20	.15	10–24
25	.15	25–39
30	.25	40–64
35	.25	65–89
40	.05	90–94
45	.03	95–97
50	.02	98–99

more accurate way to assign numbers on the wheel would be to pick five numbers randomly spaced around the wheel. In fact this would not be necessary if the wheel were fair and evenly balanced. For the sake of clarity let's just assign numbers sequentially to each possible sales level and assume a fair wheel. Table 16.2 shows the number assignments for this example.

Now all we have to do is spin the wheel 30 times, record the 30 numbers that come up, and find and record the sales levels that correspond to the numbers. In Table 16.3 the results of the simulation are tabulated. The simulation resulted in the following distribution of sales.

Sales	Days	Percentage
10	2	6.666
15	1	3.333
20	6	20.000
25	2	6.666
30	11	36.666
35	7	23.333
40	1	3.333
45	0	0
50	0	0
	30	100.000

Let's see what the profit would have been under the current strategy and the two proposed strategies. The profits are calculated by multiplying the assumed ingredient amounts by $.10 and subtracting the result from the sales multiplied by $.20. Obviously no more can be sold than has been prepared. Therefore if a simulated sale is greater than the amount prepared, it is assumed the same amount is sold as is prepared.

Table 16.3 SIMULATED LEMONADE SALES FOR 30 DAYS

DAY	RANDOM NO.	SALES	DAY	RANDOM NO.	SALES
1	89	35	16	94	40
2	67	35	17	36	25
3	57	30	18	41	30
4	83	35	19	4	10
5	41	30	20	63	30
6	63	30	21	18	20
7	20	20	22	2	10
8	59	30	23	49	30
9	62	30	24	21	20
10	88	35	25	9	15
11	60	30	26	68	35
12	52	30	27	53	30
13	68	35	28	22	20
14	23	20	29	80	35
15	20	20	30	36	25

Table 16.4 LEMONADE INVENTORY STRATEGY COMPARISONS FOR 30-DAY SIMULATION

SALES	DAYS	PROFITS			
		25 GLASSES	30 GLASSES	35 GLASSES	40 GLASSES
10	2	$-1.00	$-2.00	$-3.00	$-4.00
15	1	.50	0	-.50	-1.00
20	6	9.00	6.00	3.00	0
25	2	5.00	4.00	3.00	2.00
30	11	27.50	33.00	27.50	22.00
35	7	17.50	21.00	24.50	21.00
40	1	2.50	3.00	3.50	4.00
		$61.00	$65.00	$58.00	$44.00

Table 16.4 shows the profit results for the current strategy, the two proposed strategies, and one additional strategy—25 glasses per day. The results of the simulation show us that the current strategy is better than the other three.

Example 2: Multiple Stages

The previous example was a simple, single-phase system. Only one random number was required for each iteration. The problem can be made more realistic (and more complex) by viewing it as a three-phase system in which the temperature distribution depends on whether or not the sun shines and the sales distribution depends on the temperature. In this

Table 16.5 LEMONADE STAND MULTISTAGE PROBABILITIES

CLOUD CONDITIONS	PROBABILITY OF CONDITION	TEMPERATURE PROBABILITY TABLE
Sunny	60%	I
Partly Cloudy	30%	II
Cloudy	10%	III

TEMPERATURE RANGE	TEMPERATURE PROBABILITY TABLES		
	I	II	III
75–79	10%	20%	50%
80–84	60%	70%	45%
85–89	20%	5%	5%
90+	10%	5%	0%

SALES PROBABILITIES

NUMBER OF GLASSES	TEMPERATURE RANGES			
	75–79	80–84	85–89	90+
10	30%	20%	10%	0%
15	25%	30%	20%	10%
20	20%	20%	30%	20%
25	15%	15%	20%	30%
30	5%	10%	10%	20%
35	5%	5%	10%	15%
40	0%	0%	0%	5%

type of system three random numbers are required to arrive at a sales figure for one day. First we must simulate cloud conditions, which will tell us which temperature distribution to use. We then simulate the temperature for the day, which will tell us which sales distribution to use. The last simulation for the day will be for the actual sales.

For this example assume that ingredients must be purchased the evening before the day on which they are to be sold. This way cloud conditions would not be known in advance.

Table 16.5 contains the probability distributions for cloud conditions, temperature, and sales. Using our wheel of fortune analogy we can depict the various distributions with eight wheels, as shown in Figure 16.3.

A table of random numbers (such as the one in Appendix E) offers a much more practical means of simulation. In Table 16.6 random number ranges have been specified for each of the distributions. After constructing this table we need only select three random numbers for each day and determine that day's sales. This has been done for 30 days in Table 16.7.

Taking the daily sales generated by the simulation, a little simple arithmetic will yield the results of alternative purchasing strategies. In

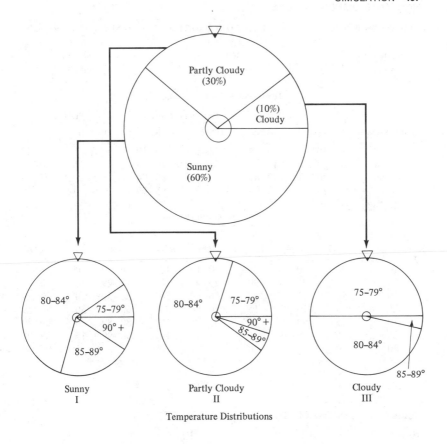

Temperature Distributions

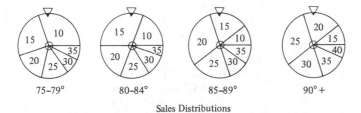

Sales Distributions

Figure 16.3   Multistage examples.

this example the alternative strategies are to purchase ingredients for 20, 25, 30, 35, or 40 glasses. From Table 16.8 it can be seen that the best strategy is to purchase for 20 glasses. Now that we understand the technique of simulation, let's look at some applications.

Table 16.6 LEMONADE STAND MULTISTAGE PROBABILITIES AND RANDOM NUMBER RANGES

CLOUD CONDITIONS	PROBABILITY OF CONDITION	RANDOM NUMBERS (RN)
Sunny	60%	0–59
Partly Cloudy	30%	60–89
Cloudy	10%	90–99

TEMP. PROBABILITY TABLES

| TEMP. RANGE | SUNNY | | PARTLY CLOUDY | | CLOUDY | |
	DIST. I	RNs	DIST. II	RNs	DIST. III	RNs
75–79	10%	0– 9	20%	0–19	50%	0–49
80–84	60%	10–69	70%	20–89	45%	50–94
85–89	20%	70–89	5%	90–94	5%	95–99
90+	10%	90–99	5%	95–99	0%	—

SALES PROBABILITIES

NUMBER OF GLASSES	75–79	RNs	80–84	RNs	85–89	RNs	90+	RNs
10	30%	0–29	20%	0–19	10%	0– 9	0%	—
15	25%	30–54	30%	20–49	20%	10–29	10%	0– 9
20	20%	55–74	20%	50–69	30%	30–59	20%	10–29
25	15%	75–89	15%	70–84	20%	60–79	30%	30–59
30	5%	90–94	10%	85–94	10%	80–89	20%	60–79
35	5%	95–99	5%	95–99	10%	90–99	15%	80–94
40	0%	—	0%	—	0%		5%	95–99

Table 16.7 LEMONADE STAND SIMULATION RESULTS

DAY NO.	RN 1	COND.	RN 2	TEMP.	RN 3	SALES
1	34	S	58	80–84	78	25
2	36	S	43	80–84	50	20
3	33	S	94	90+	35	25
4	54	S	79	85–89	59	20
5	83	PC	2	75–79	23	10
6	65	PC	90	85–89	42	20
7	72	PC	12	75–59	17	10
8	98	C	55	80–84	73	25
9	32	S	28	80–84	48	15
10	1	S	55	80–84	80	25
11	57	S	93	90+	29	20
12	94	C	66	80–84	18	10
13	74	PC	57	80–84	23	15
14	80	PC	24	80–84	33	15
15	36	S	52	80–84	62	20
16	32	S	85	85–89	28	15
17	83	PC	28	80–84	19	15
18	74	PC	33	80–84	33	20
19	20	S	55	80–84	13	15
20	99	C	23	75–79	93	30

Table 16.7   (*continued*)

DAY NO.	RN 1	COND.	RN 2	TEMP.	RN 3	SALES
21	4	S	78	85–89	85	30
22	99	C	66	80–84	66	20
23	68	PC	38	80–84	47	15
24	82	PC	90	85–89	17	15
25	2	S	63	80–84	93	30
26	91	C	56	80–84	39	15
27	62	PC	52	80–84	4	10
28	11	S	8	75–79	25	10
29	45	S	54	80–84	54	20
30	3	S	22	80–84	79	25

Table 16.8   LEMONADE STAND PURCHASE STRATEGY COMPARISONS

DAY NO.	SALES	PURCHASE STRATEGIES 20	25	30	35	40
1	25	$2.00	$2.50	$2.00	$1.50	$1.00
2	20	2.00	1.50	1.00	.50	0
3	25	2.00	2.50	2.00	1.50	1.00
4	20	2.00	1.50	1.00	.50	0
5	10	0	− .50	− 1.00	− 1.50	− 2.00
6	20	2.00	1.50	1.00	.50	0
7	10	0	− .50	− 1.00	− 1.50	− 2.00
8	25	2.00	2.50	2.00	1.50	1.00
9	15	1.00	.50	0	− .50	− 1.00
10	25	2.00	2.50	2.00	1.50	1.00
11	20	2.00	1.50	1.00	.50	0
12	10	0	− .50	− 1.00	− 1.50	− 2.00
13	15	1.00	.50	0	− .50	− 1.00
14	15	1.00	.50	0	− .50	− 1.00
15	20	2.00	1.50	1.00	.50	0
16	15	1.00	.50	0	− .50	− 1.00
17	15	1.00	.50	0	− .50	− 1.00
18	20	2.00	1.50	1.00	.50	0
19	15	1.00	.50	0	− .50	− 1.00
20	30	2.00	2.50	3.00	2.50	2.00
21	30	2.00	2.50	3.00	2.50	2.00
22	20	2.00	1.50	1.00	.50	0
23	15	1.00	.50	0	− .50	− 1.00
24	15	1.00	.50	0	− .50	− 1.00
25	30	2.00	2.50	3.00	2.50	2.00
26	15	1.00	.50	0	− .50	− 1.00
27	10	0	− .50	− 1.00	− 1.50	− 2.00
28	10	0	− .50	− 1.00	− 1.50	− 2.00
29	20	2.00	1.50	1.00	.50	0
30	25	2.00	2.50	2.00	1.50	1.00
		$41.00	$34.00	$22.00	$7.00	$ − 8.00

INVENTORY MODEL WITH UNCERTAIN LEAD TIME AND DEMAND

In standard inventory models we assume a known lead time (T_L) and a known usage rate (d). Needless to say these are unrealistic assumptions. Typically the delivery time (lead time) for an order will be within some range, say between 10 and 15 days. Also the demand will not remain constant. Consequently, a firm must maintain some safety stock to provide for those situations in which lead time is longer than usual or demand during lead time is higher than usual, or both.

Obviously there is some cost associated with carrying safety stock as well as a cost of running out of stock (stockout). Naturally stockouts can be avoided by carrying sufficient safety stock, and safety stock carrying costs can be eliminated by allowing stockouts to occur. The wise manager attempts to find a balance between the cost of carrying safety stock and the cost of stockouts so that their total will be a minimum. One of the tools that can be used to test various strategies is simulation.

Let's assume that the lead time for a particular item is between 10 and 15 days and follows the probability distribution in Table 16.9. Also assume that demand during lead time for the item varies between 100 units per day and 150 units per day according to the probability distribution shown in Table 16.9. The random number ranges corresponding to the probabilities have been added to each of the distributions.

Currently the reorder point for the company is 1560 units. The company is interested in determining the advisability of changing the reorder point to reduce the number of stockouts. The company proposes to simulate 5 years of operation (their records show that they have ordered this item 21 times in the past 5 years) using three strategies plus the current strategy. The three alternate strategies will be changing the reorder point to 1760, 1960, and 2160. The company has determined that each stockout costs $5 (the profit foregone from the lost sale) and that the cost of carrying inventory is $1 per unit per order period.

In order to perform the simulation we will have to establish a lead time and a usage rate for each order period. Then we multiply the usage rate by the number of days lead time to establish the total usage during lead time. This is demonstrated in Table 16.10.

Table 16.9 LEAD TIME AND DEMAND PROBABILITY DISTRIBUTIONS

	LEAD TIME			DEMAND	
DAYS	PROBABILITY	RN RANGE	UNITS/DAY	PROBABILITY	RN RANGE
10	10%	0– 9	100	5%	0– 4
11	10%	10–19	110	10%	5–14
12	25%	20–44	120	20%	15–34
13	35%	45–79	130	30%	35–64
14	15%	80–94	140	20%	65–84
15	5%	95–99	150	15%	85–99

Table 16.10   INVENTORY SIMULATION RESULTS

PERIOD	LEAD TIME RN	DAYS	USAGE RN	UNITS/DAY	TOTAL DEMAND DURING LEAD TIME
1	93	14	91	150	2100
2	52	13	98	150	1950
3	98	15	77	140	2100
4	31	12	71	140	1680
5	17	11	16	120	1320
6	63	13	95	150	1950
7	75	13	44	130	1690
8	19	11	63	130	1430
9	53	13	95	150	1950
10	75	13	98	150	1950
11	24	12	3	100	1200
12	22	12	66	140	1680
13	13	11	75	140	1540
14	90	14	77	140	1960
15	62	13	70	140	1820
16	88	14	83	140	1960
17	4	10	84	140	1400
18	87	14	50	130	1820
19	57	13	83	140	1820
20	53	13	27	120	1560
21	84	14	26	120	1680

The next step is to determine the results for each of the four strategies. When the total usage for a period is greater than the reorder point, there are stockouts. When the total usage is less, there is a stock overage. The overage results in added inventory carrying cost.

In Table 16.11 we see the ramifications of each strategy. Setting the reorder point at 1960 units results in a total cost that is considerably less than the others. Obviously the total cost cannot be further reduced, because there are no stockouts for a 2160-unit reorder point strategy.

AN INVESTMENT SIMULATION

An investor desires to add an oil company stock to his portfolio. He has narrowed his choice to Dry Hole Oil, Inc., and Blowout Oil, Inc. Both have about the same earning history and are selling for the same price per share.

An analysis of the weekly performance for both stocks reveals the following.

1. On a weekly basis Dry Hole has remained at the same price 80% of the time, gone up 10% of the time, and down 10% of the time.
2. Blowout has remained unchanged only 60% of the time, gone up 20% of the time, and down 20% of the time.
3. When Dry Hole went up it went up by $\frac{1}{8}$ 60% of the time, $\frac{1}{4}$ 25% of the time, $\frac{3}{8}$ 10% of the time, and $\frac{1}{2}$ 5% of the time.

Table 16.11 IMPACT OF INVENTORY STRATEGIES

STRATEGY PERIOD	USAGE	1560 UNDER	1560 OVER	1760 UNDER	1760 OVER	1960 UNDER	1960 OVER	2160 UNDER	2160 OVER
1	2100	540		340		140			60
2	1950	390		190			10		210
3	2100	540		340		140			60
4	1680	120			80		280		480
5	1320		240		440		640		840
6	1950	390		190			10		210
7	1690	130			70		270		470
8	1430		130		330		530		730
9	1950	390		190			10		210
10	1950	390		190			10		210
11	1200		360		560		760		960
12	1680	120			80		280		480
13	1540		20		220		420		620
14	1960	400		200					200
15	1820	260		60			140		340
16	1960	400		200					200
17	1400		160		360		560		760
18	1820	260		60			140		340
19	1820	260		60			140		340
20	1560				200		400		600
21	1680	120			80		280		480
		4710	910	2020	2420	280	4880	0	8800 units
COST		$24,460		$12,520		$6,280		$8,800	

Table 16.12 STOCK FLUCTUATION PROBABILITY DISTRIBUTION

DRY HOLE OIL COMPANY			BLOWOUT OIL COMPANY		
CHANGE	PROBABILITY	RN	CHANGE	PROBABILITY	RN
Up	.10	0– 9	Up	.20	0–19
None	.80	10–89	None	.60	20–79
Down	.10	90–99	Down	.20	80–99
AMOUNT UP			AMOUNT UP		
$1/8\%$	.60	0–59	$1/8\%$	.50	0–49
$1/4\%$	.25	60–84	$1/4\%$	.25	50–74
$3/8\%$	.10	85–94	$3/8\%$	.15	75–89
$1/2\%$	.05	95–99	$1/2\%$	.10	90–99
AMOUNT DOWN			AMOUNT DOWN		
$1/8\%$	.75	0–74	$1/8\%$	.40	0–39
$1/4\%$	.15	75–89	$1/4\%$	.30	40–69
$3/8\%$	.05	90–94	$3/8\%$	.20	70–89
$1/2\%$	.05	95–99	$1/2\%$	.10	90–99

Table 16.13 STOCK SIMULATION RESULTS

WEEK	DRY HOLE OIL COMPANY				BLOWOUT OIL COMPANY				
	DIRECTION		AMOUNT	CUM. PRICE	DIRECTION		AMOUNT		CUM. PRICE
	RN		RN	INCREASE/DECREASE	RN		RN	INCREASE/DECREASE	INCREASE/DECREASE
1	15	—			99	→	7	$\frac{1}{8}$	$-\frac{1}{8}$
2	1	←	3 $\frac{1}{8}$	$+\frac{1}{8}$	5	←	49	$\frac{1}{8}$	0
3	47	—			71	—	26	$\frac{1}{8}$	$-\frac{1}{8}$
4	27	—			95	→			
5	65	—			72	—			
6	47	—			80	→	97	$\frac{1}{2}$	$-\frac{5}{8}$
7	49	—			95	→	96	$\frac{1}{2}$	$-\frac{9}{8}$
8	77	—			95	→	51	$\frac{1}{4}$	$-\frac{11}{8}$
9	41	—			48	—			$-\frac{1}{8}$
10	7	←	46 $\frac{1}{8}$	$+\frac{1}{4}$	16	←	45	$\frac{1}{8}$	$-\frac{10}{8}$
11	11	—			45	—			
12	52	—			59	—			
13	23	—			54	—			
14	86	—			1	←	32	$\frac{1}{8}$	$-\frac{9}{8}$
15	60	—			65	—			
16	36	—			27	—			
17	35	—			13	←	22	$\frac{1}{8}$	$-\frac{8}{8}$
18	54	—			36	—			
19	13	—			11	←	61	$\frac{1}{4}$	$-\frac{6}{8}$
20	19	—			57	—			
21	42	—			91	→	16	$\frac{1}{8}$	$-\frac{7}{8}$
22	7	←	4 $\frac{1}{8}$	$+\frac{3}{8}$	66	←			
23	59	—			4		15	$\frac{1}{8}$	$-\frac{6}{8}$
24	67	—			43	—			
25	34	—			7		91	$\frac{1}{2}$	$-\frac{2}{8}$
26	91	→	27 $\frac{1}{8}$	$+\frac{1}{4}$	87	← →	78	$\frac{3}{8}$	$-\frac{5}{8}$

4. When Dry Hole went down it went down by $\frac{1}{8}$ 75% of the time, $\frac{1}{4}$ 15% of the time, $\frac{3}{8}$ 5% of the time, and $\frac{1}{2}$ 5% of the time.
5. When Blowout went up it went up by $\frac{1}{8}$ 50% of the time, $\frac{1}{4}$ 25% of the time, $\frac{3}{8}$ 15% of the time and $\frac{1}{2}$ 10% of the time.
6. When Blowout went down it went down by $\frac{1}{8}$ 40% of the time, $\frac{1}{4}$ 30% of the time, $\frac{3}{8}$ 20% of the time, and $\frac{1}{2}$ 10% of the time.

Table 16.12 summarizes this information and includes the random number ranges necessary for simulating the future performance of the two stocks.

The investor wants to hold the stock just long enough to qualify for a long-time capital gain (6 months at the time of this analysis). Consequently he believes a 6-month week-by-week simulation of the two stocks' performances will give him a better basis for a decision.

For this simulation a random number is drawn to determine if the price goes up, down, or stays the same. If the price goes up or down, another random number is selected to determine the price increase or decrease. Table 16.13 shows the results of the simulation. Dry Hole appears to be the best selection even though it has less activity than Blowout.

A MACHINE SHOP SIMULATION

The Small Time Machine Shop has 1 lathe, 1 milling machine, and 1 grinder. The shop performs small custom machining jobs on a first-come–first-served basis. These jobs may require the use of 1, 2, or all 3 machines in various sequences.

Recently the proprietor has noticed that he has been getting further and further behind in completing jobs. The backlog has been increasing by about 3 jobs each month. He thinks he may be able to increase his shop's capacity if he adds 1 more machine. He would like to add a lathe, because its cost would be less than that of a milling machine or a grinder.

In preparation for simulating the operation, the proprietor collected the historical data in Table 16.14. The shop receives an average of 25 jobs per month; so that is the number to be simulated. The procedure is to select a random number to determine the machine sequence for each job and then to select a random number for each machine in each sequence to determine the time each will spend on the job. The results are tabulated in Table 16.15 and have been plotted on the graphs in Figure 16.4.

The top part of Figure 16.4 shows the results with 1 lathe only, and the bottom when 2 lathes are employed. The jobs are shown as the numbered, crosshatched areas on the graphs and have been constrained so that all work on one machine is completed before the job moves to the next machine in its sequence. Note that with 1 lathe the shop was unable to complete 22 jobs, but with the additional lathe 25 jobs were completed with time left over.

Table 16.14 MACHINE SHOP SEQUENCE AND TIME PROBABILITY DISTRIBUTIONS

MACHINE SEQUENCE	PROBABILITY (%)	RN RANGE	MACHINE TIME (DAYS)	PROBABILITY (%)	RN RANGE
1	5	0– 4	$\frac{1}{4}$	25	0–24
2	5	5– 9	$\frac{1}{2}$	25	25–49
3	5	10–14	$\frac{3}{4}$	25	50–74
1–2	5	15–19	1	25	75–99
2–1	5	20–24			
1–3	5	25–29			
3–1	5	30–34			
2–3	5	35–39			
3–2	5	40–44			
1–2–3	10	45–54			
1–3–2	10	55–64			
2–1–3	10	65–74			
2–3–1	10	75–84			
3–1–2	10	85–94			
3–2–1	5	95–99			

Table 16.15 MACHINE SHOP SIMULATION RESULTS

JOB	RN	SEQUENCE	LATHE (1) RN	LATHE TIME	MILL (2) RN	MILL TIME	GRINDER (3) RN	GRINDER TIME
1	65	2–1–3	55	$\frac{3}{4}$	78	1	12	$\frac{1}{4}$
2	54	1–2–3	71	$\frac{3}{4}$	64	$\frac{3}{4}$	3	$\frac{1}{4}$
3	80	2–3–1	8	$\frac{1}{4}$	43	$\frac{1}{2}$	3	$\frac{1}{4}$
4	85	3–1–2	46	$\frac{1}{2}$	90	1	75	1
5	1	1	87	1				
6	83	2–3–1	38	$\frac{1}{2}$	43	$\frac{1}{2}$	38	$\frac{1}{2}$
7	24	2–1	83	1	39	$\frac{1}{2}$		
8	59	1–3–2	14	$\frac{1}{4}$	51	$\frac{3}{4}$	70	$\frac{3}{4}$
9	70	2–1–3	87	1	80	1	0	$\frac{1}{4}$
10	39	2–3			15	$\frac{1}{4}$	42	$\frac{1}{2}$
11	42	3–2			15	$\frac{1}{4}$	65	$\frac{3}{4}$
12	56	1–3–2	49	$\frac{1}{2}$	3	$\frac{1}{4}$	46	$\frac{1}{2}$
13	28	1–3	4	$\frac{1}{4}$			27	$\frac{1}{2}$
14	19	1–2	10	$\frac{1}{4}$	3	$\frac{1}{4}$		
15	50	1–2–3	43	$\frac{1}{2}$	1	$\frac{1}{4}$	13	$\frac{1}{4}$
16	23	2–1	37	$\frac{1}{2}$	71	$\frac{3}{4}$		
17	52	1–2–3	85	1	96	1	84	1
18	62	1–3–2	88	1	31	$\frac{1}{2}$	74	$\frac{3}{4}$
19	74	2–1–3	0	$\frac{1}{4}$	64	$\frac{3}{4}$	39	$\frac{1}{2}$
20	11	3					27	$\frac{1}{2}$
21	27	1–3	2	$\frac{1}{4}$			81	1
22	82	2–3–1	28	$\frac{1}{2}$	18	$\frac{1}{4}$	21	$\frac{1}{4}$
23	86	3–1–2	31	$\frac{1}{2}$	63	$\frac{3}{4}$	7	$\frac{1}{4}$
24	30	3–1	65	$\frac{3}{4}$			54	$\frac{3}{4}$
25	15	1–2	80	1	85	1		

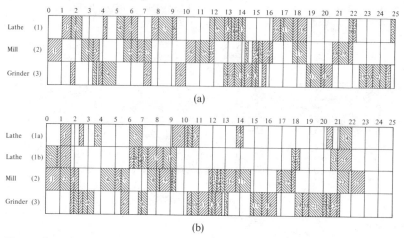

Figure 16.4 Graphical simulation. (a) One lathe; (b) Two lathes.

A WORD ON APPLICATIONS

The examples of simulation in this chapter are not good real-life examples. Most of them could have been handled as easily by using simple statistical techniques. They were employed here only to show the *approach* to simulation.

Real simulation applications in industry are highly complex and almost always require a computer. Also, the number of iterations used in industry application runs into the thousands, not the unrealistic few used in this chapter's examples. For example, a computer program designed to simulate an automatic baggage-handling system for airports has been used to simulate an entire day's arrival and departure schedule for some of the largest airports in the nation. The number of baggage cars is varied until a satisfactory response time is found. The systems are so complex that the numerous probability distributions are unknown and can be developed only through simulation.

Our hope is that these simple examples will serve to demonstrate the procedures involved in simulation, so that you can add this powerful tool to your bag of analytical tricks, for it represents an approach to decision making that can be used as an alternative when the precise, deterministic methods fail to adequately describe the problem. It is for this reason that it has been called by some "the method of last resort" for the management scientist, which can be relied when all else fails.

SUMMARY OF KEY CONCEPTS

Simulation. A model of reality.

Stochastic model. A model in which the outputs or results are not strictly predictable from the inputs but behave according to probability distributions.

Deterministic model.   A model that relies on fixed parameter values.

Discrete model.   A model that permits only a limited number of values for the variables.

Continuous model.   A model that permits variables to assume *any* value within the bounds of the model.

Monte Carlo simulation.   A process that employs random numbers drawn from probability distributions to simulate or model a system or process.

PROBLEMS

1. Two basketball players, Slim and Stretch, have career free-throw averages of .85 and .90, respectively. Simulate a 20-shot free-throw contest between them. Start at the top of column 1 in the random number table and select consecutive random numbers. The players alternate shots, with Slim shooting first.

2. The Albion Bar sells between 25 and 55 pitchers of beer each day. Profit is $1 per pitcher. Simulate 10 days of sales and calculate profit. Begin with the second random number column. The demand and probabilities are as follows.

D	P (D)
25	.05
30	.05
35	.10
40	.20
45	.25
50	.20
55	.15

3. It costs the Acme Company $10 per case to carry ethyl alcohol in inventory for 1 year. Each lost sale costs the company $30 per case. The company presently orders once each quarter, with a reorder level of 75 cases. It has been suggested that the reorder level be raised to 85 cases to reduce stockouts. Using the following demand during lead-time distribution, simulate 2 years' operation and determine if the new reorder level is cheaper than the old. Start at the top of the third random number table column.

D (cases)	P (D)
80	.15
85	.10
90	.05
95	.02

4. The Acme Company has a new supplier of alcohol who is cheaper but less dependable on deliveries. They believe their reorder level should be raised to 90 cases from 85 cases because of the lead-time

variations. The usage during lead time in cases per day and lead-time distributions are as follows. Simulate 2 years of operation and see if the 90-case reorder level saves money. Inventory and stockout costs are the same as in problem 3. Start at the top of random number column 4.

D (cases/day)	P (D)	L (days)	P (L)
15	.68	≤4	.65
16	.15	5	.10
17	.10	6	.15
18	.05	7	.05
19	.02	8	.05

Demand is never less than 15 cases per day, and delivery is never less than 4 days.

5. A local respiratory clinic's records show that 60% of their patients are women. Twenty percent of their female patients and 30% of their male patients have been found to have a new strain of flu.
   a. Determine what percentage of the next 20 patients will have this new flu by using probabilities.
   b. Simulate 20 arriving patients starting with random number 31, column 1 for sex, and random number 31, column 2 for flu, and compare the results with (a).

6. History shows that on a particular par 3 golf hole at a local country club a golfer has a 30% probability of hitting the green with his tee shot, a 50% probability of hitting the sand trap, and a 20% probability of going into the lake in front of the green. If he goes into the trap, he has an 80% probability of hitting his next shot onto the green and a 20% probability of remaining in the trap. When a ball goes into the lake, the golfer must add 1 penalty stroke and hit the next shot from the edge of the lake. His chance of hitting this shot into the lake again is 10%; onto the green, 60%; and into the trap, 30%. Once on the green the golfer may take 3 putts to hole out, 20%; 2 putts, 70%; or 1 putt, 10%. Simulate 10 golfers playing this hole and calculate the mean score. Start with column 7 in the random number table and assign each golfer one eight-digit random number. Each digit represents 1 shot.

Chapter 17

WAITING LINES (QUEUES)

INTRODUCTION

It often seems we spend a large percentage of our lives waiting in lines. We wait to register for classes, to check out at the supermarket, to get a table at a restaurant. We turn away, if we have a choice, when the wait seems too long. When there is more than one line, we choose the shortest or fastest moving one. Of course we do not always have the choice of turning away or switching.

To most of us the cost of waiting in line is measured in relative inconvenience, but in reality, waiting lines are economic in nature. Airlines, trucking companies, manufacturers, and many other organizations try to minimize the total of waiting cost, on the one hand, and the cost of providing service on the other.

In this chapter we will concentrate primarily on the economic aspects of queues and on the various methods used for the solution of queuing problems. First we will explore the graphical method, in which the horizontal axis of the graph will represent time and the results will be determined through observation. Next we will refine the graphical model by assuming some probabilistic relationships in the model and employing Monte Carlo simulation to obtain a solution. (See Chapter 16 for a more detailed discussion of simulation.) Finally we will examine the deterministic approach to queuing problems. This is simply a mathematical technique for finding the steady-state (average) conditions of queuing systems which meet certain requirements.

WAITING-LINE TERMINOLOGY

Before we go on let's agree on some terms and definitions. Any system that has units, or customers, waiting for service is a *waiting line* or *queuing system*. Queue (pronounced "Q") is the British word for waiting line. We will refer to the people, trucks, cars or other objects that wait in lines to be served, loaded, checked out, or unloaded as *arrivals* or *customers*. These customers may be from either finite or infinite populations. Much of the development of queuing theory has been directed at industrial production and manufacturing applications, where the units in the queues are *things*, rather than people. Our focus will be on more people-related systems with which nontechnical business students should be more familiar. The analyses are the same; only the the contexts are different.

The individuals or machines that perform the service for which the arrivals are waiting are referred to as *servers*. The place where the service takes place is the *service facility*. A service facility may be a *single channel*, as in a grocery store with a single checkout counter, or it may be a *multichannel* facility, such as a turnpike toll plaza with several toll booths. Examples of several different types of facilities are shown in Figure 17.1.

The *queuing discipline* refers to the way in which arrivals are admitted to the service facility. Most cases with which we are familiar are first-come–first-served systems. At many grocery stores there is a special express checkout for short processing-time arrivals. Some other disciplines are reservations first and special handling or emergency, such as a hospital has for emergency cases.

Customers arrive at a service facility according to some *arrival distribution*. This distribution may range from a very controlled situation where a predetermined number of customers arrives at a constant rate to a situation where neither the number of customers nor the rate at which they arrive can be controlled. Some of the more common arrival distributions are the exponential, the Poisson, and the Erlang distributions.

There are other characteristics of customers that affect the queuing model. Patience or impatience, and line switching in multichannel facilities, can make a difference in queuing decisions.

When we speak about arrival distributions we are referring to either *arrival rates* (number of customers per time period) or *arrival time* (the number of time units between arrivals). Arrival rate is the reciprocal of arrival time. The rates at which arrivals are served may also be described by exponential, Poisson, and Erlang distributions.

The *queuing system* includes the waiting line(s) and the service facilities. There may be one or several waiting lines and a single server, or there may be a single waiting line and one or several servers. There may also be several stages of service within a queuing system. For example,

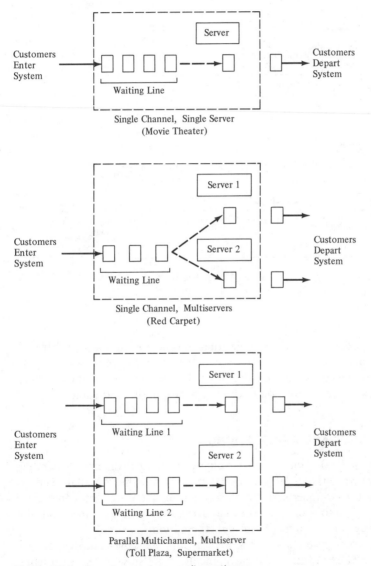

Single Channel, Single Server
(Movie Theater)

Single Channel, Multiservers
(Red Carpet)

Parallel Multichannel, Multiserver
(Toll Plaza, Supermarket)

Figure 17.1 Queuing system configurations.

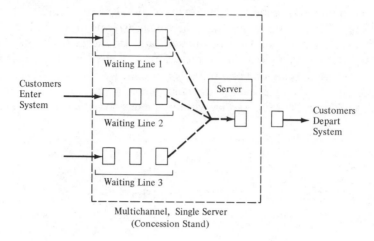

Multichannel, Single Server
(Concession Stand)

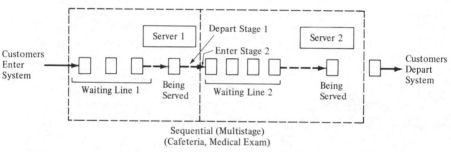

Sequential (Multistage)
(Cafeteria, Medical Exam)

Figure 17.1 (*continued*)

when new recruits in the army get their physical examinations there are several stages—eye check; ear, nose, and throat check; reflex check; heart and lung check; and medical history. Recruits line up at each stage, are processed, then move on to the line awaiting the next stage.

APPROACHES AND APPLICATIONS

There are several approaches to solving queuing problems, depending on the characteristics of the model or system. One popular method, especially for complex systems, is simulation. Here we "spin the wheel of fortune," so to speak, to represent arrivals and service rates, and plot the progress of the arrivals through the system.

In simpler systems we may take a purely mathematical approach to solving the problem. We have mentioned "solving the problem." What are we solving for? What do we have to know to get the answers?

Remember earlier we mentioned that we wanted to minimize the total of waiting cost and serving cost. Consequently, we would like to know the average number of customers waiting in line and the average time spent waiting. We also need to know the cost per time unit for waiting and the cost for service.

CONSTANT ARRIVALS AND SERVICE

The simplest queuing system is the single-channel system with constant arrival and service rates.

Let's look at a situation where the *arrival rate* (A) is constant at 6 arrivals per hour, equally spaced, and where the single server processes customers at a *service rate* (S) of 12 units per hour. This means that 1 customer arrives every $\frac{1}{6}$ of an hour and is processed in $\frac{1}{12}$ of an hour.

We can determine by inspection that there is no waiting line. The server processes the first arrival in $\frac{1}{12}$ of an hour and has $\frac{1}{12}$ of an hour spare time before the next arrival. The server, then, is busy only 50% of the time. The percentage of time that the server is busy is called the *utilization rate*. In terms of the arrival rate and the service rate, the utilization rate (U) is calculated as follows.

$$U = \frac{A}{S} \times 100$$

Figure 17.2 illustrates the first example.

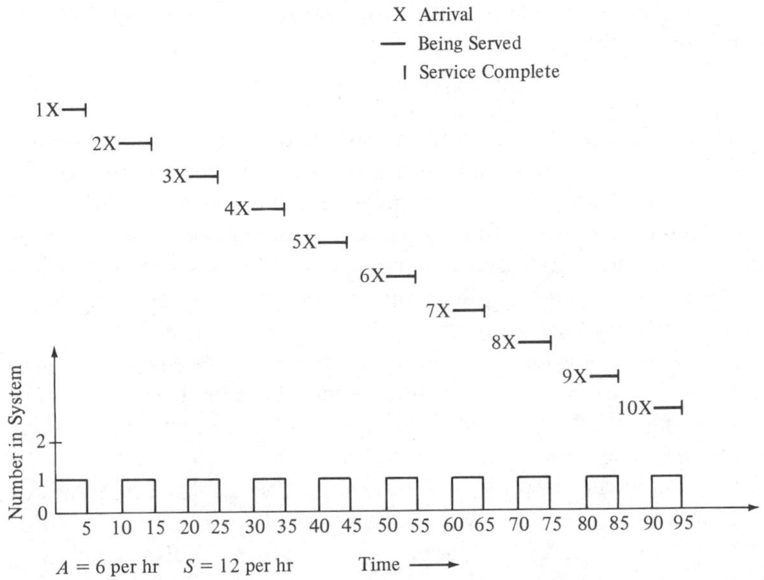

X Arrival
— Being Served
| Service Complete

$A = 6$ per hr $S = 12$ per hr   Time $\longrightarrow$

Figure 17.2   Graphical simulation with constant arrival and service rates.

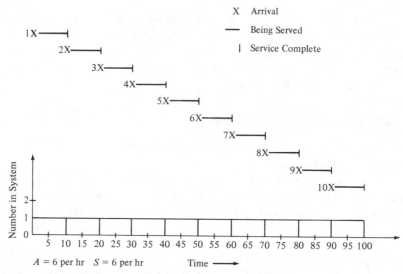

Figure 17.3   Graphical simulation with arrival rate equal to service rate.

Figure 17.3 shows a queuing system with one server having a constant service rate of 6 customers per hour and customers arriving at the rate of 6 per hour. In this system the customer is processed as soon as she or he arrives. As soon as one customer has been processed the next arrives but is not required to wait. The server has no spare time; so the utilization rate is

$$U = \tfrac{6}{6}(100) = 100\%$$

It should be obvious by now that when the arrival rate is greater than service rate, a waiting line will form. When the arrival and service rates are constant and the arrival rate is greater, the waiting line will continue to increase in length until either: (1) the service rate increases (perhaps by the addition of another server), or (2) the arrival rate decreases (as customers, seeing the long line, turn away; or as the manager locks the door to terminate arrivals).

Figure 17.4 illustrates a system where the arrival rate is 6 customers per hour but the service rate is only 4 customers per hour. The figure shows only 10 arrivals. We have "locked the door" on additional arrivals, but the server continues to work until all 10 arrivals have been served.

The first does not have to wait, but the second arrives 5 minutes before the first has been processed and must wait in line for 5 minutes before being served. Each additional arrival waits 5 additional minutes so that the tenth arrival waits $(10 - 1) \times 5 = 45$ minutes $[(10 - 1)$ because

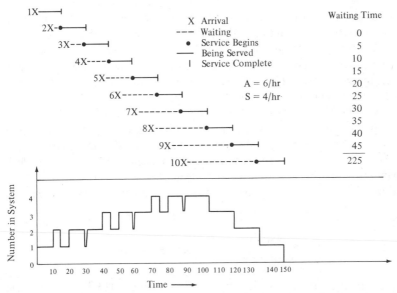

Figure 17.4 Graphical simulation with arrival rate greater than service rate.

only 9 arrivals wait)]. The average waiting time is the sum of the waiting times (225) divided by the number of customers (10), or $22\frac{1}{2}$ minutes.

We can calculate the average number of customers in the system by totaling the number of customers in the system in each 5-minute period and dividing the number of 5-minute periods.

$$\frac{75}{30} = 2.5 \text{ customers}$$

In the same way we can calculate the average number in line by totaling the number waiting in each period and dividing by the number of periods.

$$\frac{45}{30} = 1.5$$

For this problem (with no idle time for the server) the number in line is exactly 1.0 less than the number in the system. If the server had idle time, this is not true, as we shall see presently.

If we continue this model for 8 hours, how many customers will enter the system? Simple. If 6 arrive every hour, then $6 \times 8 = 48$ total arrivals. How many of these arrivals will be completely served? Again, simple. If 4 can be served each hour, then $4 \times 8 = 32$ arrivals served. How long will the thirty-second arrival wait? Because the first arrival does not wait and each additional arrival waits 5 minutes more than the previous arrival, the thirty-second arrival waits $(32 - 1) \times 5 = 155$ minutes.

What is the average waiting time? Because no one who is not going to be served is likely to wait, there will be only a total of 32 customers entering the system. The waiting time of the first (0) plus the waiting time of the last (155) divided by 2 is 77.5 minutes.

Assume the arrivals are mechanics arriving at a parts counter to have parts orders filled by a clerk. The clerk is paid $40 per day, and mechanics are paid $80 per day. How many clerks should be employed?

First of all, what is the cost under the present conditions? The clerk costs $40, and the lost time of the mechanics is 77.5 minutes average waiting time, multiplied by the number of arrivals in the system (32).

$$77.5 \times 32 = 2480 \text{ minutes}$$

$$\frac{2480 \text{ minutes}}{60 \text{ minutes/hour}} = 41.333 \text{ hours}$$

Mechanics are paid $10 per hour; so $41.333 \times 10 = \$413.33$ is the waiting cost.

$$
\begin{array}{r}
\$413.33 \\
+ \quad 40.00 \\
\hline
\$453.33/\text{day}
\end{array}
$$

If we add 1 more clerk, the service rate becomes 8 customers per hour. This means there will be no waiting time, and our cost of clerks has increased only $40, for a total cost of $80. We need go no further because adding more clerks cannot decrease waiting time.

VARIABLE ARRIVAL RATE, CONSTANT SERVICE RATE

Now we will explore a somewhat more complex situation. We will vary the arrival rates and service rates to observe the effect on our models. First, we will vary the arrival rate while holding the service rate constant.

Some of the early work in waiting-line theory was based on calls entering a telephone exchange; so a telephone model is appropriate here.

Assume that a small town has a very basic telephone system. All lines terminate at the local exchange. A single operator receives calls and makes the connections manually. It always takes the operator 30 seconds (.5 min) to make a connection. However, calls come in according to the probability distribution shown in Table 17.1. If a call comes while the operator is processing a previous call, there will be a busy signal, and the caller will hang up and place the call later.

There will be no waiting line in this system, only uncompleted calls. The objective of the problem is to determine the minimum number of

Table 17.1 ARRIVAL DISTRIBUTION

TIME BETWEEN CALLS ($1/A$) (MINUTES)	PROBABILITY
.1	.05
.2	.05
.3	.20
.4	.30
.5	.10
.6	.10
.7	.05
.8	.05
.9	.05
1.0	.05

operators to employ in order to reduce uncompleted calls to zero (or nearly so).

To determine how many calls are uncompleted, we will use simulation. Because we know the probability distribution of the time between arrivals, we can employ a table of random numbers (such as the one in Appendix E). Using the last two digits of each number to determine the time between arrivals. We see that there is a 5% probability that there will be .1 minute between 2 calls. If any random number between 00 and 04 comes up, we assume .1 minute between 2 calls. Also, .2 has a probability of 5%; so we assign the next 5% of the random numbers (05–09). If one of those numbers comes up, we will assume .2 minutes between 2 calls.

To better illustrate the concept, let's imagine a large wheel of fortune (such as the one we used in Chapter 16) separated into 100 segments. We can assign one segment per percent probability for each possible occurrence. Figure 17.5 is such a wheel set up for the probability distribution for this problem.

Now let's simulate 25 calls. Assume the first call is attempted at time zero. We spin the wheel to find the elapsed time before the next call attempt, and it lands on 03. This corresponds to .1 minute. Continuing the same drill we get the results in Table 17.2.

Figure 17.6 is a plot of the attempted calls, showing calls processed and uncompleted calls. Each call attempted while another is being processed is uncompleted. From the figure we see that 10 calls were uncompleted, calls 2, 4, 6, 8, 12, 14, 16, 19, 21, and 24.

Now we add another operator and see how many calls will be uncompleted. Again we will simulate 25 calls. Spinning the wheel we get the time between arrivals in Table 17.3.

Figure 17.7 is a plot of the two-operator model. Note that only one call, number 12, was not completed. By adding one operator the percentage of uncompleted calls dropped from 40% to 4%.

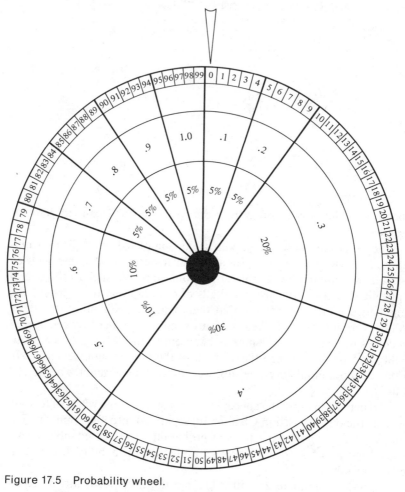

Figure 17.5   Probability wheel.

Table 17.2 SIMULATION RESULTS

CALL NO.	RN	TIME	CALL NO.	RN	TIME	CALL NO.	RN	TIME
1	—	0	9	30	.4	17	54	.4
2	03	.1	10	78	.6	18	91	.9
3	51	.4	11	73	.6	19	42	.4
4	26	.3	12	18	.3	20	46	.4
5	09	.2	13	22	.3	21	30	.4
6	49	.4	14	38	.4	22	95	1.0
7	70	.6	15	34	.4	23	81	.7
8	56	.4	16	37	.4	24	36	.4
						25	46	.4

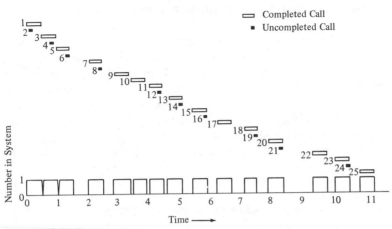

Figure 17.6 Graphical simulation of single-operator phone system.

Table 17.3 TWO-OPERATOR SIMULATION RESULTS

CALL NO.	RN	TIME	CALL NO.	RN	TIME	CALL NO.	RN	TIME
1	—	0	9	34	.4	17	52	.4
2	56	.4	10	14	.3	18	31	.4
3	53	.4	11	05	.2	19	37	.4
4	01	.1	12	01	.1	20	39	.4
5	85	.8	13	83	.7	21	18	.3
6	62	.5	14	80	.7	22	57	.4
7	42	.4	15	98	1.0	23	78	.6
8	88	.8	16	63	.5	24	96	1.0
						25	86	.8

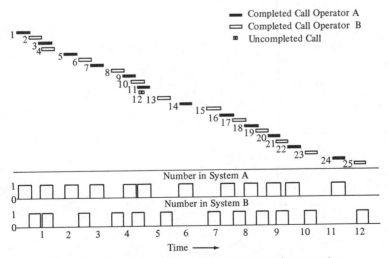

Figure 17.7 Graphical simulation of two-operator phone system.

CONSTANT ARRIVAL RATE, VARIABLE SERVICE RATE

Imagine a system in which customers arrive at a fixed rate of 20 per hour (exactly 3 minutes between arrivals) and the rate of service varies according to the probability distribution shown in Table 17.4. If we simulate 20 customers we merely have to plot the arrivals at 3-minute intervals. The service rate for each arrival is simulated using a random number table.

The results of this simulation are shown in Table 17.5. Plotting the results gives us Figure 17.8. The profile at the bottom of the figure shows how the system behaves over time. The profile reveals a trend toward a

Table 17.4 SERVICE TIME/RATE PROBABILITY DISTRIBUTION

SERVICE TIME (MINUTES)	SERVICE RATE (CUSTOMERS/HOUR)	PROBABILITY	RANDOM NUMBER RANGE
1	60	.05	0– 4
2	30	.20	5–24
3	20	.50	25–74
4	15	.20	75–94
5	12	.05	94–99

Table 17.5 SIMULATION DATA

ARRIVAL NO.	SERVICE RN	TIME
1	88	4
2	34	3
3	14	2
4	05	2
5	01	1
6	83	4
7	80	4
8	98	5
9	63	3
10	52	3
11	31	3
12	37	3
13	39	3
14	18	2
15	57	3
16	78	4
17	96	5
18	86	4
19	97	5
20	51	3

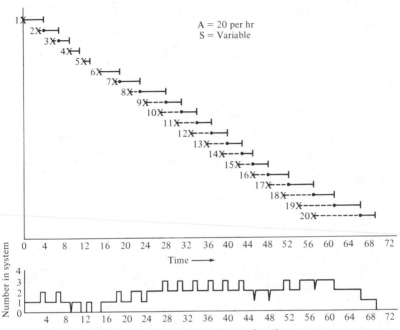

Figure 17.8   Constant arrival rate, variable service time.

growing waiting line. After the 20th arrival we terminate further arrivals and service the four remaining units in the line.

VARIABLE ARRIVAL RATE, VARIABLE SERVICE RATE

Let's look at a single-channel model where customers arrive and are serviced according to probability distributions. Table 17.6 shows the time between arrivals distribution and the random number range for each possible time. Table 17.4 shows the distribution of service times and the random number range for each (the same used in the last example).

Table 17.6   ARRIVAL TIME/RATE PROBABILITY DISTRIBUTION

TIME BETWEEN ARRIVALS (MINUTES)	ARRIVAL RATE (CUSTOMERS/HOUR)	PROBABILITY	RANDOM NUMBER RANGE
1	60	.15	0–14
2	30	.30	15–44
3	20	.40	45–84
4	15	.10	85–94
5	12	.05	95–99

Table 17.7 SIMULATED ARRIVAL DATA

ARRIVAL NO.	ARRIVAL		SERVICE	
	RN	TIME	RN	TIME
1	—	0	88	4
2	49	3	34	3
3	67	3	14	2
4	06	1	05	2
5	30	2	01	1
6	95	5	83	4
7	01	1	80	4
8	10	1	98	5
9	70	3	63	3
10	80	3	52	3
11	66	3	31	3
12	69	3	37	3
13	76	3	39	3
14	86	4	18	2
15	56	3	57	3
16	84	3	78	4
17	54	3	96	5
18	91	4	86	4
19	66	3	97	5
20	08	1	51	3

When both arrivals and service times occur according to a probability distribution, we must "spin the wheel" twice for each arrival, once to determine the arrival time and once to determine the service time for that arrival. If we simulate 20 arrivals and 20 services and assume that the first occurs at time zero, we can develop a table of arrival and service times like the ones shown in Table 17.7.

If these arrivals and services are plotted as in Figure 17.9, what do we learn about the system? First of all, we can see that waiting time tends to get longer and longer as time progresses. We could, of course, have predicted this by analyzing the arrival distribution and the service distribution. If we calculate the expected values (means) of these distributions, we see that the average service time is longer than the average arrival time. The calculations are shown in Table 17.8.

If this system were allowed to operate indefinitely, the waiting line would continue to get longer and longer, and the average waiting time would be infinite. Let's say we only allow the system to operate for 8 hours. How could we find the average length of the waiting line, the maximum length of the waiting line, the average waiting time, and the maximum waiting time? We could simulate the system for an 8-hour period and get a fairly good approximation of waiting-line length and waiting time. Better still, we could simulate several 8-hour days (the

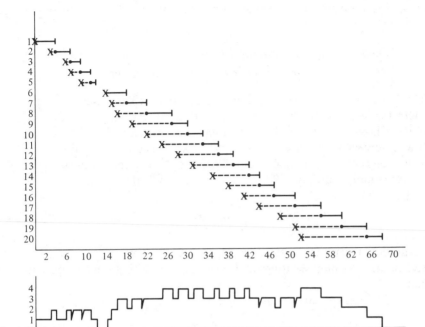

Figure 17.9   Variable arrival rate and service time.

Table 17.8   ARRIVAL AND SERVICE TIME DISTRIBUTIONS

ARRIVAL TIME	PROBABILITY		SERVICE TIME	PROBABILITY	
1	.15	.15	1	.05	.05
2	.30	.60	2	.20	.40
3	.40	1.20	3	.50	1.50
4	.10	.40	4	.20	.80
5	.05	.25	5	.05	.25
	Mean Time Between Arrivals (*MTBA*)	2.60		Mean Service Time (*MST*)	3.45

more the better) and find the averages. The ultimate result of repeated simulations would yield the average arrival and service rates found in Table 17.8.

Knowing this, we can estimate the number of customers arriving during an 8-hour period. If customers arrive at an average of 1 every 2.6 minutes, the average arrival rate is

$$1/2.6 = .385 \text{ arrivals/min} \times 60 \text{ min/hr} = 23.1 \text{ arrivals/hr}$$
$$23.1 \text{ arrivals/hr} \times 8 \text{ hrs} \approx 185 \text{ customers}$$

In the same manner the average service rate and number of customers serviced is approximated.

$$1/3.45 = .29 \text{ customers/min} \times 60 \text{ min/hr} = 17.4 \text{ customers/hr}$$
$$17.4 \text{ customers/hr} \times 8 \text{ hrs} \approx 139 \text{ customers}$$

The 185th customer arrives just as the facility closes. Consequently the 140th through the 184th arrivals (45 customers) were in line at the end of the 8-hour period. The 140th customer has waited in line the longest. If we know when he arrives in the system, we can subtract the time from 8 and determine how long he waits. To find out when the 140th customer arrives, simply multiply 139 times the average arrival time

$$139 \text{ arrivals} \times \frac{1}{23.1} \text{ hrs/arrival} = 6.02 \text{ hrs}$$

(assuming arrivals are at the average rate), and 8 hours − 6.02 hours = 1.98 hours maximum waiting time. The average waiting time is approximately

$$\frac{\text{max} + \text{min}}{2} = \frac{0 + 1.98}{2} = .99 \text{ hrs}$$

The average number of customers in the waiting line can be estimated by averaging the maximum and minimum number in the line.

$$\frac{\text{max} + \text{min}}{2} = \frac{0 + 45}{2} = 22\frac{1}{2} \qquad \text{(average number of customer in line)}$$

What would happen if another server were added to the system? If we assume that the two servers working together can process a customer twice as fast as the single server, then the average service rate will be doubled. (And, of course, the average service time will be halved). The new service rate will be 34.8 customers per hour. Consequently, the waiting line will not continue to get longer and longer because fewer arrive (23.1) than are serviced (34.8). If both servers are not always occupied, the service rate will be increased but not necessarily doubled.

With this situation one would expect that there would be no waiting line in the system at any time, but this is not so. Look at the two probability distributions in Figure 17.10. Note that the two distributions overlap. This means there is some probability that short arrival times occur in conjunction with long service times, resulting in a situation where one or more customers must wait in line for short periods.

So far we have dealt with *discrete distributions* only. In reality arrivals and service rates will be described by continuous distributions where an infinite number of occurrences can take place rather than just a few, as in

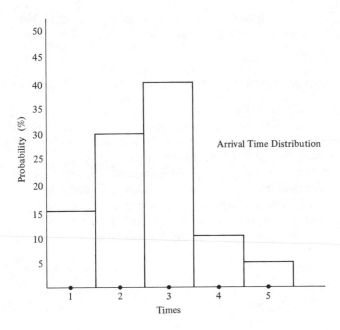

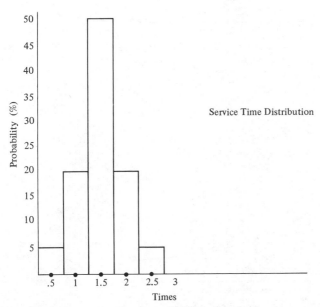

Figure 17.10   Arrival and service time distributions.

our past examples. The following sections of this chapter will deal with Poisson-distributed arrivals and negative-exponential-distributed service times.

SOLVING QUEUING PROBLEMS BY FORMULA

Some queuing problems can be solved analytically when certain conditions are met by the system. The formulas discussed in this section can be applied to single channel single server systems to determine steady-state or average conditions. In other words, the formulas will provide information about the queuing system after it has stabilized. They will tell us nothing about the system during start-up or shutdown. In order for the formulas to work, we must also assume that service is on a first-come-first-served basis and that no arrival leaves the system before being served.

In the following formulas these conventions will be used.

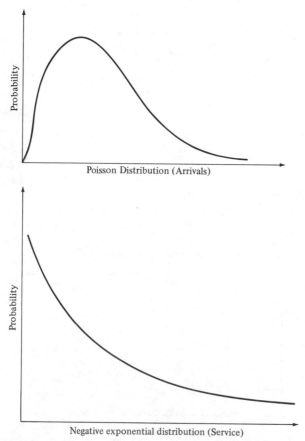

Figure 17.11   Arrival and service distributions.

A is the mean of the Poisson arrival distribution and will be called simply the "arrival rate" (in arrivals per hour). It is the reciprocal of the mean time between arrivals ($A = 1/MTBA$).

S is the mean of the negative exponential service rate distribution and will be called simply the "service rate" (in customers per hour). It is the reciprocal of the mean service time ($S = 1/MST$). (Figure 17.11 illustrates a Poisson and an exponential distribution.)

U is the utilization factor (A/S or $MST/MTBA$)—the average portion of time that the service facility is busy. In order for our equations to be valid, U must lie in the range $0 < U < 1$.

If we want to find the average length of time spent in the queuing system (T_S), we may do so by solving the equation

$$T_S = \frac{1}{S - A}$$

(Note that $U < 1$ implies $A < S$, for if we violate this requirement, we will obtain negative values for T_S.) If we want to calculate the average time in the waiting line (T_Q), we need only multiply the average time in the system (T_S) by the utilization factor (U)

$$T_Q = UT_S = \left(\frac{A}{S}\right)\left(\frac{1}{S - A}\right) = \frac{A}{S(S - A)}$$

The total time in the system will equal the sum of the time spent waiting in line and the time spent being served.

$$T_S = T_Q + MST$$

$$= UT_S + S$$

$$= \frac{A}{S(S - A)} + S$$

$$= \frac{A + (S - A)}{S(S - A)}$$

$$= \frac{1}{S - A}$$

To find the average number of customers in the system (N_S) we can multiply the average time in the system (T_S) by the arrival rate (A).

$$N_S = AT_S = \frac{A}{S - A}$$

To find the average number of customers in the waiting line (N_Q), we merely multiply the average number of customers in the system (N_S) by the utilization factor (U)

$$N_Q = UN_S = \left(\frac{A}{S}\right)\left(\frac{A}{S-A}\right) = \frac{A^2}{S(S-A)}$$

One last relationship is the probability that there are exactly n customers in the system (P_n). This probability is calculated by

$$P_n = (1 - U)U^n$$

where U is the utilization factor.

If, for example, the utilization factor U were equal to .5 and we desired to know the probability that there were exactly 2 customers in the system, we would calculate this by

$$P_2 = (1 - .5)(.5)^2 = (.5)(.25) = .125$$

or 12.5%.

By the same token we can calculate the probability that the server is idle (no customers in the system) by

$$P_0 = (1 - .5)(.5)^0 = (.5)(1) = .5$$

or 50%.

This is a perfectly logical relationship; because U is the probability that the server is busy, $1 - U$ is the probability the system is empty.

APPLYING THE FORMULAS

Example 1: A Doctor's Office

Dr. Walter "Happy" Goodfellow, M.D., is a general practitioner with an established, one-man practice. He schedules office visits at 15-minute intervals and has observed that the actual arrivals are Poisson distributed.

His average patient requires 12 minutes of Happy's actual time. These service times do vary and are distributed in a reasonable approximation to a negative exponential distribution. From these data we wish to determine the average wait per patient, the average number in the waiting room, and the probability that there will be more than 4 patients waiting at any time. (There is limited seating in Happy's waiting room.)

Using our steady-state equations, we find

$$A = \frac{1}{MTBA} = \frac{1}{15 \text{ min}} = 4/\text{hr}$$

$$S = \frac{1}{MST} = \frac{1}{12 \text{ min}} = 5/\text{hr}$$

$$U = \frac{A}{S} = \frac{4}{5} = \frac{MST}{MTBA} = \frac{12}{15} = .8 \text{ (no units)}$$

The average time in the system is

$$T_S = \frac{1}{S - A} = \frac{1}{5 - 4} = 1 \text{ hr}$$

The average time waiting is

$$T_Q = UT_S = (.8)(1) = .8 \text{ hr} \quad \text{or} \quad (.8)(60) = 48 \text{ min}$$

We can check these values by adding the average time spent waiting (T_Q) to the average length of service (MST) to obtain the average time in the system (T_S).

$$48 \text{ min} + 12 \text{ min} = 60 \text{ min} = 1 \text{ hr}$$

The average number in the system is

$$N_S = AT_S = (4/\text{hr})(1 \text{ hr}) = 4 \text{ patients}$$

The average number in the waiting room is

$$N_Q = UN_S = (.8)(4) = 3.2 \text{ patients}$$

Dr. Goodfellow's percentage of idle time is

$$P_0 = (1 - U)U^0 = 1 - .8 = 20\%$$

The probability that there will be more than 4 waiting is the same as the probability of more than 5 in the system, or

$$
\begin{aligned}
P_{N>5} &= 1 - [P_0 + P_1 + P_2 + P_3 + P_4 + P_5] \\
&= 1 - [(1 - U)(U^0) + (1 - U)(U^1) + (1 - U)(U^2) \\
&\quad + (1 - U)(U^3) + (1 - U)(U^4) + (1 - U)(U^5)] \\
&= 1 - [.2 + .16 + .128 + .1024 + .08192 + .065536] \\
&= 1 - .738 = .262
\end{aligned}
$$

So there will be more than 4 patients waiting over $\frac{1}{4}$ of the time.

Example 2: A Loading Dock

Let's assume that a central freight and forwarding company has a mean arrival rate of 3 trucks per hour at its loading dock and that a single dockhand can load or unload a truck in an average of 30 minutes. Also assume that arrivals are Poisson, service times are negative exponential, and that addition of more dockhands linearly reduces the average service time. (This means that two workers double the service rate, three triples it, etc.) Truck drivers are paid $15 per hour, and dockhands are paid $7 per hour. What is the optimum number of dockhands that should be employed?

ANALYSIS

What do we know about the system? First we know the arrival rate of customers (trucks). We also know the service *time* per dockhand. Remember that to make the formulas work we need the service *rate*, the reciprocal of the service time.

What do we want to know about the system? We want to know the number of dockhands that will minimize the total cost of idle time for truck drivers and wages for dockhands. Note that truck drivers are idle while they are waiting in line and while their trucks are being loaded or unloaded.

All we have to do to find the total daily cost for each number of dockhands is to substitute the mean service rate for the number of dockhands into the N_S equation and multiply this by 8 hours and then by \$15, and to this the number of dockhands multiplied by 8 hours then by \$7.

For 1 dockhand we find that N_S is negative ($U > 1$)

$$N_S = \frac{A}{S - A} = \frac{3}{2 - 3} = -3$$

This means the line, over time, will be infinitely long. This will not do because the job will never get done. So let's try 2 dock hands.

$$N_S = \frac{3}{2(2) - 3} = \quad 3 \qquad \text{(average number of trucks in system)}$$

$$3 \times 8 \times \$15 = \$360 \qquad \text{(cost of idle drivers)}$$
$$2 \times 8 \times \$7 = \underline{\quad 112} \qquad \text{(cost of 2 dockhands)}$$
$$\$472 \qquad \text{total}$$

Three dock hands

$$N_S = \frac{3}{3(2) - 3} = \quad 1 \qquad \text{(idle drivers)}$$

$$1 \times 8 \times \$15 = \$120 \qquad \text{(cost of drivers)}$$
$$3 \times 8 \times \$7 = \underline{\quad 168} \qquad \text{(cost of 3 dockhands)}$$
$$\$288 \qquad \text{total}$$

Four dock hands

$$N_S = \frac{3}{4(2) - 3} = \quad .6 \qquad \text{(idle drivers)}$$

$$.6 \times 8 \times \$15 = \$ \ 72 \qquad \text{(cost of drivers)}$$
$$4 \times 8 \times \$7 = \underline{\quad 224} \qquad \text{(cost of 4 dockhands)}$$
$$\$296 \qquad \text{total}$$

Five dock hands

$$N_S = \frac{3}{5(2) - 3} = \quad .43 \qquad \text{(idle drivers)}$$

$$.43 \times 8 \times \$15 = \$\ 51.60 \qquad \text{(cost of drivers)}$$
$$5 \times 8 \times \$7 = \underline{280.00} \qquad \text{(cost of 5 dockhands)}$$
$$ \$331.60 \qquad \text{total}$$

Six dock hands

$$N_S = \frac{3}{6(2) - 3} = \quad .33 \qquad \text{(idle drivers)}$$

$$.33 \times 8 \times \$15 = \$\ 40.00 \qquad \text{(cost of drivers)}$$
$$6 \times 8 \times \$7 = \underline{336.00} \qquad \text{(cost of 6 dockhands)}$$
$$ \$376.00 \qquad \text{total}$$

Total cost is a minimum when 3 dockhands are employed. Figure 17.12 illustrates the cost behavior of this system.

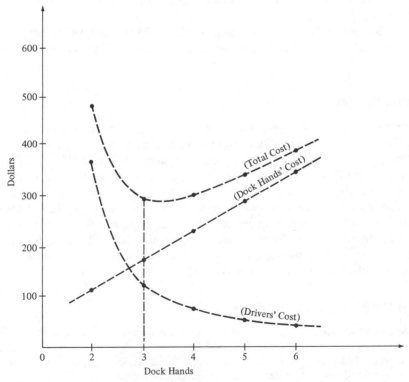

Figure 17.12   Cost versus number of servers.

Example 3: A Computer Service Bureau

A computer service bureau receives jobs to run at an average rate of 5 per hour and is able to process jobs at an average of 6 per hour. A prospective customer has made a commitment to use the service if she can be guaranteed an average turnaround of $\frac{1}{2}$ hour or less for each job. The addition of this new customer will raise the average arrival rate of jobs to 6 per hour. Service capability can be added to the bureau's computer at a cost of $100,000 per additional job per hour. The new customer will add $75,000 per year to income. If the bureau must have a 15% per year return on investment, should sufficient computer capacity be added to acquire the new customer?

We must first determine how much additional computer capacity must be added to assure $\frac{1}{2}$ hour or less turnaround time for an arrival rate of 6 jobs per hour. Turnaround time (T_S) includes time waiting to be processed (T_Q) plus processing time (MST).

The requirement for acquiring the new customer is $T_S \leq .5$. Because $T_S = 1/(S - A)$ and $A = 6$, $1/(S - 6) \leq .5$, then S must be at least 8. In the original system S was equal to 6 jobs per hour; so the capacity to process 2 additional jobs per hour must be added. The cost is $2 \times \$100,000 = \$200,000$.

The return on this investment would be $75,000/200,000 = .375$, or 37.5%. This is certainly favorable, and the bureau should make the investment.

CONCLUSION

The treatment of queuing theory in this chapter has been very basic. Steady state solution equations were presented for only the single-channel single-server model. When more complex systems are involved, the mathematics are more complicated and beyond the scope of this text. Computer simulation of complex systems is much more common than the use of mathematical approaches, because conditions during system start-up and shutdown are often critical and because the rather rigid requirements for frequency distributions are often not met and the equations do not apply. The simulation technique we have discussed has no such restrictions and can be used for any system.

SUMMARY OF KEY CONCEPTS

Arrivals (customers). The people or objects that enter a queuing system and subsequently wait in the queue for service.

Servers. The people or machines that provide the service in a queuing system (e.g., toll booth attendants, grocery store checkers, etc.).

Service facility. The place where the service takes place (checkout counter).

Single channel.   One service facility only.

Multichannel.   More than one service facility.

Queuing discipline.   The way in which arrivals are admitted to the service facility.

Arrival distribution.   The probability distribution that describes the frequency with which customers arrive in the system.

Constant distribution.   The interval between arrivals is constant.

Exponential, Poisson, and Erlang distributions.   The most common distributions encountered in queuing theory.

MTBA.   Mean time between arrivals (expected value of the arrival distribution).

A.   Arrival rate in units per time period ($1/MTBA$).

MST.   Mean service time (expected value of service time distribution).

S.   Service rate in units served per time period ($1/MST$).

Queuing system.   The waiting line(s) and the service facility(ies).

Steady state.   Condition of a system after start-up and before shutdown fluctuations.

Utilization factor (U).   The probability of the server being occupied at any point in time ($U = A/S$).

Time in system (T_S).   The average time an arrival spends in the queue plus time being served [$T_S = 1/(S - A)$].

Waiting time (T_Q).   The average time each arrival spends in the queue [$T_Q = A/[S(S - A)] = U T_S$].

Customers in system (N_S).   The average number of customers in the queue plus those being served [$N_S = A/(S - A) = A T_S$].

Customers in queue (N_Q).   The average number of customers in the queue awaiting service [$N_Q = A^2/[S(S - A)] = U N_S$].

P_N.   The probability of there being exactly N customers in the system [$P_N = (1 - U)(U)^N$].

P_0.   The probability of a server being idle at any point in time ($P_0 = 1 - U$).

PROBLEMS

1. Monroe Scullins sells license plates at the county tax office. Customers arrive at the rate of 1 every 5 minutes exactly, and it takes Monroe exactly 6 minutes to process the customer. The office opens at 1:00 P.M., and the line is closed at 3:00 P.M. Using graphical analysis, determine when Monroe gets to go home. Also determine how many customers are in line at 3:00 P.M.

2. At the Last National Bank a drive-in teller completes a transaction every 5 minutes. Cars arrive at the rate of 1 every 3 minutes until the queuing space, which accommodates 10 cars, is filled. Using graphical analysis, determine the following.
   a. How long does it take the queuing space to fill?
   b. How many customers are turned away during the first hour after the queue is filled?

3. A local free clinic is open 4 hours each day and experiences the patient arrival distribution that follows. The doctor allots exactly 15 minutes

to each patient. Using graphical simulation for 1 day and beginning with the first number in column 1 of the random number table, find the following.

a. The doctor's percent idle time.

b. The maximum number of patients in line.

c. The average number of patients in line.

Time Between Arrivals (min)	P (time)
5	.10
10	.25
15	.50
20	.15

4. During the rush hour airliners arrive at the holding pattern over Slocum International Airport at the rate of 1 every 5 minutes. The rate at which the airliners are able to land and clear the runway is described by the following distribution. How long must the last airliner to arrive stay in the holding pattern? Use graphical simulation and begin with the first number in column 2 of the random number table.

Time Between Landings (min)	P (time)
4	.05
5	.25
6	.45
7	.15
8	.10

5. The Casa de Belleza Beauty Shop has 1 operator and experiences the customer arrival distribution that follows. There is room for only 4 customers in the waiting area. Thirty percent of the customers get a shampoo and set, and the rest get a set only. A shampoo takes 20 minutes, and a set takes 15 minutes. The owner/operator can hire another operator for $40 per day. If the profit on a shampoo is $3 and on a set $2 and the shop is open 10 hours per day, should the new operator be hired? Base your decision on a 1-day graphical simulation, starting with the last number in column 1 of the random number table and proceed up the column.

Time Between Arrivals (min)	P (time)
10	.50
15	.30
20	.20

6. Cars being processed through the Astro Deluxe Car Wash go through two operations—washing and drying. The customer arrival distribution and the service time distributions for washing and drying are as

shown in the following table. Use graphical simulation for 1 hour, starting with the bottom number in column 2 of the random number table and proceeding upward to determine the following.

a. Total arrivals.

b. Maximum number of cars in each queue.

c. Average number of cars in each queue.

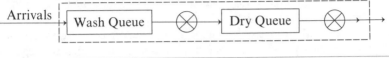

TIME BETWEEN ARRIVALS (MINUTES)	P (TIME)	SERVICE TIME (WASH)	P (TIME)	SERVICE TIME (DRY)	P (TIME)
4	.2	4	.2	3	.3
5	.7	5	.3	4	.4
6	.1	6	.5	5	.3

7. The Dry Gulch, New Mexico, post office has instituted a "red carpet" waiting system. If the postmistress (A) is free, she handles the next customer. If she is busy, her assistant (B) handles the next customer.

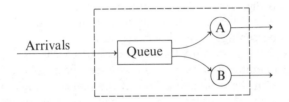

If both are busy, the customer waits in the queue and proceeds to whichever station first becomes free. Graphically simulate the system for 1 hour.

TIME (MINUTES)	PERCENTAGE OF ARRIVALS	PERCENTAGE OF A'S SERVICE	PERCENTAGE OF B'S SERVICE
1	50	20	10
3	40	40	20
5	10	40	70

a. Find A's idle time.

b. Find B's idle time.

c. Find the maximum number in the queue.

d. Find the average number in the queue.

In the random number table start at the top and take arrivals from the third column, A's service from the fourth column, and B's service from the fifth column.

8. Billy Joe Bob Schwartz is planning the grand opening of a one-pump service station. He expects the mean time between arrivals to be 5 minutes (Poission) and the average length of service to be 4 minutes (negative exponential). Based on these figures, calculate the following.
   a. The average number of customers in line.
   b. The average length of time spent in the system.
   c. What percentage of the time is Billy Joe Bob idle?
   d. What is the probability that there will be more than 2 customers in the station at once?

9. If the arrivals in a single-channel single-server queuing system are Poisson with an average of 8 per hour and service times are negative exponential with an average of 10 per hour, find the following steady-state values.
   a. What is the mean time between arrivals ($MTBA$)?
   b. What is the mean service time (MST)?
   c. What is the arrival rate (A)?
   d. What is the service rate (S)?
   e. How long will the average unit spend in the shop (counting both waiting and being serviced)?
   f. How much of that time is spent waiting?
   g. How much is spent being serviced?
   h. What is the average number of units in the system?
   i. What is the average number of units in the queue?
   j. What percentage of the time is the server idle?
   k. What is the probability that there are exactly 2 units in the queue?

10. A small manufacturer of painted wooden chests of drawers has a bottleneck in the production flow at the painting function. He can build the units at an average rate of 5 per hour (Poisson distributed), and his painter can only paint them at an average rate of 3 per hour (negative exponential). A large inventory of unpainted units has therefore begun to accumulate. He plans to hire a second painter, which would double the painting rate to 6 per hour. If he does this, answer the following about the steady-state system in the paint shop.
    a. What is the mean time between arrivals ($MTBA$)?
    b. What is the mean service time (MST)?
    c. What is the arrival rate (A)?
    d. What is the service rate (S)?
    e. How long will the average unit spend in the paint shop (counting both waiting and being painted)?
    f. How much of that time is spent in waiting?
    g. How much is spent being painted?
    h. What is the average number of units in the system?
    i. What is the average number of units in the queue?
    j. What percentage of the time are the painters idle?

 k. What is the probability that there are more than 2 units waiting to be painted?

11. A student organization is having a "dog wash" to raise money. Through a series of trials, the students have determined that 1 worker can wash a dog in 30 minutes; 2 workers, in 15 minutes; 3 workers, in 10 minutes; 4 workers, in $7\frac{1}{2}$ minutes; etc. (Each additional worker adds 2 per hour to the service rate). The dogs are expected to arrive at the dog wash at an average rate of 11 per hour.

 a. What is the hourly service rate (S) for 3 workers?

 b. How many workers must be on hand in order to bring the utilization factor (U) below 1.0?

 c. How many must work in order to keep the average time in the system (TS) below 15 minutes?

 d. If 6 students work, calculate average time in the system (TS).

 e. Find the average time waiting in line (TQ) in minutes. (6 students)

 f. Find the average number of customers in the system (NS). (6 students)

 g. Find the average number in the line (NQ). (6 students)

 h. What is the probability that there are exactly 2 customers in line at a given time? (6 students)

 i. What is the probability of 3 or more in the system at once? (6 students)

12. On the average, grain trucks arrive at an unloading dock at the rate of 3 every 4 hours, 24 hours per day every day. The rate at which dockhands can unload the trucks is calculated by

$$S = .5D - .05D^2$$

where D is the number of dockhands on duty at one time. Dockhands are paid \$40 per day for an 8 hour shift. The unloading company must pay the trucking company \$750 each day multiplied by the average number of trucks in the waiting line. How many dockhands should be employed on each shift? (3 shifts per day) (Assume Poisson arrivals and negative exponential service times.)

Chapter 18

CONCLUSION

Unless you were peeking ahead to see how the book ends, you now have reached the end of the substantive material in this text. You were told in the introduction what to expect and what you should get from the course. Now that you have it, more or less, what are you going to do with it? We hope that the material you have studied has made some sense to you, and that you are a better-educated person and a better problem solver. You may have even decided to pursue management science as a major. Whether or not you plan to increase your depth of knowledge in the field, it may be interesting to explore the role management science may play in the business world in the years to come.

THE FUTURE AND MANAGEMENT SCIENCE

Efficient Use of Diminishing Resources

There is no question that the natural resources of the world are being used up. The days of cheap energy and cheap raw material are gone.

Many of these resources are irreplaceable; so the world must "make do" with what is left. The overriding thrust of management science is the use of quantitative techniques to optimize or, in other words, to do the very best that you can do in light of the constraints placed on you by the market, the government, and the world in general. In short, management science is concerned with efficiency.

For example, the linear programming technique is often used to find the most profitable product mix given a set of resource and environmental constraints. Probability may be equated with desirability of a product in the market. The numerical results we obtain from quantitative models allow us to refine the decision-making process and gain a better perspective of the system we are studying.

The message is simple and clear: We cannot afford the luxury of waste any longer. Quantitative techniques can help us be less wasteful.

Government Controls

While natural resources are diminishing, governmental controls on business and industry are proliferating. This means that constraints on how we do business and how we produce and market goods and services are becoming more numerous. Management science encompasses techniques for organizing and systematizing the decision process. Systematically including new constraints in our decision models will aid business and industry in dealing with new government regulations and guidelines.

New Technology

New technology and new ways of doing business will introduce more complex decision processes. Simply keeping up with the numerous variables and their interrelationships will make the use of mathematical models imperative. "Seat of the pants" and "gut feel" decision making will be too dangerous with complex systems that must be finely tuned to be effective and efficient.

Capital Formulation Problems

If the current trend in new capital formulation continues, there will be more and more corporations competing for investment capital, and the government will be competing for a larger and larger share. Our forecasting techniques will have to be more accurate, and the investing public will demand to see the numbers before they will commit their venture capital.

Social Pressures

The public is becoming ever more sensitive to the efficiency of public institutions. There is no reason to believe the public will change this attitude. All management science techniques are aimed at achieving the best results from a system given the constraints of the environment within which the system exists. Both government and industry will find it necessary to employ these techniques and to educate the public as to their efforts.

COMPUTERS AND MANAGEMENT INFORMATION SYSTEMS AND THEIR IMPACT ON MANAGEMENT SCIENCE

Coping with the Information Explosion

It is always difficult to make the proper decision when there is insufficient information. The problem is often compounded when there is *too much* information. Today's manager has at his or her fingertips literally thousands of information sources. The computer has made data storage and data retrieval, not to mention data manipulation, ridiculously easy compared to the situation of 25 years ago. Maybe it is too easy. Sorting the wheat from the chaff, the significant information from the irrelevant, is a major task in itself.

Every student, at one time or another, has faced a test problem in which too much information is given. That type of problem was always more difficult than the type in which just the right amount of information is available. The modern business decision maker faces this dilemma every day.

The answer to coping with the information explosion is the systemization of the decision process. The management scientist can develop algorithms and decision rules that can focus on the significant data for problem solution and bypass the extraneous data. She or he can help design management information systems that can enable the matching of the ability to use information with the growing ability to collect, store, and retrieve data.

Complexity of Systems

Just because there is an explosion of information does not mean that much of the available information is not significant and useful. It is merely confusing. More significant information means more complex decision models. Using computers will enable us to deal with these systems and the vast amount of data associated with and impinging on them. We have seen how complex decision models can be segmented into a series of simpler models. The computer may not help us further simplify systems, but it does allow us to deal with the computational tasks.

Available Catalogued Algorithms

Practically any university computer system, and many industrial and commercial systems, has libraries of computer programs for solving a wide variety of management science problems. Most common among these are linear programming, transportation, Markov, simulation, inventory, and regression and correlation programs.

The user of these programs usually has only to input the data and call up the particular program that is desired. Normally the output formats are designed for ease of understanding, and the user need not know a great deal about programming in order to use the packages effectively. The trick, of course, is to understand enough about the various algorithms to choose the proper one and to correctly interpret the results.

The Generalist Versus the Management Science Specialist

A growing trend in business education is for the management generalist to learn more and more about quantitative techniques. Management science is not a panacea that can be used to solve all problems, but the perceptive student realizes that quantitative techniques are valuable tools to aid in intelligent decision making. To ignore these valuable tools is to intentionally handicap oneself in the world of business and industry.

The management science specialist may find him- or herself in the position of in-house consultant to various other departments in the organization. As such she or he must speak the languages of finance, marketing, accounting, and management as well as the language of management science and mathematics.

The message, then, is that the generalist should not avoid or ignore quantitative methods, and the management science specialist should be well versed in the other subdisciplines of business administration to achieve the highest level of effectiveness.

The "Proper" Place for the Management Scientist in the Organization

OR DEPARTMENT/IN-HOUSE CONSULTANT

As we mentioned, many organizations maintain operations research departments. The members of the OR departments are often temporarily assigned to other departments within the organization for specific tasks or projects. This arrangement has the advantage of assigning the most proficient individual in a particular area to a specific project requiring that proficiency. There are, of course, disadvantages. Temporary assignments violate the principle of unity of command. In other words, the management scientist finds him- or herself being directed by someone other than the supervisor who must appraise his or her performance and recommend raises and promotions. Also, the management scientist is unlikely to work in a department long enough to gain an in-depth knowledge of that department's operations.

ASSIGNMENT OF MANAGEMENT SCIENTISTS TO INDIVIDUAL DEPARTMENTS

In many cases operational departments within an organization may have one or more quantitatively proficient personnel assigned permanently. Here the management scientist helps other members of the department with their quantitative problems. This arrangement has the advantage of having quantitative individuals who are very familiar with the department operations but is disadvantageous for the management scientist. She or he is the department oddball who is somewhat out of the mainstream.

THE OUTSIDE CONSULTANT

Smaller organizations may be hardpressed to justify the full-time employment of a management scientist, but there simply may not be enough work to keep one busy. In this case the firm may rely on outside management science consultants to solve specific problems.

In order to be an effective outside consultant, a management scientist must have a great deal of experience as well as depth and breadth of knowledge. For the experienced practitioner, consulting can be a very lucrative business. Employing outside consultants is also advantageous for business firms, because very-high-quality assistance can be obtained without the expense of a full-time high-level employee.

As you see, there is no universal "proper" place for a management scientist in the organization. In different situations and different organizations, the relationship varies. Only one thing is certain, and that is that there is a place in every organization for the well-trained management scientist.

ACCEPTANCE OF MANAGEMENT SCIENCE

The acceptance of management science techniques for decision making has been a slow process. The use of these techniques has been restricted mainly to large, progressive organizations that have sophisticated management. The reason for the lack of acceptance in the past has been primarily due to a lack of understanding of the techniques by upper management.

Because almost every business administration curriculum now contains a requirement for one or more courses in management science, we can expect the collective level of understanding to increase significantly with each succeeding generation of top managers. Consequently, the efficiency of decision making in industry, government, and nonprofit organizations should show continuing improvement.

Appendix A

THE BINOMIAL PROBABILITY DISTRIBUTION

BINOMIAL PROBABILITY DISTRIBUTION

$$P(d/n, p) = C_d^n p^d (1 - p)^{n - d}$$

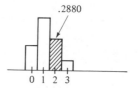

Example

$$P(d = 2/n = 3, p = .4) = .2880$$

					$n = 2$					
d \ p	.01	.02	.03	.04	.05	.06	.07	.08	.09	.10
0	.9801	.9604	.9409	.9216	.9025	.8836	.8649	.8464	.8281	.8100
1	.0198	.0392	.0582	.0768	.0950	.1128	.1302	.1472	.1638	.1800
2	.0001	.0004	.0009	.0016	.0025	.0036	.0049	.0064	.0081	.0100
	.11	.12	.13	.14	.15	.16	.17	.18	.19	.20
0	.7921	.7744	.7569	.7396	.7225	.7056	.6889	.6724	.6561	.6400
1	.1958	.2112	.2262	.2408	.2550	.2688	.2822	.2952	.3078	.3200
2	.0121	.0144	.0169	.0196	.0225	.0256	.0289	.0324	.0361	.0400
	.21	.22	.23	.24	.25	.26	.27	.28	.29	.30
0	.6241	.6084	.5929	.5776	.5625	.5476	.5329	.5184	.5041	.4900
1	.3318	.3432	.3542	.3648	.3750	.3848	.3942	.4032	.4118	.4200
2	.0441	.0484	.0529	.0576	.0625	.0676	.0729	.0784	.0841	.0900

$n = 2$ (Continued)

d \ p	.31	.32	.33	.34	.35	.36	.37	.38	.39	.40
0	.4761	.4624	.4489	.4356	.4225	.4096	.3969	.3844	.3721	.3600
1	.4278	.4352	.4422	.4488	.4550	.4608	.4662	.4712	.4758	.4800
2	.0961	.1024	.1089	.1156	.1225	.1296	.1369	.1444	.1521	.1600

	.41	.42	.43	.44	.45	.46	.47	.48	.49	.50
0	.3481	.3364	.3249	.3136	.3025	.2916	.2809	.2704	.2601	.2500
1	.4838	.4872	.4902	.4928	.4950	.4968	.4982	.4992	.4998	.5000
2	.1681	.1764	.1849	.1936	.2025	.2116	.2209	.2304	.2401	.2500

$n = 3$

	.01	.02	.03	.04	.05	.06	.07	.08	.09	.10
0	.9704	.9412	.9127	.8847	.8574	.8306	.8044	.7787	.7536	.7290
1	.0294	.0576	.0847	.1106	.1354	.1590	.1816	.2031	.2236	.2430
2	.0003	.0012	.0026	.0046	.0071	.0102	.0137	.0177	.0221	.0270
3	.0000	.0000	.0000	.0001	.0001	.0002	.0003	.0005	.0007	.0010

	.11	.12	.13	.14	.15	.16	.17	.18	.19	.20
0	.7050	.6815	.6585	.6361	.6141	.5927	.5718	.5514	.5314	.5120
1	.2614	.2788	.2952	.3106	.3251	.3387	.3513	.3631	.3740	.3840
2	.0323	.0380	.0441	.0506	.0574	.0645	.0720	.0797	.0877	.0960
3	.0013	.0017	.0022	.0027	.0034	.0041	.0049	.0058	.0069	.0080

	.21	.22	.23	.24	.25	.26	.27	.28	.29	.30
0	.4930	.4746	.4565	.4390	.4219	.4052	.3890	.3732	.3579	.3430
1	.3932	.4015	.4091	.4159	.4219	.4271	.4316	.4355	.4386	.4410
2	.1045	.1133	.1222	.1313	.1406	.1501	.1597	.1693	.1791	.1890
3	.0093	.0106	.0122	.0138	.0156	.0176	.0197	.0220	.0244	.0270

	.31	.32	.33	.34	.35	.36	.37	.38	.39	.40
0	.3285	.3144	.3008	.2875	.2746	.2621	.2500	.2383	.2270	.2160
1	.4428	.4439	.4444	.4443	.4436	.4424	.4406	.4382	.4354	.4320
2	.1989	.2089	.2189	.2289	.2389	.2488	.2587	.2686	.2783	.2880
3	.0298	.0328	.0359	.0393	.0429	.0467	.0507	.0549	.0593	.0640

	.41	.42	.43	.44	.45	.46	.47	.48	.49	.50
0	.2054	.1951	.1852	.1756	.1664	.1575	.1489	.1406	.1327	.1250
1	.4282	.4239	.4191	.4140	.4084	.4024	.3961	.3894	.3823	.3750
2	.2975	.3069	.3162	.3252	.3341	.3428	.3512	.3594	.3674	.3750
3	.0689	.0741	.0795	.0852	.0911	.0973	.1038	.1106	.1176	.1250

$n = 4$

d \ p	.01	.02	.03	.04	.05	.06	.07	.08	.09	.10
0	.9606	.9224	.8853	.8493	.8145	.7807	.7481	.7164	.6857	.6561
1	.0388	.0753	.1095	.1416	.1715	.1993	.2252	.2492	.2713	.2916
2	.0006	.0023	.0051	.0088	.0135	.0191	.0254	.0325	.0402	.0486
3	.0000	.0000	.0001	.0002	.0005	.0008	.0013	.0019	.0027	.0036
4	.0000	.0000	.0000	.0000	.0000	.0000	.0000	.0000	.0001	.0001

n = 4 (continued)

p d	.11	.12	.13	.14	.15	.16	.17	.18	.19	.20
0	.6274	.5997	.5729	.5470	.5220	.4979	.4746	.4521	.4205	.4096
1	.3102	.3271	.3424	.3562	.3685	.3793	.3888	.3970	.4039	.4096
2	.0575	.0669	.0767	.0870	.0975	.1084	.1195	.1307	.1421	.1536
3	.0017	.0061	.0075	.0094	.0115	.0138	.0163	.0191	.0222	.0256
4	.0001	.0002	.0003	.0004	.0005	.0007	.0008	.0010	.0013	.0016

	.21	.22	.23	.24	.25	.26	.27	.28	.29	.30
0	.3895	.3702	.3515	.3336	.3164	.2999	.2840	.2687	.2541	.2401
1	.4142	.4176	.4200	.4214	.4219	.4214	.4201	.4180	.4152	.4116
2	.1651	.1767	.1882	.1996	.2109	.2221	.2331	.2439	.2544	.2646
3	.0293	.0332	.0375	.0420	.0469	.0520	.0575	.0632	.0693	.0756
4	.0019	.0023	.0028	.0033	.0039	.0046	.0053	.0061	.0071	.0081

	.31	.32	.33	.34	.35	.36	.37	.38	.39	.40
0	.2267	.2138	.2015	.1897	.1785	.1678	.1575	.1478	.1385	.1296
1	.4074	.4025	.3970	.3910	.3845	.3775	.3701	.3623	.3541	.3456
2	.2745	.2841	.2933	.3021	.3105	.3185	.3260	.3330	.3396	.3456
3	.0822	.0891	.0963	.1038	.1115	.1194	.1276	.1361	.1447	.1536
4	.0092	.0105	.0119	.0134	.0150	.0168	.0187	.0209	.0231	.0256

	.41	.42	.43	.44	.45	.46	.47	.48	.49	.50
0	.1212	.1132	.1056	.0983	.0915	.0850	.0789	.0731	.0677	.0625
1	.3368	.3278	.3185	.3091	.2995	.2897	.2799	.2700	.2600	.2500
2	.3511	.3560	.3604	.3643	.3675	.3702	.3723	.3738	.3747	.3750
3	.1627	.1719	.1813	.1908	.2005	.2102	.2201	.2300	.2400	.2500
4	.0283	.0311	.0342	.0375	.0410	.0448	.0488	.0531	.0576	.0625

n = 5

	.01	.02	.03	.04	.05	.06	.07	.08	.09	.10
0	.9510	.9039	.8587	.8154	.7738	.7339	.6957	.6591	.6240	.5905
1	.0480	.0922	.1328	.1699	.2036	.2342	.2618	.2866	.3086	.3280
2	.0010	.0038	.0082	.0142	.0214	.0299	.0394	.0498	.0610	.0729
3	.0000	.0001	.0003	.0006	.0011	.0019	.0030	.0043	.0060	.0081
4	.0000	.0000	.0000	.0000	.0000	.0001	.0001	.0002	.0003	.0004

	.11	.12	.13	.14	.15	.16	.17	.18	.19	.20
0	.5584	.5277	.4984	.4704	.4437	.4182	.3939	.3707	.3487	.3277
1	.3451	.3598	.3724	.3829	.3915	.3983	.4034	.4069	.4089	.4096
2	.0853	.0981	.1113	.1247	.1382	.1517	.1652	.1786	.1919	.2048
3	.0105	.0134	.0166	.0203	.0244	.0289	.0338	.0392	.0450	.0512
4	.0007	.0009	.0012	.0017	.0022	.0028	.0035	.0043	.0053	.0064
5	.0000	.0000	.0000	.0001	.0001	.0001	.0001	.0002	.0002	.0003

	.21	.22	.23	.24	.25	.26	.27	.28	.29	.30
0	.3077	.2887	.2707	.2536	.2373	.2219	.2073	.1935	.1804	.1681
1	.4090	.4072	.4043	.4003	.3955	.3898	.3834	.3762	.3685	.3602
2	.2174	.2297	.2415	.2529	.2637	.2739	.2836	.2926	.3010	.3087
3	.0578	.0648	.0721	.0798	.0879	.0962	.1049	.1138	.1229	.1323
4	.0077	.0091	.0108	.0126	.0146	.0169	.0194	.0221	.0251	.0284
5	.0004	.0005	.0006	.0008	.0010	.0012	.0014	.0017	.0021	.0024

$n = 5$ (Continued)

d \ p	.31	.32	.33	.34	.35	.36	.37	.38	.39	.40
0	.1564	.1454	.1350	.1252	.1160	.1074	.0992	.0916	.0845	.0778
1	.3513	.3421	.3325	.3226	.3124	.3020	.2914	.2808	.2700	.2592
2	.3157	.3220	.3275	.3323	.3364	.3397	.3423	.3441	.3452	.3456
3	.1418	.1515	.1613	.1712	.1811	.1911	.2010	.2109	.2207	.2304
4	.0319	.0357	.0397	.0441	.0488	.0537	.0590	.0646	.0706	.0768
5	.0029	.0034	.0039	.0045	.0053	.0060	.0069	.0079	.0090	.0102

	.41	.42	.43	.44	.45	.46	.47	.48	.49	.50
0	.0715	.0656	.0602	.0551	.0503	.0459	.0418	.0380	.0345	.0312
1	.2484	.2376	.2270	.2164	.2059	.1956	.1854	.1755	.1657	.1562
2	.3452	.3442	.3424	.3400	.3369	.3332	.3289	.3240	.3185	.3125
3	.2399	.2492	.2583	.2671	.2757	.2838	.2916	.2990	.3060	.3125
4	.0834	.0902	.0974	.1049	.1128	.1209	.1293	.1380	.1470	.1562
5	.0116	.0131	.0147	.0165	.0185	.0206	.0229	.0255	.0282	.0312

$n = 6$

d	.01	.02	.03	.04	.05	.06	.07	.08	.09	.10
0	.9415	.8858	.8330	.7828	.7351	.6899	.6470	.6064	.5679	.5314
1	.0571	.1085	.1546	.1957	.2321	.2642	.2922	.3164	.3370	.3543
2	.0014	.0055	.0120	.0204	.0305	.0422	.0550	.0688	.0833	.0984
3	.0000	.0002	.0005	.0011	.0021	.0036	.0055	.0080	.0110	.0146
4	.0000	.0000	.0000	.0000	.0001	.0002	.0003	.0005	.0008	.0012
5	.0000	.0000	.0000	.0000	.0000	.0000	.0000	.0000	.0000	.0001

	.11	.12	.13	.14	.15	.16	.17	.18	.19	.20
0	.4970	.4644	.4336	.4046	.3771	.3513	.3269	.3040	.2824	.2621
1	.3685	.3800	.3888	.3952	.3993	.4015	.4018	.4004	.3975	.3932
2	.1139	.1295	.1452	.1608	.1762	.1912	.2057	.2197	.2331	.2458
3	.0188	.0236	.0289	.0349	.0415	.0486	.0562	.0643	.0729	.0819
4	.0017	.0024	.0032	.0043	.0055	.0069	.0086	.0106	.0128	.0154
5	.0001	.0001	.0002	.0003	.0004	.0005	.0007	.0009	.0012	.0015
6	.0000	.0000	.0000	.0000	.0000	.0000	.0000	.0000	.0000	.0001

	.21	.22	.23	.24	.25	.26	.27	.28	.29	.30
0	.2431	.2252	.2084	.1927	.1780	.1642	.1513	.1393	.1281	.1176
1	.3877	.3811	.3735	.3651	.3560	.3462	.3358	.3251	.3139	.3025
2	.2577	.2687	.2789	.2882	.2968	.3041	.3105	.3160	.3206	.3241
3	.0913	.1011	.1111	.1214	.1318	.1424	.1531	.1639	.1746	.1852
4	.0182	.0214	.0249	.0287	.0330	.0375	.0425	.0478	.0535	.0595
5	.0019	.0024	.0030	.0036	.0044	.0053	.0063	.0074	.0087	.0102
6	.0001	.0001	.0001	.0002	.0002	.0003	.0004	.0005	.0006	.0007

$n = 6$ (Continued)

d \ p	.31	.32	.33	.34	.35	.36	.37	.38	.39	.40
0	.1079	.0989	.0905	.0827	.0754	.0687	.0625	.0568	.0515	.0467
1	.2909	.2792	.2673	.2555	.2437	.2319	.2203	.2089	.1976	.1866
2	.3267	.3284	.3292	.3290	.3280	.3261	.3235	.3201	.3159	.3110
3	.1957	.2061	.2162	.2260	.2355	.2446	.2533	.2616	.2693	.2765
4	.0660	.0727	.0799	.0873	.0951	.1032	.1116	.1202	.1291	.1382
5	.0119	.0137	.0157	.0180	.0205	.0232	.0262	.0295	.0330	.0369
6	.0009	.0011	.0013	.0015	.0018	.0022	.0026	.0030	.0035	.0041
	.41	.42	.43	.44	.45	.46	.47	.48	.49	.50
0	.0422	.0381	.0343	.0308	.0277	.0248	.0222	.0198	.0176	.0156
1	.1759	.1654	.1552	.1454	.1359	.1267	.1179	.1095	.1014	.0938
2	.3055	.2994	.2928	.2856	.2780	.2699	.2615	.2527	.2436	.2344
3	.2831	.2891	.2945	.2992	.3032	.3065	.3091	.3110	.3121	.3125
4	.1475	.1570	.1666	.1763	.1861	.1958	.2056	.2153	.2249	.2344
5	.0410	.0455	.0503	.0554	.0609	.0667	.0729	.0795	.0864	.0938
6	.0048	.0055	.0063	.0073	.0083	.0095	.0108	.0122	.0138	.0156

$n = 7$

d \ p	.01	.02	.03	.04	.05	.06	.07	.08	.09	.10
0	.9321	.8681	.8080	.7514	.6983	.6485	.6017	.5578	.5168	.4783
1	.0659	.1240	.1749	.2192	.2573	.2897	.3170	.3396	.3578	.3720
2	.0020	.0076	.0162	.0274	.0406	.0555	.0716	.0886	.1061	.1240
3	.0000	.0003	.0008	.0019	.0036	.0059	.0090	.0128	.0175	.0230
4	.0000	.0000	.0000	.0001	.0002	.0004	.0007	.0011	.0017	.0026
5	.0000	.0000	.0000	.0000	.0000	.0000	.0000	.0001	.0001	.0002
	.11	.12	.13	.14	.15	.16	.17	.18	.19	.20
0	.4423	.4087	.3773	.3479	.3206	.2951	.2714	.2493	.2288	.2097
1	.3827	.3901	.3946	.3965	.3960	.3935	.3891	.3830	.3756	.3670
2	.1419	.1596	.1769	.1936	.2097	.2248	.2391	.2523	.2643	.2753
3	.0292	.0363	.0441	.0525	.0617	.0714	.0816	.0923	.1033	.1147
4	.0036	.0049	.0066	.0086	.0109	.0136	.0167	.0203	.0242	.0287
5	.0003	.0004	.0006	.0008	.0012	.0016	.0021	.0027	.0034	.0043
6	.0000	.0000	.0000	.0000	.0001	.0001	.0001	.0002	.0003	.0004
	.21	.22	.23	.24	.25	.26	.27	.28	.29	.30
0	.1920	.1757	.1605	.1465	.1335	.1215	.1105	.1003	.0910	.0824
1	.3573	.3468	.3356	.3237	.3115	.2989	.2860	.2731	.2600	.2471
2	.2850	.2935	.3007	.3067	.3115	.3150	.3174	.3186	.3186	.3177
3	.1263	.1379	.1497	.1614	.1730	.1845	.1956	.2065	.2169	.2269
4	.0336	.0389	.0447	.0510	.0577	.0648	.0724	.0803	.0886	.0972
5	.0054	.0066	.0080	.0097	.0115	.0137	.0161	.0187	.0217	.0250
6	.0005	.0006	.0008	.0010	.0013	.0016	.0020	.0024	.0030	.0036
7	.0000	.0000	.0000	.0000	.0001	.0001	.0001	.0001	.0002	.0002

n = 7 (Continued)

d \ p	.31	.32	.33	.34	.35	.36	.37	.38	.39	.40
0	.0745	.0672	.0606	.0546	.0490	.0440	.0394	.0352	.0314	.0280
1	.2342	.2215	.2090	.1967	.1848	.1732	.1619	.1511	.1407	.1306
2	.3156	.3127	.3088	.3040	.2985	.2922	.2853	.2778	.2698	.2613
3	.2363	.2452	.2535	.2610	.2679	.2740	.2793	.2838	.2875	.2903
4	.1062	.1154	.1248	.1345	.1442	.1541	.1640	.1739	.1838	.1935
5	.0286	.0326	.0369	.0416	.0466	.0520	.0578	.0640	.0705	.0774
6	.0043	.0051	.0061	.0071	.0084	.0098	.0113	.0131	.0150	.0172
7	.0003	.0003	.0004	.0005	.0006	.0008	.0009	.0011	.0014	.0016

	.41	.42	.43	.44	.45	.46	.47	.48	.49	.50
0	.0249	.0221	.0195	.0173	.0152	.0134	.0117	.0103	.0090	.0078
1	.1211	.1119	.1032	.0950	.0872	.0798	.0729	.0664	.0604	.0547
2	.2524	.2431	.2336	.2239	.2140	.2040	.1940	.1840	.1740	.1641
3	.2923	.2934	.2937	.2932	.2918	.2897	.2867	.2830	.2786	.2734
4	.2031	.2125	.2216	.2304	.2388	.2468	.2543	.2612	.2676	.2734
5	.0847	.0923	.1003	.1086	.1172	.1261	.1353	.1447	.1543	.1641
6	.0196	.0223	.0252	.0284	.0320	.0358	.0400	.0445	.0494	.0547
7	.0019	.0023	.0027	.0032	.0037	.0044	.0051	.0059	.0068	.0078

n = 8

	.01	.02	.03	.04	.05	.06	.07	.08	.09	.10
0	.9227	.8508	.7837	.7214	.6634	.6096	.5596	.5132	.4703	.4305
1	.0746	.1389	.1939	.2405	.2793	.3113	.3370	.3570	.3721	.3826
2	.0026	.0099	.0210	.0351	.0515	.0695	.0888	.1087	.1288	.1488
3	.0001	.0004	.0013	.0029	.0054	.0089	.0134	.0189	.0255	.0331
4	.0000	.0000	.0001	.0002	.0004	.0007	.0013	.0021	.0031	.0046
5	.0000	.0000	.0000	.0000	.0000	.0000	.0001	.0001	.0002	.0004

	.11	.12	.13	.14	.15	.16	.17	.18	.19	.20
0	.3937	.3596	.3282	.2992	.2725	.2479	.2252	.2044	.1853	.1678
1	.3892	.3923	.3923	.3897	.3847	.3777	.3691	.3590	.3477	.3355
2	.1684	.1872	.2052	.2220	.2376	.2518	.2646	.2758	.2855	.2936
3	.0416	.0511	.0613	.0723	.0839	.0959	.1084	.1211	.1339	.1468
4	.0064	.0087	.0115	.0147	.0185	.0228	.0277	.0332	.0393	.0459
5	.0006	.0009	.0014	.0019	.0026	.0035	.0045	.0058	.0074	.0092
6	.0000	.0001	.0001	.0002	.0002	.0003	.0005	.0006	.0009	.0011
7	.0000	.0000	.0000	.0000	.0000	.0000	.0000	.0000	.0001	.0001

	.21	.22	.23	.24	.25	.26	.27	.28	.29	.30
0	.1517	.1370	.1236	.1113	.1001	.0899	.0806	.0722	.0646	.0576
1	.3226	.3092	.2953	.2812	.2670	.2527	.2386	.2247	.2110	.1977
2	.3002	.3052	.3087	.3108	.3115	.3108	.3089	.3058	.3017	.2965
3	.1596	.1722	.1844	.1963	.2076	.2184	.2285	.2379	.2464	.2541
4	.0530	.0607	.0689	.0775	.0865	.0959	.1056	.1156	.1258	.1361

$n = 8$ (Continued)

d \ p	.21	.22	.23	.24	.25	.26	.27	.28	.29	.30
5	.0113	.0137	.0165	.0196	.0231	.0270	.0313	.0360	.0411	.0467
6	.0015	.0019	.0025	.0031	.0038	.0047	.0058	.0070	.0084	.0100
7	.0001	.0002	.0002	.0003	.0004	.0005	.0006	.0008	.0010	.0012
8	.0000	.0000	.0000	.0000	.0000	.0000	.0000	.0000	.0001	.0001

	.31	.32	.33	.34	.35	.36	.37	.38	.39	.40
0	.0514	.0457	.0406	.0360	.0319	.0281	.0248	.0218	.0192	.0168
1	.1847	.1721	.1600	.1484	.1373	.1267	.1166	.1071	.0981	.0896
2	.2904	.2835	.2758	.2675	.2587	.2494	.2397	.2297	.2194	.2090
3	.2609	.2668	.2717	.2756	.2786	.2805	.2815	.2815	.2806	.2787
4	.1465	.1569	.1673	.1775	.1875	.1973	.2067	.2157	.2242	.2322
5	.0527	.0591	.0659	.0732	.0808	.0888	.0971	.1058	.1147	.1239
6	.0118	.0139	.0162	.0188	.0217	.0250	.0285	.0324	.0367	.0413
7	.0015	.0019	.0023	.0028	.0033	.0040	.0048	.0057	.0067	.0079
8	.0001	.0001	.0001	.0002	.0002	.0003	.0004	.0004	.0005	.0007

	.41	.42	.43	.44	.45	.46	.47	.48	.49	.50
0	.0147	.0128	.0111	.0097	.0084	.0072	.0062	.0053	.0046	.0039
1	.0816	.0742	.0672	.0608	.0548	.0493	.0442	.0395	.0352	.0312
2	.1985	.1880	.1776	.1672	.1569	.1469	.1371	.1275	.1183	.1094
3	.2759	.2723	.2679	.2627	.2568	.2503	.2431	.2355	.2273	.2188
4	.2397	.2465	.2526	.2580	.2627	.2665	.2695	.2717	.2730	.2734
5	.1332	.1428	.1525	.1622	.1719	.1816	.1912	.2006	.2098	.2188
6	.0463	.0517	.0575	.0637	.0703	.0774	.0848	.0926	.1008	.1094
7	.0092	.0107	.0124	.0143	.0164	.0188	.0215	.0244	.0277	.0312
8	.0008	.0010	.0012	.0014	.0017	.0020	.0024	.0028	.0033	.0039

$n = 9$

	.01	.02	.03	.04	.05	.06	.07	.08	.09	.10
0	.9135	.8337	.7602	.6925	.6302	.5730	.5204	.4722	.4279	.3874
1	.0830	.1531	.2116	.2597	.2985	.3292	.3525	.3695	.3809	.3874
2	.0034	.0125	.0262	.0433	.0629	.0840	.1061	.1285	.1507	.1722
3	.0001	.0006	.0019	.0042	.0077	.0125	.0186	.0261	.0348	.0446
4	.0000	.0000	.0001	.0003	.0006	.0012	.0021	.0034	.0052	.0074
5	.0000	.0000	.0000	.0000	.0000	.0001	.0002	.0003	.0005	.0008
6	.0000	.0000	.0000	.0000	.0000	.0000	.0000	.0000	.0000	.0001

	.11	.12	.13	.14	.15	.16	.17	.18	.19	.20
0	.3504	.3165	.2855	.2573	.2316	.2082	.1869	.1676	.1501	.1342
1	.3897	.3884	.3840	.3770	.3679	.3569	.3446	.3312	.3169	.3020
2	.1927	.2119	.2295	.2455	.2597	.2720	.2823	.2908	.2973	.3020
3	.0556	.0674	.0800	.0933	.1069	.1209	.1349	.1489	.1627	.1762
4	.0103	.0138	.0179	.0228	.0283	.0345	.0415	.0490	.0573	.0661
5	.0013	.0019	.0027	.0037	.0050	.0066	.0085	.0108	.0134	.0165
6	.0001	.0002	.0003	.0004	.0006	.0008	.0012	.0016	.0021	.0028
7	.0000	.0000	.0000	.0000	.0000	.0001	.0001	.0001	.0002	.0003

$n = 9$ (Continued)

d \ p	.21	.22	.23	.24	.25	.26	.27	.28	.29	.30
0	.1199	.1069	.0952	.0846	.0751	.0665	.0589	.0520	.0458	.0404
1	.2867	.2713	.2558	.2404	.2253	.2104	.1960	.1820	.1685	.1556
2	.3049	.3061	.3056	.3037	.3003	.2957	.2899	.2831	.2754	.2668
3	.1891	.2014	.2130	.2238	.2336	.2424	.2502	.2569	.2624	.2668
4	.0754	.0852	.0954	.1060	.1168	.1278	.1388	.1499	.1608	.1715
5	.0200	.0240	.0285	.0335	.0389	.0449	.0513	.0583	.0657	.0735
6	.0036	.0045	.0057	.0070	.0087	.0105	.0127	.0151	.0179	.0210
7	.0004	.0005	.0007	.0010	.0012	.0016	.0020	.0025	.0031	.0039
8	.0000	.0000	.0001	.0001	.0001	.0001	.0002	.0002	.0003	.0004

	.31	.32	.33	.34	.35	.36	.37	.38	.39	.40
0	.0355	.0311	.0272	.0238	.0207	.0180	.0156	.0135	.0117	.0101
1	.1433	.1317	.1206	.1102	.1004	.0912	.0826	.0747	.0673	.0605
2	.2576	.2478	.2376	.2270	.2162	.2052	.1941	.1831	.1721	.1612
3	.2701	.2721	.2731	.2729	.2716	.2693	.2660	.2618	.2567	.2508
4	.1820	.1921	.2017	.2109	.2194	.2272	.2344	.2407	.2462	.2508
5	.0818	.0904	.0994	.1086	.1181	.1278	.1376	.1475	.1574	.1672
6	.0245	.0284	.0326	.0373	.0424	.0479	.0539	.0603	.0671	.0743
7	.0047	.0057	.0069	.0082	.0098	.0116	.0136	.0158	.0184	.0212
8	.0005	.0007	.0008	.0011	.0013	.0016	.0020	.0024	.0029	.0053
9	.0000	.0000	.0000	.0001	.0001	.0001	.0001	.0002	.0002	.0003

	.41	.42	.43	.44	.45	.46	.47	.48	.49	.50
0	.0087	.0074	.0064	.0054	.0046	.0039	.0033	.0028	.0023	.0020
1	.0542	.0484	.0431	.0383	.0339	.0299	.0263	.0231	.0202	.0176
2	.1506	.1402	.1301	.1204	.1110	.1020	.0934	.0853	.0776	.0703
3	.2442	.2369	.2291	.2207	.2119	.2027	.1933	.1837	.1739	.1641
4	.2545	.2573	.2592	.2601	.2600	.2590	.2571	.2543	.2506	.2461
5	.1769	.1863	.1955	.2044	.2128	.2207	.2280	.2347	.2408	.2461
6	.0819	.0900	.0983	.1070	.1160	.1253	.1348	.1445	.1542	.1641
7	.0244	.0279	.0318	.0360	.0407	.0458	.0512	.0571	.0635	.0703
8	.0042	.0051	.0060	.0071	.0083	.0097	.0114	.0132	.0153	.0176
9	.0003	.0004	.0005	.0006	.0008	.0009	.0011	.0014	.0016	.0020

$n = 10$

	.01	.02	.03	.04	.05	.06	.07	.08	.09	.10
0	.9044	.8171	.7374	.6648	.5987	.5386	.4840	.4344	.3894	.3487
1	.0914	.1667	.2281	.2770	.3151	.3438	.3643	.3777	.3851	.3874
2	.0042	.0153	.0317	.0519	.0746	.0988	.1234	.1478	.1714	.1937
3	.0001	.0008	.0026	.0058	.0105	.0168	.0248	.0343	.0452	.0574
4	.0000	.0000	.0001	.0004	.0010	.0019	.0033	.0052	.0078	.0112
5	.0000	.0000	.0000	.0000	.0001	.0001	.0003	.0005	.0009	.0015
6	.0000	.0000	.0000	.0000	.0000	.0000	.0000	.0000	.0001	.0001

$n = 10$ (Continued)

d \ p	.11	.12	.13	.14	.15	.16	.17	.18	.19	.20
0	.3118	.2785	.2484	.2213	.1969	.1749	.1552	.1374	.1216	.1074
1	.3854	.3798	.3712	.3603	.3474	.3331	.3178	.3017	.2852	.2684
2	.2143	.2330	.2496	.2639	.2759	.2856	.2929	.2980	.3010	.3020
3	.0706	.0847	.0995	.1146	.1298	.1450	.1600	.1745	.1883	.2013
4	.0153	.0202	.0260	.0326	.0401	.0483	.0573	.0670	.0773	.0881
5	.0023	.0033	.0047	.0064	.0085	.0111	.0141	.0177	.0218	.0264
6	.0002	.0004	.0006	.0009	.0012	.0018	.0024	.0032	.0043	.0055
7	.0000	.0000	.0000	.0001	.0001	.0002	.0003	.0004	.0006	.0008
8	.0000	.0000	.0000	.0000	.0000	.0000	.0000	.0000	.0001	.0001

	.21	.22	.23	.24	.25	.26	.27	.28	.29	.30
0	.0947	.0834	.0733	.0643	.0563	.0492	.0430	.0374	.0326	.0282
1	.2517	.2351	.2188	.2030	.1877	.1730	.1590	.1456	.1330	.1211
2	.3011	.2984	.2942	.2885	.2816	.2735	.2646	.2548	.2444	.2335
3	.2134	.2244	.2343	.2429	.2503	.2563	.2609	.2642	.2662	.2668
4	.0993	.1108	.1225	.1343	.1460	.1576	.1689	.1798	.1903	.2001
5	.0317	.0375	.0439	.0509	.0584	.0664	.0750	.0839	.0933	.1029
6	.0070	.0088	.0109	.0134	.0162	.0195	.0231	.0272	.0317	.0368
7	.0011	.0014	.0019	.0024	.0031	.0039	.0049	.0060	.0074	.0090
8	.0001	.0002	.0002	.0003	.0004	.0005	.0007	.0009	.0011	.0014
9	.0000	.0000	.0000	.0000	.0000	.0000	.0001	.0001	.0001	.0001

	.31	.32	.33	.34	.35	.36	.37	.38	.39	.40
0	.0245	.0211	.0182	.0157	.0135	.0115	.0098	.0084	.0071	.0060
1	.1099	.0995	.0898	.0808	.0725	.0649	.0578	.0514	.0456	.0403
2	.2222	.2107	.1990	.1873	.1757	.1642	.1529	.1419	.1312	.1209
3	.2662	.2644	.2614	.2573	.2522	.2462	.2394	.2319	.2237	.2150
4	.2093	.2177	.2253	.2320	.2377	.2424	.2461	.2487	.2503	.2508
5	.1128	.1229	.1332	.1434	.1536	.1636	.1734	.1829	.1920	.2007
6	.0422	.0482	.0547	.0616	.0689	.0767	.0849	.0934	.1023	.1115
7	.0108	.0130	.0154	.0181	.0212	.0247	.0285	.0327	.0374	.0425
8	.0018	.0023	.0028	.0035	.0043	.0052	.0063	.0075	.0090	.0106
9	.0002	.0002	.0003	.0004	.0005	.0006	.0008	.0010	.0013	.0016
10	.0000	.0000	.0000	.0000	.0000	.0000	.0000	.0001	.0001	.0001

	.41	.42	.43	.44	.45	.46	.47	.48	.49	.50
0	.0051	.0043	.0036	.0030	.0025	.0021	.0017	.0014	.0012	.0010
1	.0355	.0312	.0273	.0238	.0207	.0180	.0155	.0133	.0114	.0098
2	.1111	.1017	.0927	.0843	.0763	.0688	.0619	.0554	.0494	.0439
3	.2058	.1963	.1865	.1765	.1665	.1564	.1464	.1364	.1267	.1172
4	.2503	.2488	.2462	.2427	.2384	.2331	.2271	.2204	.2130	.2051
5	.2087	.2162	.2229	.2289	.2340	.2383	.2417	.2441	.2456	.2461
6	.1209	.1304	.1401	.1499	.1596	.1692	.1786	.1878	.1966	.2051
7	.0480	.0540	.0604	.0673	.0746	.0824	.0905	.0991	.1080	.1172
8	.0125	.0147	.0171	.0198	.0229	.0263	.0301	.0343	.0389	.0439
9	.0019	.0024	.0029	.0035	.0042	.0050	.0059	.0070	.0083	.0098
10	.0001	.0002	.0002	.0003	.0003	.0004	.0005	.0006	.0008	.0010

n = 100

d \ p	.01	.02	.03	.04	.05	.06	.07	.08	.09	.10
0	.3660	.1326	.0476	.0169	.0059	.0021	.0007	.0002	.0001	.0000
1	.3697	.2707	.1471	.0703	.0312	.0131	.0053	.0021	.0008	.0003
2	.1849	.2734	.2252	.1450	.0812	.0414	.0198	.0090	.0039	.0016
3	.0610	.1823	.2275	.1973	.1396	.0864	.0486	.0254	.0125	.0059
4	.0149	.0902	.1706	.1994	.1781	.1338	.0888	.0536	.0301	.0159
5	.0029	.0353	.1013	.1595	.1800	.1639	.1283	.0895	.0571	.0339
6	.0005	.0114	.0496	.1052	.1500	.1657	.1529	.1233	.0895	.0596
7	.0001	.0031	.0206	.0589	.1060	.1420	.1545	.1440	.1188	.0889
8	.0000	.0007	.0074	.0285	.0649	.1054	.1352	.1455	.1366	.1148
9	.0000	.0002	.0023	.0121	.0349	.0687	.1040	.1293	.1381	.1304
10	.0000	.0000	.0007	.0046	.0167	.0399	.0712	.1024	.1243	.1319
11	.0000	.0000	.0002	.0016	.0072	.0209	.0439	.0728	.1006	.1199
12	.0000	.0000	.0000	.0005	.0028	.0099	.0245	.0470	.0738	.0988
13	.0000	.0000	.0000	.0001	.0010	.0043	.0125	.0276	.0494	.0743
14	.0000	.0000	.0000	.0000	.0003	.0017	.0058	.0149	.0304	.0513
15	.0000	.0000	.0000	.0000	.0001	.0006	.0025	.0074	.0172	.0327
16	.0000	.0000	.0000	.0000	.0000	.0002	.0010	.0034	.0090	.0193
17	.0000	.0000	.0000	.0000	.0000	.0001	.0004	.0015	.0044	.0106
18	.0000	.0000	.0000	.0000	.0000	.0000	.0001	.0006	.0020	.0054
19	.0000	.0000	.0000	.0000	.0000	.0000	.0000	.0002	.0009	.0026
20	.0000	.0000	.0000	.0000	.0000	.0000	.0000	.0001	.0003	.0012
21	.0000	.0000	.0000	.0000	.0000	.0000	.0000	.0000	.0001	.0005
22	.0000	.0000	.0000	.0000	.0000	.0000	.0000	.0000	.0000	.0002
23	.0000	.0000	.0000	.0000	.0000	.0000	.0000	.0000	.0000	.0001
24	.0000	.0000	.0000	.0000	.0000	.0000	.0000	.0000	.0000	.0000

d	.11	.12	.13	.14	.15	.16	.17	.18	.19	.20
0	.0000	.0000	.0000	.0000	.0000	.0000	.0000	.0000	.0000	.0000
1	.0001	.0000	.0000	.0000	.0000	.0000	.0000	.0000	.0000	.0000
2	.0007	.0003	.0001	.0000	.0000	.0000	.0000	.0000	.0000	.0000
3	.0027	.0012	.0005	.0002	.0001	.0000	.0000	.0000	.0000	.0000
4	.0080	.0038	.0018	.0008	.0003	.0001	.0001	.0000	.0000	.0000
5	.0189	.0100	.0050	.0024	.0011	.0005	.0002	.0001	.0000	.0000
6	.0369	.0215	.0119	.0063	.0031	.0015	.0007	.0003	.0001	.0001
7	.0613	.0394	.0238	.0137	.0075	.0039	.0020	.0009	.0004	.0002
8	.0881	.0625	.0414	.0259	.0153	.0086	.0047	.0024	.0012	.0006
9	.1112	.0871	.0632	.0430	.0276	.0168	.0098	.0054	.0029	.0015
10	.1251	.1080	.0860	.0637	.0444	.0292	.0182	.0108	.0062	.0034
11	.1265	.1205	.1051	.0849	.0640	.0454	.0305	.0194	.0118	.0069
12	.1160	.1219	.1165	.1025	.0838	.0642	.0463	.0316	.0206	.0128
13	.0970	.1125	.1179	.1130	.1001	.0827	.0642	.0470	.0327	.0216
14	.0745	.0954	.1094	.1143	.1098	.0979	.0817	.0641	.0476	.0335
15	.0528	.0745	.0938	.1067	.1111	.1070	.0960	.0807	.0640	.0481
16	.0347	.0540	.0744	.0922	.1041	.1082	.1044	.0941	.0798	.0638
17	.0212	.0364	.0549	.0742	.0908	.1019	.1057	.1021	.0924	.0789
18	.0121	.0229	.0379	.0557	.0739	.0895	.0998	.1033	.1000	.0909
19	.0064	.0135	.0244	.0391	.0563	.0736	.0882	.0979	.1012	.0981

$n = 100$ (Continued)

d \ p	.11	.12	.13	.14	.15	.16	.17	.18	.19	.20
20	.0032	.0074	.0148	.0258	.0402	.0567	.0732	.0870	.0962	.0993
21	.0015	.0039	.0084	.0160	.0270	.0412	.0571	.0728	.0859	.0946
22	.0007	.0019	.0045	.0094	.0171	.0282	.0420	.0574	.0724	.0849
23	.0003	.0009	.0023	.0052	.0103	.0182	.0292	.0427	.0576	.0720
24	.0001	.0004	.0011	.0027	.0058	.0111	.0192	.0301	.0433	.0577
25	.0000	.0002	.0005	.0013	.0031	.0064	.0119	.0201	.0309	.0439
26	.0000	.0001	.0002	.0006	.0016	.0035	.0071	.0127	.0209	.0316
27	.0000	.0000	.0001	.0003	.0008	.0018	.0040	.0076	.0134	.0217
28	.0000	.0000	.0000	.0001	.0004	.0009	.0021	.0044	.0082	.0141
29	.0000	.0000	.0000	.0000	.0002	.0004	.0011	.0024	.0048	.0088
30	.0000	.0000	.0000	.0000	.0001	.0002	.0005	.0012	.0027	.0052
31	.0000	.0000	.0000	.0000	.0000	.0001	.0002	.0006	.0014	.0029
32	.0000	.0000	.0000	.0000	.0000	.0000	.0001	.0003	.0007	.0016
33	.0000	.0000	.0000	.0000	.0000	.0000	.0000	.0001	.0003	.0008
34	.0000	.0000	.0000	.0000	.0000	.0000	.0000	.0001	.0002	.0004
35	.0000	.0000	.0000	.0000	.0000	.0000	.0000	.0000	.0001	.0002
36	.0000	.0000	.0000	.0000	.0000	.0000	.0000	.0000	.0000	.0001
37	.0000	.0000	.0000	.0000	.0000	.0000	.0000	.0000	.0000	.0000

d \ p	.21	.22	.23	.24	.25	.26	.27	.28	.29	.30
0	.0000	.0000	.0000	.0000	.0000	.0000	.0000	.0000	.0000	.0000
1	.0000	.0000	.0000	.0000	.0000	.0000	.0000	.0000	.0000	.0000
2	.0000	.0000	.0000	.0000	.0000	.0000	.0000	.0000	.0000	.0000
3	.0000	.0000	.0000	.0000	.0000	.0000	.0000	.0000	.0000	.0000
4	.0000	.0000	.0000	.0000	.0000	.0000	.0000	.0000	.0000	.0000
5	.0000	.0000	.0000	.0000	.0000	.0000	.0000	.0000	.0000	.0000
6	.0000	.0000	.0000	.0000	.0000	.0000	.0000	.0000	.0000	.0000
7	.0001	.0000	.0000	.0000	.0000	.0000	.0000	.0000	.0000	.0000
8	.0003	.0001	.0001	.0000	.0000	.0000	.0000	.0000	.0000	.0000
9	.0007	.0003	.0002	.0001	.0000	.0000	.0000	.0000	.0000	.0000
10	.0018	.0009	.0004	.0002	.0001	.0000	.0000	.0000	.0000	.0000
11	.0038	.0021	.0011	.0005	.0003	.0001	.0001	.0000	.0000	.0000
12	.0076	.0043	.0024	.0012	.0006	.0003	.0001	.0001	.0000	.0000
13	.0136	.0082	.0048	.0027	.0014	.0007	.0004	.0002	.0001	.0000
14	.0225	.0144	.0089	.0052	.0030	.0016	.0009	.0004	.0002	.0001
15	.0343	.0233	.0152	.0095	.0057	.0033	.0018	.0010	.0005	.0002
16	.0484	.0350	.0241	.0159	.0100	.0061	.0035	.0020	.0011	.0006
17	.0636	.0487	.0356	.0248	.0165	.0106	.0065	.0038	.0022	.0012
18	.0780	.0634	.0490	.0361	.0254	.0171	.0111	.0069	.0041	.0024
19	.0895	.0772	.0631	.0492	.0365	.0259	.0177	.0115	.0072	.0044
20	.0963	.0881	.0764	.0629	.0493	.0369	.0264	.0182	.0120	.0076
21	.0975	.0947	.0869	.0756	.0626	.0494	.0373	.0269	.0186	.0124
22	.0931	.0959	.0932	.0858	.0749	.0623	.0495	.0376	.0273	.0190
23	.0839	.0917	.0944	.0919	.0847	.0743	.0621	.0495	.0378	.0277
24	.0716	.0830	.0905	.0931	.0906	.0837	.0736	.0618	.0496	.0380

$n = 100$ (Continued)

d \ p	.21	.22	.23	.24	.25	.26	.27	.28	.29	.30
25	.0578	.0712	.0822	.0893	.0918	.0894	.0828	.0731	.0615	.0496
26	.0444	.0579	.0708	.0814	.0883	.0906	.0883	.0819	.0725	.0613
27	.0323	.0448	.0580	.0704	.0806	.0873	.0896	.0873	.0812	.0720
28	.0224	.0329	.0451	.0580	.0701	.0799	.0864	.0886	.0864	.0804
29	.0148	.0231	.0335	.0455	.0580	.0697	.0793	.0855	.0876	.0856
30	.0093	.0154	.0237	.0340	.0458	.0580	.0694	.0787	.0847	.0868
31	.0056	.0098	.0160	.0242	.0344	.0460	.0580	.0691	.0781	.0840
32	.0032	.0060	.0103	.0165	.0248	.0349	.0462	.0579	.0688	.0776
33	.0018	.0035	.0063	.0107	.0170	.0252	.0352	.0464	.0579	.0685
34	.0009	.0019	.0037	.0067	.0112	.0175	.0257	.0356	.0466	.0579
35	.0005	.0010	.0021	.0040	.0070	.0116	.0179	.0261	.0359	.0468
36	.0002	.0005	.0011	.0023	.0042	.0073	.0120	.0183	.0265	.0362
37	.0001	.0003	.0006	.0012	.0024	.0045	.0077	.0123	.0187	.0268
38	.0000	.0001	.0003	.0006	.0013	.0026	.0047	.0079	.0127	.0191
39	.0000	.0001	.0001	.0003	.0007	.0015	.0028	.0049	.0082	.0130
40	.0000	.0000	.0001	.0002	.0004	.0008	.0016	.0029	.0051	.0085
41	.0000	.0000	.0000	.0001	.0002	.0004	.0008	.0017	.0031	.0053
42	.0000	.0000	.0000	.0000	.0001	.0002	.0004	.0009	.0018	.0032
43	.0000	.0000	.0000	.0000	.0000	.0001	.0002	.0005	.0010	.0019
44	.0000	.0000	.0000	.0000	.0000	.0000	.0001	.0002	.0005	.0010
45	.0000	.0000	.0000	.0000	.0000	.0000	.0000	.0001	.0003	.0005
46	.0000	.0000	.0000	.0000	.0000	.0000	.0000	.0001	.0001	.0003
47	.0000	.0000	.0000	.0000	.0000	.0000	.0000	.0000	.0001	.0001
48	.0000	.0000	.0000	.0000	.0000	.0000	.0000	.0000	.0000	.0001

d	.31	.32	.33	.34	.35	.36	.37	.38	.39	.40
14	.0000	.0000	.0000	.0000	.0000	.0000	.0000	.0000	.0000	.0000
15	.0001	.0001	.0000	.0000	.0000	.0000	.0000	.0000	.0000	.0000
16	.0003	.0001	.0001	.0000	.0000	.0000	.0000	.0000	.0000	.0000
17	.0006	.0003	.0002	.0001	.0000	.0000	.0000	.0000	.0000	.0000
18	.0013	.0007	.0004	.0002	.0001	.0000	.0000	.0000	.0000	.0000
19	.0025	.0014	.0008	.0004	.0002	.0001	.0000	.0000	.0000	.0000
20	.0046	.0027	.0015	.0008	.0004	.0002	.0001	.0001	.0000	.0000
21	.0079	.0049	.0029	.0016	.0009	.0005	.0002	.0001	.0001	.0000
22	.0127	.0082	.0051	.0030	.0017	.0010	.0005	.0003	.0001	.0001
23	.0194	.0131	.0085	.0053	.0032	.0018	.0010	.0006	.0003	.0001
24	.0280	.0198	.0134	.0088	.0055	.0033	.0019	.0011	.0006	.0003
25	.0382	.0283	.0201	.0137	.0090	.0057	.0035	.0020	.0012	.0006
26	.0496	.0384	.0286	.0204	.0140	.0092	.0059	.0036	.0021	.0012
27	.0610	.0495	.0386	.0288	.0207	.0143	.0095	.0060	.0037	.0022
28	.0715	.0608	.0495	.0387	.0290	.0209	.0145	.0097	.0062	.0038
29	.0797	.0710	.0605	.0495	.0388	.0292	.0211	.0147	.0098	.0063
30	.0848	.0791	.0706	.0603	.0494	.0389	.0294	.0213	.0149	.0100
31	.0860	.0840	.0785	.0702	.0601	.0494	.0389	.0295	.0215	.0151
32	.0833	.0853	.0834	.0779	.0698	.0599	.0493	.0390	.0296	.0217
33	.0771	.0827	.0846	.0827	.0774	.0694	.0597	.0493	.0390	.0297
34	.0683	.0767	.0821	.0840	.0821	.0769	.0691	.0595	.0492	.0391

$n = 100$ (Continued)

d \ p	.31	.32	.33	.34	.35	.36	.37	.38	.39	.40
35	.0578	.0680	.0763	.0816	.0834	.0816	.0765	.0688	.0593	.0491
36	.0469	.0678	.0678	.0759	.0811	.0829	.0811	.0761	.0685	.0591
37	.0365	.0471	.0578	.0676	.0755	.0806	.0824	.0807	.0757	.0682
38	.0272	.0367	.0472	.0577	.0674	.0752	.0802	.0820	.0803	.0754
39	.0194	.0275	.0369	.0473	.0577	.0672	.0749	.0799	.0816	.0799
40	.0133	.0197	.0277	.0372	.0474	.0577	.0671	.0746	.0795	.0812
41	.0087	.0136	.0200	.0280	.0373	.0475	.0577	.0670	.0744	.0792
42	.0055	.0090	.0138	.0203	.0282	.0375	.0476	.0576	.0668	.0742
43	.0033	.0057	.0092	.0141	.0205	.0285	.0377	.0477	.0576	.0667
44	.0019	.0035	.0059	.0094	.0143	.0207	.0287	.0378	.0477	.0576
45	.0011	.0020	.0036	.0060	.0096	.0145	.0210	.0289	.0380	.0478
46	.0006	.0011	.0021	.0037	.0062	.0098	.0147	.0212	.0290	.0381
47	.0003	.0006	.0012	.0022	.0038	.0063	.0099	.0149	.0213	.0292
48	.0001	.0003	.0007	.0012	.0023	.0039	.0064	.0101	.0151	.0215
49	.0001	.0002	.0003	.0007	.0013	.0023	.0040	.0066	.0102	.0152
50	.0000	.0001	.0002	.0004	.0007	.0013	.0024	.0041	.0067	.0103
51	.0000	.0000	.0001	.0002	.0004	.0007	.0014	.0025	.0042	.0068
52	.0000	.0000	.0000	.0001	.0002	.0004	.0008	.0014	.0025	.0042
53	.0000	.0000	.0000	.0000	.0001	.0002	.0004	.0008	.0015	.0026
54	.0000	.0000	.0000	.0000	.0000	.0001	.0002	.0004	.0008	.0015
55	.0000	.0000	.0000	.0000	.0000	.0000	.0001	.0002	.0004	.0008
56	.0000	.0000	.0000	.0000	.0000	.0000	.0000	.0001	.0002	.0004
57	.0000	.0000	.0000	.0000	.0000	.0000	.0000	.0001	.0001	.0002
58	.0000	.0000	.0000	.0000	.0000	.0000	.0000	.0000	.0001	.0001
59	.0000	.0000	.0000	.0000	.0000	.0000	.0000	.0000	.0000	.0001

	.41	.42	.43	.44	.45	.46	.47	.48	.49	.50
21	.0000	.0000	.0000	.0000	.0000	.0000	.0000	.0000	.0000	.0000
22	.0000	.0000	.0000	.0000	.0000	.0000	.0000	.0000	.0000	.0000
23	.0001	.0000	.0000	.0000	.0000	.0000	.0000	.0000	.0000	.0000
24	.0002	.0001	.0000	.0000	.0000	.0000	.0000	.0000	.0000	.0000
25	.0003	.0002	.0001	.0000	.0000	.0000	.0000	.0000	.0000	.0000
26	.0007	.0003	.0002	.0001	.0000	.0000	.0000	.0000	.0000	.0000
27	.0013	.0007	.0004	.0002	.0001	.0000	.0000	.0000	.0000	.0000
28	.0023	.0013	.0007	.0004	.0002	.0001	.0000	.0000	.0000	.0000
29	.0039	.0024	.0014	.0008	.0004	.0002	.0001	.0000	.0000	.0000
30	.0065	.0040	.0024	.0014	.0008	.0004	.0002	.0001	.0001	.0000
31	.0102	.0066	.0041	.0025	.0014	.0008	.0004	.0002	.0001	.0001
32	.0152	.0103	.0067	.0042	.0025	.0015	.0008	.0004	.0002	.0001
33	.0218	.0154	.0104	.0068	.0043	.0026	.0015	.0008	.0004	.0002
34	.0298	.0219	.0155	.0105	.0069	.0043	.0026	.0015	.0009	.0005
35	.0391	.0299	.0220	.0156	.0106	.0069	.0044	.0026	.0015	.0009
36	.0491	.0391	.0300	.0221	.0157	.0107	.0070	.0044	.0027	.0016
37	.0590	.0490	.0391	.0300	.0222	.0157	.0107	.0070	.0044	.0027
38	.0680	.0588	.0489	.0391	.0301	.0222	.0158	.0108	.0071	.0045
39	.0751	.0677	.0587	.0489	.0391	.0301	.0223	.0158	.0108	.0071

					$n = 100$ (Continued)					
p d	.41	.42	.43	.44	.45	.46	.47	.48	.49	.50
40	.0796	.0748	.0675	.0586	.0488	.0391	.0301	.0223	.0159	.0108
41	.0809	.0793	.0745	.0673	.0584	.0487	.0391	.0301	.0223	.0159
42	.0790	.0806	.0790	.0743	.0672	.0583	.0487	.0390	.0301	.0223
43	.0740	.0787	.0804	.0788	.0741	.0670	.0582	.0486	.0390	.0301
44	.0666	.0739	.0785	.0802	.0786	.0739	.0669	.0581	.0485	.0390
45	.0576	.0666	.0737	.0784	.0800	.0784	.0738	.0668	.0580	.0485
46	.0479	.0576	.0665	.0736	.0782	.0798	.0783	.0737	.0667	.0580
47	.0382	.0480	.0576	.0665	.0736	.0781	.0797	.0781	.0736	.0656
48	.0293	.0383	.0480	.0577	.0665	.0735	.0781	.0797	.0781	.0735
49	.0216	.0295	.0384	.0481	.0577	.0664	.0735	.0780	.0796	.0780
50	.0153	.0218	.0296	.0385	.0482	.0577	.0665	.0725	.0780	.0796
51	.0104	.0155	.0219	.0297	.0386	.0482	.0578	.0665	.0735	.0780
52	.0068	.0105	.0156	.0220	.0298	.0387	.0483	.0578	.0665	.0735
53	.0043	.0069	.0106	.0156	.0221	.0299	.0388	.0483	.0579	.0666
54	.0026	.0044	.0070	.0107	.0157	.0221	.0299	.0388	.0484	.0580
55	.0015	.0026	.0044	.0070	.0108	.0158	.0222	.0300	.0389	.0485
56	.0008	.0015	.0027	.0044	.0071	.0108	.0158	.0222	.0300	.0390
57	.0005	.0009	.0016	.0027	.0045	.0071	.0108	.0158	.0223	.0301
58	.0002	.0005	.0009	.0016	.0027	.0045	.0071	.0108	.0159	.0223
59	.0001	.0002	.0005	.0009	.0016	.0027	.0045	.0071	.0109	.0159
60	.0001	.0001	.0002	.0005	.0009	.0016	.0027	.0045	.0071	.0108
61	.0000	.0001	.0001	.0002	.0005	.0009	.0016	.0027	.0045	.0071
62	.0000	.0000	.0001	.0001	.0002	.0005	.0009	.0016	.0027	.0045
63	.0000	.0000	.0000	.0001	.0001	.0002	.0005	.0009	.0016	.0027
64	.0000	.0000	.0000	.0000	.0001	.0001	.0002	.0005	.0009	.0016
65	.0000	.0000	.0000	.0000	.0000	.0001	.0001	.0002	.0005	.0009
66	.0000	.0000	.0000	.0000	.0000	.0000	.0001	.0001	.0002	.0005
67	.0000	.0000	.0000	.0000	.0000	.0000	.0000	.0001	.0001	.0002
68	.0000	.0000	.0000	.0000	.0000	.0000	.0000	.0000	.0001	.0001
69	.0000	.0000	.0000	.0000	.0000	.0000	.0000	.0000	.0000	.0001

Appendix B

THE CUMULATIVE BINOMIAL DISTRIBUTION

CUMULATIVE BINOMIAL PROBABILITY DISTRIBUTION

$$P(d \geq X/n,\, p) = \sum_{d=X}^{n} C_d^n p^d (1-p)^{n-d}$$

Example

$$P(d \geq 2/n = 3,\, p = .40) = .3520$$

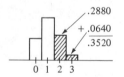

						$n = 2$				
d \ p	.01	.02	.03	.04	.05	.06	.07	.08	.09	.10
1	.0199	.0396	.0591	.0784	.0975	.1164	.1351	.1536	.1719	.1900
2	.0001	.0004	.0009	.0016	.0025	.0036	.0049	.0064	.0081	.0100
	.11	.12	.13	.14	.15	.16	.17	.18	.19	.20
1	.2079	.2256	.2431	.2604	.2775	.2944	.3111	.3276	.3439	.3600
2	.0121	.0144	.0169	.0196	.0225	.0256	.0289	.0324	.0361	.0400

$n = 2$ (Continued)

d \ p	.21	.22	.23	.24	.25	.26	.27	.28	.29	.30
1	.3759	.3916	.4071	.4224	.4375	.4524	.4671	.4816	.4959	.5100
2	.0441	.0484	.0529	.0576	.0625	.0676	.0729	.0784	.0841	.0900
	.31	.32	.33	.34	.35	.36	.37	.38	.39	.40
1	.5239	.5376	.5511	.5644	.5775	.5904	.6031	.6156	.6279	.6400
2	.0961	.1024	.1089	.1156	.1225	.1296	.1369	.1444	.1521	.1600
	.41	.42	.43	.44	.45	.46	.47	.48	.49	.50
1	.6519	.6636	.6751	.6864	.6975	.7084	.7191	.7296	.7399	.7500
2	.1681	.1764	.1849	.1936	.2025	.2116	.2209	.2304	.2401	.2500

$n = 3$

d	.01	.02	.03	.04	.05	.06	.07	.08	.09	.10
1	.0297	.0588	.0873	.1153	.1426	.1694	.1956	.2213	.2264	.2710
2	.0003	.0012	.0026	.0047	.0072	.0104	.0140	.0182	.0228	.0280
3	.0000	.0000	.0000	.0001	.0001	.0002	.0003	.0005	.0007	.0010
	.11	.12	.13	.14	.15	.16	.17	.18	.19	.20
1	.2950	.3185	.3415	.3639	.3859	.4073	.4282	.4486	.4686	.4880
2	.0336	.0397	.0463	.0533	.0608	.0686	.0769	.0855	.0946	.1040
3	.0013	.0017	.0022	.0027	.0034	.0041	.0049	.0058	.0069	.0080
	.21	.22	.23	.24	.25	.26	.27	.28	.29	.30
1	.5070	.5254	.5435	.5610	.5781	.5948	.6110	.6268	.6421	.6570
2	.1138	.1239	.1344	.1452	.1562	.1676	.1793	.1913	.2035	.2160
3	.0093	.0106	.0122	.0138	.0156	.0176	.0197	.0220	.0244	.0270
	.31	.32	.33	.34	.35	.36	.37	.38	.39	.40
1	.6715	.6856	.6992	.7125	.7254	.7379	.7500	.7617	.7730	.7840
2	.2287	.2417	.2548	.2682	.2818	.2955	.3094	.3235	.3377	(.3520)
3	.0298	.0328	.0359	.0393	.0429	.0467	.0507	.0549	.0593	.0640
	.41	.42	.43	.44	.45	.46	.47	.48	.49	.50
1	.7946	.8049	.8148	.8244	.8336	.8425	.8511	.8594	.8673	.8750
2	.3665	.3810	.3957	.4104	.4252	.4401	.4551	.4700	.4850	.5000
3	.0689	.0741	.0797	.0852	.0911	.0973	.1038	.1106	.1176	.1250

$n = 4$

d	.01	.02	.03	.04	.05	.06	.07	.08	.09	.10
1	.0394	.0776	.1147	.1507	.1855	.2193	.2519	.2836	.3143	.3439
2	.0006	.0023	.0052	.0091	.0140	.0199	.0267	.0344	.0430	.0523
3	.0000	.0000	.0001	.0002	.0005	.0008	.0013	.0019	.0027	.0037
4	.0000	.0000	.0000	.0000	.0000	.0000	.0000	.0000	.0001	.0001
	.11	.12	.13	.14	.15	.16	.17	.18	.19	.20
1	.3726	.4003	.4271	.4530	.4780	.5021	.5254	.5479	.5695	.5904
2	.0624	.0732	.0847	.0968	.1095	.1228	.1366	.1509	.1656	.1808
3	.0049	.0063	.0079	.0098	.0120	.0144	.0171	.0202	.0235	.0272
4	.0001	.0002	.0003	.0004	.0005	.0007	.0008	.0010	.0013	.0016

$n = 4$ (Continued)

d \ p	.21	.22	.23	.24	.25	.26	.27	.28	.29	.30
1	.6105	.6298	.6485	.6664	.6836	.7001	.7160	.7313	.7459	.7599
2	.1963	.2122	.2285	.2450	.2617	.2787	.2959	.3132	.3307	.3483
3	.0312	.0356	.0403	.0453	.0508	.0566	.0628	.0694	.0763	.0837
4	.0019	.0023	.0028	.0033	.0039	.0046	.0053	.0061	.0071	.0081

	.31	.32	.33	.34	.35	.36	.37	.38	.39	.40
1	.7733	.7862	.7985	.8103	.8215	.8322	.8425	.8522	.8615	.8704
2	.3660	.3837	.4015	.4193	.4370	.4547	.4724	.4900	.5075	.5248
3	.0915	.0996	.1082	.1171	.1265	.1362	.1464	.1569	.1679	.1792
4	.0092	.0105	.0119	.0134	.0150	.0168	.0187	.0209	.0231	.0256

	.41	.42	.43	.44	.45	.46	.47	.48	.49	.50
1	.8788	.8868	.8944	.9017	.9065	.9150	.9211	.9269	.9323	.9375
2	.5420	.5590	.5759	.5926	.6090	.6252	.6412	.6569	.6724	.6875
3	.1909	.2030	.2155	.2283	.2415	.2550	.2689	.2831	.2977	.3125
4	.0283	.0311	.0342	.0375	.0410	.0448	.0488	.0531	.0576	.0625

$n = 5$

	.01	.02	.03	.04	.05	.06	.07	.08	.09	.10
1	.0490	.0961	.1413	.1846	.2262	.2661	.3043	.3409	.3760	.4095
2	.0010	.0038	.0085	.0148	.0226	.0319	.0425	.0544	.0674	.0815
3	.0000	.0001	.0003	.0006	.0012	.0020	.0031	.0045	.0063	.0086
4	.0000	.0000	.0000	.0000	.0000	.0001	.0001	.0002	.0003	.0005

	.11	.12	.13	.14	.15	.16	.17	.18	.19	.20
1	.4416	.4723	.5016	.5296	.5563	.5818	.6061	.6293	.6513	.6723
2	.0965	.1125	.1292	.1467	.1648	.1835	.2027	.2224	.2424	.2627
3	.0112	.0143	.0179	.0220	.0266	.0318	.0375	.0437	.0505	.0579
4	.0007	.0009	.0013	.0017	.0022	.0029	.0036	.0045	.0055	.0067
5	.0000	.0000	.0000	.0001	.0001	.0001	.0001	.0002	.0002	.0003

	.21	.22	.23	.24	.25	.26	.27	.28	.29	.30
1	.6923	.7113	.7293	.7464	.7627	.7781	.7927	.8065	.8196	.8319
2	.2833	.3041	.3251	.3461	.3672	.3883	.4093	.4303	.4511	.4718
3	.0659	.0744	.0836	.0933	.1035	.1143	.1257	.1376	.1501	.1631
4	.0081	.0097	.0114	.0134	.0156	.0181	.0208	.0238	.0272	.0308
5	.0004	.0005	.0006	.0008	.0010	.0012	.0014	.0017	.0021	.0024

	.31	.32	.33	.34	.35	.36	.37	.38	.39	.40
1	.8436	.8546	.8650	.8748	.8840	.8926	.9008	.9084	.9155	.9222
2	.4923	.5125	.5325	.5522	.5716	.5906	.6093	.6276	.6455	.6630
3	.1766	.1905	.2050	.2199	.2352	.2509	.2670	.2835	.3003	.3174
4	.0347	.0390	.0436	.0486	.0540	.0598	.0660	.0726	.0796	.0870
5	.0029	.0034	.0039	.0045	.0053	.0060	.0069	.0079	.0090	.0102

$n = 5$ (Continued)

d \ p	.41	.42	.43	.44	.45	.46	.47	.48	.49	.50
1	.9285	.9344	.9398	.9449	.9497	.9541	.9582	.9620	.9655	.9688
2	.6801	.6967	.7129	.7286	.7438	.7585	.7728	.7865	.7998	.8125
3	.3349	.3525	.3705	.3886	.4069	.4253	.4439	.4625	.4813	.5000
4	.0949	.1033	.1121	.1214	.1312	.1415	.1522	.1635	.1752	.1875
5	.0116	.0131	.0147	.0165	.0185	.0206	.0229	.0255	.0282	.0312

$n = 6$

d \ p	.01	.02	.03	.04	.05	.06	.07	.08	.09	.10
1	.0585	.1142	.1670	.2172	.2649	.3101	.3530	.3936	.4321	.4686
2	.0015	.0057	.0125	.0216	.0328	.0459	.0608	.0773	.0952	.1143
3	.0000	.0002	.0005	.0012	.0022	.0038	.0058	.0085	.0118	.0158
4	.0000	.0000	.0000	.0000	.0001	.0002	.0003	.0005	.0008	.0013
5	.0000	.0000	.0000	.0000	.0000	.0000	.0000	.0000	.0000	.0001

d \ p	.11	.12	.13	.14	.15	.16	.17	.18	.19	.20
1	.5030	.5356	.5664	.5954	.6229	.6487	.6731	.6960	.7176	.7379
2	.1345	.1556	.1776	.2003	.2235	.2472	.2713	.2956	.3201	.3446
3	.0206	.0261	.0324	.0395	.0476	.0560	.0655	.0759	.0870	.0989
4	.0018	.0025	.0034	.0045	.0059	.0075	.0094	.0116	.0141	.0170
5	.0001	.0001	.0002	.0003	.0004	.0005	.0007	.0010	.0013	.0016
6	.0000	.0000	.0000	.0000	.0000	.0000	.0000	.0000	.0000	.0001

d \ p	.21	.22	.23	.24	.25	.26	.27	.28	.29	.30
1	.7569	.7748	.7916	.8073	.8220	.8358	.8487	.8607	.8719	.8824
2	.3692	.3937	.4180	.4422	.4661	.4896	.5128	.5356	.5580	.5798
3	.1115	.1250	.1391	.1539	.1694	.1856	.2023	.2196	.2374	.2557
4	.0202	.0239	.0280	.0326	.0376	.0431	.0492	.0557	.0628	.0705
5	.0020	.0025	.0031	.0038	.0046	.0056	.0067	.0079	.0093	.0109
6	.0001	.0001	.0001	.0002	.0002	.0003	.0004	.0005	.0006	.0007

d \ p	.31	.32	.33	.34	.35	.36	.37	.38	.39	.40
1	.8921	.9011	.9095	.9173	.9246	.9313	.9375	.9432	.9485	.9533
2	.6012	.6220	.6422	.6619	.6809	.6994	.7172	.7343	.7508	.7667
3	.2744	.2936	.3130	.3328	.3529	.3732	.3937	.4143	.4350	.4557
4	.0787	.0875	.0969	.1069	.1174	.1286	.1404	.1527	.1657	.1792
5	.0127	.0148	.0170	.0195	.0223	.0254	.0288	.0325	.0365	.0410
6	.0009	.0011	.0013	.0015	.0018	.0022	.0026	.0030	.0035	.0041

d \ p	.41	.42	.43	.44	.45	.46	.47	.48	.49	.50
1	.9578	.9619	.9657	.9692	.9723	.9752	.9778	.9802	.9824	.9844
2	.7819	.7965	.8105	.8238	.8364	.8485	.8599	.8707	.8810	.8906
3	.4764	.4971	.5177	.5382	.5585	.5786	.5985	.6180	.6373	.6562
4	.1933	.2080	.2232	.2390	.2553	.2721	.2893	.3070	.3252	.3438
5	.0458	.0510	.0566	.0627	.0692	.0762	.0837	.0917	.1003	.1094
6	.0048	.0055	.0063	.0073	.0083	.0095	.0108	.0122	.0138	.0156

$n = 7$

	.01	.02	.03	.04	.05	.06	.07	.08	.09	.10
1	.0679	.1319	.1920	.2486	.3017	.3515	.3983	.4422	.4832	.5217
2	.0020	.0079	.0171	.0294	.0444	.0618	.0813	.1026	.1255	.1497
3	.0000	.0003	.0009	.0020	.0038	.0063	.0097	.0140	.0193	.0257
4	.0000	.0000	.0000	.0001	.0002	.0004	.0007	.0012	.0018	.0027
5	.0000	.0000	.0000	.0000	.0000	.0000	.0000	.0001	.0001	.0002

	.11	.12	.13	.14	.15	.16	.17	.18	.19	.20
1	.5577	.5913	.6227	.6521	.6794	.7049	.7286	.7507	.7712	.7903
2	.1750	.2012	.2281	.2556	.2834	.3115	.3396	.3677	.3956	.4233
3	.0331	.0416	.0513	.0620	.0738	.0866	.1005	.1154	.1313	.1480
4	.0039	.0054	.0072	.0094	.0121	.0153	.0189	.0231	.0279	.0333
5	.0003	.0004	.0006	.0009	.0012	.0017	.0022	.0029	.0037	.0047
6	.0000	.0000	.0000	.0000	.0001	.0001	.0001	.0002	.0003	.0004

	.21	.22	.23	.24	.25	.26	.27	.28	.29	.30
1	.8080	.8243	.8395	.8535	.8665	.8785	.8895	.8997	.9090	.9176
2	.4506	.4775	.5040	.5298	.5551	.5796	.6035	.6266	.6490	.6706
3	.1657	.1841	.2033	.2231	.2436	.2646	.2861	.3081	.3304	.3529
4	.0394	.0461	.0536	.0617	.0706	.0802	.0905	.1016	.1134	.1260
5	.0058	.0072	.0088	.0107	.0129	.0153	.0181	.0213	.0248	.0288
6	.0005	.0006	.0008	.0011	.0013	.0017	.0021	.0026	.0031	.0038
7	.0000	.0000	.0000	.0000	.0001	.0001	.0001	.0001	.0002	.0002

	.31	.32	.33	.34	.35	.36	.37	.38	.39	.40
1	.9255	.9328	.9394	.9454	.9510	.9560	.9606	.9648	.9686	.9720
2	.6914	.7113	.7304	.7487	.7662	.7828	.7987	.8137	.8279	.8414
3	.3757	.3987	.4217	.4447	.4677	.4906	.5134	.5359	.5581	.5801
4	.1394	.1534	.1682	.1837	.1998	.2167	.2341	.2521	.2707	.2898
5	.0332	.0380	.0434	.0492	.0556	.0625	.0701	.0782	.0869	.0963
6	.0046	.0055	.0065	.0077	.0090	.0105	.0123	.0142	.0164	.0188
7	.0003	.0003	.0004	.0005	.0006	.0008	.0009	.0011	.0014	.0016

	.41	.42	.43	.44	.45	.46	.47	.48	.49	.50
1	.9751	.9779	.9805	.9827	.9848	.9866	.9883	.9897	.9910	.9922
2	.8541	.8660	.8772	.8877	.8976	.9068	.9153	.9233	.9307	.9375
3	.6017	.6229	.6436	.6638	.6836	.7027	.7213	.7393	.7567	.7734
4	.3094	.3294	.3498	.3706	.3917	.4131	.4346	.4563	.4781	.5000
5	.1063	.1169	.1282	.1402	.1529	.1663	.1803	.1951	.2105	.2266
6	.0216	.0246	.0279	.0316	.0357	.0402	.0451	.0504	.0562	.0625
7	.0019	.0023	.0027	.0032	.0037	.0044	.0051	.0059	.0068	.0078

$n = 8$

	.01	.02	.03	.04	.05	.06	.07	.08	.09	.10
1	.0773	.1492	.2163	.2786	.3366	.3904	.4404	.4868	.5297	.5695
2	.0027	.0103	.0223	.0381	.0572	.0792	.1035	.1298	.1577	.1869
3	.0001	.0004	.0013	.0031	.0058	.0096	.0147	.0211	.0289	.0381
4	.0000	.0000	.0001	.0002	.0004	.0007	.0013	.0022	.0034	.0050
5	.0000	.0000	.0000	.0000	.0000	.0000	.0001	.0001	.0003	.0004

$n = 8$ (Continued)

d \ p	.11	.12	.13	.14	.15	.16	.17	.18	.19	.20
1	.6063	.6404	.6718	.7008	.7275	.7521	.7748	.7956	.8147	.8322
2	.2171	.2480	.2794	.3111	.3428	.3744	.4057	.4366	.4670	.4967
3	.0487	.0608	.0743	.0891	.1052	.1226	.1412	.1608	.1815	.2031
4	.0071	.0097	.0129	.0168	.0214	.0267	.0328	.0397	.0476	.0563
5	.0007	.0010	.0015	.0021	.0029	.0038	.0050	.0065	.0083	.0104
6	.0000	.0001	.0001	.0002	.0002	.0004	.0005	.0007	.0009	.0012
7	.0000	.0000	.0000	.0000	.0000	.0000	.0000	.0000	.0001	.0001

d \ p	.21	.22	.23	.24	.25	.26	.27	.28	.29	.30
1	.8483	.8630	.8764	.8887	.8999	.9101	.9194	.9278	.9354	.9424
2	.5257	.5538	.5811	.6075	.6329	.6573	.6807	.7031	.7244	.7447
3	.2255	.2486	.2724	.2967	.3215	.3465	.3718	.3973	.4228	.4482
4	.0659	.0765	.0880	.1004	.1138	.1281	.1433	.1594	.1763	.1941
5	.0129	.0158	.0191	.0230	.0273	.0322	.0377	.0438	.0505	.0580
6	.0016	.0021	.0027	.0034	.0042	.0052	.0064	.0078	.0094	.0113
7	.0001	.0002	.0002	.0003	.0004	.0005	.0006	.0008	.0010	.0013
8	.0000	.0000	.0000	.0000	.0000	.0000	.0000	.0000	.0001	.0001

d \ p	.31	.32	.33	.34	.35	.36	.37	.38	.39	.40
1	.9486	.9543	.9594	.9640	.9681	.9719	.9752	.9782	.9808	.9832
2	.7640	.7822	.7994	.8156	.8309	.8452	.8586	.8711	.8828	.8936
3	.4736	.4987	.5236	.5481	.5722	.5958	.6189	.6415	.6634	.6846
4	.2126	.2319	.2519	.2724	.2936	.3153	.3374	.3599	.3828	.4059
5	.0661	.0750	.0846	.0949	.1061	.1180	.1307	.1443	.1586	.1737
6	.0134	.0159	.0187	.0218	.0253	.0293	.0336	.0385	.0439	.0498
7	.0016	.0020	.0024	.0030	.0036	.0043	.0051	.0061	.0072	.0085
8	.0001	.0001	.0001	.0002	.0002	.0003	.0004	.0004	.0005	.0007

d \ p	.41	.42	.43	.44	.45	.46	.47	.48	.49	.50
1	.9853	.9872	.9889	.9903	.9916	.9928	.9938	.9947	.9954	.9961
2	.9037	.9130	.9216	.9295	.9368	.9435	.9496	.9552	.9602	.9648
3	.7052	.7250	.7740	.7624	.7799	.7966	.8125	.8276	.8419	.8555
4	.4292	.4527	.4762	.4996	.5230	.5463	.5694	.5922	.6146	.6367
5	.1895	.2062	.2235	.2416	.2604	.2798	.2999	.3205	.3416	.3633
6	.0563	.0634	.0711	.0794	.0885	.0982	.1086	.1198	.1318	.1445
7	.0100	.0117	.0136	.0157	.0181	.0208	.0239	.0272	.0310	.0352
8	.0008	.0010	.0012	.0014	.0017	.0020	.0024	.0028	.0033	.0039

$n = 9$

d \ p	.01	.02	.03	.04	.05	.06	.07	.08	.09	.10
1	.0865	.1663	.2398	.3075	.3698	.4270	.4796	.5278	.5721	.6126
2	.0034	.0131	.0282	.0478	.0712	.0978	.1271	.1583	.1912	.2252
3	.0001	.0006	.0020	.0045	.0084	.0138	.0209	.0298	.0405	.0530
4	.0000	.0000	.0001	.0003	.0006	.0013	.0023	.0037	.0057	.0083
5	.0000	.0000	.0000	.0000	.0000	.0001	.0002	.0003	.0005	.0009
6	.0000	.0000	.0000	.0000	.0000	.0000	.0000	.0000	.0000	.0001

					$n = 9$ (Continued)					
d \ p	.11	.12	.13	.14	.15	.16	.17	.18	.19	.20
1	.6496	.6835	.7145	.7427	.7684	.7918	.8131	.8324	.8499	.8658
2	.2599	.2951	.3304	.3657	.4005	.4348	.4685	.5012	.5330	.5638
3	.0672	.0833	.1009	.1202	.1409	.1629	.1861	.2105	.2357	.2618
4	.0117	.0158	.0209	.0269	.0339	.0420	.0512	.0615	.0730	.0856
5	.0014	.0021	.0030	.0041	.0056	.0075	.0098	.0125	.0158	.0196
6	.0001	.0002	.0003	.0004	.0006	.0009	.0013	.0017	.0023	.0031
7	.0000	.0000	.0000	.0000	.0000	.0001	.0001	.0002	.0002	.0003

	.21	.22	.23	.24	.25	.26	.27	.28	.29	.30
1	.8801	.8931	.9048	.9154	.9249	.9335	.9411	.9480	.9542	.9596
2	.5934	.6218	.6491	.6750	.6997	.7230	.7452	.7660	.7856	.8040
3	.2885	.3158	.3434	.3713	.3993	.4273	.4552	.4829	.5102	.5372
4	.0994	.1144	.1304	.1475	.1657	.1849	.2050	.2260	.2478	.2703
5	.0240	.0291	.0350	.0416	.0489	.0571	.0662	.0762	.0870	.0988
6	.0040	.0051	.0065	.0081	.0100	.0122	.0149	.0179	.0213	.0253
7	.0004	.0006	.0008	.0010	.0013	.0017	.0022	.0028	.0035	.0043
8	.0000	.0000	.0001	.0001	.0001	.0001	.0002	.0003	.0003	.0004

	.31	.32	.33	.34	.35	.36	.37	.38	.39	.40
1	.9645	.9689	.9728	.9762	.9793	.9820	.9844	.9865	.9883	.9899
2	.8212	.8372	.8522	.8661	.8789	.8908	.9017	.9118	.9210	.9295
3	.5636	.5894	.6146	.6390	.6627	.6856	.7076	.7287	.7489	.7682
4	.2935	.3173	.3415	.3662	.3911	.4163	.4416	.4669	.4922	.5174
5	.1115	.1252	.1398	.1553	.1717	.1890	.2072	.2262	.2460	.2666
6	.0298	.0348	.0404	.0467	.0536	.0612	.0696	.0787	.0886	.0994
7	.0053	.0064	.0078	.0094	.0112	.0133	.0157	.0184	.0215	.0250
8	.0006	.0007	.0009	.0011	.0014	.0017	.0021	.0026	.0031	.0038
9	.0000	0000	.0000	.0001	.0001	.0001	.0001	.0002	.0002	.0003

	.41	.42	.43	.44	.45	.46	.47	.48	.49	.50
1	.9913	.9926	.9936	.9946	.9954	.9961	.9967	.9972	.9977	.9980
2	.9372	.9442	.9505	.9563	.9615	.9662	.9704	.9741	.9775	.9805
3	.7866	.8039	.8204	.8359	.8505	.8642	.8769	.8889	.8999	.9102
4	.5424	.5670	.5913	.6152	.6386	.6614	.6836	.7052	.7260	.7461
5	.2878	.3097	.3322	.3551	.3786	.4024	.4265	.4509	.4754	.5000
6	.1109	.1233	.1366	.1508	.1658	.1817	.1985	.2161	.2346	.2539
7	.0290	.0334	.0383	.0437	.0498	.0564	.0637	.0717	.0804	.0898
8	.0046	.0055	.0065	.0077	.0091	.0107	.0125	.0145	.0169	.0195
9	.0003	.0004	.0005	.0006	.0008	.0009	.0011	.0014	.0016	.0020

					$n = 10$					
	.01	.02	.03	.04	.05	.06	.07	.08	.09	.10
1	.0956	.1829	.2626	.3352	.4013	.4614	.5160	.5656	.6106	.6513
2	.0043	.0162	.0345	.0582	.0861	.1176	.1517	.1879	.2254	.2639
3	.0001	.0009	.0028	.0062	.0115	.0188	.0283	.0401	.0540	.0702
4	.0000	.0000	.0001	.0004	.0010	.0020	.0036	.0058	.0088	.0128
5	.0000	.0000	.0000	.0000	.0001	.0002	.0003	.0006	.0010	.0016
6	.0000	.0000	.0000	.0000	.0000	.0000	.0000	.0000	.0001	.0001

$n = 10$ (Continued)

d \ p	.11	.12	.13	.14	.15	.16	.17	.18	.19	.20
1	.6882	.7215	.7516	.7787	.8031	.8251	.8448	.8626	.8784	.8926
2	.3028	.3417	.3804	.4184	.4557	.4920	.5270	.5608	.5932	.6242
3	.0884	.1087	.1308	.1545	.1798	.2064	.2341	.2628	.2922	.3222
4	.0178	.0239	.0313	.0400	.0500	.0614	.0741	.0883	.1039	.1209
5	.0025	.0037	.0053	.0073	.0099	.0130	.0168	.0213	.0266	.0328
6	.0003	.0004	.0006	.0010	.0014	.0020	.0027	.0037	.0049	.0064
7	.0000	.0000	.0001	.0001	.0001	.0002	.0003	.0004	.0006	.0009
8	.0000	.0000	.0000	.0000	.0000	.0000	.0000	.0000	.0001	.0001

	.21	.22	.23	.24	.25	.26	.27	.28	.29	.30
1	.9053	.9166	.9267	.9357	.9437	.9508	.9570	.9626	.9674	.9718
2	.6536	.6815	.7079	.7327	.7560	.7778	.7981	.8170	.8345	.8507
3	.3526	.3831	.4137	.4442	.4744	.5042	.5335	.5622	.5901	.6172
4	.1391	.1587	.1794	.2012	.2241	.2479	.2726	.2979	.3239	.3504
5	.0399	.0479	.0569	.0670	.0781	.0904	.1037	.1181	.1337	.1503
6	.0082	.0104	.0130	.0161	.0197	.0239	.0287	.0342	.0404	.0473
7	.0012	.0016	.0021	.0027	.0035	.0045	.0056	.0070	.0087	.0106
8	.0001	.0002	.0002	.0003	.0004	.0006	.0007	.0010	.0012	.0016
9	.0000	.0000	.0000	.0000	.0000	.0000	.0001	.0001	.0001	.0001

	.31	.32	.33	.34	.35	.36	.37	.38	.39	.40
1	.9755	.9789	.9818	.9843	.9865	.9885	.9902	.9916	.9929	.9940
2	.8656	.8794	.8920	.9035	.9140	.9236	.9323	.9402	.9473	.9536
3	.6434	.6687	.6930	.7162	.7384	.7595	.7794	.7983	.8160	.8327
4	.3772	.4044	.4316	.4589	.4862	.5132	.5400	.5664	.5923	.6177
5	.1679	.1867	.2064	.2270	.2485	.2708	.2939	.3177	.3420	.3669
6	.0551	.0637	.0732	.0836	.0949	.1072	.1205	.1348	.1500	.1662
7	.0129	.0155	.0185	.0220	.0260	.0305	.0356	.0413	.0477	.0548
8	.0020	.0025	.0032	.0039	.0048	.0059	.0071	.0086	.0103	.0123
9	.0002	.0003	.0003	.0004	.0005	.0007	.0009	.0011	.0014	.0017
10	.0000	.0000	.0000	.0000	.0000	.0000	.0000	.0001	.0001	.0001

	.41	.42	.43	.44	.45	.46	.47	.48	.49	.50
1	.9949	.9957	.9964	.9970	.9975	.9979	.9983	.9986	.9988	.9990
2	.9594	.9645	.9691	.9731	.9767	.9799	.9827	.9852	.9874	.9873
3	.8483	.8628	.8764	.8889	.9004	.9111	.9209	.9298	.9379	.9453
4	.6425	.6665	.6898	.7123	.7340	.7547	.7745	.7933	.8112	.8281
5	.3922	.4178	.4436	.4696	.4956	.5216	.5474	.5730	.5982	.6230
6	.1834	.2016	.2207	.2407	.2616	.2832	.3057	.3288	.3526	.3770
7	.0626	.0712	.0806	.0908	.1020	.1141	.1271	.1410	.1560	.1719
8	.0146	.0172	.0202	.0236	.0274	.0317	.0366	.0420	.0480	.0547
9	.0021	.0025	.0031	.0037	.0045	.0054	.0065	.0077	.0091	.0107
10	.0001	.0002	.0002	.0003	.0003	.0004	.0005	.0006	.0008	.0010

					$n = 100$					
p \ d	.01	.02	.03	.04	.05	.06	.07	.08	.09	.10
1	.6340	.8674	.9524	.9831	.9941	.9979	.9993	.9998	.9999	1.0000
2	.2642	.5967	.8054	.9128	.9629	.9848	.9940	.9977	.9991	.9997
3	.0794	.3233	.5802	.7679	.8817	.9434	.9742	.9887	.9952	.9981
4	.0184	.1410	.3528	.5705	.7422	.8570	.9256	.9633	.9827	.9922
5	.0034	.0508	.1821	.3711	.5640	.7232	.8368	.9097	.9526	.9763
6	.0005	.0155	.0808	.2116	.3840	.5593	.7086	.8201	.8955	.9424
7	.0001	.0041	.0312	.1064	.2340	.3936	.5557	.6968	.8060	.8828
8	.0000	.0009	.0106	.0475	.1280	.2517	.4012	.5529	.6872	.7939
9	.0000	.0002	.0032	.0190	.0631	.1463	.2660	.4074	.5506	.6791
10	.0000	.0000	.0009	.0068	.0282	.0775	.1620	.2780	.4125	.5487
11	.0000	.0000	.0002	.0022	.0115	.0376	.0908	.1757	.2882	.4168
12	.0000	.0000	.0000	.0007	.0043	.0168	.0469	.1028	.1876	.2970
13	.0000	.0000	.0000	.0002	.0015	.0069	.0224	.0559	.1138	.1982
14	.0000	.0000	.0000	.0000	.0005	.0026	.0099	.0282	.0645	.1239
15	.0000	.0000	.0000	.0000	.0001	.0009	.0041	.0133	.0341	.0726
16	.0000	.0000	.0000	.0000	.0000	.0003	.0016	.0058	.0169	.0399
17	.0000	.0000	.0000	.0000	.0000	.0001	.0006	.0024	.0078	.0206
18	.0000	.0000	.0000	.0000	.0000	.0000	.0002	.0009	.0034	.0100
19	.0000	.0000	.0000	.0000	.0000	.0000	.0001	.0003	.0014	.0046
20	.0000	.0000	.0000	.0000	.0000	.0000	.0000	.0001	.0005	.0020
21	.0000	.0000	.0000	.0000	.0000	.0000	.0000	.0000	.0002	.0008
22	.0000	.0000	.0000	.0000	.0000	.0000	.0000.	.0000	.0001	.0003
23	.0000	.0000	.0000	.0000	.0000	.0000	.0000	.0000	.0000	.0001

	.11	.12	.13	.14	.15	.16	.17	.18	.19	.20
1	1.0000	1.0000	1.0000	1.0000	1.0000	1.0000	1.0000	1.0000	1.0000	1.0000
2	.9999	1.0000	1.0000	1.0000	1.0000	1.0000	1.0000	1.0000	1.0000	1.0000
3	.9992	.9997	.9999	1.0000	1.0000	1.0000	1.0000	1.0000	1.0000	1.0000
4	.9966	.9985	.9994	.9998	.9999	1.0000	1.0000	1.0000	1.0000	1.0000
5	.9886	.9947	.9977	.9990	.9996	.9998	.9999	1.0000	1.0000	1.0000
6	.9698	.9848	.9926	.9966	.9984	.9993	.9997	.9999	1.0000	1.0000
7	.9328	.9633	.9808	.9903	.9953	.9978	.9990	.9996	.9998	.9999
8	.8715	.9239	.9569	.9766	.9878	.9939	.9970	.9986	.9994	.9997
9	.7835	.8614	.9155	.9508	.9725	.9853	.9924	.9962	.9982	.9991
10	.6722	.7743	.8523	.9078	.9449	.9684	.9826	.9908	.9953	.9977
11	.5471	.6663	.7663	.8440	.9006	.9393	.9644	.9800	.9891	.9943
12	.4206	.5458	.6611	.7591	.8365	.8939	.9340	.9605	.9773	.9874
13	.3046	.4239	.5446	.6566	.7527	.8297	.8876	.9289	.9567	.9747
14	.2076	.3114	.4268	.5436	.6526	.7469	.8234	.8819	.9241	.9531
15	.1330	.2160	.3173	.4294	.5428	.6490	.7417	.8177	.8765	.9196
16	.0802	.1414	.2236	.3227	.4317	.5420	.6458	.7370	.8125	.8715
17	.0456	.0874	.1492	.2305	.3275	.4338	.5414	.6429	.7327	.8077
18	.0244	.0511	.0942	.1563	.2367	.3319	.4357	.5408	.6403	.7288
19	.0123	.0282	.0564	.1006	.1628	.2424	.3359	.4374	.5403	.6379
20	.0059	.0147	.0319	.0614	.1065	.1689	.2477	.3395	.4391	.5398

				$n = 100$ (Continued)					
p d	.11	.12	.13	.14	.15	.16	.17	.18	.19	.20
21	.0026	.0073	.0172	.0356	.0663	.1121	.1745	.2525	.3429	.4405
22	.0011	.0034	.0088	.0196	.0393	.0710	.1174	.1797	.2570	.3460
23	.0005	.0015	.0042	.0103	.0221	.0428	.0754	.1223	.1846	.2611
24	.0002	.0006	.0020	.0051	.0119	.0246	.0462	.0796	.1270	.1891
25	.0001	.0003	.0009	.0024	.0061	.0135	.0271	.0496	.0837	.1314
26	.0000	.0001	.0004	.0011	.0030	.0071	.0151	.0295	.0528	.0875
27	.0000	.0000	.0001	.0005	.0014	.0035	.0081	.0168	.0318	.0558
28	.0000	.0000	.0001	.0002	.0006	.0017	.0041	.0091	.0184	.0342
29	.0000	.0000	.0000	.0001	.0003	.0008	.0020	.0048	.0102	.0200
30	.0000	.0000	.0000	.0000	.0001	.0003	.0009	.0024	.0054	.0112
31	.0000	.0000	.0000	.0000	.0000	.0001	.0004	.0011	.0027	.0061
32	.0000	.0000	.0000	.0000	.0000	.0001	.0002	.0005	.0013	.0031
33	.0000	.0000	.0000	.0000	.0000	.0000	.0001	.0002	.0006	.0016
34	.0000	.0000	.0000	.0000	.0000	.0000	.0000	.0001	.0003	.0007
35	.0000	.0000	.0000	.0000	.0000	.0000	.0000	.0000	.0001	.0003
36	.0000	.0000	.0000	.0000	.0000	.0000	.0000	.0000	.0000	.0001
37	.0000	.0000	.0000	.0000	.0000	.0000	.0000	.0000	.0000	.0001

	.21	.22	.23	.24	.25	.26	.27	.28	.29	.30
1	1.0000	1.0000	1.0000	1.0000	1.0000	1.0000	1.0000	1.0000	1.0000	1.0000
2	1.0000	1.0000	1.0000	1.0000	1.0000	1.0000	1.0000	1.0000	1.0000	1.0000
3	1.0000	1.0000	1.0000	1.0000	1.0000	1.0000	1.0000	1.0000	1.0000	1.0000
4	1.0000	1.0000	1.0000	1.0000	1.0000	1.0000	1.0000	1.0000	1.0000	1.0000
5	1.0000	1.0000	1.0000	1.0000	1.0000	1.0000	1.0000	1.0000	1.0000	1.0000
6	1.0000	1.0000	1.0000	1.0000	1.0000	1.0000	1.0000	1.0000	1.0000	1.0000
7	1.0000	1.0000	1.0000	1.0000	1.0000	1.0000	1.0000	1.0000	1.0000	1.0000
8	.9999	1.0000	1.0000	1.0000	1.0000	1.0000	1.0000	1.0000	1.0000	1.0000
9	.9996	1.9998	1.9999	1.0000	1.0000	1.0000	1.0000	1.0000	1.0000	1.0000
10	.9989	.9995	.9998	.9999	1.0000	1.0000	1.0000	1.0000	1.0000	1.0000
11	.9971	.9986	.9993	.9997	.9999	.9999	1.0000	1.0000	1.0000	1.0000
12	.9933	.9965	.9983	.9992	.9996	.9998	.9999	1.0000	1.0000	1.0000
13	.9857	.9922	.9959	.9979	.9990	.9995	.9998	.9999	1.0000	1.0000
14	.9721	.9840	.9911	.9953	.9975	.9988	.9994	.9997	.9999	.9999
15	.9496	.9695	.9823	.9900	.9946	.9972	.9986	.9993	.9997	.9998
16	.9153	.9462	.9671	.9806	.9889	.9939	.9967	.9983	.9992	.9996
17	.8668	.9112	.9430	.9647	.9789	.9878	.9932	.9963	.9981	.9990
18	.8032	.8625	.9074	.9399	.9624	.9773	.9867	.9925	.9959	.9978
19	.7252	.7991	.8585	.9938	.9370	.9601	.9757	.9856	.9918	.9955
20	.6358	.7220	.7953	.8547	.9005	.9342	.9580	.9741	.9846	.9911
21	.5394	.6338	.7189	.7918	.8512	.8973	.9316	.9560	.9726	.9835
22	.4419	.5391	.6320	.7162	.7886	.8479	.8943	.9291	.9540	.9712
23	.3488	.4432	.5388	.6304	.7136	.7856	.8448	.8915	.9267	.9521
24	.2649	.3514	.4444	.5386	.6289	.7113	.7828	.8420	.8889	.9245
25	.1933	.2684	.3539	.4455	.5383	.6276	.7091	.7802	.8393	.8864

d \ p	.21	.22	.23	.24	.25	.26	.27	.28	.29	.30
				$n = 100$ (Continued)						
26	.1355	.1972	.2717	.3561	.4465	.5381	.6263	.7071	.7778	.8369
27	.0911	.1393	.2009	.2748	.3583	.4475	.5380	.6252	.7053	.7756
28	.0588	.0945	.1429	.2043	.2776	.3602	.4484	.5378	.6242	.7036
29	.0364	.0616	.0978	.1463	.2075	.2803	.3621	.4493	.5377	.6232
30	.0216	.0386	.0643	.1009	.1495	.2105	.2828	.3638	.4501	.5377
31	.0123	.0232	.0406	.0669	.1038	.1526	.2134	.2851	.3654	.4509
32	.0067	.0134	.0247	.0427	.0693	.1065	.1554	.2160	.2873	.3669
33	.0035	.0074	.0144	.0262	.0446	.0717	.1091	.1580	.2184	.2893
34	.0018	.0039	.0081	.0154	.0276	.0465	.0739	.1116	.1605	.2207
35	.0009	.0020	.0044	.0087	.0164	.0290	.0482	.0760	.1139	.1629
36	.0004	.0010	.0023	.0048	.0094	.0174	.0303	.0499	.0780	.1161
37	.0002	.0005	.0011	.0025	.0052	.0101	.0183	.0316	.0515	.0799
38	.0001	.0002	.0005	.0013	.0027	.0056	.0107	.0193	.0328	.0530
39	.0000	.0001	.0002	.0006	.0014	.0030	.0060	.0113	.0201	.0340
40	.0000	.0000	.0001	.0003	.0007	.0015	.0032	.0064	.0119	.0210
41	.0000	.0000	.0000	.0001	.0003	.0008	.0017	.0035	.0068	.0125
42	.0000	.0000	.0000	.0001	.0001	.0004	.0008	.0018	.0037	.0072
43	.0000	.0000	.0000	.0000	.0001	.0002	.0004	.0009	.0020	.0040
44	.0000	.0000	.0000	.0000	.0000	.0001	.0002	.0005	.0010	.0021
45	.0000	.0000	.0000	.0000	.0000	.0000	.0001	.0002	.0005	.0011
46	.0000	.0000	.0000	.0000	.0000	.0000	.0000	.0001	.0002	.0005
47	.0000	.0000	.0000	.0000	.0000	.0000	.0000	.0000.	.0001	.0003
48	.0000	.0000	.0000	.0000	.0000	.0000	.0000	.0000	.0000	.0001
49	.0000	.0000	.0000	.0000	.0000	.0000	.0000	.0000	.0000	.0001

	.31	.32	.33	.34	.35	.36	.37	.38	.39	.40
1	1.0000	1.0000	1.0000	1.0000	1.0000	1.0000	1.0000	1.0000	1.0000	1.0000
2	1.0000	1.0000	1.0000	1.0000	1.0000	1.0000	1.0000	1.0000	1.0000	1.0000
3	1.0000	1.0000	1.0000	1.0000	1.0000	1.0001	1.0000	1.0000	1.0000	1.0000
4	1.0000	1.0000	1.0000	1.0000	1.0000	1.0000	1.0000	1.0000	1.0000	1.0000
5	1.0000	1.0000	1.0000	1.0000	1.0000	1.0000	1.0000	1.0000	1.0000	1.0000
6	1.0000	1.0000	1.0000	1.0000	1.0000	1.0000	1.0000	1.0000	1.0000	1.0000
7	1.0000	1.0000	1.0000	1.0000	1.0000	1.0000	1.0000	1.0000	1.0000	1.0000
8	1.0000	1.0000	1.0000	1.0000	1.0000	1.0000	1.0000	1.0000	1.0000	1.0000
9	1.0000	1.0000	1.0000	1.0000	1.0000	1.0000	1.0000	1.0000	1.0000	1.0000
10	1.0000	1.0000	1.0000	1.0000	1.0000	1.0000	1.0000	1.0000	1.0000	1.0000
11	1.0000	1.0000	1.0000	1.0000	1.0000	1.0000	1.0000	1.0000	1.0000	1.0000
12	1.0000	1.0000	1.0000	1.0000	1.0000	1.0000	1.0000	1.0000	1.0000	1.0000
13	1.0000	1.0000	1.0000	1.0000	1.0000	1.0000	1.0000	1.0000	1.0000	1.0000
14	1.0000	1.0000	1.0000	1.0000	1.0000	1.0000	1.0000	1.0000	1.0000	1.0000
15	.9999	1.0000	1.0000	1.0000	1.0000	1.0000	1.0000	1.0000	1.0000	1.0000
16	.9998	.9999	1.0000	1.0000	1.0000	1.0000	1.0000	1.0000	1.0000	1.0000
17	.9995	.9998	.9999	1.0000	1.0000	1.0000	1.0000	1.0000	1.0000	1.0000
18	.9989	.9995	.9997	.9999	.9999	1.0000	1.0000	1.0000	1.0000	1.0000
19	.9976	.9988	.9994	.9997	.9999	.9999	1.0000	1.0000	1.0000	1.0000
20	.9950	.9973	.9986	.9993	.9997	.9998	.9999	1.0000	1.0000	1.0000

$n = 100$ (Continued)

d \ p	.31	.32	.33	.34	.35	.36	.37	.38	.39	.40
21	.9904	.9946	.9971	.9985	.9992	.9996	.9998	.9999	1.0000	1.0000
22	.9825	.9898	.9942	.9968	.9983	.9991	.9996	.9998	.9999	1.0000
23	.9698	.9816	.9891	.9938	.9966	.9982	.9991	.9995	.9998	.9999
24	.9504	.9685	.9806	.9885	.9934	.9963	.9980	.9990	.9995	.9997
25	.9224	.9487	.9672	.9797	.9879	.9930	.9961	.9979	.9989	.9994
26	.8841	.9204	.9471	.9660	.9789	.9873	.9926	.9958	.9977	.9988
27	.8346	.8820	.9185	.9456	.9649	.9780	.9867	.9922	.9956	.9976
28	.7736	.8325	.8800	.9168	.9442	.9638	.9773	.9862	.9919	.9954
29	.7021	.7717	.8305	.8781	.9152	.9429	.9628	.9765	.9857	.9916
30	.6224	.7007	.7699	.8287	.8764	.9137	.9417	.9618	.9759	.9852
31	.5376	.6216	.6994	.7684	.8270	.8748	.9123	.9405	.9610	.9752
32	.4516	.5376	.6209	.6982	.7669	.8254	.8733	.9110	.9395	.9602
33	.3683	.4523	.5375	.6203	.6971	.7656	.8240	.8720	.9098	.9385
34	.2912	.3696	.4530	.5375	.6197	.6961	.7643	.8227	.8708	.9087
35	.2229	.2929	.3708	.4536	.5376	.6192	.6953	.7632	.8216	.8697
36	.1650	.2249	.2946	.3720	.4542	.5376	.6188	.6945	.7623	.8205
37	.1181	.1671	.2268	.2961	.3731	.4547	.5377	.6184	.6938	.7614
38	.0816	.1200	.1690	.2285	.2976	.3741	.4553	.5377	.6181	.6932
39	.0545	.0833	.1218	.1708	.2301	.2989	.3750	.4558	.5378	.6178
40	.0351	.0558	.0849	.1235	.1724	.2316	.3001	.3759	.4562	.5379
41	.0218	.0361	.0571	.0863	.1250	.1739	.2330	.3012	.3767	.4567
42	.0131	.0226	.0371	.0583	.0877	.1265	.1753	.2343	.3023	.3775
43	0075	.0136	.0233	.0380	.0594	.0889	.1278	.1766	.2355	.3033
44	.0042	.0079	.0141	.0240	.0389	.0605	.0901	.1290	.1778	.2365
45	.0023	.0044	.0082	.0146	.0246	.0397	.0614	.0911	.1301	.1789
46	.0012	.0024	.0046	.0085	.0150	.0252	.0405	.0623	.0921	.1311
47	.0006	.0012	.0025	.0048	.0088	.0154	.0257	.0411	.0631	.0930
48	.0003	.0006	.0013	.0026	.0050	.0091	.0158	.0262	.0417	.0638
49	.0001	.0003	.0007	.0014	.0027	.0052	.0094	.0162	.0267	.0423
50	.0001	.0001	.0003	.0007	.0015	.0029	.0054	.0096	.0165	.0271
51	.0000	.0001	.0002	.0003	.0007	.0015	.0030	.0055	.0098	.0168
52	.0000	.0000	.0001	.0002	.0004	.0008	.0016	.0030	.0056	.0100
53	.0000	.0000	.0000	.0001	.0002	.0004	.0008	.0016	.0031	.0058
54	.0000	.0000	.0000	.0000	.0001	.0002	.0004	.0008	.0017	.0032
55	.0000	.0000	.0000	.0000	.0000	.0001	.0002	.0004	.0009	.0017
56	.0000	.0000	.0000	.0000	.0000	.0000	.0001	.0002	.0004	.0009
57	.0000	.0000	.0000	.0000	.0000	.0000	.0000	.0001	.0002	.0004
58	.0000	.0000	.0000	.0000	.0000	.0000	.0000	.0000	.0001	.0002
59	.0000	.0000	.0000	.0000	.0000	.0000	.0000	.0000	.0000	.0001

	.41	.42	.43	.44	.45	.46	.47	.48	.49	.50
1	1.0000	1.0000	1.0000	1.0000	1.0000	1.0000	1.0000	1.0000	1.0000	1.0000
2	1.0000	1.0000	1.0000	1.0000	1.0000	1.0000	1.0000	1.0000	1.0000	1.0000
3	1.0000	1.0000	1.0000	1.0000	1.0000	1.0000	1.0000	1.0000	1.0000	1.0000
4	1.0000	1.0000	1.0000	1.0000	1.0000	1.0000	1.0000	1.0000	1.0000	1.0000
5	1.0000	1.0000	1.0000	1.0000	1.0000	1.0000	1.0000	1.0000	1.0000	1.0000

d \ p	.41	.42	.43	.44	.45	.46	.47	.48	.49	.50
6	1.0000	1.0000	1.0000	1.0000	1.0000	1.0000	1.0000	1.0000	1.0000	1.0000
7	1.0000	1.0000	1.0000	1.0000	1.0000	1.0000	1.0000	1.0000	1.0000	1.0000
8	1.0000	1.0000	1.0000	1.0000	1.0000	1.0000	1.0000	1.0000	1.0000	1.0000
9	1.0000	1.0000	1.0000	1.0000	1.0000	1.0000	1.0000	1.0000	1.0000	1.0000
10	1.0000	1.0000	1.0000	1.0000	1.0000	1.0000	1.0000	1.0000	1.0000	1.0000
11	1.0000	1.0000	1.0000	1.0000	1.0000	1.0000	1.0000	1.0000	1.0000	1.0000
12	1.0000	1.0000	1.0000	1.0000	1.0000	1.0000	1.0000	1.0000	1.0000	1.0000
13	1.0000	1.0000	1.0000	1.0000	1.0000	1.0000	1.0000	1.0000	1.0000	1.0000
14	1.0000	1.0000	1.0000	1.0000	1.0000	1.0000	1.0000	1.0000	1.0000	1.0000
15	1.0000	1.0000	1.0000	1.0000	1.0000	1.0000	1.0000	1.0000	1.0000	1.0000
16	1.0000	1.0000	1.0000	1.0000	1.0000	1.0000	1.0000	1.0000	1.0000	1.0000
17	1.0000	1.0000	1.0000	1.0000	1.0000	1.0000	1.0000	1.0000	1.0000	1.0000
18	1.0000	1.0000	1.0000	1.0000	1.0000	1.0000	1.0000	1.0000	1.0000	1.0000
19	1.0000	1.0000	1.0000	1.0000	1.0000	1.0000	1.0000	1.0000	1.0000	1.0000
20	1.0000	1.0000	1.0000	1.0000	1.0000	1.0000	1.0000	1.0000	1.0000	1.0000
21	1.0000	1.0000	1.0000	1.0000	1.0000	1.0000	1.0000	1.0000	1.0000	1.0000
22	1.0000	1.0000	1.0000	1.0000	1.0000	1.0000	1.0000	1.0000	1.0000	1.0000
23	1.0000	1.0000	1.0000	1.0000	1.0000	1.0000	1.0000	1.0000	1.0000	1.0000
24	.9999	.9999	1.0000	1.0000	1.0000	1.0000	1.0000	1.0000	1.0000	1.0000
25	.9997	.9999	.9999	1.0000	1.0000	1.0000	1.0000	1.0000	1.0000	1.0000
26	.9994	.9997	.9999	.9999	1.0000	1.0000	1.0000	1.0000	1.0000	1.0000
27	.9987	.9994	.9997	.9998	.9999	1.0000	1.0000	1.0000	1.0000	1.0000
28	.9975	.9987	.9993	.9997	.9998	.9999	1.0000	1.0000	1.0000	1.0000
29	.9952	.9974	.9986	.9993	.9996	.9998	.9999	1.0000	1.0000	1.0000
30	.9913	.9950	.9972	.9985	.9992	.9996	.9998	.9999	1.0000	1.0000
31	.9848	.9910	.9948	.9971	.9985	.9992	.9996	.9998	.9999	1.0000
32	.9746	.9844	.9907	.9947	.9970	.9984	.9992	.9996	.9998	.9999
33	.9594	.9741	.9840	.9905	.9945	.9969	.9984	.9991	.9996	.9998
34	.9376	.9587	.9736	.9837	.9902	.9944	.9969	.9983	.9991	.9996
35	.9078	.9368	.9581	.9732	.9834	.9900	.9942	.9968	.9983	.9991
36	.8687	.9069	.9361	.9576	.9728	.9831	.9899	.9941	.9967	.9982
37	.8196	.8678	.9061	.9355	.9571	.9724	.9829	.9897	.9941	.9967
38	.7606	.8188	.8670	.9054	.9349	.9567	.9721	.9827	.9896	.9940
39	.6927	.7599	.8181	.8663	.9049	.9345	.9563	.9719	.9825	.9895
40	.6176	.6922	.7594	.8174	.8657	.9044	.9341	.9561	.9717	.9824
41	.5380	.6174	.6919	.7589	.8169	.8653	.9040	.9338	.9558	.9716
42	.4571	.5382	.6173	.6916	.7585	.8165	.8649	.9037	.9335	.9557
43	.3782	.4576	.5383	.6173	.6913	.7582	.8162	.8646	.9035	.9334
44	.3041	.3788	.4580	.5385	.6172	.6912	.7580	.8160	.8645	.9033
45	.2375	.3049	.3794	.4583	.5387	.6173	.6911	.7579	.8159	.8644
46	.1799	.2384	.3057	.3799	.4587	.5389	.6173	.6911	.7579	.8159
47	.1320	.1807	.2391	.3063	.3804	.4590	.5391	.6174	.6912	.7579
48	.0938	.1328	.1815	.2398	.3069	.3809	.4593	.5393	.6176	.6914
49	.0644	.0944	.1335	.1822	.2404	.3074	.3813	.4596	.5395	.6178
50	.0428	.0650	.0950	.1341	.1827	.2409	.3078	.3816	.4599	.5398

					$n = 100$ (Continued)					
d \ p	.41	.42	.43	.44	.45	.46	.47	.48	.49	.50
51	.0275	.0432	.0655	.0955	.1346	.1832	.2413	.3082	.3819	.4602
52	.0170	.0278	.0436	.0659	.0960	.1350	.1836	.2417	.3084	.3822
53	.0102	.0172	.0280	.0439	.0662	.0963	.1353	.1838	.2419	.3086
54	.0059	.0103	.0174	.0282	.0441	.0664	.0965	.1355	.1840	.2421
55	.0033	.0059	.0104	.0175	.0284	.0443	.0666	.0967	.1356	.1841
56	.0017	.0033	.0060	.0105	.0176	.0285	.0444	.0667	.0967	.1356
57	.0009	.0018	.0034	.0061	.0106	.0177	.0286	.0444	.0667	.0967
58	.0004	.0009	.0018	.0034	.0061	.0106	.0177	.0286	.0444	.0666
59	.0002	.0005	.0009	.0018	.0034	.0061	.0106	.0177	.0285	.0443
60	.0001	.0002	.0005	.0009	.0018	.0034	.0061	.0106	.0177	.0284
61	.0000	.0001	.0002	.0005	.0009	.0018	.0034	.0661	.0106	.0176
62	.0000	.0000	.0001	.0002	.0005	.0009	.0018	.0034	.0061	.0105
63	.0000	.0000	.0000	.0001	.0002	.0005	.0009	.0018	.0034	.0060
64	.0000	.0000	.0000	.0000	.0001	.0002	.0005	.0009	.0018	.0033
65	.0000	.0000	.0000	.0000	.0000	.0001	.0002	.0005	.0009	.0018
66	.0000	.0000	.0000	.0000	.0000	.0000	.0001	.0002	.0004	.0009
67	.0000	.0000	.0000	.0000	.0000	.0000	.0000	.0001	.0002	.0004
68	.0000	.0000	.0000	.0000	.0000	.0000	.0000	.0000	.0001	.0002
69	.0000	.0000	.0000	.0000	.0000	.0000	.0000	.0000	.0000	.0001

Appendix C

AREAS UNDER THE NORMAL CURVE

ONE-TAILED AREAS UNDER NORMAL CURVE

Example

Area to the left of $Z = -2$ is .0228.
Area to the right of $Z = +1$ is .1587.

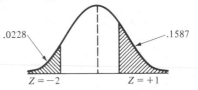

z	.00	.01	.02	.03	.04	.05	.06	.07	.08	.09
0.0	.5000	.4960	.4920	.4880	.4840	.4801	.4761	.4721	.4681	.4641
0.1	.4602	.4562	.4522	.4483	.4443	.4404	.4364	.4325	.4286	.4247
0.2	.4207	.4168	.4129	.4090	.4052	.4013	.3974	.3936	.3897	.3859
0.3	.3821	.3783	.3745	.3707	.3669	.3632	.3594	.3557	.3520	.3483
0.4	.3446	.3409	.3372	.3336	.3300	.3264	.3228	.3192	.3156	.3121
0.5	.3085	.3050	.3015	.2981	.2946	.2912	.2877	.2843	.2810	.2776
0.6	.2743	.2709	.2676	.2643	.2611	.2578	.2546	.2514	.2483	.2451
0.7	.2420	.2389	.2358	.2327	.2296	.2266	.2236	.2206	.2177	.2148
0.8	.2119	.2090	.2061	.2033	.2005	.1977	.1949	.1922	.1894	.1867
0.9	.1841	.1814	.1788	.1762	.1736	.1711	.1685	.1660	.1635	.1611
1.0	.1587	.1562	.1539	.1515	.1492	.1469	.1446	.1423	.1401	.1379
1.1	.1357	.1335	.1314	.1292	.1271	.1251	.1230	.1210	.1190	.1170
1.2	.1151	.1131	.1112	.1093	.1075	.1056	.1038	.1020	.1003	.0985
1.3	.0968	.0951	.0934	.0918	.0901	.0885	.0869	.0853	.0838	.0823
1.4	.0808	.0793	.0778	.0764	.0749	.0735	.0721	.0708	.0694	.0681
1.5	.0668	.0655	.0643	.0630	.0618	.0606	.0594	.0582	.0571	.0559
1.6	.0548	.0537	.0526	.0516	.0505	.0495	.0485	.0475	.0465	.0455
1.7	.0446	.0436	.0427	.0418	.0409	.0401	.0392	.0384	.0375	.0367
1.8	.0359	.0351	.0344	.0336	.0329	.0322	.0314	.0307	.0301	.0294
1.9	.0287	.0281	.0274	.0268	.0262	.0256	.0250	.0244	.0239	.0233
2.0	.0228	.0222	.0217	.0212	.0207	.0202	.0197	.0192	.0188	.0183
2.1	.0179	.0174	.0170	.0166	.0162	.0158	.0154	.0150	.0146	.0143
2.2	.0139	.0136	.0132	.0129	.0125	.0122	.0119	.0116	.0113	.0110
2.3	.0107	.0104	.0102	.0099	.0096	.0094	.0091	.0089	.0087	.0084
2.4	.0082	.0080	.0078	.0086	.0073	.0071	.0070	.0068	.0066	.0064
2.5	.0062	.0060	.0059	.0057	.0055	.0054	.0052	.0051	.0049	.0048
2.6	.0047	.0045	.0044	.0043	.0042	.0040	.0039	.0038	.0037	.0036
2.7	.0035	.0034	.0033	.0032	.0031	.0030	.0029	.0028	.0027	.0026
2.8	.0026	.0025	.0024	.0023	.0023	.0022	.0021	.0021	.0020	.0019
2.9	.0019	.0018	.0018	.0017	.0016	.0016	.0015	.0015	.0014	.0014

Appendix D

TABLE OF SQUARES, CUBES, ROOTS, AND RECIPROCALS

n	n^2	$\sqrt{n}$	$\sqrt{10n}$	n^3	$\sqrt[3]{n}$	$\sqrt[3]{10n}$	$\sqrt[3]{100n}$	$1/n$
1	1	1.00000	3.16228	1	1.00000	2.15442	4.64152	1.00000
2	4	1.41421	4.47214	8	1.25992	2.71439	5.84793	0.50000
3	9	1.73205	5.47723	27	1.44224	3.10720	6.69420	0.33333
4	16	2.00000	6.32456	64	1.58739	3.41991	7.36792	0.25000
5	25	2.23607	7.07107	125	1.70997	3.68398	7.93684	0.20000
6	36	2.44949	7.74597	216	1.81711	3.91481	8.43415	0.16667
7	49	2.64575	8.36660	343	1.91292	4.12123	8.87885	0.14286
8	64	2.82843	8.94427	512	1.99999	4.30881	9.28297	0.12500
9	81	3.00000	9.48683	729	2.08007	4.48134	9.65467	0.11111
10	100	3.16228	10.00000	1000	2.15442	4.64152	9.99977	0.10000
11	121	3.31662	10.48809	1331	2.22396	4.79134	10.32256	0.09091
12	144	3.46410	10.95445	1728	2.28941	4.93235	10.62633	0.08333
13	169	3.60555	11.40175	2197	2.35131	5.06571	10.91367	0.07692
14	196	3.74166	11.83216	2744	2.41012	5.19241	11.18662	0.07143
15	225	3.87298	12.24745	3375	2.46619	5.31320	11.44686	0.06667
16	256	4.00000	12.64911	4096	2.51982	5.42874	11.69578	0.06250
17	289	4.12311	13.03840	4913	2.57126	5.53956	11.93454	0.05882

(Continued)

n	n^2	$\sqrt{n}$	$\sqrt{10n}$	n^3	$\sqrt[3]{n}$	$\sqrt[3]{10n}$	$\sqrt[3]{100n}$	$1/n$
18	324	4.24264	13.41641	5832	2.62072	5.64612	12.16410	0.05556
19	361	4.35890	13.78405	6859	2.66838	5.74880	12.38531	0.05263
20	400	4.47214	14.14214	8000	2.71439	5.84793	12.59889	0.05000
21	441	4.58258	14.49138	9261	2.75890	5.94382	12.80547	0.04762
22	484	4.69042	14.83240	10648	2.80201	6.03670	13.00558	0.04545
23	529	4.79583	15.16575	12167	2.84384	6.12681	13.19972	0.04348
24	576	4.89898	15.49193	13824	2.88447	6.21435	13.38831	0.04167
25	625	5.00000	15.81139	15625	2.92399	6.29949	13.57173	0.04000
26	676	5.09902	16.12452	17576	2.96246	6.38239	13.75033	0.03846
27	729	5.19615	16.43168	19683	2.99997	6.46318	13.92440	0.03704
28	784	5.29150	16.73320	21952	3.03656	6.54201	14.09422	0.03571
29	841	5.38516	17.02939	24389	3.07228	6.61898	14.26005	0.03448
30	900	5.47723	17.32051	27000	3.10720	6.69420	14.42211	0.03333
31	961	5.56776	17.60682	29791	3.14134	6.76777	14.58061	0.03226
32	1024	5.65685	17.88854	32768	3.17477	6.83977	14.73573	0.03125
33	1089	5.74456	18.16590	35937	3.20750	6.91029	14.88765	0.03030
34	1156	5.83095	18.43909	39304	3.23957	6.97940	15.03654	0.02941
35	1225	5.91608	18.70829	42875	3.27103	7.04716	15.18253	0.02857
36	1296	6.00000	18.97367	46656	3.30189	7.11365	15.32577	0.02778
37	1369	6.08276	19.23538	50653	3.33218	7.17891	15.46638	0.02703
38	1444	6.16441	19.49359	54872	3.36193	7.24301	15.60448	0.02632
39	1521	6.24500	19.74842	59319	3.39117	7.30600	15.74018	0.02564
40	1600	6.32456	20.00000	64000	3.41991	7.36792	15.87357	0.02500
41	1681	6.40312	20.24846	68921	3.44817	7.42881	16.00476	0.02439
42	1764	6.48074	20.49390	74088	3.47598	7.48872	16.13384	0.02381
43	1849	6.55744	20.73644	79507	3.50335	7.54769	16.26088	0.02326
44	1936	6.63325	20.97618	85184	3.53030	7.60575	16.38597	0.02273
45	2025	6.70820	21.21320	91125	3.55685	7.66294	16.50917	0.02222
46	2116	6.78233	21.44761	97336	3.58300	7.71928	16.63057	0.02174
47	2209	6.85565	21.67948	103823	3.60878	7.77482	16.75021	0.02128
48	2304	6.92820	21.90890	110592	3.63419	7.82957	16.86818	0.02083
49	2401	7.00000	22.13594	117649	3.65926	7.88357	16.98451	0.02041
50	2500	7.07107	22.36068	125000	3.68398	7.93684	17.09927	0.02000
51	2601	7.14143	22.58318	132651	3.70838	7.98940	17.21252	0.01961
52	2704	7.21110	22.80351	140608	3.73246	8.04128	17.32429	0.01923
53	2809	7.28011	23.02173	148877	3.75624	8.09250	17.43464	0.01887
54	2916	7.34847	23.23790	157464	3.77971	8.14308	17.54360	0.01852
55	3025	7.41620	23.45208	166375	3.80290	8.19304	17.65123	0.01818
56	3136	7.48331	23.66432	175616	3.82581	8.24240	17.75757	0.01786
57	3249	7.54983	23.87467	185193	3.84845	8.29117	17.86264	0.01754
58	3364	7.61577	24.08319	195112	3.87082	8.33937	17.96650	0.01724
59	3481	7.68115	24.28992	205379	3.89294	8.38703	18.06917	0.01695
60	3600	7.74597	24.49490	216000	3.91481	8.43415	18.17068	0.01667
61	3721	7.81025	24.69818	226981	3.93644	8.48074	18.27107	0.01639
62	3844	7.87401	24.89980	238328	3.95784	8.52684	18.37037	0.01613
63	3969	7.93725	25.09980	250047	3.97900	8.57243	18.46861	0.01587

(Continued)

n	n^2	$\sqrt{n}$	$\sqrt{10n}$	n^3	$\sqrt[3]{n}$	$\sqrt[3]{10n}$	$\sqrt[3]{100n}$	$1/n$
64	4096	8.00000	25.29822	262144	3.99994	8.61755	18.56581	0.01563
65	4225	8.06226	25.49510	274625	4.02067	8.66220	18.66201	0.01538
66	4356	8.12404	25.69047	287496	4.04118	8.70640	18.75722	0.01515
67	4489	8.18535	25.88436	300763	4.06149	8.75015	18.85148	0.01493
68	4624	8.24621	26.07681	314432	4.08160	8.79347	18.94481	0.01471
69	4761	8.30662	26.26785	328509	4.10151	8.83636	19.03722	0.01449
70	4900	8.36660	26.45751	343000	4.12123	8.87885	19.12875	0.01429
71	5041	8.42615	26.64583	357911	4.14076	8.92093	19.21941	0.01408
72	5184	8.48528	26.83282	373248	4.16011	8.96261	19.30922	0.01389
73	5329	8.54400	27.01851	389017	4.17928	9.00392	19.39820	0.01370
74	5476	8.60233	27.20294	405224	4.19828	9.04484	19.48637	0.01351
75	5625	8.66025	27.38613	421875	4.21710	9.08540	19.57376	0.01333
76	5776	8.71780	27.56810	438976	4.23576	9.12560	19.66037	0.01316
77	5929	8.77496	27.74887	456533	4.25426	9.16545	19.74622	0.01299
78	6084	8.83176	27.92848	474552	4.27260	9.20496	19.83133	0.01282
79	6241	8.88819	28.10694	493039	4.29078	9.24413	19.91572	0.01266
80	6400	8.94427	28.28427	512000	4.30881	9.28297	19.99940	0.01250
81	6561	9.00000	28.46050	531441	4.32669	9.32149	20.08239	0.01235
82	6724	9.05539	28.63564	551368	4.34442	9.35969	20.16469	0.01220
83	6889	9.11043	28.80972	571787	4.36201	9.39759	20.24633	0.01205
84	7056	9.16515	28.98275	592704	4.37945	9.43518	20.32731	0.01190
85	7225	9.21954	29.15476	614125	4.39676	9.47247	20.40766	0.01176
86	7396	9.27362	29.32576	636056	4.41394	9.50947	20.48738	0.01163
87	7569	9.32738	29.49576	658503	4.43098	9.54619	20.56648	0.01149
88	7744	9.38083	29.66479	681472	4.44789	9.58262	20.64498	0.01136
89	7921	9.43398	29.83298	704969	4.46468	9.61878	20.72288	0.01124
90	8100	9.48683	30.00000	729000	4.48134	9.65467	20.80021	0.01111
91	8281	9.53939	30.16621	753571	4.49787	9.69030	20.87696	0.01099
92	8464	9.59166	30.33150	778688	4.51429	9.72567	20.95315	0.01087
93	8649	9.64365	30.49590	804357	4.53059	9.76078	21.02880	0.01075
94	8836	9.69536	30.65942	830584	4.54677	9.79564	21.10390	0.01064
95	9025	9.74679	30.82207	857375	4.56283	9.83025	21.17847	0.01053
96	9216	9.79796	30.98387	884736	4.57879	9.86462	21.25252	0.01042
97	9409	9.84886	31.14482	912673	4.59463	9.89876	21.32606	0.01031
98	9604	9.89949	31.30495	941192	4.61037	9.93266	21.39909	0.01020
99	9801	9.94987	31.46427	970299	4.62599	9.96633	21.47163	0.01010
100	10000	10.00000	31.62278	1000000	4.64152	9.99977	21.54369	0.01000

Appendix E

TABLE OF RANDOM NUMBERS

TABLE OF RANDOM DIGITS

(1)	78020983	98672900	95435370	82279865	77703852	68643077	84194847
(2)	62799836	76839392	39665528	58525734	42005126	80159920	47775872
(3)	69077251	81362235	55091895	29479306	58698604	47432014	89863921
(4)	42924138	25991932	46403285	00003916	65806460	09184045	56230612
(5)	67904252	66762333	74526402	65246516	98198843	27969196	78276939
(6)	00518158	08681259	05919717	92676948	21465945	78135620	25366137
(7)	28659119	73816242	29585728	47319034	90997340	92306133	89178620
(8)	25065463	75240578	68390957	46810697	47392210	20875269	50639006
(9)	89777087	83506626	95870608	97310159	91843569	14870369	26289026
(10)	39648786	77145062	77061794	77571574	45447841	41867295	63632100
(11)	64709597	74200211	82949200	27213544	78022136	18040817	11999689
(12)	78770701	99185323	07725501	42493254	84111581	63354226	94481051
(13)	43035318	94596290	79855876	37717896	24679174	82870480	04160342
(14)	22860082	09400021	86142937	04349109	95465129	82423210	86901362
(15)	51197418	75010402	99829936	41745770	21160253	40370732	10890475
(16)	36205729	09687654	20392617	38709012	82357941	89920663	96583667
(17)	81706532	41683926	81744064	72496332	45852413	41510042	59270562
(18)	60335976	66751874	98743018	73909705	00420215	62546142	13017767

TABLE OF RANDOM DIGITS (Continued)

(19)	89609554	67783235	32832968	23683296	45145956	68074367	25882942
(20)	14599297	70384951	59877973	69096648	07371213	87964556	20296405
(21)	21673902	73259865	78562255	95821475	71546025	74047690	19522910
(22)	21544717	02045810	83915992	76082695	21862440	42019817	27070131
(23)	67685106	83584521	05049223	62281393	63369178	45773246	10952135
(24)	72523457	01751728	41283621	53817470	10225742	64035436	43577246
(25)	02780047	24247813	32990015	63184243	37576871	54464026	76885101
(26)	07894108	76272078	04826469	18459394	47033013	83848030	33845233
(27)	36834972	85379822	78671259	27856342	81529739	70333182	89789197
(28)	87037620	41281502	18198099	55444344	53093062	35096837	72529136
(29)	97198996	23532700	14084833	23774627	80156020	82230029	40101552
(30)	86788852	60237036	03865980	75513106	48771218	97860149	35525257
(31)	72988427	16504307	87887846	31032770	67758376	15037115	28785070
(32)	90670685	02216885	59171444	94459625	82933111	56810920	21134232
(33)	03037914	58211707	64164664	15505851	06826368	30752510	57430646
(34)	36860892	21003362	03497097	75695039	06522731	27534781	77059405
(35)	37420735	30287109	35443370	96725306	62228225	69782511	34659097
(36)	15443066	51600913	56546061	69641750	68898719	80766697	45884073
(37)	73613148	16179734	32784033	01246152	44063816	80549373	93309713
(38)	56348944	56705989	57565227	98778654	72845309	11117456	51082552
(39)	44448592	47477509	54498633	58518168	14849323	72562179	52545637
(40)	34518878	58779276	03295704	90895207	75757172	50796746	40914281
(41)	46320953	16253307	69328462	03466965	69275729	17172909	25072571
(42)	94703060	74342953	82009214	28870903	33263852	65555037	83503446
(43)	42431376	44138939	43143090	05904583	38315251	64428619	51801088
(44)	20888546	73782881	68885067	51331987	36701983	50229807	12372319
(45)	41558953	81323431	02912719	54055548	11594770	73288701	63203128
(46)	54968232	51078163	70681930	51209145	72094815	97564736	70529818
(47)	94647362	38219969	63016507	18435704	48874303	30414035	68683883
(48)	70023499	84943715	49026004	80051045	17923781	44982650	23401104
(49)	02347401	52768916	87179978	33893370	45871807	67461103	18763591
(50)	59673690	35716195	82093313	42310061	05187393	84501331	13868769

BIBLIOGRAPHY

GENERAL REFERENCES

1. Ackoff, R. L., and M. W. Sasieni. *Fundamentals of Operations Research*. New York: Wiley, 1968.
2. Adam, Everett E., and Ronald J. Ebert. *Production and Operations Management, Concepts, Models, and Behavior*. Englewood Cliffs, N.J.: Prentice-Hall, 1978.
3. Agee, Marvin II., Robert E. Taylor, and Paul E. Torgersen. *Quantitative Analysis for Management Decisions*. Englewood Cliffs, N.J.: Prentice-Hall, 1976.
4. Anderson, D. R., D. J. Sweeney, and T. A. Williams. *An Introduction to Management Science*. St. Paul, Minn.: West, 1976.
5. Bazarra, M. S., and J. J. Jarvis. *Linear Programming and Network Flows*. New York: Wiley, 1977.
6. Bell, C. E. *Quantitative Methods for Administration*. Homewood, Ill.: Irwin, 1977.
7. Bellman, R. E., and S. E. Dreyfus. *Applied Dynamic Programming*. Princeton, N.J.: Princeton University Press, 1962.
8. Bhat, U. N. *Elements of Applied Stochastic Processes*. New York: Wiley, 1972.

9. Bierman, H., C. P. Bonini, and W. H. Hausman. *Quantitative Analysis for Business Decisions, 4th ed.* Homewood, Ill.: Irwin, 1973.

10. Bowen, Earl K. *Mathematics with Applications in Management and Economics, 3rd ed.* Homewood, Ill.: Irwin, 1972.

11. Braverman, Jerome D. *Fundamentals of Business Statistics.* New York: Academic Press, 1978.

12. Brown, Kenneth S., and Jack B. ReVelle. *Quantitative Methods for Managerial Decisions.* Reading, Mass.: Addison-Wesley, 1978.

13. Brown, R. V., A. S. Kahr, and C. Peterson. *Decision Analysis for the Manager.* New York: Holt, Rinehart and Winston, 1974.

14. Budnick, F. S., R. Mojena, and T. E. Vollman. *Principles of Operations Research for Management.* Homewood, Ill.: Irwin, 1977.

15. Buffa, Elwood S. *Operations Management: The Management of Productive Systems.* New York: Wiley Hamilton, 1976.

16. Cangelosi, V. E., P. H. Taylor, and P. F. Rice. *Basic Statistics, A Real World Approach, 2nd ed.* St. Paul, Minnesota: West Publishing Co., 1979.

17. Chase, Richard B., and Nicholas J. Aquilano. *Production and Operations Management: A Life Cycle Approach.* Homewood, Ill.: Irwin, 1973.

18. Childress, Robert L. *Mathematics for Managerial Decisions.* Englewood Cliffs, N.J.: Prentice-Hall, 1974.

19. Clark, Charles T., and Lawrence L. Schkade, *Statistical Analysis for Business Decisions, 3rd ed.* Cincinnati, Ohio: South Western, 1979.

20. Cook, T. M., and R. A. Russell. *Introduction to Management Science.* Englewood Cliffs, N.J.: Prentice-Hall, 1977.

21. Cooper, L., and D. Steinberg. *Methods and Applications of Linear Programming,* Philadelphia: W. B. Saunders Company, 1974.

22. Cooper, R. B. *Introduction to Queueing Theory.* New York: Macmillan, 1972.

23. Daellenbach, Hans G., and John A. George. *Introduction to Operations Research Techniques.* Boston: Allyn & Bacon, 1978.

24. Dantzig, G. B. *Linear Programming and Extensions.* Princeton, N.J.: Princeton University Press, 1963.

25. Denardo, E. V. *Dynamic Programming: Theory and Application.* Englewood Cliffs, N.J.: Prentice-Hall, 1975.

26. Draper, Jean E., and Jane S. Klingman. *Mathematical Analysis: Business and Economic Applications, 2nd ed.* New York: Harper & Row, 1972.

27. Eck, R. D. *Operations Research for Business.* Belmont, Calif.: Wadsworth, 1976.

28. Emerson, Lloyd S., and Laurence R. Paquett. *Fundamental Mathematics for the Social and Management Sciences.* Boston: Allyn & Bacon, 1975.

29. Eppen, Gary D., and F. J. Gould. *Quantitative Concepts for Management, Decision Making Without Algorithms.* Englewood Cliffs, N.J.: Prentice-Hall, 1979.

30. Forrester, J. W. *Industrial Dynamics.* Cambridge, Mass.: M.I.T. Press, 1961.

31. Forrester, J. W. *Urban Dynamics.* Cambridge, Mass.: M.I.T. Press, 1969.

32. Forrester, J. W. *World Dynamics.* Cambridge, Mass.: M.I.T. Press, 1971.

33. Freund, John E. *College Mathematics with Business Applications, 2nd ed.* Englewood Cliffs, N.J.: Prentice-Hall, 1975.

34. Gallagher, Charles A., Hugh J. Watson. *Quantitative Methods for Business Decisions.* New York: McGraw-Hill, 1980.

35. Gass, S. I. *An Illustrated Guide to Linear Programming*. New York: McGraw-Hill, 1970.
36. Gilligan, Lawrence G., and Robert B. Nenno. *Finite Mathematics with Applications to Life. 2nd ed.* Santa Monica, Calif.: Goodyear Publishing Co., 1979.
37. Grawoig, Dennis E., Bruce Fielitz, James Robinson, and Dwight Tabor. *Mathematics: A Foundation for Decisions*. Reading, Mass.: Addison-Wesley, 1976.
38. Green, Thad B., Sang M., Lee, and Walter B. Newsom. *The Decision Science Process, Integrating the Quantitative and Behavioral*. New York, Petrocelli Books, Inc., 1978.
39. Greene, J. H. *Production and Inventory Control, rev. ed.* Homewood, Ill.: Irwin, 1974.
40. Griffin, Walter C. *Queueing, Basic Theory and Applications*. Columbus, Ohio: Grid, Inc., 1978.
41. Gross, D., and C. M. Harris. *Fundamentals of Queueing Theory*. New York: Wiley, 1974.
42. Gulati, Bodh R. *College Mathematics with Applications to the Business and Social Sciences*. New York: Harper & Row, 1978.
43. Hadley, G. *Nonlinear and Dynamic Programming*. Reading, Mass.: Addison-Wesley, 1964.
44. Hartley, R. V. *Operations Research: A Managerial Emphasis*. Pacific Palisades, Calif.: Goodyear Publishing Co., 1976.
45. Harvey, Charles M. *Operations Research, An Introduction for Linear Optimization and Decision Analysis*. New York: North Holland, 1979.
46. Heinze, David. *Management Science: Introductory Concepts and Applications*. Cincinnati: South Western, 1978.
47. Hesse, Rick, and Gene Woolsey. *Applied Management Science*. Chicago: Science Research Associates, 1980.
48. Hillier, F. S., and G. J. Lieberman. *Introduction to Operations Research*. San Francisco: Holden-Day, 1974.
49. Hogg, Robert V., Anthony J. Schaeffer, Ronald R. Randles, and James C. Hickman. *Finite Mathematics and Calculus with Applications to Business and the Social Sciences*. Menlo Park, Calif.: Cummings, 1974.
50. Hopeman, Richard J. *Production: Concepts, Analysis, and Control, 3rd ed.* Columbus, Ohio: Merrill, 1976.
51. Ignizio, J. P., and J. N. D. Gupta. *Operators Research in Decision Making*. New York: Grane, Russak & Company, Inc., 1975.
52. Johnson, R. D., and B. R. Siskin. *Quantitative Techniques for Business Decisions*. Englewood Cliffs, N.J.: Prentice-Hall, 1976.
53. Johnson, R. H., and P. R. Winn. *Quantitative Methods for Management*. Boston: Houghton Mifflin, 1976.
54. Jolson, M. A., and R. T. Hise. *Quantitative Techniques for Marketing Decisions*. New York: Macmillan, 1973
55. Joshi, Madhukar. *Management Science: A Survey of Quantitative Decision-Making Techniques*. Belmont, Calif.: Duxbury Press, 1980.
56. Kim, C. *Quantitative Analysis for Managerial Decisions*. Reading, Mass.: Addison-Wesley, 1976.

57. Knotts, Ulysses S., Jr., and Ernest W. Swift. *Management Science for Management Decisions*. Boston: Allyn & Bacon, 1978.

58. Koshy, Thomas. *Finite Mathematics and Calculus with Applications*. Santa Monica, Calif.: Goodyear Publishing Co., 1979.

59. Kwak, No Kyoon. *Mathematical Programming with Business Applications*. New York: McGraw-Hill, 1973.

60. Lapin, L. L. *Quantitative Methods for Business Decisions*. New York: Harcourt Brace Jovanovich, 1976.

61. Laufer, Arthur C. *Operations Management*. Cincinnati: South Western, 1975.

62. Lee, Sang M. *Goal Programming for Decision Analysis*. Philadelphia: Auerbach, 1972.

63. Levin, R. I., and C. A. Kirkpatrick. *Quantitative Approaches to Management, 3rd ed.* New York: McGraw-Hill, 1975.

64. Lial, Margaret L., and Charles D. Miller. *Mathematics: With Applications to the Management, Natural, and Social Sciences*. Glenview, Ill.: Scott, Foresman, 1974.

65. Loomba, N. P. *Linear Programming: A Managerial Perspective, 2nd ed.* New York: Macmillan, 1976.

66. Luce, R. D., and H. Raiffa. *Games and Decisions*. New York: Harcourt Brace Jovanovich, 1973.

67. McLaughlin, Frank S., and R. C. Pickhardt. *Quantitative Techniques for Management Decisions*. Boston, Mass.: Houghton Mifflin, 1979.

68. Nemhauser, G. L. *Introduction to Dynamic Programming*. New York: Wiley, 1966.

69. Orlicky, J. *Material Requirements Planning: The New Way of Life in Production and Inventory Management*. New York: McGraw-Hill, 1975.

70. Raiffa, H. *Decision Analysis*. Reading, Mass.: Addison-Wesley, 1968.

71. Schlaifer, R. *Analysis of Decisions Under Uncertainty*. New York: McGraw-Hill, 1969.

72. Schriber, Thomas J. *Simulation Using GPSS*. New York: Wiley, 1974.

73. Shamblin, J. E., and G. T. Stevens. *Operations Research: A Fundamental Approach*. New York: McGraw-Hill, 1974.

74. Shore, Barry, *Operations Management*. New York: McGraw-Hill, 1973.

75. Starr, Martin K. *Production Management, 2nd ed.* Englewood Cliffs, N.J.: Prentice-Hall, 1972.

76. Taha, H. A. *Operations Research: An Introduction*. New York: Macmillan, 1971.

77. Theodore, Chris A. *Applied Mathematics: An Introduction, 3rd ed.* Homewood, Ill.: Irwin, 1975.

78. Thierauf, Robert J., and Robert C. Klekamp. *Decision Making Through Operations Research, 2nd ed.* New York: Wiley, 1975.

79. Thompson, Gerald E. *Linear Programming*. New York: Macmillan, 1971.

80. Thompson, Gerald E. *Statistics for Decisions: An Elementary Introduction*. Boston: Little, Brown, 1972.

81. Thornton, Billy M., and Paul Preston. *Introduction to Management Science: Quantitative Approaches to Managerial Decisions*. Columbus, Ohio: Merrill, 1977.

82. Trueman, R. E. *An Introduction to Quantitative Methods for Decision Making.* New York: Holt, Rinehart and Winston, 1974.
83. Turban, E., and J. R. Meredith. *Fundamentals of Management Science.* Dallas, Texas: Business Publications, 1977.
84. Van Horne, J. C. *Financial Management and Policy, 4th ed.* Englewood Cliffs, N.J.: Prentice-Hall, 1977.
85. Vollman, T. E. *Operations Management.* Reading, Mass.: Addison-Wesley, 1973.
86. Wagner, H. M. *Principles of Management Science.* Englewood Cliffs, N.J.: Prentice-Hall, 1975.
87. Wheeler, Ruric E., and W. D. Peeples, Jr. *Modern Mathematics for Business Students.* Belmont, Calif.: Brooks/Cole, 1969.
88. White, D. J. *Dynamic Programming.* San Francisco: Holden-Day, 1969.
89. Williams, Donald R. *Modern Mathematics for Business Decision-Making.* Menlo Park, Calif.: Wadsworth, 1974.
90. Williams, Donald R. *Finite Mathematics with Applications.* Belmont, Calif.: Wadsworth, 1976.
91. Williams, Donald R. *Modern Mathematics with Applications.* Belmont, Calif.: Wadsworth, 1976.
92. Wu, Nesa L'abbe', and Jack Ardin Wu. *Introduction to Management Science, A Contemporary Approach.* Chicago: Rand McNally College Publishing Co., 1980.

SELECTED REFERENCES

Chapter	Bibliography Reference Numbers
Two	10, 13, 16, 18, 26, 33, 34, 37, 42, 49, 64, 77, 87, 89, 90, 91
Three	4, 6, 9, 46, 68, 53, 54, 56, 60, 63, 67, 73, 83
Four	3, 5, 6, 9, 14, 21, 24, 27, 34, 35, 44, 45, 47, 48, 51, 56, 59, 60, 65, 78, 79, 86
Five	3, 4, 5, 6, 9, 12, 14, 24, 27, 34, 35, 44, 47, 48, 51, 56, 59, 60, 65, 78, 86
Six	5, 9, 21, 27, 29, 48, 56, 59, 60, 65, 78, 86
Seven	4, 20, 34, 45, 46, 47, 48, 53, 55, 57, 63, 78, 86
Eight	4, 14, 23, 29, 34, 62, 81, 92
Nine	10, 18, 23, 26, 28, 33, 37
Ten	50, 61, 74, 75, 84, 85
Eleven	2, 3, 4, 9, 12, 14, 15, 17, 23, 38, 39, 44, 47, 51, 53, 61, 63, 69, 73, 74, 75, 82, 84, 85, 86
Twelve	3, 4, 9, 14, 15, 34, 46, 47, 48, 51, 55, 63, 78, 86, 92
Thirteen	7, 9, 25, 27, 43, 47, 68, 86, 88
Fourteen	11, 19, 47, 51, 55, 66, 70, 71, 80, 92
Fifteen	34, 36, 46, 58, 63, 66, 67
Sixteen	23, 29, 30, 31, 32, 34, 48, 51, 55, 72, 73, 76, 92
Seventeen	1, 3, 8, 14, 22, 34, 40, 41, 48, 51, 52, 55, 73, 76, 78, 82

SOLUTIONS TO SELECTED PROBLEMS

Note: The complete solutions to all text problems are found in the *Solutions Manual*, which accompanies the text. This appendix contains only the final answers to selected problems.

1.1 A set of qualitative tools for the solution of problems through the use of objective, quantitative mathematical models. Management scientists apply these tools to problems in business and public administration.

1.2 Identify goals (problems), define objectives, generate alternative solutions, evaluate alternatives and select solutions, implement the solution, use feedback to assure that solutions are appropriate to actual problems.

1.3 Abstraction (construction), validation, prediction, evaluation, and revision (modification).

1.4 A solution which is inferior to the optimal; optimizing at too low a level (optimizing a subsystem).

1.5 Carrying the analysis past the point of diminishing returns, where the effort required to achieve a small increase in solution accuracy exceeds the usefulness of the added precision. The saucer solution has a wide range of near optimal solutions; the funnel has a very narrow margin of error about the optimum.

2.1   a. $X = 19$ b. $X = \frac{8}{5}$

       c. $X = \frac{5}{7}$ d. $X = -\frac{5}{8}$

2.3   a. $X < 6$ b. $X \geq -\frac{7}{2}$

       c. $X > 8$ d. $X \leq -\frac{10}{3}$

       e. $X \geq 18$ f. $X \leq \frac{1}{2}$

2.5   a. $Y = -3 + 2X$ b. $Y = 25 - \frac{5}{3}X$

       c. $Y = 2 + \frac{3}{2}X$ d. $Y = 1 - \frac{1}{2}X$

2.7 $A = \$3333$ $B = \$1667$

2.9   a. $(10, \quad 7, \quad 5)$ b. $\begin{pmatrix} 3 \\ 6 \\ -6 \\ 2 \end{pmatrix}$

c. $\begin{pmatrix} 4 & 6 & 5 \\ 5 & -1 & 9 \\ 4 & 11 & 3 \\ 10 & -4 & 15 \end{pmatrix}$ d. $\begin{pmatrix} 9 & -1 & 3 \\ -4 & -1 & 3 \end{pmatrix}$

e. $\begin{pmatrix} 7 & 4 \\ 2 & 2 \\ 1 & -1 \\ 6 & 3 \end{pmatrix}$ f. $\begin{pmatrix} -1 & 4 & 2 \\ 6 & 3 & 1 \\ 8 & 3 & 0 \\ 9 & 0 & 5 \end{pmatrix}$

g. $\begin{pmatrix} 8 & 8 & 12 & 4 \\ 2 & 2 & 3 & 1 \\ 14 & 14 & 21 & 7 \end{pmatrix}$ h. $(59, \quad 34, \quad 25)$

i. $\begin{pmatrix} 8 & -3 \\ 20 & 31 \end{pmatrix}$ j. $\begin{pmatrix} \frac{6}{10} & -\frac{4}{10} \\ \frac{1}{10} & \frac{1}{10} \end{pmatrix}$

k. $\begin{pmatrix} -2 & \frac{3}{2} & 5 \\ 1 & -\frac{1}{2} & -2 \\ -2 & \frac{3}{2} & 4 \end{pmatrix}$

2.11   a. $X = 4,\ Y = -\frac{5}{2}$ b. $X = \frac{36}{7},\ Y = -\frac{16}{7}$

       c. $X = 4,\ Y = -1,\ Z = 2$ d. $X = 1,\ Y = 3,\ Z = -2$

2.13   a. $-1.585, -4.415$ b. $1, -\frac{1}{3}$

       c. $-5.54, .54$ d. $\frac{1}{5}, 1$

2.15   Each point (red odd, red even, black odd, black even) has a probability of $\frac{1}{4}$.

2.17   Each outcome (e.g., red, white, blue) has a probability of $\frac{1}{27}$.

      a. $P(C) = \frac{7}{27}$ b. $P(D) = \frac{19}{27}$

      c. $P(E) = \frac{1}{9}$ d. $P(C\ \&\ D) = \frac{1}{9}$

e. $P(D \text{ or } E) = \frac{7}{9}$ f. $P(D \& \bar{E}) = \frac{2}{3}$

g. $P(D \& E) = \frac{1}{27}$ h. $P(C \text{ or } E) = \frac{1}{3}$

i. $P(C \text{ or } D) = \frac{23}{27}$

j. None of the events are mutually exclusive because each has one or more points in common with each of the others.

2.19 $X = 2.52$

2.21 a. .1937   b. .1029

     c. .1209   d. .0085

     e. .0100

2.23 a. .4095   b. .8369

     c. .8327   d. .2970

     e. .8205

2.25 a. 23%   b. 69%

     c. 7%   d. 99%

     e. 15%

3.1

.9	.76	.704	.6816	.67264	.669056
.1	.24	.296	.3184	.32736	.330944
MS_0	MS_1	MS_2	MS_3	MS_4	MS_5

3.3 $X = \frac{2}{3}, Y = \frac{1}{3}$

3.5 $X = .2, Y = .8$

3.7 R's equilibrium share $= 50\%$

3.9 A's share $= 60\%$; B's $= 0$; C's $= 40\%$

4.1 $X = 3, Y = 2, Z = 25$

4.3 $X = 1, Y = 5, Z = 45$

4.5 b. $X_1 = \frac{2}{3}, X_2 = \frac{20}{3}, Z_{\text{MAX}} = \frac{164}{3} = 54\frac{2}{3}$

     c. $X_1 = \frac{10}{3}, X_2 = \frac{4}{3}, Z_{\text{MIN}} = \frac{5}{23} = 17\frac{1}{3}$

     d. Feasible region becomes a *point* at $(\frac{10}{3}, \frac{4}{3})$.

4.7 a. Max $Z = 8R + 10S$

     ST $2R + 4S \leq 28$

              $6R + 4S \leq 48$

              $(R, S \geq 0)$

     b. $R = 5, S = 4.5, Z_{\text{MAX}} = 85$

4.9 1 cow, 6 pigs, $Z_{\text{MAX}} = \$160$

5.6 $T = 4 \text{ doz/hr}, R = 0, S_2 = 2 \text{ doz/hr}, Z = \$16/\text{hr}$

5.8 $X_1 = 7000 \text{ acres}, X_3 = 3000 \text{ acres}, S_3 = 3000 \text{ acres}$

5.13 a. $-\infty < \Delta C_1 \leq |\Delta Z_1|$ so $-\infty < C_1 \leq 23$; no change in optimum solution.

     b. $-10 \leq C_2 \leq 14$. If C_2 is reduced, Z_{OPT} is reduced and vice versa.

     c. $S_1 \leq \Delta b_1 < +\infty$; so $-8.167 \leq b_1 < \infty$, but because b_1 cannot be negative, $0 \leq b_1 \leq \infty$ is the range.

     d. $0 \leq b_2 \leq 20.99$

6.1 $X_2 = 3.083, X_3 = .833, S_1 = 20.167, Z = 21.25$

6.3 $X_1 = 40, X_2 = 20, X_3 = 66.667, S_1 = 20, S_3 = 46.667, S_6 = 66.667,$
$Z = 2,066.67$

6.5 $X_1 = 10, X_2 = 5, X_3 = 5.833, S_3 = 45, S_4 = 24.167, S_5 = 9.167,$
$S_6 = 5, S_8 = .833, Z = 1170.833$

6.7 $X_3 = 1500, X_4 = 2000, X_5 = 200, X_8 = 3300, X_{11} = 0, X_{12} = 1000,$
$X_{15} = 500, Z = \$127,700$

6.9 $X_1 = 500, X_2 = 5285, X_3 = 500, X_4 = 500, X_5 = 1000, X_6 = 500,$
$S_3 = 4785, S_5 = 400, S_9 = 1000, S_{11} = 5285$

7.1 Diana-trial, Olivia-crash, Mel-fire, Dummy-drug raid

7.3 Lucky-bacarat, Gus-poker, Slick-blackjack (Total = 19) or Lucky-blackjack, Gus-bacarat, Slick-poker (Total = 19)

7.5 Sheri-Don's, Mort-Ace's, Zelda-Cal's, Thurman-Bob's

7.7 AW-35, BW-35, BX-15, CX-15, CY-65, DY-10, DZ-55

7.9 CW-70, CX-10, DX-20, BY-50, DY-25, AZ-35, DZ-20

7.13 W_2R_1–1000, W_2R_2–1000, W_3R_2–3500, W_1R_3–4000, W_3R_3–2500, W_4R_4–5000

7.15 Ponney–4 MG/S, McWilson–2 Stat, 1 MG/S, 1 Queues Barker–4 Stat, Broberts–2 Queues, 2 Simulations No Prof–0 Stat, 1 MG/S

7.17 QX-20, None X-20, MR-40, None R-10, MD-20, SP-35, SD-15

8.1 $X_1 = 0, X_2 = 0, X_3 = 25, V_1 = 15, S_1 = 0, V_2 = 0, S_2 = 0,$
$Z = 125$

8.3 $X_1 = 52,000, X_2 = 0, X_3 = 0, X_4 = 48,000, S_1 = 0, S_2 = 0, V_3 = 0,$
$S_3 = 7,600,000, V_4 = 60,000,000, S_4 = 0$

8.5 $X_1 = 100,000, X_2 = 120,000, X_3 = 0, X_4 = 10,000, X_5 = 20,000,$
$S_1 = 0, V_2 = 3300, S_2 = 0, V_3 = 0, S_3 = 0, V_4 = 0, S_4 = 0, V_5 = 0,$
$S_5 = 20,000, V_6 = 0, S_6 = 25,000, V_7 = 0, S_7 = 0, V_8 = 0, S_8 = 0$

9.1 a. $T' = 11$

b. $B' = -4 + 10M$

c. $F' = \dfrac{1}{2\sqrt{R}}$

d. $D' = \dfrac{-2}{3L^2} - \frac{27}{2}\sqrt{L} + \frac{6}{5}$

e. $V' = 6 + 26S - 2.4S^2$

f. $Q' = -\dfrac{6}{\sqrt{N^3}} + 3 + \dfrac{5}{\sqrt{2N}}$

g. $C' = -\dfrac{7}{P^2} + 8P - 3P^2$

9.3 a. $X^* = 3, Y'' = -4$ (Max)

b. $T^* = \frac{7}{6}, S'' = 6$ (Min)

c. $P^* = 2, M'' = 2$ (Min); $P^* = -2, M'' = -2$ (Max)

d. $L^* = 3$, $E'' = -12\sqrt{3}$ (Max); $L^* = -3$, $M'' = (-12)(-\sqrt{3})$
(Min)

e. $D^* = 1$, $W'' = 8$ (Min); $D^* = 9$, $W'' = -8$ (Max)

f. $V^* = \frac{4}{3}$, $R'' = -2$ (Max); $V^* = 2$, $R'' = 2$ (Min)

9.5 a. Highest point: $X = 0$, $Y = +5$
Lowest point: $X = 4$, $Y = -11$

b. Highest point: $C = 10$, $W = 20.8$
Lowest point: $C = 2$, $W = 8$

c. Highest point: $T = -3$, $Q = 15$
Lowest point: $T = 0$, $Q = 6$

d. Highest point: $B = 2$, $Z = 18$
Lowest point: $B = 0$, $Z = 2$

e. Highest point: $Q = 5$, $P = 17$
Lowest point: $Q = 0$, $Q = 10$, $P = -8$ (tie)

9.7 $C^* = 6$, $R_{MIN} = 4$ gal/hr

9.9 $Q^* = 3$, $P_{MAX} = \$5$

10.1 a. $TC = 5 + 4Q$, $TR = 5Q$, $\mathbb{P} = -5 + Q$

b. $Q_B = 5000$ pairs/month   d. Q_B increases.

e. Q_B drops.   f. Q_B drops.

10.3 To maximize TR, $Q^* = 250$ doz/day, $P = 25¢$/doz.
To maximize $\mathbb{P}$, $Q^* = 220$ doz/day, $P = 28¢$/doz.
At breakeven, $Q_B = 128.5$, 311.5 doz/day, $P = 37¢$, $19¢$/doz.

10.5 a. To Max TR, $Q^* = 3$, $P = \$6$, $AC = \$6.67$, $TC = \$20$, $\mathbb{P} = -\$2$

b. To Min AC, $Q^* = 1$, $P = \$10$, $TR = \$10$, $AC = \$4$, $TC = \$4$,
$\mathbb{P} = \$6$

c. To Max $\mathbb{P}$, $Q^* = \frac{3}{2}$, $P = \$9$, $TR = \$13.50$, $AC = \$4.33$, $TC = \$6.50$, $\mathbb{P} = \$7$

11.1 $\$10,000$

11.3 1600 units per order, 400 units reorder level

11.5 10 orders per year

11.7 Accept discount, save $\$11,778.75$

11.9 About 3800 units

11.11 .3 months' supply

12.1 $T_E = 23$; CP-1-2-3-4-5-6

12.3 $T_E = 26$; CP-1-3-4-7

12.5 6–8 slack = 8

12.7 b. 38,   c. 1-3-5-8-9,   d. 0,   e. 9

12.9 4.551%

12.11 b. 1 week 3-4 ($400), 1 week 1-3 ($700), 1 week 4-5 ($800), $1900
total

13.1 $3700 with $1 restriction
$4100 without restriction

13.3 Maximum total profit = $29,000

13.5 Total cost = $43

14.1 a. Cut federal spending; decrease federal taxes; antiabortion.
  b. Decrease federal spending (1.5 million votes).
  c. Cut federal spending (700,000 votes).
  d. Decrease federal spending (1.1 million votes).
  e. $\alpha = .4$
  f. Decrease federal taxes (Max regret $= .7$).
  Decrease federal taxes (933,333 votes).

14.3 c. Settle out of court (expected payoff $= \$600,000$; expected regret $= \$220,000$).
  d. $EVPI = \$220,000$

14.5 c. Order small computer now; switch to large computer if 2 or more contracts are received. (expected profit $= \$13,000$)
  d. and e. Risk avoider: Expected utilities are .685, .350, .565. Optimal act is to purchase small computer.
  Risk seeker: Expected utilities are .17, .10, .17. Optimal act is a tie between small computer and time share.

14.7 b. Rent the home. (expected profit $= \$1100/$year)
  $EVPI = \$300$
  e. $P(G/PG) = .64$, $P(B/PG) = .36$, $P(G/PB) = .16$, $P(B/PB) = .84$, $P(PG) = .5$, $P(PB) = .5$
  f. If prediction is "good," rent; if "bad," sell.
  g. $EVSI = \$1230 - \$1100 = \$130$; or $EVSI = \$300 - \$170 = \$130$
  h. Efficiency $= \dfrac{EVSI}{EVPI} = \dfrac{\$130}{\$300} = 43.3\%$

15.1 a. A plays a_1; B plays b_2; $V = 3$
  b. A plays a_2; B plays b_3; $V = -1$

15.3 "Racetrack" uses aggressive approach in 60% of cases; conservative in 40%.
  "White Hat" is hardline in 80% of cases; moderate in 20%.
  "Racetrack" wins 44% of the cases.

15.5 Red positions 90% of troops at north end 44% of the time, and 10% at north end 56% of the time.
  Blue attacks the north end 48% of the time; the south end 52% of the time.
  Blue loses 122 attackers on each try.

15.7 This game reduces to a 2×2 by dominance. Solution: $a_2 = 25\%$, $a_4 = 75\%$, $b_2 = 37.5\%$, $b_4 = 62.5\%$. The value of the game is 1.25.

15.9 Daisy cuts price with $P = 0$, increases ads with $P = .4$, does both with $P = .6$, and does neither with $P = 0$. Vita Moo's corresponding probabilities are the same as Daisy's. The value of the game is $V = -.2$.

15.11 For Daisy the relative frequencies are $\frac{1}{10}$, $\frac{4}{10}$, $\frac{5}{10}$; for Vita Moo, they are $\frac{0}{10}$, $\frac{4}{10}$, $\frac{6}{10}$. The value of the game lies in the range $-\frac{8}{10} \le V \le -\frac{2}{10}$. (Compare these with the solution from 15.9.)

16.1 Slim 16 (80%); Stretch 18 (90%)

16.3 Old reorder point (75): $900
New reorder point (85): $350

16.5 a. 4.8 or approximately 5 out of 20
b. 8 of the 20 in the simulation have the flu.

17.1 Monroe leaves at 3:30.
Five customers in line at 3:00.

17.3 a. 3.5%　　　　　　　b. 2　　　　　　　c. .554

17.5 New operator would add $39 maximum and cost $40. Do not hire.

17.7 a. 14　　　　　　　　b. Wash $Q - 2$, Dry $Q - 0$
c. Wash $Q - 1.183$, Dry $Q - 0$

17.9 a. 7.5 minutes　　　　　b. 6 minutes
c. 8 arrivals/hour　　　　d. 10 customers/hour
e. 30 minutes　　　　　　f. 24 minutes
g. 6 minutes　　　　　　h. 4 customers
i. 3.2 customers　　　　　j. 20%
k. 10.24%

17.11 a. 6 customers/hour　　　　b. $N = 6$ workers
c. $N = 8$ workers　　　　　d. 1 hour
e. 55 minutes　　　　　　　f. 11 customers
g. 10.08 customers　　　　　h. 7%
i. 77.03%

INDEX